Islam

 Contemporary Issues in the Middle East

Islam

Continuity and Change
in the Modern World

Second Edition

JOHN OBERT VOLL

Syracuse University Press

Syracuse University Press Edition 1994
94 95 96 97 98 99   6 5 4 3 2 1

Publication of this book is through arrangement with
Westview Press, Inc., Boulder, Colorado 80301.

This book is part of the Mohamed El-Hindi Series on Arab Culture and Islamic Civilization and is published with the assistance of a grant from the M.E.H. Foundation.

The paper used in this publication meets the minimum requirements of American National
Standard for Information Sciences—Permanence of Paper for Printed Library Materials, ANSI
Z39.48-1984. ∞™

Library of Congress Cataloging-in-Publication Data
Voll, John Obert, 1936–
Islam, continuity and change in the modern world / John Obert
Voll. — 2nd ed.
p.   cm. — (Contemporary issues in the Middle East)
Includes bibliographical references and index.
ISBN 0-8156-2639-8
1. Islam—History.   2. Islam—20th century.   I. Title.
II. Series.
PB60.V64   1994
297'.09'03—dc20   94-22075

Manufactured in the United States of America

Dedicated to Sarah, Layla, and Michael,
whose support makes research possible

John Obert Voll is professor of history at the University of New Hampshire. He is author of the *Historical Dictionary of the Sudan,* coauthor of *The Contemporary Islamic Revival: A Critical Survey and Bibliography,* and co-editor of *Eighteenth-Century Renewal and Reform in Islam.* He has published numerous articles on modern Islam and the Middle East and Sudanese history, and in 1991 received the Presidential Medal from President Husni Mubarak of Egypt in recognition for his scholarship on Islam.

Contents

Map

Preface to the Second Edition

The growing significance of the modern and contemporary Islamic world to the global community requires that we understand not only the broad continuities and commonalities but also the new elements and local particulars of Muslim experience. The past decade was marked by many conferences discussing, and numerous books exploring, these complex dimensions of modern Islamic history. However, there continues to be a need for a single volume that tries to cover this vast picture within the perspective and framework of the views of a single person. Many people appear to have found the first edition of this book to be helpful, and it is to them that I offer this second edition.

In this new edition, I have tried to reduce those sections that appeared to be least helpful in order to provide space for coverage of the significant events of the 1980s and early 1990s. As a result, the first two chapters of the original have been combined into a single introductory chapter, and the final two chapters, as well as the bibliographical essay, have been fully rewritten. The chapters covering the eighteenth and nineteenth centuries and the twentieth century Islamic experiences up to the 1970s (chapters 3–6 in the original and 2–5 in this edition) are unrevised. Each could be rewritten on the basis of important scholarship that has been published in the past decade, but I think that the main lines of the analysis in the original edition remain valid, and more revision would mean a new book rather than a second edition of a book which still has utility.

I continue to be enriched by people who help me, either through personal encouragement or through their scholarship or both. It is essential that I note the personal and scholarly support for more than a decade of John L. Esposito, and I sadly note the passing of two friends who commented on the first edition but will not see this second edition, although I have benefited from their work in preparing it: Richard P. Mitchell and Joseph Fletcher. In addition, I want to express my continuing gratitude to my wife, Sarah, for her encouragement, and to our children, Layla and Michael, who now provide ideas as well as inspiration for my work. Because of these gifts, this book continues to be dedicated to the three of them.

Durham, New Hampshire   *John Obert Voll*
April 1993

Preface to the First Edition

Much has been written recently about the contemporary Islamic experience. However, I believe that there is still a need for a discussion of the modern history of Islam that goes beyond the current headlines, and I have tried in this book to present such a study. The world of Islam is vast and diverse, but it is important to attempt to see the full extent of that world, both in time and space. The current resurgence of Islam is not something that suddenly appeared on the world scene. It is part of a long evolution of the modern Islamic experience that has its foundations in the eighteenth century and earlier. As a result, I have tried to show both the significant elements of continuity and the significant factors of diversity.

Any book that discusses the modern development of Islam in Africa, the Middle East, Asia, and elsewhere must cover a tremendous range of subjects. There are some advantages to having such a book written by a group of scholars, each with a particular regional expertise. However, such collections frequently lack clarity and cohesiveness. The advantage of having one person write such a book is that the whole picture can be presented within a single analytic framework. It is for this reason that I have written this book by myself, and I hope that the reader will find that the advantages outweigh the problems of my attempt to cover such a broad subject.

Clearly, I owe a great debt to the many people who have aided me, either through their personal encouragement or through their scholarship. Among this large group I especially want to thank Richard P. Mitchell and Leon Carl Brown. Their scholarship, instruction, and friendship are important in whatever virtues this book may have, although they have no part in its faults. I also want to express my deep gratitude to my wife, Sarah, and my children, Layla and Michael. Their cooperation and encouragement made it possible for this book to be written—that is why it is dedicated to them.

John Obert Voll

Note on Spelling

The problem of spelling names and terms originally written in other alphabets has never been satisfactorily solved. In order to achieve some uniformity of usage without adopting the cumbersome transliteration systems of formal scholarship, I have chosen to follow the spellings found in a widely-used textbook: Arthur Goldschmidt, Jr., *A Concise History of the Middle East*, 4th ed. (Boulder, Colo.: Westview, 1991). For names and terms that do not appear in that book, I have attempted to use spellings that appear in commonly used sources for the general reader.

Islam

The World of Islam

Muslim Population
(Percent)

- 89 – 100
- 51 – 88
- 26 – 50
- 2 – 25

Central Asian republics change from
minority to majority (not keyed).

1

Introduction

Islam is a dynamic force in the contemporary world. At the end of the twentieth century and the beginning of the fifteenth Islamic century, movements of Muslim revival have increasing visibility and influence. From success in elections in Algeria and Jordan to political prominence in southeast Asia and effective expansion in Africa, North America, and Europe, the entire world of Islam shows the continuing appeal and power of the message of the Quran.

The Islamic resurgence is part of a global experience of religious revival which surprised many analysts in the 1980s. In the past, an established part of the theories of modernization was that modern development involves "the secularization of the polity" as "a prerequisite for significant social change."[1] The contemporary experience in Muslim societies shows clearly that the old assumption of a direct correlation between modernization and secularization must at least be reexamined, if not rejected.

This book is based on the assumption that the currently visible resurgence of Islam is not simply the last gasp of a dying religious tradition. The general basis for this assumption is an examination of the experience of the Islamic community in modern history which broadly concludes that the Islamic world, like other societies in the contemporary world, is in the process of major transformation. The result of that process, however, will not be identically modernized, secularized societies. The shape of global, "postmodern" society is only beginning to emerge, but it seems clear that the special identities provided by the major world religious traditions will have important roles to play in that emerging new global order.

A fundamental issue is the nature of the religious traditions in the postmodern world. It is possible that fundamentally new ideas and institutions have been given a traditional appearance by the established religions. Using this point of view, one might see the current revival of Islam as a desire to provide familiar forms for basically non-Islamic ideas and institutions. Many commentators viewed the Islamic movements of the 1970s and 1980s in that

3

way, seeing Islamic activism as primarily nationalist or socialist or economically motivated movements dressed in the garb of religion. That viewpoint seems, at heart, to deny the possibility of a truly Islamic-inspired anti-imperialism or an Islamic-oriented desire for social transformation, and it also ignores the durability of the appeal over the final decades of the twentieth century.

An alternative view, suggested by the analysis in this book, is that the Islamic community is entering a new phase, not the end, of its history. It is possible to see the current resurgence as a continuation of basic themes, even though those themes may be expressed in new ways. To ignore religious motivations and to concentrate only on the economic drives or secularized political motives is to limit unnecessarily the scope of our understanding. In the broader perspective of Islamic history, the dynamic vitality of the faith has assumed a variety of forms as historical conditions have changed. Any examination of Islam in the contemporary world must take that past experience into account if the present is to be adequately understood. Part of the visible Muslim resurgence is putting modern sentiments into Islamic garb, but the Islamic resurgence also involves the creation of new and effective forms for the continuing vitality of the Islamic message.

Three Dimensional Approach

If these new forms are to be discerned, three dimensions of the Islamic experience in the modern world must be examined. It is, of course, important to study the specific individuals and groups involved in the resurgence. Local conditions vary and every movement is in some ways unique. It is important to understand the specific conditions out of which particular groups emerged rather than simply view them as examples of some abstract model. At the same time, if these experiences are simply viewed in isolation, their broader significance in world history can be missed and even their specific aspects will be misunderstood if they are separated from the broader patterns and experiences of which they are a part.

The need for additional analytical dimensions becomes clear when one seeks to define the basic nature of the movements and the significance of the issues involved. Islamic activist movements do not occur in isolation from the rest of the world; instead, they are a part of the broader patterns of modern global interactions. A second important dimension, in addition to the specifically local, is the relationship of the various Islamic movements to the basic dynamics of modern world history. How that relationship is interpreted will depend upon the perspective of the analyst. The Islamic resurgence has been described by some as a part of the changing relationships among various regions in the world system of capitalism created by the emergence of an industrial society in the West. Others see the resurgence in the context of the changing natures of political legitimacy and social authority, while still others interpret it as a theological and social reaction to the implications that modern ideas and institutions have for traditional societies. The common factor in the many different possible approaches is the interaction of the Islamic tradition with the ideas and institutions of modern society. In this dimension, the major theme is the response of Islam to modernization and development.

Even this broader dimension may miss key elements that are involved in the contemporary Islamic experience. By concentrating on the impact of modernization, analysts sometimes attempt to fit the Islamic experience into a model that is based on the experience of Western society rather than Islamic society. For example, it is sometimes noted that Islam has not experienced a major change similar to the Protestant Reformation in Europe, and some feel that such a change is needed if Islam is to adapt successfully to the challenge of modernity. Such a view is thought provoking, but it often ignores the fundamental differences between the structures of Western and Islamic societies. The separation of church and state and secularization may be essential aspects of modernization in the West, but it is difficult to translate the meaning of these issues into Islamic society, in which religious institutionalization has not involved the formal structure of a "church."

The necessary third dimension to be examined, therefore, is Islam itself. Islamic revival is not unique to the modern era, and throughout its history the Islamic community has faced the challenge of changing conditions. For instance, militant activism has been one feature of the Islamic resurgence. Activist Islamic groups in the twentieth century can be seen as having underlying similarities because they are responding to issues of modernization, but they also can be seen as a part of a continuing Muslim tradition. They must be viewed in their Islamic as well as their modern context. The forms the Islamic experience has taken maintain a continuity that spans the gap between premodern and modern; consequently, by recognizing the Islamic dimension, one stands a better chance of avoiding the pitfalls of using only a modernization model as the basis for analysis.

All three dimensions are important, and they form the basic framework for the analysis in this book. Islam in the modern era is seen as the interaction of the specific aims and goals of individuals and groups, which are affected by particular local conditions, with the factors of the dynamics of modern change and the continuity of the Islamic experience.

The Islamic Dimension: Historical Foundations

The history of the Islamic community is a dynamic part of the Islamic experience. The early and continuing success of Islam provided a confirmation for Muslims of the message of the revelation, and the starting point for an understanding of Islam in the modern world must be the historical experience of the *ummah* (the Muslim community). The long interaction between changing conditions and the permanently established Quranic message has set patterns and ideals, and an analysis of the continuing effectiveness of that interaction is a necessary foundation for an understanding of Islam in the contemporary world.

The Islamic dimension involves the complex and rich heritage of the Islamic community. There are many significant elements which can be viewed in terms of three general themes: the historical development of the community, the common elements of the continuity of the Islamic experience, and the basic elements of diversity within the Islamic community.

The Islamic Community in History

The heart of the Islamic faith is the belief in one God who is directly involved in the affairs of humanity. God is seen as requiring submission to His will and as having made that will known to humanity through revelations to a series of prophets. For Muslims, the final and complete form of those revelations was given to the Prophet Muhammad in the seventh century. It is carefully recorded in the Quran and is the foundation of Islam. Muslims, then, are those people who accept the unique oneness of God and recognize that Muhammad was the messenger of God.

This simple foundation for faith and experience has significance for all aspects of life. The revelation did not just define a creed or a set of beliefs; it set forth the basic blueprint by which humanity should live. In this way, the Quran is the foundation for the ideal society, which Muslims believe will result from submission to God and His will. To be a Muslim is not simply a matter of individual belief; it means participating in the effort to implement God's will on earth. As one modern Muslim explains it, "Islam teaches not only that the realization of the good is possible in this world but that to bring it about here and now is precisely the duty of every man and woman."[2] In the broadest sense, the Islamic community is that community which works to implement God's will as defined in the Quran here on earth in the contexts of history and society.

The experience of the Muslim community is a key part of the Islamic message. The foundation for the Islamic awareness of historical experience is set in the Quran itself, as it "lays great emphasis on the fact that the process of history is not neutral in respect of nations and communities for it says clearly, 'God is on the side of those who fear Him and do good.'"[3] The success or failure of actual communities of Muslims becomes a major concern, with political structures, economic practices, and social customs all being relevant to the historic vocation of faithful Muslims. However, throughout Islamic history, there have been disagreements over the way God's will is to be implemented. These disagreements are the basis for a variety of styles and modes of Islamic experience, and they provide a starting point for understanding the dynamics of Islamic history.

Muhammad and His Community

The Muslim community began during the lifetime of the Prophet Muhammad, and by the time of his death in 632, the basic principles had been established. "The Muslim Community as a fabric of society, with its own principles of internal solidarity, was brought into being under his own hands even though it underwent further important developments later."[4] The Muslim community as it emerged during the life of the Prophet became a model for later Muslims as they attempted to live up to the commands of God and to create a society in accord with revelation.

The early community is not simply an utopian creation of later imagination. It was a functioning, real community, however much subsequent generations may have idealized it. In its actual experience, the community set the patterns that have guided the habits and customs of later Muslims. These patterns have provided an important element of continuity over the centuries of Islamic experience.

The keystone of the new human community in the seventh century was the Prophet. Underlying similarities in leadership styles within the Muslim world down to the present "can be traced to the days of the Prophet Muhammad, himself the model par excellence of political leadership."[5] In Muhammad, there was the distinctive unification of political, social, and religious concerns that characterizes the Islamic tradition.

Muhammad was born in Mecca, a commercial and religious center in the western Arabian Peninsula. When he was about forty, he began to have religious experiences, which took the form of visions and revelations from God for the guidance of humanity. The message preached by Muhammad on the basis of these revelations had direct bearing on the social and personal conditions of the time. In a sanctuary center of tribal polytheistic cults, he preached that there are no other gods than the one God, and in a city dominated by wealthy merchants, he preached social responsibility toward the poor and underprivileged, warning the people of the coming Day of Judgment. He gathered a small group of believers but faced great opposition from most of the people of Mecca.

After a period of persecution, Muhammad and his fellow believers moved to Yathrib, an oasis community north of Mecca. He was invited to come and be the arbitrator among the local tribes and a new community was created under his leadership. The nature of the community of believers changed from being a persecuted minority to being a self-governing community. Yathrib became known as "the city" of the Prophet or Medina, and the move from Mecca in 622 is marked by Muslims as the beginning date in the Islamic calendar. By Muhammad's death in 632 even his old enemies in Mecca had submitted to his leadership and the Muslim community included much of the Arabian Peninsula.

Muhammad personally set critical patterns of adherence to Islam. He was a religious leader and was also the major coordinator of political, economic, and military affairs. He showed a tenacious adherence to the revelation of God but, at the same time, was flexible in dealing with new conditions. His personal piety emphasized the individual's obligations in the faith while his strong sense of group interaction reinforced the sense of community unity. His conservatism is exemplified in his willingness to accept existing symbols and customs, like the pilgrimage to Mecca, if they could be understood within the framework of the revelation he received.

Soon after Muhammad's death the records of the revelations were collected and put in a standardized form. That collection, the Quran, became the fundamental source of guidance for Muslims. In addition, Muslims look to the sayings and deeds of the Prophet for guidance. Accounts of his words and actions, called *hadiths*, were gradually brought together into great collections. Although there was disagreement over the validity of particular *hadiths*, the body of the Traditions was accepted as providing an accurate picture of the general behavior pattern or Sunnah of the Prophet. In this way, the Quran and the Traditions became the basic guides for Muslims through the centuries.

The Community of the Caliphs

The first great issue faced by Muslims after Muhammad's death was defining the nature of the continuing leadership for the community. Apparently, most Muslims did not feel that the Prophet had designated a successor and, after some debate, accepted Abu Bakr, a respected early believer and a father-in-law of the Prophet, as the *khalifah* ("successor"; the term is usually rendered as "caliph" in English usage). The caliph was not regarded as a prophet but combined political, social, and military leadership with religious prestige, thus continuing the general pattern set by Muhammad.

In the first three decades after Muhammad's death, the community expanded rapidly. The armies of the community defeated the two great empires of the time in the Middle East—the Sasanid Empire, heir to the Persian imperial tradition, and the Byzantine Empire, successor to the Roman Empire in the eastern Mediterranean. In the process the small city-state was transformed into a great world empire stretching from central Asia to north Africa. The caliphs adapted the administrative structures of the earlier empires but never lost sight of the fact that they were the leaders of a community which was bound by the message of the Quran and the actions of the Prophet.

Tensions created by the rapid expansion and the transformation of the community resulted in the first civil war within Islam. The third caliph, Uthman, was killed in Medina by mutinous troops in 656 and Ali, a cousin and son-in-law of Muhammad, was named caliph by the people in Medina. Ali had been an early believer with a special reputation for bravery and piety. In addition, Ali had the distinction of being the father of Muhammad's only grandsons, Hasan and Husayn. As caliph, Ali faced the opposition of the family of Uthman, the Umayyads, and the first civil war became a conflict between the "Party of Ali" (or the Shi'at Ali) and the supporters of the Umayyads. In the minds of later Muslim interpreters, the conflict has been as the struggle between differing views of the nature of the Islamic community. For the Shi'a (the supporters of Ali), Ali represents the ideal of a community led by a divinely guided leader, drawn from the family and direct descendants of the Prophet. Mu'awiyah, in contrast, was the epitome of the practical realist who would compromise for the sake of the unity of the community.

In addition, Ali as caliph faced other opposition. Some came from other companions of the Prophet, who wanted to continue the idea of an elective caliphate and eventually, but grudgingly backed the Umayyads after their own army was defeated by Ali. A part of Ali's own army revolted against him when he started to negotiate with the Umayyads and they withdrew from his army. They are called the Kharijites, or "those who went out," and they demanded an absolute adherence to a strict interpretation of the message. They said that anyone who was an absolute follower of the will of God could be caliph, regardless of his status or ancestry. That concept challenged the legitimacy of the Shi'a, the oligarchy of the old companions and emerging learned establishment, and the pragmatism of the Umayyads. For centuries, Kharijism provided an inspiration for revolt against virtually every Muslim government.

Ultimately the Umayyads won the war and created an effective imperial organization. The majority of Muslims did not follow either the radicalism of the Kharijites or the legitimacy of the Shi'a. Instead, the majority position, which came to be called Sunni Islam, accepted the customary tradition, practice, and consensus (the *sunnah*) of the early community as being itself guided by God. In this first conflict and definition of positions, one can see the beginnings of the basic styles or modes of Islamic experience: the pragmatic adapters, the conservatives, the fundamentalists, and those who emphasize personal spiritual power.

The first civil war was only a brief pause in the dynamic growth of the Islamic community. Under the Umayyads a vast imperial organization was created with the caliph at the center. The Umayyads faced many challenges and were finally overthrown by the Abbasids in the middle of the eighth century, but this change of caliphal dynasties did not stop the continued expansion and development of the Islamic community. The period of the great caliphates of the Umayyads and the Abbasids was the time of the great flowering of medieval Islamic civilization. The ideal of political unity under the caliph was maintained and closely approximated historical reality. The processes of defining the Islamic tradition and absorbing many cultural elements created the dynamic sociocultural synthesis of Islamic civilization. This era saw the formalization of the great structure of Islamic law (the *shari'ah*), the development of the Islamic philosophical tradition, and the general agreement on the content of the Traditions of the Prophet.

The political unity of the Abbasid caliphate began to crumble by the middle of the tenth century. The empire may have been too large to maintain for long with the available technology. The contradiction between a hierarchically organized imperial structure and the more egalitarian message of the Islamic revelation may also have been a factor. The caliphate was no longer the sole focus of Muslim loyalty. There was now the whole emerging vision of an Islamically based social order with a system of law, philosophy, and personal piety that could function without the direction of an imperial leader. The core group of the community was no longer the group around the caliph, it was the emerging social grouping of those learned in Islamic knowledge, called the *ulama* ("learned people"), and other pious articulaters of the Islamic message.

The Abbasid caliphate continued, fulfilling a generally symbolic role, until the Mongol destruction of their capital, Baghdad, in 1258, but effective leadership in military and political affairs was taken over by military commanders, called sultans. The political system of the Muslim community was gradually transformed from the formal unity of the early caliphate to the political fragmentation of the rule by regional military commanders. Although the political unity of the Abbasid caliphate crumbled, the imperial experience reinforced the enduring feeling of the essential unity of the Islamic community and the importance of the social and political dimensions of the revelation.

The New Islamic Society of the Sultans

The new Islamic society, which emerged in the era of the sultanates, had a number of distinctive features. For all practical purposes, the state passed into the hands of the strongest military commanders. Between the tenth and the fifteenth centuries, a bewildering array of military states emerged. Some were large and others were little more than small garrisoned city-states. Some were built around adherence to Shiʿite Islam, but most ruled under the banner of Sunni Islam. The legacy of this period is a tradition of the firm control of state structures by pragmatic military commanders. The state was not, however, a secular institution; it was subordinate to the ideals of the Islamic faith and part of a broader sense of Islamic community involving a cosmopolitan social order that transcended the boundaries of any particular state.

The development of this cosmopolitan Islamic social order involved the emergence of important groupings and institutions not directly tied to the state. The ulama assumed an increasingly influential position as a professional class within the community. There is no specially ordained clergy in Islam, but the learned people have a distinctive position on the basis of their knowledge. The formalization of Islamic law standardized the Islamic learning that identified the ulama, but the structure of the law was not monolithic. In the Sunni tradition, four systems of legal thought—Hanafi, Maliki, Shafiʿi, and Hanbali—were recognized as valid. During the sultanate period, special educational institutions (*madrasahs*) became focal points for the ulama. Scholars traveling from school to school and from region to region provided a cosmopolitan sense of unity. A scholar like Abu Abdallah ibn Battuta in the fourteenth century could travel through many different states from west Africa to southeast Asia and still maintain a "consciousness . . . of the entire Dar al-Islam [House of Islam] as a social reality."[6]

A second important social organization is related to the development of the piety and religious practices of the masses. In the early days of Islam, there were mystics who had lived reclusive lives of piety and asceticism. The tradition of personalized, mystic piety, which is called Sufism, gradually developed a theological-philosophical structure of thought. At first, most ulama were suspicious of Sufism but the teachings of Abu Hamid al-Ghazali (d. 1111) integrated Sufism into mainstream Sunni thought. This was followed by the articulation of a full-scale elaboration of Sufi theology along monistic or pantheistic lines by Muhyi al-Din Ibn al-Arabi (d. 1240).

Sufi social organizations, called *tariqahs*, began as informal groups of disciples gathered around particularly famous Sufi guides. By the twelfth century, these groups became more formally organized, and *tariqahs* became large-scale, popular associations based on pious devotional traditions. There was no central organization for all *tariqahs*, but many individual orders, like the Qadiriyyah, spread throughout the Islamic world. Like the networks of schools and traveling scholars, the *tariqahs* provided a means of integration and identity that transcended the boundaries of the separate military states and helped to give a cosmopolitan structure to the transcontinental social order of Islam.

The evolution of the Islamic social order emphasized the ideal of a community that is integrated as a whole through personalized associations. Although there were rich and poor, leaders and followers, elites and masses, the social groupings did not create entities (like class, church, or state) that stood "between the individual and the community of the faithful" as a whole.[7] The sense of belonging to the *ummah* became a central feeling, and for the Sunni majority, that sense had a higher claim than loyalty to a particular state. That tradition of social order has helped to shape modern sociopolitical development in the Islamic world.

Islamic Dynamism in the Sixteenth and Seventeenth Centuries

The development of the new cosmopolitan social order was accompanied by dramatic expansion so that by the end of the fifteenth century the world of Islam had doubled in size since the days of the Umayyads. The global Islamic community experienced a brilliant political and cultural florescence in the sixteenth and seventeenth centuries, the most visible aspect of which was a broad band of militarily strong, wealthy, and expansive imperial systems. The largest of these states have been called "gunpowder empires" because they were the product of harnessing gunpowder technology for military and political goals. That technology involved a transformation of government that "led to the rise of central governments and the decline of feudal lords . . . The states that successfully made the transition to the gunpowder age were those that strengthened their administrative and commercial classes at the expense of the landowning aristocracy."[8] The special structure of the new Islamic society initially aided that transition since the landowning aristocracy had less power in the sultanate system of rule.

The largest of the gunpowder sultanates were the Ottoman Empire in the Mediterranean region, the Safavid state in Iran, and the Moghul Empire of

India. However, the network of Islamic states spread from Philippines and southeast Asia to the city-states of the east African coasts and the large states of central and west Africa, like the Songhai Empire. Coping with the diversity of peoples and cultures that had become part of the Islamic world set the tone for this era. Each region had its own distinctive ways of dealing with sociocultural pluralism, but the overall sense of Islamic community provided a common foundation. The two alternative approaches were a tolerant openness and a more strict exclusivism. During the sixteenth and seventeenth centuries, both approaches were used but there was a gradual shift in emphasis. The expansion and early consolidation of the great states were associated with a more tolerant acceptance of diversity. By the end of the seventeenth century, there was a reaction to the compromises that were involved, and the dominant mood began to shift in the direction of greater exclusivism.

This shift can be seen in the development of the different states. Following the Ottoman conquest of Constantinople in 1453, Sultan Mehmet II gave special recognition to the patriarch of the Greek Orthodox Church, giving him civil as well as religious authority over Orthodox Christian subjects of the empire. In this way, the *millets* or religious communities began to be organized in a "system of autonomous self-government under religious leaders" that eventually was extended to all major non-Muslim groups in the empire.[9] There was a similar openness among Muslim in the empire. Popular Sufi orders allowed practices that were not strictly Islamic but these orders were usually suppressed only if they engaged in antigovernmental activities. Within the schools of the ulama, a wide range of intellectual subjects was covered, thus following "the most broadminded traditions of sunni Islam."[10]

During the sixteenth century, an effort was made to organize and codify the system more formally. Suleyman I, the great sultan of the century, centralized the system while the ulama, fearing that the openness was diluting the Islamic message, began to limit intellectual speculation in the schools. On the popular level, heterodox religious groups came under tighter controls both out of a desire to purify popular practice and to defend the empire from the threat of internal subversion in the face of the growing Shi'ite power of the Safavid state in Iran.

In the Ottoman experience, the continuing interaction of the different styles of Islam is visible. The pragmatic adaptationists created new ways of action, the conservatives preserved the gains that had been made in the past, and the fundamentalists kept the responses to change within the bounds of what was clearly Islamic. In the centuries of great dynamism, there was a gradual shift in emphasis from the flexibility of the early days to a more conservative and sometimes fundamentalist vision of the Ottoman Empire as the greatest Sunni state.

The same general dynamic is visible elsewhere in the Islamic world. The sixteenth century was a time of great Islamic expansion in India under the Moghul sultans. Babur, a central Asian military adventurer, defeated the medieval sultanates of northern India, partly by using gunpowder technology. His grandson, Akbar, who became emperor in 1556, built an effective administrative structure, which combined the diverse elements within his empire. The majority of the population in the new empire was non-Muslim, and Akbar's state was built on a tolerant acceptance of religious diversity. Akbar even attempted to create an eclectic court religion, which would combine the teachings of the major religious traditions of his subjects. This effort paralleled a popular religious trend that worked within the framework of local devotional practice and Sufi pantheism to combine Hindu and Muslim ideas and practices.

Some Muslims saw these developments as a threat to the basic Islamic message and the ability to create a truly Islamic social order. Some ulama and other teachers responded in a variety of ways. One of the most important responses was the activism of the leaders of a noncompromising *tariqah*, the Naqshbandiyyah. A major figure in this *tariqah*'s revivalism was Ahmad Sirhindi (1564–1624), who lived at the end of the tenth century of Islamic history and became known as the Renewer (*Mujaddid*) of the second thousand years. From its base in India, the Naqshbandiyyah revivalist spirit spread throughout much of the Islamic world, and it may have played a role in inspiring revivalist feelings in Ottoman areas.

The reaction against the eclecticism of Akbar and the syncretism of the popular devotional movements spread to the highest levels of government. Sultan Aurangzeb (1618–1707) made the exclusivist spirit the basis for Moghul imperial policy. During his reign, the transition from a dominant spirit of accommodation to a fundamentalist spirit reached a climax.

This transition took a variety of forms throughout the Islamic world. In the far west of the Islamic world, there was the transition from the relatively open, cosmopolitian court of the Moroccan sultan Ahmad al-Mansur (r. 1578–1603) to the more fundamentalist attitudes of Moroccan rulers like Muhammad ibn Abdallah (r. 1757–1790) and Mawlay Suleyman (r. 1792–1822). At the other end of the Islamic world, in the East Indies, the relatively syncretist mood of southeast Asian Sufism was challenged by more strict teachers like Abd al-Ra'uf al-Sinkili (d. after 1693).[11]

The nature of the great flourishing of Islam during the sixteenth and seventeenth centuries was not radical innovation, nor were the old traditions ultimately questioned. Marshall G. S. Hodgson suggests that "it was a florescence within established lines of tradition, rather perfecting than launching them. . . . Perhaps we may say that this florescence was not one of *origination* . . . but rather one of *culmination* in a culture already long mature."[12] In the context of the continuing visible success of the Islamic community, there was little need to question the basic traditions.

Common Themes and Diverse Interpretations

Islam is a distinctively identifiable part of world history, but it is not monolithic. While the most visible aspect of the Islamic dimension is the experience of the Sunni-dominated community, as articulated by the political and cultural elites, it is not the totality of the experience of Muslims. Within the broad framework of the shared basic Islamic message, there is a luxuriant diversity. Part of the dynamism of the Islamic experience has been the continuous interaction between common themes and diverse interpretations and applications of those themes.

Common Themes

All Muslims, regardless of their particular interpretations, accept certain common elements of faith. The first of these is symbolized in the acceptance of the statement that "there is no god but the one God." However it may be defined, Islam means submission to the divine, and that principle is expressed in a clear monotheism.

The full statement of Islamic belief that is accepted by all Muslims adds the affirmation, "and Muhammad is the messenger of the one God." This addition has two important corollaries. It means that God's revelation through Muhammad is the real word of God and that Muhammad is in some ways a significant person in the history of the world.

This revelation in its exact words is believed to be recorded in the Quran. Although there are diverse interpretations, there are no disagreements over the wording of the Quran. The Quran is the crucial sign of the revelation. In the revelation, Muhammad is instructed to say, "Even if humanity and the spiritual forces joined together, aiding each other, in order to produce something like this recitation [the Quran], they would not produce anything like it."[13]

The experience of the Quran surrounds Muslims in a variety of ways. Its recitation is a common sound in the Islamic world; it is visually present in the decoration of buildings; and its phrases are a part of the long literary tradition. Indeed, its very syntax and grammar are the basis for linguistic study and usage. The Quran overrides sectarian and geographic divergences and is a vital element in the continuity of Islamic history.

The second corollary involves the definition of Muhammad's role. The revelation is in the word, not specifically in the person of the Prophet. The tone is set in the Quran by the statement: "And what is Muhammad, except simply a messenger? Before him there have been other messengers who have passed away."[14] The role of the messenger is, however, crucial when the message is from God. As a modern Arab writer notes, "recourse to testimony is one, if not the only, foundation of the Muslim religion; for the word of God is transmitted by a witness, the veracious Prophet."[15] Without a full acceptance of the integrity of Muhammad, the validity of the Quran would be suspect. The continuing strength and power of this position could be seen in the near universal condemnation by Muslims of the novel by Salman Rushdie, *The Satanic Verses,* in 1989, because the novel was seen as questioning the integrity of the Prophet and the authenticity of the Quran.[16]

Another common theme is the idea of unity (*tawhid*), which, on the most general level, is the principle of the unitary nature or oneness of God. In specific terms, there may be disagreement over the implications of *tawhid,* but Muslims across a full spectrum of views see the principle as a key one in terms of human life. A modern Shi'i philsopher states, "To the Muslim, the idea of unity does not just mean the assertion that there is only one God sitting in heaven instead of two or three . . . On the social plane Unity expresses itself in the integration of human society."[17] Similarly, a major Sunni fundamentalist thinker says that "*Tawhid* is that which gives Islamic civilization its identity, which binds all its constituents together and thus makes of them an integral, organic body which we call civilization."[18]

These common themes emphasize the moral and ethical dimensions of the revelation. Muslims are to build and work in a moral, divinely guided community, and the *ummah* (the Islamic "community") is an important focus of Muslim identity and loyalty. Although there are disagreements over specific aspects of the nature of the community, the moral dimension of Islam and the critical importance of the community of believers are common themes within the Islamic tradition.

The oneness of God, the Quran, the significance of Muhammad, and the community are basic elements in the continuity and unity of the Islamic dimension. Different perceptions of these elements and diverse historical experiences create varying manifestations of Islam. However, this diversity is more often expressed in local variations and overlapping interpretations than in formal schisms and sectarian distinctions.

Diversity Within the Sunni Tradition

The ideals and organizations of the majority of Muslims fit within the broad patterns of Sunni Islam. However, within these boundaries there is great scope for diversity of approach and emphasis. Even on the basic question of the meaning of the oneness of God, differing aspects of the divine are emphasized by different Sunni groups. Two poles of the interpretive spectrum are emphasis on the immanence of God and emphasis on God's transcendence. Although no Muslim loses all sense of either aspect of God, there is a tendency to focus on one or the other. The Sufi traditions concentrate on the closeness of God to the individual believer and the legalistic ulama place greater weight on divine transcendence. Within the Sunni community, when Sufism has moved in the direction of a more overt pantheism, there has been resistance, just as extreme legalism has often aroused a more mystical response. A similar diversity can be seen in approaches to Quranic interpretation.

The life of Muhammad has received great attention in the Sunni tradition. Major efforts to collect the Traditions of the Prophet culminated in the ninth century when six great collections of *hadith*s were compiled and came to be accepted as the standard body of the Traditions. However, these collections are not canonical and their authority comes from a flexible consensus in the community rather than an official institutional validation.

The information provided by the records of the early community is the basis for the Sunni definition of the just society. The early community is accepted by Sunni Muslims as being a special example of the way the *ummah* should be, and later Sunni revivalists have modeled their actions on those of the *salaf* ("pious ancestors"). This community provides a relatively concrete basis for the ideal even though great diversity in interpreting the experience is possible.

Sunni Muslims are in full agreement that the message of unity provides the foundation for social integration and that this means that the legal basis for society is Islam. However, as the Islamic legal system evolved, a number of accepted schools emerged rather than one single, authoritative statement of the law. By the time of the rule by sultans, four Sunni schools of law (*madhhab*s) had come to be accepted as equally authoritative, despite the disagreements among them. These schools are not separate "sects" or "denominations," but, rather, emphasize different moods and techniques of law and interpretation.

Each school starts from the bases of the Quran and the Traditions. The Hanafi school traces its development back to Abu Hanifa (d. 767), and gives some emphasis to personal reasoning and free judgment in legal interpretation. Because of its relative flexibility, it became the school of a number of major states and was officially recognized by the Ottoman and Moghul rulers. It is thus widespread in the central and eastern parts of the Islamic world. The Maliki school, which traces back to Malik ibn Anas (d. 795), places greater stress on using the Traditions as a basis for legal interpretation and is more conservative in mood. It became the dominant school in much of Islamic Africa. Muhammad al-Shafiʿi (d. 820), the founder of the Shafiʿi

school, developed a more formal science of jurisprudence, which characterizes his school, by combining a strict usage of Traditions with a formal
methodology of analogical analysis. This school became important in the
Arabic-speaking areas of the eastern Mediterranean. The fourth school is the
Hanbali. It is the most strict in its insistence upon an adherence to the specific
terms of the Quran and the Traditions, and it allows very little scope for individual reasoning or analogy. This school has often been associated with fundamentalism and is currently dominant in Saudi Arabia. The law schools reflect
the fact that Sunni Islam is not monolithic. It is the product of diversity developing within the framework of the great common themes of Islam.

The Special Case of Shiʿism

The major division within Islam is between the Sunnis and the Shiʿites. At
the heart of the split is disagreement over the nature of the *ummah* and the
full meaning of the revelation. The Sunni majority tradition has the authority
of being confirmed by the historical experience of the community, while the
Shiʿi Islamic tradition has often been at odds with the actual historical experience. The Shiʿi tradition developed as an alternative vision and, in the days
of the caliphs, presented a basis for opposition to the emerging Sunni political and social establishments. When Abbasid unity crumbled in the tenth
century, successful Shiʿi movements built the large Fatimid empire in Egypt
and north Africa and a number of smaller states. However, the firm establishment of the sultanate system was accompanied by a reassertion of Sunni
dominance in most of the Islamic world.

In the framework of the great common themes, the Shiʿites tend to emphasize the immanent aspects of the divine, especially in terms of leadership
for the community as being centered in the figure of the Imam. In the Shiʿite
view, Muhammad *did* designate a successor and that person was Ali. The
validity of the succession of the first three caliphs was denied, and the community is believed to have been in error. The importance of a designated
successor or Imam was explained in terms of the continuing human need for
guidance in understanding and applying the revelation. "The interpretation
of the divine revelation by the Imam . . . was regarded as the right guidance
needed by the people at all times."[19]

For most Shiʿites, there was a line of twelve Imams who provided this
guidance, even though none of the Imams gained significant political power.
In the tenth century, this "Twelve-Imam Shiʿism," or Imami Shiʿism believes that the twelfth Imam in the line was taken into divinely sheltered
seclusion and will return to visible leadership of humanity at some future
date as a Mahdi or messianic guide.

Diversity within Shi'ism comes over the identification of the authority of specific Imams. One group associates itself with Zayd ibn Ali, who led a revolt in 740. Among the Zaydi Shi'ites, the Imam is any member of the house of the Prophet who rises against the illegitimate rulers of an age. This tradition became established in Yemen. Another group takes as its starting point the claim of a person called Isma'il to be the legitimate seventh Imam. The Isma'ilis maintained a more revolutionary mode as the majority of the Shi'ites became more politically passive in later Abbasid times.

Significant numbers of Imami Shi'ites are in Syria, Lebanon, and Iraq, and they are the dominant majority in Iran. This dominance began when the Safavid state established Imami Shi'ism as the official religion of the Iranian state in the sixteenth century. By Safavid times, Imami basic positions had become carefully articulated. The Ja'fari school of law, whose origins are identified with the sixth Imam, Ja'far al-Sadiq, provides the basic structure for jurisprudence and differs little from the Sunni schools except in the issue of the Imamate and the choice of authentic traditions. In the area of political theory and community guidance, it was clear that "pending the return of the Hidden Imam, the possibility of absolute claim to political power (*qudra*) and authority (*wilaya*) resembling that of the Imam himself was ruled out."[20] In this situation, Imami Shi'ites accepted the idea that there are religious teachers whose piety and knowledge render them capable of independent interpretive judgment in matters of faith. These people are called *mujtahid*s, that is, people who can exercise *ijtihad* ("independent judgment"). It came to be accepted that in the absence of the Imam, people needed to follow the guidance of a living *mujtahid*.

Developments in the Safavid state reflect the broader trends of the time in the Islamic world. Early Safavid rulers created a relatively flexible state system, culminating with the rule of Shah Abbas (r. 1587–1629). However, by the mid-seventeenth century, the Shi'i ulama were asserting their own position as guides for the community and at the end of the century one of the major *mujtahid*s, Muhammad Baqir al-Majlisi, compiled a comprehensive exposition of Imami Shi'ism in strict and uncompromising terms. In the following years, as the Safavid state itself collapsed, the religious scene was dominated by a tension between two schools of thought: the Usuli, which utilized a more flexible methodology that relied on reasoned opinion and analogy, and the Akhbari, which was more fundamentalist in tone.

Diversity Through Popular Practice

The vibrant diversity of Islamic experience is not confined to the realms of the ulama and the political elites. Underlying the visible movements of thought and social structure is the general faith of the masses. The application of the great common themes in daily life is influenced strongly by local customs and traditions. There is a lively interaction in Islamic history between the cosmopolitan literate tradition and the "popular religion" of the masses. "Popular Islam" is often defined in negative terms as Islamic experience that has been "diluted" by non-Islamic practices. Traditionally strict ulama as well as modern intellectuals tend to condemn what they see as magical practices and superstitions.

One dimension of popular faith is the role of specially respected local holy men. In all of the areas which became part of the Islamic world, there were customs built around the local religious leader, and the functions performed by those leaders were taken over by Muslim guides as the communities converted to Islam. Just as there are distinctive differences between the shamans of central Asia and the village spiritual leaders in Africa, local Muslim leadership also presents a picture of diversity. In general terms these figures came to be explained in Islamic terms as *walis*, or individuals who are especially close to God.

In popular faith the immanent aspects of God tend to be stressed, and explanations tended to take Sufi forms. As a result, there was frequently a blending of Sufi teachings, tariqah structures, and local devotional practices and organizations. Popular tariqahs often became the vehicles for flexible adaptation to local conditions and helped to bring new peoples into the Islamic community. However, because of this openness, fundamentalist movements often opposed the popular practices of the Sufi groups in their efforts to "purify" religious life.

A second major theme in popular religion is continuing messianic expectations. Although the achievements of the Islamic community have been great, life for the average peasant, worker, or nomad continues to be difficult. The revelation is seen by them as a promise for a better future, a world of justice without oppression. Islam was and is a vehicle for the expression of these hopes. It is widely accepted that at the end of the current age, God will send a rightly guided leader, the Mahdi, "who will fill the world with justice, as it had been filled with injustice."[21]

The doctrine of the coming of the Mahdi is most fully developed in Shiʿi teachings. However, despite reservations on the part of the Sunni ulama, the expectation of the Mahdi is also part of popular Sunni Islam. "It was, then, in the hearts of the Muslim multitude that the faith in the Mahdi found its resting place and support . . . The more, too, the Muslim masses have felt themselves oppressed . . . the more fervent has been their longing for this ultimate restorer of the true Islam and the conqueror of the whole world for Islam. And as the need for a Mahdi has been felt, the Mahdis have always appeared."[22] Militant Islamic activism, whether Sunni or Shi'i, has often taken the form of a Mahdist movement. Within Sunni Islam there has also developed a less apocalyptic vision or revival involving a renewer or *mujaddid* who is thought to be sent by God at the beginning of each century to bring new life to Muslims.

Popular Islam presents further elements of diversity within the Islamic community. The faith of the masses has been shaped by the broad, common themes of Islam and they have looked to the great leaders of the faith as well as their local leaders for guidance. At the same time, the vigor of popular faith has helped to maintain an awareness of the problems of daily life and the special visions of hope shaped by the expectations of the masses have influenced the thinking and practices of the intellectual and political elites.

Conclusion: Basic Styles of Action

In this complex array of great themes, elements of diversity, and different moods and approaches, it is helpful to look for common patterns or styles of approach and action among Muslims. Such patterns are, of course, constructs created by the viewer to aid in understanding the complexity of the Islamic experience, and yet they can help to bring some comprehensible order to the vast subject. One framework for organization which arises from this discussion of continuity and change, of common themes and diversity, is to note the different styles of social action in the broad Islamic experiences.

In the experiences of coping with change and maintaining continuity, it is possible to define four styles of action. Other approaches might see more or fewer styles, while still others might prefer to view the experiences in very different ways. In this discussion of continuity and change in the modern world, however, the organizing framework for the presentation will be to view the three dimensions of the Islamic experience as the context for four styles of Islamic action, as have already been seen in the premodern history of the Islamic community.

The first of these styles is the adaptationist, which represents a willingness to make adjustments to changing conditions in a pragmatic manner. This style is visible in the political realism of the early caliphs and sultans and is manifested in the intellectual traditions of those thinkers who adapted Greek philosophical traditions in explaining Islamic positions. The religious openness of Akbar in Moghul India and the flexibility of popular Sufi teachers are other examples of this style.

This adaptationist style opened the way for the great syntheses that have given dynamism and social power to the Islamic community. It made it possible for Muslims to cope with many great challenges, such as the tensions arising from the first conquests, the problems associated with the collapse of the political unity of the early caliphate, and the intellectual challenges of integrating new ideas into the basic framework of the Islamic revelation.

The success of Islam brought achievements that are worth preserving, which is the motivation behind the second style, the conservative. As a great synthesis emerged, much of the learned community hoped to preserve the gains that had been made. From the very beginning, the perfection of the revelation has been seen by Muslims as requiring a reserved attitude about change that is too rapid. In this style, a mistrust of innovation tends to be the keynote.

The efforts of the conservatives have served the Islamic community well in times of turmoil, and they have helped to keep the compromises of the adaptationists within the bounds of what has become accepted as Islamic. In the long run, the conservative style of action has avoided supporting stagnation of the community by gradually accepting new circumstances as they have become part of the established order to be preserved.

The third style is the fundamentalist. The scriptures of religions that accept the concept of recording divine revelations provide a basis for a permanent standard to use in judging existing conditions. In Islam, the Quran is this unchangeable standard, and the fundamentals of the faith as presented in the Quran have a universally accepted validity within the Islamic community. The fundamentalist style insists upon a rigorous adherence to the specific and general rules of the faith and presents a critique of existing conditions by calling for a return to the fundamentals of the faith. When additional elements are accepted as authoritative, they may also be included among the fundamentals. Thus, within Sunni Islam, the Sunnah of the Prophet, as defined by the *hadith* literature, is also used as a basis for evaluating Muslim practices, as are the collections of the traditions of Ali and the Imams within Shi'i Islam.

The distinction between the fundamentalist and conservative styles is important. Fundamentalists are unwilling to accept adaptations and are more often critics than defenders of existing conditions. They frequently are political activists, and they often are disturbing elements who upset social stability and oppose the conservative establishments of Muslim society.

The fundamentalist style serves as a corrective adjustment mechanism. In the context of change and adaptation, fundamentalists work to keep the basic Islamic message in full view of the community. When adjustments to local conditions or the adoption of new ideas and techniques threaten to obliterate the unique and authentically Islamic elements, fundamentalist pressure begins to build. In one sense, the mission of Islamic fundamentalism is to keep adjustments to change within the range of those options that are clearly Islamic.

The fourth style places emphasis on the more personal and individual aspects of Islam. Although all Muslims recognize the communal implications of the revelation, there is a style which tends to subordinate legal structures and communal institutions to the personal aspects of piety and leadership by charismatic, divinely guided individuals. The Shi'i concept of the Imamate and the popular belief in the Mahdi are broad political manifestations of this style, and it is also visible in the Sufi tradition of personal piety and the importance of the local spiritual guide. This style of action permeates the whole Islamic experience, and in a general sense, the resistance of the Islamic tradition to the creation of a formal church structure and an ordained clergy is a product of this individualized spirit.

These styles are not formal, separate movements within the Islamic community but represent orientations for action within the broader Islamic experience as a whole. In any specific group or individual, the styles are combined with varying degrees of emphasis. The identification of these styles is for the purpose of providing an analytical framework for understanding the complex dynamics of the Islamic experience.

The Islamic dimension of this study includes the historical experience of the community. In that history there is a dynamic interaction between the elements of continuity and change, including the interplay between the challenge of adapting to changing conditions and the steady adherence to to fundamentals of the faith. The way these elements interact is described by observing the various styles of Islamic action and response. The heritage of the Islamic community is the foundation of the modern history of Islam.

2

The Foundations of the Modern Experience

Revival and Reform in the Eighteenth Century

The eighteenth century is often viewed as a "dark age" of Islamic history, and descriptions focus on the disintegration of the great sultanate empires and a general sense of decline. This perception is influenced by a knowledge of the subsequent Islamic experience as the nineteenth century was a period of loss of control to Western imperial powers, and the perspective is defined by a series of assumptions that have been developed as a result of knowing the later history. It has been assumed that the Islamic viewpoint represented a "traditional" world view that inevitably clashed with modern ideas and was, also inevitably, defeated by them. The implicit question in many of these discussions is, Why was Islam unable to cope with the basic dynamics of modern history?

The final quarter of the twentieth century is a time when this historical interpretation needs to be reexamined. Clearly, in view of its continuing vitality, Islam has been able to achieve at least some significant success in coping with modern conditions. The old-fashioned Western imperialist could complacently state that Islam's "gradual decay cannot be arrested by any modern palliatives however skillfully they may be applied."[1] But that statement was made when there appeared to be no way to stop European expansion. In the days when modern Islamic thought could be relatively accurately described in terms of "the intellectual confusions and the paralyzing romanticism which cloud the minds of the modernists,"[2] the decline of Muslim vitality could be emphasized. However, the resurgence of Islam at the beginning of its fifteenth century requires not just different answers to the old questions, but a reformulation of the questions.

In the process of this reexamination, the history of Islam in the eighteenth century assumes a new significance. With the current status of Islam in mind, it is clear that the elements of continuity are stronger in the modern context than has been thought. The struggles related to Western politico-

24

military control and to the influence of Western ideas have obscured but have not eliminated the basic dynamics of Islamic continuity. It is now possible to speak of the emergence of a "posttraditional" Islamic society, a society that is not simply a transplanted version of modern Western society. In that emergence, the underlying Islamic experience has been shaped in some important ways by the history of Islam in the eighteenth century. The basic question is not, Why did Islam fail? because it has not "failed." Rather, the question is a more complex one: What are the elements of the Islamic experience that continue to have vitality and how have they developed in the context of the modern global experience?

General Eighteenth-Century Themes

Local conditions, modern issues, and the Islamic continuity provide the three dimensions of the history of the Muslim world in the eighteenth century. Within this framework, it is possible to identify the general themes of the Islamic experience. Primarily, those general themes have been defined by the interaction of Islamic and modern elements, and the specific forms have been shaped by particular local conditions. Three such themes are the decentralization of political control with a realignment of the major politico-economic elements, a reorientation of the Sufi tradition, and the emergence of revivalist movements that aimed at the socio-moral reconstruction of society.

Political and Economic Realignments

The sixteenth-century florescence produced the great sultanate empires, which had a relatively high degree of political centralization. By the eighteenth century, those large states were crumbling under a variety of pressures. Although local conditions differed, some common features in that decentralization process can be identified.

One factor is that the premodern, agrarian-based imperial systems tended to alternate between periods of strong centralized power and times of greater decentralization. This cycle was described in the Islamic context by a great Muslim writer, Ibn Khaldun (d. 1406). He noted that the vigor of the victorious conquerors and the social cohesion of their supporters tend, over time, to weaken as the fruits of their success come to be enjoyed. In each of the great sultanate empires, emerging vested-interest groups came into conflict over the control of the wealth and power of the state. As powerful groups consolidated their positions, they developed a resistance to change and reform, even when the state itself was clearly being weakened. In this way, influential sections of the elite became manifestly conservative, and the states were less able to cope with change. Effective power then shifted away from the centralized control of the sultans. Ibn Khaldun's analysis was in the minds of Ottoman observers and was used by them to interpret the Ottoman troubles at the beginning of the eighteenth century.

The economic aspects of the situation are now being studied more systematically. The Western challenge to Islamic society was only beginning and was not widely felt. Growing European power resulted in some defeats of Muslim forces, but it had not yet reached the stage of open domination and clear military superiority. However, the less immediately visible impact of the emerging European economic system was already beginning to have an influence. The economic structures associated with the sultanate empires were based on state control of the flow of capital within the society, and the ability of the merchant and commercial groups to accumulate large amounts of capital was limited by the state's imposition of market controls, customs levies, and price controls. In addition, interregional trade that crossed political boundaries tended to be primarily in nonessentials and luxury goods, the major consumers of which were the political elite.

The beginnings of the transformation of the European economy provided the Middle Eastern merchants and producers with new opportunities. New markets for basic goods like foodstuffs and cotton were created, and they were beyond the control of the sultanate governments. These markets were made more appealing by the higher prices offered by European purchasers. The Islamic governments attempted to limit, if not prohibit, the export of basic goods, but they were not successful. The contraband trade with Europe grew and provided a major flow of capital that was outside the control of the Islamic governments. One result was the encouragement of commercially oriented groups that were increasingly independent in economic terms. Local notables and provincial leaders benefited from this change, and their strength increased at the expense of the central government.

The process of a diffusion of power was visible within the central institutions themselves. In the sixteenth century, the dominant figure in most states had been the sultan, but by the eighteenth century, other officials were assuming greater prerogatives. A good example is that decision-making powers in the Ottoman Empire were assumed by officials like the grand viziers, the shaykhs al-Islam, and the palace eunuchs. Such officials resisted reforms that would again centralize power in the hands of the sultan, and thus they undermined the state's ability to cope with the other problems of decentralization.

Under these circumstances, one of the most visible trends in eighteenth-

century history was the emergence of regional, provincial, and local notables who had increasing degrees of independence or at least autonomy.
Although in many cases, nominal allegiance to the sultan was maintained,
power was being effectively decentralized, and the sultanate empires were
greatly weakened—in some cases, they disappeared. The balance of effective political and economic power in many areas was shifting away from
those groups that had been dominant in the early days of the sultanate
empires.

Reorientation of the Sufi Tradition

The second general theme of eighteenth-century Islamic history was a
reorientation of at least some elements of the Sufi tradition. This reorientation was manifested in two areas: a significant evolution in the Sufi theological and philosophical positions and a further development of the
organization of the *tariqah* and its function in society.

In intellectual terms, Sufism had become widely identified with the pantheistic style of theology expressed by Ibn al-Arabi. In this formulation, God
is seen as the only reality, and the Sufi path becomes a striving for absorption into that ultimate being. Other themes reflect Neoplatonic ideas of the
eternal word and light manifested through the prophets. Such a definition of
Islam emphasized the immanent aspects of the divine and tended to accept
the validity of any religious experience. In this way, Sufism provided a
theological foundation for open accommodation to other faiths and for syncretism. Although the *tariqah* leaders on the frontiers of Islam were not
often sophisticated Sufi philosophers, the symbolism and formulations of
this style of Sufism gave them a doctrinal basis for their own adaptable
eclecticism.

During the eighteenth century, the long dialogue between representatives
of this type of mystic thought and the more strict Sunni ulama gained new
momentum. In many areas, scholars worked to reinterpret the Ibn al-Arabi
tradition in less pantheistic terms, and commentators on his most famous
works gave greater emphasis to the transcendence of God. They restated the
goal of the Sufi path in terms of the individual being in harmony with the
spirit of the Prophet rather than losing individual identity by absorption into
the absolute being. It is possible to see a shift toward the more moderate
mysticism that had been defined by al-Ghazali in the twelfth century, which
was reflected by a revived interest in the writings of that teacher.

Although much of this intellectual activity still used themes found in Ibn
al-Arabi's writings, some teachers explicitly rejected his work. This rejection was not new in the Islamic world as the more rigorous fundamentalists

had usually been quite explicit in attacking positions held by Ibn al-Arabi. The great Hanbali scholar Ahmad ibn Taymiyyah had vigorously condemned that style of Sufism in Syria, and the Naqshbandiyyah revivalism in Moghul India had included a similar attack. During the eighteenth century, the most visible example of the rejection of Ibn al-Arabi was the Wahhabi teachings in the Arabian Peninsula, and the continuing strength of that rejection is reflected in the attempt by Egyptian fundamentalists in 1978–1979 to remove the books of Ibn al-Arabi from libraries and university curricula.

The eighteenth-century developments in the *tariqah* organization were complex. Affiliation with a *tariqah* means many different things. Literally, the term *tariqah* means "path" and refers to the devotional "path" of special exercises and litanies developed by a great Sufi teacher. Becoming a member of a Sufi order involves learning this devotional path from the teacher himself or from one of his disciples. As an organization, what is called a *tariqah* may be an informal group of individuals who share a respect for some particular teacher's devotional exercises, or it may be a more formally organized association with specially appointed leaders and administrators. Some *tariqah*s are identified with important families of religious teachers, and others are tied to particular social or economic groups.

Since the twelfth century, *tariqah*s have, from time to time, provided the organizational framework for a variety of social movements. By the time of the great sultanate empires, *tariqah* affiliation had become a mass phenomenon and most people had some type of tie to a Sufi brotherhood. Groupings of soldiers, artisans, and others were integrated into the broader Islamic community through *tariqah*-style affiliations. As those structures provide the potential for mobilizing large numbers of people, *tariqah*s were at times the basis for movements of revolt. The origins of the Safavids lie in a militant *tariqah*, and the foundations of the Murabitun and Muwahhidun movements, which established medieval states in North Africa, were organizations built around the leadership of holy teachers. The ulama reaction to Akbar's religious policy was organized through the Naqshbandiyyah Tariqah.

The Naqshbandiyyah in India may have been an influential prototype for the *tariqah* development in the eighteenth century. Most activist *tariqah*s had been relatively heterodox in terms of theology, but the Naqshbandiyyah Tariqah aimed at combating compromises of the faith. Increasingly, in a wide range of areas during the eighteenth century, better organized and more activist *tariqah*s along the lines of the Naqshbandiyyah Tariqah emerged. These new groups were vehicles for purification and revival rather than for adaptation and synthesis. These organizations thus reflected, in their activism, the reorientation of Sufi thought that was taking place. The more world-negating pantheism of medieval Sufism was being replaced by organizations in which "the *emphasis* had shifted more towards the positive issues of society, whether in political, moral or spiritual terms."[3]

In the eighteenth century, intellectual and organizational trends brought forth what has been called Neo-Sufism.[4] Building on the traditions of the earlier leaders like Ibn Taymiyyah and Ahmad Sirhindi, some *tariqah*s provided the framework for movements of purification and adherence to a rigorous interpretation of the Islamic tradition. Older syncretistic and possibly heterodox styles of Sufism did not disappear, but Neo-Sufism had become an important element in the Islamic world by the end of the eighteenth century.

Spirit of Socio-moral Reconstruction

During the florescence associated with the sultanate empires, the emphasis was on the adaptationist style of Islam, but, gradually, the other styles of action set limits on the compromises formulated by the adaptionist rulers and intellectuals. The changing historical circumstances of the seventeenth and eighteenth centuries provided opportunities for more conservative and more fundamentalist elements. Local conditions meant that the process was diverse, but there was a relatively widespread spirit of socio-moral reconstruction based on a more strict adherence to the Quran and the Sunnah of the Prophet.

The general conditions within the Islamic world helped to inspire this mood. The imperial sultanates had become less effectively organized, and military defeats, the growing ineffectiveness of administration, and economic difficulties presented a picture of degeneration that inspired some people to engage in reforming action. The general tolerance of a wide diversity of local customs and their apparent acceptance, even by the ulama, aroused indignation over what was seen as a dilution of Islam. The targets for criticism were the adaptationist practices of the rulers and Sufi groups.

On the positive side, the reforming spirit called for a moral reconstruction of society. The ideal was the early Islamic community, and the program offered was, with varying details, a return to Islam as it is defined by a literal interpretation of the Quran and the Sunnah of the Prophet. Some aspects of the Islamic tradition were emphasized and others rejected. The development of Neo-Sufism is one aspect of this picture. Similarly, the concentration on the life of the Prophet and the early community meant that the study of *hadith* literature was important. In the movements that emerged in the eighteenth century, there was an apparent coming together of *hadith* scholarship and Neo-Sufism, and the prominent teachers were both *muhaddith*s ("*hadith scholars*") and participants in the new style of Sufi thought—

one of the best examples being the major eighteenth-century Indian teacher, Shah Wali Allah. There was also a tendency to rely less on the authority of the great medieval teachers and to claim the right of independent judgment (*ijtihad*) in interpreting the fundamentals of the faith.

The eighteenth century was thus a time when there was a major revivalist effort within Islam, and the lines of that effort were similar to efforts in preceding periods. Although there was already some impact from the modernizing West, that was not the primary or most visible challenge that aroused the reforming spirit. Just before the time of European dominance, a reformist-revivalist tradition had been established in the mold of the fundamentalist style of Islamic experience, and that tradition created an underlying theme for the modern Islamic experience. Social groups and associations had been created to meet the issues raised by the adaptationists within the Islamic community, and those groups had a fundamentalist mood, which has always been close to the surface in the past two centuries. Thus, the style of the eighteenth-century spirit of socio-moral reconstruction has provided the counterpoint to the adaptationists' secularizing reforms. When the latter weaken or appear to have failed, as was frequently the case by the 1970s, the more fundamentalist style emerges into full view.

During the eighteenth century, the leadership for the revivalist movements came from the scholars of Islam. The scholars were often able to inspire political figures to support them, and, when that happened, the result was the creation of new states based on their teachings. However, the eighteenth-century fundamentalist spirit was not tied to the changing political boundaries of the time. Ulama traveled widely, often disregarding politico-military rivalries, and were part of a broad, cosmopolitan network. As a result, even though the specific history of a revivalist movement in any given area might be distinctive, there were direct lines of interaction among the revivalist ulama. One such line was the gradual expansion of the Naqshbandiyyah from South Asia into the eastern Mediterranean areas; another was the influence of North African teachers in central Islamic lands. The central position within the Islamic world of the cities of Mecca and Medina and the annual pilgrimages to those holy cities made them important points of interchange. There, groups of scholars from throughout the Islamic world provided one focus for the interacting cosmopolitan network. Other important centers were the great schools in Cairo, Damascus, and the imperial capitals.

Although the pragmatic mode of adaptation did not disappear, there was a new emphasis on the fundamentalist style of action, and the eighteenth century was a time of vital interaction in the continuing definition of the nature of the Islamic community. The Islamic dimension provides the framework for the variety of experiences in the Islamic world; an examination of the "local dimension" gives substance to the generalizations about eighteenth-century Islamic themes.

Local Dimension: The Ottoman Experience

The Ottoman Empire in the eighteenth century brought together a tremendous variety of peoples. To examine the history of Islam in the context of this complex structure, it is helpful to distinguish between the experience of the imperial state itself and the Islamic movements that were not directly part of the state structure. These two aspects were interconnected in many ways, as when non-state religious teachers led revolutionary movements or when important political leaders became the patrons of "unofficial" religious leaders. However, if it is remembered that the state and the non-state experiences are simply two facets of the broader history of the empire, it is possible, for purposes of analysis, to deal with them separately.

Islam and the Ottoman Empire

The general political history of the Ottoman Empire in the eighteenth century is filled with wars, revolutions, and periods of instability. In terms of the major themes, one can consider that the eighteenth century began, in political terms, with the failure of the Ottoman armies to capture Vienna in 1683. That failure exposed the Ottoman weakness to the view of the Europeans, and in subsequent campaigns the Ottoman army collapsed. Continuing defeats in the field and military mutinies in Istanbul finally produced a reaction in the form of powerful reformist efforts. In the face of imperial disaster, conservative groups and corrupt vested interests were willing to accept some reorganization efforts that were aimed at increasing the effectiveness of the army and the efficiency of the administration. However, as soon as the immediate threat had passed, the reformers were forced out of office and were replaced by leaders who would tolerate the old inefficiencies once again. In effect, a pattern emerged that "epitomized all the glories and disasters of the Ottoman Empire in its age of disintegration. The pattern was a quick recovery from disaster followed shortly by a stalemate and subsequent collapses."[5]

There was a line of reforming administrators who attempted to revitalize the imperial structures. Some of the most famous of those reformers came from the Koprulu family, the first Koprulu to become grand vizier, the chief Ottoman administrator, having been Mehmet Pasha, who assumed that post in 1656. The eighteenth-century reforming viziers increasingly came to accept the idea that the adoption of specific European techniques might aid the empire. Such an approach can be seen in the policies of grand viziers like Husayn Koprulu (1644–1702), Damad Ibrahim (in office, 1718–1730), and Mehmet Ragib in mid-century. The culmination of this trend was the reform program of Sultan Selim III (r. 1789–1807), who made a major effort to create a "new order" (*nizam-i-jedid*).

A variety of forces worked against the success of those efforts, but mostly it was the conservative elements that worked to preserve conditions as they were. Despite the problems of the empire, its inefficiencies benefited a number of groups. Ineffective central control provided opportunities for local and provincial notables to increase their own personal power, and any reform of the central administration that was too successful would limit their control. As a result, they opposed such reforms, and the eighteenth-century political history of the empire is marked by the increasing power of those local dignitaries. Despite the reforming viziers, the process of decentralization continued throughout the century.

In addition to the local notables, there were strongly conservative elements within the central imperial organization. The bureaucrats participated in a system of buying and selling offices that profited them personally but undermined the efficiency of the administration, and efforts to reform the administrative structure met with the resistance of those officials. A similar situation was presented by the military. The heart of the Ottoman military was the Janissary Corps, and by the eighteenth century, the janissaries had become directly involved in many nonmilitary activities. They had maintained the privileges of their military elite status even though they had become an ineffective military force, and they were unwilling to accept new techniques or training that would require them to abandon their lucrative nonmilitary activities. As a result, they were also a conservative force.

The official religious leadership also fit into the same pattern. The Ottoman state had created a large hierarchy of religious offices to administer the religious aspects of the empire. In the sixteenth century, a well-organized curriculum and a careful structure of official positions had been established, and that system had created a mechanism for fruitful cooperation between the rulers and the ulama. With advancement based on long education and merit, the hierarchy had helped to strengthen the sultanate in its religious legitimacy and had provided well-trained scholars to fill a variety of positions. However, the creation of this organization "carried with it the seeds of considerable trouble for the state" since it intensified the natural conservatism of the ulama and opened the door for the corrupt practices of nepotism and the sale of offices.[6]

By the eighteenth century, these problems had become a major factor in the religious establishment. The higher, and more lucrative, offices were dominated by a few great families, and it became common for untrained men to hold major teaching positions through nepotism. The highest official in the hierarchy was the shaykh al-Islam. As the leading religious official in the empire, the shaykh al-Islam was a powerful political figure, and during the eighteenth century, the holders of that post were important conservative figures. "Ironically it was the very cohesiveness created by the hierarchical structure, which had yielded great benefits to the state in the sixteenth century . . . which from at least the eighteenth century on lent such power to the efforts of the ulema to block often necessary reforms and innovations."[7]

It should be noted that the conservatism of the establishment ulama was not based on the nature of Islam itself. In the sixteenth century, the leading figures of the emerging hierarchy had been important in the adaptations that were made by the sultans of the time. It was the structural context in which the later hierarchy found itself that was the basis for the ulama conservatism. Other Muslim leaders, those not in the upper levels of the state organization, did not maintain as conservative a style as the "high ulama" of the state did in the eighteenth century. Opposition to the practices of the official ulama sometimes came from people in the lower levels of the hierarchy and at other times from popular religious leaders outside of the state organization.

A series of events in the eighteenth century illustrate the interaction of these forces, and they give an insight into the history of Islam as it related to the development of the Ottoman state. The first of these was the "Edirne incident" of 1703, which has been called "a high water mark in the influence of the ulema in the affairs of state."[8] The major opponent of the reforming grand vizier Husayn Koprulu was the shaykh al-Islam Feyzullah. Feyzullah had been the tutor of the sultan, Mustafa II, and was appointed shaykh al-Islam when his former student came to the throne in 1695. Through Feyzullah's personal influence over the sultan and his ability to manipulate the state patronage system, Feyzullah came to dominate the government. He succeeded in driving Husayn Koprulu from office and controlled the subsequent grand viziers. He persuaded the sultan to name Feyzullah's son as his future successor in the position of shaykh al-Islam, and there were some who felt that he aspired to hold the combined posts of shaykh al-Islam and grand vizier.

Through his domination, Feyzullah roused opposition in many quarters. His rejection of the Koprulu reforms created financial problems, and a revolt was sparked in 1703 by the mutiny of janissaries who were demanding back pay. They were joined by large numbers of religious students and low-level official ulama and others who had been antagonized by Feyzullah. The rebels gained control of Istanbul and soon marched on the sultan's palace in

Edirne. In the end, Feyzullah and many of his associates were caught and killed, and the sultan himself was deposed by the dissidents.

The career of Feyzullah illustrates the potential power of the establishment ulama group. However, his personal characteristics and ambitions alienated many within the religious establishment itself, and as a result, the ulama conservatives rejected what might have been a drastic change in the role of the ulama leaders. Feyzullah was motivated by personal greed, did not present a broad program based on some organizing principle, and was unable to mobilize support beyond those who benefited directly from his patronage. He was a corrupt pragmatist rather than a conservative or a fundamentalist. The Edirne incident shows that it was possible for one of the ulama to assume a major political role. However, within the upper levels of the Ottoman official ulama, there were few after Feyzullah who seized the opportunity. "There are no ulema of political distinction in the eighteenth century who could match the influence of Feyzullah Efendi. With the Empire's frontiers contracting, and with opportunities for significant employment declining as a result, the ulema appear to have given up their political pretensions in return for security for themselves and their children."[9]

A second illustration of the forces in operation during the eighteenth century is the cycle of events associated with the Tulip Period, which ended with the Patrona Khalil revolt in 1730. The sultan who came to the throne after the Edirne incident was Ahmed III, and he ruled until 1730. After a careful manipulation of the divisions among the groups that had placed him on the throne, Ahmed III was able to revive imperial reform efforts. The leading figure in this effort was Damad Ibrahim, Ahmed's grand vizier from 1718 until 1730. Ibrahim made great efforts to become well informed of developments in Europe, and some of the new techniques were utilized. In the palace itself, some Western European fashions came into vogue, and one of the fads was the cultivation of tulips in the gardens of newly built pleasure pavilions. On the more serious side, Ibrahim's reform effort aimed at strengthening the powers of the central government, this time making use of European techniques rather than simply using the golden age of Ottoman power as a model for reform.

The policies of the Tulip Period were, however, unable to solve the basic difficulties of the empire. Revenues were increasingly lost through contraband trade, and the diversion of tax revenues by powerful local notables and provincial governors increased. Popular unrest was encouraged by inflation, rural banditry, and oppressive taxation, and the reforms attacked the interests of important conservative groups. The period was brought to an end when all the elements of opposition came together in Istanbul and overthrew both the sultan and his grand vizier in the course of the Patrona Khalil revolt of 1730.

That revolt involved a realignment of forces within the ruling elite. Prior to this period, the major support for the centralized sultanate had come from the military elite and the ulama. However, the centralizing reforms became more closely associated with European ideas and were colored by a French-influenced secularist trend. As a result, the antireform movement assumed a more clearly religious tone, and "Thus a religiously oriented anti-western movement became the second strand running across the whole history of the Turkish transformation, in contrast to the Westernist strand."[10] The ulama played an important role in defining the religious basis for the opposition and in giving it legitimacy.

In the decades that followed, there were continuing efforts to introduce Western techniques into the Ottoman system. The tradition of the reforming viziers was maintained by a series of capable administrators, and their reform efforts created a small body of men within the ruling elite who were committed to strengthening the central power. They were aided by European advisers, particularly in the military, but their efforts were constantly interrupted by the activities of the conservative forces. The experience of Claude-Alexandre Comte de Bonneval (1675–1747) is a good example. After a career of military service in European armies, he began serving the Ottoman Empire in 1729 and worked to train new-style military groups. His fortunes rose and fell with the reformist political leaders, and his military engineering school only survived him by three years, being closed because of janissary opposition in 1750.

Many factors complicated the dialogue between reformers and conservatives. Throughout the century, the empire was engaged in wars with neighboring states, and although there were a few victories, the overall results were military defeats and expensive treaties. The conflicts with the European powers played an ambiguous role in the fortunes of the reformers. On the one hand, clearly visible weakness and defeat provided a rationale for reforms that even the conservatives accepted in times of impending collapse. On the other hand, the wars provided an emotional context that allowed the conservatives to arouse significant opposition to the adoption of Western ideas and techniques, which were the tools of the enemy and therefore subversive.

The reformers were unable to diminish the power of the local notables, and the international wars gave provincial leaders an opportunity to use the government's need for their military assistance as a way of gaining concessions from the state. Increasingly, the most productive areas of the empire came under the control of men only nominally loyal, if that, to the sultan. This situation deprived the central government of needed revenues and further strengthened the forces that opposed effective centralizing reform programs.

The culmination of the eighteenth-century reform efforts and the evolution of the relationship of Islam to the Ottoman state came with the programs of Sultan Selim III, who ruled from 1789 to 1807. The Ottoman reforms arrived at a major turning point with Selim's attempts to create a "new order" (*nizam-i-jedid*). "In most ways Selim was a failure. His reforms were limited and eventually dissipated. . . . He went little beyond strictly military and technical innovations to the more fundamental political, social, economic, and judicial developments which had provided the necessary context for their successful operation in Europe. Yet in his efforts, and in the factors which defeated him, lay the seeds of modern Turkish reform."[11]

Faced with external challenges and internal disintegration, Selim III attempted to create a more effective imperial structure. The focus of his reform efforts was the military, and he worked to reform the Janissary Corps and then to create a new, modern-style military force. There were also efforts to improve the administrative structure and financial organization, but those efforts were less well organized. In the long run, the most important part of Selim's program was that under his leadership, knowledge of the West spread to a broader range of people within the empire. Also, the reformist tradition gained strength and became firmly identified with the idea of introducing Western techniques.

Selim III set a basic pattern for the modern Islamic experience. In the face of the changing conditions, the adaptationist style of the Muslim leaders became associated with a particular type of reform program, a program that involved adopting European methods. From the time of Selim to the present, political adaptationism has meant Westernizing reform.

With adaptationism in the political arena being co-opted by the Westernizers, the possibility of a more rigorously Islamic adaptationism was submerged and is reemerging only in the last quarter of the twentieth century. The identification of adaptationism with Westernization may have been inevitable, given the military strength of European states, the penetrating power of the Western economic system, and the seductive appeal of modern ideas as defined by the West.

The manifestly Islamic reactions to the changing conditions tended to be conservative, fundamentalist, or individualist in style, and the ending of Selim's program shows the continuing strength of those forces in the Ottoman Empire at the end of the eighteenth century. Selim was overthrown in 1807 by a combination of antireform forces. Local notables joined with janissaries to provide the military force for the rebellion, and the movement was given legitimacy by the ulama, who felt that the reforms ran counter to Islam. Even though Selim agreed to accept the demands of the revolutionaries and to dismantle the *nizam-i-jedid*, he was deposed. The conservative shaykh al-Islam issued a ruling that authorized his deposition on the grounds that Selim's reforms had been contrary to religion and tradition.

"Unofficial" Islam in the Ottoman Empire

Most of the religious teachers and leaders living within the Ottoman Empire were not part of the official hierachy. Learned scholars taught in a wide variety of schools that spread far beyond the official institutions for training the state ulama. There were also the Sufi leaders, whose *tariqah*s had an important impact on the political life of the empire but were largely outside of the formal Ottoman religious establishment.

The Islam of the community and the Islam of the state overlapped in some areas and competed in others, forming complementary parts of the picture of Ottoman Islamic life. Two important parts of that picture were the developing roles of the non-state ulama and the continuing evolution of the *tariqah*s. One of the heritages of Islamic society was the generally autonomous operation of Islamic structures and groups outside of state structures. Ulama and *tariqah*s in the Ottoman provinces had some lines of direct contact with the state hierachy, but they pursued their own lines of operation in the general life of the community.

The non-state ulama were the main definers of the sociolegal implications of Islam for most people. In the provinces, it was the local scholars rather than the state-appointed judges who were the most influential ulama, and they were supported by a complex network of pious endowments and other gifts. In Damascus, for example, a large number of endowed instructorships and supported religious positions had been created as early as the twelfth and thirteenth centuries.[12] Although some of them had been funded by sultans and other politico-military leaders, they had not become a part of the state system when it was formalized by the Ottomans. In the eighteenth century, the central government had some role in determining who would hold certain positions, but most of the major posts were not filled by people from the official hierarchy. That was clearly true for the muftis in each of the four schools and was also true for the lucrative instructorships in the Umayyad Mosque.

The reformist-conservative struggle that highlighted the eighteenth-century history of the official religious establishment was not as important among the non-state ulama, for whom the emphasis was more on the study of the traditional intellectual disciplines and issues raised by the internal development of Islamic society. Egypt and the Arabian Peninsula are special cases and will be examined separately, but in the rest of the "Arab provinces" of the empire, the different styles of the Islamic experience interacted in usually rather undramatic ways.

The ulama in those provinces were quite cosmopolitan in their orientation. Scholars from areas as widely separated as India and North Africa came and studied, and often settled and became well-known teachers, and similarly, the native ulama frequently traveled as a part of their education. The learned community was not parochial in its attitudes and experiences in terms of the larger Islamic world, although there was little familiarity with anything outside of the world of Islam. There was a sense of Islamic community that transcended political boundaries.

The traveling scholar was a part of a broad network of interregional ties. Two important lines of contact were through the study of the *hadith*s and the learning or "taking" of the *tariqah*s. Among the academic disciplines, the study of the Traditions of the Prophet was one that most encouraged travel. The custom was firmly established that the study of the *hadith*s was most validly accomplished by wandering from teacher to teacher, listening to their verbal transmissions of the Traditions and their comments on the great medieval collections. In the early development of *hadith* study, the focus of attention was on the *isnad*, or chain of authorities transmitting the account. This emphasis continued in later study, and scholars sought out the old traditionists, or *muhaddith,* as a way of shortening the length of their own chain of authorities. The "certification" of a scholar came not through a diploma granted by an institution, but by a permission document from his various teachers authenticating the instruction given. A scholar's credentials were general lists of his teachers and their *isnad*s. Although the study of Islamic law and other disciplines followed a similar pattern, there was less emphasis on the need for travel in order to gain prestige or a major reputation. As a result, *hadith* studies played an important role in the cosmopolitanism of the eighteenth-century ulama.

Initiation into a *tariqah* was another element of interregional contact. During the eighteenth century in the Arab provinces of the Ottoman Empire, the development and expansion of the *tariqah*s was the area of most visible change. Among the ulama there was a growing sense of the desirability of a redefinition of the Sufi tradition. Although few of the ulama rejected Sufism, there were many who were active in an effort to bring it more in line with a stricter interpretation of Islam. One manifestation of this effort was the growth or expansion of certain *tariqah*s among the ulama. The two most important were the Naqshbandiyyah and the Khalwatiyyah.

The Naqshbandiyyah spread from India to the eastern Mediterranean world in the seventeenth and eighteenth centuries, and it carried with it some of the fundamentalist tone associated with the Indian Naqshbandiyyah revival. The leaders of the order insisted upon a careful adherence to Islamic law and clearly disassociated themselves from the heterodox tendencies and latitudinarianism of the older, popular Turkish brotherhoods. As a clearly Sunni order that was relatively free from the excesses of the orders of the masses, the Naqshbandiyyah Tariqah had a strong appeal among the ulama, both within and outside of the religious establishment.

That *tariqah* spread to the Ottoman territories through a number of channels. Earlier groups had been associated with the Turks in Central Asia, but two main lines entered in the seventeenth and eighteenth centuries, both arising out of the activist Indian tradition. The most prominent line was associated with Ahmad Sirhindi, who was active in opposing syncretism in Akbar's time. The chief propagator of this *silsilah,* or line of transmission, was Murad al-Bukhari (1640–1720), a student of the son of Ahmad Sirhindi. Murad al-Bukhari traveled widely in the eastern Mediterranean areas and gained a reputation for piety and learning. He initiated many ulama in a number of areas, and Sultan Mustafa II gave him special grants of land and other sources of income. He settled in Damascus, and his wealth and reputation laid the foundation for a prominent place for his descendants among the ulama of that city. By the end of the century, his family had provided many of the Hanafi muftis in the city, and some members were important teachers. The Muradi family had close associations with Abd al-Ghani al-Nablusi (1641–1731), a leading Sufi writer and a member of the Naqshbandiyyah.

The other major Naqshbandiyyah line spread through Mecca. Its propagator was Taj al-Din ibn Zakariya (d. 1640), a contemporary of Ahmad Sirhindi and a fellow student with him of Muhammad Baqi billah. Taj al-Din settled in Mecca, and his students established the Naqshbandiyyah in Yemen and elsewhere. Through this line, the Naqshbandiyyah spread to Egypt.

The Khalwatiyyah Tariqah has a longer history in Arab lands. Its origins are obscure, but it arose in the general area of western Iran and eastern Turkey. It was distinguished by its emphasis on individual asceticism and withdrawal for meditation. In its early days, it appears to have had strong links with the Shi'i tradition and to have placed little emphasis on conforming to the rules of Islamic law. It may also have been related to movements of popular unrest and local religious practice. Because of its encouragement of individual actions of piety, it did not maintain a single line of organization but, rather, split into a number of suborders that shared little more than a common tradition of devotional practices and litanies.

A variety of suborders of this *tariqah* spread through the Ottoman lands, and it gradually moved away from its Shi'i connections and antinomian tendencies. As a part of this evolution, it became increasingly popular among the ulama and propertied classes. By the eighteenth century, the order was one of the most widely accepted among the ulama, and during that century, it became an important vehicle for the emerging Neo-Sufism. A key figure in this development was Mustafa ibn Kamal al-Din al-Bakri, who died in 1748. Mustafa al-Bakri was a student of both Abd al-Ghani al-Nablusi, the famous Sufi teacher and Naqshbandi in Damascus, and Abd al-Latif al-Halabi, a leading Khalwatiyyah shaykh in Aleppo. Al-Bakri thus combined the *tariqah* of Ottoman ulama respectability with the reinterpretation of the

Sufi theology of Ibn al-Arabi and the more activist mood of the Naqshban-diyyah. He was a tireless traveler in the eastern Mediterranean regions, and he had many students in Syria, Jerusalem, Egypt, and the Arabian Penin-sula. His own special branch of the Khalwatiyyah, the Bakriyyah, became the parent of activist *tariqah*s throughout the Islamic world. By the end of the eighteenth century, the revivalist Khalwatiyyah had inspired orders throughout the Ottoman territories and beyond into Islamic Africa.

In the central parts of the Ottoman Empire, the development of the *ta-riqah*s and the activities of the non-state ulama did not produce many openly political movements, and the representatives of the fundamentalist style of Islam tended to be more moderate and less activist than in other areas. The Hanbali scholars of Damascus, for example, were important teachers of tra-dition and carried on the distinctive strictness of their school. At the same time, in contrast to the Hanbalis in the Arabian Peninsula, they tended not to be militant revivalists. In these areas, the Neo-Sufism of the ulama created a tone that consolidated fundamentalist tendencies among the nonstate reli-gious leadership. Although there was a strong conservative spirit among these teachers, the general style for coping with changing conditions when major challenges arose, was to opt for a more fundamentalist than adapta-tionist style of Islam, even though the latter was increasingly the dominant style of the politico-military leadership.

The culmination of these tendencies in the Ottoman areas outside of Egypt and the Arabian Peninsula can be seen in the career of Khalid al-Naqsh-bandi, who died in Damascus in 1827.[13] He was born in the Kurdish area of northern Iraq and combined many of the tendencies of his day. His educa-tion was the result of wide travels and he had a cosmopolitan awareness of the Islamic world of his time. He studied not only in the major cities of the eastern Mediterranean, but also in India, where he was initiated into Ahmad Sirhindi's line of the Naqshbandiyyah Tariqah. He returned to Iraq and Syria where he had a long and successful career as a teacher and *tariqah* leader.

His life was characterized by support for rigorous fundamentalism. He had close ties to ulama who were sympathetic to this style of Islam, like the Muradi family in Damascus, but he frequently aroused the hostility of the conservative ulama by accusing them of laxness and of diluting Islamic pu-rity. In so doing, Khalid helped to confirm the fundamentalist tone of specif-ically Islamic solutions to the challenges of change at the beginning of the nineteenth century. It has been suggested that the Khalidi branch of the Naqshbandiyyah helped to establish the Sufi shaykhs as key figures in the movements of popular opposition that occurred later.[14] The revivalist orien-tation and sociopolitical concerns for the purity of the community made the great shaykhs a natural focus for such movements. Naqshbandis in the line of Khalid were important in leading the Kurdish nationalist movements and in organizing Islamic opposition to the nineteenth-century Russian expansion into Islamic areas.

The main themes of eighteenth-century Islamic history are visible in the Ottoman experience. Political and economic realignments saw the forces of decentralization become stronger, and the official ulama played an important role in that decentralization as a conservative force. The reorientation of the Sufi tradition was especially noticeable among the non-state ulama, although it did have some impact within the official state religious hierarchy. An important feature of the reorientation was the expansion of the two major Neo-Sufi orders, the Naqshbandiyyah and the Khalwatiyyah/Bakriyyah as study of the *hadith*s helped to provide a basis for a spirit of socio-moral reconstruction. Among the religious leaders in the government, that mood took the form of opposition to Westernizing tendencies and reformism. Although much of the opposition to reform can be traced to individual and group interests, the Islamic spirit of revival was also present. In the interaction of these styles, important foundations were laid for future attitudes. In coping with the changing conditions, adaptationism came to be identified with adopting Western techniques and the secularizing of the reformers. As a result, more specifically Islamic reactions tended to assume a conservative or fundamentalist style. It was to be a long time before this eighteenth-century pattern would be broken and a more effectively Islamic adaptationism would emerge.

Egypt: A Special Ottoman Case

The Ulama and Egyptian Society

The history of Islam in Egypt during the eighteenth century presents a picture that diverges somewhat from the main lines of the Ottoman experience centered in Istanbul. Egypt was a province of the Ottoman Empire, but the increasing forces of decentralization provided opportunities for virtually autonomous rule by the politico-military elite. Control of Egypt was mainly in the hands of the Mamluks, the political heirs of the old slave-soldier aristocracy that had ruled Egypt before the Ottoman conquest in 1517. In this system, the "rulers and ruled formed different ethnic and linguistic units."[15] The Mamluks were a faction-ridden ruling elite that engaged in a great deal of internal conflict, and their struggles for power in the eighteenth century increasingly created general conditions of instability, which was reflected by a number of popular revolts among the urban and rural Egyptian masses. There was an Ottoman governor, but his position was weak because he lacked an effective military force and had to rely upon his personal ability for political manipulation.

Those factors provided the framework for the major political and economic realignments that took place. The expansion of the European system of trade and exchange brought changing patterns of economic enterprise to Egypt during the eighteenth century, and the accompanying commercial revival helped to provide resources for a variety of groups. In the process, the "Mamluk *beys* emerged as the political elite in alliance with a number of rich merchants who formed the economic elite after a series of internecine struggles between their rivals, the Janissaries and other feudal military groups."[16]

The ulama emerged during the century as a distinctive sociopolitical force. As Mamluk factional strife increased, the ulama were called upon more frequently to act as mediators. They not only arbitrated among the Mamluk factions, but they also acted as a link between the ruling elite and the general population. Frequently, the ulama were called upon by the people to intervene with the rulers in order to correct some injustice or to reduce oppressive measures.

The actual power of the ulama was defined by certain special conditions. They did not control any military forces themselves, and their ability to influence the direction of affairs depended upon their personal persuasive powers. They were not, in other words, an organized political faction with military power, and their influence rested upon their ability to direct public opinion and to persuade the rulers. By making use of the Friday sermons and their own individual followings, they could mobilize popular demonstrations in support of or in opposition to government policies. In terms of the ulama self-image, they believed that "it was not their duty to act directly to maintain law and order, that is to take the initiative, for they were not the governors. . . . Their function was to assist the governors by offering advice and good offices."[17]

During this time of significant change, that role of mediation was of growing importance. The Mamluk leaders came to rely more and more on the ulama, and the religious leaders showed a growing willingness to participate in politics. When the French occupied Egypt in 1798, they needed the aid of the ulama to an even greater extent than the Mamluks had. Napoleon created a special council composed entirely of ulama, "who were to help him legislate, maintain order, and act as an intermediary between the French authorities and the people."[18] The defeat of the French by British and Ottoman forces by 1801 provided further opportunities for the ulama to function in the political arena, and one of the leading ulama, Umar Makram, became the major spokesman for local opinion. He was able to mobilize the ulama and other local leaders to reject the Mamluk leadership, secure the deposition of the Ottoman governor, and gain the appointment of Mehmet Ali as the new governor.

The actions of Umar Makram and the successful nomination of Mehmet Ali by the Egyptian ulama represent a climax in the political development of the religious leaders, as after the appointment of the man they had supported, the ulama withdrew from such an active political role. In line with long-standing habits, the ulama were unwilling to take a direct role in the government except in crises. When there was strong leadership. as there was under Mehmet Ali, the political activity of the ulama declined.

The sociopolitical role of the Egyptian ulama has a particular tone, and the eighteenth-century pattern is important in terms of its implications for later history. The ulama were not organized into a unified institution, although there were some influential organizations such as the great Islamic university of al-Azhar. It was as molders of public opinion and as an informal force in society that they had their real power. The ulama kept that style of informal organization, even when they may have had an opportunity to assume more direct political power. In this way, they made it possible for a strong, nonulama leader to gain control and begin the process of reconstructing the institutions of a strong central government. Mehmet Ali's leadership soon became identified with modernizing reform, and the tensions already seen during the rule of the Ottomans were to build in Egypt between Westernizing adaptationism and more conservative religious leadership. However, in Egypt, the ulama had tentatively withdrawn from the political arena, and thus they had weakened their ability to resume a more active political. role.

That style of operation has been an important feature of the modern development of Islam in Egypt. The religious leadership had, and sometimes still has, the ability to influence the mood of public opinion, but there is still no formal organization for direct political action or for a direct governmental role for the ulama. Religious sentiment operates in the context of a religiously "unincorporated" society.

Al-Azhar: Egypt's Religious Establishment

Cairo has long been a great center for Islamic education. During the era of the early sultanates, the Mongol conquests and other turbulent events had undermined, if not destroyed, the effective influence of many of the great medieval educational institutions in the eastern part of the Middle East, but the Mamluk sultans had provided patronage for many schools in Egypt.

Following the Ottoman conquest in 1517, many of those schools lost control of their endowments, but the great school of al-Azhar, centrally located in Cairo, was able to win support from the new rulers. Gradually, al-Azhar came to dominate the educational scene, and by the eighteenth century, it had developed a great reputation throughout the Islamic world and attracted students from many lands.

The teachers and other ulama associated with al-Azhar formed a religious establishment within Egyptian Islam, and those ulama who held official posts in Egypt could not match the reputation and popular influence of the shaykhs of al-Azhar. During the eighteenth century, the university was a focal point for much of the political activity of the Egyptian ulama, and the shaykh al-Azhar, or leader of the university, was a major figure in both religious and political life.

The role of al-Azhar as a community of scholars is illustrative of the distinctive character of Egyptian Islamic life. Because the university attracted scholars from so many different areas, it became an important center of Islamic cosmopolitanism. Students who returned from Cairo to their homelands were an important factor in the diffusion of ideas within the Islamic world. In that way, for instance, Neo-Sufism spread into Africa as disciples of Mustafa al-Bakri and the revitalized Khalwatiyyah Tariqah introduced those ideas to the founders of influential orders in North and West Africa.

At the same time, the university itself was curiously parochial. The principal teachers were local shaykhs who had themselves been trained in the university, and the cosmopolitanism was largely a feature of the ulama who came to the university to learn rather than a result of the travels of many of the Azhari teachers. The teachers tended to draw back from activist fundamentalism or social radicalism, and during the upheavals of the eighteenth century, the university stood for stability rather than for revolution. Although it acted to oppose excessive oppression on the part of the ruling class, it also helped to control the more activist popular opposition to the status quo. Militant Islamic activism of either a fundamentalist or a mesianic character tended to arise outside of either the Egyptian or the official Ottoman religious establishment.

Nonestablishment Religious Life

Spreading beyond the core of the ulama of al-Azhar was a broad spectrum of religious life, but it is difficult to draw sharp lines of definition because the various parts of the Islamic community were in constant interaction. The local religious establishment itself was not a closed corporation. "The social background of the Egyptian ulama differed from that of the ulama of the rest of the Ottoman Empire, for there was no aristocratic hereditary caste of high as against lesser ulama. . . . Most of the prominent ulama were of fallah, peasant, origins."[19] The educational system provided by al-Azhar was a means of genuine social mobility and helped to keep the religious leaders aware of the needs and views of the masses. However, the more prominent ulama tended not to be spokesmen for positions that would challenge the politico-social system as a whole.

From time to time, individuals and groups that expressed a more radical position emerged to represent the views of the general population. The great nineteenth-century Egyptian historian, Abd al-Rahman al-Jabarti, describes an incident early in the eighteenth century that illustrates the complex interaction of the various Islamic groups in Egypt.[20] A man began preaching to the people in one of the mosques, and he vigorously condemned the practices of some of the *tariqah*s in venerating Sufi "saints." His message was basically that of a vigorous fundamentalist, and it soon attracted a number of followers. As a group armed with clubs moved through the streets, some people went to al-Azhar to seek the opinion of the ulama there, and two major shaykhs at the university said that the preacher was in error. The preacher then demanded a debate in the court of the *qadi,* the official Ottoman Islamic judge in Egypt. When the *qadi* saw the size of the crowd, he went to the military authorities, and after much discussion, the preacher was suppressed by the armed forces. In this incident, the conservatism of the Azhar shaykhs is evident. One also can see the complex lines of interaction among the different groups and the care that was taken in dealing with a popular street preacher.

Popular religious views were more frequently presented through the *tariqah*s. There, too, it was not simply a matter of the ulama on one side and the lower classes on the other. A prototype of the popular *tariqah* in this era was the Bayyumiyyah, which was established by Ali al-Bayyumi (1696–1769), a *hadith* scholar and, initially, a follower of one of the branches of the revivalist Khalwatiyyah. The Bayyumiyyah Tariqah made significant departures from the Khalwatiyyah spirit and appealed more directly to the lower classes. Bayyumi's ecstatic form of Sufism was condemned by many of the more conservative ulama, but, at the same time, the shaykh al-Azhar thwarted attempts by those ulama to ban the weekly tariqah meetings. In his writings, Bayyumi maintained "the legitimacy of the developing religious counterculture," and they reflect the fact that the popular orders sometimes defended the lower classes.[21]

For most Egyptians, religious life was centered around the activities of daily life. Local teachers and festivals were focal points of attention, and customs were shaped by indigenous traditions as well as by Islamic teachings. The practices of popular Islam were a combination of elements that were believed to be Islamic by the people and usually tolerated by the ulama, even when they appeared to contradict a strict interpretation of the Quran and the Sunnah of the Prophet. It was only in times of crisis or special political oppression that the official institutions attempted to influence the religious life of the masses.

Religious life in Egypt was thus a series of overlapping elements. The ulama establishments, the *tariqah*s, and the local practices all interacted in various ways. In general terms, the Azhar-oriented establishment was conservative, and the *tariqah*s might have supported fundamentalist activism or continuation of the daily routines. Rigorous activism tended to be related to but outside of the religious establishment itself. This pattern of activist, nonestablishment organizations continues throughout the modern history of Islam in Egypt and can be seen in the rise of the Muslim Brotherhood in the twentieth century.

Egypt and the Larger Islamic World

Cairo was a major religious and intellectual crossroads during the eighteenth century, and the cosmopolitan community of visiting scholars and local teachers played an important role in the development and spread of ideas. That role was particularly important in the two key areas of the emergence of Neo-Sufism and the continuing trends in *hadith* scholarship.

Scholars went to Cairo from many parts of the Islamic world, both as students and as pilgrims on their way to Mecca and Medina, and that cosmopolitan group interacted with the local establishment in a variety of ways. Some of the scholars came into conflict with the local conservatives, and others were accepted as a part of the establishment.

The Egyptian scholars played a significant role in the eighteenth-century interest in *hadith* studies. There was a long tradition of *hadith* scholarship in Cairo, and many of the major reference works in *hadith* studies had been compiled by great Egyptian teachers in the late Middle Ages. The work of Ahmad Ibn Hajar al-Asqalani (d. 1449), for example, has been described as "the final summation of the science of *hadith*,"[22] and his commentaries on the major collections of the Traditions were known throughout the Islamic world. Later scholars of the Traditions in Egypt also had international reputations. The name of Zakariya al-Ansari (d. 1520) appears in the chain of transmission of many of the *muhaddith*s of the eighteenth century, and a key figure leading up to the eighteenth-century interest in *hadith* study was Muhammad al-Babili (d. 1666). Al-Babili attracted many students, including some who became the major figures in the emerging fundamentalist mood of the eighteenth century. Those students included the great Hanbali mufti of Damascus, Abu al-Muwahib ibn Abd al-Baqi, and the important Neo-Sufi shaykh in Medina, Ibrahim al-Kurani. Thus, the foundations for *hadith* studies were well laid in Cairo.

During the eighteenth century, the changing economic conditions gave added impetus to Cairene *hadith* scholarship as the revival of commercial activity increased the importance of the merchant classes who patronized the *hadith* scholars. Informal discussion groups provided a place where local scholars could gather together with people outside the religious establishment and with itinerant scholars, and there was a general rise in the standards of religious scholarship and in the methods of critical analysis.[23]

A high point was reached with the work of Muhammad Murtada al-Zabiti (d. 1791), one of the major scholars of his day. He was born in India and studied in many major centers of learning. He studied *hadith* in India with one of the great scholars of the time, Shah Wali Allah al-Dihlawi, and then continued his studies in Yemen, especially in the city of Zabid. After further travel, he settled in Cairo and became one of that city's leading intellectuals. His massive works in many fields brought him widespread fame, and his scholarship in disciplines related to *hadith* study were of great importance in providing a climax to the developments of the period.

Al-Zabidi was not simply a traditionist as he was also active in the redefinition of Sufism. One of his best-known works was a commentary on al-Ghazali's work, which gave added impetus to the movement away from the Ibn al-Arabi tradition within Sufi thought in the direction of formulations more in accord with a stricter style of Islam. Just as al-Zabidi combined Indian and Egyptian traditions of *hadith* scholarship, he also joined together the Neo-Sufism of Shah Wali Allah in India, the Naqshbandiyyah ideas that had developed in both India and the Arabian Peninsula, and the Khalwatiyyah-inspired Neo-Sufism of the eastern Mediterranean.

Egyptian Neo-Sufism in the eighteenth century was the product of many forces, but the most visible element was the Khalwatiyyah tradition as defined by Mustafa al-Bakri. The Khalwatiyyah/Bakriyyah tradition was rigorist in tone and aimed at a strict adherence to the rules of the Quran and the Sunnah. The order's leaders, at least, were involved in a careful study of the *hadith*s, and, in this way, the growth of the order paralleled the intellectual trends of the time. Al-Bakri's students included men who became some of the major *hadith* teachers later in the century. His leading deputy, or *khalifah,* in Egypt was Muhammad ibn Salim al-Hifnawi (d. 1767). Al-Hifnawi taught *hadith* and other subjects in al-Azhar and eventually became shaykh al-Azhar. In addition, he initiated many people into the Khalwatiyyah *Tariqah*. Al-Hifnawi and his fellow students of al-Bakri met students from all over the Islamic world and brought them into the Bakriyyah tradition. However, the relative individualism of the Khalwatiyyah style meant that what emerged was a large cluster of related suborders rather than a single, centrally organized *tariqah*. Included in the list of suborders were the Rahmaniyyah, found in Algeria and Tunisia, and the Tijaniyyah, founded by a student of one of al-Hifnawi's *khalifah*s.

The circle of *hadith* scholars and *tariqah* shaykhs around al-Hifnawi was one that was sought out by many visiting ulama, and it appears to have been influential in shaping their thought. One of the early intellectual leaders of Islamic revivalism in West Africa, Jibril ibn Umar, found his way into the Hifnawi circle while he was in Cairo. This was also true of a major scholar from India, Abd al-Rahman al-Aydarus.

The Bakriyyah was thus an important part of Egyptian Neo-Sufism in the eighteenth century. It was not, however, the only element. Muhammad Murtada al-Zabidi was only one of a long line of scholars that had gone to Cairo from the eastern parts of the Islamic world. Many of those scholars were associated with the revivalist Naqshbandiyyah tradition, which helped to reinforce the reformist currents set in motion by the Khalwatiyyah activity. The Yemeni line of the Naqshbandiyyah was introduced into Egypt by Ahmad al-Banna al-Dimyati (d. 1715). He had studied *hadith* in Mecca and had been initiated into the Naqshbandiyyah order there. Other scholars associated with the Naqshbandiyyah, like al-Zabidi, also helped to present its revivalist ideas to the Egyptian cosmopolitan circles.

A third element in Egyptian Neo-Sufism was the influence of the North African teachers. The most apparent role of the North African ulama in Cairo was as students and visitors who traveled through the city and carried ideas back to their homelands. However, those North Africans may also have made a significant contribution to the nature of Neo-Sufism as it emerged by the end of the century. In North Africa in the fifteenth and sixteenth centuries, Sufism had become effectively organized as popular associations as the veneration of holy men provided a focus for the mobilization of large numbers of people. There was less emphasis on the need for a disciple to follow a long and arduous path and more on the personal attachment to an individual holy man. The great shaykhs and their organizations became an important factor in North African society.

It is possible to say that in the eastern Mediterranean, Sufism tended to be a more individual pursuit while in North Africa it became "collectivized."[24] In the new-style organizations, the validating principle was the special sanctity of the teacher rather than the legitimacy of his *silsilah,* or chain of authorities. Rather than seeking a metaphysical union with a pantheistically defined God, North African Sufis concentrated more intensely on the Prophet. By the eighteenth century, some North African *tariqah* leaders stressed that the purpose of the Sufi devotions was union with the spirit of the Prophet rather than union with God. They claimed validity for their *tariqah* on the basis of permission given to them directly by the Prophet.

North African scholars traveling through Cairo were familiar with those ideas. Although the excesses of "saint worship" were rejected by the Neo-Sufis, the ideas of more effective mass *tariqah* organizations and a less pantheistic orientation for the Sufi path were appealing to the new spirit. By the end of the eighteenth century, Neo-Sufism in Cairo appeared to be combining the more fundamentalist content of the Khalwatiyyah and Naqshbandiyyah traditions with the forms of North African Sufism. This combination was appealing to many and helped to provide the foundations for the activist revivalist orders that emerged early in the nineteenth century.

The Islamic Center: Mecca and Medina

The center of the cosmopolitan world of Muslim scholars and believers is the homeland of Islam, the two cities of Mecca and Medina. Even though the Haramayn (literally, "the two sanctuaries") are on the fringes of the great political units, their centrality is emphasized by the practice of facing Mecca while praying and the requirement of making a pilgrimage to Mecca. During the hajj or pilgrimage, Muslims from all parts of the Islamic world gather. Scholars often stay for relatively long periods, teaching and studying, and some settle permanently. As a result, the Haramayn is a key point in the international exchange of Islamic ideas and inspiration.

The history of the Haramayn in the eighteenth century can be traced on two interacting levels of action. On the one hand, there is the political history of the two cities, which were dominated by local power establishments and their relations with the Ottoman Empire, of which they were a peripheral part. On the other hand, there is the history of the cosmopolitan scholarly community, which was more directly involved with the broader evolution of Islamic thought and society. At times, the two levels seem to have been separate, and at other times, they have directly influenced each other.

Islam and Local Politics

Because of the distinctive position of the holy cities in the minds of Muslims, their rulers had to have some religious prestige. At the same time, since the days of the Umayyad caliphate, western Arabia had been unable to mobilize sufficient military power to be fully independent for long periods of time. The cities were usually under at least the nominal control of a sovereign from outside the Hijaz, the western section of the Arabian Peninsula. The title of protector or servant of the sanctuaries was taken by those outside rulers, and it was felt that the title added to their prestige. Since the sixteenth century, that role had been filled by Ottoman sultans.

The influence and prestige of the local leaders in the Hijaz set limits to the effectiveness of the control by the outside rulers, and the Ottomans never fully displaced the religious leaders as political controllers in the area. By the eighteenth century, as a part of the trend of decentralization within the empire, the Ottoman position was quite weak, and the situations in Mecca and Medina were different.

Mecca had had a long tradition of virtual political independence within the framework of loose outside control. As early as the tenth century, descendants of the Prophet, called sharifs, had been the controllers of Mecca, and for nearly a thousand years, the leading political figure in the city had been the grand sharif. The family of the early grand sharifs grew over the centuries, and the rival clans that developed within it became a firmly established aristocracy. Although the clans fought among themselves, they were able to keep the office of grand sharif within their local aristocracy. By the eighteenth century, the three major groups competing for power were the Abdallah, Zayd, and Barakat clans.

The Sharifian clans had great religious prestige, but they were primarily political interest groups. Although they were patrons of scholars and writers, they were not often directly involved in scholarly activity, and they opposed ideas and policies that would introduce significant changes in the management of the pilgrimage and in the sociopolitical context of Mecca. As a result, they were usually vigorously conservative in their style of Islam.

The situation in Medina was different as no great dynasty or single family dominated the political scene. There was a sense of city pride and a number of great families, some of whom traced their lineage back to the early Medinese supporters of the Prophet. In political terms, the great families had less power to withstand the control of the outside rulers than did the sharifs of Mecca, so the provincial governor and his garrison played a correspondingly greater role. The major Medinese families were supported by a wide variety of endowments, and they tended to monopolize the administrative positions within the mosques and other sites of religious importance. Although less independent than Mecca, Medina maintained a high degree of local autonomy, and both cities prospered from imperial subsidies and gifts from pious Muslims throughout the world of Islam.

The "establishment" in Medina was not as closed as that in Mecca. Immigrant scholars could settle, and over time, their families would be able to join the dominant oligarchy. As a result, the general style of the Medinese was not as conservative as was the case in Mecca. There was a greater sense of adapting to the changing political framework of the outside rulers and a greater willingness to incorporate newcomers into the structure of local power. The cosmopolitan scholarly community in Medina was often more lively and more directly involved in local affairs. There was also a tendency for scholars to settle in Medina rather than in Mecca.

The Scholarly Community

Mecca and Medina were major centers for study in the eighteenth century. The subjects studied were almost exclusively the basic religious disciplines, but in those, the teachers of the Haramayn had great importance for the whole world of Islam. There, as elsewhere in the Muslim world, scholars of *hadith* and teachers involved in the reorientation of the Sufi tradition had a special prominence, and the interregional communication taking place among the scholars in the Hijaz may have been an important catalyst in the evolution of those ideas. It is clear that study in Mecca and Medina had an impact on the scholars who went for instruction and then returned to their homelands.

At the heart of the cosmopolitan community of scholars in the holy cities was a core group of resident teachers, and they formed a continuing tradition of learning throughout the century. The key figures in that group were connected by close student-teacher ties or were fellow students together. They shared common academic interests and were initiated into the same *tariqah*s. They were not, however, a formally structured organization.

Twelve of the most prominent teachers in the Haramayn from the middle of the seventeenth century to the second half of the eighteenth were major figures in that informal scholarly grouping, and they came from many different backgrounds. Two were born in India, two in Morocco, three came from Kurdish areas in northern Iraq, and five were born in either Mecca or Medina, but only one of those came from a long-established family. However, all were involved in *hadith* scholarship, and all had *tariqah* affiliations with orders that were involved in the development of Neo-Sufism. Each of them was either a student or a teacher of at least three of the rest of the group.

Within the group there was a tendency to go beyond a simple acceptance of the medieval commentaries in *hadith* studies, and the members appear to have encouraged an examination of the earliest sources. As a result, they often rejected the idea that it was necessary to engage in *taqlid* (accepting the conclusions of previous scholars) and instead used their own critical efforts in an analysis of the sources (that is called using *ijtihad*). One example of that emphasis is the stress that at least some of them gave to the study of compilations of *hadith*s that were earlier than the standard collections, which dated from the ninth century and were usually the basis for *hadith* study.

The careful study of the Traditions of the Prophet was a part of a concern that those teachers had for the purifying of society by eliminating practices that were not approved by the Quran or the Sunnah. Students of these men described them with terms like "the Mujaddid [Renewer] of the Haramayn" and the "bearer of the banner of the Sunnah in Medina." Although these men were not militant activists, they were generally more fundamentalist than conservative or adaptationist in style.

That fundamentalist tone is reflected in the type of Sufism these men believed in. Although none of them totally rejected Sufism, they were not involved in the more popular or pantheistic styles of mysticism. The emerging nature of Neo-Sufism is reflected in the changing positions of this group between the mid-seventeenth century and the end of the eighteenth. The great seventeenth-century teacher, Ahmad al-Qushashi (d. 1661), had accepted some of the major theological formulations of Ibn al-Arabi, although he had opposed *tariqah* syncretism—al-Qushashi and his students were primarily associated with *tariqah*s as devotional practices and litanies rather than as social associations. Three generations of students later, scholars within the prominent group of twelve were emphasizing the study of al-Ghazali rather than Ibn al-Arabi, and they were beginning to establish *tariqah*s that were large-scale organizations as well as traditions of devotional practice.

Within the core of the cosmopolitan group of scholars, the main lines of Neo-Sufism were being defined. The Naqshbandiyyah perspective was combined with the North African style of organization to produce the reforming orders of the late eighteenth and early nineteenth centuries. Mustafa al-Bakri, the chief figure in the revivalist Khalwatiyyah, studied *hadith* and other subjects with at least three of those leading Haramayn teachers. In turn, he initiated into the Khalwatiyyah one of the group's Medinese scholars and students, Muhammad ibn Abd al-Karim al-Samman, who later established the Sammaniyyah Tariqah, an order of the activist, Neo-Sufi type.

A similar interaction can be seen in terms of the Indian ulama. A number of the members of the Haramayn group were affiliated with the Naqshbandiyyah through a chain of authorities going back to Ahmad Sirhindi. The major teacher of that line in India during the eighteenth century was Shah Wali Allah al-Dihlawi. Wali Allah studied *hadith* with the Haramayn group and later became one of the most significant teachers in India. One of his students was Muhammad Murtada al-Zabidi, who studied in Arabia with members of the group himself and went on to become one of the leading scholars of *hadith* in the eastern Mediterranean region. Many people in the cosmopolitan Haramayn group later became his students.

The Haramayn cosmopolitan scholarly tradition may not have been the cause of eighteenth-century Islamic revivalism, but it had connections with most such movements in addition to the ties with al-Bakri, Wali Allah, and al-Zabidi. Abd al-Ra'uf al-Sinkili (d. after 1693), an opponent of Sufi excesses in the East Indies, studied with early teachers in the group. Late in the century, the founders of activist Neo-Sufi *tariqah*s like the Tijaniyyah, the Sammaniyyah, the Sanusiyyah, and the Khatmiyyah were associated with the group. Teachers who laid the foundations for the holy war in West Africa and the jihad movement of Ahmad Brelwi in India also had some contacts with this Haramayn tradition. The best known of the movements established by students of those teachers was the rigorously fundamentalist one that was led by Muhammad ibn Abd al-Wahhab, whose followers came to be called the "Wahhabis."

In the eighteenth century, Mecca and Medina were clearly more than places of pilgrimage. They were important centers for the cosmopolitan world of Islamic scholarship, and movements associated with the scholars of the Haramayn were crucial to the development of Neo-Sufism and the revivalism of the time.

Wahhabis: Rigorous Fundamentalism at the Center

The spirit of socio-moral reconstruction reached a peak in the eighteenth century with the fundamentalist movement established by Muhammad ibn Abd al-Wahhab (1703–1792). The followers of this teacher call themselves the Muwahhidun, that is, believers in *tawhid,* but they are more commonly known as the Wahhabis. Because of the movement's general fame and its location at the center of Islam, the Wahhabi movement has come to represent the prototype of rigorous fundamentalism in the modern Islamic experience.

Since the eighteenth century, the term *Wahhabism* has become "a kind of umbrella term—the 'Wahhabi idea'— . . . summed up as a reassertion of monotheism and equality of men combined with varying degrees of reinterpretation of the actual positive legacy of the Islamic tradition for the reconstruction of Muslim society."[25] That "idea" has its clear foundations in the eighteenth-century Islamic experience. Wahhabism built on the existing

currents of thought and carried them to their culmination in militant fundamentalism. In this sense, the Muwahhidun were not typical of the eighteenth-century revivalists or the later movements that grew out of their
work, but represented the polar end of the spectrum that runs from fundamentalism to open adaptationism and syncretism.

The career of Muhammad ibn Abd al-Wahhab and his works combine the
major themes of the fundamentalist style of eighteenth-century Islam. He
was born in central Arabia to a family of teachers attached to the Hanbali
school. He was trained in the most strict of the Sunni schools of law and
then went to Mecca and Medina for more education. In the Haramayn, his
major teachers included Muhammad Hayat al-Sindi, one of the key figures
in the cosmopolitan revivalist group. He received rigorous training in the
study of *hadith* and was frequently reminded of the gap between the ideal
community that was described by the traditions and the society that he saw
around him.

After further travels, he returned to his homeland, the Najd region in
central Arabia. There he began to preach, calling upon the people to abandon the practices of popular religion and adhere strictly to the Quran and the
Sunnah. For some time he met with opposition, but eventually one of the
local chieftains, Muhammad ibn Saud of Dariyah, accepted his call. The
alliance that was formed between the fundamentalist teacher and the warrior
chief produced a militant Islamic state, and it expanded rapidly in the Arabian Peninsula. The momentum created by the combination of religious enthusiasm and military skill was maintained after the deaths of the original
leaders. The Saudi-Wahhabi forces raided the Shi'i holy cities in southern
Iraq in 1802 and captured Mecca in 1803, and the first decade of the nineteenth century was the high point of the first Saudi state. The Ottoman
leaders became concerned about the new challenge to their authority and
sent the newly created Egyptian army against the Saudis. In the war that
ensued, there was a direct conflict between forces created by the new Westernizing adaptations of rulers, which were characteristic of the nineteenth
century, and forces created by the dynamism of eighteenth-century Islamic
revivalism. The Saudi-Wahhabi forces were defeated, and by 1818, the first
Saudi state had been brought to an end. However, the foundations had been
laid for the twentieth-century emergence of a successor fundamentalist state.

Basic Positions

The teachings of Muhammad ibn Abd al-Wahhab reflect both the general
traditional themes of the Muslim fundamentalists and the more specific concerns arising out of the eighteenth-century experience. He carried the rein-

terpretation of the Sufi tradition to a logical fundamentalist conclusion and vigorously rejected the whole structure of the Sufi devotional practices as being unwholesome innovations. He proclaimed that veneration for any human, however saintly, constituted *shirk* or polytheism. Anyone who participated in such practices was declared an unbeliever and subject to the death penalty for leaving Islam. In the absoluteness of his rejection of Sufism, he went beyond virtually all other Muslim fundamentalists—both those who had preceded him and those who succeeded him in later generations. However, the example of the Wahhabi movement gave an added impetus to the element of eighteenth-century socio-moral reconstructionism that objected to the syncretistic tone of later medieval Sufism.

Muhammad ibn Abd al-Wahhab replaced the pantheistic style of Sufi theology with a renewed emphasis on the interpretation of *tawhid,* the oneness of God, that stressed God's transcendence. In that interpretation, there was emphasis on strict obedience to the word of God and on the full responsibility of the individual believer. The "Sufi path" was to be accepted only if it meant a striving to purify the heart from vices and sin in order to obey more fully the commands of God.[26]

In that context, it was the obligation of the believer to think for himself, rather than accept blindly the words of others. Muhammad ibn Abd al-Wahhab wrote that men should examine their condition and the condition of the people of the age who simply took their faith from their fathers and borrowed prevailing local customs. He reminded his readers that it would do them no good if, after death, they told the questioning angels, "I heard the people saying something, so I said it, too."[27]

Implicit in that position is a rejection of the unquestioning acceptance of the medieval scholarly authorities, and blind *taqlid* or imitation was rejected in examining the importance of the Quran and the Sunnah. The position of the shaykh and his followers was that it was not obligatory for any Muslim to follow any persons in their faith except the Prophet himself. The Quran and the Sunnah were the two fundamental and binding sources for Islamic faith and law, and anything beyond those two sources was binding only insofar as it reflected the clear meaning of the revelation.

The followers of Muhammad ibn Abd al-Wahhab denied that that position meant a rejection of the works of the earlier teachers, but they did object to placing such works on the same level as the Quran and the Sunnah in being required guides for the believer. In this way, the Wahhabi position insisted on the right of an informed independent analysis of the fundamental sources of the faith (*ijtihad*). Although they did not feel that total *ijtihad* was necessary, they believed that it was of continuing importance in special cases. In this recognition of *ijtihad,* the movement reflected concerns that were a part

of traditional fundamentalism and eighteenth-century socio-moral reconstructionism, and that recognition was one of the features that distinguished
the movement from the conservative style of Islam.

Impact of Wahhabism

In addition to laying the foundations for the twentieth-century Kingdom of
Saudi Arabia, the eighteenth-century Wahhabi movement had a broad impact. It provided a striking example at the center of the Islamic world of
rigorous fundamentalism in practice, and by its success, the movement was
able to show Muslims from other areas that militant purification was possible. In this way, it gave added emphasis to the eighteenth-century mood of
socio-moral reconstruction along strictly Islamic lines.

Some caution must be exercised, however, in assessing the direct impact
of Wahhabism. It has been common at times to assert that any teacher who
happened to go to Arabia in the eighteenth century and who returned to
his home full of fundamentalist enthusiasm was somehow influenced by
the Wahhabis. That assertion is clearly an underestimation of the role of the
scholars of the Haramayn, and it ignores the broader Islamic trends of the
century. It is worth noting, for example, that many of the revivalist movements that had emerged by the end of the century did so in the framework of
Neo-Sufi thought and organization rather than by following the Wahhabi
attitude.

It is clear, even with those reservations, that Wahhabism was a significant
element in the Islamic world, and its example was important at the time.
The movement's ideas were viewed favorably by a reformist Moroccan sultan, Mawlay Suleyman, and they helped him define the bases for his opposition to Sufi practices. Other contemporaries were also directly affected. In
the long run, the teachings and writings of Muhammad ibn Abd al-Wahhab
and his followers provided an inspiration for twentieth-century Muslim
thinkers, particularly in the movement that came to be called the Salafiyyah.
In those later movements, the ideal of a comprehensive program of social
and political fundamentalism and a rigorous opposition to Sufism were fully
developed and the debt to the Wahhabis acknowledged. In this way, the
Wahhabi movement can be seen as a prototype of the rigorous fundamentalism that is a part of the twentieth-century Islamic experience.

Islam in the Indian Ocean Region

Modern scholarship often makes distinctions between arbitrarily defined
regions and calls them the Middle East, South Asia, and Southeast Asia.

Although such distinctions are a convenience for some kinds of analysis, they create boundaries that did not exist within the eighteenth-century Islamic world. The whole Indian Ocean region was, especially in terms of the cosmopolitan ulama groups, a loosely integrated unit. Trade, political contacts, and wandering scholars provided the means for a significant interaction among the various parts of the region. Thus, although there were special local conditions that shaped the Islamic experience, it is important to keep the broader regional networks in mind.

The largest single unit within the region was the Moghul Empire, but since it was a land-based imperial system, it did not dominate the region in political terms. Groupings of small sultanates and city-states provided the political context for much of the region, and important clusters of them were in the islands and peninsulas of Southeast Asia, the southern Arabian Peninsula, and along the East African coast. Those groups interacted along the sea-lanes, and by the eighteenth century, there was a new element of growing importance that also tended to be based on the oceanic lines of communication. That new element was the development of the great European trading companies, which had the military support of the emerging Western imperial systems. European powers had become a factor in the Indian Ocean region when the Portuguese intruded during the fifteenth and sixteenth centuries, but that Portuguese challenge had been successfully contained. During the eighteenth century, it was the British, French, and Dutch who were the growing European commercial and military forces in the region.

Within the Islamic community, the major lines of communication were outside of the state systems themselves. There was a constant movement of scholars throughout the region, following the lines of trade. One factor was the travel to and from Mecca and Medina, which brought Muslims from South and Southeast Asia to the central Islamic lands. In the opposite direction, there was a movement of scholar-missionaries from Arabia and India to the more removed sections of the region. Within this framework, there were great ulama and merchant families that maintained a network of contacts throughout the region.

One of the underlying dynamics of eighteenth-century history was the gradual fragmentation of the region. Significant regional interaction continued long after the end of the century, but it was more restricted than it had been earlier. An important factor in this change was the gradual consolidation of influence and then control by the European powers. As the European economic "world system" became more important, the lines of local trade were disrupted, and the older economic networks that had supported the Islamic interaction were replaced by networks that were Europe oriented.

These broad changes produced a climate in which the conservative style of Islam was weakened. In reaction to the changing circumstances, the other

Islamic styles assumed an increasing importance. Fundamentalist and adaptionist styles interacted, and in some cases, there was also a tendency for withdrawal into a more individualized, passive Islam. That latter trend was sometimes encouraged by the adaptationists, who began to accept some of the secularizing implications of the Western ideas.

Moghul India and Shah Wali Allah

During the eighteenth century, the Moghul Empire collapsed as an effective system of political control in India. The last years of the reign of Aurangzeb were filled with revolts, and following his death in 1707, wars of succession and the rise of local and provincial powers brought an end to the politico-military unity that had been created by Moghul rule. Hindu and Sikh princes competed with local Muslim commanders and Afghan and Persian invaders for dominance within the subcontinent, but no single local power was able to establish a long-lasting position of strength. In the long run, a foreign power, Great Britain, assumed control over much of India, but during the eighteenth century, the British were simply one of a large number of competitors. Their ultimate victory would not have been clear to many, if any, informed observers of the time.

The Muslim response to the changing situation was dominated by the career and works of Shah Wali Allah al-Dihlawi (1702–1762), in whom one can see the interaction of the broader themes of eighteenth-century Islamic history with the special local conditions in India. Wali Allah represents an important climax point for Indian Islam. On the one hand, his career was a high point in the evolution of Islam that had been set in motion by the rise of the Moghuls and the emergence of Naqshbandiyyah revivalism, and on the other hand, his work provided the foundation for virtually every major Muslim movement in India since that time.

Like other eighteenth-century Islamic revivalists, Wali Allah was not primarily concerned with the challenge of the modernizing West, and his reformism arose out of the interaction between the changing local conditions and the Islamic dimension. In that way, the starting point for Islamic thought in modern India was inspired more by "indigenous" factors than by "foreign" ones. This quality of having arisen from within the Islamic tradition rather than simply being a reaction to the modern West gives a special character to Islamic revivalism in the context of modern history.

Two great issues set the framework for Wali Allah's work: the decline of the Muslim community as a whole in India and the disunity and conflict within that community. In dealing with the first issue, Wali Allah was a vigorous fundamentalist and reaffirmed the authenticity of the Islamic revelation. However, in dealing with disputes among Muslims, his goal appears to have been one of reconciliation, and his major formulations attempted to create positions that could unify Muslims holding diverse views.

Wali Allah mistrusted syncretistic trends, and, in that, he continued the Naqshbandiyyah opposition to tolerant religious universalism. He was in a direct line from Ahmad Sirhindi in his opposition to compromises with non-Islamic practices, and he attacked the rulers for not imposing punishments in accord with Islamic law and accused the local Sufi teachers of encouraging idolatry. In addressing all classes of Muslims he said, "O children of Adam, you have wrecked your morals, made your living miserable and drifted into the care of Satan. . . . You have adopted such vicious customs as have corrupted true faith. . . . You behave and indulge in frivolous acts like the ignorant communities."[28]

Wali Allah did not organize a formal movement or create a special association. The structures that he developed were schools for instruction, through which he hoped to provide the basis for a revitalization of Islamic thought and, by this means, restore the Islamic position within India. He himself looked to various Muslim commanders to lead the military struggle. When those failed, his successors began to create more directly politico-military organizations. Thus, the militant activism of the fundamentalists in the early nineteenth century followed Wali Allah's ideas but went beyond his own type of organizational activity.

In dealing with the problem of Muslim disunity, Wali Allah utilized many of the major eighteenth-century themes. His style, in terms of interpretation, was fundamentalist, but his goal was reconciliation, not condemnation. Wali Allah was active in the development of Neo-Sufi ideas. The Naqshbandiyyah teachings of Ahmad Sirhindi had created a school of thought that opposed the ideas of Ibn al-Arabi, and the main disagreement centered on the meaning of the oneness of God. Ibn al-Arabi's relatively pantheistic idea of the unity of being (*wahdat al-wujud*) had been opposed by Sirhindi, who had proposed the idea of unity in the manifestations of God (*wahdat al-shuhud*). That idea emphasized God's transcendence rather than the mystic unity of God and the material universe. In the seventeenth century, those positions had become identified with political factions and had been the slogans for two different concepts of the empire. A war of succession to the Moghul throne that began in 1657 had pitted two brothers against each other, with one representing the syncretistic spirit of the earlier sultan, Akbar, and the other, the fundamentalist reaction of Ahmad Sirhindi. Aurangzeb, the latter, had won, and the tone of Moghul policy had become more fundamentalist.

In the context of the collapse of Muslim political unity, it was important to reconcile the two positions. Wali Allah argued persuasively that the two concepts were basically different metaphors describing the same underlying reality. Through this line of thought, the broader range of Sufi thought in India was reintegrated into a single intellectual structure, and the extremes of pantheistic speculation were reduced. At the same time, Wali Allah worked to have *tariqah* practices conform more closely to the prescriptions of the Quran and the Sunnah. "To check the spiritual decadence of Islam in his age, he completed the work begun by Shaykh Ahmad Sirhindi, the channelling of the streams of Sufi spiritual heritage into traditional Islam. This also involved a composition of Sufism's internal differences of practice, and a synthetic merging together of the various Sufi disciplines of India into one."[29]

That merging was an important part of the development of Neo-Sufism in the eighteenth century. Wali Allah carried forward the reinterpretation of the teachings of Ibn al-Arabi and made it possible to reject pantheistic extremes without fully rejecting Sufism. In his preaching on moral rectitude, he laid the foundation for the more militant Neo-Sufi groups, and his role was similar to that of Mustafa al-Bakri. It is, in fact, worth noting that Wali Allah and Mustafa al-Bakri shared at least one teacher; they both studied with Abdallah ibn Salim al-Basri, one of the members of the revivalist scholarly group in the Haramayn.

The eighteenth-century emphasis on the study of *hadith* is also reflected in the work of Wali Allah. His *hadith* studies, like his interpretations of Sufism, show his dual concern with reconciling divisions within the Muslim community and bringing Islamic practice more into line with the Islamic ideal.

One of the lines of division was the separation of the Sunni Muslims into the different schools of law. Although there was mutual recognition among the scholars in the different schools, the differing interpretations sometimes led to vigorous disputes. In his work, Wali Allah subordinated the study of law to the discipline of *hadith* studies. Like Muhammad ibn Abd al-Wahhab, Wali Allah rejected the practice of *taqlid* if it meant blind adherence to the teachers within the law schools' traditions. Instead, he believed that *ijtihad* was necessary, and the only two unquestioned sources for Islamic law, according to that position, are the Quran and the Sunnah. Thus, the study of the traditions takes precedence over imitation of the earlier jurists' writings. That belief was made clear when Wali Allah was once asked what was his *madhhab* or legal school. He replied, "I try my best to combine all the points of agreement in all the schools, and in matters of variance I adhere to what is proved by the genuine *hadith*—which, thank God, I can do."[30]

Wali Allah is an important figure in the development of the attitude toward the study of the *hadiths*. One aspect of the Naqshbandiyyah revival was the development of a rigorist tradition in the study of *hadith* that was associated with Abd al-Haqq al-Dihlawi (1551–1642), who had introduced new methods of *hadith* transmission and popularized *hadith* study. Wali Allah developed ties with that tradition and then studied with some of the major revivalist *muhaddiths* in Mecca and Medina. Like other scholars in those groups, Wali Allah did not accept the standard ninth-century *hadith* collections as infallible or not open to question and analysis.

Wali Allah's position is shown not only in his general acceptance of the idea of the continuing validity of *ijtihad* but also in the *hadith* material that he studied. Like some of his teachers and fellow students in Mecca and Medina, he gave preference in his *hadith* analysis to the *hadith* collections that were earlier than the standard ninth-century compilations. In doing so they gave special precedence to the *Muwatta* of Malik ibn Anas, the founder of the Maliki law school. Wali Allah's position that Malik's work was the foundation of the science of *hadith* is similar to the statement of a West African who studied and taught *hadith* in Medina a little later. That scholar called the Muwatta the "first source" and the most widely used of the ninth-century collections the "second source."[31]

The line of interaction between the *hadith* studies led by Wali Allah in India and those conducted by the scholars in Mecca and Medina continued throughout the century. Muhammad Murtada el-Zabidi, one of the leading *hadith* scholars in the later part of the century, was a student of Wali Allah before settling in Egypt. Wali Allah also had an important impact on the later development of Islam in India. His work in reformulating Islam on a basis broader than that of the traditional schools of thought made possible a wider range of adaptation than the more strict fundamentalism of the Wahhabis. His influence may have been an important factor in the relatively early development in India of a modernist adaptationism that was Islamic in its orientation. He thus inspired both fundamentalism and adaptation within later Indian Islam.

The Transformation of Southeast Asia

The islands and peninsulas of Southeast Asia are at the eastern periphery of the Indian Ocean region within the Islamic world, and the Islamic experience in the area is distinctive and clearly influenced by local conditions. However, despite the distance to the central Islamic lands, the major trends of eighteenth-century Islam had an impact on the Southeast Asian Muslim communities.

From the perspective of modern history, a key element in the eighteenth-century experience was the development of European imperialism. However, it is possible to miss significant aspects of the Islamic experience in the area if one concentrates on the activities of the Dutch East India Company and the other European groups. The ultimate domination of the area by the Dutch, British, and French was not yet evident during the eighteenth century. Modern Western historians sometimes find it convenient to think of non-Western societies in the eighteenth century as stagnant, crumbling structures, falling almost without effective resistance in the face of the European expansion. But even in Southeast Asia, where the local states were quite small compared with the Ottoman or Moghul imperial systems, that assumption is not a very accurate one.

The general picture is probably more correctly presented by a Dutch historian, J. C. van Leur, who has noted that the eighteenth century "did not know any superior Occident, nor any self-isolating Orient no longer progressing with it. It knew a mighty East, a rich fabric of a strong, broad weave with a more fragile Western warp thread inserted in it at broad intervals."[32] There were a number of important factors that interacted. Clearly, there was a "Western thread," but there were also local elements whose evolution was not governed simply by the European encroachment. This discussion of the Islamic history of Southeast Asia in the eighteenth century will focus on the experience of the territories within modern Indonesia.

At the beginning of the eighteenth century, there were a large number of smaller states competing for power as the coming of Islam in the preceding centuries had provided the foundations for sultanates that were scattered throughout the islands. In addition, European forts and trading centers had been established. The Portuguese had been a factor since the sixteenth century, when they had conquered Malacca, a key commercial and military center. However, by the eighteenth century, the major European power was the Dutch East India Company, which had built a number of settlements, especially on the island of Java. Dutch naval power and commercial activity were an important part of the shifting scene.

Islam was firmly established in the islands although it was not universal and Indonesian Islam exhibited distinctive characteristics. During the long centuries of the introduction and spread of Islam throughout the islands, its propagators had made significant adaptations to the local conditions. It had been introduced by merchants and itinerant teachers who had been willing to take on at least some of the coloring of the local religious customs. The pre-Islamic culture had been strongly influenced by Hinduism and Buddhism, which meant that the more pantheistic styles of Islam had the greatest success. As the older monarchies had begun to convert to Islam, they, too, had maintained forms and moods that reflected the Hindu past. Therefore, Indonesian Islam was distinctively adaptationist.

That Islamic experience was challenged in the seventeenth and eighteenth centuries on two fronts. One was the growing power of the Dutch. and the other was the development of a fundamentalist style of Islam. Those factors operating together helped to shape the form taken by Indonesian Islam in the nineteenth and twentieth centuries.

The expansion of Dutch control in Indonesia was gradual. Although there was some increase in the amount of land that was under the direct control of the Dutch, the primary method of expansion was to exert influence on and then to dominate the existing states. In this way, the Dutch controlled most of the sultans and other local rulers by the end of the eighteenth century. Although some local rulers fought the Dutch expansion, at times successfully, the traditionally political institutions were increasingly unable to resist effectively. Dutch commercial and military power was gradually replacing adaptationist Islam as the basis for the ability of the old-style monarchies to remain in existence.

The form and context of the local Indonesian states were very different from those of the Ottoman Empire. There was, however, a general similarity in that the adaptationism of the rulers became identified with the expansion of Western ideas. Opposition to this identification often took the form of fundamentalist Islam, and it was the nonadaptationist style that assumed the duty of preserving an authentic identity. "If colonialism created the conditions in which an oppositional, identity-preserving, willed Islam could and did flourish, scripturalism [i.e., fundamentalism] . . . provided the content of such an Islam."[33]

The emergence of fundamentalism was not simply the product of Dutch expansion as it also evolved within the context of Indonesian Islam as the area interacted with the broader Islamic world. Themes and interactions similar to, and sometimes influenced by, those found elsewhere can be seen in the experience of Indonesia at this time.

The theological foundations for the adaptationist mysticism of Indonesian Islam were the ideas of Ibn al-Arabi and similar Sufi writers. By the mid-seventeenth century, some Indonesian ulama had become convinced that the pantheism of that Sufism was not in accord with the Quran and the Sunnah, and the attack on that style of mysticism had received a strong impetus when a scholar from India arrived in the sultanate of Atjeh in Sumatra. That teacher, Nur al-Din al-Raniri (who stayed in Atjeh from 1637 to 1644) had strongly opposed the implications of the idea of *wahdat al-wujud* ("unity of being") as presented by Ibn al-Arabi. In his fundamentalist attack, he had been supported by the sultan, and he had an impact on later Indonesian Islam.

Al-Raniri's theme had been carried on by an Indonesian scholar named Abd al-Ra'uf al-Sinkili (d. sometime after 1693). That scholar had studied for nineteen years in Arabia, where he had been a student of Ahmad al-Qushashi and Ibrahim al-Kurani, two figures in the Haramayn revivalist group. Although he had not been as extreme in his polemics as al-Raniri, he had worked diligently to eliminate the extremes of pantheistic mysticism. He had returned to Indonesia with the permission of his Medinese teachers to propagate the Shattariyyah Tariqah with devotional practices that were more in accord with a fundamentalist style of Islam. His studies and translations became major works in the literature of the more strict Muslims in Indonesia.

The positions of al-Raniri and al-Sinkili represent a withdrawal from the kind of Sufism that had developed as a result of the adaptationism on the local level. That withdrawal was also a movement away from the theological positions of Ibn al-Arabi and often entailed a direct attack on his ideas, which reflects the general development of Neo-Sufism in the general Islamic world.

In the eighteenth century, others among the best-known ulama continued that position, reflecting the later stages of Neo-Sufism in the central Islamic lands. In Sumatra, that continuation is visible in the works of Shihab al-Din ibn Abdallah Muhammad and his son, Muhammad. "Shihabuddin's aim was to criticize current excesses in the practice of mysticism,"[34] and one vehicle he used was to attack the ideas of *wahdat al-wujud* and to reemphasize the transcendence-oriented meaning of the doctrine of *tawhid*. His son was affiliated with a Neo-Sufi *tariqah* that found its way to Indonesia in the second half of the eighteenth century, the Sammaniyyah, which had been established by Muhammad ibn Abd al-Karim al-Samman, the student of Mustafa al-Bakri. Muhammad ibn Shihab al-Din prepared a Malay translation of a life of al-Samman and aided in the spread of this new type of *tariqah*.

The major propagator of the Sammaniyyah Tariqah was Abd al-Samad al-Palimbani, who lived for a long time as a student and teacher in Mecca. His best-known work was a translation of the writings of al-Ghazali, which reflects the interest in the Sufi theologian's work in Neo-Sufism. Al-Palimbani also wrote a summary of some lectures that were given in Mecca in 1763 by Ahmad al-Damanhuri, an Egyptian scholar who claimed, like Shah Wali Allah, to be proficient in all the law schools, judging on the basis of tradition rather than on simple imitation of earlier scholars. Another work dealt with holy war and urged believers to combat infidels. This last treatise inspired writings that circulated during holy wars against the Dutch in the nineteenth and twentieth centuries.

Through the works of these teachers and others like them, the foundations of the modern Islamic experience in Indonesia were built. As European powers came increasingly to dominate the area, this more fundamentalist style of Islam often provided the rationale for resistance. Opposition was not usually organized in the traditional courts of the old rulers as they tended to adapt to the changing circumstances and became client-states and part of the colonial ruling system. As a result, activist Islam tended to take the form of non-state associations, and through this type of organization, large numbers of people could be mobilized. Large-scale resistance also did not arise out of the popular religious practices of the villagers. Only when the population was inspired by a more fundamentalist rationale could they be aroused to action. The potential division between state-oriented, Western-influenced leadership and fundamentalist Islam that began to emerge in the eighteenth century is a continuing feature in the Islamic history of Southeast Asia.

South Arabia: A Linking Area

The small states and communities of the southern and eastern shores of the Arabian Peninsula were an important focal point in the linking together of the Islamic regions of the Indian Ocean basin as Muslim scholars and merchants from this area moved throughout the region and provided an important means for tying the scattered parts of the Indian Ocean basin together. Those scholars and merchants also connected those Muslim communities to the broader Islamic world.

The cities and towns of Yemen and the Hadramaut were natural stopping points for pilgrims coming from the east and south, and students often stopped and studied with the local ulama on their way to or from Mecca and Medina. The ports were also convenient focal points in the pattern of trade, and merchants and ulama from these areas traveled widely, taking with them their goods and ideas. These itinerants from the southern part of Arabia were a common part of Islamic life throughout the Indian Ocean basin. They helped to spread Islam, and they also established branches of their families in many areas.

During the eighteenth century, there were opportunities for local political forces and economic groups to expand their influence. In the sixteenth century, Portuguese naval power had disrupted the old political and economic networks by controlling the key harbor locations and being a major force. However, by the eighteenth century, the Muslim rulers had been able to defeat the Portuguese and to reassert local control. Although other European powers were beginning to enter the area, they were still not a dominant force, and the British and the French appeared often as potential allies as well as enemies. The British, for example, cooperated with Persian forces in driving the Portuguese out of Hormuz at the mouth of the Persian Gulf.

Local rulers were able to maintain a high degree of independence, and in some cases, they expanded the areas under their control. In southern Arabia there were two states with distinctive Islamic traditions. In Yemen, the Zaydi form of Shiʿi Islam had been established in medieval times. A line of Zaydi imams led the community, sometimes as an independent state and sometimes under the overlordship of an outside power. There was a long history of Ottoman attempts to establish power over the imams of Yemen, which continued throughout the eighteenth century. However, in the context of Ottoman decentralization, the imams were largely in control.

The Zaydis were primarily the mountain and highland peoples, and the majority of the population in the coastal plains and lowland areas was Sunni and affiliated with the Shafiʿi law school. The two groups both competed and cooperated. In the cities of the plains, a tradition of respected scholarship developed, which was especially centered in the mosques of Zabid and the surrounding areas. During the eighteenth century, there was a general fluctuation in the areas under the control of the imam and the areas that were on the fringes of the control of the Ottoman governors and the Meccan sharifs.

The other distinctive political context was in Oman. The Ibadi branch of the Kharijite movement had been firmly established in Oman early in Islamic history, and like the Zaydis in Yemen, the Ibadis had alternated through the centuries between independence and some type of external control. The Ibadi community was traditionally led by an elected imam. During the sixteenth century, the Portuguese established forts along the Omani coast and were a dominant force, but the Ibadi imams of the seventeenth century drove the Portuguese out and began a significant military and commercial expansion along the East African coast. In the middle of the eighteenth century, Oman was threatened by invasion from Iran but overcame that threat under the leadership of Imam Ahmad ibn Said, who turned the scattered Omani-influenced territories into a flourishing sea-based empire. He founded the Bu Said dynasty, which has ruled Oman since that time. After the death of his son and successor, the Bu Said rulers ceased using the title of imam and generally were known as sayyids or sultans.

The Bu Said dynastic state had religious prestige because of its ties to the Ibadi tradition, but it was not an elective imamate of the style most in accord with Ibadi beliefs. As a result, from time to time, Ibadi groups would elect an imam, and the more fundamentalist groups would challenge the dynastic state. During the eighteenth century, the sultanate faced a growing challenge from Wahhabi expansion, and there were problems in dealing with the increasing power of the European states in the Indian Ocean. The Omani sultans solved these difficulties by adapting to the changing conditions. In

1798, the sultan signed a treaty with Great Britain, which granted the British an exclusive role in Omani foreign relations in exchange for British protection and support for the dynasty. This arrangement preserved the sultanate and is the basis for the modern history of Oman.

Along the rest of the Arabian coast, from Yemen in the southwest to Kuwait in the northeast, the eighteenth century was the time when the modern states emerged as distinct political entities. Between Yemen and Oman, a cluster of small princedoms and city-states led by people who were considered saints emerged. In 1732, the territory around Aden and Lahej became independent from the control of the imam of Yemen. This feat was accomplished by the founder of the long-lasting Abdali dynasty of Lahej. Similarly, in the Persian/Arab Gulf coasts of the peninsula, leaders of migrating tribal groups established a long chain of city-states, which were dominated by aristocratic clans. The current ruling families of Kuwait Qatar, Bahrain, and many of the constituent parts of the United Arab Emirates emerged at that time. Like Oman, most of these states established special relations with Great Britain, which helped to ensure dynastic continuity and, through the local autonomy allowed by the arrangements, to insulate the areas from many of the developments of modern Middle Eastern history. As a result, these states entered the era of their independence in the last third of the twentieth century with social and political institutions that were still fundamentally similar to those that were created in the eighteenth century.

The relatively parochial political developments should not obscure the important role of the cosmopolitan community of scholars of southern Arabia. In some ways, the high degree of local autonomy made it possible for ulama and merchants to roam freely while maintaining ties with their homelands, and the great religious families of Yemen and the Hadramaut in particular established branches in many areas. A good example is the experience of the Aydarus family, one of a number of families that developed a reputation for both piety and scholarship. The family was Sufi but avoided identification with the more ecstatic and pantheistic styles—the founder of the family in the fifteenth century, for example, had studied the teachings of al-Ghazali. The family was supported by pious endowments in their original home of Tarim. Abu Bakr al-Aydarus (d. 1508) had moved to Aden, where he had established a branch of the family and had become the "patron saint" of the city. During the sixteenth century, a number of family members had settled in India, where they became wealthy scholars and influential religious teachers in the palaces and courts. By the eighteenth century, there were prominent branches of the family all the way from the cities of East Africa to the islands of Southeast Asia, and children in the family moved freely from one area to another in search of education and employment.

The Aydarus family provided one of the more remarkable itinerant scholars of the eighteenth century, Abd al-Rahman ibn Mustafa al-Aydarus (1723–1778). He was born in South Arabia and studied and traveled widely in India, living there for ten years. He traveled extensively in the eastern Mediterranean regions and settled in Egypt, and he studied with many of the major teachers in the revivalist group in Mecca and Medina and was an active scholar in the Naqshbandiyyah. His students included some of the leading figures in late-eighteenth-century Neo-Sufism, and he may well have been an important link among those scholars. Through him, for example, one can see a connection between the great Naqshbandiyyah family in Syria, the Muradis, and the Khalwatiyyah students of Mustafa al-Bakri in Egypt such as Muhammed al-Hifnawi.

In the career of Abd al-Rahman al-Aydarus, one has a microcosm of the role of the southern Arabian scholars in the eighteenth century. They were links that brought together scholars and ideas from many parts of the Islamic world. The schools of Zabid flourished during this period, and education there had an impact. Muhammad Murtada al-Zabidi, for example, felt that his instruction in Zabid was of such importance that he often referred to himself as "al-Zabidi" (i.e., a person from Zabid) even though he was born in India. The history of South Arabia in the eighteenth century thus emphasizes the importance of that era as a foundation for modern history and shows the interconnected and cosmopolitan nature of the eighteenth-century Islamic world.

Islamic Africa in the Eighteenth Century

Another great region of interaction within the eighteenth-century Islamic world was Muslim Africa. Like the Indian Ocean basin, this was a vast area with distinctive local conditions, and it was involved in a broad, regional network of exchange. The East African coast was part of the Indian Ocean network, and it was tied to the rest of the Islamic world through southern Arabia. The rest of Muslim Africa had a different orientation. The major lines of interaction spread in a great oval. There was the line across the North African coast and the north-south lines to the sub-Saharan Sudanic areas. There was also by the eighteenth century the beginnings of significant east-west travel along the pilgrim routes stretching through the savanna areas just south of the desert. A focal point in this network was Egypt, through which most African Muslim scholars passed on pilgrimage and to which many went for study. The movement of scholars and ideas within this large oval made the area a special, interconnected region with diverse local conditions.

Within the area, there were many major developments that were conditioned by local circumstances. Along the Mediterranean coast, the Muslim communities had a long tradition of adherence to the faith, and in that area, the eighteenth century was a time of further evolution of long-standing institutions and customs. In the southern half of the oval, Islam had not been as firmly established, and the expansion and consolidation of Islam were important factors. However, despite these differences, there was much mutual interaction, and the developments in the older Islamic areas influenced and inspired trends in the newer Islamic areas.

Ottoman North Africa

During the sixteenth century, Ottoman control had extended to the coastal regions of North Africa in the areas of modern Libya, Tunisia, and Algeria, but by the eighteenth century, the provincial garrisons had assumed a significant degree of autonomous control. However, the sultan in Istanbul continued to have some influence. "Even on the distant borders of the Maghreb the sultan exercised sufficient political control throughout most of the eighteenth century to maintain the integrity of the Empire in this tumultuous zone. What disorganized the eighteenth century politics of the Ottoman frontier in the western Mediterranean was the rise of the modern western nation state and not the actions of the Maghreb corsair communities."[35]

The European challenge to the Islamic communities of North Africa was not, in the eighteenth century, a threat in ideological terms. It was, rather, a continuation of the long politico-military struggle for control in the western Mediterranean, and the main lines of that conflict had long been in terms of military power. In this context, the role of Islam had been and remained one of helping to mobilize the local forces to oppose European military expansion. In the eighteenth century, the new element was the growing economic involvement of Europe, which helped to alter the structure of local power but was not yet a major challenge to Islam as a faith.

Operating within the context of both victories and defeats, the main lines of the Islamic development were primarily inspired locally. The most important feature of Islamic life was the development of the Sufi *tariqahs* and their role in society. There was no dramatic break with the past, but orders with a more Neo-Sufi orientation were emerging by the end of the eighteenth century.

These general movements were part of an assertion of local identity in Islamic terms, not only against European forces but also against the ruling military elite, which was primarily recruited outside of the area. The movement took different forms in Libya, Tunisia, and Algeria. The basic social framework included the foreign military elite, local ulama and Sufi saints, and the great tribal organizations. In each of the three areas, the interaction took a different form.

In Libya, the Karamanli family created a dynasty within the military elite that lasted from 1711 until 1835. Its center was in Tripoli where the local religious establishment was small and relatively weak. There were resident teachers that traveling ulama would meet and mention in their accounts but the strongest local forces were the tribes. Ottoman control beyond the coastal cities was limited, and the Karamanli leaders faced frequent resistance from the various tribes. Religion did not provide a significant force for local mobilization or organization until the nineteenth century, when the Sanusiyyah Tariqah was established in the country.

The situation was significantly different in Tunisia. There, an ulama elite dominated the religious scene, and there were important Islamic institutions under their control. The city of al-Qayrawan had been a center of Islamic learning from the days of the first Muslim conquests, and although its prestige and prosperity had declined by the eighteenth century, it was still in many ways the leading Islamic center in the country and a place scholars went to from many parts of the Muslim world. There were also judgeships and other religious posts, many of which were centered in Tunis, the largest city.

In political terms, Tunis and the surrounding areas came under the control of a dynasty of Ottoman commanders established in 1705 by Husayn ibn Ali (d. 1740). In contrast to other military elites in the area, the Husaynid dynasty aided in the gradual assimilation of the Turkish troops, and "by the beginning of the nineteenth century the process was complete and the Husainid dynasty had become a Tunisian dynasty."[36] An important part of this process was the interaction of the local Tunisian religious establishment with the foreign military class.

The Tunisian ulama were the most prominent spokesmen for the general population, and the affiliation that was of greatest importance was not membership in a Sufi order but adherence to the Maliki law school. The official school of the Ottoman Empire was the Hanafi, and there was a history of tension between the local Maliki establishment and non-Tunisian Hanafi appointees to religious posts. By the eighteenth century, support for the Maliki institutions had become a symbol of the assertion of a special local identity. The Husaynids were able to win the support of the Maliki establishment by patronage and gradually reduced the antagonism between the adherents of the two schools in Tunisia.[37]

The characteristics of the Tunisian ulama and their relationship with the dynasty were shaped by the nature of the religious organization in Islam.

The law schools were not formal associations but schools of thought and traditions of learning. As a result, adherence to the Maliki school did not mean that there was a formal churchlike structure to provide institutional support for or place constraints upon individual scholars in their dealings with the rulers. In Tunisia, the major organized religious institutions were the various educational institutions and local mosques. The mainstays of the Maliki establishment were the Zaytuna University Mosque in Tunis, and the various mosques in the religious center of al-Qayrawan. By endowing new instructorships and refurbishing the buildings, the political leadership was able to win support from the religious establishment without creating an independent, nationally organized religious association.

The success of the political elite in their religious policy helped to create a relatively conservative mood within the religious establishment in Tunisia, and it reinforced the unincorporated nature of the ulama groupings and reduced the susceptibility of the Tunisian Muslim community to more fundamentalist organizations and ideas. That situation was to provide the foundation for a distinctive tone for modern Islam in Tunisia.

The Algerian experience during the eighteenth century was also different. There, the military ruling elite tended to remain apart from the local population, and the local Islamic leadership was also of a different character. Although the Maliki school was the dominant *madhhab* in Algeria as well as Tunisia, it did not provide the major focus for Islamic affiliation in Algeria. The major Muslim leaders in Algeria were associated with Sufi *tariqahs*, and centers built up around local saints, their families, and their tombs. These centers were quite well organized, and their involvement in the life of the people was comprehensive. In contrast to the ulama of Tunisia, the Algerian religious leaders belonged to formal associations that had the capacity to mobilize large segments of the population for political and military as well as religious purposes.

The eighteenth century was a time of major religious organizational activity in Algeria. New religious orders were created, older ones were revitalized, and increasingly by the end of the century, these orders came to assume a Neo-Sufi tone. As the military rulers became more oppressive in their demands upon the population, "these fraternities catalysed the discontent of the population and gave a formidable religious interpretation to its anti-Turkish sentiments."[38]

Some of the leading orders illustrate the ties of Algeria to the broader world of Neo-Sufism. In the first half of the century, orders with virtual political independence controlled a number of areas. As in the case of the Tayyibiyyah in the northwest, the creation of the order did not involve much in the way of a fundamentalist style. A more revivalist and militant tradition was created by Ahmad al-Darqawi (1760–1823), an ascetic teacher who preached against the exploitation of piety by the established orders. His followers became involved in a wide range of politico-religious activity. Although his own establishment was in Morocco, his influence soon spread to western Algeria where, in 1805, one of his local deputies led an attack on the Turkish rulers. He himself did not organize a formal brotherhood, but all across North Africa, Darqawiyyah derivatives had emerged by the end of the eighteenth century, and many of his followers had established close ties with Neo-Sufi teachers in the eastern Mediterranean area.

By the end of the century, Algeria was prepared for the vigorous activism of the Islamic revivalist style that emerged in the following century. The older orders were involved in a wide range of popular practices that could arouse fundamentalist opposition. However, most of the organized revivalism used the forms of the older orders, and Neo-Sufi ideas provided the inspiration.

Morocco

Morocco never came under direct Ottoman control, and Islamic institutions there also had a distinctive character. Political leadership was in the hands of groups with strong ties to the local population rather than being an alien military elite. During the sixteenth and seventeenth centuries, the older medieval institutions of central control had crumbled, and in the anarchic conditions, a number of small states had arisen. Many of those states had been formed by local religious leaders, and respect for local saints, or marabouts, had become a major factor in North African religious life. In times of political disorganization, these marabouts became major political figures.

There is a long tradition in the region of political activism related to religion. Two great medieval empires had their origins in religious orders, and the militance of those two groups, the Murabitun and the Muwahhidun, was tied to a spirit of religious revivalism combined with political activism. In the fifteenth and sixteenth centuries, local saint veneration had become firmly integrated into the formulations of Sufism and *tariqah* structures. One aspect of this "maraboutism" was a common belief that the spiritual power of the holy man could be inherited by his descendants, so the dynastic principle came to be accepted. It was natural for special reverence to be paid to the descendants of the Prophet Muhammad, and sharifs had played an important role in the religiopolitical life of the country. These trends had culminated in the Sharifian empire of the Saʿdian dynasty, which united most of Morocco in the sixteenth century.

It was the collapse of Saʿdian power that opened the way in the seventeenth century for the resurgence of small, marabout-led states. By the end of that century, one of the states, led by a Sharifian family, had reestablished relatively strong central control and established the Alawite dynasty, which is still on the Moroccan throne.

The eighteenth-century Moroccan political system thus had rulers with special religious prestige and close ties to the structures of the local Islamic community. The sultans were important religious figures and could utilize Islamic sentiments to mobilize the population. At the same time, the Moroccan sultans recognized the potential political power of the other religious groups and worked to co-opt or limit the influence of the marabouts.

In the context of eighteenth-century Islam, the sultans tended to support the more fundamentalist positions, as they were being developed by the Neo-Sufists, as a way of curtailing the influence of the local *tariqahs*, which could be accomplished by campaigns against the "non-Islamic" practices of the local saints. During the century, the sultans were often associated with this revivalist viewpoint, but there were some problems with this association since, by the end of the century, the idea of establishing Neo-Sufi *tariqah*s as vehicles for fundamentalist reform resulted in new orders in Morocco that could sometimes challenge the authority of the sultan. This problem arose during the reign of Sultan Suleyman. "Himself a strictly orthodox Muslim, Mawlay Sulayman was influenced after 1810 by Wahhabism, which led him to take a firm stand against maraboutism, at the very time when both the recently-founded order of the Darqawa and the earlier order of the Wazzaniyya [the Tayyibiyyah] were undergoing a great expansion in Morocco."[39]

The general development of Sufi organization and Islamic studies in North Africa had an impact on the broader Islamic world. Scholars from North Africa not only went to the eastern Mediterranean to study, but some remained and became prominent teachers. Those scholars from North Africa, or the Maghrib, made contributions in the two important areas of *hadith* studies and Neo-Sufism.

Scholars of *hadith* from the Maghrib were an important part of the cosmopolitan community of scholars in Mecca and Medina, and they were also often associated with revivalist ideas. An early scholar in this group was Muhammad ibn Muhammad ibn Suleyman (1626–1683). Born in Morocco, he received an education in the *hadiths* from the major scholars of his day in the Maghrib and was also initiated into local Sufi orders. After further studies in Cairo and the holy cities, he traveled widely and became an associate of the Ottoman grand vizier, Ahmad Koprulu. In Mecca he soon became a major political force, dominated the grand sharif for a time, and instituted a number of "radical reforms designed to improve the lot of the foreign elements and the poorer classes in Mecca at the expense of the old aristocracy."[40] With the fall of his patron, the grand vizier, he went to Damascus where he continued to teach and attract students from many areas.

Most of the major teachers of *hadith* in Mecca, Medina, and Damascus in the early eighteenth century studied *hadith* under Muhammad ibn Suleyman. In his works on *hadith*, he combined study of the ninth-century collections with a study of Malik's *Muwatta* and may have been an important influence in that orientation of eighteenth-century *hadith* studies.

A later North African scholar of similar importance was Muhammad Ibn al-Tayyib (1698–1757), who was born in Morocco and taught most of his life in Medina. In order to advance the study of the *hadith*s, he studied lexicography extensively. As a result of that emphasis, he inspired his best-known student, Muhammad Murtada al-Zabidi, and through him had a substantial impact on the intellectual developments of the day.

Late in the eighteenth century teachers from North Africa were also important in creating activist *tariqah*s that utilized the ideas of Neo-Sufism. The *tariqah* tradition of being well-organized, popular associations that had developed in the Maghrib was an influence in the organizational form that Neo-Sufism took and in the process, a Moroccan scholar named Ahmad ibn Idris (d. 1837) was an important figure. Initiated into activist *tariqah*s in North Africa, he taught for many years in Mecca. "His biographer says that he based his Sufi practice solidly on the Qur'an and Sunna, accepting only these as *usul* (foundations) and rejecting *ijma* (consensus) except that of the Companions upon which the Prophet's Sunna is based."[41] That statement reflects both the more fundamentalist style of Sufism and the emphasis on a knowledge of *hadith*. His expertise in the Traditions of the Prophet was widely known. When Ahmad's reformism brought him into conflict with the conservative establishment in Mecca, it was as a *muhaddith* that he was examined publicly by a panel of ulama. (A favorable account of his disciple-biographer notes that he was able to confound his critics and emerged with an enhanced reputation.)[42]

Ahmad ibn Idris was eventually forced out of Mecca and moved to Asir, between Mecca and Yemen. There he established a community that in many ways was similar to the marabout-led communities of North Africa, and his descendants remained virtually independent rulers of the area until after World War I. In that community, one can see a combination of fundamentalist concepts and the more politically activist organizational ideas of North African maraboutism. The followers of Ahmad ibn Idris were to establish a number of *tariqah*s that became significant elements in nineteenth-century Islamic revivalism, including the Sanusiyyah in Libya, the Khatmiyyah in the Sudan, and the *tariqah* line that produced the Salihiyyah in Somalia.

Ottoman North Africa and Morocco were important contributors to the general history of eighteenth-century Islam, and that century also saw the creation of local Islamic institutions that would distinguish those countries in the modern era. Those local institutions ranged from the confirmation of a conservative style of religious leadership in Tunisia to the emergence of activist religious brotherhoods in Algeria and Morocco.

Islam in Sudanic Africa

In the vast belt of territories that stretch from the Atlantic to the Indian Ocean basin, between the Sahara and the heavily forested areas, Islam played a dynamic role in the eighteenth century. This savanna region is often called "the sudan" or Sudanic Africa, using the traditional Arabic name of *bilad al-Sudan* ("land of the blacks"). In Sudanic Africa, Islam was introduced at different times in different sections, but it was generally a clearly present element by late medieval times. It was spread by wandering merchants and teachers as well as by soldiers, and Islam in Sudanic Africa shares many of the features of Islam in Southeast Asia.

When Islam came into the area, there were already established political structures and social institutions. As a result, the main themes of Islamic history in Sudanic Africa deal with the interaction between Islam and the existing basic elements. In this interaction there were two main phases.

The first phase was while Islam was gradually spreading southward from the established Muslim communities on the Mediterranean coast. Special impetus was given to that expansion in the western areas by the Murabitun and Muwahhidun activist Muslim movements, which had been established in Morocco in the eleventh and twelfth centuries. Islam had a distinctive role in Sudanic societies during this phase, which lasted until the eighteenth century in most areas. It was, in many ways, a special class cult. It was the religion of the commercial and clerical classes who traveled widely within the region, and Islam was the faith of the interregional cosmopolitan elements. In addition, Islam became a special religion of dynasties or imperial structures in many parts of Sudanic Africa. Rulers combined the cosmopolitan advantages of Islam and the Muslim groups with particular local, non-Islamic customs and rituals and so gave their rule legitimacy among the majority of their non-Muslim or barely Islamized subjects.

The basic Islamic style, on the part of the converting rulers and the Muslim teachers and traders, was adaptationism. "Religious life was characterized by accommodation or, more correctly, by a dualism or a parallelism of the old and the new—the African idea of harmony of society maintained itself over against any idea of Islamic exclusiveness. Consequently, Islam's challenge to traditional life was largely neutralized."[43] This was the period of the "mixers," who combined pagan and Islamic practices. Although there were a few protesters, like Muhammad ibn Abd al-Karim al-Maghili (d. 1504), the general tone, even of the ulama, was either adaptationist or, once the compromise had been set, conservative.

By the eighteenth century, dynamic new themes were emerging in Sudanic Islam. As Islamic consciousness spread beyond the limited class base of the first phase, it was possible to organize movements that called for a more rigorous adherence to Islam, with fewer compromises in all areas, especially the political realm. The century was "the birth time of the theocracies, which in a series of revolutions engulfed almost the whole Sudan before European control was imposed."[44] The leaders in this new consciousness were drawn from the ulama and were teachers who were inspired by a vision of a more clearly Islamic society. During the eighteenth century, those scholars created a tradition of a militant, more fundamentalist Islam in the Sudanic belt. Although not always victorious themselves, they paved the way for the holy wars that characterized Islam in the Sudanic areas during the nineteenth century.

In West Africa, there was at least some memory of the medieval theocratic traditions of the Murabitun and the Muwahhidun. In Futa Jallon, a highland area in modern Guinea, some of the earliest efforts in the Islamic transformation took place. There, a scholar named Ibrahim Musa (sometimes called Karamoko Alifa, d. 1751) proclaimed a holy war against the local rulers and took the title of *almami,* meaning "the imam" or leader. He and a revivalist warrior, Ibrahim Sori, who became the almami in 1776, created a revivalist state with active schools as well as militant armies. However, the almamis in Futa Jallon did not succeed in creating an effectively cohesive state, and the "theocratic republic" was always troubled by internal division as well as by external attack. The revivalism of Futa Jallon did succeed in spreading to other areas, inspiring similar movements.

In Futa Toro, in the Senegal area, a similar state was created. After studying in Futa Jallon, Suleyman Bal preached against the local rulers in Futa Toro and announced that an almami should rule there too. He himself refused the post, but another scholar, Abd al-Qadir, was named almami in 1776. Although he was killed in 1806, the imamate continued until the French occupation. In other areas, similar movements led toward holy wars and the creation of theocratic states.

During this time, another feature of Sudanic Islam was being consolidated as the traditions of scholarship and respected local holy men were being combined with the introduction and expansion of some of the great Sufi *tariqahs.* The oldest of the major brotherhoods in West Africa is the Qadiriyyah, and its introduction and spread there was associated with a prominent religious family, the Kunta. Ahmad al-Bakka'i al-Kunti (d. 1504) was the first major figure in that family, and his influence extended from Timbuctoo to the Atlantic. Ahmad's son Umar is reported by Kunti historians to have had close ties with a famous scholar with strict views, Muhammad al-Maghili, and a major teacher in Cairo, Abd al-Rahman al-Suyuti. Whether or not those three scholars actually had close personal connections, the Kunta clearly identified themselves with the rigorous fundamentalist style of Islamic scholarship represented by al-Maghili. They combined that scholarly activity with an affiliation with the Qadiriyyah.

The real spread of that combination of scholarship and Sufism through the Kunti family occurred in the eighteenth century under the leadership of al-Mukhtar al-Kunti (1729–1811). He was "widely renowned for his sanctity and scholarship throughout West and North Africa, and to him is attributed the revival of the Qadiriyya and the Maliki *madhhab* (school of jurisprudence) in much of West Africa."[45] Al-Mukhtar created a vast confederation of tribal groups and supporters with real influence in political, economic, and religious affairs. Through his work and that of his followers and associates in the order, the Qadiriyyah was active in many parts of West Africa and was tied to the forces of revival. There were Qadiriyyah centers with at least some ties to the Kunti leaders in Futa Jallon, Futa Toro, and later militant revivalists like Uthman dan Fodio.

Tariqah leaders in West Africa were not isolated from the development of Neo-Sufism in the central parts of the Islamic world. Scholars on pilgrimage had contacts with Neo-Sufi leaders and brought back with them their ideas and affiliations. Jabril ibn Umar, the major teacher of Uthman dan Fodio for example, studied in Cairo with Muhammad Murtada al-Zabidi and Yusuf al-Hifnawi, the brother of the Khalwatiyyah leader in Egypt, Muhammad al-Hifnawi. Early in the nineteenth century, the Tijaniyyah began to spread in the area, and it brought with it its style of Neo-Sufism.

In this way, the eighteenth-century mood of socio-moral reconstruction was clearly visible in western Sudanic Africa. The combination of traditions of scholarly study and Sufi organization played an important role in the development of the Islamic community there and created the activist foundations for the militancy that was a major feature of Islam in the following century.

In the eastern sections of Sudanic Africa, there was less militant activism, even though some of the same basic issues were present. In some states, the rulers were Islamic, but they still maintained pre-Islamic practices in an adaptationist mixture that was accepted by the local Muslim teachers. As in West Africa, Islam in this area tended to be most closely identified with particular classes. As a result, the issue of the relationship between local practices and the Islamic message was important in the east as well as in the west. However, the major sources of Islamic influence were Egypt and the Arabian Peninsula, and the spirit of militant revivalism and the marabout political institutions were not a significant part of the messages coming from the centers in Egypt and the Haramayn. The more conservative spirit of al-Azhar was reflected in some of eastern Sudanic Islam.

An Islamic state, the Funj sultanate, had been established in the Nile valley during the sixteenth century, but although officially Islamic, many older practices of political ritual and organization had been continued there. Gradually, the Nilotic Sudan came under increasing Islamic influence. Scholars who had studied in the Haramayn or in Egypt established school communities and introduced a more accurate study of the fundamentals of the faith. Early in the seventeenth century, for example, Ibrahim al-Bulad Ibn Jabir was the first to teach the standard textbooks of Maliki law in Funj territory. Around the same time, some of the major *tariqah*s, like the Qadiriyyah, had been introduced. However, the product of this growing Islamization was still a relatively tolerant style of Islam, open to substantial adaptation to local customs and practices. Local scholar-saint dynasties emerged and were the major focuses for both Islamic learning and popular religious practices.

By the end of the eighteenth century, the development of Neo-Sufi ideas had begun to penetrate into the Funj territories, first through Sudanic pilgrims who had studied under Neo-Sufi figures in the Haramayn. The Khalwatiyyah of Mustafa al-Bakri was introduced into the Sudan through the Sammaniyyah, which had been established in the Haramayn by al-Bakri's disciple, Muhammad ibn Abd al-Karim al-Samman. Ahmad al-Tayyib ibn Bashir, a pilgrim from the Sudan, was initiated into that *tariqah* in Medina and carried the order back to the Sudan in 1800. There he had success in winning the allegiance of some of the major established families, and the *tariqah* expanded rapidly. This Sammaniyyah branch in the Sudan included the late nineteenth-century militant fundamentalist, Muhammad Ahmad, the Sudanese Mahdi.

Other significant Neo-Sufi groups to enter the Sudan at this time were associated with Ahmad ibn Idris, the popular Neo-Sufi teacher in the Haramayn from North Africa. One of his students was Muhammad al-Majdhub al-Sughayyir (1796–1833). That man was a member of one of the major Sudanese holy families, and on his return to the Sudan, he reorganized the family *tariqah* along more activist lines. The other major Sudanese order to follow the tradition of Ahmad ibn Idris is the Khatmiyyah, which was introduced into the Sudan early in the nineteenth century by Muhammad Uthman al-Mirghani.

Sudanese Islam was thus entering a new phase by the end of the eighteenth century. The new style of teachers was more firmly committed to a more rigorous adherence to Islam than the earlier religious leaders had been. However, the preaching of those new scholars did not result at that time in a militant holy war, as happened in West Africa. Instead, the indigenous development of Islam was stopped by the Egyptian conquest of the Sudan around 1820, which introduced a totally new element since the conquering Egyptian army was the product of the modernizing reforms of Mehmet Ali. The more standard pattern of Sudanic Islamic evolution was thus abruptly replaced by the problems of dealing with modernization as well as Islamizing trends.

Emergence of Modern Shi'i Patterns in Iran

Political Context

Safavid power was crumbling in Iran by the beginning of the eighteenth century, and in the context of the resulting political struggle and military attacks, important developments were taking place within Shi'ism. Those developments created the basis for the role of religion and religious leadership in modern Iranian history.

The political and military history of Iran during the century began with the increasingly ineffective Safavid state's facing a series of revolts. Those revolts culminated in an invasion by Afghans, who captured the Safavid capital of Isfahan in 1722 and ruled for seven years. In reaction, a great leader of the Afshar tribe, Nader Khan, organized the support that was still loyal to the Safavid house. He succeeded in defeating the Afghans and restored the Safavid shah to the throne. However, Nader was the real power in the state, and he finally assumed the throne himself as Nader Shah in 1736. He built a large conquest empire that controlled all of Iran, brought a stop to the Ottoman advances, and successfully invaded northern India. However, his abilities were military rather than administrative, and he did not create a stable imperial system. His harsh measures of control soon created opposition, and he was killed in 1747. Following his death, various tribal and military groups competed for control in the chaotic situation. After half a century, in which there was virtually no central control in Iran, one of those groups, the Qajars, emerged victorious. In 1795, Aga Muhammad, the Qajar leader, was proclaimed shah and centralized control was reestablished in Iran.

Shiʿism and the Iranian Identity

Until the time of the Safavids, Shiʿism had not been explicitly identified with the Persian cultural tradition, although it had been one aspect of the Islamic experience in Iran. The proclamation of Twelver Shiʿism as the religion of the Safavid state and the subsequent conversion of the majority of the population to Shiʿism during the Safavid era were major turning points in the history of Islam in Iran. The Safavids "presided over the fusion of Shiʿism with the Iranian national consciousness."[46]

The Safavid form of this fusion placed great importance on the state and the role of the monarch, and during the Safavid era, Shiʿi Islam was both state supported and state supporting. The shah assumed a special role as an agent of the hidden imam and thus had a religiously based authority. In establishing an "official" religion, the Safavids created a government-related group of ulama. Before the Safavid period, there had been relatively few Shiʿi ulama in Iran, so the emerging ulama class of "imported" scholars and new local teachers was, initially, tied quite closely to state patronage.

By the end of the eighteenth century, an independent group of Shiʿi ulama had emerged. The leading figures were scholars whose independent interpretations had been accepted by the majority of the population. These *mujtahid*s as they were called, stood outside of the organization of the state, and the foundation of their authority was independent from the patronage of the state. The non-state ulama became a major religious force, which competed with the government religious establishment and the shah himself. As the state structure weakened, the *mujtahids* played a more prominent role until, under the last Safavid shahs, great *mujtahids* like Muhammad Baqir al-Majlisi came to dominate the political system itself.

With the collapse of the Safavid monarchy, the Shiʿi ulama essentially liberated themselves from the monarchical institution. In the absence of effective central control, Shiʿism was able to become the basic Islamic expression of the Iranian identity without reference to a particular monarchical structure. "The eighteenth century was, then, a period in which Shiʿism, its learning and institutions, defied political and social decay to maintain its dominance in Iran."[47] The stage was thus set for the modern dual elements of monarch and *mujtahid,* sometimes cooperating but more often in conflict.

Conflict over Definition

The most visible challenge in the eighteenth century to the special Shiʿi tradition in Iran came from some of the political leadership. Nader Shah made a major effort to redefine the place of Shiʿi Islam within the Islamic world by working to gain recognition from the major Sunni powers. There are many possible reasons why he made that effort. It could have been because he wanted to unify the Islamic world under his leadership, or it could have been a justification for his suppression of the Shiʿi ulama, both state and non-state, as a part of his efforts to strengthen the monarchy. He may also have been inspired by his own religious convictions and background, in which there were at least some Sunni elements.

Whatever his reasons, Nader Shah attempted to integrate a redefined Shiʿism into the Sunni tradition. He rejected the Shiʿi condemnation of the first three caliphs and enforced that position within his realm. In addition, he tried to secure Ottoman recognition of Twelver Shiʿism as a fifth Sunni school of law, to be called the Jaʿfari school after the sixth imam, Jaʿfar al-Sadiq. The whole pattern of Shiʿism as built on the idea of the imamate was to be replaced. Neither the Sunni Ottomans nor the major Shiʿi teachers of the time accepted Nader's redefinition, although he was able, through military force, to "persuade" a few teachers to agree with his ideas. Clearly, the monarchy was not accepted as a vehicle for interpreting the faith, and in the long run, Nader's efforts only deepened the gap between the ulama and the monarchy.

The results of Nader's attempt reaffirmed the Shiʿi emphasis on the Islamic style that concentrated on the role of individualistic leadership, and the role of the imamate in the Shiʿi tradition was a continuing affirmation of that distinctive style. The adaptationist efforts of Nader Shah failed to change this orientation.

Among the Shiʿi ulama themselves, that orientation was also reaffirmed in a series of doctrinal conflicts that had long-term significance. By the beginning of the eighteenth century, two major schools of Shiʿi thought had emerged, the Akhbari and the Usuli, and many of the leading teachers settled in the Shiʿi holy cities in Iraq in order to avoid the growing political and military disorders in Iran. Those cities, Najaf and Karbala, are the sites of the tombs of Ali and Husayn and are major centers of Shiʿi devotion and study.

The heart of the controversy between the Akhbaris and the Usulis was the role of the ulama in guiding the people. The Akhbari position emerged as a type of Shiʿi fundamentalism as that school held that the Quran and the Traditions from the Prophet and the imams were sufficient guidance for the community. The function of the ulama should be simply searching through the sources for solutions to problems. The Akhbaris felt that there was no need for scholars to use independent judgment (*ijtihad*) and that, in fact, *ijtihad* was an unsound innovation. This doctrinal position cut at the very heart of the evolving role of the Shiʿi *mujtahid*s as guides for the community. In its fundamentalism, the Akhbari school was a move away from the charismatic, individualized style of leadership in Shi'ism.

The Akhbari group dominated the intellectual studies in the Shi'i holy cities for a good part of the eighteenth century. By the end of the century, however, the Usuli position had emerged as victorious, largely as a result of the efforts of Aga Muhammad Baqir Bihbihani (1705–1803). The Usuli position reaffirmed the importance of the role of the *mujtahid* as the guide for the community. In the absence of the imam, the community needed some guidance in coping with changing conditions, and the Usulis asserted that the learned scholar was capable of authentic independent judgment and that such a scholar was a necessary agent of the hidden imam. As such, every person should accept the direction of a *mujtahid*.

The Usulis recognized that there might be a variety of interpretations among the *mujtahids* as a result of changing conditions or different viewpoints. Thus, although the judgment of the *mujtahid* must be followed by his supporters, "it established no precedent and believers are forbidden to follow the rulings of a deceased mujtahid in place of a living one."[48] The victory of the Usuli position by the end of the eighteenth century affirmed the importance of the living *mujtahids* as the necessary guides for all believers.

The political implications of that position form a major part of the modern history of Iran. Since the Islamic message is valid in all areas of life, the political guidance of the *mujtahid* is, at least in theory, as binding as his social and doctrinal guidance. "The monarch was theoretically bound, no less than his subjects, to submit to the authoritative guidance of a *mujtahid* and in effect to make the state the executive branch of ulama authority."[49] Although it is possible for the ulama and the monarchy to cooperate, when there is an assertion of a strong monarchical role in society, it is possible that *mujtahid* and monarch will come into conflict. In many ways, it is possible to say that the Usuli triumph in the eighteenth century created the necessary foundation for the triumph of the Ayatollah Khomeini in this century.

There was a third school of Shi'i thought at the time that went beyond the Usuli in terms of the role of the charismatic leader. This school was established by Ahmad al-Ahsa'i (1741–1826), and his followers came to be called the Shaykhis. He may have come from an Akhbari background, rejecting the idea that legal reasoning limits the direct charismatic authority of the imams. Stressing the continuing metaphysical position of the imam as a guide for humanity, a doctrine of human access to the imam through a particular intermediary was developed. Thus, the Shi'i style of charismatic individualism was maintained, but the general validity of the *ijtahid* of the ulama was denied. In the early nineteenth century, al-Ahsa'i and his followers clashed with the major ulama leaders and the Shaykhi teachings were declared heretical. However, the Shaykhis had established the basis for a continuing charismatic messianism and played a role in the later messianic revolts.

The messianic strand in Iranian Islamic history helped to reinforce the significance of the Usuli victory. The main popular spokesmen for the faith were not within the political structure but outside of it, in a position to mobilize large-scale support for opposition movements. Islamic leadership became, in this way, a major check on the power of the monarch in Iran.

Conclusion

Throughout the Islamic world, the eighteenth century was a significant period, and developments during the century helped to determine the shape that Islamic movements would take in the following centuries. One significant feature that emerges from a study of the eighteenth-century Islamic experience is that Islam became a basis for the assertion of an authentically indigenous identity, which was often in opposition to the emerging political structures. That situation occurred from Southeast Asia through Iran and the Ottoman Empire to the states of West Africa. In some cases, there was a relatively conservative resistance to reforms instituted by political leaders; in other cases, fundamentalist movements, which aimed at a socio-moral reconstruction, were created.

In contrast, many governments in the Islamic areas emerged as the leading forces for adaptationism, and increasingly, adaptationism meant coming to an accommodation with the new forces, both economic and military, of the modernizing West. This trend only strengthened the nonestablishment character of many of the activist Islamic movements.

A look at the eighteenth-century Islamic experience helps to emphasize the importance of the Islamic dimension of modern Muslim history. That Islamic world was not simply a stagnant, inert mass on which the West imposed its control and ideas, and the reformism and revivalism that are visible in the modern Islamic world are not simply the result of contact with the West. Authentically Islamic movements of self-criticism and revivalism were already emerging in the eighteenth century, and the special characteristics of those movements are an important part of the interaction between Islam and the challenges of modern history. Although the role of the modernizing West is important, the role of the forces that have arisen out of the Islamic dimension of the modern Muslim experience cannot be ignored.

3

European Domination and Islamic Response

The Islamic world faced a major challenge during the nineteenth century. Expanding Western European states and economies played an increasing role in determining events, both on a global scale and within Islamic societies. By the end of the century, many Muslim territories were under direct European control, and much of the rest of the Muslim world was dominated by the West. The basis for this European capacity for domination was the transformation of Western society through the processes of modernization. In the past, world civilizations had competed, with advances and defeats usually being determined by local quantitative differences in power, but the bases of power were fundamentally the same. However, the emerging modern society in the West had a qualitatively different type of power, enabling physically small states like England to dominate large parts of the globe.

The interaction of this new basic life-style with the older lifestyles and world views is a fundamental theme of modern world history, and it provides the second major dimension that is required for understanding the history of Islam in the modern world. The Islamic dimension and the modern dimension represent the framework within which local Islamic histories develop.

At times, the Islamic-Western interaction has resulted in fruitful cooperation, but the prevailing tone in the nineteenth century was one of conflict. Rather than partnerships emerging, the primary arrangement was domination-subordination. The context for the Islamic experience was thus often one of struggle, and the new Western ideas and techniques were seen as being in competition with the Islamic ideals. From a strict Islamic standpoint, adaptation in this context gave the appearance of surrender. It was not until the end of the nineteenth century that significant efforts were made to create an Islamically oriented adaptationism.

Part of the problem for Muslims was a growing awareness of Western power and the feeling that the strength of the modern ideas and institutions was in fact qualitatively different from the Islamic sources of power. For a community whose historical experience tended to reinforce the idea that

84

"God is on the side of those who fear Him and do good," the visible strength of the modernizing West posed grave problems, and at times, it created a sense of unease. It has been said that "the fundamental spiritual crisis of Islam in the twentieth century stems from an awareness that something is awry between the religion which God has appointed and the historical development of the world which He controls."[1] This crisis arose out of the nineteenth-century history of the Islamic world.

Conflict and spiritual crisis are only part of the story. In addition, building on the eighteenth-century foundations, there is a theme of socio-moral reconstruction, and that effort utilizes lessons learned from the interaction with the West but remains authentically Islamic. Although the nineteenth and early twentieth centuries were dominated by the mood of spiritual crisis, this other theme has continued to build. By the final third of the twentieth century, it has assumed many forms, but it is no longer clearly subordinate—as it seemed to be in the nineteenth century—to the theme of crisis.

In the diversity of the Islamic experiences during the nineteenth century, some general trends can be discerned. There was a continuing momentum of the eighteenth-century developments that gave inspiration to Islamic activist movements in many areas. There were also substantial efforts to introduce Western techniques in the creation of more effective state structures. The success of both of those efforts was limited in the nineteenth century in the face of growing European dominance, and as that fact became clear, efforts were made to redefine Islam in order to meet the challenges. Along with that redefinition, other activities developed, sometimes in conjunction with and sometimes in competition with Islamic sentiments. These activities involved more clearly secularist attitudes, ideas of radical reform, and nationalism.

Three general types of evolution can be seen within that framework. One centered around the efforts of adaptationist Westernizers; the second began with an eighteenth-century style of militant reaction to the Western expansion and then, after defeat, there were efforts at reorientation. In the third type of evolution, there was a continuation of an eighteenth-century type of activity, which was not dominated by the West for some time but was finally affected by European imperial control. In addition to these experiences with the imperialist West, there were a few areas, particularly in Africa and China, where Islamic revivalism emerged outside of the context of interaction with European imperialism.

Adaptationist Westernizers and Nineteenth-Century Islam

The nineteenth century was a time of dramatic reform programs. Those were frequently undertaken by colorful, strong personalities, some of the

best known of whom were Mehmet Ali in Egypt and Mahmud II, the reforming Ottoman sultan. Those men were not the only ones in the Islamic
world who tried to create modern-style armies and administrative structures,
but they are the most visible of a major type of Muslim leader that was
emerging during the century. The reform programs took place in a still functioning political system, which was bureaucratically organized and accepted
as legitimate by a majority of the population. The personnel within that
apparatus was a distinct official class whose fortunes were tied to the continued effective existence of the state.

The leaders worked under a variety of challenges to restructure a government and to increase its role in society in order to cope with new problems.
The techniques and methods used by the rulers were not determined by past
tradition alone; they were willing to adapt and adopt whatever appeared to
have the potential for strengthening their government and meeting their
goals. In the nineteenth century, the source of most of the ideas for this type
of reform was the West. Although there had been a long history of interaction with Western states, there had not been a period of fundamental intellectual preparation for political change. Rather, in those established
bureaucratically organized governments, "selected members of the existing
political class experimented in a piecemeal, pragmatic fashion with Western-
inspired reforms."[2]

The ideas and techniques were relatively new to both the reformers and
the society, but the role of the political elite was basically a continuation of
the adaptationist style of Islam. None of the reformers renounced Islam, but
they were not primarily concerned with doctrinal issues or with creating
religiously oriented roles for themselves. Like the early caliphs and the Umayyads, they made use of the available techniques in a pragmatic way in
order to strengthen the state. Similarly, like the Umayyads, they were sometimes criticized by the more conservative and fundamentalist Muslims for
the compromises that were implicit in their adaptations.

In his analysis of one of those early Westernizing reformers, L. Carl
Brown proposes a useful general framework for viewing the adaptationist
style of reformers who operated within the context of bureaucratic governments.[3] He suggests that in the bureaucratic states, the first, pragmatic stage
is similar in countries like Egypt, the central Ottoman Empire, Tunisia, Morocco, and Iran. It is only after the first reformist efforts have been initiated
by members of the political elite that a "reformist ideology" can develop.
After the first phase, the experience varies. The existing political elites may
break down in the process, creating major crisis situations. A second possibility is that reform continues to be imposed from the top by a small dominant group. In that case, "an expanded state is left to dominate a people now

stripped of traditional political patterns and left only to demonstrate the violent swings of political activity associated with 'mass society.'"[4] In a third pattern, the reforms create a gradually expanding circle of participants, and, through evolutionary processes, a modernizing society emerges with a minimum of violence. Some aspects of each of these types of experience can be seen in the developing Islamic experience of the nineteenth century.

If one focuses on the modern Islamic experience, the details of the reform programs and the political history are not as important as the developing interaction of the Islamic styles. In the larger bureaucratic states, the adaptationist reformers were clearly the dominant group. After early clashes, the more conservative Muslims tended to be cowed into submission. They could at times influence the pace of reform, but even that strength declined as the reforms undermined the old bases of conservative power. In the long run, as reformism became established, the conservatives began to assume the role of preservers of the early reforms. An interesting example of that phenomenon is the history of the fez, the headgear of North African origin. There was conservative opposition to its adoption as a part of the army uniform during the period of the early Ottoman military reforms, but, a century later, the prohibition of the fez aroused conservative opposition.

Effective, organized opposition to reform, in Islamic terms, was largely the product of a fundamentalist style of activity. In addition, by the end of the nineteenth century, the currents set in motion by the early reforms had begun to produce "ideologies of reform" that sometimes went beyond the positions of the later rulers. Intellectual adaptationism created a theme of Islamic modernism that sometimes supported and sometimes opposed government policies, and nationalism and socialism also began to appear as alternative orientations. A final element that limited the power of the reformist rulers was the European powers, as European political interference and economic activity had a major impact on the outcome of the indigenous reform programs. In some cases, as in Egypt, European military occupation or political dominance meant that the ability to initiate government policy effectively passed into foreign hands.

The Central Ottoman Empire

The reform programs of the nineteenth century in the central Ottoman Empire had some foundations on which to build. The more traditional reforms of the preceding century had opened the way for at least a small portion of the ruling elite to accept Western techniques, and the work of Sultan Selim III had helped to create a small core of able men who had some experience with Westernizing reforms. At the same time, the abrupt end of

Selim's *nizam-i-jedid* showed the continuing power of the conservative forces within the state.

Mahmud II emerged from the conflicts at the end of Selim's reign as the new sultan. He was interested in pursuing a reform program but had to work very cautiously in order to avoid the same fate as Selim. Mahmud managed to survive by balancing a variety of forces and by gradually infiltrating men who shared his goals into the upper levels of the religious establishment and the Janissary Corps. In addition, he was able to avoid serious defeat at the hands of the Europeans and the various semi-independent provincial notables. Having organized his support, Mahmud began a more dramatic reform effort in 1826, and the first target of this program was the Janissary Corps, which revolted and was crushed. By 1826 Mahmud had substantial support for the abolition of the janissaries, since even the conservative religious leaders saw their ineffectiveness as a threat to the empire.

For the conservative ulama, the destruction of the janissaries was a serious blow, even though they had supported it, because their destruction meant that there was no longer a military force that could act to support the ulama's interests. As a result, Mahmud was able to undermine the sources of the ulama strength with greater effectiveness than his predecessors. The religious establishment gradually lost its administrative autonomy, and control over the pious endowments increasingly passed out of the hands of the conservative ulama. The establishment of new schools meant that the government elite was increasingly drawn from people whose education was significantly different from that of the ulama.

The role of Islam in the Ottoman state was changing, and, with that change, the ulama increasingly lost effective influence. The reforming leadership did not reject Islam, and it was usually careful never to go beyond what would be tolerated by the majority of the Muslims. Islam was, after all, the ultimate basis for the legitimacy of the Ottoman sultanate. The ulama generally had two options. Most remained basically conservative, trying to slow the pace of change and to keep it within clearly Islamic bounds. Unfortunately, "the majority of the ulema shut themselves off from the contemporary world in their medieval medreses [*madrasahs*] and courts of Holy Law."[5] The other option was to accept the inevitability of change and to make an active effort to reconcile tradition with reform through an active involvement in the political realm.

In the period following the death of Mahmud II in 1839, there were some important examples of ulama participation in the reform efforts. Although their participation was limited in scope, these men helped to open the door for attempts to adapt Islam to the new conditions, and the period is often called the era of the Tanzimat or "reorganizations." In general terms, the reorganizations were efforts to restructure Ottoman public life and to create a more effectively centralized empire. The Tanzimat took place in the context of a growing European involvement in Ottoman affairs and the continuing relative weakness of the empire. It was, however, a significant effort in reformist programs of modernization, and it created a modern-educated class and effectively restructured the imperial system in more modern terms.

The Tanzimat resulted in some changes in the specifically Islamic institutions, and the imperial religious establishment was brought under greater bureaucratic control. The office of the shaykh al-Islam continued to have importance, but during the Tanzimat, the position was held by men drawn from the lower levels of the ulama rather than from a few great religious families, as had been the case earlier.[6]

A few ulama made a direct and important contribution to the Tanzimat. The most famous of those was Ahmad Cevdet Pasha (1822–1895), who was trained in the traditional religious curriculum but had also studied modern subjects. He was respected by both the reformers and the leading ulama, and as a result, he was a logical choice when the reforming grand vizier, Mustafa Rashid Pasha, requested the shaykh al-Islam to name a religious scholar to assist in the drafting of the legal codes. Cevdet was the major figure in the creation of the Majalla, a vast formulation of a civil code that combined Islamic legal principles with new legal ideas. In this effort and in other ways, Cevdet was an influential figure in the Tanzimat, and his attitude reflects the best of constructive conservatism in Ottoman Islam. "Cevdet was essentially conservative. . . . This conservatism did not blind him to reality. . . . He recognized the need for bringing the Ottoman legal and judicial system into step with the times, but he advocated the modification and adaptation of the indigenous Muslim law instead of the importation of alien law wherever that was possible."[7] The narrow vision of most of the Ottoman ulama, however, is reflected in the fact that Cevdet was forced to leave the ulama establishment and become a part of the administrative structure in order to accomplish his goals.

The period of the Tanzimat saw the end of the first phase of reformism, and the simple pragmatic adoption of techniques was placed in a broader framework of emerging intellectual formulations. In this intellectual activity at the end of the nineteenth century, there was a vibrant diversity, but three main themes can be seen, and Islam provided some of the framework for each of them.

The first theme was a criticism of the Tanzimat for not going far enough, and it was expressed in the writings of a diffuse group, sometimes called the Young Ottomans. Those men were strongly influenced by European liberal thinking and feared that the Tanzimat represented political maneuvers to create the foundations for an absolutist government. Namik Kemal, one of the leading figures in this movement, wrote of one of the imperial decrees establishing the basis for the Tanzimat that on the surface, "one would think it to have been made as a surety for the life, property, and honour of every individual. But the truth of the matter is that it was proclaimed for the purpose of securing the life of the state."[8]

This liberal critique of the reform program had its Islamic dimension. The Young Ottomans appealed to the egalitarian principles in the Islamic tradition and justified liberalizing reforms in Islamic terms. Their goal was a constitutional and parliamentary system with the restoration of Islamic law. "This would not, however, mean a simple rejection of Westernization and a return to the immediately preceding past; what was needed was a return to the true spirit of early Islam, which recognized the sovereignty of the people and the principle of government by consultation."[9] The Young Ottomans were early representatives of a style of Islam that is common in the modern era—a style that is essentially adaptationist but appeals to a fundamentalist style of reasoning.

The second theme was more directly Islamic in nature. As it became obvious that the reform programs were unable to stem the tide of the growing European dominance, some thinkers advocated a more rigorous reliance upon Islamic principles as the first line of defense. With the death of some of the major Tanzimat leaders, growing financial problems, and a difficult international situation by the 1870s, there was a tendency to place greater stress on the Islamic basis of the state and the need for effective Muslim unity. News of defeats of Muslims elsewhere and their mistreatment by non-Muslim governments aroused a greater sensitivity to the need for greater Muslim cooperation throughout the world of Islam.

The Islamic reaction to these conditions took two forms in the Ottoman Empire. One was to emphasize the role of the Ottoman ruler as the leading Muslim figure in the world. It was felt that he was not just the sultan and head of the empire but also the caliph and spokesman for Muslims throughout the world. Sultan Abdulhamid II, who came to the throne in 1876, actively pursued a policy based on this Pan-Islamic ideal, established ties with Muslims in many areas, and attracted leading figures to Istanbul. In areas far beyond the borders of the empire, there were Muslims who looked to the sultan-caliph for help. In the long run, the concrete results of the Pan-Islamic policies were limited, but a broader sense of Islamic unity was fostered. The second type of Islamic reaction was a growing willingness to defend Islam intellectually. European scholars denigrated Islam, Muslims began to debate with them, and in the process of those discussions, Muslim intellectuals began to create an intellectual framework for Islamic modernism.

A leading figure in both the intellectual defense of Islam and the development of Pan-Islamic ideas was Jamal al-Din al-Afghani (1839–1897), whose influence was not limited to the central Ottoman lands. He traveled and taught in Iran and Egypt and spent some years in Europe. He preached the necessity of Islamic revival and unity and vigorously affirmed that Islam was fully compatible with reason and modern science. For a time, he was among the intellectuals who were supported by Abdulhamid II in Istanbul but his political ideas were ultimately too revolutionary for the regime of Abdulhamid.

The third theme in the emerging intellectual framework in the later part of the nineteenth century was the increasing absolutism of the Ottoman ruler, which is especially associated with the policies of Abdulhamid II. In many ways, that sultan was a culmination of the Tanzimat even though he represented a repudiation of its liberal constitutional ideals. He was faced with many crises and took dramatic, authoritarian measures. "He developed a structure of personal control that, with the centralized system of administration created by the Tanzimat, made possible a far more extensive and complete autocracy than anything ever achieved previously by the greatest of the sultans."[10] Modernizing reform, as the rule of Abdulhamid illustrates, gives added power to the instruments of state control. It can create the conditions for autocracy as well as for democracy.

Islam's role in Abdulhamid's autocracy was to provide legitimacy. Abdulhamid consciously identified himself with the emerging Pan-Islamic themes, and he received support from a wide variety of people who were persuaded that the secularism inherent in many of the Westernizing reforms was a growing threat to Islam. This support came not only from the conservative and fundamentalist elements; even someone with real commitment to reform, such as Ahmad Cevdet, gave support in many ways to Abdulamid's autocratic policies.

The culmination of nineteenth-century Ottoman history came with the rise of the Young Turk movement, which ultimately captured control of the state by revolution in 1908. Resistance to Abdulhamid developed among the new generation of modern-educated people that had been created by the continuing reforms and development. There was real diversity within the movement that overthrew Abdulhamid. The basic themes of the nineteenth century manifested themselves in terms of plans for the future of the empire. Liberal constitutionalism was the most widely accepted platform, but there was disagreement over whether the empire should be strongly centralized—thus continuing in a different form the trends toward autocracy—or whether it should become a more decentralized federation. Because Pan-Islamic policies were associated with the sultan, they were not as visible in the Young

Turks' programs, but there was still a strong element of looking to Islam to provide the basic identity of the state.

That issue of basic identity was complicated by the emergence of nationalist feelings even within the Ottoman educated elite. For some of them, ethnic and linguistic heritages were becoming more important than religious communal ties. That nationalist sentiment had long been an important aspect of the attitudes of the non-Muslim subject peoples who opposed the Ottoman imperial centralization, but now the two major Muslim elements within the empire also began to experience nationalist stirrings. The Arabic-speaking Ottomans began to speak of the Arab fatherland, and among the Turkish educated people, there was an emphasis on the Turkish nature of the ruling elite within the empire. For a time, Turks with that sentiment hoped to unify the larger world of the Turkish-speaking peoples, which stretched from the Balkans to Central Asia. The most realistic focus for this nationalist feeling was to focus on the Turkish-speaking heartland of the empire in Anatolia. Within the Young Turk movement, one can thus see the beginnings of the complex issue of the relationship between nationalist sentiments and Muslim religious loyalties.

The Ottoman Empire at the end of the nineteenth century exemplifies the major issues of Islam at the time. Reform involved adapting to Western techniques and ideas, and believing Muslims had to decide what impact this had on their faith. The possibilities of both liberalism and autocracy that were inherent in the Westernizing reforms were reflected in the Islamic responses. The first phase of a relatively simple, pragmatic reformism was replaced by efforts to redefine Islam in terms of the rapidly changing conditions. The reassertion of Islamic authenticity, the restatement of Islam in terms of modern rationalism, and the subordination of Islam to other approaches were common themes in the Islamic experience at the time, and they were manifested in the movements within the Ottoman Empire.

In terms of Islamic styles, adaptationism was a major force, in both political and intellectual terms. The majority of the Muslims within the empire may have been basically conservative in style, but conservatism was forced to accept a continually changing reality. Within the Ottoman Empire itself, there were few major movements that were explicitly fundamentalist, although a fundamentalist tone was present in a number of ways. The Quran and the Sunnah were often cited as validation for positions that were progressive or reactionary. The traditional modes of the individualistic style of Islam were not a prominent aspect of the changing Ottoman experience, but personalized faith might have aided acceptance of the secularist implications of the reforms, and emphasis on charismatic leadership might have given messianic dimensions to nationalism and the various opposition movements.

Islam and Nineteenth-Century Egypt

Egypt in the nineteenth century was still officially a part of the Ottoman Empire, but it was virtually independent of direct Ottoman control. Following the French invasion of Egypt in 1798, a strong ruler, Mehmet Ali, emerged as the ruler. He was a military adventurer who had gone to Egypt with the Ottoman army and used the strength of his character and the chaotic local conditions to soon become the Ottoman governor and ruler. He instituted a vigorous program of reform that aimed at creating a modern state capable of withstanding foreign control. The period of his rule (1805–1849) was an era of pragmatic reforms in Egypt, and those reforms transformed the basic political and economic structures along Westernizing reformist lines.

Under his successors, the reform programs continued but in a more flamboyant, less austere manner. His son, Said (r. 1854–1863), and grandson, Isma'il (r. 1863–1879), rebuilt cities, extended transportation systems, expanded educational facilities, and generally pursued active reformist policies. However, their extravagance created grave financial problems, which led to a European control of Egyptian finances. When Isma'il encouraged local discontent, he was deposed, and Egyptian opposition developed under the influence of students of Jamal al-Din al-Afghani and dissatisfied military officers. The resulting revolt, under the leadership of Ahmad Urabi, led to the British occupation of Egypt in 1882. For the rest of the century, Egypt was still nominally a part of the Ottoman Empire and ruled by autonomous governors, but those governors were under the firm, if technically indirect, control of the British. For all practical purposes, the ruler of Egypt after 1882 was Lord Cromer, the British agent and consul general in Cairo until 1907. Cromer continued programs of economic and administrative reform but was distinctly autocratic in style. In a sense he became the Abdulhamid of the Nile without Islamic regalia.

Within this general political framework, the Islamic experience developed in ways that were roughly parallel to the developments in the central Ottoman Empire. The ulama establishment maintained a basically conservative style, neither mobilizing effective resistance to the reforms nor fully accepting them. By the second half of the century, there were significant efforts toward "ideologies of reform," and the two key themes were the emergence of Egyptian nationalism and the formulation of Islamic modernism. Individual religious leaders played important roles in those activities even though the majority of the ulama were less active.

The ulama had helped to bring Mehmet Ali to power, but they soon became dependent upon him as his reforms reduced their financial and administrative independence. The modernizing programs of Mehmet Ali and his successors "dealt a heavy blow to the ulama. Politically and economically they were rapidly displaced by the new bureaucracy, and the new foreign merchant class. Intellectually they were outdistanced by the new westernized intelligentsia."[11] The ulama remained an important factor in influencing public opinion, but they basically used their position to encourage obedience to those in power. They did not attempt to assume direct political control but used their position to preserve tradition as best they could under the rapidly changing conditions of the time.

The ulama did, however, produce a number of men that were crucial in the formulation of modern Egyptian thought. Rifaʿa al-Tahtawi (1801–1873) had a sound traditional education in the Islamic disciplines, and at al-Azhar, he had been influenced by Shaykh Hasan al-Attar, a religious teacher who had had a relatively cosmopolitan experience and was sympathetic to the reform program of Mehmet Ali. Al-Tahtawi went to Paris with a major diplomatic mission as its religious teacher and gained a familiarity with French life and thought. In Egypt, al-Tahtawi was an important figure in the development of a new educational system and made a great contribution by encouraging translations and language instruction. Through his own translations he became, for many Egyptians, an instructor in European ideas, but he was not simply a transmitter of ideas. He also worked to provide a basic intellectual framework in which Islamic and European ideas could be integrated. He supported reform but, at the same time, encouraged continued adherence to the basic teachings of Islam. In this way, he helped to lay the foundations for Islamic modernist thought. He was also enthusiastic about the historic glories of Egyptian civilization and wrote that within the universal Islamic community, there were special national communities that were deserving of loyalty. Thus, he also helped to build the foundations for Egyptian nationalism. It is significant that this important formulation came from someone drawn from the ulama class but it is also significant that like Ahmad Cevdet in Istanbul, the positions al-Tahtawi held were outside of the ulama establishment.

In Egypt itself, Islamic developments tended to avoid militant activism, and the great Muslim leaders of the nineteenth century, like al-Tahtawi, accepted the existing political framework. There was, however a point when that acceptance might have changed as the potential for a militant religious activism appeared in conjunction with the Urabi movement of 1879–1882. Jamal al-Din al-Afghani, the itinerant advocate of Islamic revival and unity went to Egypt in 1871 and taught there for eight years. He soon attracted a circle of followers, many of whom were students at al-Azhar, and the inherent political activism of his message led many of them to take an active part in political events during the last years of Isma'il's reign and after his deposition. However, following Urabi's defeat and the British occupation, the leading religious activists went into exile and soon reverted to more politically passive roles.

The leading Egyptian follower of Al-Afghani was Muhammad Abduh (1849–1905), another Egyptian with basic ulama training who became a leading intellectual. He was inspired by al-Afghani and took part in the upheaval associated with the Urabi movement. In exile, he worked with al-Afghani in publishing and plotting, but by 1888, he was back in Cairo and basically accepted the politico-military realities of the British occupation. His goal became the reformulation of Islamic thought and the revitalization of Islamic society through integrating modern and Islamic ideas and techniques.

Abduh soon was able to put many of his ideas into practice through a series of public positions that he held. He was made a judge and in 1899 became the mufti of Egypt, the head of the religious court system. In that position, he worked to reform the religious courts, and his legal rulings reinterpreted Islamic law in terms of modern conditions. In addition, he helped to reform the structure and curriculum of al-Azhar University. In his scholarly work, he provided a reinterpretation of Islam, explaining how Islam could provide a moral basis for a modern society. In that analysis, he used themes that had already been developed in the eighteenth century but put them in a contemporary context. He felt that a basic purpose in his life was "to liberate thought from the shackles of *taqlid,* and understand religion as it was understood by the elders of the community before dissension appeared; to return, in the acquisition of religious knowledge, to its first sources, and to weigh them in the scales of human reason . . . and to prove that, seen in this light, religion must be accounted a friend of science."[12] In that statement of purpose, one can see the call for independent judgment (*ijtihad*) and the fundamentalist desire to return to the basic sources of the faith, as well as a vindication of modernist rational thought and science.

Muhammad Abduh was the leading Muslim thinker of his day, and his work had an influence on Islamic thought far beyond the boundaries of Egypt. His heritage was, however, a mixed one. On the one hand, his reaffirmation of the truth of Islam helped to inspire intellectual fundamentalist movements in the twentieth century. On the other hand, his acceptance of reason provided justification for a rationalism by some thinkers that went beyond what he himself might have accepted as legitimate. Clearly, with Muhammad Abduh, modernist thought had become firmly established in the Islamic experience.

At the same time that Islamic modernist thought was developing, the modern form of Egyptian nationalism was emerging. During the nineteenth century, there was a growing awareness of the special heritage of Egyptian civilization as archaeological discoveries opened the world of ancient Egypt to modern eyes. Men like al-Tahtawi and Muhammad Abduh had a special feeling for the Egyptian homeland, but their views were tempered by a special loyalty to the Islamic tradition. However, in the second half of the century, there were intellectuals who placed less emphasis on the Islamic heritage in Egypt and were concerned with freeing Egypt from foreign control.

That new sense of nationalism was a part of the Urabi movement, but at the time the potential nationalists were divided. There were Egyptian military officers, like Ahmad Urabi himself, who resented the privileges of the Turkish military officers who dominated the Egyptian army. There were also the Islamically oriented reformers, who followed al-Afghani's ideas, and the supporters of the idea of a constitutional parliamentary regime. Following the defeat of the Urabi movement and the British occupation, overt nationalism was less visible, but in the last decade of the century, there was a revival of nationalist activity. That revival was led by a French-educated Egyptian lawyer, Mustafa Kamil (1874–1908), an effective orator and a skilled political propagandist. His primary goal was to rid Egypt of the British occupation forces, and he thus appealed more to sentiments of national pride than to religious loyalties.

Mustafa Kamil identified nationalism with modernization. In 1906 he wrote: "We have realized for over a century now that nations cannot lead an honorable life unless they follow the path of Western civilization. We were the first oriental people to shake hands with Europe, and we shall certainly continue along the path we have taken."[13] Kamil did not ignore Islam, but he viewed it in the light of modern nationalistic sentiments. He gave some support to Pan-Islamic causes, but as a way of removing foreign control from Egypt. He was not a well-organized political theorist, but he appears to have thought of Islam largely in individualistic terms, implicitly accepting the secularism of much of modern thought. For him, religion was an individual matter of personal faith and morals, so he was an early believer in one type of individualistic Islam that evolved in the modern context. That type allowed a personalizing of religion and a separation of it from the realm of economics and politics. In that belief, Kamil was in sharp contrast to the emerging Islamic modernist thought.

Kamil led the Hizb al-Watani (National party) until his death. Before World War I, that group was largely an organization of the modern-educated elite rather than a mass party. However, the nationalist movement did help to awaken Egyptians to more political issues and paved the way for a mass nationalist party following the war.

In Egypt, the first phase of reform was followed by a period in which great efforts were made to respond intellectually and actively to the changing conditions. Militant revolt was not, however, a viable possibility following the British occupation, so significant militant opposition did not occur until after World War I. Under the leadership of Muhammad Abduh and Mustafa Kamil, Islamic modernism and Egyptian nationalism emerged as influential intellectual forces. In Islamic terms, the styles of Islam most visible at the end of the century were intellectual adaptationism with a fundamentalist shading in Muhammad Abduh and an individualist shading in Mustafa Kamil.

Islam and Reform in Tunisia

During the nineteenth century, Tunisia went from a relatively autonomous province of the Ottoman Empire to the status of a French protectorate, but it remained a monarchy and reflected the trends that were taking place in Egypt and the central Ottoman Empire. A first phase of pragmatic, if somewhat haphazard, reforms was undertaken by Ahmad Bey, who ruled from 1837 until 1855. New schools were established, military modernization was undertaken, and there was a general attempt to expand the role of government while maintaining the traditional structures. Under pressure from modern-educated Tunisians and European powers, a constitutional regime had been established by 1860. However, financial mismanagement led to increasing problems, and tax increases and economic problems created the conditions for a major tribal revolt in 1864, which spread to urban areas. Ulama participated in that revolt in an effort to regain some of their financial privileges, which had been lost through the reform program. The revolt was put down, but the financial problems were not solved, so in 1869, a European commission took control of Tunisian finances.

The need for more effective reform programs was clearly visible when one of the leading nineteenth-century Muslim reformist thinkers, Khayr al-Din Pasha, became the Tunisian prime minister in 1873. Although he was forced to resign in 1877, he succeeded in creating a coherent reformist framework for later Tunisians. Despite the reforms, however, Tunisia was unable to avoid increasing European domination, and in 1881, French military forces occupied the country and established a protectorate. Although the monarchy was formally preserved, real political control was in French hands. The first phase of pragmatic reform had been followed by the emergence of a reforming ideology, but the end result, in political terms, was foreign control.

The role of Islam in this history is similar to its role in Egypt and Istanbul. The ulama establishment was basically conservative in its style, but it gradually accepted reforms and seldom participated directly in the opposition movement. Instead, the ulama relied on their political skills to limit the changes and to remove reformers from positions of power, but in the long run, the ulama accepted a reorganization of religious finances and Zaytuna University. Major reform leaders had ties with the ulama, but no major figure emerged from the Tunisian ulama to shape the ideologies of reform in the manner of Ahmad Cevdet in Istanbul or Muhammad Abduh in Egypt.

The leading figure in nineteenth-century Tunisian reformism was Khayr al-Din Pasha, a Mamluk of Circassian origin who went to Tunis in 1840. He was active in the reforms of Ahmad Bey and had substantial experience in dealing with Europeans. He reached the peak of his power in 1873–1877, when he was the Tunisian prime minister. Both as a political leader and as a writer he was a key figure in the development of reformist ideology. His influence spread beyond Tunisia, as is reflected in the fact that after his resignation as prime minister in 1877, he went to Istanbul where he became grand vizier of the Ottoman Empire for a short time in the early days of Abdulhamid II's reign. However, his favorable attitude toward a constitutional regime soon clashed with the emerging autocracy there, and he retired.

Khayr al-Din was knowledgeable in both European affairs and Islamic learning. His basic goal was to reform Islamic society in a way that would profit from European experience but remain true to the Islamic heritage. He believed that "there is no reason to reject or ignore something which is correct or demonstrable simply because it comes from others."[14] One of the key parts of his reform program was an emphasis on education that combined traditional Islamic learning with a knowledge of the West, and while he was prime minister, he established Sadiki College, which attempted to do just that. That college and his own influence shaped the next generation of Tunisian leaders. Khayr al-Din was clearly an Islamic adaptationist who worked to create a modern but still Islamic society.

Following the establishment of French control, there was a period of quiet adjustment for the Tunisian educated elite. However, like Muhammad Abduh in Egypt, most of that Tunisian elite felt that direct resistance to the French was useless and worked to reform society within the framework of French control. Followers of Khayr al-Din and graduates of Sadiki College found their way into minor administrative posts, and a group known as the Young Tunisians emerged. With the Young Tunisians, there was an effort to move from passivity to self-assertion.

Unlike the contemporary Young Turks or the Egyptian nationalists, the Young Tunisians tended to avoid revolutionary activity and militant opposition to European control. They assumed more of a linking role, trying to explain the French to the Tunisians and represent Tunisian interests to the French. An example of this effort was the establishment of the Khalduniyyah school in 1896, which attempted to instruct people with a more traditional religious education in the modern ideas. Although Sadiki College emphasized European language instruction, the Khalduniyyah school gave greater emphasis to instruction in Arabic.

In the Young Tunisian movement, there was a relatively broad spectrum of religious views. The predominant mood was one that saw Islam in primarily personal terms with the broader issues of social structure and communal identity being governed by modern ideas. The group moved in the direction of an individualized style of Islam within the framework of a modern, secularist orientation.

A more rigorously Islamic position also developed under the influence of the Pan-Islamic politics of Abdulhamid and the teachings of Muhammad Abduh. A leading figure in that trend was Abd al-Aziz al-Thaʿalibi, a person with a thorough religious training but with a fundamentalist rather than a conservative style. For al-Thaʿalibi, modernism was a tool for strengthening Islam rather than an end in itself. He aroused ulama opposition in Tunisia by his attacks on the existing religious practices, and his emphasis on the Islamic identity of Tunisians ran counter to the assimilationism of most of the Young Tunisians. He was thus an adaptationist with strong fundamentalist leanings. When the Young Tunisians were suppressed by the French in 1912, following a series of relatively minor frictions between the government and the intellectuals, it was al-Thaʿalibi's more militant nationalist tone that survived.

Within all the Ottoman-related areas there was a general pattern that was repeated with local variations, as can be seen in the experiences of the central Ottoman Empire, Egypt, and Tunisia. The main impetus for reform came from the dominant political elite, and it was adaptationist in style and oriented toward Western ideas. At first, that impetus took the form of pragmatic reform programs initiated by rulers like Mahmud II, Mehmet Ali, and Ahmad Bey. Such reforms were accelerated and took a more organized form by the middle of the century in the hands of leaders like Ahmad Cevdet, Ismaʿil, and Khayr al-Din Pasha In religious terms, the efforts did not constitute a rejection of Islam but, rather, were an attempt to integrate Islamic ideas and Western techniques.

By the end of the century, the process had gone further, and a variety of ideologies of reform had emerged. Two main types can be identified. One was more secular in orientation and emphasized the Westernizing dimensions of reform. This type provided a foundation for nationalist feelings and, in religious terms, adopted a more individualized style of Islam. Islam was seen as a primarily personal matter, and the Western secularizing assumptions of a separation of religion and politics were accepted. The other ideology of reform was Islamic modernism. Because of the Pan-Islamic policies of Abdulhamid, it was an important political factor, and in the case of thinkers like Muhammad Abduh, the emphasis was placed on social reform and a reorientation of religious attitudes. The two types of reform ideology were adaptationist with an individualist tone and adaptationist with a more fundamentalist tone. However, in those Ottoman states, fundamentalism did not emerge as the organizing principle for militant activist movements.

Morocco: Traditional Monarchy

Outside of the Ottoman Empire, there were two states that maintained their independence within the Islamic world, Morocco and Iran. In these cases, the governments were less effectively organized in bureaucratic terms but maintained monarchical institutions that were closely tied to the local conditions. In both of these states, the reform efforts were less well organized, and the non-state structures were much stronger.

The sultans of Morocco ruled over a loosely controlled area. Government structures were less comprehensive, a great deal of political power was in the hands of the great tribal chiefs and local religious notables, and the extent of the sultan's control depended upon his ability to secure the cooperation of those local magnates. In doing so, the sultan relied upon the military forces at his personal disposal, and those made available to him by his allies. The armed forces of the central government were never as clearly dominant in Morocco as they were in the Ottoman areas in the eastern Mediterranean. The Moroccan monarch, however, had an additional source of strength in his religious prestige among the general population. As a sharif, he benefited from the respect given to holy men and the tradition of special respect accorded to the monarchical sharif.

During the nineteenth century, there was constant tension in Morocco created by internal struggles for power and the growing expansion of European political and economic influence. Because the sultan was unable, in the long run, to prevent the European expansion, he faced religiously inspired opposition. In this context, it was difficult for any nineteenth-century Moroccan monarch to initiate effective Western-inspired reform programs. No figure similar to Mahmud II emerged, and those reforms that were attempted tended to be haphazard ant halfhearted. The most vigorous effort was made by Sultan Hasan, who ruled from 1873 to 1894. He hoped to check European expansion through the adoption of Western techniques, especially in the military, but the general structure of society could not adjust rapidly enough. The result was the way was opened for a further expansion of European influence. Following Sultan Hasan's death, weak leadership, internal revolts, and a vigorous French expansionism created the conditions for the loss of Moroccan independence. In 1911, the French intervened in a revolt, and they established a protectorate in 1912.

The Islamic dimension of that history is complex. The dominant religious institutions were the monarchy itself and the great religious orders and marabout centers. The formal ulama class had some influence in the urban areas, as teachers and scholars, but they were not important as a focus for religious identity and loyalty. As a result, they tended to follow the lead at various times of either the *tariqah* leaders or the sultan.

In contrast to the political passivism of the ulama establishments in the Ottoman areas, the marabouts and the *tariqah*s had a tradition of political activism in Morocco, and they were frequently rivals of the sultans for control of various areas within the country. This context provides an important framework for the Islamic experience of Morocco during the nineteenth century.

Sultans in the late eighteenth century had taken a number of important religious initiatives. Sultan Muhammad ibn Abdallah (r. 1757–1790) had encouraged a revival of religious scholarship and had worked to reform the curriculum of the major Islamic university of Qarawiyin. In scholarship, he had emphasized the study of *hadith*s and had supported a fundamentalist tone. His son, Mawlay Suleyman (r. 1792–1822) attacked the popular religious practices of the marabouts and the tariqahs, and he sent a delegation to Mecca in 1812 for discussions with the Wahhabis and accepted many of their interpretations. The sultans were thus directly involved in the development of revivalist ideas in the evolution of Moroccan Islam. This was one way of asserting their control over the marabout forces.

During the nineteenth century, the major form of action taken by the sultans against the religious orders was military efforts to limit their control. From time to time, local saints were important figures in supporting revolts against the ruling sultans. There were also cases in which the sultans recognized the local autonomy of the religious leaders and thus secured them as allies. That situation was true in the case of the leaders of the Tayyibiyyah who dominated the hinterlands of Tangiers. At the end of the century, the sultans gave some encouragement to scholars who had been influenced by the teachings of Muhammad Abduh that criticized some of the Sufi practices. However, that encouragement did not place significant restraints on the influence of the *tariqah*s.

The basic position of the sultans was a conservative one as they attempted to maintain their leadership role within Morocco. To accomplish that goal, they sometimes utilized adaptationist styles, but in a haphazard manner, just as they sometimes supported fundamentalist ideas. However, too rigorous a fundamentalist position might undermine their own prestige based on their position as sharifs, and they were either unwilling or unable to become vigorous reforming adaptationists in the manner of Mahmud II or Mehmet Ali.

The other major set of Moroccan Islamic institutions, the *tariqah*s and the marabouts, maintained a similarly ambiguous conservative style. At the end of the eighteenth century, Neo-Sufi ideas had been brought to Morocco, and Moroccans had played an important role in the development of Neo-Sufism in the central Islamic lands. However, the basic patterns of mass organization were already in opposition to at least some of the patterns of the popular religious practices associated with Moroccan Sufism. As a result, Neo-Sufi revivalism had a greater impact on the ulama of Morocco than on its marabouts.

The Tijaniyyah Tariqah was the major Neo-Sufi order in Morocco. It was established by Ahmad al-Tijani (1737–1815), a scholar born in southern Algeria. He had studied *hadith* in Fez and joined major Moroccan orders before going on a pilgrimage to Mecca in 1772. While on pilgrimage, he had studied with Mahmud al-Kurdi, a leading member of the revivalist Khalwatiyyah in Cairo, and then with Muhammad ibn Abd al-Karim al-Samman in Medina. When al-Tijani returned to North Africa, he announced that he had received special authorization from the Prophet to establish a new *tariqah,* which reflected the Neo-Sufi emphasis on a mystical relationship with the Prophet rather than on union with God. In Fez, al-Tijani was welcomed by the reform-minded Sultan Suleyman, possibly as a result of the sultan's opposition to the older Sufi brotherhoods. Many government officials became affiliated with the Tijaniyyah. Although the order was influential, it did not become the basis for a large-scale, transtribal movement of Islamic revivalism in Morocco, although it did in other parts of Africa.

Al-Tijani taught that the Tijaniyyah was the culmination of the *tariqah*s and he required initiates to give up their membership in other orders. He also said that it was forbidden for Tijanis to visit living saints or the tombs of dead ones, reflecting a fundamentalist theme.[15] The rigorous exclusivism of the order meant that although there were branches of the brotherhood in many areas, the Tijaniyyah did not spawn a host of distinctive suborders in a manner similar to Mustafa al-Bakri's Khalwatiyyah. The cohesiveness of the Tijaniyyah tradition was characteristic of a number of Neo-Sufi orders that emerged early in the nineteenth century.

During the nineteenth century, the Tijaniyyah in Morocco remained quite closely tied to the monarchy. The major centers of the order developed in

Algeria around the family of the founder. In Algeria, the Tijaniyyah came to cooperate quite closely with the French, but the Moroccan branch was less willing to aid the French after the establishment of the protectorate. The Tijaniyyah was thus an order within the developing Neo-Sufi tradition, but it was not particularly involved in instigating activist movements with a countrywide political significance.

Most of the other major *tariqah*s in Morocco continued in the marabout tradition, and they had a significant but localized influence. Because of the nature of the spiritual authority of both the sultans and the marabouts, there was always either potential or open competition. The marabouts succeeded in maintaining their local positions, and the sultans were able to keep the influence of any given Sufi teacher localized. As a result, the *tariqah*s were not able to organize any large-scale resistance movements as *tariqah*s elsewhere did. Rather than resisting the expanding influence of the French, the major Moroccan orders tended to cooperate with the Europeans as a way of resisting the power of the sultans. Such cooperation was true from time to time, of the Tayyibiyyah and the Darqawiyyah, and after the protectorate was established, the old-style orders were a major source of Moroccan collaboration with the French.

By the end of the nineteenth century, the impetus for Islamic reformism had passed from the people who were influenced by Neo-Sufism to those who were influenced by the emerging ideas of Islamic modernism as expressed by Jamal al-Din al-Afghani and Muhammad Abduh. This school of thought came to be called the Salafiyyah, meaning those who follow the pious ancestors (*salaf*).

One of the earliest people to introduce Salafiyyah ideas into Morocco was a scholar, Abdallah ibn Idris al-Sanusi (d. 1931). He came into contact with those ideas during a pilgrimage in 1870 and, on his return to Morocco was named by the reformist sultan, Hasan, to a royal council of prominent scholars. Al-Sanusi advocated a literal interpretation of the Quran and a strict adherence to the Sunnah, and he opposed local Sufi practices. A second, more active figure in promoting Salafiyyah ideas was Abu Shuʿayb al-Dukkali (1878–1937). He studied in Egypt and taught for a time in Mecca, and after his return to Morocco, under the French protectorate, he was active as a judge and a legal scholar. Abu Shuʿayb helped to reform the curriculum at the major Moroccan Islamic university and to spread Salafiyyah opposition to popular Sufism. He and his student, Mawlay al-Arabi al-Alawi, were major forces in educating the emerging nationalist Moroccans, and they provided the intellectual foundations for the more politically active Salafiyyah type of movement that emerged following World War I.

The Moroccan Salafiyyah provides a contrast, then, to the more conservative style of the major Islamic institutions in that country. Neither the *tari-qah*s nor the sultans were able to create an effective adaptationist reformism, and they were not significant sources for ideologies of reform. That role was thus left to the ulama and the educated groups, who laid the foundations for a modernizing ideology within the framework of fundamentalist modernism.

The Qajar Dynasty: Monarchy in Shi'i Society

In Iran during the nineteenth century, the monarchy operated within the framework of a Shi'i society and had much less direct religious legitimation than the sultanate in Morocco. By the time of the Qajar unification of Iran at the end of the eighteenth century, Shi'i political thought had quite clearly defined all government other than that led by the imam as illegitimate. Believers were to accept the existing regime as necessary for public order and stability, but religious guidance in all matters, including political ones, was to come from the *mujtahid*s and ulama in general rather than from the political rulers.

There were inherent tensions in a sociopolitical order of that type. One basic line of tension was between the political rulers and the religious leadership. Even though the Iranian ulama generally accepted the monarchy, they worked to limit its powers and to restrain the arbitrary rule of the Qajar shahs. In this effort, they had strong allies in other major segments of the population. The leaders of the great tribes and the major ethnic minority groups also resisted a strengthening of the powers of the central government and frequently cooperated with the ulama. In some cases, *mujtahid*s were among the leading spokesmen for those ethnic groups whose religion was Shi'i Islam. Some of the minority groups were Sunni Muslims, but even they would at times cooperate with the *mujtahid*s to limit the shah's control. Another social group with similar goals was the merchants of the bazaars or city markets. Control of the traditional economy was in their hands, and any expansion of the power of the central government often meant increased state supervision in the bazaars. The bazaar merchants were one of the leading groups of lay supporters of the ulama, tied to them by common background and a firm adherence to Iranian Shi'i Islam. The ulama, tribal and ethnic groups, and bazaar merchants represented an informal alliance of forces to act as a check upon the monarchy and to limit its ability to initiate and implement policies that would significantly alter the structure of Iranian society.

The strength of those forces and the general weakness of the Qajar shahs meant that nineteenth-century reform efforts in Iran were not very effective. No clearly dominant reformer emerged, and most of the reform efforts were considered by the general population to be foreign interference in Iranian affairs. Opposition to efforts to create a more effective central government could be either the traditional Shiʿi opposition to monarchical "tyranny" or the opposition to foreign ideas that would undermine the Islamic foundations of society. By the end of the nineteenth century, those sentiments had succeeded in keeping the monarchy weak but had been unable to stop European military and economic expansion.

The problems faced by the modernizing reformers in Iran are illustrated by the fate of the major reform efforts during the century. In the early years, Abbas Mirza, the crown prince, worked to introduce military reforms, although without parallel administrative and financial reorganization. He had some success, but military defeats at the hands of the Russians destroyed much of his work. He died in 1833, before his father's death, and never came to the throne. Although he had tried to win ulama support, their call for a jihad during the Russian wars had limited his ability to negotiate, and their opposition to foreign techniques had laid him open to the charge of departing from the Islamic faith.

In the middle of the century, a grand vizier under Nasiruddin Shah, Mirza Taqi Khan, called Amir Kabir (in office, 1848–1851), attempted major administrative and legal reforms. The ulama considered those reforms to be attempts to limit their role in society, and they were able to arouse popular opposition to them and to support the court intrigues of the grand vizier's enemies. The result was that Amir Kabir was dismissed and then murdered in 1851. "After his fall, only Mirza Husayn Khan Sipahsalar among Qajar ministers contemplated any serious reform, and the demand for reform was to be associated with that for a form of government consultative at least in appearance."[16] Attempts to expand the power of the monarchy were increasingly associated with concessions to the Europeans, and "reform" came to have a religious and an antimonarchical tone.

The Shiʿi ulama in Iran emerged as the spokesmen for the nation instead of the interests of the state, which helped to set a conservative and religious foundation for Iranian nationalism as it emerged in the modern era. In addition, the ulama became the allies of the proponents of liberal reform because of the shared aim of wishing to limit the power of the monarch, but this alliance did not result in the creation of a modernist Islamic ideology. The interpretive freedom given to the *mujtahid*s by the traditional Shiʿi theology, as it had developed in the eighteenth century, made adjustments and alliances possible without intellectual adaptationism of a modernist type.

That fact had an impact on the development of modernizing reformist thought. By the end of the century, a group of Iranians who had received a modern education and experience began to play a more important role in

Iranian history. Through journalism and their political activism, they had an impact on the formulation of the antimonarchical positions. However, the integration of modern and Islamic ideas was always tentative, reflecting the ulama-liberal interaction that produced an alliance but no synthesis.

An extreme case of the loose integration is that of Mirza Malkum Khan (1833–1908). Malkum Khan was from an Armenian Christian background but was himself a Muslim, although the depth and nature of his commitment to Islam was sometimes suspect. He was involved in organizing secret societies, was active in the political plotting of the second half of the nineteenth century, and was a strong supporter of the Westernizing reforms in Iran. He called the ulama ignoramuses but recognized the need for their cooperation if the reform programs were to be implemented successfully. Thus, whatever cooperation existed was in the form of an alliance rather than a successful integration of ideas. In 1889–1890 he published a newspaper, *Qanun*, which, along with his other writings, helped to introduce Iranians to the modern concepts of government. Although the ulama might not have agreed with him, they utilized concepts such as a constitutionally elected assembly in their cooperation with the Westernizing reformers against the power of the monarchy.

The relationship between Malkum Khan and the ulama emphasizes a basic aspect of the development of Islamic thought in Iran. The ulama and the Westernized intellectuals were able to avoid, for a critical period, dealing with the problems of the ideological implications of modernization in an Islamic society. The possibility of an antimonarchical alliance based on the common political interest of limiting the power of the shah allowed the ulama to be a key focus for nationalist sentiments, and even political reformism, without having to develop an Islamic modernism or a fundamentalist Islam in modern garb. For example, in the days of the constitutional movement in 1906 and later, it was possible for scholars like Muhammad Husayn Naʿini (1860–1936) to defend the constitutional cause in terms that basically reaffirmed traditional Shiʿi political theory with little reference to that cause's modern ideological context or implications.

Similarly, the Westernized intellectuals were able to treat the alliance with the ulama as a "marriage of convenience and necessity." Modernizers like Malkum Khan recognized that their views were counter to those of the ulama and opposed by most of them. However. the intellectuals' response was generally to conceal or at least understate their "real" positions rather than to attempt to develop an effective bridge in intellectual terms between the Islamic and the Westernizing positions.

Although Jamal al-Din al-Afghani inspired efforts to integrate Islamic and Western ideas elsewhere, he did not have significant success in Iran where his role was more that of a political agitator. His followers had some impact in the political intrigues at the end of the century—one of them murdering Nasiruddin Shah in 1896—but the main thrust of Islamic thought remained dominated by the *mujtahids* rather than by the new Muslim modernists.

The central theme in the development of religious activism was the relationship between the ulama and the state. However, another line of eighteenth-century religious development was also important for a time during the nineteenth century. The charismatic messianism of the Shaykhi movement provided the impetus for a movement of religious revolt in the middle of the century, and the Shaykhi teachers encouraged a popular expectation of the coming of the Mahdi. In 1844, Ali Muhammad, a student of a major Shaykhi teacher, declared himself to be the Bab (Gateway) to the Truth and the initiator of a new prophetic age. The Bab soon clashed with the ulama because of his criticism of their practices and then his followers began to revolt, coming into conflict with the state as well as with the religious leadership in Iran. The Bab gained a relatively large following in a short time, which illustrates the potential religious activism of large segments of the population. However, the government suppressed the movement and executed the Bab and other leaders. In exile, the remnants of the movement continued the tradition in a more politically passive form, and the major surviving element followed Baha'Allah in the establishment of the Baha'i religious tradition. Within Iran, the followers of the Bab, the majority of whom became part of the Baha'i group, remained a persecuted religious minority but had little direct role in Iranian affairs after the suppression of the original movement.

The more significant evolution of Iranian religious activism and nationalism took place through the activities of the ulama and other groups in their interaction with the monarchy. The character of this development is illustrated by two major events. One was the successful opposition to a tobacco concession granted by the shah to a British firm in 1890, and the other was the constitutional movement of 1905–1906. In both of these cases, the shah was seen as the tool of growing foreign control in Iran and the supporter of corrupt and tyrannical governmental practices. Large-scale opposition emerged, and the alliance of the ulama, the bazaar merchants, and the new educated class was able to force the shah to accept the popular demands. The common goals of the three major elements in the alliance were a limitation of the powers of the monarchy and an elimination of foreign influence in Iran. Characteristically, however, the success of the opposition movements was based on an alliance of diverse forces rather than on a common ideology of reform.

In 1906, the alliance succeeded in forcing the shah to accept a constitution with an elected parliament. The haphazard Westernizing reform efforts of the nineteenth century had created a group of Iranians with a modern education who, through their writings, were able to provide the conceptual terminology for the constitutional movement. However, the reforms had not built a structure of modernized institutions to support those ideas. The monarchy itself was weak, and the state, in contrast to the states in other Muslim areas, could not provide an effective focus for the modernizing efforts.

With the success of the constitutional movement, the divisions within the alliance came to the fore. In addition to the continuing threat of Russian and British imperial ambitions, the new regime had to cope with significantly different perceptions of what the nature of the government should be. Three competing viewpoints had emerged. The modern-educated group worked to create a basically secularized, democratic regime, although at least some in this group realized the need to give some recognition to Islam in order to maintain the support of the majority of the population. The second group was drawn from the ulama. Although they resisted many of the secularizing tendencies of the modernizers, they continued to support the constitutional cause. They felt that a constitutional government would be a way of limiting the tyranny of the rulers and, through the assembly or parliament, would provide a vehicle for the defense of Islamic ideals. In this way, the basic themes of Shi'i political theory could be reconciled with the existing reality. A clear statement of this constitutionalist viewpoint was presented in a significant book by Muhammad Husayn Na'ini (1860–1936), and that work had a long-term impact on the political thought of the majority of the Iranian ulama. Significantly, the book was not an exposition of a new, modernist Shi'ism but, rather, a reaffirmation of traditional Shi'i political theory in a different context.[17]

The modernist tendency in the constitutionalist movement was clearly adaptationist and, in its religious aspect, accepted the individualized nature of religion in a secularized context. The constitutionalist ulama were more conservative, but there was some willingness to accept adaptationism in terminology. The third group was more clearly fundamentalist in style. Shaykh Fadl Allah al-Nuri led those people who felt that there could be no dilution of Islamic law, and he and his supporters joined forces in an attempt by the shah to overthrow the constitutional regime, which triumphed briefly in 1908. Shaykh Fadl Allah allowed the execution of well-known religious laymen, and when the constitutionalists returned to power, Shaykh Fadl Allah was executed. This fundamentalist effort represents an additional theme in the development of Iranian Islam in the modern era. Shaykh Fadl Allah was one of a series of militant ulama who opposed secularist compromises and were willing to become political activists in support of their position.

Summary

The Islamic state systems that survived in the nineteenth century had a variety of experiences. In each of them, there were attempts at modernizing reform programs, but those attempts were more coherent in the central Ottoman Empire, Egypt, and Tunisia than in Morocco and Iran. In all cases, the expanding European power played a role that both encouraged and ultimately thwarted the reform efforts. By the end of the century, a more Islamic reaction had developed. Some of the reformers maintained a semblance of Islamic loyalty, but increasingly, in their view, Islam was to be a personal matter. This viewpoint recognized the implicit secularism of the Westernizing reforms and gave rise to a new form of the individualistic style of Islam, which is well illustrated by the Egyptian nationalism of Mustafa Kamil.

A more specific Islamic orientation developed through the work of scholars like Muhammad Abduh in Egypt and the Salafiyyah movement, which grew out of that trend of Islamic modernism, and an adaptationist style with an Islamic emphasis developed. That style provided a vehicle for integrating Western and Muslim ideas. In Iran, the integration was more in terms of a political alliance than an intellectual synthesis. As a result, the constitutionalist ulama there were more conservative in style, and that situation created an opening for a more explicitly fundamentalist position. This potential for a nationalism with a more fundamentalist tone was realized later in the twentieth century in Iran and had its counterparts in the Moroccan Salafiyyah and al-Thaʿalibi in Tunisia. This more militant Islam provides a link between the eighteenth-century activism and the resurgence of Islamic sentiments in the last quarter of the twentieth century.

Militant Reaction and Reorientation

In those areas of the Islamic world where the governments were less effective, nineteenth-century events followed a different pattern. The resistance to Western expansion and internal decline produced vigorous Islamic reactions, that followed the eighteenth-century patterns, and there was less effort to introduce modernizing reforms of institutions because of the weakness of the local rulers. By the end of the century, the more traditional Islamic reactions had clashed with the European imperial expansion directly and had been defeated. In the aftermath of that defeat, significant efforts were made to adjust to the new circumstances, and Islamic reformism, modernist adaptationism, and nationalism emerged as the major ideological styles.

Islam in Nineteenth-Century India

At the beginning of the nineteenth century, India was in turmoil. After a century of revolt and warfare, the Moghul Empire was no longer an effective governing structure, the Indian subcontinent was divided into warring states, and the British were gradually expanding their influence and control. Within the Muslim community, the most important intellectual force was the tradition of the great eighteenth-century thinker, Shah Wali Allah. His followers and descendants were, at the beginning of the nineteenth century, the source of most of the dynamic developments taking place within Indian Islam.

In the face of this disintegrating situation, Muslims began to react with a vigor that was characterized by a fundamentalist militancy. During the first half of the century, a number of activist groups raised the banner of holy war, and others supported programs of Islamic revivalism. In tone and in general intellectual content, these movements were direct continuations of the eighteenth-century trends. However, by mid-century, the ability of these groups to win their battles had declined, and a great rebellion that spread throughout much of India in 1857 became a major watershed. After the British had crushed the revolt, British domination of all of India was clear, and few militant groups arose. Instead, major efforts were made in the direction of adapting to the new reality. Those efforts took the forms of an Indian Islamic modernism, a conservative revivalism, and the beginnings of Muslim nationalism in India.

The political dimension of Shah Wali Allah's ideas took concrete form in the movement established by Ahmad Brelwi (1786–1831). Ahmad had been a student of Wali Allah's oldest son, and his reformist ideas rested on the foundations of that major tradition of scholarship. Ahmad Brelwi was upset by the deepening decline of Muslim fortunes, believed that the decline was due to a departure from the faith, and opposed the popular religious practices and compromises with local Hindu customs. He gained widespread respect and followers through active preaching tours, and after a pilgrimage to Mecca in 1821, he organized a special religio-political state and initiated a holy war to restore Muslim rule in India. He was killed in battle in 1831, and much of his army was scattered, although his followers were able to continue a limited preaching of fundamentalist reform.

The movement of Ahmad Brelwi is often called a Wahhabi movement, but he probably received no direct inspiration from the teachings of Muhammad ibn Abd al-Wahhab. However, Ahmad Brelwi clearly was within the tradition of eighteenth-century socio-moral reconstructionism. Through Shah Wali Allah's teachings, he had direct ties to the broader movements of eighteenth-century Islam, and in his opposition to popular Sufi practices and syncretism, he was part of the developing Neo-Sufi tradition. That fact is possibly reflected in some of his specific teachings . Like his near contemporary, Ahmad al-Tijani, he claimed direct inspiration from the Prophet Muhammad, which provided the foundation for uniting the major *tariqah*s into the Muhammadiyyah Tariqah. That Neo-Sufi theme of using a *tariqah* based on direct contact with Muhammad and calling itself the Muhammadiyyah Tariqah was a part of a number of contemporary movements, including the orders established by students of Ahmad ibn Idris. In addition, Ahmad Brelwi also placed emphasis on the importance of the *hadith*s and opposed the authority of the four medieval schools of law if that authority required *taqlid*.

Eighteenth-century themes provided the basic foundations for this movement of Islamic revival in India. Ahmad Brelwi attempted to meet the challenges of the early nineteenth century with tools that had been created in the previous century, and his defeat helped to show that those tools were not sufficient in the changing circumstances.

Ahmad Brelwi's movement was largely influential in central and northwest India, and there were similar movements in other parts of India at the same time. One of Ahmad Brelwi's students, Mir Nithar Ali, commonly called Titu Mir (1782–1831), established his own movement in Bengal. He organized Muslim peasants in opposition to the Hindu landlords and British commercial interests and attempted to reform the popular religious customs. He soon clashed with British forces and was killed in 1831.

Another militant movement at the time was the Fara'idiyyah, which was established by Hajji Shariat Allah (1764–1840), a teacher who had studied in Mecca for almost twenty years. There he may have come into direct contact with Wahhabi ideas, and he was clearly influenced by the more general socio-moral reconstructionism of the time. He initiated a vigorous reform movement in Bengal, and many of his key themes were common contemporary ones: an emphasis on the oneness of God and a rejection of those popular religious customs that ran counter to a strict interpretation of the Quran and the Sunnah. He also supported the cause of Muslim peasants against the landlords and British commercial interests. His son, Dudu Miyan (1819–1862), succeeded him as leader of the movement and gave it a careful organizational structure. Dudu Miyan created what was essentially a separate government for members of the Fara'idiyyah and soon clashed with the authorities. After he was arrested in 1847, the movement weakened without his leadership, and it gradually became just one of many religious movements in the area.

The era of large-scale militant Muslim movements reached a climax in the general Indian uprising against the British in 1857. What began as a mutiny among both Muslim and Hindu troops in the British army soon became a widespread series of revolts against the British. Many different groups participated, and the character of the opposition depended upon local conditions. Although Muslim religious leaders participated, the uprisings did not represent a unified Islamic opposition to imperial rule. The ulama in Delhi were persuaded to declare the revolt a holy war, and some scholars established a religious state in Thana Bhawan. The leader of that latter group was Imdad Allah (1815–1899), a noted Sufi teacher who fled after the rebellion to Mecca, where he became a popular teacher and had an influence upon the later Indian Muslim reform movements.

The British were able to crush the uncoordinated revolts, and the 1857 rebellion marks a major turning point in the history of Indian Islam. Although small-scale militant Islamic groups continued to revolt from time to time, the major Islamic movements after 1860 assumed a different form and most Muslim leaders accepted the reality of the British military dominance. Like Muhammad Abduh in Egypt, they set out to revive and reform Islam within the context of foreign control. Militant Muslim revivalism had failed, and the need now was for ways to adjust to Western domination and modern ideas.

The leading figure in this reorientation of Indian Islam was Sayyid Ahmad Khan (1817–1898). Sayyid Ahmad had worked as a young man for the East India Company, and after 1857, he strove to reconcile the Indian Muslims and the British. In intellectual terms, he attempted to integrate Western and Islamic thought because he believed that a Muslim adjustment to the modern intellectual realities was absolutely essential. He said, "If people do not shun blind adherence, if they do not seek that Light which can be found in the Qur'an and the indisputable Hadith, and do not adjust religion and the science of today, Islam will become extinct in India."[18]

In order to carry out his program, Sayyid Ahmad worked to translate Western works into Indian languages, helped to organize special education committees, and established a modern institution of higher education for Muslims—the Muhammadan Anglo-Oriental College in Aligarh, which became a major center for Islamic modernist education in India. His general approach to integrating modern scientific thought with Islam is stated in his axiom that nature, which is the work of God, is identical with the Quran, which is the word of God. Through his writings and life work, he created the intellectual foundations for Islamic modernism in India. He also helped to revive the communal morale of Muslims, and he resisted nationalist pressures to have Muslims join the emerging Hindu-dominated Indian nationalist movement. By helping to revive Muslim pride and by encouraging Muslim separatism, he opened the way for Muslim nationalism and the creation of the state of Pakistan.

The implications of the positions taken by Sayyid Ahmad Khan led to a variety of developments, either reacting in opposition or developing the positions further. The work of an associate of Sayyid Ahmad's, Chiragh Ali (d. 1895), illustrates the radical potential of the new modernism. Chiragh Ali rejected the whole structure of medieval society as outmoded. He engaged in a vigorous defense of Islam against the criticism of Christian missionaries and other Europeans, but he did so on the basis of an analysis and interpretation of the Quran rather than by defending existing Muslim practices. In the defense, he presented arguments through the vehicle of a rational historical analysis, saying that "Islam exists as a religion distinct from a social system, though Muslims in various phases of their history confused the individual or cumulative experience of their social systems with the Quran."[19]

That development produced what has been called "speculative fundamentalism."[20] In that style, a modernist adaptationism is combined with a rejection of all classical sources of Islamic law and thought except the Quran itself. Positions are supported by a rigorous, if speculative, analysis of the Quran, and everything else in the Islamic tradition is viewed in its historical context. It was possible for Chiragh Ali, and others like him, to argue that Muhammad did not set up a formal legal system and did not require his followers to do so; thus, Muslims are free to develop legal systems that are in accord with the specific conditions of their own times and are not bound by systems developed by Muslims in other times or places. This speculative fundamentalism opened the way for a radically modernist form of Islam.

The position of Sayyid Ahmad Khan was not accepted by all of the major Muslim teachers and the richness of Indian Muslim thought at the end of the nineteenth century and the breadth of the foundations provided by Shah Wali Allah are clearly visible in the variety of the more conservative positions that had emerged by the end of the century. New educational institutions were a leading part of the more traditional revival. In 1867, an Islamic school was established at Deoband by scholars in the tradition of Wali Allah. Although some of the scholars had participated in the ulama militancy led by Imdad Allah in 1857, their goal now was to revive a rigorous study of the traditional Islamic disciplines and to provide a link between the Muslim community and its traditional identity. The Deoband school was relatively conservative in accepting the validity of the law schools and fundamentalist in rejecting compromises with Hindu customs and also in rejecting the adaptationism of Sayyid Ahmad Khan. The Deoband theological school established an international reputation and had ties with the ulama of al-Azhar in Egypt.

The more conservative style was also manifested in other important schools. The oldest and most conservative of the major schools was the Faranji Mahal in Lucknow, which maintained a traditional curriculum and was relatively aloof from the arguments of the modernists and active traditionalists. A less conservative school was the Nadwat al-Ulama, which was established in Lucknow in 1894. Its leaders attempted to find a middle path between the modernism of Sayyid Ahmad Khan and the conservativism of Deoband and hoped to provide the training necessary for the ulama to be able to reassert their role as the moral leaders of the Muslim community in India.

A more rigorous fundamentalism of a traditional rather than a "speculative" type also emerged in the late nineteenth century in the form of a group known as the Ahl al-Hadith (People of Hadith), who built on the tradition of *hadith* study that had been firmly established in India by Shah Wali Allah. The movement emphasized a reliance on the Quran and the Sunnah, and its members were unwilling to accept the teachings of the medieval scholars as binding unless they were directly based on the fundamental sources of the faith. In this belief, they were continuing the eighteenth-century trends in *hadith* scholarship and were an important link between modern and premodern developments.

In addition to adaptationists, conservatives, and fundamentalists, the nineteenth-century Indian Islamic experience produced a major movement that can be seen as an assertion of the individualist emphasis on charismatic leadership. This was the Ahmadiyyah movement, which was founded by Mirza Ghulam Ahmad of Qadiyan (1839–1908). He claimed special revelation from God and regarded himself as a prophet and the promised messiah. Although in many ways the Ahmadiyyah remained within the bounds of the Islamic tradition, other Muslims rejected the Ahmadiyyah as heretical. By the early twentieth century, the movement had become a separate religious community and had become active in missionary work outside of India.

The vigorous activity within the Indian Muslim community during the nineteenth century shows the dynamism of Islam in the early modern era. Movements both built on the Islamic foundations of the past and reacted to the changing modern conditions, and the community was not isolated within the Islamic world. Sayyid Ahmad Khan was aware of the works of Khayr al-Din Pasha in Tunisia, and Chiragh Ali read the works of al-Tahtawi in Egypt as well as the writings of Khayr al-Din. The Ahl al-Hadith were influenced by nineteenth-century Yemeni scholarship, and virtually all educated Muslims were aware of developments in Egypt and the Ottoman Empire. The second half of the nineteenth century was a time of real Islamic resurgence in India in intellectual and religious terms, although it took place in the context of foreign politico-military control. In this resurgence, all of the traditional styles of Islamic action were visible in varying forms as the Muslim community worked to meet the challenges of modern history.

Muslim Activism in Southeast Asia

During the nineteenth century, a number of dynamic tensions provided the framework for the development of Islam in Southeast Asia. The old tension between a localized, syncretic Islam and a more rigorous, cosmopolitan faith continued. The main lines of that interaction had already been set in the eighteenth century and were manifested in the reforming crusades that were led by ulama who had been on pilgrimage and the work of others who had been influenced by the cosmopolitan trends in the Indian Ocean basin. This old tension often involved conflict between the religious leaders and the established rulers. The second conflict involved the expansion of Dutch control and the local resistance to developing Western imperialism. Since the Dutch attempted to work through the local rulers and the courts, the two conflicts often merged, and the holy wars were both attempts to reform religious practice and expressions of opposition to expanding foreign control.

The general pattern of development was similar to what was taking place in India. The old local state systems were crumbling and were not able to provide effective leadership for the reformist efforts. Resistance and reform followed eighteenth-century lines rather than adopting reform programs of a Westernizing type. The more traditionally structured Islamic reactions produced militant movements, which ultimately were defeated by the forces of European imperialism. However, this phase of militant resistance was spread throughout the century, in contrast to the Indian experience, because Dutch control expanded only gradually throughout the islands of the East Indies. As the Dutch consolidated their position in an area, local militant resistance would arise and, usually after a long struggle, would be defeated. It was not until the end of the century that the Muslim communities in Southeast Asia reached the stage where most religious leaders accepted the inevitability of foreign control and initiated significant nonmilitary efforts of reform.

For the Muslims in Southeast Asia, the nineteenth century was a time of a long series of bitter and hard-fought holy wars, which had the dual purpose of reforming local religious practice and resisting the Dutch. The character of these conflicts shows that Southeast Asian Islam was not isolated from the rest of the Muslim world. As changes took place elsewhere, they were reflected in the developing attitudes in Southeast Asia.

The early holy wars still followed eighteenth-century patterns. In 1803, three scholars returned from a pilgrimage to Mecca and began a vigorous preaching mission to reform the local religious practices in Sumatra. Their active preaching upset the existing balance between the local chiefs and the religious teachers. The movement the scholars started was called the Padri movement by the Europeans and *kaum puteh* ("white ones") locally because of the requirement that men wear white, Arab-style robes, and it expanded by persuasion and force from village to village. By 1820, the Dutch became involved as they hoped to expand their power by aiding local rulers who were opposed to the *kaum puteh*. After sixteen years of fighting, the *kaum puteh* were subdued, but, during that time, the movement gradually evolved into a relatively unified Muslim front, led by the *kaum puteh,* that opposed the infidel foreigners. In the process, the ulama emerged with great prestige as the spokesmen for indigenous interests. Descendants of the *kaum puteh* leaders later became respected religious teachers who continued to support a more rigorous adherence to Islam and played an important role in the emergence of Islamic modernism in Indonesia.

A second major war in the first half of the century illustrates many of the same trends. Dutch control during the first two decades of the nineteenth century had an unsettling effect and opened the way for a growing exploitation of the local population. The Java War from 1825 to 1830 was led by a local sultan's son, Dipa Negara, who had retired from court life to engage in religious meditation. He had gained a reputation for visions and was persuaded that his mission was to purify Islam. Rebellion broke out when he was insulted by a Dutch official, and he was soon supported by many of the ulama. Some of the Javanese nobility remained loyal to the Dutch, but gradually, as in the case of the *kaum puteh,* the ulama-led movement of opposition to the compromises of court life became a holy war against the infidel foreigners. Militant revivalist Islam again provided the ideology of revolt against foreign rule, and the fundamentalist ulama gained strength among the general population as the old court nobility became identified with the Dutch.

The third great war of the nineteenth century was the result of Dutch control expanding into the area of the old, and now ineffective, sultanate of Atjeh in Sumatra. Atjeh had remained independent—although that status depended primarily on the Anglo-Dutch Treaty of 1824, which defined spheres of influence and guaranteed the independence of Atjeh—but in the second half of the century, it became clear that the Dutch intended to extend their control into the area. In an interesting illustration of the cosmopolitan, if naive, view of the Achinese sultan, he appealed to the Ottoman sultan for aid against the growing Dutch interference, and some people from the court contacted the U.S. and Italian consuls in Singapore. After a new Anglo-Dutch Treaty, the Dutch invaded Atjeh in 1873, and a long war began.

The old court and the local notables were ineffective in the resistance. The real leaders were the ulama, and the war rapidly became a holy war against Dutch aggression. Gradually, the sultan and then the local governors accepted Dutch rule, and the ulama became identified, as they had in the other conflicts, as the true representatives of local opposition to alien rule.

Although the Atjeh resistance was similar in many ways to the fundamentalist style of militant Islam visible elsewhere in the early part of the century, it also reflects late-nineteenth-century movements as well, as there was a sense of Pan-Islam as it was promoted by Abdulhamid II in Istanbul. Local enthusiasm was aroused when a Turkish warship passed through Singapore on its way to Japan, and Southeast Asian Muslims were aware of events like the Russo-Turkish War of 1877–1878 and the Mahdist uprising in the Sudan in the 1880s. All of those events helped to keep alive the hope of a general Islamic movement that would defeat the European imperialists.

Ironically, the international ties of the Muslim community were aided by the consolidation of Dutch control, and less militant but still strongly revivalist movements had emerged by the beginning of the twentieth century. On the negative side, the identification of the old ruling class with the colonial administration removed the major rival of the ulama as the leaders of the majority of the population. However, on the positive side, the Dutch improved the communications system and thus opened up previously isolated communities to Muslim influence. In addition, the expansion of the Dutch administration meant that Muslims were given subordinate clerical positions and sent to many areas where they acted as conscious or unconscious missionaries.

One major impact of a more modern communications system was a significant rise in the number of Southeast Asian Muslims going on pilgrimage. Despite restrictions imposed by the Dutch, the pilgrimage was a significant part of Muslim life in Indonesia, and in the second half of the century, the increase and improvement in steamship services made the holy cities more readily accessible. The experience of being in Mecca and Medina inspired a desire to bring local Muslim life more into accord with a strict interpretation of the Quran and the Sunnah. In this way, the popularity of the pilgrimage helped to support a fundamentalist style of reformism. In addition, a large community of Southeast Asian scholars became established in Mecca and Medina, and they participated in the major currents of Islamic thought and were an effective channel for their transmission back to their homeland.

International contacts and ties were a part of the inspiration for the militant holy war movements during the nineteenth century. These contacts were also important in the emergence of a less militant but still reformist Islam as it emerged by the end of the century. An early leader in this shift, who also provided a more modernist tone, was Shaykh Ahmad Khatib (1855–1916). He was a descendant of a Padri teacher in Sumatra and went to Mecca in 1876 where he remained and became a well-known teacher of Shafi'i law. Although he did not return to Indonesia, his students became major figures of Sumatran and Malayan reform. He was relatively traditional in his approach to legal studies and did not accept some of the ideas of Muhammad Abduh, although he was familiar with them.

Another Sumatran descendant of a Padri teacher, Shaykh Muhammad Tahir ibn Jalal al-Din (1867–1957), was more directly involved in spreading the ideas of Muhammad Abduh's Salafiyyah to Southeast Asia. He also taught in Mecca for a time after studying at al-Azhar as well as in the holy cities, Early in the twentieth century, he began publishing a newspaper called *al-Imam* in Singapore, and it circulated widely in the area. He supported and spread Abduh's ideas and opposed local popular religious practices. In legal opinions, he based his conclusions on the Quran and the Sunnah rather than utilizing traditional opinions from the law schools. He and his associates established a school with a modernist curriculum, which became a model for other schools. Muhammad Tahir was representative of a new generation of Muslim leaders who accepted the political realities of the time but continued the reformist spirit. The activities of this generation soon led to the creation of relatively large-scale organizations that were active in religiocultural affairs, education, and politics. In this way, the foundations were laid for the twentieth-century experience of Southeast Asian Islam.

During the nineteenth century, adaptationism in Southeast Asia largely took the form of collaboration with the growing Dutch power on the part of the local rulers. There was little effort at modernizing reforms, if for no other reason than the rulers did not have the power to implement them. Conservative-style Muslims were those who worked to preserve the old cultural compromises that were manifested in the local popular religious practices. Throughout the century, the conservatives were on the defensive, not so much facing the attacks of modernizing reformers as facing those of the revivalist fundamentalists.

In Southeast Asia, it was the fundamentalist style of Islam that flourished during the nineteenth century. Rigorous reformism became identified with opposition to alien rule, and in many rural areas that reformism provided the leadership that replaced the older-style religious conservatives. The holy wars led by the fundamentalists could not stem the tide of Dutch expansion, but neither could the Dutch eliminate the influence of the activist ulama. By the end of the century, though, a significant number of ulama had begun to exercise their reformist zeal against social practices and traditional ideas in a less politically militant manner. In that change, the influence of emerging Islamic modernism in the Middle East and India played a role.

The Algerian Experience

In Algeria, the domination of the French was more complete than that of the Dutch in Indonesia or the British in India. The weak Ottoman governors were replaced by French rule in the years following the French invasion in 1830, and there was no opportunity for local governments to adopt reformist programs. Opposition to European imperialism was almost entirely the work of the local religious and tribal leaders. Because the French policies undermined the very nature of Islamic society in Algeria, there was little incentive to create a reformist movement similar to Abduh's, which accepted the political realities. The Algerian religious leaders who cooperated with the French did so as political allies, preserving their own interests, rather than in an effort to create an effective synthesis of Western and Islamic ideas. It was not until the twentieth century that effective Islamic modernist or Algerian assimilationist movements developed.

The foundations for a nineteenth-century religiopolitical activism were being laid early in the century, before the French invasion. As the Turkish governors in Algiers became more ineffective and oppressive, local political leadership was assumed by marabouts and *tariqah* leaders. There were revolts by the Darqawiyyah and Tijaniyyah orders against Turkish rule, and popular support for the *tariqah* leaders made it possible for the orders to create states in the existing political vacuum. This conflict with the Turks also made it possible for some of the *tariqah* leaders to see the French as allies in the struggle. In this way, some of the major brotherhoods established alliances with the French, and that cooperation continued throughout the century. In particular, despite its Neo-Sufi origins, the Tijaniyyah in Algeria became closely associated with the European rulers. The early Tijaniyyah attempts to establish a state of their own had been thwarted, first by the Turks and then by other militant orders who opposed the French. The Tijaniyyah thus allied themselves with "the enemies of their enemies" and accepted French rule.

The most famous militant Muslim leader in nineteenth-century Algeria was the Amir Abd al-Qadir (1808–1883). Through his family and education he had direct ties to the major trends of the eighteenth-century Islamic world, and between 1830 and 1847, he led a major movement of resistance to French control. The ancestors of Abd al-Qadir had been local teachers in Algeria, and they had maintained a family devotional tradition of adherence to the Qadiriyyah Tariqah. His grandfather, Mustafa ibn Muhammad al-Hasani (1747–1798), had reorganized the family order along Neo-Sufi lines after studying in the eastern Mediterranean, in particular with Muhammad Murtada al-Zabidi in Cairo. On his return to Algeria, Mustafa had enlarged the activity of his family's branch of the Qadiriyyah, and the family center became a well-known place of learning. Mustafa's son, Muhyi al-Din (1776–1834), had continued this revival and had gained a large following among many of the major tribes.

Abd al-Qadir, Muhyi al-Din's son, grew up in the context of this revived *tariqah*. He went with his father to the eastern Mediterranean where he studied *hadith* in Damascus and is said to have been initiated into the Naqshbandiyyah Tariqah by the revivalist-reformer, Khalid al-Naqshbandi. On his return to Algeria, Abd al-Qadir began to assume a position of leadership in his family's order.

Following the French invasion, tribesmen in western and central Algeria turned to Muhyi al-Din for resistance leadership. He finally agreed to guide the jihad and soon turned over its direct leadership to Abd al-Qadir, who was both an able military commander and an effective political organizer. Abd al-Qadir soon established a militant movement that was both an army and a state. He showed himself to be a fundamentalist in spirit but willing to accept new techniques if they would make his army and administration more effective. He consciously modeled his creation on the community of the Prophet and the early caliphs, but he did not encourage messianist enthusiasm. Through a long series of campaigns and negotiations, he fought the French for almost two decades. Finally, internal divisions within Algeria and the military power of the French defeated him.

Abd al-Qadir was not the only religious teacher to oppose the French as a number of local preachers also organized resistance movements. However, some of the most important of those were men who proclaimed themselves to be the Mahdi and refused to cooperate with Abd al-Qadir. Their opposition diluted Abd al-Qadir's strength, since he had to subdue them as well as fight the French. In addition, Tijaniyyah rivalry with Abd al-Qadir's family brought that order into conflict with the amir's forces. Thus, internal divisions were one factor that weakened the Algerians' ability to stop the French expansion.

After the final defeat of Abd al-Qadir in 1847, there were other resistance movements, but none had the large-scale support or the effectiveness of the earlier movement. Most of the revolts were led by religious figures, and Islam became clearly identified as a major source of opposition to imperialism. However, the collaboration with the French by some of the major *tariqah*s did not make the relationship between Islam and opposition to foreign rule as clear as it was in some other parts of the Islamic world.

There were clearly socioeconomic political reasons for revolt, but French power made revolution on those pragmatic grounds impractical. After the defeat of Abd al-Qadir, most revolts had to be based on an ideology that could transcend the material realities. Politically passive Sufism and even traditional revivalism, if it was based on prudent fundamentalism, could not provide the inspiration for revolt. Building on the teachings of Abd al-Qadir, prudent fundamentalism advocated emigration from the infidel-controlled areas if a successful holy war were not possible. Adaptationism, conservatism, and fundamentalism did not provide the basic Islamic style for continued opposition to the French. It was the individualistic style of Islam, which emphasized charismatic and messianic leadership, that provided the vision necessary for revolt in the face of French power.

For almost half a century after Abd al-Qadir's defeat, what has been called a "general apocalyptic awareness"[21] provided the basis for some religious activism. That sentiment accepted the possibility of establishing a realm of just rule through charismatically led revolutionary movements aided by divine intervention. A number of revolts of this type took place, but by the end of the century, the spirit had begun to fade. The apocalyptic vision had been kept alive in a number of local religious centers, but gradually, the French succeeded in destroying this institutional base. "Once this network was disrupted apocalyptic action disintegrated into banditry, civil disorder, passive resistance or resignation."[22]

In Algeria, the Muslims faced not only the overwhelming military power of European imperialism, but also a growing community of European settlers who came to dominate local politics and the economy. That domination severely limited the options that were open to Muslims who were willing to undertake even intellectual adaptationism. Islamic society in Algeria was disrupted, and it was not until much later that Algerian Muslims began to develop effective "ideologies of reform." In contrast to the rich diversity seen in Muslim India and Indonesia, there was little beyond efforts at simple survival within the Algerian Muslim community. With adaptationism apparently blocked and other styles of Islamic action stymied, Algerian Islam acted with passive resistance or resignation, waiting for new opportunities, which would be provided by the changing conditions created by World War I and the events of the interwar era.

Russian Expansion and Islam

Muslim communities in the Eurasian steppes faced the expanding Russian Empire. In a process that began in the sixteenth century and was essentially completed by the end of the nineteenth, a variety of Muslim groups came under Russian control. These groups can be divided into four general types, within which there was substantial diversity.

In the Volga River area and the Crimea Peninsula, Muslims had long been in contact with Russia, and they were the earliest to be conquered. By the nineteenth century, overt military resistance had virtually ceased, and large-scale Russian immigration was rapidly changing the demographic character of those areas. The major themes of the Islamic experience there were related to adapting to clearly permanent incorporation into the Russian Empire. In addition, the relative success of the Russian efforts to convert Tatar Muslims to Christianity provided an added challenge. In this context, Tatar Muslims of all classes were open to efforts of Islamic revival in the framework of a modernist style of Islam.

At the beginning of the nineteenth century, a second group of Muslim communities were coming under Russian control in the Caucasus region between the Black and Caspian seas. There, Russian expansion met militant Muslim opposition, and the local groups retained special ethnic and linguistic identities that would become the foundation for later nationalist sentiments.

The third and fourth groups were in Central Asia, in the general area called Turkestan. In the northern part of that area, the Kazakhs had only recently converted to Islam and had remained a largely nomadic society. The Russians were able to win the cooperation of a substantial proportion of the old tribal nobility, and Russo-Kazakh cooperation was an important theme. However, great tensions had arisen by the end of the nineteenth century as a result of a growing number of Russian settlers taking over the pasturelands of the nomads.

In the southern part of Turkestan, Islam was a long-established feature of the urban culture, and great cities like Bukhara and Samarkand had been centers of Islamic learning since the days of the Abbasid empire. Some of their commercial wealth and cultural life had crumbled as a result of a long series of invasions during the later medieval period, but in the early years of the nineteenth century, there were still relatively well-organized states led by the khans of Bukhara, Khiva, and Khokand. During the century, Russia established diplomatic ties with those states, and then, as control of the Kazakh areas was established, the khanates were drawn into the Russian Empire as relatively autonomous regions. In the khanates, the Russians felt that the older, conservative style of Islam could keep the Muslim communities backward, and the Russians supported the old institutions. Because of this induced isolation, reformism and nationalism were delayed.

In all of these areas, Muslim political institutions were either ineffective in the long run or nonexistent. As a result, there could be no reforms of the style instituted by Mahmud II or Mehmet Ali. In this way, the Russian Muslim experience was closer to that of Algeria or India. Governmental reform programs were guided by European rulers and were intended to increase Western control rather than to create modern Islamic states. Islamic developments in the nineteenth century thus took place outside of the government structures.

As was the case in other areas, initial Islamic activism took relatively traditional forms. One of the most dramatic movements of this type was in the Caucasus region of Dagestan, where, during the seventeenth and eighteenth centuries, there had been a flowering of Islamic thought. Scholars from Dagestan had traveled widely and had participated in the major trends of eighteenth-century Muslim thought. They were part of the cosmopolitan community of scholars in Mecca and Medina and were noted teachers in Damascus, Aleppo, and elsewhere. During this time, the Naqshbandiyyah was introduced into Dagestan, and under a series of activist leaders, it provided an organizational vehicle for uniting the local peoples against the Russians. This Naqshbandiyyah movement reached a climax under the leadership of Imam Shamil, who was able to maintain a holy war against the Russians for twenty-five years. His final defeat came in 1859.

Opposition to Russian control in the other areas conquered during the nineteenth century was less well organized and less successful. The groups in Turkestan were poorly armed and localized in attitude. Only the tribal and traditional khans had large potential organizations, but after some initial resistance, which was quickly brought to an end by the overwhelming Russian military force, the old political elites tended to accept the military realities. When revolts did occur, they were usually led by local religious preachers, who would collect a small band of followers and be quickly subdued. Typical of those was an uprising in Andizhan, in eastern Turkestan, in 1898. There, a local Sufi leader, Muhammad Ali (known as Ishan Madali), gained a special reputation for piety and organized an effort to overthrow the Russians in the whole region. His men, armed with charms and cudgels, were stopped in two days.

The last great uprising under the czarist regime, which occurred in 1916, continued to have the same weaknesses of the nineteenth-century movements. The Russian government issued a decree conscripting non-Russian workers for war labor. Coming in the midst of the unsettled conditions of World War I, this measure became the catalyst for widespread revolts throughout all of Russian Turkestan. There was, however, virtually no coordination in the uprisings, although in some areas the opposition assumed the form of a holy war against the infidels. The military weakness of the Muslim populations was again clearly shown. Despite the facts that Russia was in the midst of its World War I efforts and the uprisings took place in many areas in a vast region, the rebellion was totally suppressed in a few months.

By 1916, other less militant movements were emerging within the Muslim communities under Russian control. The traditional means of protest were being replaced by activities of revival and reform that were better suited to the modern conditions. By the end of the nineteenth century, a vigorous Islamic intellectual revival had begun to take place, and it took a number of religious and cultural forms. Islamic thought and education had been strongly conservative, but some intellectuals began to break away from the old conservatism, which avoided any change in order to preserve Islamic traditions in the face of the challenges posed by Russian rule. In these developments, Muslims in the Volga region and the Crimea provided much leadership.

Even in the different context of Russian control, participants in the revivalist movement developed positions and ideas that were similar to those found elsewhere in the Islamic world. One of the early leaders in this break with the traditional conservatism was Shihab al-Din Marjani (1818–1889), a teacher and writer in Kazan in the Volga basin. He rejected *taqlid* and advocated direct study of the Quran and the Sunnah, and he worked to reform the educational curriculum. Although he hoped to return to a pure form of Islam, he believed that that was compatible with modern scientific ideas. Through his work, he provided a basis for Islamic modernism in Russian and inspired a wide range of Muslim intellectuals.

An important part of this religiocultural revival was the modernization of the national languages. Some scholars were convinced that important factors in the backwardness of the Muslim peoples of Russia were their ignorance of their own languages and the absence of a literature in those languages that could bring Islamic culture and new ideas to the general population. Abd al-Qayyum Nasiri (1824–1904) helped develop and popularize a Tatar literary language based on local dialects. Elsewhere efforts to modernize Azeri Turkish and Kazakh resulted in the publication of books and newspapers and stimulated a literary florescence.

These developments were joined together in the work of Isma'il Gasprinski (1851–1914), a Crimean Turk who had had a modern education and traveled widely in Europe and the Islamic world. He was an active journalist, working in Paris and Istanbul, and he began publication, in Russia, of a Turkish-language newspaper called *Tarjuman* in 1883. He hoped to provide a vehicle for bringing modern ideas to Russian Muslims and also for unifying those Muslims. Influenced by the ideas of Pan-Slavism, he was an early advocate, if not the initiator, of Pan-Turkish ideas, and he used his writings as a means of developing a common Turkish language, which he hoped would replace the variety of Turkish languages and dialects. Although he did not succeed in this endeavor, his Pan-Turkish ideas were influential not just in Russia but also among the emerging Young Turks in the Ottoman Empire. His goals of providing a sense of general Turkish identity and creating a common literary language became the basis for the curriculum of the schools he established. In those schools, the aim was also to introduce the Russian Muslim communities to modern ideas. This broad combination of themes was to be the "new foundation" (*usul jadid*). Gasprinski's model schools were imitated throughout Russia and inspired educational efforts in Turkey and Iran. On the basis of this inspiration, the advocates of the whole general movement of Muslim religiocultural reform came to be called Jadids.

Gradually, Jadidism took more political forms, especially after the Russian Revolution of 1905. Muslim political parties were organized, and some secret revolutionary groups were established. Inspired by the Young Turks Young Bukharan and Young Khivan associations were created. In this activism, there was great diversity, ranging from those people who advocated cooperation with liberal Russian groups to those who supported radical revolutionary goals or regional nationalist programs.

By World War I, the Muslim communities under Russian control were exhibiting a real vitality. The major style was modernist adaptationism, and the conservatism of the old ulama and political elites was on the defensive and tied to czarist autocracy. There was, however, little overt secularism and the intellectual vitality was tied to the religiocultural revival of the late nineteenth century. Islam was a key part of the identity being asserted by the various movements, and this Islamic sentiment was influenced by and adapted to modern ideas. In Jadidism, there was less of a fundamentalist tone than was found in the Salafiyyah or similar movements elsewhere in the Islamic world. However, the Islamic dimension was a crucial component in the emerging nationalist identities of the Muslim peoples of Russia.

Summary

In large parts of the Islamic world during the nineteenth century, direct European control was established, and in those areas, the politically oriented reformist pattern was not possible. In India, Southeast Asia, Algeria, and Russia, special patterns of Islamic development emerged. The first phase was not, as it had been in the states that maintained at least a formal independence, an attempt at pragmatic, modernizing reform. The first phase was, rather, a more religious and traditional resistance to the advancing European power. With varying degrees of speed, these militant movements were crushed. Muslims were then forced to face directly the challenge of European control, in intellectual as well as in political terms. The result was an Islamic revival with varying degrees of strength, weakest in Algeria and probably strongest in India. Efforts to create an Islamic modernism provided new intellectual foundations for religious thought in the modern context. This work often combined with the emerging nationalist sentiments, which often were influenced by and had some influence upon the development of Islamic modernist and nationalist movements elsewhere. In this way, although local experiences were distinctive, there was still some sense of the broader cosmopolitan unity of the Islamic world.

Imperialism and Revivalism Without Modernism

Direct European invasion and control were not the only types of imperialism that affected Muslim communities in the nineteenth century. Non-European states, some Muslim and some non-Muslim, also expanded or reestablished their rule over Muslim groups. This activity produced Islamic responses that were more traditional in nature and did not lead directly to the development of Islamic modernist ideas. In addition, there were some areas into which European powers were expanding in which the traditional structures of society remained relatively intact. In those areas as well, the Islamic response followed the older patterns rather than producing a modernist adaptationism.

In these areas, like Somalia or the Nilotic Sudan, the activist movements frequently had direct ties with eighteenth-century developments or followed long-standing patterns of sociopolitical action. In the late nineteenth century, Islamic activism in those areas assumed a form that from the perspective of the twentieth century, might be seen as proto-nationalism. However, taken in their own terms, those movements were assertions of local identity and autonomy that used traditional bonds of religion and tribe or ethnic group as a basis for unity of action. If, at times, they became a component of an emerging nationalist movement, they did so without passing through a stage of significant ideological redefinition.

Mecca and Medina

One of the first areas of the Islamic world to face expansion by modernized Islamic armies was the Arabian Peninsula. At the beginning of the nineteenth century, the Wahhabi movement reached a peak of its power with the conquest of Mecca and Medina. This culmination of eighteenth-century fundamentalism led to the invasion of Arabia by the armed forces of Mehmet Ali as the Ottoman sultan asked Mehmet Ali to bring an end to the

Wahhabi expansion and threats to Ottoman prestige and security. In 1812, the Egyptian army reconquered the two holy cities, and by 1818, the Wahhabi state had been crushed. After a vicious series of punitive measures, the Egyptians withdrew to the western areas of the peninsula, where they maintained control until almost mid-century, when direct Ottoman control was restored.

The Egyptian occupation and the restoration of Ottoman control did not mean the creation of a new political system. The old arrangement of a formal imperial control with the sharifs of Mecca and the notables of Medina handling local affairs was reconstituted. The Egyptian commanders and the later Ottoman governors were, however, in a position to ensure that the grand sharif was a relatively cooperative person. In view of the threat that Wahhabism had posed, any sharif or local notable who showed tendencies toward fundamentalist reformism was viewed as a potential enemy.

The situation reinforced the normal conservatism of the local religious establishments, and it also gave them added support in dealing with those ulama in the cosmopolitan scholarly community who became too popular or were visibly active in calling for reforms. The local religious notables were able to get Egyptian and then Ottoman support when they wanted to limit the activities of Neo-Sufi teachers like Ahmad ibn Idris. That scholar faced a series of public examinations and finally felt it necessary to leave the holy cities. He settled in Asir, between Mecca and Yemen, where his descendents established a virtually independent religiopolitical regime.

Despite the limitations, the international community of scholars continued to be an influential intellectual center. Through traveling students and pilgrims, the Haramayn continued to act as a distribution point for ideas. However, that international scholarly group was no longer in the forefront of Islamic thought. Its teachers continued to work and rework the themes that had been developed in the eighteenth century, and although those ideas could still inspire Islamic revival efforts, the efforts were now more traditional in style. Shaykh Ahmad Khatib, the Sumatran scholar who taught Shafi'i law in Mecca after 1876, is a good example of the change in the Haramayn. His approach to legal studies was very traditional, and he had strong reservations about modernist ideas, but his students who returned to Southeast Asia became major figures in the Islamic reform movements there. In a way, the Haramayn became a refuge for the more conservative thinkers who sought to escape the emerging modernism of Cairo or India— for example, for some prominent Egyptians who taught in Mecca, such as Muhammad Basyuni and Mustafa Afifi.

In the second half of the nineteenth century, Meccan religious leaders did become directly involved in movements that were more modern in style, but they did so without a significant redefinition of their Islamic intellectual framework. They were active in the emerging Pan-Islamic movements and eventually were involved in nationalist activities, often giving them an Islamic dimension.

Throughout the nineteenth century, the Haramayn continued its role as an incubator for activist Neo-Sufi movements. Early in the century, Haramayn scholars played a role in the development of the Sammaniyyah Tariqah, which spread in Africa; the development of the Tijaniyyah; and the education of leaders of the Padri movement in Indonesia. The scholars had at least some impact on Ahmad Brelwi, the Indian Muslim activist, and on leaders of holy wars in West Africa. The followers of Ahmad ibn Idris, the North African Neo-Sufi teacher in Mecca, produced a group of orders that were influential in the African Islamic revivals, including the Sanusiyyah in North and Central Africa, the Khatmiyyah in the Nilotic Sudan, and the Ahmadiyyah in South Arabia and East Africa. In the second half of the century, a second generation of scholars in the tradition of Ahmad ibn Idris provided education and inspiration for people who were active in the Pan-Islamic movement as well as the leader of the holy war in Somalia at the beginning of the twentieth century. Thus, although the intellectual community in the Haramayn was no longer in the forefront of the new style of thought in the Islamic world, it remained an active and influential part of the cosmopolitan world of Islamic activism.

Mecca provided an environment that could arouse Pan-Islamic feelings especially among the pilgrim scholars, and it remained one of the few places that seemed beyond the control of the Europeans. One European who lived in Mecca late in the nineteenth century wrote, "The fact of students from all regions living together keeps the consciousness of the wide diffusion of their religion, and puts away the idea that is brought by many youths from Frank-ruled lands that the Moslems are condemned for an indefinite time to servitude."[23] In this manner, Mecca inspired the emerging Islamic reform efforts, even though it did not participate directly in them.

The holy cities were not untouched by the effects of modernization in the Middle East. The introduction of printed texts of the great ninth-century collection of *hadith*s by Muhammad ibn Isma'il al-Bukhari, for example, had an effect on the manner of instruction in the Traditions of the Prophet. The improvement of transportation systems brought larger numbers of pilgrims, and on the political level, the increasing centralization of the administration of the Ottoman Empire, especially in the autocratic days of Abdulhamid II, meant that Istanbul was able to exert more control in the area. The building of the Hijaz Railroad from Damascus to Medina in the first years of the twentieth century was a concrete manifestation of both of those factors since it not only facilitated the flow of pilgrims, but also made the dispatch of imperial troops easier.

The major new mood in Mecca came from the ruling sharifs rather than from the scholarly community. Members of the leading Sharifian families traveled widely and became familiar with Ottoman politics. Some received a modern type of education in the schools in Istanbul, and most were aware of the major political currents of the time. In this context, the leading sharifs began to operate in the new political style and participated in Ottoman parliaments and societies; some even had contacts with secret revolutionary groups.

The leading figures in this development were members of the Awn clan of sharifs, led by Husayn ibn Ali (1852–1931), a grandson of the grand sharif who had been appointed by the Egyptian occupation forces in 1827. Husayn ibn Ali was born in Istanbul and circulated freely in the official and court circles. Following the Young Turk Revolution in 1908, he secured the appointment of grand sharif of Mecca, and he worked to establish autonomous, if not independent, power. His growing mistrust of Ottoman intentions led him finally in 1916 to revolt against the sultan with the aid of the British. He attempted to assume the title of king of the Arab countries, and after World War I, he claimed the title of caliph. In his actions, one can see the foundations for Arab nationalism, but his goals were probably more clearly religious and personal than nationalistic. He provides a good example of the transition to the more modern forms of action without a stage of intellectual modernism.

In Mecca and Medina during the nineteenth century, the currents of the previous century clearly continued to flow with vigor. In the cosmopolitan scholarly community, a fundamentalist style of Islam was gradually becoming more conservative. At the same time, the conservative establishment found itself faced with new political realities, and it gradually assumed a vigorous political adaptationism that was conservative in intellectual content but modernizing in the form that its political activism took.

Localized Revivalism in the Western Indian Ocean Basin and the Arabian Peninsula

In a number of areas in the western Indian Ocean basin and the Arabian Peninsula, special local conditions produced a variety of Muslim activist movements during the nineteenth century. Those movements tended to lack the cosmopolitan flavor of the Meccan experience, but some of the elements of the Meccan pattern can be seen in them. The economic and political conditions of the region were being changed by the growing European imperial involvement, and new and more modernized regional powers played a role. However, the interaction between modernized and local forces did not result in significant intellectual reorientations. Islamic activism followed lines that had been set in the eighteenth century rather than moving in the direction of an Islamic modernism. By the end of the century, this activism had created religiously based movements of "national" unity, or Islamically based political forms, that provided the foundations for local states in the twentieth century.

Wahhabis. The first Wahhabi state had been crushed by the Egyptian invasion of the Arabian Peninsula and the outside imperialist force that these fundamentalists faced was Middle Eastern rather than European. The Egyptian occupation of the central parts of the peninsula was not long lasting, and the interaction was primarily military. This conflict did not pose an intellectual or a religious challenge to Wahhabi fundamentalism.

The Wahhabi forces, led by the Saud family, were soon able to reestablish control in the Najd, the central region of the peninsula. Led by Turki ibn Abdallah, who ruled from 1823 to 1834, a vigorous fundamentalist state was recreated. Under Turki and his son, Faysal (d. 1865), the "second" Saudi state was a major local power, but it did not have the international significance of the earlier state. Turki and Faysal were guided by a firm adherence to the religious traditions of their family and movement, but they were also relatively pragmatic in setting their political goals. They did not insist on a vigorous expansionism as one description of Faysal emphasizes. "Farsighted enough to realise that he could not convert the whole world to Wahhabism, and that if he tried he would again bring ruin on his people and himself, the Imam Faisal played a lower bid. He was a devout Wahhabi, but, instead of attacking Karbala, he received a British diplomat in his capital."[24]

The period of rule by Turki and Faysal was important in the development of Wahhabism. Following the defeat at the hands of Mehmet Ali's armies, the movement could have faded and become simply part of the historical record. However, those two leaders were able to rekindle and confirm the adherence of many of the tribes to their movement, and that adherence survived the subsequent disintegration of the state at the end of the century.

Another important aspect of this era is that the basic Wahhabi ideas were more fully defined and applied in the administration of the state. Major teachers, including Turki and Faysal, wrote letters defining the Wahhabi position on a wide range of specific issues. Those letters and a number of decisions and opinions, which were carefully collected, provided the state with a more clearly defined ideological basis. In this definition, there was a realistic application of fundamentalist ideas to existing conditions, but there was no adaptationist attempt to combine with modern ideas. There was little need for such a combination because of the limited nature of the involvement of modernized forces in the area.

During the period, there was significant intellectual activity that was associated with the movement but was not directly religious. There were a number of sound historians who focused on the history of Wahhabism, and an active group of poets emerged. A description of the work of those poets by a major Egyptian intellectual and scholar of the twentieth century, Taha, provides conclusions that can be applied to the movement as a whole at the time.

> It cannot be said that they brought about a renaissance of poetry or that they created what had not existed before, but at least they returned in their poetry to the ancient style and gave us in the twelfth and thirteenth [Islamic] century that sweet Arab song, which had not been heard in the memory of living men. This song, whose authors did not imitate the city folk nor force themselves to search for new and strange expressions, was conceived in liberty and borne along by all the greatness, the yearning for the highest ideal, and the strong longing for the revival of ancient glory, which filled its soul.[25]

After Faysal's death in 1865, the Saudi state began to crumble in the face of rivalry among members of the ruling family and attacks from enemies. By the end of the century, the state had been defeated, and the Saudi princes living as political refugees. A grandson of Faysal, Abd al-Aziz (1880–1953), created a third state in this fundamentalist tradition, the twentieth-century Kingdom of Saudi Arabia. He began the process in 1902 when he led a small band of soldiers and recaptured the old Saudi capital of Riyadh.

There was thus another revival of the Wahhabi movement at the beginning of the twentieth century. Like the second revival, it did not involve a departure from the fundamentalist ideals of the movement. There was little intellectual or doctrinal adaptationism, but there was a real element of pragmatic adaptationism in the political realm. This fundamentalist revival was little influenced by the emerging Islamic modernism, but it came to have an impact on that modernism by encouraging a fundamentalist tone in the Salafiyyah, who were impressed by the success of Abd al-Aziz.

The Wahhabi experience in the nineteenth century built the foundation for an active and influential twentieth-century state. In an area where contact with the forces of the modernized Middle Eastern states and European imperialism was comparatively limited, a rigorous fundamentalist style was maintained, although it came to be tempered by a political adaptationism. By maintaining this style through the difficulties of the nineteenth century, the Wahhabi movement was able to emerge early in the twentieth century as the leading example and exponent of fundamentalist activism in the Islamic world.

Oman. In Oman, there was a similar continuation of a fundamentalist Muslim style but with a significant variation from the Wahhabi experience as pragmatism in the political realm became separated from the fundamentalist tradition in institutional terms. The tradition of the special Ibadi imamate continued as the major focus of the fundamentalist loyalties, but the imamate came to be a rival of the ruling sayyids of the Bu Said dynasty. In the Saudi state, the religious teachers supported the ruler, and the rulers were able to maintain a combination of roles of leading the religious movement and the state; in Oman, a significant tension developed between the two roles.

During the first half of the nineteenth century, the rulers of Oman were successful in expanding Omani power. Under Said ibn Sultan, who ruled from 1804 until 1856, a vast, sea-based empire was created. Omani control extended well down the East African coast, and a major center was firmly established in Zanzibar. The port of Muscat, in Oman, was an important trading center in the western Indian Ocean basin. However, Said faced the growing involvement of Britain in the area, and because of its naval power, that country soon assumed the role of permanent supervisor of much of the region. Said became a firm ally of Britain and, through pragmatic measures, maintained Omani independence and commercial prosperity. He tended, however, to be a merchant prince and political realist rather than claiming a religious basis for his authority. The more conservative Ibadi teachers opposed this style of rule and attempted to take control of the state following Said's death.

Between 1856 and 1868, the fundamentalist opposition gained strength while Said's successors proved to be weak leaders. In 1868, the fundamentalists, led by a major teacher, Said ibn Khalfan al-Khalili, and Azzan ibn Qays, a member of a branch of the ruling family, revolted and gained control of the government. They attempted to create an imamate that would control both religion and the state, and the tone of government policy was strictly fundamentalist. For a brief period, the coastal commercial centers and the inland areas were effectively ruled by the same person. However, the new regime was not able to cope with the problems of declining trade and did not secure British recognition. Tribes in the interior came under attack by Wahhabi warriors, and general unrest began to increase. By 1871, Turki, a son of Said, was able to organize forces sufficient to overthrow the imamate and reestablish a more pragmatic regime.

In the restored state, the rulers continued to follow more pragmatic policies, but Oman was no longer a major regional power. It was closely tied to

British imperial power, although independent in terms of internal policy, and the monarchs faced regular tribal revolt and continuing fundamentalist resistance. At the end of the century, Sultan Faysal ibn Turki attempted to be more independent of British guidance but was forced to submit in 1899. That sultan's efforts were diplomatic, and he did not attempt to declare his independence through modernizing reforms.

The fundamentalist elements continued within the framework that had been firmly established during the century. Some of their leaders were relatively effective political organizers, but virtually none of them made any attempts at a further development of Ibadi ideas. The fundamentalism became a conservative fundamentalism, committed to the establishment of a traditionally defined imamate. The fundamentalists' response to British influence and the political adaptationism of the sultans was to elect a new imam, and the twentieth century began with this type of action. In 1913, Salim ibn Rashid al-Kharusi was elected imam, and he gained control of much of the inland territory. The dynamics of the nineteenth century had set the stage for twentieth-century Omani history.

South Arabia. During the nineteenth century, the centers of Muslim learning in southern Arabia lost some of the prominence they had had in the preceding era. It was a time of turmoil, with military adventurers and British imperialism playing important roles. The British took control of the port of Aden in 1839 and gradually built up a network of alliances with the local rulers to protect their position in the port, which imposed an anarchic stability on the region, and no local ruler could merge as a dominant force. A major complicating factor was the ties of the local communities throughout the Indian Ocean basin. South Arabians prospered as military leaders and as scholars in regional states, especially in India, and those mercenary soldiers often brought their wealth, expertise, and sometimes their troops back to South Arabia, where they added an element of instability.

The great scholarly and religious families continued to be influential in local affairs, but their schools did not attract as wide a range of students as in previous centuries. Sound conservative scholarship, sometimes with a Sufi tone and sometimes with a more fundamentalist style, characterized the work of the South Arabian ulama. There was, however, little intellectual adaptationism and not much participation in the intellectual movements of the time.

By the end of the century, South Arabia was divided into the city of Aden, which was an active commercial center dominated by the British, and the rural areas, which were led by local chieftains who were tied by treaties to the British. The old traditions of Islamic scholarship were preserved, but in both the political and the intellectual realms, the style was increasingly conservative. The only exception to that trend was in Aden itself, where modern commercial life was creating a whole new way of life, but British control suppressed any potential tendencies of independent political or intellectual life there. Essentially, in South Arabia, there was direct and indirect imperialism with little revivalism of either a fundamentalist or an adaptationist style.

Yemen and Asir. In the regions of Yemen and Asir, the principal imperialist forces in the nineteenth century were the Ottoman Empire and Egypt. At the beginning of the century, neither area was under direct outside control, but the reformist and centralizing policies in Istanbul soon led the Ottoman leaders to attempt to reestablish control in western and southern Arabia. After a long series of campaigns, that goal was largely achieved. The Zaydi imam in Yemen was forced to accept Ottoman troops and recognize Ottoman suzerainty, and the various groups in Asir submitted.

At the beginning of the twentieth century, especially after the Young Turk Revolution in 1908, the Ottoman control crumbled in the face of revived political activism in both regions. In Yemen, the Zaydi imamate had never been destroyed, and in 1891, highland tribesmen had followed an imam who had not accepted the Ottoman control. That man, Muhammad ibn Yahya of the Hamid al-Din family, provided a focus for the antiforeign sentiments and opposition to Ottoman rule. Although the Ottomans were able to maintain control in some of the urban areas, Yemeni resistance continued. In 1904, there was a resurgence of opposition under Muhammad's son, Yahya, who was able to force the Ottomans to grant him recognition. A treaty establishing the Imam Yahya's control in the highlands, but leaving the coastal areas in Ottoman hands, was signed in 1911. The state established by Yahya was committed to a rigorous application of Islamic law. In his public positions, the imam was clearly fundamentalist in his style, so the Yemeni "national" resurgence was closely tied to Zaydi fundamentalism. With the collapse of the Ottoman Empire during World War I, Imam Yahya extended his control to the coastal areas with a Sunni majority, but he maintained his own fundamentalist style in setting policy.

The attempt to establish a fundamentalist Islamic state without political or intellectual adaptationism was not possible in many parts of the Islamic world by the end of the nineteenth century as such states were usually destroyed by the expansion of more modernized Islamic states or by European powers. However, Imam Yahya succeeded because of a combination of factors. The relative isolation of his domain and the difficulty of military operations in Yemen gave him some protection. The collapse of the Ottoman Empire eliminated the major regional enemy, and the reviving Wahhabi state was unable to expand its control into Yemen.

The experience of Asir was in contrast to that of Yemen. A local dynasty of religious leaders was led by descendants of the Neo-Sufi teacher, Ahmad ibn Idris. Until the end of the nineteenth century, the Idrisi family had a primarily religious role, but the local political leadership was discredited by the successful reestablishment of Ottoman control and the Idrisis gradually assumed a more active political role. The key figure in that increased role was Muhammad ibn Ali al-Idrisi (1876–1923), a great grandson of Ahmad. He had wide experience, having been educated at al-Azhar and the San-usiyyah center in Libya and having lived for a time in the Sudan. When he returned to the Asir, he organized an effective local administration.

Muhammad al-Idrisi was committed to a rigorous adherence to Islam, but he was also a skillful and cosmopolitan diplomat. He had ties with Italians and British and was able to balance Ottoman, Yemeni, and Meccan political forces. He led a revolt against the Ottomans in 1910 and was the first independent Arab leader to sign a treaty of alliance with the British during World War I. Following that war, he preserved his independence by cooperating with the expanding Saudi power at the expense of Grand Sharif Husayn in Mecca and Imam Yahya. After Mohammad al-Idrisi's death, his successors were not able to maintain the same independent position. Asir became first a Saudi protectorate and then, in 1934, was formally incorporated into the Saudi kingdom.

The Neo-Sufi tradition of Ahmad ibn Idris provided the foundations for a movement of resistance against Ottoman imperial control. In style, this movement maintained the fundamentalism of its origins, tempered by a pragmatic adaptationism in terms of political operation. It would not appear, however, that Muhammad ibn Ali al-Idrisi made any major efforts toward an intellectual reorientation of the tradition of his ancestor, despite his education in Egypt at the end of the nineteenth century. The political adaptationism of the Idrisi movement did not extend to creating a protonationalist mood among its followers. As a result, the Asir revolts did not eventually lead to an Asiri nationalism.

Among the best known of the nineteenth-century scholars in southwestern Arabia was Muhammad al-Shawkani (1760–1834). He was a Yemeni teacher trained in the Zaydi tradition, but his ideas had an impact far beyond that limited circle. His works were known to and cited by Chiragh Ali in India and Hasan al-Banna, founder of the Muslim Brotherhood in Egypt, for example, and his historical studies and biographical works continue to be widely used. Al-Shawkani's impact remained that of a single scholar rather than setting in motion a more general movement. The major themes of his scholarship are fundamentalist in tone. He vigorously rejected *taqlid* and what he thought was slavish adherence to the medieval law schools and so provided a justification for *ijtihad* that was useful to Sunni as well as Zaydi scholars. In intellectual terms, his influence was greater outside of Yemen than in his homeland, and he was unable to create the foundations for an Islamic modernism in southwestern Arabia.

The East African Coast. The political situation in the Indian Ocean coastal areas of Africa was fluid during the nineteenth century. Sea-based powers established positions of control in the cities and on the islands of the coast, but the inland areas were not effectively subjugated by the coastal states. Early in the century, the sultans of Oman created their empire, which controlled many major ports in East Africa. By the end of the century, Omani rule had been replaced by the European powers, with Britain, France, Germany, Italy, and Portugal all getting at least some territory. Although the foreign rulers affected trade and economic relations, there was little modernizing restructuring of local societies, except in the sense of a growing integration into the global network of Western capitalism.

Islam's role in those changing conditions was complex. On the one hand, Islam, like the foreign imperialists, came from the outside and was centered in the ports and commercial centers. On the other hand, it made significant progress in converting the hinterland tribesmen in some areas, and by the end of the century, it was providing a unifying ideology for resistance to European rule.

Before the nineteenth century, even in areas like Somalia, where many inland tribesmen had been Muslim for a long time, Islamic life had been basically tied to tribal organizations and customs. It was an adaptationist Islam, and it had made substantial compromises with local conditions. During the nineteenth century, some of the spirit of Neo-Sufism spread in the region. The result was the establishment of a number of orders whose base of support was intertribal and whose style was more fundamentalist. These *tariqah*s were active in establishing educational and social centers and taught a reformist Islam in the Neo-Sufi pattern.

Among the most prominent of those orders were the Shadhiliyyah, the Qadiriyyah, and the Salihiyyah. The Shadhiliyyah was led by Shaykh Muhammad Ma'ruf (1853–1905), a sharif in the Comoro Islands of South Arabian origin. He was initiated into the Yashrutiyyah branch of the Shadhiliyyah, an order that had its center in Palestine and was active in the Pan-Islamic movement supported by the Ottoman sultan. Under Muhammad Ma'ruf's leadership, the Yashrutiyyah was active in establishing centers and doing missionary work in the whole eastern coastal region. Although the leaders of the brotherhood sometimes attacked the policies of the local rulers and occasionally faced European controls, the order did not become a major political force. Rather, its significance was in consolidating the position of a more rigorous Islam in the region.

The Qadiriyyah played a similar role, and its most important figure in East Africa was Shaykh Uways al-Barawi (1847–1909). The Qadiriyyah tradition was more flexible and less influenced by Neo-Sufi ideas, and the Uwaysiyyah, a suborder created by Shaykh Uways, was less reformist than the Yashrutiyyah. The Uwaysiyyah approved of the practices associated with special respect for local holy men and was less rigorous in restricting the popular religious practices. However, Shaykh Uways was an active preacher and organizer, and he was especially influential in the Somali areas, where the Uwaysiyyah provided a major vehicle for action that could transcend tribal loyalties. He was an effective revivalist but not a fundamentalist reformer. As a result, he came into conflict with a more fundamentalist group and, in 1909, was murdered by one of its members.

That rival order was the Salihiyyah, which was led by Muhammad Abdallah Hasan (1864–1921) of Somaliland. Muhammad Abdallah, called Mad Mullah by his British opponents, was the leader of the revivalist *tariqah* that led a major anti-imperialist holy war at the beginning of the twentieth century. The origins of the movement are clearly within the Neo-Sufi tradition. While on pilgrimage, Muhammad Abdallah had been initiated into the Salihiyyah by its founder, Muhammad ibn Salih (1854–1917), the religious heir of one of the major students of Ahmad ibn Idris. When Muhammad Abdallah returned to his homeland, he began to preach against the local popular religious practices and created an effective religiopolitical organization. In his reformism, he soon clashed with the Uwaysiyyah, and in his political militance, he came into conflict with the British, whose domination of Somalia was growing. For more than two decades, he led a militant resistance movement against the British and other imperialists.

Although Muhammad Abdallah was fundamentalist in style, he was willing to adapt in political terms when compromises were necessary. For one period during the holy war, for example, he signed a treaty with the Italians and was willing to accept their nominal protection as a way of forestalling the British advances. In this way, he was a political pragmatist although he was not willing to assume an adaptationist style in ideology. Because of his ability to organize a movement that transcended tribal differences, he is seen by many as a proto-nationalist, laying the foundations for a later Somali nationalism.

In East Africa, the nineteenth century was a time of considerable Islamic activism, much of it inspired by eighteenth-century Neo-Sufi traditions. Although the mood was often revivalist and reformist, little effort was expended in creating Islamic modernist positions. When late-nineteenth-century Islamic developments influenced East African affairs, that influence was more in the form of an activist Pan-Islam than of an Islamic modernism. In some areas, that activism helped create the basis for later nationalist movements.

The Sanusiyyah Tariqah

One of the most vigorous and widespread movements inspired by the Neo-Sufi tradition was the Sanusiyyah Tariqah, which was established by Muhammad ibn Ali al-Sanusi (1787–1859), a North African scholar who was a student of Ahmad ibn Idris and a major thinker in his own right. In his work, al-Sanusi combined the major themes and movements of late-eighteenth-century Islam. As a student in North Africa, he had studied with the founders of the Darqawiyyah and Tijaniyyah Tariqahs and was already a well-known teacher before he went on a pilgrimage to Mecca. He was an expert in Islamic law and *hadith* and often clashed with the conservative religious establishments because of his fundamentalism. In Egypt, he clashed with the ulama of al-Azhar, especially over his advocacy of the right of *ijtihad*. Similarly, as a leading follower of Ahmad ibn Idris, he came into conflict with the conservatives in Mecca.

After the death of his teacher, al-Sanusi moved to the area of modern-day Libya, leaving a well-organized group of followers in the holy cities and the surrounding tribes. In Libya, he created a growing network of educational and social centers, which provided a basis for unity among the scattered and often conflicting tribes of the region. He was committed not only to the reform of local religious practice but also to the missionary expansion of Islam. As a result, members of the Sanusiyyah were sent into a number of areas in Central and West Africa. The result of al-Sanusi's work was the creation of a vast, loosely structured community that was based on a fundamentalist style of ideology. In terms of sociopolitical dynamics, al-Sanusi and his successors were brilliant adaptationists, creating a structure that could integrate tribal communities without destroying the underlying foundations of the social order. In intellectual terms, however, al-Sanusi must be viewed as a culmination of Neo-Sufism rather than a precursor of Islamic modernism.

The Sanusi leaders were fully aware of the threat by the European expansion in the Islamic community. Although they were not as fanatically anti-Christian as the late-nineteenth-century French propagandists suggested, they were not willing to accept European expansionism without a struggle. At first, the major areas of the Sanusiyyah were relatively isolated, but by the end of the century, a series of clashes with French forces had limited and then reduced the areas under Sanusi influence in Central Africa. Finally, in 1911, the Italian invasion of Libya brought European imperialism directly into the Sanusi homeland. At first, the Sanusiyyah joined forces with the remaining Ottoman troops in opposing the Italians, but the sultan soon withdrew his troops, and the order was left as the only organized opposition to the Italian invasion. In this way, the Sanusiyyah became a focus for modern Libyan nationalism.

The anti-imperialist struggle gave the Sanusiyyah a modern function, despite the fact that its ideology remained largely free of Islamic modernist ideas. Like revivalist movements elsewhere, political pragmatism and the struggle against imperialism led to political adaptationism, but intellectual fundamentalism continued.

Mahdism and Revivalism in the Sudan

The Islamic experience in the Nilotic Sudan was a special case in the interaction between imperialism and local Islamic communities, and in some ways, it was similar to the experiences in India, Algeria, and Southeast Asia. A previously strong Islamic state was already in the process of disintegration by the end of the eighteenth century as the Funj sultanate was wracked by civil wars and had lost effective control in much of the area. As in those other states, it was at this point of political disintegration that outside forces invaded and gained control of the region.

But in contrast to the cases of India, Algeria, and Southeast Asia, the conquering force was an Islamic state, Egypt, rather than a European one. In this way, the Sudanic situation was similar to those of the states and groups in the Arabian Peninsula that faced Egyptian and Ottoman expansionism. However, unlike the grand sharifate of Mecca and the imamate in Yemen, the Funj sultanate tradition was not strong enough to maintain itself in the face of outside control. Egyptian rule created a new political system in the Sudan, and the old political order disappeared. The new structures were influenced by the reformist experience of Egypt, and Westernizing reformism thus came to the Sudan through Muslim but non-Sudanese hands.

The impact of this distinctive experience upon the development of Islam in the Sudan was profound. Neo-Sufi revivalism had begun to enter the Sudan during the last years of the Funj rule, particularly through the Sammaniyyah and the Khatmiyyah Tariqahs. After the Egyptian invasion in 1820, the traditional Muslim revivalists did not face a crumbling regime that had accepted local popular religious practices but, rather, a government that itself seemed to encourage Islamic reformism. Whatever the religious position of Mehmet Ali may have been in Egypt, the Egyptian government in the Sudan assumed an overtly Islamic role. During the conquests, the commanders had proclaimed themselves to be representatives of the caliph-sultan. After consolidation of Egyptian control, the government worked to create an ulama establishment that could counter the influence of the local religious teachers whose influence was tied to popular religious customs.

Neo-Sufi teachers faced a choice: They could support this new, apparently Islamic government and, in that way, combat popular religious practices, or they could oppose the "foreign" rulers but, in that way, support the local teachers whom they might otherwise oppose. The latter course was chosen by at least two major groups. The Sammaniyyah held aloof from the new rulers and often criticized their policies, and in the process, the order became rather thoroughly "sudanized"—i.e., it adopted local customs and practices. The Majdhubiyyah, the order of Muhammad al-Majdhub al-Sughayyir, a student of Ahmad ibn Idris, took part in the early revolts against the Egyptians and remained a potential source of militant opposition.

The major religious group to cooperate with the Egyptian regime was the Khatmiyyah Tariqah. The founder of this order was Muhammad Uthman al-Mirghani (1793–1853), a member of a scholarly Meccan family who had been a major student of Ahmad ibn Idris. He had traveled widely in the Sudan during the last days of the Funj, and his son, Hasan, became the head of the *tariqah* there in the early days of Egyptian rule. In contrast to most of the orders in the Sudan, the Khatmiyyah was effectively centralized in its activities throughout the Sudan rather than being confined to a specific locality. This "nationwide" organization was aided by the establishment of the more centralized political regime with which the order cooperated.

By the final quarter of the century, substantial dissatisfaction with Egyptian rule had developed in the Sudan. Although there were many reasons for the dissatisfaction, it was the leaders who articulated the unrest most effectively, and the opposition Neo-Sufis played a crucial role. Although most of the Sammaniyyah shaykhs hat adapted themselves to local practices, the fundamentalist message continued as a part of their tradition. A Sammaniyyah teacher, Muhammad Ahmad (1848–1885), began to preach against the corruption of the faith that he saw around him, and in 1881, he declared himself to be the expected Mahdi. He led a holy war against the Egyptian regime and its local allies, and among his early strong supporters were not only people from his own *tariqah,* but also the leaders of the Majdhubiyyah. By the time of his death in 1885, the Mahdist movement, or Mahdiyyah, had gained control of much of the Sudan, and a fundamentalist regime had been established. His successor, the Khalifah Abdallahi (1846–1899), maintained the independent Mahdist state until the British and Egyptian armies conquered the Sudan in 1899.

The Mahdist state in the Sudan was a factor in Islamic activism throughout the Islamic world. Although the writings of the Mahdi were not widely circulated and few Muslims had direct contact with the regime, knowledge of the success of the Mahdists helped to inspire activism elsewhere. Muslims in Indonesia, West Africa, Mecca, and elsewhere heard of the Mahdist movement, and many felt that it marked the beginning of the Islamic revival that would defeat the infidels' imperialism.

In local terms, the Mahdist movement had great significance. Although it was militarily defeated in 1899, it provided an experience of "national" independence that many twentieth-century Sudanese nationalists could remember, and it also created a movement that transcended tribal and local loyalties and could be a basis for later nationalism. In that respect, the Mahdist movement was similar to the Khatmiyyah. The development of Islam during the nineteenth century gave the Sudan two "nationwide" organizations, and those two groups provided popular support for the two styles of nationalism that emerged in the Sudan during the twentieth century—one supporting union with Egypt, and the other supporting an independent Sudan.

In general terms, the Sudanese Islamic experience has been characterized by two extensions of the Neo-Sufi tradition. The Mahdiyyah maintained a more rigorous fundamentalism in both intellectual and political terms, and the Khatmiyyah was more adaptationist in its political activities but did not depart significantly from the intellectual formulations of its founder.

Summary

In many areas of the Islamic world, a pattern developed that was different from the pattern in areas that came under direct European control. In some areas, there was contact with a variety of imperialisms that did not fully disrupt the traditional structures of society or break the influence of an eighteenth-century type of activism. In a third pattern of Islamic development, the traditional responses continued to have validity and support which was made possible by the type of imperialism faced.

In that third pattern, the phase of traditional resistance may have come later or was not as completely defeated. There might have been political adaptationism in the course of a struggle or in creating a functioning government, but there was little activity aimed at redefining Islam in modern terms. Instead, the phase of the development of Islamic modernism was either bypassed or postponed, and the traditional Islamic activism became a kind of proto-nationalism rather than a modernizing reformism.

Revivalism Without European Imperialism

European expansion was clearly a dominant feature of the nineteenth-century experience of the Islamic world. However, despite what seems to be the almost universal character of that imperialism, there were areas in the Islamic world where developments were only peripherally affected. In those areas, the internal dynamics of the movements worked themselves out to a significant extent before European intervention played a significant role, and the primary characteristic of Islamic activism was an assertion of Islamic identity in opposition to elements that were primarily premodern. The two major areas where this situation prevailed were in West and Central Africa and among the Muslim communities in China.

West and Central Africa

The early nineteenth century was a time of tremendous activism among the Muslim communities in West and Central Africa. Developments during the eighteenth century had prepared the way for a wide variety of movements to bring about an Islamic revolution in the region. Prior to the nineteenth century, Islam in those areas had been only one element in a complex network of relationships, and the chief characteristic was an adaptationism that accepted a mixing of Islamic and non-Islamic elements. However, by the end of the eighteenth century, the revolutions in Futa Jallon and Futa Toro and the expansion of more dynamic Sufi orders had signaled the coming of a new era.

The new dynamism may have been indirectly affected by the changing patterns of trade that were created by European activities, but it was primarily an activism that operated in circumstances that were not affected by European expansionism. The great issues were the purification of Islamic practice and the creation of more clearly Islamic political regimes, and it was the eighteenth-century mood of socio-moral reconstruction that dominated. It was not until the end of the century that expanding European control became a major factor. By then, most of the early activist movements had settled into a more conservative phase or were disintegrating because of internal divisions following the death of the early leaders whose charisma had held the movements together.

The first great wave of Islamic revolutionary movements is associated with the Islamic revivalism of Uthman dan Fodio (1754–1817) in northern Nigeria and the central Sudanic areas. Uthman had ties with the Qadiriyyah tradition in the region, and his teacher had studied under Neo-Sufi leaders like Muhammad Murtada al-Zabidi and Yusuf al-Hifnawi in Egypt. Uthman preached vigorously against the local religious practices, which had been accepted by the local ulama and rulers. He soon became convinced that this older establishment was essentially pagan and began, by 1786, to organize holy wars in opposition to its domination.

The reforming holy war of Uthman dan Fodio spread rapidly, and by 1809, a large theocratic empire had been created. Uthman himself soon withdrew from direct leadership in favor of his son, Muhammad Bello, and brother, Abdallah ibn Muhammad. The dream of a purely Islamic state was not realized, but the new political order that emerged was clearly Islamic and was based on the fundamentalist ideology of its founder. However, particularly after the death of Uthman, the founding ideology could not prevent internal rivalries, and the theocratic empire became a group of warring princes who were more interested in preserving their own interests than in continuing the effort to purify the faith. When the British and other European powers moved into the area at the end of the century, the dynasties accepted foreign control with little resistance. In Nigeria, they became a part of the British system of indirect rule, through which the princes maintained local autonomy.

The early activism was infectious and soon spread beyond the borders of Uthman's state. In Adamawa to the east, a teacher with revivalist inclinations, Modibbo Adama (d. 1847), heard of the holy war and went to Uthman. He was given the banner of jihad and returned to his homeland where he succeeded in establishing a revivalist state. Similarly, a vigorous teacher from Masina to the west, Shaykh Hamad (Ahmad Lobbo), participated in the early days of the jihad of Uthman and then returned home. As a result of a holy war in the Masina region in 1810–1818, he succeeded in establishing a vigorously Islamic, fundamentalist state. Following his death in 1844, his successors maintained a fundamentalist spirit. Although his grandson was defeated by another militant Muslim leader, al-Hajj Umar, in 1862, the Masina theocracy survived until the French conquest in 1893.

As Uthman dan Fodio's warriors moved east, they met the forces of another revivalist teacher, Muhammad Amin al-Kanemi (d. 1835). Al-Kanemi was a highly respected teacher in the state of Bornu, and the crisis created by the attacks from the west allowed him to take control of the state from the old ruling dynasty. An effective ruler, he created a state on a more fundamentalist style of Islam. Under his successors, the Islamic spirit was maintained, and the state remained independent until conquered by a Muslim military adventurer, Rabih al-Zubayr, in 1893. When the British established control in the Bornu area, the descendants of al-Kanemi were incorporated into the structure of indirect rule.

By the middle of the nineteenth century, the major theater of militant activism had shifted further to the west, and the leading figure was al-Hajj Umar Tal (1794–1864). Born in Futa Toro, he had been raised in the tradition of theocratic militancy there. He had traveled widely, and while on pilgrimage in Mecca he had been initiated into the Tijaniyyah Tariqah. On his return, he had stayed in the court of Muhammad Bello in Sokoto, where he had married Bello's daughter, and he had spent some time in Masina with Shaykh Hamad. In this way, he combined a familiarity with the Neo-Sufi tradition with the experience of the new revolutionary states in Central Africa. After his return to his homeland, he declared a jihad in 1852 and soon created a large conquest empire based on the ideals of Islamic revival. Although he clashed with the French at times, he accepted a demarcation of spheres of action and carried on his holy war against the African states to the east rather than continuing a war against the French.

Al-Hajj Umar was killed in 1864 before he could fully consolidate his regime. His conquests did, however, confirm the dominance of a more militant Islam in much of West Africa. His successors faced internal divisions which made effective resistance to French expansion impossible, and the state was conquered in a series of campaigns that ended with the defeat of Umar's son, Ahmad al-Shaykh (Amadu Seku), in 1893. Like the other militant Islamic states of the region, the empire of Umar was drawn together by a fundamentalist vision, but after the passing of the original inspiring leader, it was unable to maintain effective unity.

The second half of the nineteenth century was a period of a high level of religious enthusiasm and activism in the Muslim communities of West and Central Africa. Many people expected the arrival of the Mahdi or a great renewer. In every area, there were local teachers who directed this enthusiasm in the direction of expanding and consolidating the position of Islam in society. This was done in a style that usually had a fundamentalist tone, although the degree of willingness to accept local customs varied widely. Although there were great leaders of holy wars, like Uthman dan Fodio and al-Hajj Umar, there were also local leaders who were less militant.

In the Senegal area, there was a remarkable array of local religious leaders. One of the best known was Ma Ba (d. 1867), a scholar born in Futa Toro whose revivalist efforts soon brought him into conflict with the French. The holy war that Ma Ba declared in 1862 was primarily against local "compromising" Muslims, and for a period of time, the French remained neutral but were eventually drawn into the conflict. It was, however, a local non-Muslim chief who defeated and killed Ma Ba in 1867. Other leaders rose and fell in the following years, and the French gradually expanded the area under their control. Internal divisions and local rivalries meant that even militant Islam was not a sufficiently integrative force to unite the area in opposition to the French.

In the end, the French victory aided rather than hindered Islam in the region. By destroying the old political structures and imposing a kind of unity, the French opened the way for Muslim preachers to spread throughout the countryside, and groups that had remained stubbornly outside of the Islamic world were converted. A forerunner of this new mode was Ahmad Bamba (d. 1927), who began in 1886 to organize a suborder of the Qadiriyyah called the Murids. In that order, there was a great deal of flexible adaptation to local customs and a willingness to cooperate with the French. The order encouraged manual labor, especially agricultural, and the Murid communities played an important role in the development of agriculture in Senegal under French rule. After the militance of the early years, a more adaptationist and less fundamentalist Islam was emerging. The success of the Murids did not, however, eliminate the more fundamentalist style of Islam, which was firmly established as a significant element in West African Islam.

In Mauritania, the Qadiriyyah was an important part of the developing Islamic experience. In an area that was a polical anarchy and dominated by tribal groups with particularist attitudes, the order came to play an important role as mediator. The leadership of the order was provided by the revivalist tradition established within the Qadiriyyah by al-Mukhtar al-Kunti in the eighteenth century. A student of al-Kunti, Shaykh Sidiyyah al-Kabir (1775–1868), established a wide network of *tariqah* centers and followers in Mauritania. Although he was not a militant leader of a holy war, his work also represents a major step in the more rigorous Islamization of the region and illustrates the ability of Islam to provide an identity that could transcend local and tribal loyalties.

Another major Qadiriyyah shaykh in Mauritania was Muhammad Mustafa Ma'al-'Aynayn (1831–1910). His father had been a student of al-Mukhtar al-Kunti but had broken with that tradition of the Qadiriyyah and had established his own suborder called the Fadliyyah. Ma'al-'Aynayn studied with his father and then went on the pilgrimage. During that trip, he established good relations with the Moroccan sultan, and he maintained an interest and involvement in Moroccan affairs for the rest of his life. He became increasingly disturbed by European expansion and eventually organized opposition to the French in both Morocco and Mauritania. Through his followers, he set up a virtually independent state with the help of the Moroccan sultans. With the failure of the sultans to resist the French in the first years of the twentieth century, he made an effort to claim the throne for himself, but his army was defeated by the French, and he died in 1910. "If Ma'al-'Aynayn accelerated the coming of nationalism in both Morocco and Mauritania, he was unfortunately unable to cope with foreign military technology or diplomatic pressures. . . . Although both Morocco and Mauritania would like to claim him as one of their national leaders, he clearly belongs to the era before mass nationalism in the Maghrib."[26]

During the latter part of the nineteenth century, there were also a number of leaders who claimed some religious legitimacy for their movements but were primarily military adventurers. They were able to utilize at least some of the more modern style of weapons that were being introduced into the area, and their military acumen gave them brief moments of success. Two of the most famous of these were Samori Ture (1830–1900) and Rabih al-Zubayr (1845–1900). Rabih began his career as a slave raider in the Nilotic Sudan. He became a supporter of the Sudanese Mahdi but soon moved into Central Africa, where he created a well-disciplined army and set himself up as a ruler in the region of Chad. Although he had contacts with the Mahdist movement, he was not a religious reformer; his aims were that of a military opportunist. When he was defeated by the French in 1900, his state collapsed.

Samori Ture was of greater long-term significance although he, too, appears to have been primarily a military adventurer. In the Mandinka area of West Africa, he created a short-lived conquest empire, which provided a vehicle for transcending localist loyalties among the Mandinka tribes. His religious ties were much stronger than those of Rabih. Samori Ture declared himself to be an almami and worked to encourage Islamic education and the elimination of non-Islamic practices in the areas that he conquered. His conquests broke the power of the local non-Muslim and compromising Muslim leadership, thus aiding the evolution of a more rigorous Islam. He was defeated by French forces in 1898 and died in exile. During the twentieth century, he has become a symbol of Mandinka opposition to European imperialism, but he was not himself the creator of a nationalist movement.

The nineteenth-century history of Islam in West and Central Africa shows the expansive dynamism of Islam. The major movements were fundamentalist in style, working to create societies that were in accord with the Quran and the Sunnah. Conservatism was associated with preserving the old compromises with local customs, and in virtually all areas, that style of Islam was significantly reduced in influence. By the end of the century, fundamentalism, because of its successes, had taken on a more conservative tone, and the descendants of the holy warriors had accepted imperialist protection in order to preserve the state structures created by the early jihads. The experience of contact with the West had little impact on the ideology of West and Central African Islam. Throughout the century, the general conditions were determined more by local factors than by European expansion until finally, at the end of the century, the European armies imposed control throughout the region. However, by the time of this conquest, the initial momentum of Islamic revivalism in most areas had been slowed by internal rivalries and dynastic disputes. In many ways, the imposition of European control provided an opportunity for Islam rather than a limitation. By destroying or controlling the rival local institutions, the social disunity that had hindered Islam previously was reduced. In the new context, Islam expanded rapidly through peaceful means rather than as the result of the militant holy wars that characterized much of the nineteenth-century experience.

Islamic Activism in China

The spirit of militant Islamic activism affected virtually all Muslim communities during the nineteenth century, and even the relatively isolated Muslim groups in China were aroused. In China, some of the issues involved were similar to those found elsewhere. In particular, Chinese Muslims faced the issue of how much compromise with local custom was possible. There had been Muslims in China for many centuries. Initially, they were non-Chinese groups who had come as merchants or, as in the Central Asian territories of China, as wandering nomads. As foreign groups, the problems of integration with the local cultures were not significant. However, under the Mongol and Ming dynasties, from the thirteenth to the sixteenth centuries, many of the communities had become Sinicized. Some Muslims held high positions in the imperial court, and it had become possible to speak of Chinese Muslims rather than simply Muslims living in China.

The establishment of the Manchu dynasty in the seventeenth century had brought a regime to power that was less tolerant of Muslims than previous rulers had been. At the same time, the normal internal evolution of the Chinese Muslim community had led to the question of how much compromise with Chinese traditions was possible for someone who claimed to be a Muslim. In Kansu Province, where there was a significant Muslim population a revivalist group had emerged during the eighteenth century. This group called the New Sect, had been led by Ma Ming-hsin and had called for a reform of local religious practices. The group had been influenced by the general Sufi developments, and its teachings had emphasized distinctive Muslim practices and had called for a rejection of many compromises with local customs. Conflict between the New Sect and the older establishment, often called the Old Sect, had led to fighting and New Sect revolts in 1781 and 1783. Although the New Sect was proscribed after 1783, its followers continued to be active in the Kansu area.

During the nineteenth century, the Chinese empire faced a variety of revolts. The efficiency of the imperial adminstration declined, and increasingly oppressive measures led to widespread popular unrest that manifested itself in further uprisings. With the imperial forces occupied in fighting revolts at the center of the empire, Muslim communities on the periphery took the opportunity to revolt as well.

There was a large Muslim community in the southern province of Yunnan, along the Burmese border. That community composed from 20 percent to 30 percent of the population and was subject to much social and political discrimination. In 1855, a rebellion broke out under the leadership of Tu Wen-hsiu, who named himself Sultan Suleyman of a new Muslim state. The central government was unable to send troops to mount an effective campaign until other more central rebellions had been crushed. The Muslims state therefore lasted until 1873, when Manchu troops finally defeated Tu.

In Kansu, the New Sect produced a dynamic leader, Ma Hua-lung, who led his followers into rebellion in 1862. Again shielded by rebellions closer to the center, the followers of Ma Hua-lung gained control of a number of cities in the province. It was only after a long and difficult campaign that the imperial armies were able to crush this rebellion, also in 1873. In both Kansu and Yunnan, the Muslim revolts were the result of many factors, but they represented movements of self-assertion on the part of the Muslim communities that had been largely adaptationist up to that time. A vigorous activism with fundamentalist overtones helped to make the revolts possible.

A third major Muslim revolt within the Chinese empire was not so directly related to issues of cultural assimilation. In the far western territories of the Manchu state, the boundary between Turkish groups in China and those beyond China's control was very vague. When the news of the Muslim revolts to the east reached the Muslims in Sinkiang, they were encouraged to revolt as well. In 1862–1863, small-scale uprisings were quickly crushed, but the unrest grew. The Chinese governors were unprepared for a large-scale uprising, and Muslim rebels soon were able to win dramatic victories. The revolt was uncoordinated in the early years, with various local commanders attempting to set up their own states. During the struggles among these Muslim leaders, one of them appealed to a Central Asian khan for aid, and in 1865, the khan of Khokand sent a force under the command of Yaqub Beg (1820–1877), who soon established himself as the ruler of much of the area. His independence was recognized by both Britain and Russia, and it was not until 1877 that Chinese imperial forces could restore Manchu control in the area.

Those three revolts and a large number of smaller outbreaks during the nineteenth century were reactions against Chinese imperial administration. Although they were affirmations of a separate identity in the face of imperialism, the empire involved was not European and, in terms of its impact on those Muslim peoples, was not an inspiration for modernizing reforms. The Muslim communities were relatively small and had few resources at their command, and with the reestablishment of imperial control, the possibility of a separate, politically independent existence was destroyed. Although the revolts were assertions of identity, they did not serve as proto-nationalist movements because of the weakness of the communities involved. Instead, most Chinese Muslims began to integrate their opposition efforts with the efforts of other Chinese who opposed the Manchu dynasty. By the beginning of the twentieth century, the Muslims had begun the process of redefining their role within China, which involved a withdrawal from separatist ideas and the adapting of Islamic modernist ideas to the Chinese context.

Conclusion: Nineteenth-Century Islam in Perspective

The nineteenth century was an era of dynamic evolution in the Islamic world. For those Western observers who see the resurgence of Islam in the later twentieth century as a new phenomenon, a study of nineteenth-century history should give a new perspective. Islamic civilization has never been stagnant or unchanging. In the face of a variety of challenges, nineteenth-century Islamic communities engaged in a wide range of activities that were aimed at both creative preservation and active adaptation. In some cases, the efforts were successful, and in others, there was failure. The most visible failure was the attempt to stop European military and economic expansion. By the end of the century, virtually all of the Islamic world was under some form of European control.

The three basic dimensions of the modern Islamic experience provided the conditions for the relative successes and failures in the nineteenth century. The Islamic dimension provided the starting point. In virtually all parts of the Islamic world, it was the ideas, emotions, and structures that had developed during the eighteenth century that were the base for the early nineteenth-century responses to historical change. In particular, Neo-Sufism and the general mood of socio-moral reconstructionism opened the way for vigorous reformism and militant fundamentalist activism.

The second dimension was provided by the expanding West. European military and economic expansion presented the prospect and then the actuality of a loss of Muslim control, and the implications of the modern Western ideas challenged the formulations of the general Islamic ideological framework. The results of the interaction of those two dimensions was determined by special local conditions, which were the necessary third dimension of modern Islamic history.

A number of patterns emerged from that interaction of elements. One pattern was dominated by the adaptationist Westernizers and developed in those areas that were able to maintain at least nominal political independence throughout the century. The first phase of this pattern was set by rigorous and pragmatic reforms that were possible only when Muslim rulers were part of an effectively functioning and politically independent regime. This phase was followed by a phase in which "ideologies of reform" emerged. Those took a variety of forms, sometimes mutually supportive and at other times competitive. In particular, Islamic modernism tried to provide an intellectual basis for integrating Muslim and modern Western ideas in all realms of activity, while Muslim secularists accepted the individualization and separation of religion that was implicit in much of Western thought. A third basic position was represented by the emergence of nationalist ideals that accepted ethnic and linguistic bases for identity rather than emphasizing the religious identity. The role of each of those positions depended upon local conditions, so that in Iran, there was an emphasis on a religiously based reformism and nationalism, with little modernist success, while in Egypt, both modernism and nationalism emerged as important intellectual orientations.

A second pattern developed in those areas where Muslim governments were already crumbling and the leaders were not in a position to institute reform programs. In such areas, European control was rapidly and firmly established. The first phase involved primarily fundamentalist rather than reformist resistance, and that was followed by military defeat and then efforts at redefinition and reorientation in the context of foreign control. That second phase was characterized by a vigorous intellectual activity in many areas, with Islamic modernism and nationalism being the two dominant forces and a variety of more fundamentalist or conservative positions also evolving. In India, Russia, and Southeast Asia, the final decades of the nineteenth century were a time of intense activity, while in Algeria, the crushing French control meant there was less opportunity for either Islamically oriented or nationalist activity.

The interaction of imperialism and revivalism without modernism provided the basis for the third important nineteenth-century pattern. In a number of areas, the underlying social conditions and the nature of the imperialist challenge led to a revivalist activism that did not involve either Westernizing reform programs or Islamic modernism. In those areas, leaders who based their authority on nonmodern, Islamic foundations were able to create relatively successful movements of resistance, and in some cases, they created the foundations for a twentieth-century state. Although not basically nationalist themselves, those movements can be viewed as having a proto-nationalist nature. The foundations of the twentieth-century states of Saudi Arabia, Oman, and Yemen and the monarchies of Jordan and Iraq are found in such movements. In addition, at least some of the nationalist identity in the Sudan, Somalia, and Mauritania rests on similar movements. In other areas, like China and West and Central Africa, the religious revivalist movements did not face European imperialism directly until after the initial dynamism of the movements had declined, so it was the more conservative successors who faced and then accepted European control without a major reformist or modernist effort. In that pattern of experience, there was often a pragmatic adaptationism in diplomatic and political terms but a rigorous adherence to a usually fundamentalist style in ideology.

In all of the patterns, the four basic styles of Islamic experience interacted. In general, because of the dramatically changing conditions, the conservative style was weakest, struggling to halt or at least retard the process of change with little success. Adaptationism was most visible in political terms early in the century and in the great reform programs and pragmatic responses of the leaders throughout the century. Adaptationism also became a major style of intellectual activity with the emergence of Islamic modernism and nationalism. Through movements characterized by charismatic leadership and in the emergence of a Muslim "secularism," the individualist style of Islam experienced a significant evolution, and the fundamentalist style was at the heart of much of the resistance to European expansion and even gave a particular tone to many of the adaptationist policies. The reaffirmation of the fundamentals of Islam provided inspiration for modernists and nationalists as well as for those who rejected all compromise with the West. The nineteenth-century experience clearly shows continuity not only with the earlier traditions of Islam, but also with the movements and issues of the late twentieth century.

4

Twentieth-Century Islam

Dominant Majorities in the Middle East and Africa

Introduction

The widespread European imperial presence in the Islamic world did not produce Muslim stagnation. Although few areas were not dominated by the Western powers at the time of World War I, the dynamism visible in Islam throughout the nineteenth century continued in the twentieth. The era from World War I until the middle of the 1960s was a time of significant and dramatic changes within the Islamic world, in both political and ideological terms. Many independent states emerged during the period, and a variety of ideological developments occurred. Those events were accompanied by militant revolutions and gradual evolutionary changes that transformed the face of the Islamic world.

From Community to State

One of the most dramatic reorientations that accompanied the twentieth-century transformations was a redefinition of the basic operating unit. Throughout Islamic history, the transnational sense of community had been a key element of Islamic identity. The community (*ummah*) had been the major general focus of loyalty. Tribal groupings, dynastic states, and other local organizations had been of great importance, but they had not provided the framework for special ideological orientations as the local and regional groups had been viewed within the broader context of the Islamic faith and community. Even when empires had assumed a distinctive religious character, as in the case of the Safavid support of Shi'ism or the Zaydi imamate in Yemen, the transnational nature of the ideology had not been forgotten. No one had assumed that only an Iranian could be an Imami Shi'i believer or that only a Yemeni could be Zaydi or that only an Ottoman could be Sunni.

152

During the twentieth century, two developments have worked to modify that situation. One is the evolution of nationalism in the Islamic world, and the other is the increasing importance of the structure of the state in society. These two trends often support each other, as an independent nation-state has been the goal of many intellectuals and political activists. In the process, the ideals of the cosmopolitan Islamic community have not been forgotten, but they have had to share the stage with the interests of the nation and the state. The *ummah,* the nation, and the state have become sometimes competing and sometimes complementary focuses of loyalty for Muslims.

Thinking of the state or the nation as something other than a unit subordinate to Islam emerged as a part of the interaction with the West. The process began in the nineteenth century when literary movements among Turkish- and Arabic-speaking groups gave rise to a sense of communities identified by language and culture rather than by religion. Special regional heritages and distinctive ethnic-linguistic traditions provided the basis for a new kind of group awareness. Although Islam was often a part of this awareness, the new sense of "nation" often crossed the boundaries of religious communities. In the Egyptian nationalism of Mustafa Kamil, for example, the special Egyptian Christian community, the Copts, was included in the population of the "Egyptian nation," and non-Egyptian Muslims were outside of it. Another case is the early development of Arab nationalism in Syria and Lebanon. There, Christian Arabs played an important role in defining the Arab nation's goals. In that new sense of nation, the loyalty of political activists was to the national community rather than to the transnational *ummah.* There was thus the potential for competition between the nation and the *ummah,* although there was also the possibility of one loyalty strengthening the other.

Although nationalism is a powerful force, the state has emerged as the most effective basic operating unit within the Muslim world—a vivid example of the influence of the West and of European imperialism in the Islamic world, because the boundaries of the emerging Muslim states were drawn by the imperialists. It has been observed that these boundaries had little relationship to local circumstances. Devised as balance-of-power compromises, many cut across ethnic, linguistic, and cultural units. Although the political units created were artificial, they defined the territory for the modern states in the Islamic world. A measure of the strength of the state systems created in this manner is that even after independence, virtually no state structure has gone out of existence in Muslim areas. There have been attempts to combine states, using the emotional appeal of nationalism, but few of those attempts have had significant long-term success.

The states defined by those boundaries were the major theaters for nationalist and anti-imperialist activities. As the Muslim areas became independent, it was in the form of those new states, and the new state system incorporated older institutions in some cases and created new centers of loyalty in others. Monarchies associated with more traditional religious contexts became identified with the new states and their corresponding nationalisms. In this way, for example, the sultans in Morocco became Moroccan kings, and the leader of the Sanusiyyah Tariqah became the leader of Libyan national resistance and later the first king of an independent Libya in 1952. Increasingly, the shahs in Iran, especially after the overthrow of the Qajar dynasty in 1925, appealed to explicitly Iranian rather than Islamic sentiments. In other areas, the "artificial" states gave the identity for Sudanese or Iraqi or Nigerian nationalisms, to list only a few of the many movements.

The tendency for the state to be the major political actor was reinforced by the global political context of the twentieth century, in which effective recognition was given not to religious communities or to traditional groupings but to states. The experience of being controlled by Europe and the process of gaining independence created both nations and states as alternatives to the *ummah* in providing group identity and ideological bases for social and political organizations.

A clear example of the changing nature of political symbols and organization is the resolution of the issue of the caliphate. The office of the caliph had ceased to be an effective symbol of the political unity of the *ummah* by the time of the Mongol destruction of Baghdad in 1258, but in the late eighteenth century, the Ottoman sultans began to revive the title. In areas that were lost to European control, the Ottomans negotiated, as a part of a series of peace treaties, for recognition of the Ottoman ruler as the "spiritual leader" of the Muslims in those territories. This distinction between temporal and spiritual leadership was acceptable to the Western negotiators because it was familiar to them, although it was not a significant part of the Islamic tradition. The Ottomans hoped that this concession would keep the way open for restoration of Ottoman rule when conditions changed. Abdulhamid II utilized the role of caliph in implementing his Pan-Islamic policies.

Muslims outside of the Ottoman Empire welcomed the revival of the caliphate, and their enthusiasm was heightened by the gradual elimination of most other independent Muslim rulers by the end of the nineteenth century, making the Ottoman sultan (and caliph) the single most important ruler in the Muslim world. The caliphate can be seen as a major symbol for the political hopes of the *ummah* as a transnational Islamic community. The weakness of that symbol as a basis for actually mobilizing Muslims became apparent during World War I when few Muslims answered the call to holy war issued by the Ottoman sultan-caliph.

Following World War I and the defeat of the Ottoman Empire, a nationalist regime was established in Turkey, which first abolished the office of sultan in 1922 and then abolished the caliphate in 1924. In India, a movement developed in support of the caliphate. Between 1919 and 1925, the Khilafat movement was able to mobilize substantial support in conjunction with the emerging Indian nationalist movement. However, Indian Muslim attempts to intervene in Turkish political affairs only alienated the nationalist leadership in Turkey, and soon after the abolition of the caliphate, the movement in India collapsed. Efforts elsewhere to keep the caliphate alive resulted only in a series of conferences that resulted in no agreement upon an effective course of action, and those efforts gained little popular attention or support. From time to time after 1924, other Muslim rulers attempted to assume the title of caliph, but those claims were more closely associated with personal, dynastic, or national politics than with a transnational sense of the *ummah*. The Muslim world had become a series of states, and the sense of Islamic unity, though maintaining a substantial emotional appeal, was a shared sentiment rather than an organizational basis for specific programs.

Lines of Evolution and Transformation

Because of the importance of the state structures, the general lines of political evolution in the twentieth century provide an important framework for understanding the general experience. Sociopolitical institutions developed in a variety of ways, but there were some experiences that were common to many, but not all, Muslim states.

The pattern of political evolution can be traced in three phases. The first was the struggle for independence from direct or indirect European control. Few areas had been able to escape some significant form of Western political or military intervention and domination, and in those areas that did, like Yemen, old institutions and relationships remained relatively intact but depended upon remaining isolated from global affairs. In most of the Islamic world, the more traditional means of resistance had failed to stop European expansion, and the spirit of opposition gradually assumed new forms—the most common being a growing sense of nationalism. This nationalism meant an affirmation of special local cultural identities through political movements, and Islam was an important component, especially in mobilizing popular support. During this first phase, the common goal of the elimination of foreign domination meant that Islamic activism and nationalism were mutally supportive.

The second phase came with the achievement of independence. The unit that became independent was a state rather than a religious or a national community, and the potential for tension existed among nation, state, and *ummah*. The organizers of the independence movements became the new rulers, so there was continuity between the two phases. However, the basic goals gradually changed from anti-imperialism to national unity and development. In this context, tensions often arose, and they led to political instability in some areas.

In states in which a consensus on national goals and the nature of the basic structures was not achieved, or where the institutions of the new states could not cope with the challenges posed by independence, there has been a third phase. Either through revolution or coup, the initial ruling group (and their general ideological approach) has been overthrown. The postindependence regimes introduced a reorientation of policies and ideology, and they usually initiated programs that aimed at a basic sociopolitical transformation through methods that reflected a more modern and radical style. By the middle of the 1960s, many of the major Islamic countries had experienced this third phase, while in others, like Jordan and Morocco, the independence regimes remained in power. Other states, like Yemen, which had remained independent, experienced a revolution that brought to power regimes that were inspired by the "third-phase" experience elsewhere.

Parallel to this political evolution, there was an evolution in the dominant type of ideological approach to the challenges of the modern era. The failure of the more traditional resistance movements added to the appeal of a more adaptationist approach, which was strengthened by the apparent success of a vigorous Westernizing reform program in Turkey following World War I. The leader of that effort, Mustafa Kemal Ataturk, succeeded in winning a war for national independence in 1919–1922, and his secularist modernization program provided a dramatic example for other leaders and reformers in the Islamic world.

Nationalist leaders in many areas supported programs of reformism and modernization. Elite group and class interests kept most of them from proposing a program of radical social transformation, but the general mood included an increasing popularity for Westernizing reforms. As a result, when states achieved independence, their leaders were committed to adaptationist programs, and frequently the new state structures were direct copies of Western political models. In many areas, the monarchies and parliamentary regimes created during the twentieth century were unable to solve the problems of the new states. Often the new structures became vehicles for preserving dynastic, factional, or class interests as leaders resisted ideas that involved making major changes in the socioeconomic order.

The ideology of this type of leadership went a step beyond the thinking of most of the late-nineteenth-century movements in a willingness to accept Western ideas. There was less conscious effort to integrate the Islamic heritage with modern ideas and techniques, and more attention was paid to creating modernized nation-states. When the heritage of the past was important, it was as a support for a nationalist movement or a postindependence national unity, and the development of a more specifically Islamic orientation was left in the hands of people who maintained a fundamentalist style. In the early part of the century, those fundamentalists were admired, but they increasingly came to be considered as obstacles to modernization. The dominant group, especially in the political realm, was the nationalist-Westernizers.

The nationalist-Westernizers were political activists but not often very radical in their social and economic programs. Following World War II, a younger generation emerged that felt that this approach was a failure and advocated a more radical adaptationism, one that would bring about a revolutionary transformation of society. The most frequently used label for this new ideology was "socialism," often used with a qualifying adjective, as in "Arab socialism." This ideological position was clearly committed to modernization and involved an acceptance of secularism. Religion was to be a matter for personal faith, and the old religious structures were to be clearly separated from politics. The role of religion in this context was to support radicalism: Islam as a revolutionary faith could be cited as a support for contemporary revolutionary ideology, and Islam as part of a great heritage could provide support for national unity. In many cases in the emerging radical ideology following World War II, if Islam was not openly rejected, it was subordinated to the emerging socialism.

By the 1960s, the dominant ideological position was that of modernizing reformism, and there had been a transition from the nationalist-Westernizers to modernizing nationalist-socialists in many areas. In either form, this modernizing reformism was largely secularist in approach and tended to put Islam in a subordinate position. By 1965, the more radical approach seemed to be sweeping the Islamic world. The most prominent leaders were men like Gamal Abd al-Nasir (Nasser) in Egypt, Ahmad Ben Bella in Algeria, Sékou Touré in Guinea, and Sukarno in Indonesia. They were clearly identified as spokesmen for a new radicalism rather than as representatives of Islam. Even more conservative or fundamentalist leaders were initiating programs that had the appearance of moving in a radical direction, as can be seen in the land reform programs of Mohammad Reza Shah Pahlavi in Iran. Yet, by the end of the 1960s, that surge had faltered, and the way had been paved for the new approaches that were to become characteristic of the 1970s.

In intellectual terms, there was a long evolution. Beginning with an Islamically oriented modernism, the Islamic world adopted an increasingly secularist and radical position, which reached a climax in the middle of the 1960s. This development ran parallel to the political experience of moving from nationalist resistance to independence and then, in some areas, to post-independence regimes.

The Islamic Dimension

In those transitions, Islam played a number of different roles. Adaptationism was clearly the dominant style of Islam from World War I until the mid-1960s, and three interrelated types of adaptationism were important during that period. Islamic modernism was the first type, continuing the dynamic trends of the nineteenth century. However, it became involved in apologetics and often sterile arguments, so the general tone shifted from intellectual activism and rationalism to a rather vague historical romanticism. The more vigorous thinkers within the Islamic modernist group split and moved in two directions. One line built on the adopted Western ideas and emphasis on reason and helped to create the secularist-reformist position; the other concentrated on the reaffirmation of Islam and became increasingly fundamentalist in style.

The second type of adaptationism was the secular reformism and nationalism that came to dominate most Islamic countries between the two world wars and later, and the third was the more radical reformism of the post-World War II era. In each of these three types, the Islamic element was progressively weakened or subordinated, and these types of adaptationism encouraged the emergence of a more individualist Islam. On the one hand, Islam was seen as a personal matter, to be separated from politics. On the other, the older Islamic style that looked to charismatic, individualized leadership helped to support the emergence of dramatic, reformist leaders. The old messianic expectations could find new forms, and the Mahdi could appear in the guise of the "father of the country" or its revolutionary savior.

The conservative style of Islamic experience was much less visible during the first two-thirds of the twentieth century. Clearly, in times of accelerating change in all aspects of life, the conservative position is a difficult one to define since the "radical" position rapidly becomes the conservative one, and leaders who are the heroes of change can suddenly be charged with conservative obstructionism. Thus, the nationalist-Westernizers of the interwar period often considered the Islamic modernist positions as conservative, but in the postindependence revolutions, those nationalist-Westernizers, were overthrown as conservative obstacles to progress.

On a broader social level, the general conservatism of everyday life must be remembered as habits and social customs change less rapidly than government structures and constitutions. There is a gradual transformation of everyday life that is sometimes invisible to the participant. This universal kind of conservatism is, in the Muslim world, tied to Islamic values and symbols and provides an Islamic foundation for the more dramatic and visible elements of modern history. On the political level, this type of conservatism meant that as political activism changed from an elite phenomenon to mass movements, its character assumed a more religious tone and nationalist and radical slogans and symbols had a different significance on the level of the masses than among the Western-educated elite. This more religious substratum began to be more effectively mobilized by the expansion of modern means of communication. At first, the Westernizing and radical reformers were able to control this process of mobilization, but one element of the changing conditions of the 1970s was that with more effective communications, it is possible for the political elite to lose control of the general population that makes up the religious substratum. This loss of control is clearly seen in the emergence of the Islamic revolution in Iran.

In the 1970s, the style of Islam that was able to mobilize the religious substratum was the fundamentalist style. The conservative style preserved the potential for religious mobilization, but conservatives, by definition and spirit, will not take the initiative. so the fundamentalist style has continued to be an effective force during the twentieth century, although it has been obscured at times by the successes of the adaptationist reformers. Fundamentalist activism did not succeed in stopping European expansion, but a few bastions were maintained. Some people saw the success of the Wahhabi movement in reestablishing the Saudi state as a counterexample to the Turkish reform program of Ataturk. In addition, in intellectual terms, a rigorous affirmation of Islam appealed to some and was supported by anti-European sentiments, which was why a more fundamentalist student of Muhammad Abduh, Muhammad Rashid Rida, was well-known, and his works were widely read in the Islamic world.

In the years before World War II, a new format for fundamentalism began to emerge: the private, sometimes secret, association. In contrast to most previous fundamentalist movements, these associations were not always led by ulama, and they often appealed to a wide range of people who had significant experience with a more modern life-style. The most famous of this new style of group is the Muslim Brotherhood (al-Ikhwan al-Muslimun), which was established in 1928 by Hasan al-Banna in Egypt. Some of these associations, like the Salafiyyah-inspired movements in North Africa, were directly associated with, if not the core of, the emerging nationalist move-

ments, but in other areas, they became the opponents of the nationalist political elite.

In the years following World War II, the growing influence of radical
reformism undermined the influence of the fundamentalist groups, and both
the fundamentalist states and the associations came to be considered reactionary. They were the "enemies" of the radical regimes, and it became
popular to see such fundamentalist organizations as rearguard groups fighting a losing battle in the face of the increasing secularization of society. As
the events of the 1970s show, this loss of influence did not destroy fundamentalism; it only obscured the continuing appeal of fundamentalism for a
wide range of Muslims who were facing the challenges of modern history. A
more fundamentalist style of Islam was a leading element in the decline of
radical socialism by the end of the 1960s.

The Local Dimensions

The tremendous diversity of conditions within the Islamic world meant
that the strengths and weaknesses of various types of experience and the
lines of evolution varied, and many elements were involved. The eighteenth-
and nineteenth-century foundations often set limits to the twentieth-century
experience and provided initial motivations. Another element was the different ways the European powers dealt with the Muslim populations under their
control. The Russians treated them as subordinate groups but part of the
whole state system, while the British often utilized techniques of "indirect
rule," thereby preserving the older forms of social and political organization.
The imperial boundary lines were another important element since they defined which groups of people would have to interact with each other in anti-
imperialist nationalism and in postindependence nation building.

Within the boundaries of those states, there are three types of socio-political environments for Muslim communities, and those environments are a
crucial element in defining both the specific challenges faced and the way
they are met. Slightly more than two-thirds of the world's Muslims live in
political units in which Muslims are the clearly dominant majority, making
up 85 percent or more of the population.[1] In those dominant majority states,
Islam is closely associated with the national identity and, often, with the
structure or ideology of the state. Key issues are the relationship between
modern and Islamic ideas and structures, how the Islamic element of the
national identity should manifest itself, and the definition of appropriate political and social institutions that will be in accord with the faith of the
citizens.

A second type of political environment is that in which Muslims are either a strong minority or a weak majority of the population, between 26 percent and 84 percent of the people. Although this category only accounts for 10 percent of the world's Muslims, it is important because there frequently is instability and conflict in such states. Outside of the three distinctive states of Lebanon, Malaysia, and Albania, all of the states in this group are on the frontiers of the Islamic world in Africa. Because of the boundaries created during the time of imperial control, many of those states face major problems of national integration, and Islam is a major factor in that integration.

In the third political environment, Muslims make up 25 percent or less of the total population of the state, and almost one-quarter of the world's Muslims are in this category. There are Muslims scattered in small communities in many different countries, but these weak Muslim minorities are not necessarily numerically small as the Muslim communities in India, the Soviet Union, and China are three of the ten largest state Muslim populations in the world. These "weak minority" communities face special problems of adjustment in the modern world, and their Islamic experience has been distinctive.

Dominant Majority Areas in the Arab East

The Arabic-speaking people in the eastern Mediterranean areas, often called the Arab East, emerged during the twentieth century as an active and important element in the Islamic world. The Arabs had been the first Muslims, and the first Islamic empire, the Umayyad, had been dominated by an Arab elite. However, the emergence of the great cosmopolitan Islamic community had reduced the distinctiveness of the Arab Muslims as a separate people. Many of the newly converted people in the Middle East experienced Arabization as well as Islamization, and the old centers of the Egyptian, Mesopotamian, and Syrian civilizations became part of the Arabic-speaking world. The Arab strand became a major cultural dimension within the broader Islamic civilization rather than a special ethnic identity. Arabic was the language of religious scholarship, regardless of the ethnic background of the writers of communities involved.

A significant sense of Arab identity had emerged in the nineteenth century as a part of a literary revival in cities like Beirut and Damascus—often inspired by the works of Christian Arabs who sought a more clearly national identity not defined solely by religion—but it was not until the early twentieth century that Arab nationalist sentiments began to be clearly formulated. The pioneer areas in that formulation were modern Syria, Lebanon, Iraq, and Palestine in the Fertile Crescent. Arabic literary revival was a part of the emergence of Egyptian nationalism as well, but a sense of belonging to a larger Arab world, as opposed to membership in the Islamic community, developed only gradually in Egypt. However, the Arab East was a vigorously interacting intellectual area, and there was a great exchange of ideas among scholars in Cairo, Damascus, Jerusalem, Baghdad, and other centers.

In this area, where Muslims were and are the clearly dominant majority, the great issues were those of liberation and modernization. (The special circumstances of the Lebanese and the Palestinians are in some ways part of this experience and in other ways need to be viewed as nondominant majority communities.) There were a variety of options open to the Islamic communities of the Arab East, and local conditions shaped the choices and developments within the framework of the continuing styles of Islamic experience. The clearly dominant style was adaptationism, which took many forms, but the other styles played significant roles as well.

Adaptationist Style: Islamic Modernism and Secularism in the Arab East

Followers of Abduh. During the first two-thirds of the twentieth century, the adaptationist style took a number of forms. At the beginning of the century, the major intellectual tone was one of Islamic modernism. Gradually, however, as nationalist movements gained strength, a more secularist orientation emerged. In the Arab East, this secularism did not represent a rejection of Islam so much as a reinterpretation of Islam's role in modernizing societies. This secularism "believed that society and religion both prospered best when the civil authority was separate from the religious, and when the former acted in accordance with the needs of human welfare in this world."[2] This was an adaptationism with an individualist tone, and at times, the implicit individualist style of earlier Sufi thought helped to shape the views of these thinkers.

The Islamic modernist position was equally adaptationist but did not accept the separation of religion and polity. In this perspective, the more traditional view of Islam as being directly relevant in all aspects of life and society was maintained. However, the distinction between the two positions was seldom absolutely clear, as these two threads of Islamic thought have influenced each other and interacted throughout the twentieth century. In the Arab world, both positions arose primarily out of the developments set in motion by Jamal al-Din al-Afghani and Muhammad Abduh as most of the leading Muslim intellectuals of the early twentieth century were, in some way, students of those two men.

In the years following Abduh's death, one group built primarily upon his emphasis on the absolute truth of Islam in its essentials and moved in the direction of an increasingly fundamentalist position. The leading figure in this was Muhammad Rashid Rida (1865–1935), a Syrian who went to Cairo to study and became the leading successor to Abduh as a prominent religious teacher. He began the publication of a journal, *al-Manar,* in 1898, and it became the leading organ of Islamic reformist ideas. It was widely read in the Islamic world and was a major factor in shaping Muslim thought from North Africa to Southeast Asia. Rida emphasized the importance of basing modern Islam on the faith of Muhammad and his immediate companions, the elders or *salaf,* and from this emphasis came the name by which this school is known, the Salafiyyah.

Rida hoped to be able to create an Islamic progressive group that would provide a middle ground between what he saw as the stagnant conservatism of the old Muslim universities and the traditionalist ulama on the one hand and the excessive secularism of the Westernizers on the other. However, under his leadership, the Salafiyyah itself moved out of the "middle ground" in the direction of a more rigorous rejection of modernizing adaptationism. Following World War I, Rida gave strong support to the Wahhabi revival in Arabia, and in terms of the trends of thought in Egypt and elsewhere in the modernizing Arab East, he was losing touch with the new generations of intellectuals. Although the conservative ulama had been a major "enemy" in the early days of *al-Manar,* the opponent by the time of Rida's death was almost exclusively the emerging Islamic secularists. "So artificial and outdated to the young men who grew up following Abduh's death did Rida's thought seem that it failed to meet the new demands of life exposed to the increasing impact of Western civilization."[3]

The failure to create a dynamic middle ground in adaptationism had significant consequences, because in the interwar period, the more extreme alternatives of a more vigorous secularism, often associated with nationalism, and a militant fundamentalism became the leading movements in the Arab East. The solutions proposed by Rida and the Manar school were not realizable under the conditions of the times. Rida felt that the full application of Islamic law in society required the restoration of the caliphate at a time when the transition from *ummah* to state made such a restoration impossible, and he and his followers felt that nationalism undermined the sense of Islamic solidarity. Although they accepted nationalism as a part of the effort to gain liberation from foreign control, they did not approve of its positive ideological aspects at a time when nationalism was becoming the dominant popular sentiment.

Outside of Egypt, the Islamic modernists who followed Abduh moved in the direction of nationalist ideas rather than fundamentalist ones. Muhammad Kurd Ali (1876–1952), a Kurd from Damascus, was active in journalism and became involved in the emerging Arab nationalist movement in Syria during World War I. His primary contributions, however, were in the area of scholarship. He helped to found the Arab Academy in Damascus, and his historical studies and literary criticism were influential in reviving awareness of the Arabs' great past.

Abd al-Qadir al-Maghribi (1867–1956) was an associate of Kurd Ali and had studied with al-Afghani in Istanbul. He also emphasized a scholarly rather than a political life but was an important figure in the intellectual climate that encouraged an Arab sense of identity. In religious thought, he developed the line of rational analysis set in motion by Abduh. For example, in his Quranic commentary, he utilized a philological exegesis that rejected both the literalist and the spiritual allegorical approaches, insisting instead that interpretation should be based on an understanding of Arabic grammar and metaphor.

A more directly nationalist role was played by Amir Shakib Arslan (1869–1946), an associate of Rashid Rida from the Druze Mountain area in Syria. Arslan started from a position of rigorous loyalty to Islam but saw the Arabs as the core of Islam. He believed that "because of the special place of the Arabs in the *umma,* Arab nationalism could be reconciled with Islamic unity in a way impossible for any other—even more, that a revival of the *umma* needed a revival of the Arabs."[4] In that belief, he and Rida were in general agreement, but Arslan refused to accept the idea of European control. He was in the Ottoman parliament from 1913 to 1918 and then lived in exile, actively supporting the various movements of Arab nationalism through publications and negotiations. Although dedicated to Islam, his career shows the tendency of many of his contemporaries to ignore intellectual and social issues and to concentrate on political activities. In so doing, he was characteristic of the emerging nationalist elite that became the dominant force in Arab countries.

The Nationalist Context. Following World War I, the conditions surrounding the development of nationalism became more complex. At the beginning of the century, there had been a growing awareness of an Arab identity among the Arabic-speaking peoples within the Ottoman Empire. Although that sentiment had not been well defined in terms of its goals, there had been some sense of an Arab nation and a hope that that nation could gain political autonomy, if not independence. This feeling tended to be confined to the communities of Southwest Asia, since identity and loyalty elsewhere in the Arabic-speaking world were based on Islam or on special local institutions like the sultanate in Morocco or the emerging awareness of a special Egyptian heritage.

In Southwest Asia, the situation was abruptly changed by the World War I settlement. Separate political units were created by the European negotiators, and the boundaries of Iraq, Syria, Lebanon, Jordan, and Palestine were drawn. Until that moment, nationalist sentiments had been regional in their perspective, and nationalist movements associated with the newly created political entities had not existed. As a result, in addition to the issue of the relationship between the Islamic community and the Arab nation, there now arose the problem of defining the relationship between movements of Arab nationalism and resistance to foreign control in the newly created states (opposing the French in Syria and Lebanon and the British in Iraq, Jordan, and Palestine). A sense of Arab unity continued to be a strong emotional force, but opposition movements began to be organized within the limits of the new borders, and efforts of regional scope became less effective than more localized ones.

In the emerging nationalist movements, the emphasis on local conditions meant a withdrawal from a more rigorous attachment to Islamic unity. Although most spokesmen still saw Islam as a factor in their identity, they assumed a more secularist position in interpreting its role, and nationalist proclamations often were explicitly secularist in tone. The proclamation of the leaders of a Syrian revolt against the French in 1925, for example, was the product of both urban-educated and tribal leadership. It called upon all Syrians to fight for "the complete independence of Arabic Syria . . . and the application of the principles of the French Revolution and the rights of Man."[5]

Nationalist writers emphasized the Arab character of Islam and saw Arab unity as being necessary for any later Pan-Islamic unity. In the same vein, an Arab nationalist intellectual, Abd al-Rahman al-Bazzaz, said in 1952 at the end of a long ideological evolution: "Islam, although it is a universal religion suitable for all peoples and has in fact been disseminated among many nations and races, is undoubtedly a religion revealed first to the Arabs themselves. In this sense, it is their own special religion."[6] In another work, the same author speaks of Muhammad as the hero of Arab nationalism and of Islam "as the religion which enabled the Arab nation to assert its place in the world."[7] Those statements show the evolution of Arab-Muslim-nationalist thought from the earlier positions of men like Shakib Arslan in the direction of a more secular orientation of Islam serving the nation rather than the nation serving Islam.

In Egypt, the development of nationalism had come earlier than in Syria and Iraq, with the Urabi movement in 1879–1882 and then the National party of Mustafa Kamil. Although the Afghani-Abduh group participated in some of this activity, it was not an explicitly Islamic modernist movement, and the two lines of development were sometimes competitive. Abduh, for example, criticized some of Urabi's ideas, and later he and his associates thought of Kamil as a demagogue.

An effective mass nationalist movement did not emerge in Egypt until the end of World War I, and when it did, it was led by an associate of Abduh, Sa'd Zaghlul (1857–1927). Zaghlul had been educated at al-Azhar, studied with al-Afghani, participated in the Urabi movement, and then, like Abduh, had cooperated with the British after some initial doubts. However, at the end of the war, he became the leading spokesman for Egyptian nationalist aspirations, more in the tradition of Mustafa Kamil than of Abduh. Faced with uncompromising British officials, his attempts to present Egyptian hopes for independence were thwarted, and he won widespread support in Egypt for his proposal to send an Egyptian *wafd* ("delegation") to London to present Egypt's case either there or at the Paris Peace Conference. When the British sent Zaghlul and some associates into exile in 1919, popular demonstrations soon turned into the largest popular revolution in modern Egyptian history. Although the revolution was suppressed, Zaghlul was able to organize a large-scale nationalist party, called the Wafd, on his return from exile. As a political leader, Zaghlul concentrated on the issue of liberation rather than on reform, and his basic unit was the Egyptian nation, regardless of religious differences, rather than the *ummah*. In that sense, he was the heir to Mustafa Kamil rather than to Muhammad Abduh.

The nationalist theme within the Abduh tradition is more closely identified with Ahmad Lutfi al-Sayyid (1872–1963), a close associate of Muhammad Abduh. Lutfi al-Sayyid was part of a group of moderate nationalists who established the Ummah party in 1907, which was a rival to Kamil's party and was supported by many intellectuals. Lutfi al-Sayyid became a leading figure in the group through his position as editor of the party's newspaper, *al-Jaridah*. After World War I, many of the people from this group established the Liberal Constitutionalist party, a rival of Zaghlul's Wafd. However, Lutfi al-Sayyid and his group were distinguished from Kamil and Zaghlul more on the basis of their relative political moderation and their concern with intellectual issues than on the basis of their being less secularist in their approach. They went the opposite direction from Rashid Rida in developing Abduh's ideas, and they emphasized the importance of reason and the necessity of coming to terms with modern ideas.

Lutfi al-Sayyid and his group were aware of and felt a part of the Egyptian nation as a distinct entity. For them, Islam was a component of Egyptian society and had an important role to play, but they tended not to be concerned with the problems of defending Islam as such or with its reformation. Lutfi al-Sayyid felt that religion was a necessary foundation for social values and important in any society. Islam was to perform that role in Egypt, but other faiths were suitable in other areas. He stated: "I am not one of those who insist that a religion or a specific ethical system should be taught for its own sake. But I say that general education must have *some* principle which should guide the student from beginning to end, and this is the principle of good and evil, with all its moral implications. There is no doubt that theories of good and evil are numerous and disparate, but each nation should teach its sons its own beliefs in the matter."[8]

Following a variety of different lines, nationalism in the Arab East represented a form of adaptationism that did not oppose Islam but subordinated it. Islam played a role as a component part of the emerging national identity, whether Arab or Egyptian. Many Arab thinkers played a role in helping to define the meaning of nationalism in the context of the changing conditions of the twentieth century, and the basic positions begun by the followers of Abduh and others early in the century represent a standard orthodoxy in interpreting nationalism that was maintained until more radical forms of nationalism became dominant in the 1950s.

A person who represents a culmination of this era of nationalist thought is Sati' al-Husri (1879–1968). He was born in Aleppo, Syria, and served as an official in the Ottoman Ministry of Education. During World War I, he supported the Arab revolt against the Ottomans, and from 1921–1941, he was an educator and an official in Iraq. Following World War II, he served as the head of the cultural section of the newly formed Arab League. Through his wide-ranging activities and many writings, he became one of the most influential definers of Arab nationalism. He felt that the basic elements of national identity were language and common historical experience, and he emphasized the importance of including Egypt within the Arab world and advocated a secular Arab nationalism. He believed that Islamic universalism could create problems for Arab nationalism if people stressed Muslim unity before Arab unity was achieved. In his view, religion could not create a political sense of community; it could only strengthen one already built on the basic ties of language and history. According to al-Husri's position, as was the case with most nationalists in this era, the prime focus was on liberation and unity, and little attention was given to issues of social reform or economic development. As a result, with the achievement of independence, this type of nationalism began to appear conservative, or at least supportive of existing socioeconomic structures. In the period following World War II, nationalism began to assume a more radical form, joining with the evolution of secularist intellectual thought in the Arab East.

Liberal Secularism. Sometimes under the influence of Muhammad Abduh and at other times emerging directly from the influence of Western thought, a wide range of more explicitly secular thinkers dealt with issues other than nationalism, although they were at times drawn into the political arena. The early part of the twentieth century was a period of intellectual experimentation, and one of the chief characteristics of intellectual secularism in the Arab East is that no well-organized, dominant movement has emerged.

One of the leading secularists was Qasim Amin (1863–1908), a friend of Abduh but whose acceptance of reason led him away from Abduh's religious emphasis. Amin's most famous works dealt with the position of women in Islamic society. He vigorously advocated the emancipation of women and supported education for them so that they could become independent and contributing members of society. He also was an advocate of individual freedom of expression, and his positions on that subject show the profound secularism of his thought: "Real freedom consists in the individual's being able to express any opinion, preach any creed, to propagate any doctrine," and "In a truly free country no one should be afraid to renounce his fatherland, to repudiate belief in God and his prophets, or to impugn the laws and customs of his people."[9]

Following World War I, that liberal secularism flourished in the Arab East, and in Egypt, it was associated with the circle of intellectuals that developed around Ahmad Lutfi al-Sayyid. They were active writers, scholars, and often were involved in politics through the activities of the Liberal Constitutionalist party. Among the many men in this group, Taha Husayn (1889–1973) gained the greatest international reputation as a leading Arab writer and intellectual. He had a traditional religious training, studied at the new Egyptian University, and received a doctorate from the Sorbonne. He taught classical literature in Egypt and was, at various times, a leading government figure in educational and cultural affairs.

In his thinking, Taha Husayn provides a good introduction to the liberal secularist ideas of the time. He was profoundly aware of his Egyptian homeland and its special heritage. In his book, *The Future of Culture in Egypt,* he argued that Egyptian civilization was essentially Western rather than "oriental" and that Islam was an element within the Egyptian identity but not its sole or primary feature. By accepting the secularist assumptions of religion as a separable aspect of society, dealing with individual emotional needs, Islam was placed on a level equal to other faiths rather than being seen as the only true faith. He applied the analytical methods of historical criticism to materials of the Islamic heritage, which created a major crisis for him. In a study of "pre-Islamic" Arabic poetry, he argued that it had in fact been written during Islamic times, and that stand aroused substantial opposition among the more conservative Muslims because it suggested that the critical method might cast doubts on the authenticity of texts that are basic to the Islamic tradition. He later wrote more inspirational religious works, which were not as rigorously critical but were aimed at reshaping religious symbols in a way that would attract modern Egyptians. He hoped that this approach would affect even the most conservative of Muslims. He wrote, for example, that al-Azhar "will fail unless the culture that it propagates throughout the Islamic world is attuned to the personality of the modern Muslim molded nowadays by secular education and modern life. There is no point in al-Azhar's waging war against the twentieth century."[10]

Much of this same spirit is reflected in the works of Taha Husayn's contemporaries, most of whom were active in both governmental and educational institutions. Muhammad Husayn Haykal (1889–1956) combined moderation in practical politics with intellectual efforts toward long-range ideological reform. In his historical studies, which included biographies of Muhammad and one of the early caliphs, he tried to present religious symbols in a way that could appeal to the more traditional Muslims while operating within the framework of modern rational analysis. For him, reason was "to be the basis of faith with the individual able to approach the Quran and God as he wished."[11] Tawfiq al-Hakim (b. 1899) has been especially active as a writer and dramatist, helping to give new forms to modern Arabic presentations, and Ahmad Amin (1886–1954) helped to redefine modern Muslim awareness of early Islamic history.

The dangers of historical analysis were illustrated by the work of another intellectual in the group, Ali Abd al-Raziq (1888–1966). He had studied at al-Azhar and Oxford and was a judge in the religious court system. In 1925, he published a book, *Islam and the Principles of Government*, which argued that Muhammad had not established a formal system of government and that no such system was defined in the Quran or the Sunnah. Therefore, the caliphate was a product of special historical circumstances and not an inherent part of the faith. Ali said: "The truth is that the Muslim religion has nothing to do with the caliphate, which the Muslims generally recognize. The caliphate is not at all a religious office; neither are the offices of *qadi* and other posts of the state. All these are simply administrative offices with which religion is not concerned."[12] This line of thought was necessary for the legitimation of a parliamentary, constitutional regime of the type supported by the liberal secularists. However, since the book was published at the time of the whole caliphate issue, it caused a great furor, and Ali Abd al-Raziq lost his job. The book provided the foundation for a long series of analyses of the relation between Islam and politics, which helped to formulate the secularist position in clearer terms.

The ideas of the liberal secularists in Egypt were reflected elsewhere in the Arab East, but the special conditions in Egypt gave them a special place there. Following World War I, Egypt had become at least nominally independent with a constitutional monarchy. Although British military forces remained in the country and British officials intervened regularly in local politics, there was a wide scope for political and intellectual activity. The rivalry between the monarch, the Wafd party, and other groups, such as the Liberal Constitutionalist party, presented the opportunity for developing a diversity of views. In this relatively flexible situation, it was possible for the moderate or "liberal" position to flourish. However, there tended to be a greater polarization in political and intellectual activities in areas like Iraq and Syria, where difficulties of national unity and integration were greater, and the choice appeared more clear-cut between collaboration with the enemy or a more radical position of opposition. Under those conditions, the liberal secularist position was not as easy to maintain, and people tended to adopt either a conservative nationalist position or a more radical secularist one.

Radical Secularism. In the years following World War II, the older styles of nationalism and liberal secularism began to be viewed by the newer generation of Arabs as being too conservative to meet the challenges of the times. Although the nationalists and liberals had gained independence, little apparent progress had been made in necessary social and economic reforms, and the political structures appeared ineffective. As a result, a new style of nationalism that was associated with a more radical approach to the problems of Arab societies gained in importance in the two decades after World War II. These emerging perspectives also have their roots in the interwar era, although at that time, they were not viewed as significant.

Some of the basic characteristics of the new viewpoints included a more clearly materialist perspective, often Marxist in approach, and a willingness to reject even an emotional role for traditional faith. There were also efforts to create organizations that would be better integrated and more effective than the personal factions and diffuse schools of thought of the old nationalists and liberals, and there was also a more conscious attempt to deal with socioeconomic problems. The emphasis of the liberal position had been on individual freedom, especially in intellectual matters, and the winning of political independence. There had also been an implicit assumption that political independence could be gained without significant social and economic reform and that those would follow naturally after independence, without direct government intervention. The new radicals rejected those assumptions.

When the new perspective became more important, it had to include a definition of the role of Islam because if it were to gain any kind of mass support, it could not simply reject the faith of the majority of the population. In this way, the Islamic context had an impact on the evolution of radical thought, and at the same time, the redefinition of the role of Islam in a radical context was an important feature of the developing Islamic experience.

In the early years of the century, the radical groups were small discussion groups, informally organized and occasionally publishing short-lived journals. In Egypt, one such group was led by Isma'il Mazhar (1891–1962), a brother-in-law of Ahmad Lutfi al-Sayyid. Mazhar accepted scientific positivism and criticized traditionalist and modernist positions alike for being unable to break away from metaphysical modes of thought, From 1927 to 1931, he published a journal called *al-Usur,* which became a vehicle for the expression of agnostic and more radically secularist ideas. In its pages, even the liberal secularists came in for vigorous attack. One writer, discussing Ali Abd al-Raziq's *Islam and the Principles of Government,* for example, said, "Why did he not say clearly and directly that the sources of authority in Islam are no longer valid and that democratic principles are superior to the Islamic?"[13] When economic problems forced Mazhar to suspend publication of the journal, he withdrew from active public life.

Associates of Mazhar in other parts of the Arab East continued their activity. In Beirut, for two years after the discontinuation of *al-Usur,* Ibrahim Haddad published *al-Duhur,* which attempted to perform the same role as Mazhar's journal but with less success. An Iraqi poet, Jamil Sidqi al-Zahawi (1863–1936), published in both of those journals. Al-Zahawi was a strong supporter of the emancipation of women and became part of a group in Iraq that had greater long-term significance than either Mazhar's or Haddad's. That group was led by Husayn al-Rahhal.

Husayn al-Rahhal has been called the Iraqi Qasim Amin and the first of the Marxists of Iraq.[14] He had traveled in Europe, witnessing the Communist Spartakusbund rebellion in Berlin in 1919, had been a student in Iraq during the 1920 revolution, and had spent some time in India. He was influenced by a variety of teachers, particularly a Marxist Armenian, and while a law student in Baghdad, he formed an informal Marxist study group in 1924. In 1924–1925, that group published *al-Sahifah,* which was primarily an intellectual journal espousing historical materialism and opposing tradition. One issue on which the group concentrated was the liberation of women, and it is worth noting that al-Rahhal's sister, Aminah al-Rahhal (b. 1919), was one of the first women in Baghdad to go unveiled, as was a member of the Central Committee of the Iraqi Communist party in 1941–1943.

The position of the al-Rahhal group regarding Islam was clear. They said that Islamic law had been "formulated for a society that existed more than a thousand years ago" and that change would take place regardless of Islamic law. They also believed that "the era when people believed in the divine guidance of natural events was gone" and that "it is not religion that moves social life but social life that moves religion."[15] When the journal was suppressed because of traditionalist opposition and political pressure, al-Rahhal formed Nadi al-Tadamun (the Solidarity Club), which for two years was active in propagating radical secularist ideas among students and in organizing student demonstrations.

One incident illustrates some of the dynamics of the developing Islamic intellectual climate. In 1927, Anis al-Nusuli, a secondary school teacher, published a history of the Umayyads for use in schools, and the book made some uncomplimentary comments about Ali, the cousin and son-in-law of the Prophet. Shi'i leaders demanded that al-Nusuli be punished, and teachers who protested were dismissed, so members of Nadi al-Tadamun helped to organize student demonstrations in support of al-Nusuli. In this incident, the extreme sensitivity on the part of the more conservative Muslims to historical reinterpretation can be seen, as it was seen in Egypt in reaction to the books by Taha Husayn and Ali Abd al-Raziq.

Following demonstrations in 1928 on another issue, the government disbanded al-Rahhal's club, and he retired from active involvement in political or intellectual affairs. However, he had introduced a generation to Marxist and radical secularist thought, and out of his circle came some of the leadership for the major radical groups that emerged in Iraq in the 1930s, especially the Communist party and the al-Ahali group.

In those two groups, radical secularism was more effectively organized. By the time of World War II, the Communist party had become a well-organized, if small, force on the Iraqi political scene, and it provided a focal point for organizing movements on a non-Islamic basis and was able to attract workers and intellectuals. It represented a viable option for people who felt that ties with traditional religion, however modified by new interpretations, would not provide an effective basis for coping with the problems of modern Iraq.

A major concern of the radical secularists was socioeconomic reform, and in 1932, a group of intellectuals and professionals began the publication of *al-Ahali,* which aimed at bringing about a socioeconomic transformation to improve the material and intellectual life of the people. The group was more populist than communist in its orientation, but it was secularist in its approach to religion. In 1936, it worked with General Bakr Sidqi in a coup that took control of the government, hoping that its members could implement their ideals. They were soon disenchanted with Sidqi's dictatorial methods, and their paper was suppressed in 1937. At that point, the group broke up, and some of its more Marxist following joined the Communist party. The non-Marxists in the al-Ahali group eventually reorganized themselves as the National Democrats in 1946, and by that time, they had taken on a more liberal position. In the course of the struggles within the National Democrat party, the noncommunist position was even more clearly affirmed by the end of the 1940s. The party thus provided a more populist and moderate option within the spectrum of Iraqi politics.

The evolution of the al-Ahali group into a more nationalist part with populist and socialist ideas represents the line of development that was necessary for radical secularism if it was to gain political power. Specifically socialist and communist organizations that did not make this kind of transition had difficulty winning mass support or political power. The early Socialist and Communist parties in the Arab East were often led by people from non-Muslim and minority groups, and such parties had to bridge the gap between themselves and the Muslims if they were to have success. This is illustrated by the experience of the Communist party in Syria. There, Khalid Bakdash, a communist of Muslim-Kurdish origin, revitalized the party, and when Soviet policy favored Arab nationalist causes, as in the mid-1930s, and again in the 1950s, Bakdash and his party prospered. However, at times, Soviet policy hindered his efforts, as was the case when Russia supported the Zionist cause in the creation of the state of Israel.

Socialist and communist thinking faced obstacles in both nationalism and Islam because they emphasized a broad sense of community as opposed to the idea of class struggle. Class warfare was seen by most Arabs as dividing the *ummah* and the nation at a time when unity was needed to eliminate foreign control. In addition, socialism and communism appeared to imply a cooperation with foreign powers, which ran counter to both nationalist and Muslim sentiments. Thus, in the years before and just following World War II, radical secularist movements performed the function of introducing new ideas of social consciousness into the Arab East at a time when liberal nationalism and Islamic modernism were not greatly concerned with socioeconomic reform. Therefore, radical secularism had an appeal and influenced subsequent nationalist and Islamic thought despite its difficulties.

Synthesis of Socialism and Nationalism. The ideology that emerged as dominant in the Arab East was neither radical secularism nor liberal nationalism but a synthesis of the two, which took a number of forms and has often been called "Arab socialism." In this development, the secularist adaptationism of the first half of the century was transformed from being basically intellectual movements into party organizations, movements with mass appeal, and groups actually in control of governments. The emergence of Arab socialists to positions of political power in the Arab East is associated with the third phase of political development, in which the ruling groups that had achieved independence were displaced by new revolutionary groups. In Syria, the revolution began in 1949 with a series of military coups and reached a climax in 1958 when a union between Syria and Egypt was created by Arab socialist leaders in both countries. The rejection of the old regime in Egypt came with the revolution in 1952. At that time, the Wafd, the monarchy, and the old liberal nationalist parties were all removed by a military coup that brought to power a group of young officers led by Gamal Abd al-Nasir (Nasser). In Iraq, the monarchy created by the British was overthrown in 1958.

The oldest of these movements is the Socialist Arab Ba'th party, organized in Syria during World War II. It grew out of informal discussion groups led by Michel Aflaq (b. 1910), the son of a Greek Orthodox merchant, and Salah al-Din Baytar (1911–1980), a Syrian Muslim. Both men were born in Damascus, received some education in France where they came into contact with the Communist party, and taught school for a time in Syria. They became disillusioned with communism, because it ignored the special needs and identity of the Arabs, and by the older nationalist leaders in their country, because they ignored the need for reform. In 1943, the two organized the Ba'th party on the basis of a socialist program of internal reform and a unity program for all Arabs. The party rejected ideas of class struggle as being divisive in the Arab nation and was vigorously anticommunist. Branches of the party were established in Jordan (1948), Lebanon (1949), and Iraq (1950), and an attempt was made to maintain a unified leadership, although the party has been plagued by factionalism throughout its history.

The Ba'th was a growing force in Syrian politics in the 1950s. The power of the old nationalist politicians, who had gained control at independence in 1945–1946, had been broken by a series of military coups in 1949, and a four-year period of more stable military rule had followed. Between 1954 and 1958, there was an era of civilian parliamentary rule in which the Ba'th and Khalid Bakdash's Communist party emerged as major forces. Fearing a communist takeover, the Ba'th persuaded Nasser, the leader of the revolutionary regime in Egypt, to join with Syria in the United Arab Republic (UAR) in 1958. The unity experiment failed, and Syria became independent again in 1961 under a coalition of conservative and radical groups. In a coup in 1963, military officers and the Ba'th took control of Syria, and, in an almost parallel coup in Baghdad, they gained control in Iraq for a few months. Internal party divisions led to another coup in Syria in 1966, which brought to power a group of younger and more radical Ba'th members, and Aflaq and Baytar went into exile. A similar group within the Ba'th gained control in Iraq in 1968. This new generation of Ba'th leadership, the Neo-Ba'th, proposed programs of state-controlled economy and land reform that were more radical than those of Aflaq and Baytar. The Neo-Ba'th continued the basic themes of the original party: emphasis on Arab unity and nationalism, the need for a social and economic transformation in Arab society, and opposition to foreign control of either the state or ideology.

With the Ba'th party, socialism emerged as an ideology that was distinctively tied to the Arab nation. Ba'th leaders insisted that theirs was not a borrowed ideology but one that arose out of the Arab tradition. The older radicalism was transformed, and all subsequent movements in this tradition had to show their independence from the domination of foreign ideas or face the charge of being "tools" of outside powers. Radicalism had become "Arabized."

In this context, the relationship between radicalism and Islam had to be more fully defined. The religious tradition of the majority of the Arabs could not simply be rejected in the name of scientific thought or historical materialism, in the manner of the earlier radical secularists. For Ba'th thinkers, Islam is part of the Arab consciousness, and the early experience of Islam is seen as the first great Arab revolution and its teachings of equality and brotherhood as the foundation for a true socialist society. Aflaq believed that "the Ba'th party, while secular in orientation, embodies a renaissance of the Arab spirit similar to that embodied in Islam," and urged Arabs to emulate the life of the Prophet because "Muhammad was the epitome of all the Arabs; so let all Arabs today be Muhammad."[16] The early Arab socialists, like the Ba'th members, thus began the process of making Islam acceptable to radicals and radicalism acceptable to Muslims.

The second major Arab socialist movement was that led by Gamal Abd al-Nasir (Nasser, 1918–1970) in Egypt. In organization and style, Nasser's movement was very different from that of the Ba'th. It originated in an informal group of military officers who took control of the Egyptian government in 1952 and was not a formal political party. The Ba'th emphasized collective leadership, and Nasserism revolved around the leadership of a strong individual. It was these differences that made the union of Egypt and Syria in 1958–1961 unworkable, despite the fact that both Nasser and the Ba'th were committed to the ideal of Arab unity. In addition, the Ba'th emphasized the importance of developing a clear and consistent ideology, and Nasserism maintained an attachment to pragmatic adaptationism, even during its more doctrinaire phase in the 1960s.

The basic principles of Nasserism gradually emerged out of the experience of the young officers after they assumed power. The great themes were the same as those of the Ba'th: Arab liberation and unity and a radical socialist transformation of society. One of the major intellectuals in the movement, Muhammad Haykal, has said that Nasserism symbolizes "the direction of liberation, social transformation, the people's control of their own resources, and the democracy of the people's working forces."[17] At first, the young officers appeared to be an extension of Egyptian nationalism opposing the ineffectiveness and corruption of the old regime. However, in 1955–1956, Nasser emerged as the most successful anti-imperialist leader in the Arab world and soon became the chief spokesman for Arab nationalism, bringing Egypt fully into the Arab nationalist orbit. Similarly, the new revolutionary regime had a vision of eliminating social and economic injustice, but a full definition of that ideal as a socialist program was not reached until the proclamation of the National Covenant in 1962. Through the nationalist successes and the general internal progress made in Egypt under Nasserite reform programs, Arab socialism became widely accepted as a popular, mass sentiment.

In Nasserism, there was a strong emphasis on the indigenous nature of the ideology and the program. Nasser himself was a devout, practicing Muslim and encouraged an analysis of the Islamic bases for socialism. The older liberal secularist and communist ideas were seen as foreign, and Islam provided a starting point for an independent socialist ideology. The Islam of Nasserism did, however, reject those institutions and intellectual habits that were associated with traditional society. This Islamic dimension in this Arab socialism emphasized social justice and equality, sought social transformation, and was not necessarily acceptable to conservatives and fundamentalists in the Arab East. However, the great prestige of Nasser as a revolutionary nationalist and as the leading spokesman for the Arab cause helped to popularize the idea of Islam as being associated with Arab socialism. In Nasserism this association had a mutual influence because although interpretations of Islam were clearly shaped by radical attitudes, the emerging radicalism of Nasserism was influenced by the Islamic sense of community as opposed to class struggle and the Islamic sense of moral worth and values as opposed to the materialism of much of modern radicalism.

By the middle of the 1960s, Arab socialism in various forms appeared to be the most dominant ideology in the Arab East. Nasserism and the Ba'th were the two leading exponents of that view, but there were many other movements based on similar principles in other areas. Most discussion of Islam at the time saw Islam's future within the Arab socialist framework. Traditional, conservative, and fundamentalist movements were often seen as final efforts of the old styles of the Islamic experience that would eventually have to accommodate themselves to this new dynamic force or face destruction. Arab socialist regimes existed in Syria, Egypt, and Iraq. In 1962, a military group overthrew the imam in Yemen and espoused those ideals; opposition to the Saudi monarchy was couched in Arab socialist terms; there were active movements of that nature in Lebanon, Jordan, and South Arabia; and the emerging Palestinian national movement expressed itself in Arab socialist terms. However, by the end of the 1960s, the picture was clearly changing, and internal divisions and reorientations of socialist thought and practice were preparing the way for the new mood of the 1970s.

In purely Islamic terms, the rise of Arab socialism performed an important function. Adaptationist secularism, as it emerged after World War I, had been largely influenced by Western ideas, and especially in its radical form, that secularism had seemed somehow foreign to the Islamic society of the Arab East. However, in the hands of the Arab socialist intellectuals and leaders, radical secularism and the awareness of the need for social transformation became an indigenous ideology. The integration of radicalism with nationalism and Islam was an important step on the path to the "radical fundamentalism" that would emerge in the 1970s. In broader terms, that integration set the intellectual framework for the Islam of the modernizing world.

Fundamentalism in the Arab East

The most visible alternative to modernizing adaptationism was a fundamentalist style of Islam, which was the path followed by Rashid Rida after the death of Muhammad Abduh. However, during the first two-thirds of the twentieth century, Islamic fundamentalism in the Arab East was more closely associated with concrete organizations than with general intellectual schools of thought, and two movements were the clearly dominant forces: the Saudi monarchy in association with the revived Wahhabi movement and the Muslim Brotherhood. The appeal of both was built on the continuing strength of Islam in social life and on the apparent failure of the more secularist modernizing movements to solve the problems of Islamic society.

The Saudi Experience. The revival of the Saudi state and the Wahhabi movement during the twentieth century was the achievement of Abd al-Aziz (Ibn Saud, 1880–1953). In the first twenty-five years of this century, he gained control of much of the Arabian Peninsula and then succeeded in consolidating his conquests into the Kingdom of Saudi Arabia. In this revival, the dramatic leadership abilities of Abd al-Aziz gave focus to the new state, and the cement was the ideology provided by the Wahhabi tradition. As in the past, the ulama and the warrior combined in a movement that secured the allegiance of tribesmen and townspeople.

Until around 1930, the emerging state remained in a relatively traditional form. It was an enlarged patriarchal state with religious ties that transcended tribal loyalties, and the program was one of rigorous fundamentalism working to purify Islamic practice, with little awareness of any challenge from modern ideas. During this era, Abd al-Aziz created a powerful military instrument called the Ikhwan (Brothers), made up of tribal warriors who had been encouraged by their religious teachers to leave their tribes and settle in agricultural communities. There they received religious and military training and formed a well-organized core for the Saudi military. The Ikhwan were fully committed to the fundamentalist cause and were a major force in the Saudi military expansion. However, by the mid-1920s, they began to pose problems for the new state because they opposed any compromises with surrounding states. They soon clashed with British forces in the newly created state of Iraq, and they threatened Abd al-Aziz's efforts to gain diplomatic recognition. When Abd al-Aziz negotiated treaties with his neighbors, many of the more fanatical Ikhwan revolted and the organization was defeated in 1928–1930.

Following the putting down of the Ikhwan revolt, the Saudi state entered an era of stability and consolidation. Those Ikhwan who had remained loyal to the king remained a part of the state, and Ikhwan-style zeal was an important sentiment, but Saudi expansionism ceased. The policy of Abd al-Aziz was to make whatever adjustments were necessary for political survival in the modern world but to keep the Saudi society based on the fundamentalist spirit. Thus, he was not averse to the introduction of some modern means of communication and weaponry, but the Quran and the Sunnah represented the law and the constitution of the state.

In the early days following World War I, the new Saudi state gained some prestige throughout the Islamic world. It was one of the few areas that retained political independence, and, in contrast to Turkey under Mustafa Kemal Ataturk, the Saudis remained vigorously and visibly Islamic. However, as nationalist and secularist currents became stronger and as the Kingdom of Saudi Arabia became a stable, patrimonial state, its international popularity tended to fade. The element that brought Saudi Arabia back into international prominence was the discovery of oil in its territories.

The development of the oil industry in Saudi Arabia, especially after World War II, brought tremendous sums of money into the country, which transformed the whole context of the kingdom. As a relatively poor and puritanical state on the fringes of world affairs, Saudi Arabia had not had to face the challenges of modern history in as direct a manner as other countries, but as a wealthy oil-producing country, it could not avoid many problems. Abd al-Aziz and then his son and successor, Saud (1902–1969), tried to maintain the old spirit of the patrimonial state, but they were unable to control the corruption and inefficiency that came in the wake of too much money for the system to handle. It became clear that the troubles were of major crisis proportion by the end of the 1950s.

Pressures for reform built and resulted in Saud's younger but more experienced brother, Faysal (1905–1975), being named prime minister. Faysal had some success in reorganizing the state's finances, but tensions soon arose between him and the king, and he resigned. Saud assumed direct leadership again and appointed a cabinet that included men drawn from the small group of modern-educated Saudis who were inspired by the more radical reform programs in other parts of the Arab world. The leading members of the royal family and the Wahhabi ulama began to feel that the whole structure of the Saudi-Wahhabi monarchy was threatened, and that feeling was emphasized by the 1962 overthrow of the imam in Yemen by republican forces inspired by Arab socialism. It was clear that a government dedicated to a decisive reform of the patrimonial monarchy was necessary if the fundamentalist spirit of the state was to be preserved. In a series of actions, the leading royal and religious notables secured the abdication of Saud and the accession of Faysal to the throne in 1963. In this process, some of Faysal's major supporters were a group of his half brothers, whose mothers came from the Sudayri family.

Under King Faysal, the Saudi state entered a new era, and the keystone of the new policies might be called "pragmatic fundamentalism." The basic foundations for law and loyalty continue to be the Quran and the Sunnah, but the operating structures reflect the changing conditions in Saudi society and the Islamic world. The initial basic document of this pragmatic fundamentalism is the ten-point program announced by Faysal, at that time prime minister, in 1962. This program promised the reorganization of provincial and central governments; a restructuring of the judiciary organization; improvements in social welfare, financial, and economic development; and the abolition of all slavery. The spirit of this program is shown in the fourth point, dealing with the ulama; "Inasmuch as the texts of the Koran and Traditions are fixed and limited, while modern times and the experience of the people in worldly affairs are constantly changing rather than being limited, and in view of the fact that our youthful state is ruled according to the letter and spirit of the Koran and Traditions, it has become imperative for us to give greater attention to jurisprudence and for our jurists and Ulema to play a positive and effective part in the discussion of important matters of State."[18] This point then included a proposal for the formation of an advisory judicial council made up of jurists and ulama.

In some ways the program reflects the facts that Arab socialism was rising to prominence in much of the Arab East, and restructuring and development were recognized as being necessary. However, the foundation of Faysal's reformism remained the fundamentalist tradition. In the Saudi program, even more than in Arab socialism, there is an emphasis on the indigenous quality of the ideology. Faysal said, "We want our nation to be in the vanguard and not in the rear-guard. We do not want to be mere imitators and satellites. On the contrary, we are capable of leading, guiding and steering the helm if we hold fast to God's Book and His Prophet's Sunnah."[19] Pragmatic fundamentalism was thus emerging as an alternative to Arab social- ism, and during the 1960s, there was conflict and competition between the two styles. In the heyday of Arab socialism, however, many people were willing to believe that Faysal's program was simply defensive reform and that the future lay elsewhere. Many in the Arab East considered the Saudi position to be reactionary.

By the end of the 1960s, Faysal was emerging as one of the leading figures in the Arab and Islamic world. Much of his prominence was based on the enormous wealth that the country's oil was providing, but also, as Arab socialist movements began to falter because of internal divisions and an inability to solve the pressing problems of modernizing societies, Saudi pragmatic fundamentalism was emerging as an important example. One fac- tor was the development of nationalism, or the lack of it, in Saudi Arabia. In contrast to other areas, the political boundaries created following World War I did not come to define a unit of overriding nationalist loyalty. The Saudi identity was primarily dynastic in local terms and identified with Pan-Arab and Pan-Islamic ideals in the larger theaters of action. In this way, the Saudi monarch could emerge as a spokesman for the Arab cause and could be active in encouraging the coordination of policy among Muslim states. In this role, Faysal became a well-known and respected international figure.

The Muslim Brotherhood. In the areas more directly affected by the ex- pansion of European imperialism and ideas, fundamentalism did not disap- pear as an important factor, but, given the fact that the political institutions and ruling elites were dominated by adaptationist modernizers, the funda- mentalist style emerged in a new format. Traditional holy wars and the old- style organizations had little appeal, and the new fundamentalism created popular associations that were dedicated to a strict adherence to the Quran and the Sunnah. The most famous of those groups in the Arab East is the Muslim Brotherhood.

Inspired by fundamentalist ideals, the Muslim Brotherhood grew directly out of the challenge modernizing secularism posed to Islamic values. It was established in Egypt by Hasan al-Banna (1906–1949), a schoolteacher with a background of individual and family religious studies and a modern-ori- ented education. He became persuaded that the weakness of Islamic society could be cured only by a return to the sources of its strength, the Quran and the Sunnah. As a student and then as a teacher in Ismailia in the Suez Canal zone, he organized study and discussion groups that provided the basis for the formal organization of the Brotherhood in 1928. The organization set up schools, became active in a variety of social and cultural affairs, and soon gained a wide following throughout Egypt; in the absence of effective pro- grams for social reform by the state and the liberal nationalists, the Brotherhood was increasingly drawn into the political arena. The cause of liberation soon engaged its attention, and it gave its support to the Palestinians. After World War II, it emerged as a revolutionary force with a program for social transformation that rivaled that of the communists and as a militant organization capable of engaging in terrorist as well as propagandistic actions. Hasan al-Banna himself was murdered in 1949 as the Brotherhood's involvement in terrorism and counterterrorism increased. The organization had ties with the young officers led by Nasser and had some influence within the new regime until rivalries led to conflict. Some members of the Brotherhood attempted to kill Nasser in 1954, and the organization was suppressed. After 1954, the Brotherhood remained active in Egypt as an underground association. In 1965, Nasser's government announced the discovery of a plot by the Brotherhood to overthrow the regime, and many arrests were made; three executions followed, including that of Sayyid Qutb, a prominent writer in the movement.

Organizations similar to the Muslim Brotherhood appeared in other countries, and they were at least inspired by, if not organizationally connected with, the Brotherhood in Egypt. The most active groups were in Syria and Jordan, and there were others in Iraq, Lebanon, and Palestine. The basic positions of all of these groups were similar.

The essential message of the Muslim Brotherhood is simple. Hasan al-Banna summarized the meaning of Islam: "First, the rules of Islam and its teachings are comprehensive, organizing the affairs of the people in this world and the next. Second, the foundation of Islamic teachings is the Book of God Almighty and the Sunnah of His Messenger, the blessings of God and His peace be upon him. Third, Islam as a general faith regulates all matters of life for every race and community, in every age and era."[20] In this vigorous affirmation of the universal validity of Islam, the Brothers viewed themselves as a part of the revivalist movements of the modern period, in line with al-Afghani, Abduh, and Rashid Rida. However, the Brotherhood sought to implement the revival rather than to engage in intellectual speculations. The Brotherhood was thus fundamentalist in its style, but it demanded adherence to the Quran and the Sunnah, not a return to the conditions of the seventh century.

The role of the organization was clearly stated in a message sent to the membership by Hasan al-Banna in 1943: "My Brothers: you are not a benevolent society, nor a political party, nor a local organization having limited purposes. Rather, you are a new soul in the heart of this nation to give it life by means of the Qurʿan, you are a new light which shines to destroy the darkness of materialism through knowing God; and you are the strong voice which rises to recall the message of the Prophet."[21] The organization was to be the vehicle for establishing an Islamically moral society and a truly Muslim government.

In its early years in Egypt, the Muslim Brotherhood was one of the few groups that advocated a vigorous social transformation and major socioeconomic reforms. In later years, some of its leading writers began to use the terminology of the times and spoke of the Brotherhood program as being Islamic socialism. One such writer was a leader of the Brotherhood in Syria, Mustafa al-Siba'i (b. 1910), who believed that Islamic socialism was "an integral part of the credo of the Muslim, who can but apply it. It constitutes a more rapid and more effectual method than any other socialism for the reform of our society."[22]

The Muslim Brotherhood appealed to more than the religiously faithful rural people and the urban lower classes. In terms of its activist members and leaders, it was a very strong movement of students, civil servants, teachers, office workers, and professionals. The appeal of the society was not to conservatives so much as to people who had already had a significant contact with Westernizing ideas and institutions. For those people, the message of the Brotherhood could provide an identity and a tie with their traditions, and the Brotherhood succeeded in creating a fundamentalism that could have an appeal in a modernizing world. Although many intellectuals and governments in the Arab East have opposed the Brotherhood as a reactionary and politically dangerous movement, it represents a successful modernization of the fundamentalist style of the Islamic experience.

The cases of Saudi Arabia and the Muslim Brotherhood in Egypt show that the fundamentalist style has continued to have some effect in the twentieth century. However, for the first two-thirds of the century, that style was overshadowed by the growing dominance of the adaptationist styles of secularism and nationalism. At the high tide of Arab socialism in the 1960s, fundamentalists were seen as an echo of the past rather than as the wave of the future.

The Changing Face of Conservatism

One of the remarkable phenomena of modern Muslim history is the flexibility exhibited by the conservative style of the Islamic experience. In a period of rapid and dramatic changes, the protectors of the existing order had to be nimble to keep up, and as new ideas and institutions became established and accepted, they soon became the objects of care and concern for the conservatives rather than the proposals of the innovators and adaptationists. Conservatism in this context is the result of a relatively rapid acceptance of any emerging consensus. In the Arab East, the most prominent conservative elements are the older Islamic institutions, the most famous of which is al-Azhar, and the various monarchies. In the latter, there are two types: those that were created following World War I and those that were based on older traditions in the Arabian Peninsula.

Al-Azhar University: The experience of al-Azhar can be taken as representative of the older Islamic institutions that survived the changes of the twentieth century. Some, like the large-scale *tariqah* organizations and independent ulama instructorships and foundations, gradually disappeared, and others, like al-Azhar, survived. The majority of the ulama associated with al-Azhar resisted the intellectual currents of change as they were taking place. At the same time, many of the leading intellectual adaptationists had some association with the institution. One link between those conservative ulama and the developing intellectual community in Egypt and the rest of the Arab world was the rector of the university. Often he played some role in the actual process of redefinition of the Islamic tradition in modern terms, meeting resistance from his conservative colleagues and. at least at times, helping to slow the pace of intellectual change among the adaptationists.

Muhammad Abduh had been active in working to reform the curriculum and teaching methods of al-Azhar, and those efforts as well as his ideas had been opposed by the majority of the teachers. Yet, in the interwar era, his teachings gained wide acceptance and later provided the basis for much of the scholarly thought of al-Azhar. The appointment of one of his followers Mustafa al-Maraghi (1881–1945), as shaykh al-Azhar in 1928 was opposed by most of the ulama as he was in favor of major reforms. His first term in the post lasted only a year, but he then served again from 1935 to 1945 with much wider support. Al-Maraghi had previously been a grand *qadi* in the Sudan, where he was active in modernizing the Islamic legal structure and its applications.

The rector from 1929 to 1935 was Muhammad al-Ahmadi al-Zawahiri (1878–1944), whose book advocating Islamic reform had been burned by order of the shaykh al-Azhar in 1904. During al-Zawahiri's term the curriculum of al-Azhar was greatly expanded to include "modern" subjects. Similarly, after al-Maraghi's death, the next rector was Mustafa Abd al-Raziq (1885–1947), an active student of Abduh whose philosophical works had been opposed by the conservative ulama early in the century but whose ideas were a solid part of the "Azhar orthodoxy" by the second half of the twentieth century.

The conservative but flexible role of al-Azhar continued after the 1952 revolution, and the emerging dominance of Arab socialism in its Nasserite form was gradually reflected in the official position of the university. In 1958, Mahmud Shaltut (d. 1964) was named rector. During the 1930s, he had been dismissed from the faculty of al-Azhar for his modernist views, and in the 1950s he had helped to create a more conservative definition of Islamic socialism, which supported the new revolutionary position, indirectly rebutting the more fundamentalist views of the Muslim Brotherhood writers. He emphasized the comprehensive and universal character of the Islamic message and argued that Egyptian socialism conformed to the Islamic tradition. In his view, mankind could find no "more perfect, more complete, more useful, more profound socialism than that decreed by Islam."[23] Thus, gradually, the conservatism of al-Azhar made it the protector of the newly emerging "orthodoxy"—at first, the consensus of liberal nationalism and modernism and, then, the dominant Arab socialist perspective.

"New Monarchies" and Changing Conservatism. During the first two-thirds of the twentieth century, new monarchies were created in a number of areas, and they were often the product of diplomatic negotiation rather than nationalist or fundamentalist revolutions, although they all had some roots in past institutions. These new monarchies were associated with modernist and adaptationist ideas at the time of their creation, but they soon became identified as bastions of conservatism and faced opposition from the more radical groups as they emerged. The ability of these monarchies to adapt and cope with the emerging challenges determined how long they survived, and the key element was not so much the vitality of the monarchical ideology as the ability of the individuals who occupied the thrones.

Three twentieth-century monarchies emerged out of the experience of one of the prominent sharif families in Mecca, the Hashimites, which had come to prominence through the activities of Husayn ibn Ali, who was the grand sharif of Mecca after the Young Turk Revolution in 1908. The family was active in Ottoman politics in Istanbul in the era of the Young Turks, and Husayn's sons, Abdallah (1882–1951) and Faysal (1883–1933), both served in the Ottoman parliament. During World War I, the family provided the leadership for the Arab revolt against the Ottomans and thus became the leading standard-bearers for Arab nationalism. Thus, although the prestige of the family was based on their religious position as descendants of the Prophet and leaders in the holy city, they were active in the adaptationist movements of the time.

Sharif Husayn's goal had been the creation of an Arab monarchy that would lead a united state in the Arab East, but that was not possible in the conditions following World War I. Instead, Husayn was recognized as the King of the Hijaz, and in 1921, his son Faysal was named king of the newly created state of Iraq, and Abdallah became the ruler of Transjordan. The history of each of these monarchies illustrates, in different ways, the gradual transition to conservatism in an effort to preserve the institutions that had been created.

King Husayn faced the rising Saudi power in the Hijaz and mishandled his diplomatic relations so that he became isolated and unable to call upon the support of his former allies, the British. His Arab nationalism also gave him no added support, and he attempted to return to a religiously based position of power. In 1924, the leader of the Arab revolt declared himself to be caliph of Islam, but that did not stop the Saudi advance, and they conquered the Hijaz in 1925. Husayn spent his remaining years in exile and died in 1931.

The other Hashimite monarchies fared better. Having been created by the British, they continued to have British support and gradually emerged as independent states. Faysal had been the major military commander from the family during the Arab revolt and had widespread support among the nationalists in the Arab East. He had been named king of Syria by a nationalist congress at the end of the war, but that was opposed by the French in 1920. In 1921, he became the king of Iraq. The combination of his religious prestige, his nationalist reputation, and his effective leadership skills made it possible for him to balance nationalist demands and British requirements, which gave Iraq a period of political stability that culminated in its formal independence and admission to the League of Nations in 1932.

Under Faysal's leadership, the Iraqi monarchy became the leading instrument for creating an Iraqi identity and a national integration. Just before his death, Faysal wrote, "In Iraq there is still—and I say this with a heart full of sorrow—no Iraqi people but unimaginable masses of human beings, devoid of any patriotic idea. . . . Out of these masses we want to fashion a people."[24] To do so, he encouraged a reconciliation among the disparate groups— Sunni and Shiʻi, Arab and Kurd—that composed the Iraqi population.

Following Faysal's death, the Hashimite leadership was weaker, and the army emerged as a source of antimonarchical leadership in alliance with secular groups like al-Ahali. The military coup of Bakr Sidqi in 1936 and a revolution led by Rashid Ali in 1941 had republican overtones, and the Hashimite leadership turned away from the emerging nationalist and secularist groups. During and following World War II, Prince Abdul Illah (1913– 1958), the regent for the young king, Faysal II (1935–1958), increasingly turned to the tribal chieftains and the British for support. By the 1950s, the self-preservation efforts of the monarchy had transformed it from the leading liberal nationalist institution into the bastion of the older traditional elements of society and the foreign imperial power that dominated Iraq. Under these circumstances, the Iraqi monarchy was swamped by the rising tide of Arab socialism and was overthrown in 1958, and its old religious prestige, which had initially been tied to modernizing movements, was lost in the process. Leadership in religious affairs reverted to the Shiʻi ulama of Najaf and Karbala and to the more conservative urban Sunni ulama.

The most successful Hashimite monarchy was the one established in Jordan. In 1921, Abdallah ibn Husayn was named the prince of the territories east of the Jordan River in British-controlled Palestine. He had already had a career as an effective politician within the Ottoman parliament and the Arab revolt, and he had had some ties with Rashid Rida. The British created his princedom in order to lessen his opposition to the French expulsion of his brother, Faysal, from Syria. Abdallah's new state was a purely artificial unit, but he set rapidly to work to create a viable state. He never cut his ties with the British, but he was able to attract many of the old nationalists to his service, and his religious prestige helped him to win the support of the largely Sunni nomadic tribes. His social policies were conservative, but he remained dedicated to the Arab nationalist cause and emerged after World War II as one of the leading figures in the pre-Arab socialist movement for Arab unity. His army, the Arab Legion, was relatively small but one of the most effective military forces in the Arab East. It performed well during the Arab-Israeli War of 1948–1949 and enabled Abdallah to annex the West Bank territories in Palestine that had not been taken over by Israeli forces. In that action, he alienated many Arab nationalists and was murdered in 1951.

The monarchy created by Abdallah was not itself a religious institution, but part of the king's prestige rested upon his religious position and his visible devotion to the faith. He survived and strengthened the monarchy by adroit maneuvering, remaining conservative enough to win the support of the tribesmen who were the core of his military and nationalist enough to be acceptable to the modern-educated groups within his kingdom. His son, Talal, reigned only briefly, and his grandson, Husayn (b. 1935), became king in 1952. The same adept ability to balance forces proved to be Husayn's greatest strength, and the Jordanian monarchy survived a wide range of challenges and remained in power in 1980. It adopted programs of vigorous modernization but never came under the control of radical Arab socialist forces. By the mid-1960s, it was seen as a major conservative force, trying to preserve the old political structures in the midst of rapid modernization. At the same time that the Saudi monarchy was moving toward pragmatic fundamentalism, the Jordanian monarchy could be said to represent a modernizing conservatism.

In Egypt, the foundations of the monarchy went back to the time of Mehmet Ali at the beginning of the nineteenth century. Virtually independent governors within the Ottoman Empire, Mehmet Ali and his successors had been the leading exponents and implementers of Westernizing reform. Following the British occupation in 1882, the rulers had been forced into a position of accepting British domination, and the initiative for both reform and nationalism had passed into the hands of other groups. As a part of the

World War I settlement, Egypt was made an independent monarchy by treaty in 1922, and a descendant of Mehmet Ali, Fuad (1868–1936), became the first king of Egypt.

The palace was now simply one of a number of competing forces in the Egyptian political scene. Leadership in the nationalist cause was in the hands of Saʿd Zaghlul and the Wafd party, and leadership in liberal and secularist thought was also outside of the palace. Fuad worked to establish the power of the monarchy firmly, but his major weapons were simply the structures of the state and British support. Neither he nor the institution had any particular religious prestige, but Islam was seen as a possible tool for increasing royal powers. As a result, Fuad attempted during the conflict over the caliphate to be named caliph, but support for that was never strong. Instead, Fuad and his successor, Faruq (1920–1965), attempted to gain religious support for their basically secular regimes by allying themselves with al-Azhar. The relatively conservative but modernist scholars who became rectors of al-Azhar preferred the monarchy to the Wafd or the more secularist intellectuals, but that support did not create religious prestige for the kings; it only gave them a way of influencing public opinion. In the long run, the inability of the monarchy to handle the growing problems of Egypt, especially under the inept and corrupt Faruq, opened the door for the 1952 revolution. The monarchy thus encouraged the conservative style of modernism in Islamic thought and had undergone a reversal in its position from being the vanguard of modernizing reform under Mehmet Ali to being one of the major obstacles to progress under Faruq.

Among the "created monarchies" in the Arab East, the one with the greatest religious identification was in Libya, which was created in 1949–1952. The first king was Idris ibn al-Mahdi (b. 1890), a grandson of Muhammad ibn Ali al-Sanusi, the founder of the Sanusiyyah Tariqah. Idris was one of the leading figures in the Sanusi order and in its conflict with Italian imperialism. During the first half of the century, the Sanusiyyah became the core of Libyan nationalism, and its heroes were the heroes of Libyan national existence. Under those conditions, Sanusi activity went in two directions simultaneously. On the one hand, it became increasingly activist in political terms, and on the other, it was more concerned with unifying resistance forces and maintaining some semblance of social life under the conditions of severe Italian repression than it was with a fundamentalist purification of Libyan society. Following World War II, the order emerged as a politically activist but ideologically conservative movement. Given the fact that there were no other "national" institutions in Libya, it was logical that the United Nations commission that "created" an independent Libya would turn to the Sanusiyyah for the leadership of the new state.

At the beginning of the century, the Sanusiyyah was involved in both nationalist activities and Islamic revivalism. The leader of the order at that time was Ahmad al-Sharif (d. 1933), a cousin of Idris who left the leadership of the order in Libya in the hands of Idris while he went to Istanbul during World War I. For a time, he cooperated with the Ottoman royal family and then aided Mustafa Kemal Ataturk in the Turkish war for independence. There was talk that he might be named caliph, and he was active in trying to reconcile Pan-Islamic ideals with the emerging Turkish nationalist reformism. However, after the abolition of the caliphate, he was asked to leave Turkey, and he spent the rest of his life in study and piety in Mecca and Medina. With his death, the Sanusiyyah order became fully involved in nationalist activities, and its underlying ideology became increasingly conservative.

After Libyan independence, the monarchy was the center of the new country's political life. Idris had great prestige as the leader of the nationalist struggle and of the major religious organization in Libya. He insisted on careful programs of economic development and worked to create national institutions, such as a parliament and an army, but he did not encourage ideological development of either an Islamic or a secularist type. As a result, the Islamic aspect of the regime became simply a justification for the existing and emerging monarchical order, and "Sanusism" became defined as the programs of social and economic development initiated by the monarchy. Those programs were often sound but did little to provide an ongoing ideological inspiration for the emerging Libyan national feeling. Ultimately, that inspiration was provided from the outside by the ideas of Arab socialism and, later, radical fundamentalism. The monarchy led the country through the hard days of its early poverty and then through the days of its growing wealth as a result of oil in the 1960s. In many ways, it survived the challenges of Arab socialism during the 1960s, and when the monarchy was overthrown in 1969, it was by a movement that was closer to the radical fundamentalism of the 1970s than to the Arab socialism of the previous decade.

The experience of the "new" monarchies emphasizes one aspect of modern conservatism in the Arab East: Conservatism does not mean trying to maintain society as it was before significant modernization but, rather, trying to slow the pace of change and preserving institutions that may have been created relatively early in the process of modernization. In general, conservatism supports an evolutionary development of society rather than revolutionary social change. Ironically, the changing face of conservatism means that it cannot be identified with a particular ideology. In Jordan, for example, it is associated with liberal nationalism, and in Egypt after the establishment of Arab socialism, it supported that ideology, defending it against opponents who desired the revolutionary overthrow of the Nasserite regime.

"Old" Monarchies. The style of conservatism that hopes to avoid any significant change can be seen in some of the monarchical systems in the Arab East. In Yemen, South Arabia, and Oman, rulers attempted by isolationism and strict controls to avoid change. In each of those areas, the prestige of the monarchy was buttressed by local Islamic traditions, but even in those isolated corners of the Arab world, change could not be stopped. As no emerging ideological alternatives of a more conservative nature were available, growing contact with the modern world produced an Arab socialist revolution in Yemen in 1962, and when South Arabia gained its independence in 1967, even the conservative hinterlands of Aden joined in supporting the new, radical secularist regime that had created the People's Republic of South Yemen. In Oman, the major problem for much of the century was the division of the country into coastal areas controlled by the sultan and inner areas under the control of an Ibadi imam. After revolts early in the century, a compromise was worked out and defined in a treaty in 1920, which established the principle of noninterference by the sultan in the affairs of the tribes of the interior. However, during the 1950s, imams led revolts against Sultan Said ibn Taymur, whose long reign lasted from 1932 until 1970. Sultan Said successfully unified the country, but even after the discovery of oil and growing government revenues, he resisted any modernization of his country. By the late 1960s, it appeared that the only alternative to the medieval rule of Said was the rule of radical revolutionaries, who began activities in the province of Dhofar. However, Said was overthrown in 1970 by his son, Qabus, who initiated a more active program of economic development and social reform.

In the other small states of the Arabian Peninsula, a more pragmatic conservatism has emerged. In Kuwait, Bahrain, Qatar, and the small shaykhdoms that became the United Arab Emirates (UAE) in 1971, the old ruling families have worked to maintain their monarchical systems while encouraging rapid economic modernization. They have been greatly assisted in this endeavor by the tremendous revenues from the sale of oil. None of these states are explicitly religious in character, but all, in varying forms, depend upon respect for the Islamic tradition to buttress the existing political order. By a judicious financial support of Islamic and radical causes, they have managed to avoid revolutions.

The old monarchies that were explicitly religious in nature—the Zaydi imamate in Yemen and the Ibadi imamate in Oman—have been destroyed. The more flexible monarchies of tribal origin have been able to utilize the oil wealth and a pragmatic conservatism to preserve their existence.

Summary

In the tremendous variety of Islamic experience in the Arab East, a number of factors should be clear. In the first place, there is nothing inherently conservative about Islam, and conversely, conservatism may be dynastic or pragmatic, but it is not inherently Islamic except in the sense that what the conservatives were trying to preserve was premodern Islamic society. Second, although many of the pre-twentieth-century types of movements proved to be ineffective in the context of the twentieth century, the basic styles of the Islamic experience—the adaptationist, fundamentalist, conservative, and individualist—continued to provide the framework within which most people in the Arab East operated.

Finally, when Muslims were the dominant majority in a society, the basic issues were those of liberation and modernization within an Islamic framework, and the extreme secularists made little headway in their attempts to create a framework that would ignore or reject the Islamic tradition. However, when radical secularism adapted itself to the local conditions and became defined as an indigenous movement, it made significant progress. By the mid-1960s, it appeared to be dominant, eclipsing the fundamentalist and conservative movements.

Dominant Majorities in the Northern Tier

The three modern states of Turkey, Iran, and Afghanistan form the northern tier of countries in the Middle East where the Muslims are the dominant majority, and their populations represent about one-eighth of the world's Muslims. In those areas, the traditions of Islam are deeply rooted as much of the area was brought into the Muslim world in the early centuries of Islamic history. However, the local ethnic and linguistic traditions do not have the same identity with the origins of Islam as they do in the Arab East. Turkish and Persian emerged as important Muslim languages, but they represent special cultural traditions within the Muslim world. The northern tier was the homeland of great imperial traditions in both premodern and modern times, and that fact is reflected in the twentieth-century experience. As was the case in Egypt, the political units that emerged had some historical validity. In contrast to Egypt, however, these three areas maintained formal independence throughout the nineteenth century.

Adaptationism: Political Leaders as Reformers

During the first half of the twentieth century, the experience of the northern tier countries was almost unique in the Islamic world. Having maintained their political independence, their political leaders were able to initiate programs of reform and modernization that had a substantially indigenous character. The experience of those countries provides a way of seeing the potential of Islam operating in the modern world in the absence of direct European control.

At the end of World War I, important reformist leaders emerged in each of the three countries, and the contrasting results of their efforts show the importance of the foundations laid in the previous centuries and the special local conditions. Each of the three leaders was committed to the rapid modernization of his country and, because of political independence, was able to have his program become the official government policy. The success or failure of the program depended more upon local forces than outside interference.

Turkey. The most dramatic and successful of those reformers was Mustafa Kemal Ataturk (1881–1938), who created the modern Turkish republic out of the ruins of the Ottoman Empire. In many ways, he represents the culmination of the long history of Ottoman reform and modernization efforts. In Turkey at the end of World War I, there was a large group of modern-educated, experienced officials and a sound awareness of the meaning of the reform efforts. However, the experience of the autocracy of Abdulhamid II's rule and the defeat of the empire during the war had eliminated many of the possible ideological options that could be used as the basis for the twentieth-century state. Ottomanism, in either a centralizing or a federalist form, was no longer possible. The empire no longer existed, and most of it had experienced nationalist revolts or European occupation. Pan-Islam was also seen as a discredited basis for policy after the failure of the call to holy war during World War I and the lack of effective cooperation among Muslim leaders. The idea of uniting all Turkish-speaking peoples was a romantic sentiment held by a few Young Turks who continued to work among the peoples of Central Asia, but their efforts came to nothing. The remaining effective option was to build a new state based on the patriotism of the Turkish-speaking people in the Anatolian Peninsula, where foreign occupation was still limited.

At the end of World War I, even that option seemed weak, and only scattered resistance movements existed. However, the invasion of Anatolia by the Greek army and the rise of Mustafa Kemal as an inspiring mobilizer provided the impetus for the creation of a Turkish nationalist movement that defeated the Greeks and forced the European Allied powers to recognize Turkish independence. The war for independence in 1919–1922 succeeded where the Egyptian and Iraqi revolutions of 1919 and 1920 failed; Turkey was not to be a European-occupied or -dominated area. In this situation, the reformist ideals of Kemal and his associates could be put into practice. The clear victory of the Muslims of Turkey over the European states gave a special prestige and visibility to the Turkish reform effort, which was undertaken in the area of the old center of Muslim attention, the realm of the Ottoman sultan-caliph.

In terms of the modern Islamic experience, the Kemalist reform program was a vigorous application of adaptationism to the Westernizing secularist style. The old institutions of Islamic politics and society were systematically eliminated rather than being reformed. The office of the sultanate was abolished in 1922, the caliphate in 1924, and the old Islamic legal structure was eliminated in a series of reforms during the following decade. The formal organizations of *tariqah*s were outlawed, pious foundations were brought under direct government control, and religious education was taken out of the hands of the traditional ulama. The Arabic script used for writing Ottoman Turkish was replaced by an alphabet that used Latin letters, and there was a major effort to "purify" the language by eliminating words borrowed from Arabic and Persian. In this way, the language and literature of the new Turkey was cut off from the earlier Islamic literary traditions. Even reference to Islam as the religion of the state, which had been included in the first republican constitution, was eliminated in 1928.

In the place of the old political system, the Kemalist reformers worked to create a modernized parliamentary republic. The keystone of the system in terms of the legitimation of political authority was that it was to be based on the will of the people. This principle was first stated by the Grand National Assembly, the organization of the Turkish independence movement, in 1920: "The real authority is the national will. There is no power superior to the Grand National Assembly."[25] The new slogan was Sovereignty Belongs to the Nation, and the principle of republicanism was one of the six principles of Kemalism. That basis of political authority meant a transformation of the ideological foundations of the state, and the old system, in which God is the sovereign and the real authority is God's, not the people's will, was eliminated.

The other principles of Kemalism were also related to that basic transformation: Nationalism directed the focus of loyalty to the new nation-state, populism emphasized the importance of the people as opposed to the elite, revolutionism supported the willingness to accept constant transformation, and statism defined the role of the government in the economy. The remaining principle, secularism, spoke directly to the role of religion, and the Kemalist program was explicitly secularist. The secularism of the Turkish republic aimed at bringing an end to all of the old institutions of the faith, and it excluded formally religious considerations from the political arena and rejected social distinctions based on religion. However, the program did not reject Islam or oppose religion in general; rather, it aimed at making adherence to Islam a personal, individual matter in an environment where a person was not obliged to follow some externally established set of rules and doctrines. It was a secularist rather than an atheistic program of modernizing reform.

As a nationalist program, Kemalism worked to "nationalize" Islam by making it more Turkish in order that all Turks could understand their faith without having to resort to professional interpreters. In this effort, the language of the faith was an important key. Through Kemal's leadership, the call to prayer and mosque sermons came to be given in Turkish rather than in Arabic. In addition, he worked to have the Quran translated from Arabic into Turkish, something that aroused much conservative opposition. In a curious reflection of fundamentalism, Kemal said: "The Turk believes in the Book, but he does not understand what it says to him. First of all, he himself must understand directly the Book that he so seeks."[26] In this way, the secularist adaptationism of Kemal worked to create a modern, individualistic Islamic style.

In the broadest political terms, the basic question raised by the secularist policy of Turkish reform was, "Is Islam conceivable in a democratically constituted state?"[27] Turkish secularism implied that Islam was not comprehensive or directly applicable to all aspects of life, a position rejected by fundamentalists, and that continuity with past institutions and formulations was unnecessary, a position objectionable to conservatives. However, if one examines the twentieth-century Turkish experience, the answer to the question must be in the affirmative. In Turkey, Muslims live in a democratically constituted state but have remained clearly Muslim in terms of their own self-identification and by most nonextremist Islamic standards.

The Kemalist program was a liberal secularist transformation rather than a socialist revolution, and it provided the foundations for the evolution of a modernizing parliamentary democracy, with major social changes taking place without a socially destructive revolution. Although Mustafa Kemal concentrated political control in his own hands, he also created a political party, the Republican People's party (RPP), that carried on his program after his death. Following World War II, the one-party state changed to a multiparty one when the Democratic party (DP) was created in 1946.

The DP won the general elections of 1950 and took control of the government by peaceful, democratic means. In this process, Islam played some role. The narrow restrictions placed upon religion had not been fully accepted by many Turks, especially in the rural areas. Part of the DP program, which was later implemented, was to expand the programs of religious instruction and to end the use of Turkish translations of the call to prayer and the Quran. Those features were factors in the DP's electoral popularity. In 1948, the Nation party was formed, and it had a more clearly religious program that advocated Islamic revival and the substantial relaxation, if not the elimination, of the secularist aspects of Turkish policies. An indication of the continuing strength of at least a modified adherence to the Kemalist tradition of secularism is that although the DP won 53 percent of the votes, the Nation party received only 3 percent in the 1950 elections.

The Nation party was significant as it represented a continuing minority of people in Turkey who advocated a greater adherence to Islamic traditions, and it was the first manifestation of an organized fundamentalist political party within the Turkish political system. Although it was outlawed in 1954 for attempting to use religion for political purposes, it was succeeded by the Republican Nation party, which won almost 5 percent of the votes in the 1954 elections. At the same time, there was renewed activity on the part of illegal activist *tariqah*s, such as the Tijaniyyah and the Naqshbandiyyah. None of this activity, however, represented a significant challenge at the time to the dominant Kemalist secularism, even in the less rigorous form espoused by the DP.

The major challenge to the Kemalist political system came from the developing policies of the DP itself, which increasingly limited its political opposition and appeared to be moving in the direction of a one-party, dictatorial state. As a result, the leaders of the armed forces took control of the government in 1960 and brought an end to the Democratic party. The new military rulers asserted their loyalty to the Kemalist program and, in contrast to many of their contemporaries elsewhere, rapidly moved to restore civilian control of the government. A new constitution was formulated by a special constituent assembly and the second Turkish republic came into existence in 1961. One of the primary concerns of the framers of the new constitution was to create safeguards against the possible emergence of a dictatorial or one-party rule, and there were complex arrangements for proportional representation and a recognition of opposition views. However, those safeguards made it difficult for a single party to win a clear majority in the parliament, and the second republic was plagued by political fragmentation rather than by dictatorial single-party rule. Its inability to cope with political disintegration was one of the reasons why it was brought to an end by military officers in 1980.

Kemalist secularism was preserved in the 1960s, and Islam continued to function in a democratically constituted state. The progress of liberal secularism was not overtaken by radical secularism, and the initial strength of Kemalism provided sufficient momentum for survival. In contrast to the secularism in the Arab East, Kemal's secularism, from the very beginning, was closely identified with indigenous interests and did not have to undergo the process, which occurred in the Arab East, of trying to adapt secularism to local conditions. However, after the 1960 revolution, the stability of the Turkish political system was not as secure, and a variety of new ideas began to emerge. In some ways, Kemalism was becoming the established view to be preserved by "conservatives" rather than the radical ideology it had been in the days following World War I.

Governmental Reformism in Iran. The reform programs initiated by the rulers of Iran during the twentieth century never secured as broad a base of support as the those of the Kemalists in Turkey. In Iran, the organized conservative and fundamentalist religious leaders, as well as the more radical modern-educated groups, provided continuing and often effective opposition from two different perspectives. Between the two, the monarchy represented modernizing reformism that was neither Islamic enough to satisfy the ulama nor liberal enough to satisfy the educated classes. The foundations for this situation had been clearly laid during the nineteenth century, and the major themes were the efforts to create an effectively modernized Iran, to limit the potential tyranny of the shah, and to restrict, if not eliminate, foreign influence in Iranian affairs.

In the constitutional movement at the beginning of the century, the ulama, along with their allies, the traditional merchants, joined forces with the small, but articulate, group of modern-educated Iranians. This alliance succeeded in imposing some limits on the shah's power, but the constitutionalists were unable to agree on many points, including the role of Islam in the new political system. Neither they nor the shah was able to prevent foreign troops and agents from substantial interference in the country during World War I, and they also could not prevent the discovery of oil in Iran in 1908 or the exploitation of Iran's oil resources by the British-owned Anglo-Persian Oil Company (APOC).

At the end of World War I, Iran appeared to be lapsing into another era of internal anarchy and foreign domination. However, in 1921, the commander of the most effective military unit in the Iranian army, Reza Khan (1878–1944), joined forces with a modern-educated intellectual, Ziya ud-Din Tabatabai, to take control of the government. Ziya was soon forced out, and Reza became the commander of the armed forces, then war minister, prime minister, and finally, in 1925, he was crowned shah. As Reza Shah Pahlavi, he ruled Iran until 1941.

Reza initiated a program of rigorous reform and has often been compared with his contemporary, Ataturk. However, in many ways he was closer to Mehmet Ali in Egypt. He worked to create a strong, modernizing dynastic state rather than a nationalist, parliamentary regime, and to some extent, this line of development was the product of Iranian conditions at the time. When he assumed power, there was the possibility that he would declare Iran to be a republic, but the rapid mobilization of opposition to that step by the ulama made the republican option appear impossible.

In his reform program, Reza concentrated on creating a strong central government. He built a national army and used it to crush tribal and provincial forces, bringing about an effective, if militarily imposed, national unity. He expanded the modern means of transportation and communication, enlarged the government administrative structure, initiated a large number of social and legal reforms, and developed the system of modern education. Although this program hastened the process of modernization in Iran, its implementation depended more upon coercion than upon persuasion, and the program remained tied to the monarchy rather than expanding to be a national cause or ideology.

In the area of religion, Reza was not so much a secularist as a leader who attempted to bring religious institutions and leaders under the control of the state. There was little, if any, ideological dimension to this effort, The basic structure of Shi'i theology and political theory remained based on the principles of the imamate and the importance of the *mujtahids,* but once Reza had established himself in power, there was little that the ulama could do to utilize that religious tradition to oppose him. In the face of active suppression, they assumed a subdued political quietism while Reza progressively narrowed their legal, educational, and economic roles in Iranian society. Although he made some compromises with religious sensibilities, in general, as one religious leader recalled in 1967, Reza "did not even go through the motions of appealing to the religious."[28] Instead, he made some effort to create a structure of religious officialdom that was subservient to the state, and the ulama in that group appeared to be the major figures of the era in religious terms.

As a part of his policy of strengthening the monarchy, Reza worked to revive an awareness of the pre-Islamic Persian tradition as he hoped that an explicitly Persian nationalism would counter the influence of the religious leaders. In the long run, the only significant impact of this activity was to reinforce the Shi'i doctrines that maintained the illegitimacy, in Islamic terms, of any monarchy other than that of the imam himself. Nevertheless, Reza strengthened the monarchy as a power in Iran. The creation of a strong military made it possible for him to have firm control of the country, and when he was overthrown, it was by Russian and British forces rather than by internal opposition.

Reza was deposed in 1941 when British and Russian troops occupied Iran, and he was succeeded by his son, Mohammad Reza Shah Pahlavi

(1919–1980), who was young and inexperienced. Between 1941 and 1953, Iran passed through a period of active political development. A variety of groups, representing the full range of the Iranian political spectrum, struggled for power, and much of that political development was made possible by the development of modern education and communications during the Reza era. In the struggle, the major groups were activist ulama of a fundamentalist style, liberal and middle-class nationalists, well-organized radical secularists, and the groups associated with the monarchy and the armed forces. For a brief period in 1951–1953, the nationalists won control under the leadership of Mohammad Mosaddiq, and the government nationalized the Anglo-Iranian Oil Company (APOC had changed its name in 1935) but was unable to establish permanent political dominance. With the support of the military and others, Mohammad Reza Shah assumed full control of the government in 1953, and the monarchy reassumed its dominant position in Iran.

Mohammad Reza Shah continued the basic governmental reform efforts of his father, but in a more organized manner. Like his father, the shah's program stood between the more radical expectations of the modern-educated class and the conservative ideals of the ulama. Although he faced some opposition from both groups, including a series of major demonstrations in 1963 led by important ulama, he was able by co-option and coercion to keep the monarchy in firm control of Iran through the decade of the 1960s.

The year 1963 was an important turning point in the development of the shah's program of reforms. Up to that point, his primary concerns had been the consolidation of the power position of the monarchy, but it then became necessary to expand the base of support for the monarchy as well as to pay greater attention to programs of social and economic development. The result was the proclamation of the White Revolution in 1963, which was a cluster of specific programs that aimed at accelerating the process of the socioeconomic modernization of Iran, with the most important "principle" being the land reform that had begun in 1962. That and other "principles," like profit sharing for factory workers and the nationalization of forest resources, reflect the popularity at the time of more radical socialist ideas.

The White Revolution was proclaimed in the same year that Faysal in Saudi Arabia announced his ten-point program of pragmatic fundamentalism. However, in contrast to the Saudi program, the shah's reforms in general and the White Revolution in particular did not represent a significant reorientation of Islamic thought. In his speech from the throne delivered to the opening of a new Majlis session on 6 October 1967, in which he assessed the White Revolution, there was only the briefest mention of Islam and the high ideals of the faith were generally alluded to but not concretely related to the principles of the revolution. Shi'i Islam remained basically as it was before Mohammad Reza Shah, who put forth no new theology of Islamic rule and no principle of secularism in an Islamic society.

The vague theology of the reformist monarchy was supplemented by Mohammad Reza Shah, however, in two ways. First, he continued and expanded his father's attempts to identify the Iranian monarchy with the traditions of the pre-Islamic Persian Empire. Two major events symbolized this effort to stress the idea of monarchical continuity and the strength of the current dynasty and, not accidentally, to show that the dynasty was Persian in a special way and not dependent upon the Islamic institutions that were controlled by the sometimes dissident ulama. Those two events were the ceremonies accompanying the coronation of the shah and Queen Farah in 1967 and the huge festival commemorating "the 2500th anniversary" of the Iranian empire in 1971.

The second way in which Mohammad Reza Shah supplemented the monarchist ideology was by claiming that he had a special divine mission to rule. He reported that he had had special visions of major Islamic figures and that his life had been miraculously saved on a number of occasions. However, neither the divine mission nor the ancient Persian tradition represented a fully articulated basis for a monarchy when the dominant majority of the people were Muslims. His reformist monarchy survived as long as he remained an adept and realistic political manipulator and leader in control of a strong military force, which was clearly the case from 1953 until at least the end of the 1960s.

The reformist monarchy of the Pahlavi dynasty was neither explicitly secularist nor essentially religious. It replaced the inept Qajar dynasty and created a strong central government in a country with many diverse elements, and through its programs of modernization, it succeeded in controlling and balancing those elements for more than half a century. That monarchy, which reached the peak of its power during the 1960s, represented an important stage in the development of an Islamic country but did not, itself, represent a significant redefinition of the Islamic experience.

Reformism and the Afghan Monarchy. Afghanistan had long been a homeland for military empires, but a more "national" monarchy did not emerge until the eighteenth century. At that time, a major tribal chieftain established the Durrani dynasty and a conquest empire, and despite internal feuds and tribal divisions, the dynasty was able to establish an Afghan kingdom. The nineteenth century was a time of great turmoil, and dynastic and tribal conflicts and the growing expansion of the British and Russian Empires encroached on Afghan territory. One branch of the dynasty established itself as the amirs of Kabul, and that family gradually expanded its power until Abd al-Rahman Khan (1844–1901) effectively unified the country. Facing a strong Russian threat, Abd al-Rahman allied himself with the British, who recognized him as the ruler of Afghanistan in return for his accepting British control of Afghan foreign affairs. During his reign, the boundaries of contemporary Afghanistan were defined in a series of treaties. His son, Habib Allah, ruled from 1901 until 1919 during a time of relative internal stability, and the position of the dynasty was firmly consolidated.

The stage was set for Afghanistan's postwar modernizing reformer, King Amanallah (1892–1960). Habib Allah was murdered in 1919 under circumstances that are still disputed, although various imperialist plots have been suspected. During Habib Allah's reign, some efforts had been made to reduce British control, and a small movement in favor of national independence and modernizing reform had developed. A key figure in that movement was Mahmud Tarzi (1865–1933), who lived in the eastern Mediterranean area where he had come into contact with Jamal al-Din al-Afghani and the Young Turks. Tarzi returned to Afghanistan during the days of Habib Allah and published a newspaper, which attacked both European imperialism and the conservative Muslim resistance to change. His daughter married Habib Allah's son, Amanallah, and through his son-in-law, many of Tarzi's ideas became government policy in the years after World War I.

Amanallah's first major act was to demand full independence for Afghanistan from the British. He declared a holy war, united general Afghan opinion behind him, and succeeded in winning British recognition of Afghan independence in both internal and foreign affairs. Afghanistan, like Turkey and Iran, was able to secure national independence early in the twentieth century, and that independence opened the way for the initiation of a government-led program of modernization. Amanallah attempted to modernize the army and to build a modern system of education. He expanded the transportation and communications system and worked to reorganize the structure of the central government. In all of those efforts, he used many foreign advisers.

Those reforms rapidly aroused opposition within Afghanistan. The modernization program directly undermined the power of both the great tribal leaders and the religious notables, and as a result, religiotribal revolts soon broke out. The resistance was primarily conservative in style, objecting to change. The dominant form of Islam in the country is Sunni, so there were not the doctrinal antimonarchical tones that there were in Iran, but the religious leaders saw Amanallah as a threat to their position and their faith. Amanallah did not develop a formal ideology of reform but, rather, was similar to the early-nineteenth-century reformers in his pragmatic approach.

However, he was an enthusiast who moved more rapidly than was practical. He was unable to create a nationalist loyalty to reform as Ataturk did, nor did he create a strong army to implement his reforms by coercion as Reza did. Mahmud Tarzi observed, "Amanallah has built a beautiful monument without a foundation."[29]

In 1928, Amanallah's army was unable to stop a major tribal revolt, and rebellion soon spread. A military adventurer captured Kabul, Amanallah was forced to flee from the country, and he spent the rest of his life in exile. The anarchy soon produced a reaction, and another member of the royal family, Muhammad Nadir (d. 1933), was able to reestablish control. He set in motion a policy that was committed to Afghan independence and open to gradual modernization, but he avoided dramatic reforms that would anger the conservatives. He cooperated with the great tribal notables and worked to placate the religious leaders He had succeeded in creating a sufficiently stable situation so that when he was murdered in 1933, the throne passed to his son, Muhammad Zahir (b. 1913), without incident. Muhammad Zahir continued to follow the restrained policies of his father and introduced reforms when they were possible without too great offense being given to the tribal and religious leaders.

This spirit of conservative reform remained the hallmark of Muhammad Zahir's policy, but it meant that a new, modern-educated class developed slowly. That class became an important force in Afghan politics as its discontentment with the slow pace of modernization grew and later led to the emergence of a more radical group. However, the dominant power for setting the tone of government policy remained with the more conservative tribal and religious leaders. Following World War II, Afghanistan followed a policy of careful neutralism in international affairs, although after the British withdrawal from India, relations with Russia became closer, and increasing Soviet aid gave an impetus to both the modernization programs and the more radical groups in Afghanistan. In 1953, General Muhammad Daoud Khan became prime minister. Under his leadership, Afghanistan attempted to reject the southern border of the country, the Durand line, which had been drawn by the British at the end of the nineteenth century, and that attempt aroused nationalist feelings that provided popular support for the government. During the decade of Daoud's leadership, the government remained paternalistic in style but accelerated the process of modernization in economic and social areas. Pressures also built for greater political modernization, and an alliance of educated groups and religious leaders helped to bring about a new constitutional regime in 1963.

In the constitution promulgated in 1964, Islam was declared the religion of Afghanistan, and the monarchy was confirmed, although members of the royal family were prohibited from participation in political parties. In defining the role of Islam, a more liberal approach emerged. In the legal system, no law was to be repugnant to the basic principles of Islam, but Islamic law was to be applied only in cases not covered by other laws. In other words, an Islamic modernism that recognized *ijtihad* provided the basic religious tone for this constitution. The new regime was intellectually satisfying to many, but in the following decade, the many divisions within Afghan society manifested themselves, which led to political instability.

The decade of the 1960s was a time of liberal experiment in Afghanstan, and there was a departure from paternalistic, "strong-man" modernization with a conservative tone. Like the White Revolution in Iran and the Saudi pragmatic fundamentalism initiated in 1963, the constitutional regime was an effort to provide a more modern structure in a society in which the majority of the Muslims were still quite conservative in their views. In Afghanistan, this modernizing effort only provided an opening for divisive forces to reduce the effectiveness of the central government and slow the pace of effective modernization.

Radical Adaptationism in the Northern Tier

The emergence of more radical thought in the northern tier was limited by the existence of reformist, independent governments. Although some modern-educated Muslims felt that their governments were not initiating sufficiently drastic reforms or moving as rapidly as they would like, the fact that the governments were clearly independent made opposition more difficult. In the nationalist mood of the time, radical criticism of government policy was easily viewed as an attack by "foreign" elements and ideas, and in addition, many of the intellectuals realized that attacking the government would aid the conservatives rather than hasten the transformation. A final element is that the reformist approaches of the government had an appeal to the more radical intellectuals, and few could fully resist the idea of an "indigenous" and activist reform effort. It was not until the government reform efforts either faltered or became more conservative, trying to protect past achievements rather than creating new ones, that significant radical groups emerged.

The relationship between the radical groups and Islam was relatively limited. As a part of their desire for social transformation, the radicals usually viewed the leaders and institutions of Islam as backward and obstacles to progress. In the northern tier countries, there was little radical effort to redefine Islam in modern terms, as the radicals were content with making vague generalizations about Islam as a socialist or revolutionary religion, if

Islam was not simply rejected as a conservative social force. In this way, northern tier radicalism tended to have few direct ties with local religiocultural traditions. The closest ties came when some groups espoused the cause of communal nationalism, but, as happened in Iran with the communist group that supported Azerbaijan autonomy, the "main line" radical groups were associated with Russian communism and were often the objects of nationalist suspicion.

Radicalism and Communism in Turkey. The major factor governing the history of radicalism in Turkey was the existence of a successful, already relatively radical program that was government policy after the establishment of Ataturk's regime. Before that time, there had been small socialist groups and parties that had had only limited success in the days of the Young Turks, but the generally chaotic conditions at the end of World War I provided an opportunity for more extensive activities. Intellectuals and workers who had been in Europe and Russia returned and formed a number of small parties that made some progress, but they were soon overtaken by the emergence of the Kemalist nationalist movement. In the Anatolian Peninsula, a more active alternative to that movement emerged in the form of the Green Army, a group that brought together a number of local resistance groups fighting against the Greeks. At first the nationalist movement cooperated with those groups, but finally, when it was clear that the Green Army could not be controlled by the Grand National Assembly, it was defeated by Kemalist forces.

The Green Army combined a variety of intellectuals and military adventurers, and it proposed a radically new economic order with state ownership of the means of production. At the same time, it asserted that its program did not conflict with Islam or the national cause. "In short, the Green Army stood for an amalgam of rather radical socialism with Islamic and nationalistic overtones."[30] Other communist and socialist groups at the time did not have a military organization and made less of a point of relating their ideas to Islam. In the end, they, too, were outlawed, and formal communist and socialist organizations disappeared.

Many of the major figures in those groups were integrated into the Kemalist movement and given positions in the government. They assisted in the definition of Kemalism, and they moved to a more nationalist position. In the early 1930s, one such group was associated with a periodical called *Kadro,* which helped to define the statist economic policy of the government. Those group members who remained in some Communist party organization assisted in the process of the disintegration of their groups by engaging in a number of factional disputes.

When the radical leftist Turks again succeeded in organizing themselves on the political scene, it was during the years of party politics following World War II. At that time, at least from a radical perspective, Kemalism had become relatively conservative, and it was possible to identify a radical position that was more clearly distinguished from government policy than had been the case in the days of Ataturk. That position was emphasized during the days of Democratic party rule, and following the establishment of the second republic, the Turkish Workers' party was formed. By that time, radical parties were no longer necessarily tied to the Soviet Union, and the Workers' party appealed to some intellectuals and labor union groups. Although it never became a large party, it received around 3 percent of the votes in the general elections of 1965 and 1969, but that was only a reflection of the emergence of a reasonably well-organized and active extreme left in the Turkish political spectrum. The religious position of that new left was one of militant opposition to traditional Islamic influence in society, but because that opposition took a basically anti-Sunni form, the radical left drew some support from the Shi'i minority groups in Turkey as well as from the more radical labor unions and intellectuals.

Radicalism, in contrast to Kemalism, did not produce a redefinition of Islam or a reorientation of its role in society. However, by the 1960s, it did begin to free itself from the stigma of association with a foreign power. It emerged at that time as a Turkish force advocating more active changes in society and became a major style of criticism of the Kemalist tradition as it was becoming more conservative. Increasingly in the 1960s, the new left engaged in militant activities and occasional terrorism, thus presenting a challenge to Turkish political stability. Although the Workers' party was outlawed in 1971, the radical position had become firmly established by that time.

Radicalism and Islam in Iran. The government's reform program in Iran was both less radical in its orientation and less successful in winning the support of the modern-educated class in Iran than the one in Turkey, which gave greater opportunity for an independent secularist radicalism in Iran. However, there were still grave problems for this position, which were posed by the strength of the independent state and the powerful appeal of nationalism and Islam as alternative bases for an ideology of reform. Radicalism faced the problems of identification with a foreign power and of an inability to mobilize mass support on the basis of its ideology.

In this context, three strands of a more secularist approach have interacted in Iran during the twentieth century. The most coherent of these, at least in organizational terms, is the development of communism and a socially radical secularism. The second is a politically oriented liberal nationalism, which is vigorously opposed to foreign influence in Iran and aware of the need for socioeconomic reform but more conservative than the communist approach in terms of actual programs. A third strand is the development of a more intellectually oriented reinterpretation of the Iranian heritage and the needs of modern Iran.

The communist movement in Iran emerged during the last years of World War I. A group called Adalat was organized among the Persian workers in Baku, in the Russian Caucasus region, and in 1918, they stormed the Iranian consulate there. The group received Russian help in becoming active within Iran, it joined forces with a local nationalist movement in the northern province of Gilan, and soon helped in establishing the "Persian Soviet Socialist Republic."

The fortunes of the Gilan movement illustrate the problems of organized communism in Iran. By associating themselves with the liberal nationalist Jangali movement in Gilan led by Kuchek Khan, the communists were able to gain a basis for support, but the communist ability to maintain that support weakened rapidly. The dependence of the local communists upon the Soviet Union raised doubts in the minds of nationalist Iranians, and the weakness of that reliance upon a foreign state was shown by the collapse of the Gilan movement when Soviet policy shifts resulted in the withdrawal of Soviet military aid. The other major communist difficulty was ideological: Opposition to religion is not popular in Iran, but communist enthusiasts frequently press the issue. In the case of the Gilan movement, the alliance with Kuchek Khan was broken soon after it was formed and one of the principle reasons was the vigorous antireligious campaign of the new communist leaders. They closed mosques, forbade religious instruction, and enacted other measures that alienated not only the conservative population but Kuchek Khan himself.

The twin obstacles of ideology and ties to a foreign power remained for communism in Iran, but the rapid growth of the more secularist, educated class and the appeal to the emerging labor groups gave organized communism a larger potential basis for support. The rigid controls of the era of Reza Shah limited the ability of the communists to take advantage of this changing situation, but the collapse of Reza's regime and the occupation of northern Iran by Russian forces provided the opportunity for the organization of the Tudeh party. The Tudeh offered a program of radical socioeconomic reform that had substantial appeal, but following World War II, a branch of the party became involved in the Azerbaijan separatist movement, and the old problems of being tied to the policy of a foreign power again weakened communism's appeal in a time of nationalist fervor. However, by careful alliance with nationalist causes and by providing a challenge to the established order, organized communism in Iran has been able to attract a wide range of adherents.

The relationship between Islam and communism in Iran is complex. Although the antireligious aspects of communist ideology, when openly espoused, created problems for groups like the Gilan leaders and the Tudeh, tactical alliances between communists and religious leaders have often been possible, and those alliances became an increasingly important aspect of Iranian politics as the monarchy became stronger. By the mid-1960s, the Tudeh had been outlawed for some time, and it was possible to conclude that "although the prospects for a renewed Communist assault on the Iranian system may be remote, Communist radicalism remains a source of ideological attraction."[31] At that time, however, it seemed clear that the major rival of communism in challenging the Iranian sociopolitical system was a nationalist and noncommunist left. As was true in many areas of the world at that time, it was indigenous secular socialism rather than religious revival that seemed to be the most important developing sociopolitical force.

The second strand of the more secularist approach in Iran is liberal nationalism, which has been a less well-organized but more popular force in Iran than communism, and its strength grew as the modern-educated class became larger. Beginning in the late nineteenth century, liberal nationalists worked to create a democratic and an independent Iran. They played a role in the constitutionalist movement at the beginning of the century but were unable to provide organized and effective leadership in the face of the strength of the conservative forces, foreign intervention, and their own internal divisions. During the era of Reza Shah, they were forced into opposition, and their liberal aims of limiting the power of an autocratic monarchy threw them into alliance again with the more conservative elements of society.

Following World War II, the liberal nationalists emerged as a major political force. Strengthened by the growth of the modern-educated classes and their identification with the nationalist cause, the liberal nationalists came to power in 1950 under the leadership of Mohammed Mosaddiq, a widely respected politician with great popular support. However, he was unable to establish a firmly coordinated political movement, and liberal nationalism remained a loose alliance of sometimes competing groups. The issue that helped bring them to power was the nationalization of the Anglo-Iranian Oil Company, but the pressures created in the subsequent dispute soon led to the collapse of the alliance and the reestablishment of the monarchy as the dominant political force.

By the 1960s, the liberal nationalists had begun to organize opposition to the shah but faced many difficulties. The shah's White Revolution included many programs they advocated, but his increasingly autocratic rule made it difficult for them to support him, and at the same time, the shah's repressive measures prevented any large-scale, effective organization of opposition. Those difficulties provided a practical reason for adopting a less secularist tone. Shi'i Islam presented a sound and fully articulated ideological basis for opposition to the expanding power of the monarchy, and a movement emerged that was a synthesis of the more liberal religious leaders with the more religiously inclined liberal nationalists. This was the Freedom movement, and its leadership included Mahdi Bazargan, an engineer who was also a writer on religious topics, and a leading *mujtahid,* Ayatollah Mahmud Taliqani. Through the thinking of such men, an ideological position developed that advocated radical socioeconomic reform in the framework of the Islamic tradition. In this way, the foundations were beginning to be laid for a fully indigenous and Islamic radicalism that was compatible with the traditions of modernizing liberal nationalism.

This ideological position was clearly less secularist than the earlier liberal nationalism, and it maintained the comprehensive validity of Islam in all areas of life. In the early 1960s, men like Bazargan and Taliqani were stressing the importance of the active involvement of the ulama in political affairs, and they were also working to reformulate the Islamic tradition in terms that would be comprehensible and acceptable to modern-educated Muslims. The old Westernizing liberalism was becoming transformed into a more Islamic movement, and in that transformation, people like Taliqani provided a link between the liberal nationalist tradition and the more fundamentalist religious leaders who were also taking a more active role, like Ayatollah Khomeini.

The third strand of the Islamic experience in twentieth-century Iran might be called secularist thought. In literature and scholarly studies, a wide variety of thinkers have worked to analyze the Persian and Islamic traditions, utilizing modern critical techniques in a lively and dynamic manner. Although communists and liberal nationalists have a strong political orientation, there is also a modernizing tradition that is not directly involved in politics, although it has political implications. Only a few such writers can be mentioned.

Ahmad Kasrawi Tabrizi (1890–1946) began his career as a religious teacher but soon became a lawyer, judge, and then history teacher. His historical studies covered political and literary history and had a major influence on the thinking of the emerging educated classes. He became a vigorous critic of social institutions and religious practices and felt that popular Shi'i practices hindered constructive progress, he supported representative government and a cooperative style of capitalism based on social welfare, and he believed that he was presenting an ideological path that was not a new religion but the successor to and a continuation of Islam. He was murdered by religious extremists in 1946.

A sharp contrast to Kasrawi is provided by Seyyed Hossein Nasr, who received a modern technical education at the Massachusetts Institute of Technology, studied the history of science at Harvard University, and taught for a number of years at the University of Tehran after his return to Iran in 1958. In his work, Seyyed Hossein presents a vigorous modern form of the Sufi tradition that has an appeal to many non-Muslims, and his approach to Shi'ism is in philosophical rather than in political terms. In works like *Ideals and Realities of Islam*, he argues that the diversity of Islam is part of its strength. "Sunnism and Shi'ism are both orthodox interpretations of the Islamic revelation contained providentially within Islam in order to enable it to integrate people of different psychological constitutions into itself."[32] Rather than writing a sociohistorical critique of Islam, Nasr's wide range of works presents a reaffirmation of Islam in mystical-philosophical terms.

The wide spectrum of positions is visible in the literary activities of the major Iranian writers, as their views range from sharp social criticism of religious conservatism to glorification of the Islamic and Persian traditions. Through the journalistic and literary activities of such authors, educated Iranians were made aware of social problems and Western ideas, and through those writings, the scope of Islamic thought in Iran was articulated and broadened.

Modernist and modernizing thought in Iran thus took many forms. Social and political radicalism and secularist thinking were often in opposition to the policies of the reformist monarchy, and in contrast to Kemalist Turkey, official reformism was unable to prevent or co-opt most intellectual movements that developed in the context of the modern conditions. Thus liberal and secularist modernism sometimes cooperated with the more explicitly Islamic movements, and each influenced the other in many ways. However, secularist thought did not change the essential nature of the Shi'i interpretations, and by the 1960s, there was a tendency for religiously influenced syntheses to emerge.

Radicalism in Afghanistan. During the twentieth century, radical secularist movements in the northern tier were least well organized in Afghanistan, and there, the more traditional loyalties and structures remained strong. Ironically, however, it was only in Afghanistan that the radicals actually assumed power in the years before 1980, which was due as much to the special conditions in the country and its international position as it was to any strength of the radicals themselves.

Early reformism under the leadership of King Amanallah, even though relatively moderate, was more extreme than most Afghans were willing to accept, and after Amanallah's fall, the more conservative reformism of the ruling dynasty generally moved rapidly enough to keep pace with the desires of the small educated class. There was a quiet republican sentiment among some in that class that was supported by the traditional tribal reservations about strong central government. That sentiment had few visible results until the period of parliamentary politics that began with the promulgation of the 1964 constitution.

In the more open political arena of the parliamentary constitutional regime of the 1960s, a more articulate and active secularist movement emerged. The careful cooperation of the Soviet Union with the Afghan government had made a procommunist radicalism possible despite Afghan suspicions of foreign interference. Small parties and newspapers presented a variety of more secularist views, and the most important of these groups were associated with the Democratic People's party, or Khalq. That group split into two factions during the 1960s. One group centered around Nur Muhammad Taraki and the newspaper he published in 1966 called *Khalq*; the other group was more revolutionary in its pronouncements, but its major figures were active in the parliament of the time. This second faction was called Parcham after its weekly publication, and the major figures in it were Babrak Karmal and Dr. Anahita, a woman deputy from Kabul. The differences among these radicals were more over methods than ideology.

The doctrinal positions of both factions of the Khalq and the other radical secularists were pragmatic. There was little philosophical opposition to religion or presentation of theological atheism; the emphasis was on social transformation. The key parts of the radical program were land reform, changing the structure of ownership, liberation of women, and reduction of the power of religious and tribal organizations. This position appealed to many people in the emerging educated groups. Although the country continued to be dominated by the old elites, the moderate and conservative reformism of the monarchy could not inspire the students or the modern-educated classes. Already in the 1960s, although it was not clear at the time, the political and ideological spectrum was beginning to be divided into a vigorous radical minority and a relatively nonadaptationist Islamic position, with the moderate center unable to build an effective political position.

Summary. In the northern tier, radicalism developed in the context of governmental reformism within the independent states. When a government's programs were dynamic and successful, the radical position was preempted, but in those periods when governments remained conservative or became authoritarian, the radicals provided a secularist alternative. In contrast to the experience in the Arab East, however, the radical alternative in the northern tier was not successful in creating a visibly Islamic radicalism. The Tudeh and Khalq groups represented a secular and non-Islamic dimension of ideology within countries with dominant Muslim majorities.

Fundamentalism in the Northern Tier

During the twentieth century, both old and new forms of Islamic fundamentalism have been active. Some groups appear to be direct heirs of earlier traditions, and others have taken on the new form of activist associations similar to the Muslim Brotherhood. In either case, the success of the movements depends upon the ability of the reformist governments to control them. The appeal of the fundamentalists is based on the continuing vitality of the Islamic tradition, which is often preserved by the more conservative forces, and the inability of the modernizers to solve pressing problems within the northern tier societies. In this context, it must be emphasized that Islamic fundamentalism is not a conservative mood attempting to prevent change. Rather, in the context of the twentieth century, it represents an alternative program of social transformation and competes with the modernizers. When modernization programs are dynamic and provide a foundation for realistic hopes for progress, fundamentalist movements are less successful in their appeal for mass support.

Neo-Sufi Orders. Despite the programs of government reformers and their efforts to limit the strength of the older Islamic organizations, some of the Neo-Sufi orders have continued to command allegiance in northern tier countries. In Turkey, that allegiance has taken the form of secret and often terrorist activities. During the period of multiparty politics following World War II, some of the old organizations took advantage of the relaxation of Kemalist secularism to renew their public activities, and the best-known case was the revival of Tijaniyyah activity. The order had been encouraged by Abdulhamid II as a part of his Pan-Islamic policy, although it did not develop a large following in Turkey. Following the ban on Sufi orders in 1925, the Tijaniyyah, like the other orders, disappeared from public view, but in 1949, members of the order began publicly demanding a greater role for Islam in the Turkish republic. In a demonstration in the Grand National Assembly, members recited the then-illegal Arabic call to prayer, and the order gained prestige when the Arabic version was restored in the following year. At the same time, an Ankara business man, Kemal Pilavoglu, a member of the order, published books and led an attack on public monuments as being images prohibited by Islam. The destruction of statues of Ataturk and other acts of violence led to Pilavoglu's trial and conviction in 1952. Although the Tijaniyyah organized some demonstrations at the time, its importance rapidly declined after the imprisonment of its leader. The decline of the Tijaniyyah did not, however, mean the end of Turkish fundamentalist activism, only that it has taken different forms in subsequent years.

The other area where older-style organizations have continued to have influence is Afghanistan. There, great religious families associated with *tari-qah*s and the old social order have been prominent in leading the opposition to modernizing reforms. One of these families was the Mujaddidi, a family associated with the Naqshbandiyyah, which had come to Afghanistan following World War I. That family had been active in Muslim revolts against communist rule in Central Asia and was a vigorous opponent of modernizing reform programs. Members of the family were involved in the dismantling of Amanallah's programs in the 1930s and were leaders in the conservative faction during the parliamentary era of 1963–1973. Another great family was the Gaylani, descendants of Abd al-Qadir al-Gaylani, the founder of the Qadiriyyah. In the period following the overthrow of Amanallah, the great religious families were more conservative than fundamentalist in style, and they were able to slow the pace of reform sufficiently so that more militant action was not necessary. However, the fundamentalist potential is clearly shown by the fact that when a radical regime came to power in the 1970s, these religious families provided much of the leadership for the emerging revolutionary groups. The transition from conservative to fundamentalist has also been a transition in organizational form from a clan- and *tariqah*-oriented structure to a more modern style of association or liberation movement.

Modern Fundamentalist Associations. One of the most dramatic aspects of fundamentalism in the northern tier is its ability to develop a variety of organizational formats to cope with changing political and social conditions. During the first two-thirds of the twentieth century, the ideological content of fundamentalism remained relatively constant but was expressed through political parties, private associations, and terrorist groups. It was not until the end of the 1960s that there were significant efforts at a redefinition of the core of the faith in fundamentalist terms.

Different groups proposed radical alterations of the existing social order, and they sometimes came into conflict with conservatives as well as with modernizing secularists. As a result, they usually drew their support from groups in society whose lives had been significantly altered by the process of modernization but who felt that they were not participating in the benefits of such development. In many cases, this element was reinforced by a sense that personal and cultural identity was being destroyed without an effective new identity being created. It is thus possible to say that fundamentalist associations in the northern tier have often been the products of moderniza-tion rather than remnants of an older social order.

Fundamentalist Groups in Turkey. The success of the Kemalist reform program and the ability of the reformist government to control, if not sup-press, fundamentalist sentiments means that for many years, observers felt that Kemalist secularism had been almost completely successful. However, the attachment of the Turks to Islam remained strong, and as secularist control loosened, Islamic fundamentalism found new ways of expressing itself.

One of the oldest groups maintaining opposition to secularist trends was the group led by Said Nursi (1867–1960). Originally a member of Ittihad-i Muhammadi, an Islamically oriented group in the days of the Young Turk Revolution, he later organized the Followers of Nur (Light). He called for the reestablishment of an Islamic state that would be based on Islamic law and ruled by the ulama. Following his death in 1960, the movement lost much of its dynamism, but it was felt to be a viable threat, and successive governments took strong measures against the group.

With the development of a multiparty political system following World War II, a number of parties emerged whose programs called for a revival of Islamic values in politics and society. Although those groups have never been as large as the two major parties, they have come to represent a significant part of the Turkish political scene, showing the continuing strength of fundamentalism.

The oldest of these parties is the Nation party, which was established in 1948. It has gone through a number of organizational changes as a result of combination with other parties or, at times, of being outlawed for anti-Kemalist activities. In its form as the Republican Peasants' Nation party, formed in 1958 by the merger of the Republican Nation party and the Peasant party of Turkey, it was the only party other than the Republican People's party to survive the 1960 revolution as a separate party. In the 1961 elections, the Republican Peasants' Nation party received 14 percent of the votes, but, as other parties became established, it received only 2.2 percent in the 1965 elections. As the party's fortunes declined, it looked for new leadership, which it found in Alparslan Turkes (b. 1917), who reorganized the party as the National Action party in 1969. During the 1970s, under Turkes's leadership, the emphasis of the party's program shifted from Islamic to Turkish nationalist themes. Special militant youth squads were organized, and they attacked leftists and others, which was part of the development of political terrorism on the Turkish scene.

During the 1960s, other small parties were created, and they espoused a wide range of economically conservative programs and joined those with an emphasis on religion. Within the major parties, there were also more religiously oriented factions. During the decade, there was a tendency for those groups both to compete and to cooperate, and out of that situation there emerged a relatively strong religious party led by a former member of the Justice party, Necmettin Erbakan (b. 1926). In its first form, the National Order party, organized in 1970, it was outlawed for antisecular activities, but Erbakan soon reorganized it as the National Salvation party, which won almost 12 percent of the votes in the 1973 elections. The party gave priority to "strengthening moral values" and opposed "wild liberalism,"[33] and it received at least some support from the remnants of the Naqshbandiyyah and the followers of Nursi.

The diversity of the religiously oriented parties in Turkey is illustrated by the Turkish Unity party, which was formed in 1966. Its party emblem contains twelve stars representing the twelve Shi'i imams, and its original appeal was to the Shi'i minority in central Turkey. In the 1969 elections, it won almost 3 percent of the votes and gained eight seats in parliament. In contrast to the Sunni parties, whose economic programs favor free enterprise or state capitalism, the Turkish Unity party moved in the direction of more socialist platforms and eventually joined forces with the leftist groups in the Turkish Labor party.

In Turkey, the vigorous reaffirmation of Islam thus took the form of activist political parties, which was possible in the framework of a multiparty system. It was not until late in the 1960s that some of the associations began to engage in more militant and directly revolutionary actions. The dominance of Kemalist secularism limited their ability to win widespread support, so they moved outside of the regular political arena in some cases.

Religious Activism in Iran. In Iran during the twentieth century, one of the major features of the Islamic experience has been the interaction between the religious leadership and the institutions of the state. In this interaction, the ulama have played a leading role, supported by the teachings of Shi'i Islam, and the major themes involved have been opposition to foreign interference and to monarchical absolutism. Because of Iranian independence, both the monarchy and the religious leadership were able to act with greater freedom than was the case in countries that remained under direct European control.

Ulama activism played a prominent part in three major episodes of twentieth-century Iranian history before the Islamic revolution of the 1970s. The first of these was the constitutional movement early in the century, when the religious leaders joined forces with other groups to gain a constitution. However, following World War I, the dictatorship of Reza Shah was able to suppress most of the effective political activity by the ulama. They had succeeded in demonstrating the political inadvisability of creating a republic in the 1920s and were a conservative force that set some limits upon Reza's programs.

It was only after the overthrow of Reza in 1941 that specifically religious forces began to play an overt political role, and that revival is associated with a new fundamentalist association the Fida'iyyan-i Islam, and activist religious leader, Abu al-Qasim Kashani (d. 1962). The new revivalists were not closely associated with the religious establishment and were often critical of the political quietism of the major *mujtahids*. Although the revivalists reflected the ideological principles of Shi'i Islam, the movements were less traditional in format.

The Fida'iyyan was formed in Tehran in 1945 as a militant group dedicated to the enforcement of the rules of the faith and to opposing secularism. The leading figure in the movement was a young religious teacher, Mujtaba Nawwab Safawi (1923–1955), who had had some technical education and had worked briefly for the Anglo-Iranian Oil Company. He was an effective orator and a charismatic leader. He was not a skilled religious scholar but used general Islamic themes as the basis for opposition to the government and foreign influence. His followers were drawn from the lower-middle-class and the lower-class urban population, and he mobilized them into an effective urban guerrilla corps dedicated to creating an Islamic state and society.

Like the Muslim Brotherhood in Egypt and fundamentalist groups elsewhere, the Fida'iyyan emphasized the universal and comprehensive validity of Islam. One of its publications explained, for example, "We believe that Islam comprises and regulates all human affairs and could solve all problems which the world is facing today."[34] There was an emphasis on the unification of all Muslims and an avoidance of sectarianism by returning to the original form of Islam as practiced by the Prophet and his companions. To accomplish this, the Fida'iyyan called for a holy war against those people who had departed from the faith, ant the group committed a series of murders, including the killing of the secularist intellectual Kasrawi in 1946 and various government officials. The group was suppressed in 1955, and the major leaders were executed. The movement itself declined after that, but the theme of militant fundamentalism had been firmly established.

The most prominent individual in the revival of militant Islam in Iran after World War II was Abu al-Qasim Kashani. He often defended the Fida'-iyyan, and they worked together, but he was not the leader of the organization. He was one of the less socially prominent ulama who developed a large popular following because of his vigorous defense of Islam and his militant opposition to imperialism. He had been educated in Iraq and was involved in anti-British activity there during and following World War I. He was not politically active during the era of Reza's rule but emerged as a spokesman for militant Islam after World War II. He became the speaker of the parliament during the Mosaddiq era and helped to organize mass support for the nationalist movement. However, by 1953, he had begun to oppose the secularism of the liberal nationalists and feared that Mosaddiq was working to establish an unconstitutional dictatorship As a result, Kashani broke with Mosaddiq and gave his support to the over throw of the nationalist regime in 1953.

Kashani was familiar with the works of al-Afghani and Abduh as well as having studied the traditional religious disciplines. However, he was more action oriented than philosophical in his approach to Islam. He believed that Islam and modernization were compatible but that purification of the Islamic society was necessary, and he rejected secularist approaches as an imperialist method for weakening Islam. He said: "Islam warns the Muslims to resist foreign dominance and exploitation and that is why the imperialists try to confuse Muslims by advocating separation of religion from politics. According to Islamic theories of government the religious leaders are required to guide the people in social as well as political affairs."[35]

The reestablishment of monarchical power in Iran in 1953 brought an end to the second major episode of religious activism and also laid the foundations for the third. In 1963, when the shah proclaimed the White Revolution, religious leaders again became politically active. The leading *mujtahid* from the end of World War II until 1961 had been Ayatollah Burujirdi (1909–1961), a politically quietist scholar whose inclinations helped to dampen religious activism in the 1950s. However, following his death, the emerging religious leaders were more willing to assume an active political role in opposing the monarchy, and some of the leading figures in this spirit were Ayatollah Ruhollah Khomeini and Ayatollah Shariat Madari. It was Khomeini who was the most active in leading the antishah demonstrations in 1963.

The significance of the 1963 demonstrations remains subject to debate. The shah and others who favored the reform programs as outlined in the White Revolution maintained that Khomeini and others opposed the reforms because they objected to the land reforms, which would reduce their economic power. Supporters of Khomeini argue that the real reason for the opposition was to oppose the growing U.S. influence in Iran and to prevent autocratic rule and the violation of the constitution. Whatever the reasons, the 1963 demonstrations were crushed, and the shah imposed substantial restrictions on the religious leaders. However, like the opposition to the tobacco concession in the nineteenth century, the 1963 movement brought the religious leadership into the center of the opposition to the monarchy, and from that time on, the ulama were to provide most of the leading spokesmen for the opposition movement.

Although the monarchical reforms appeared to be increasingly successful in the 1960s, the forces of militant Islam were gaining organizational experience and were reemerging as a major political force after a long period of quietism. Although observers in the 1960s felt that the role of the ulama was declining in the face of the monarchical reform programs, the foundations were being laid for the Islamic revolution of the 1970s.

Summary

During the first two-thirds of the twentieth century, the dominant Islamic style in the northern tier was a modernizing adaptationism. To many people, both participants and observers, modernizing reformism was triumphant by the 1960s, and the political independence of the three countries made it possible for the governments themselves to set the tone. With varying degrees of emphasis on secularism, modern political structures were created that appeared to be increasingly divorced from traditional Islam. A new type of Islamic society was emerging, and parliaments, modern economic sectors, and religious faith had their greatest influence in terms of an individual's personal life. This trend was reinforced by the intellectual developments, as modern-educated Muslims adopted a variety of secularist positions, ranging from a radical rejection of Islam to a vague identification of Islam as a source of morality.

At the same time, however, the general conservatism of personal life among the majority preserved a respect for the Islamic tradition, and by the 1960s, there were indications that that respect could provide the basis for a more active and overt role for Islam in society. The very process of modernization itself helped to create new forms for the expression of Islamic faith through political parties, study groups, and militant associations. Islam remained a dynamic element in society, despite the apparent success of Westernizing secularism.

Dominant Majorities in the Maghrib

A third major area of dominant Muslim majorities in the Islamic world is the "Arab West" or the Maghrib, the area of modern Tunisia, Algeria, and Morocco, and many of the challenges of the modern experience are clearly visible in that area. The great issue of the meaning of modernizing adaptationism was highlighted by the experience of French rule. In the Maghrib, instead of adaptationism being a matter of what techniques might be utilized and how an indigenous modernizing reformism might be defined, it became an issue of defending a distinctive identity against the threat of assimilation into Western culture. In the nineteenth-century, Islam had played a role in defining the special identity of society in the Maghrib against outside forces, and that role is an important part of the area's twentieth-century history.

Adaptationism in the Maghrib ran the risk of losing contact with the community if it went too far in the direction of a modernizing secularism. At the same time, religiously oriented nationalists could not separate themselves too rigidly from the modern-educated intellectuals without running the risk of pushing them into an assimilationist position or weakening the nationalist cause in the face of the great pressures of French domination. Therefore, neither radical secularism nor extreme fundamentalism emerged as a significant force in the Maghrib. Other difficulties faced those religious leaders who maintained a conservative style of Islam. Those who came to accept the existing conditions of French rule and collaborated with them wrote their own obituaries as important leaders. That was especially true of the leaders of the established *tariqahs,* who were open to attack on the grounds of both fundamentalist opposition to popular religious practices and nationalist resentment toward collaborationism.

Within this framework, the Islamic experience in the Maghrib has been closely tied to the three major stages of political evolution—the struggle for independence, the new state of independence, and the "postindependence" regime. In each of these stages, Islam has played an important but sometimes different role. The key issues that have emerged are the relationship of Islam to nationalism and the role of Islam in formulating a basic sense of national unity and ideology in the independent states.

Islam and the Struggle for Independence

French control took different forms in each of the three countries. As a result, the specific path to independence varied, but at least some general aspects were shared throughout the region, with events in one country often having an impact on developments in another. In general terms, there were common key factors. The French attitude of cultural superiority in each country forced people who were willing to cooperate with them to cut all ties of identity with their own culture or to accept a clearly subordinate position or, in the case of traditional notables, to be treated as benighted but useful museum pieces. In each country, the French exhibited a clear unwillingness to adapt or compromise unless forced to do so, making violent demonstrations and conflict a necessary part of nationalism.

Islam and Tunisian Nationalism. The period following World War I was a decisive one in shaping the nature of Tunisian nationalism and Islam's role in the struggle for independence. Many of the key groups of the past were no longer significant forces in political terms. The monarchy, which had been the leading reformist institution in the nineteenth century, had become simply a puppet institution under the French system of control. The ulama continued their quietist conservatism, cooperating with the French to a degree that made them unable to assume a role of nationalist leadership, even if they had chosen to do so. The liberal intellectuals of the Young Tunisian movement had been crushed in the suppression before and during World War I. Their assimilationist attitudes had some echo following the war but were increasingly impractical in the face of French cultural arrogance and political intransigence. What remained was the Islamically oriented nationalist position of men like Abd al-Aziz al-Thaʿalibi, who could appeal to the relatively conservative middle class and at least some of the increasing educated class.

At the end of the war, al-Thaʿalibi organized the Destour party, which demanded independence for Tunisia. Although al-Thaʿalibi and his associates were influenced by Salafiyyah ideas coming from Egypt, their party did not take a significant position in terms of Islamic reform. The party was radical in terms of its demands to the French but basically conservative in its social orientation, and it defined Tunisian nationalism in terms of Islamic and Arabic traditions. The Destour party was more of a mass movement than the Young Tunisians had been, and it laid the foundations through a nationwide organization for a mass nationalist party. However, its leadership tended to be confined to the urban Islamic middle class, which was centered in Tunis. In its approach, it relied on legalistic debate rather than on mass mobilization, and thus it did not have the strength to succeed in overcoming the restrictions imposed on the party's activities by the French.

The crucial role of Islam in mobilizing mass support for nationalism can be seen in the events that brought about the effective demise of the Destour party. The Destour presented itself as a defender of Islam, but by the late 1920s, it was the younger and more militant Tunisians who had had a modern education who were most effective in that role. Some of those younger men joined the Destour party but soon attempted to go beyond its conservative legalism. One of their major figures was Habib Bourguiba (b. 1903), a graduate of Sadiki College, which had been established by Khayr al-Din Pasha in the nineteenth century. Although Bourguiba had studied in France and was convinced of the need for major social reform in Tunisia, he vigorously defended the veil for women when that custom was attacked by a French socialist, saying that the Frenchman was trying to deprive Tunisians of their distinctive national identity. Bourguiba and his colleagues recognized the importance of modern ideas but rejected the idea of assimilation or "naturalization."

The issue of naturalization gave the younger nationalists a cause that enabled them to be united with the more religiously conservative majority of Tunisians. In 1923, the French made it possible for Tunisian Muslims to become French citizens, but few Tunisians took advantage of the opportunity because of the religious implications: It meant that a French Muslim would be tried in the French civil courts rather than in Islamic courts, which many Tunisians felt amounted to apostasy. In 1932, a mufti ruled that a naturalized Muslim could not be buried in a Muslim cemetery, which led to a series of demonstrations, and naturalized Tunisians were buried in Muslim cemeteries under armed guard only to be secretly exhumed later. Bourguiba vigorously supported the Muslim case in his newspaper, *L'Action Tunisienne,* which had begun publication in 1931. Since the leaders of the Destour party did little in this campaign and the conservative ulama remained quiet or compromised with the French on the issue, the younger nationalists could claim, as they did, that it was the modern-educated, nationalist youth and not the old conservatives who were the true defenders of Islam.

The young militants led by Bourguiba soon captured the leadership of the nationalist movement. The Destour Executive Committee censured Bourguiba when he led a demonstration on the burial issue in 1933, so he and his friends soon called their own party congress and created the Neo-Destour party in 1934. From then on, it was the Neo-Destour that led the struggle for independence, and not content with legal debates, the party created a mass organization that was able to mobilize the Tunisian people. After a long struggle, during which Bourguiba spent at least ten years in French jails, Tunisia became independent in 1956.

The thinking of the Neo-Destour leaders was clearly modern in orientation, but those men never adopted a definitely antireligious position. Bourguiba believed that a modernizing transformation of Tunisian society was necessary but that to accomplish this, a real sense of national solidarity was needed. That theory was especially true in the days of the struggle for independence. The value system common to all Tunisians was provided by Islam, and thus it had a crucial role both in obtaining independence and in providing unity in the struggle for modernization. One French administrator described these two dimensions of the Neo-Destour: "The Neo-Destour has often been reproached for its two faces: western and democratic before westerners, Islamic and xenophobic when it addresses its troops. The theorists of the party are nonetheless sincere in their love of Cartesianism. But, in a party of the people, they must speak the passionate language of the people."[36]

The key feature of Islam in Tunisia during the preindependence period was not that there was a modernist interpretation that emerged but, rather, that Islam provided the symbols and the vocabulary for a mobilization of the people in opposition to foreign rule. The instrument for that mobilization was a mass political party led by modern-educated men who were committed to the independence and modernization of Tunisia. Although accused by conservatives of atheism or hypocrisy, the extent of the identification of Neo-Destourian nationalism with Islam in the popular mind can be seen in the reported comment of an old Zaytuna shaykh in 1958, who said, "Whoever does not believe in the word of Bourguiba does not believe in the word of God or his Prophet."[37] It was not until after independence that a significant conflict between Neo-Destourian reformism and Islam arose, and even then the result was neither a radical secularism nor a vigorous fundamentalism.

Islam and Algerian Nationalism. The emergence of nationalism was a more complex process in Algeria. Although Tunisia had a relatively distinctive local identity, Algeria was not a separate area with special local characteristics before the time of the French conquest. In many ways, Algerian nationalism developed not as a movement to recover a lost national identity but as a movement to create and assert a special identity in the face of the destructive forces of French colonialism. Virtually no other area in the Islamic world faced such a concerted effort to destroy the basic social order. That effort not only took the form of a political and cultural offensive, but also utilized the establishment in the country of a large European settler population. In this context, the struggle was to define the meaning of being an Algerian, a process in which Islam played a significant role.

By the end of the World War I, there were few effective Algerian institutions around which nationalism could develop. The state was a French creation and an instrument of foreign control as well as settler domination. Tribal leaders had long been crushed into submission during almost a century of direct French rule, and most religious leaders collaborated with the French in a conservative effort to preserve what was left of their position in society. As in Tunisia, nationalism had to come from the emerging educated class. One possible tie to the older traditions of resistance was quickly broken when the election of a grandson of the Amir Abd al-Qadir to a government council was annulled and he went into exile in 1920.

The first organized Algerian nationalist movement in the twentieth century was established in France in 1926 under the leadership of Messali al-Hajj. Many Algerians had gone to work in France and Messali's organization, Étoile Nord-Africaine, served as a combination labor union and political association for those workers. Messali demanded complete independence for Algeria, and, although the organization's program initially had a Marxist orientation, it soon came to emphasize Islamic and Arabic nationalist themes. This change was at least partly the result of Messali's contacts with Arab nationalists like Shakib Arslan while Messali was in exile in 1930.

Messali was allowed to return to Algeria in 1936 when the Popular Front government came to power in France, and he began to organize a mass political movement, which became the Parti du Peuple Algérien (PPA). The PPA program denounced ideas of assimilation and demanded the recognition of Arabic as an official language as well as supporting more general themes of Islamic unity. Messali was attacked by French communists, and the man who had once been a member of the Communist party became a vigorous Muslim nationalist. Radicalism could not be combined, in French-dominated Algeria, with emerging Algerian nationalism.

The Islamic element of the expression of Algerian identity is even more visible in the career of Abd al-Hamid Ibn Badis (Ben Badis, 1889–1940). He came from a relatively wealthy, pro-French family, and in his early years, he was a quiet religious teacher. However, in 1925, he began to publish a newspaper that espoused the cause of Islamic reform. He was strongly influenced by the ideas of Muhammad Abduh and Rashid Rida, and he worked to spread the teachings of the Salafiyyah in Algeria. He and some of his friends succeeded in mobilizing a number of the Algerian ulama and, in 1931, organized the Association of Algerian Ulama. The major themes of that organization and Ben Badis's journal, *al-Shihab,* were opposition to the *tariqah* leaders and the practices of popular Islam and a condemnation of assimilationism. Ben Badis advocated a modernist interpretation of the Quran and was active in encouraging a revival of both Arabic and Islamic elements in Algerian culture, and the ulama association established schools for that purpose. These activities played a significant role in affirming the Arab and Islamic identity of Algeria. The Salafiyyah ulama were not, however, political militants until the outbreak of the Algerian revolution in 1954. Although the association was important in defining the basis for Algerian nationalism, it took no overt actions hostile to French rule.

The challenge to an Islamic and Arabic Algeria was clearly manifested by a third major Algerian movement, which spread following World War I, that accepted the principle of assimilation. As early as 1912, a party of Young Algeria had been formed by French-educated Muslims who accepted the idea of French rule and assimilation into French culture. What they worked for was full equality within a France that included Algeria. The major threat to this ideal was, ironically, the French settler community in Algeria, which opposed any measures that would reduce their privileged position. Time after time, they succeeded in forcing the French government to reject proposals that would have made assimilation possible.

After World War I, one of the leading figures in the assimilationist group was Farhat Abbas (b. 1899), whose writings express the assimilationist position clearly. He believed that the future of Algeria lay with France, and he rejected all ideas of Algerian independence. Two distinctive requests the assimilationists made were that they be able to maintain their Muslim legal status in personal matters of marriage and inheritance and that eventually, Arabic would become an officially recognized language. They were not, however, thinking in politically nationalist terms but hoped to preserve some element of their cultural identity.

The clash between the assimilationist and Islamic positions was clearly expressed in a famous and often-quoted exchange between Abbas and Ben Badis. Abbas wrote in 1936:

> If I had discovered an Algerian nation, I would be a nationalist and I would not blush for it as though it were a crime. . . . Yet I will not die for the Algerian homeland, because such a homeland does not exist. I have not found it. I have questioned history, I have asked the living and the dead, I have visited the cemeteries; no one has told me of it. . . . We have once and for all dispersed the storm clouds of fantasy in order to tie for ever our future to that of the work of France in this land.[38]

The response of Ben Badis a few months later was equally clear and stressed the importance of Islam in the definition of Algeria: "History had taught us that the Muslim people of Algeria were created like all the others. They have their history, illustrated by noble deeds; they have their religious unity and their language. . . . This Muslim population is not France; it cannot be France, it does not want to be France."[39]

French intransigence finally did what the ulama and the nationalists had been unable to do. After years of disappointment, the assimilationists finally came to the conclusion that no matter how moderate and compromising they were, they would never gain equality in a French-ruled Algeria, so Farhat Abbas gradually moved to a position of seeking first autonomy and then independence for Algeria. The elimination of the assimilationist position was dramatically illustrated when Abbas told the French Assembly in 1946, "The Algerian personality, the Algerian fatherland, which I did not find in 1936 amongst the Moslem masses, I find there today."[40] The political evolution of Algeria had effectively removed the possibility of a secularized, individualist style of Islam.

After World War II, a new configuration of nationalist movements emerged, and there was less emphasis upon reformist Islam and more on the political drive for independence. Following the death of Ben Badis, the Association of Algerian Ulama had less political visibility, and the most prominent organizations were the Union Democratique du Manifeste Algérien (UDMA), formed as a relatively moderate and modernist political action group by Farhat Abbas in 1946, and the Mouvement pour le Triomphe des Libertes Democratiques (MTLD), the militantly nationalist organization created by Messali al-Hajj as the successor to his banned PPA. However, French repression, a continued unwillingness to compromise, and the corruption of even the few electoral rights the Algerians had combined to discredit the political methods. The UDMA's moderation had gained it nothing, and the MTLD began to split into factions, with some members unwilling to follow Messali's increasingly autocratic leadership. Some younger members with military experience opted for violent rather than political activism.

The young militants were the nucleus for what was to emerge as the major movement of Algerian nationalism, the Front de Libération Nationale (FLN). Originally formed by dissidents from the older movements and ex-soldiers with military experience, the FLN led a major armed uprising in 1954, and that led to the long Algerian war for independence. Among its early and most durable leaders was Ahmad Ben Bella (b. 1916), a young man who had had both a French and a Quranic education and had served in the French army during World War II. He had joined the MTLD after the war. Although Farhat Abbas joined the FLN during the course of the Algerian war for independence and there were other major figures in the movement, it was Ben Bella who emerged as the leader of the independent Algeria in 1962.

During the Algerian revolution, ideology was less important than the effort to defeat the French. The basic ideological themes expressed by the FLN leaders were a mixture of traditional nationalist ideals and a growing utilization of socialist and radical terminology. However, Islam played an important role as one of the identifying pillars of Algerian society, which the FLN was both creating and defending. The revolution was not a time for reflection or redefinition; it was a time for mobilization, and in that, Islam was a key factor.

French efforts to undermine the local culture were seen as attacks on Islam, which in the minds of the nationalist revolutionaries was identified with the Algerian nation. Ahmad Ben Bella, for example, recalled the moment when "deep in my heart, I felt myself becoming a rebel."[41] That was when he was fourteen; a French teacher had denounced the Prophet Muhammad as an imposter, and Ben Bella had been punished for arguing with him. Even the radical ideologue of the revolution, Frantz Fannon, saw French efforts to unveil Algerian women as a plot to destroy the Algerian nation.[42] Islam was thus a vital force in providing the symbolism and emotion of the Algerian revolution. It was complementary to, rather than competing with, nationalism.

Resistance and Islam in Morocco. The connection between Islam and the resistance to European rule in Morocco was a major aspect of the emergence of nationalism there. Following World War I, there were two major movements of a very different character, and they illustrate the potential lines of the Islamic nationalist efforts. The first and, at the time, the most visible was the active military resistance to the establishment of Spanish control in the northern part of Morocco. There, a major tribal family organized a movement that led to the establishment of an independent republic in the Rif. In many ways, this movement was a transition from a more traditional to a modern-style activist movement. A great tribal leader, Abd al-Karim al-Khattabi (d. 1920), first worked with Spanish officials in an effort to win autonomy for his people. His sons were given modern educations as well as training in traditional tribal leadership, and his son Muhammad organized effective military opposition when the Spanish refused to compromise. By 1922, he had succeeded in driving the Spanish out of much of northern Morocco, and he declared the foundation of an Islamic republic. The official policy of this regime was outlined in a statement in 1925, which claimed the right of self-determination and the goal of combining the basic teachings of Islam with the scientific and industrial achievements of the West. In 1926, the new republic came into conflict with the French and was defeated. However, the Rif republic emphasized the possibility that traditional leadership could create a state that would combine Islamic values and modernization, a pattern that was to emerge again when Morocco became independent in 1956.

The other movement that emerged following World War I had greater similarity to the beginnings of nationalist movements in the other Maghrib states. Islamic reformism of the Salafiyyah type had come to Morocco early in the century, and following the war, active study groups developed in Rabat and Fez. The Moroccan Salafiyyah was strongly opposed to the practices of the *tariqah*s and eager to support Arabic and Islamic education. The leading figures in that effort were Mawlay al-Arabi al-Alawi and Abu Shuʿayb al-Dukkali, but it was their students who gradually transformed the Salafiyyah spirit into a nationalist movement. That transformation was possibly inevitable because the "religious" positions had political implications, and an attack on the leaders of the orders was an attack on the chief supporters of the French regime. It was easy to equate the doctrinal corruption of the Sufis with their collaboration with infidel imperialists, and similarly, the effort to establish schools with an Arab-Islamic curriculum could provide a focus for feelings of national identity.

The leading figure in the politicization of the Salafiyyah was Allal al-Fasi, a student of Mawlay al-Arabi who was actively dedicated to the cause of

Islamic reform. As his thinking developed, al-Fasi became convinced that independence was an essential first step in Islamic reform, and under his leadership, the basic theological positions of the Salafiyyah remained relatively stable while its political activism gradually grew. The issue that gave impetus to this development was the Berber Decree of 1930, by which the French removed certain Berber tribes from the jurisdiction of Islamic law and replaced it with French law and tribal custom. Religious protest and political opposition were combined in demonstrations organized by Salafiyyah groups, but the need for organization was recognized in the process, and a series of less formal groupings produced the National Action Bloc by 1932.

The intellectuals involved in the religionationalist party ranged from people with relatively conservative religious ideas and Salafiyyah supporters to modern-educated intellectuals. Although the party was initially an elite grouping, it began to develop mass support. It took a number of organizational forms, and its leaders were often jailed or exiled. One of the more modern-oriented leaders, Ahmad Balafrej, reorganized the party during World War II while al-Fasi was in exile, and the new party was called the Istiqlal (Independence) party. Al-Fasi became its leader when he returned to Morocco in 1946, and the party grew rapidly.

It was not, however, only the Istiqlal party that led the fight for independence as it developed a political consciousness among many Moroccans and helped to tie the drive for independence to the more traditional symbols and ideals of Islam. However, in contrast to the Neo-Destour party in Tunisia, the Istiqlal faced a traditional institution whose strength had not been destroyed by the experience of imperial rule: the sultanate. Although the sultan was little more than a puppet of the French, the office retained considerable religious prestige, and nationalists were willing to recognize the sultan as a symbol of the Moroccan nation. That fact became a very important element in the Moroccan struggle for independence.

The development of the sultanate as an important nationalist symbol was associated with the career of Muhammad ibn Yusif (1909–1961), or Muhammad V. He was chosen by the French to succeed his father in 1927, and they assumed that he would be quiet and docile. However, within the limits of strict French control, Muhammad gave quiet encouragement to the nationalist cause. Popular demonstrations welcoming him during a visit to Fez in 1934, and his willingness to receive visits from nationalists, as well as his support for the idea of independence during World War II, helped to cement the ties between him and the Istiqlal. Muhammad became even more active after the war, making symbolic protests against French rule, and after 1951, he began to refuse to sign decrees prepared by the French. In 1953, the

French deposed him and sent him into exile, providing a clear issue around which all Moroccans could be mobilized. Serious outbreaks of violence finally persuaded the French to recall Muhammad in 1955, and he became King Muhammad V of an independent Morocco in 1956.

Thus in Morocco, the two major vehicles expressing nationalist aspirations were a religiously oriented nationalist party and a monarchy whose prestige in society rested firmly on Islamic grounds. Islam provided the symbol for mass mobilization and, even more, provided at least some of the institutional structure for an independent Morocco. It was a nationalist Islam rather than a developing modernist style or fundamentalism that was the most significant element of the Muslim experience in Morocco in the days of the struggle for independence.

Islam in the Independent Maghrib

After the winning of independence, there was a remarkable political stability in the Maghrib, despite the violence of the liberation struggle. There was, however, a significant evolution in each state from the independence-achieving regime to the postindependence one. In this transition, the key issues relating to the Islamic experience involved the problems of modernization and nation building. In particular, once the common enemy was removed, debate arose over the appropriate ideological and programmatic foundations for modernization. During the 1960s, the major development in this area was the evolution of a more secularist socialism, often of a radical style, that advocated revolutionary social transformation. This ideological approach became a powerful force by the middle of the decade but then declined in importance. Parallel to that process was a decline and then a revival of a more visibly Islamic orientation.

The most dramatic but perhaps most confusing case is the experience of Algeria. The war for independence came to an end in 1962, and the FLN began to disintegrate into its constituent parts. In the early days, before old-style politicians like Farhat Abbas joined the FLN, its program had advocated a radical social transformation as well as freedom from France. In the brief conflict among FLN leaders in 1962, one of the spokesmen for the early group, Ahmad Ben Bella, emerged as the leader of independent Algeria.

Ben Bella was aware of the value of Islam as a symbol for national unity and took care to identify Algeria as an Islamic state by taking symbolic Islamic actions. For example, when he went to the United Nations in 1962, he refused to allow the serving of alcoholic beverages at a reception Algeria gave to celebrate its admission to the United Nations. He told his adviser:

"Even if it is the custom, I am not going to do it. Algeria is a Moslem country. She will offer hospitality according to her own traditions."[43] However, Ben Bella's actual line of policy was more clearly a secularist style of socialism, with Islam playing a subordinate role. Islam, in the emerging ideology of Ben Bella, was to be a support for socialism rather than an independent force.

In that move, Ben Bella went beyond the ideas of most of the FLN members, and at the first national FLN congress in 1964, the delegates supported a less revolutionary style of socialism whose guidelines would be the traditional Islamic principles. Ben Bella's increasing identification with a more "scientific socialism" was one of the factors that undermined his support within the FLN and Algeria. That factor and internal rivalries within the ruling elite led to his overthrow in 1965 by a leading FLN military commander, Houari Boumedienne (1925–1978), and with that change of leaders, the emphasis shifted away from an internationally oriented socialist policy to a more pragmatic reformism that placed greater stress upon Arabization and Islamic values.

In contrast to many of the countries in the Arab East, the "old" socially conservative nationalist leadership in Algeria had already been eliminated by the time of independence. The independence-achieving regime was closer in tone to the postrevolutionary regimes in Iraq and Egypt than to the initial nationalist regimes. The 1965 coup was, in many ways, a pulling back from the more doctrinaire socialism that was common elsewhere in the developing world at the time. The government of Boumedienne remained committed to social transformation and anti-imperialism, but the mood reflected the fact that Boumedienne had been a student at al-Azhar and an Arabic teacher before joining the FLN.

It is in this political context that there was a continuing discussion of Islam and its nature. Even the radicals did not condemn Islam, and the Ben Bella and Boumedienne attitudes had their parallels in more intellectual works. A close associate of Ben Bella was Amer Ouzegane (b. 1920), a self-educated man who had been a member of the French Communist party but had been expelled in 1948 for nationalist deviation. He was an active ideologue in the FLN and helped to frame a number of its more radical proclamations. He was a sharp critic of the Communist party for its failure to support the Algerian revolution but blended Marxism and Islamic nationalism in his thinking. "We are seeking a symbiosis . . . between Islam and Marxist-Leninism," he said and noted that his communist friends did not understand that "the secret of progress in Arab and Moslem countries, and of the destruction of colonialism and feudalism, lay precisely in the symbiosis of Islam and of progressivist theories."[44]

A less radical orientation is seen in the works of Malek Bennabi (b. 1905), who became a prominent educator after independence. In his works, he maintained that Algeria had fallen under imperialist control because Algerian Muslims had allowed themselves to stagnate in both religious and scientific areas, and he advocated Islamic revival along with the adoption of Western science. He believed that "the common cause of error of both Modernists and Reformists . . . is that neither one nor the other has gone to the source itself of their inspiration. . . . The reformists have not really returned to the origins of Islamic thought, nor have the Modernists gone to the roots of occidental thought."[45]

In independent Tunisia, some of that same duality of approach can be seen, with the primary effort being the creation of an effectively modern Tunisia. A well-informed observer in 1962 noted that in Tunisia, "Religion is not the most important of the problems, and Islam is taken for granted since the Tunisians are Muslims."[46] The context and spirit of the role of Islam are defined in the new state's constitution, in which the principles of Islam are given as the basis for law and polity, but there is no insistence upon the letter and rule of traditional structures of Islamic law. In many ways, the independent state of Tunisia is the direct heir of Khayr al-Din Pasha and his efforts to blend modern and Islamic elements into a new synthesis.

As happened in Algeria, the old, conservative nationalists had been ousted from power before independence. In Tunisia, that happened as early as 1934 with the creation of the Neo-Destour party. The new nationalist leadership was committed to at least the ideal of a modernizing social transformation, and after independence, the leadership moved gradually in the direction of a more radical socialism. That trend was emphasized when the more conservative nationalist elements joined with Salah Ben Youssef (d. 1961) in his effort to overthrow Bourguiba as leader of the nationalist movement and the Neo-Destour party in the period from 1955 to 1960. Bourguiba was aided by the younger, more radical elements of the party, especially Ahmad Ben Salah, a strong labor union leader. During the 1960s, great efforts were made to establish a more centrally planned economy, and measures such as enforced creation of agricultural cooperatives and collectives were undertaken. This more radical phase was brought to an abrupt end in 1969 when Ben Salah was dismissed from his many powerful positions, and policy then assumed a less doctrinaire, socialist orientation. A major factor in the evolution was the resistance of many Tunisians to the more radical secularist spirit of the Neo-Destourian socialism.

In specifically Islamic terms, the main line of development was the growing strength of an individualized style of Islam as religion was increasingly accepted as a personal matter. It remained of importance as an element in the Tunisian identity, but in a form that was closer to the role of religion in a more secularized, modern society than in a premodern Islamic culture. The old Muslim structures and leadership groups were replaced. Religious education, for example, which had been dominated in the past by the great mosque schools of Zaytuna and al-Qayrawan, passed into the hands of the theological faculty in the University of Tunis, which was led by a committed but modernist Muslim scholar. There was no Islamically sanctioned monarchy to provide a focus for the more traditional visions, and even the powerless monarchical office of the bey was abolished soon after independence with no popular protest.

The Islamic position of Bourguiba's government was modernist and reformist. The goal was to transform Tunisians' religious attitudes as a part of the overall process of modernization without arousing popular opposition. Bourguiba attempted to present himself not as a secularizer, similar to Ataturk, but as a Muslim reformer in the tradition of Abduh. He was most successful in reforming specific structures, customs, and practices that could be considered as not being an inherent part of Islam. He reorganized the whole structure of religious endowments; transformed the laws of personal status, marriage, and the role of women; and removed independent religious control in education and the court system. However, the limits of this reform program were shown when Bourguiba attempted to change something that was an essential and basic part of Islam: the fast of Ramadan. Bourguiba attempted to persuade Tunisians that the month-long fast hindered the effort to build a strong and wealthy economy and society. In 1960, he recommended that the fast not be undertaken, but few Tunisians followed his lead, and there were many protests against his proposal. The effort was soon dropped, showing that Tunisian Muslims were willing to accept a wide range of secularist changes in Islamic practices but were unwilling to tamper with the basic fundamentals.

Even the Ramadan issue did not produce a significant fundamentalist movement. The dominant style of Islam in the era of independence has been one of secularist adaptationism, which experimented with but withdrew from a more radical position. The effort to provide a synthesis of modern and Islamic principles can be seen in the works of a number of younger Tunisians during the 1960s and is illustrated in the writings of Mohammed Taalbi. He noted, for example, that "a medieval restoration is not the desired solution" but that a vague sense of Islam simply as a factor of cohesion puts it "at the mercy of every demogogue." For Taalbi, the hope of Islam rests with Muslim scholars "trained in the disciplines of European universities" who are "concerning themselves in greater number with the history of ideas in Muslim civilization and are attempting to define the importance of the spiritual values which have modelled its humanism."[47]

In Morocco, the political scene has been dominated by the religiously prestigious monarchy as Muhammad V was the symbol of the nation and of national resistance. As a result, in contrast to the experiences in Algeria and Tunisia, the major nationalist political party, the Istiqlal, did not become the ruling group in the independent state. During the 1960s, there were active political parties, but they were under the strict control of the king—first, Muhammad V, who died in 1961, and then his son, Hasan II. In Islamic terms, the major development was the modernization of the leading institution, the monarchy. A parliamentary regime was established, but Hasan II assumed the role of the primary political leader of the country as well as being its symbol. He was able to disband parliament in 1965 and ruled directly until 1970.

The monarchy relied upon the traditional loyalty to the king, who was both the leading religious figure and the major politician of the country. In moves similar to the White Revolution in Iran and the emergence of pragmatic fundamentalism in Saudi Arabia, Hasan II made the monarchy the leading force for the economic modernization of society while attempting to avoid social revolution. In that effort, traditional Islamic themes were balanced with a reformist appeal. The two sides of the king's policy are illustrated by the various positions of women in the royal family. The king's wife remained hidden from view, acting in a very traditional manner, but the king's sister, Princess Lalla Aicha, was one of the leaders in the movement for the liberation of women, and she was appointed the Moroccan ambassador to Great Britain in 1965. That illustration is typical of the royalist policy of balancing Islamic and modern forces without creating a synthesis of the ideas involved.

The major political organizations did not fare well during the 1960s. The older Istiqlal leadership was challenged soon after independence by younger, more radical nationalists, and the result was the creation of the Union Nationale des Forces Populaires (UNFP), led by Mehdi Ben Barka, in 1959. Ben Barka was kidnapped and killed while in exile in 1965, and the leader of the old Istiqlal, Allal al-Fasi, died in 1967, which left the major potential opposition to the king without prominent leaders. The dominant theme of the opposition parties was to challenge the increasing power of the monarchy, but there was little in their programs that represented significant developments in Islamic thought during the period.

It is outside of the political arena that major intellectual issues involving Islam have been dealt with. The major themes inspired by the political context involve the debate over the preservation and the dismantling of the traditional monarchical structure. However, the broader themes seen in the rest of the Maghrib also appear in Moroccan thought: the issues relating to a reconciliation of the modern and the traditional, the Islamic and the Western. Some of the major lines in the intellectual activity can be seen in the works of Abdallah Laroui, whose views represent an intellectual nationalism influenced by a modified Marxism. He emphasizes the importance of historical awareness, but not as part of an effort to create an artificial traditionalism since a self-conscious awareness of traditional means "traditionalization at the hands of an elite that, finding itself in a position of self-defense, changes its role."[48] He thus rejects false traditionalization while recognizing the importance of the historical experience.

If one moves beyond the turmoil of politics, the major Islamic issues have not been developed in the framework of radical secularism or extremist fundamentalism. The Islamic experience has concentrated more on creating an integration of modernism and Islam, which has taken a variety of forms, as in Destourian socialism and Moroccan monarchism. What one analyst has said, comparing Ouzegane and Bennabi, describes the alternatives presented by the intellectual efforts of the Maghribi Muslims in general: "Both believe that Islam and modernism are compatible," but for one perspective "religion is only a means to realize modernism," and for the other, "the religious is an end in itself and a basic and permanent dimension of the Moslem character."[49] The choice that is made between those two alternatives will shape the future of Islam in the Maghrib.

5

Twentieth-Century Islam

Eastern World, Nondominant Majorities, and Minorities

The Eastern Muslim World: Dominance and Struggle

Almost half of the world's Muslims live in the Indian subcontinent and Southeast Asia. The Islamic communities in the region are large but vary in their position within the broader society from being dominant majorities in Pakistan, Bangladesh, and Indonesia to being a strong minority in Malaysia to being a weak minority in the contemporary Republic of India. All of these communities have been involved in struggles for independence and have had to find some answer to the issue of the relationship between Islam and nationalism. The issue is more complex in the eastern region than it is in the Middle East and North Africa because there are "traditional" and local cultural identities that are not clearly Islamic. In addition to having to define the relationship between Islam and modernity, Muslims have also had to define their identity in relation to other nonmodern or modernizing traditions. In this way, even where Muslims are a dominant social majority, Muslim self-consciousness has operated in a pluralistic context.

The complexity of the issues gave rise to a luxuriant growth of Islamic movements and ideas covering the full spectrum of styles of Islamic experience. No single book can give an adequate introduction to the large number of groups and individuals who have been important in defining the modern Islamic experience in this region; in this work, only the main themes are identified, and an indication is given of the major types of movements.

Islam in British India

The vibrant vitality of nineteenth-century Islam continued in the twentieth century. Although the Muslims had been politically dominant in the days of the Moghul Empire, they remained a minority in the Indian subcontinent. As

231

a result, in the twentieth century, the relationship of the Muslims to the Hindu majority was an issue that was added to the problem of defining the relationship with modern ideas, and the two lines of development constantly interacted. Nationalism and modernism became the two themes that helped to define and create the variety of the Indian Muslim experiences, and each style of Islamic experience dealt with those themes in the era leading up to independence from British rule.

Adaptationist Reformism. Under British rule, adaptationism was limited to the intellectual areas and the developing definition of nationalism. Until independence was won following World War II, there was no scope for "applied adaptationism" in social or political reform programs. In both nationalism and Islamic modernism, the key adaptationist line of development can be seen as the heritage of Sayyid Ahmad Khan.

It was the emerging modern-educated Muslims who provided the leadership for the adaptationist movements in twentieth-century Muslim India. The most significant general line of evolution was the development of a modernist Islamic assertion of a Muslim identity associated with a major Muslim intellectual, Muhammad Iqbal, and the Muslim League developed as an organizational expression of that identity. Eventually, that line led to the creation of Pakistan as an independent Muslim state.

Modern nationalism had begun in India late in the nineteenth century outside of the Muslim community. The modern-educated classes had begun to work for a greater role in Indian government, and in the process of advance and disappointment, the Indian National Congress was formed in 1885 to express Indian aspirations. Leadership in the Congress was largely drawn from Hindu Indians, and two wings of Congress soon developed. A moderate, liberal group aimed at a modernized, self-governing India structured along Western parliamentary lines, and it emphasized Indian "national" unity and attempted to bridge religious communal differences. However, the other major faction within the Congress was militantly Hindu and sought independence on the basis of past Hindu glories and future Hindu leadership. In this context, the issue of nationalism as a potential rival of Islam was soon clearly raised, and modern-educated Muslims were faced with the choice of participating in the nationalist movement, which was at best secularist and non-Islamic and, at worst, militantly non-Islamic in some of its forms.

Sayyid Ahmad Khan set the tone for many of the educated Muslims by not participating in the Congress. He did not urge opposition to the new nationalist movement, but he and his followers withheld their support. They believed that in a truly democratic state, the majority would rule and this, in the Indian context, would ultimately mean the end of the Muslim community there.

It gradually became apparent that nonparticipation was not sufficient. When reforms that recognized separate Muslim electorates were being instituted, the Muslim League was organized in 1906 to present Muslim views. For many years, the Muslim League worked to secure and maintain Muslim communal rights within the broader society. The league's solution to the problem raised by a Hindu-oriented or a majoritarian nationalism was to seek recognition for the Muslims as a special community whose representation and existence would be guaranteed within the future independent state. The league was able to cooperate with the Congress in this framework, and the two groups held joint meetings and coordinated many of their activities during World War I. The league was temporarily eclipsed by the rise of the Khilafat movement when the enthusiasm for the caliphate reached a peak. The Khilafat movement captured popular imagination, received support from the Congress, and gave its support to the noncooperation campaign of the Congress in the 1920s. However, by the end of the decade, the Khilafat movement was effectively dead as a political force in India.

As the early generation of Muslim League leaders began to pass from the scene, the new leadership expressed more militancy. The old league had been relatively conservative in approach, but during the 1930s, it became more nationalistically assertive, and the key figure in the revival of the league was Muhammad Ali Jinnah (1876–1948). He started as a member of the moderate wing of the Indian National Congress but had joined the Muslim League in 1913 and was one of the architects of Congress–Muslim League cooperation. He had remained aloof from the political turmoil of the 1920s but had become increasingly disillusioned about the prospects for special communal guarantees and separate electoral bodies for Muslims in an India dominated by the Congress. He assumed leadership of the league in 1934 and led it to a position that made it, by World War II, the generally recognized spokesman for Indian Muslims.

Jinnah gradually became persuaded that only a separate and an independent state for the Muslims would guarantee their rights, and he developed the idea of the "two nation theory." He felt that "Hinduism and Islam represent two distinct and separate civilizations and, moreover, are as distinct from one another in origin, tradition and manner of life as are nations of Europe."[1] When the Congress was unwilling to cooperate with the league in the elections of 1937 and 1939, Jinnah was convinced that separatism was necessary, so in 1940, the League formally identified its goal as an independent Muslim state in those areas where Muslims formed a majority. The name for this state had been suggested earlier by students at Cambridge University: Pakistan, formed from the names of Punjab, Afghania, Kashmir, Sind, and Baluchistan and suggesting words meaning "land of the pure."

The goal of a separate Muslim state was finally recognized by the British, and in 1947, British India was partitioned into two independent states. The partition was accompanied by large-scale communal violence and a massive exchange of population. Certain territories were claimed by both countries, and some, such as Kashmir, became the basis for long-term tension and conflict.

Pakistan was the result of the evolving nationalist efforts of Indian Muslims, and an important aspect of that evolution is that it was the product of the modern-educated leadership within the Muslim community. The primary concern had been the protection of the community rather than a definition of what form it would take as an independent state. The modernist thinkers associated with the league were active in reformulating the philosophical foundations of Islam in the modern world, but they did little to provide a political definition of Islam for a modern state. The Pakistan movement was an assertion of an identity that everyone felt was self-explanatory, and thus, at independence, the leaders of the league had created a "state of Muslims" but had not gone very far in creating an "Islamic state."

Muhammad Iqbal (1875–1938) was the leading intellectual figure in the emerging adaptationist modernism. He was a prominent poet and scholar with a Western education, and he developed a philosophy of mystic dynamism in which Western and Islamic ideals were combined in often dramatic and poetic forms. In his most famous work, *The Reconstruction of Religious Thought in Islam,* he argued that philosophical rationality and religious intuition were complementary ways of understanding the truth, and that belief enabled him to combine a variety of perspectives. For example, in his interpretation of the problem of predestination, he developed a modern ideal of free will on the basis of doctrines similar to the idea of unity in the manifestations of God (*wahdat al-shuhud*), which had been developed by the Naqshbandiyyah teacher, Ahmad Sirhindi. Similarly, Iqbal integrated the Sufi concept of the perfect man with Henri Bergson's theory of creative evolution.[2]

Iqbal urged the exercise of *ijtihad* to bring about the necessary reconstruction of Islam in the modern world. He spoke highly of the Turkish experiment under Ataturk, but he criticized Kemalism for assimilating the idea of a separation of church and state from Europe without realizing that "it suggests a dualism which does not exist in Islam."[3] Iqbal advocated the use of *ijtihad* to help restructure Islamic law, rejecting any sense of that law as being unalterable. Iqbal combined *ijtihad* with a redefinition of *ijma* ("consensus") as a basic source of Islamic law, and he noted that traditionally the right of *ijtihad* had been limited to special individuals and that validating consensus was also restricted. However, Iqbal noted that *ijma* had not assumed the form of a permanent institution in Islamic societies because "possibly its transformation into a permanent legislative institution was contrary to the political interests of the kind of absolute monarchy that grew up in Islam."[4] Iqbal believed that the transfer of the power of *ijtihad* to a modern Muslim legislative assembly was the necessary line of evolution if life were to be restored to the Islamic legal system.

Although Iqbal was not as active in political affairs as a man like Jinnah, he was very influential and is often credited with being the founder of the idea of Pakistan. He certainly was a key figure in transforming Muslim nationalism from the struggle to win guarantees for Muslims within a larger community to the movement for an independent Islamic state. Although Islamic separatism was implicit in the position taken by those Muslims who did not join the Congress, the first major proposal for the creation of a separate Muslim state was made in an address by Iqbal to the Muslim League in 1930. Iqbal played an important role in the conversion of league leaders, especially Jinnah, to the Pakistan idea.

Iqbal was only one of a large number of Muslim scholars and activists who were involved in the reassertion of an Islamic communal and intellectual identity. A significant aspect of this modernist-nationalist evolution was that the leaders were primarily Western educated rather than coming from traditional or conservative intellectual backgrounds, which meant that although their loyalty to Islam was strong, they were not tied to particular traditions within Islam. The Islamic identity that they worked to create was a composite one, perhaps as the result of the origins of the leaders themselves Although Iqbal was of Sunni background, Jinnah came from a minority Shi'i community. One of the leading early modernist intellectuals, Amir Ali (1849–1928), who provided a vigorous glorification of Sunni historical Islam and whose works made possible a favorable appreciation of Islamic history among Westernized Muslims far beyond India, was a committed Twelver Shi'i believer. The nontraditionalism of modernist nationalism made it possible to ignore or overcome traditional divisions in the name of the emerging Indian Muslim communal identity.

Intellectual adaptationism was dominated by modernist Islamic nationalism, but there were other important threads as well. One critical distinction was between those Muslim leaders who were willing to cooperate with the Indian National Congress and those who opposed such cooperation. A leading figure among the modernist Muslims in India who remained closely associated with the Congress and ultimately rejected the Pakistan idea was Abu al-Kalam Azad (1888–1958). Azad's education was more traditionalist, and he had traveled in his early years in the Arab East where he had come into contact with the ideas of al-Afghani and Abduh. He published a journal and books that were widely read, in which he emphasized the importance of a thorough study of the Quran. Although his approach utilized modern methods of analysis, his emphasis and tone were more conservative. On the matter of *ijtihad*, for example, he replaced the legal concept of *ijtihad* with *ta'sis* ("reconsolidation"), "arguing that in modern times what is needed is not free or new legal speculation, but a consolidation of what he interprets as Islam's fundamental verities which would externalize the perfection inherent in it."[5]

Azad's more traditional orientation led him to support ideas of Pan-Islam, and he became actively involved in the Khilafat movement. He stressed the univeralism of Islam and, in this way, came to reject the identification of Islam as a basis for a localized nationalist movement. At first, that belief meant that he rejected the idea of cooperation with Hindu nationalists in India, but on the basis of an appeal to human fraternity and a sense of religious cooperation built on a study of comparative religion, Azad later became a vigorous supporter of integrated nationalism and was, for many years, elected president of the Indian National Congress. In addition to Islamic reservations about using Islam as a basis for local separatism, Azad found a positive basis for cooperation with the Congress in the community created by the Prophet Muhammad himself when he moved to Medina in 622. That *ummah* had contained both Muslims and non-Muslims and Azad believed that it provided a sound precedent for integrated efforts to create a community of Muslims and non-Muslims. Although Azad did not express a modernized secularism explicitly, his position implicitly laid the foundations for a position that would accept religion as a matter of personal faith and practice rather than as the basis for the political order.

In Iqbal and Azad, one sees the two lines of modernist adaptationism in British India. Both utilized modern critical analysis and, in many ways, supported similar efforts in reinterpreting and redefining Islam. It was the issue of nationalism that clearly separated them. For Iqbal, the issue of communal identity and preservation took precedence over Pan-Islamic and universalist ideas, and with Azad, a more secularist position on the issue of nationalism emerged because of an adherence to the more universalist aspects of the Islamic tradition.

Intellectual Conservatism. Azad's position on the issue of nationalism was shared by many of the more conservative ulama in India. In the context of British India, few Muslim leaders maintained a rigorously consistent, conservative political position of supporting British rule. Most social and intellectual conservatives, for example, the leading teachers at the Deoband school, adopted the more activist political position of support for the nationalist idea. However, they, like Azad, emphasized the importance of maintaining Islam as a universalist faith and not tying it to a specific local nationalism. Virtually all of the conservative ulama saw the importance of protecting the Muslim community in India but advocated doing so on the basis of practical alliances rather than on the basis of creating a nationalist Islamic ideology. A number of individuals and organizations represented the varieties of this viewpoint. One of the best known was the Jam'iyyat al-Ulama-i Hind, established in 1919 as part of the Khilafat excitement and in the tradition of opposition to Ahmad Khan's heritage. Many of its supporters, including its leader in the time of greatest nationalist ferment, Husayn Ahmad Madani, were associated with the Deoband. Madani argued that Muslims and non-Muslims could be partners in creating an independent state and that this would allow for the preservation of the Indian Muslim community without compromising the universalism of the Islamic teachings. Deoband and the Jam'iyyat opposed the league and the Pakistan movement right up to the day of partition.

The intellectual conservativism had had its roots in the late nineteenth century with movements like the Deoband school and the Ahl al-Hadith, and interpretive conservatism was preserved in the twentieth century by adopting what might be seen as a secularist position. Although many of its leaders became citizens of Pakistan, other became leaders of the still large Muslim community in the Republic of India.

Fundamentalist Activism. Although the liberal nationalists often were attacked by the conservative ulama, in many ways the most important challenge to the liberal nationalist, modern-educated leadership of the Muslim community came from fundamentalist Islam. Although a number of fundamentalist groups and teachers existed, the most influential were Abu al-Ala Mawdudi (b. 1903) and the organization he established in 1941, the Jama'at-i Islami.

On the great issue of nationalism, Mawdudi presented a third option, which involved the rejection of nationalism itself. In Mawdudi's view, the programs of both the Muslim League and the Indian National Congress represented a non-Islamic emphasis on nationalism and were counter to Islam. Nationalism, whether that proposed by the league or the Congress, was a selfish principle that was prohibited by Islam, and people who espoused the nationalist cause were leading Muslims away from the legitimate goal of a truly Islamic society based on universal principles. The real revolution and true independence would come when pious men of faith in all walks of life would create a spirit of moral dedication throughout society.[6] As a result, Mawdudi attacked the ulama of the Jam'iyyat al-Ulama for a nationalism that ran counter to Islam and also, in tactical terms, risked the sociocultural absorption of Muslims into Hindu society. By 1939, the chief focus of Mawdudi's attack had shifted to the leaders of the Muslim League, whose separatist nationalism seemed to him to be tantamount to unbelief.

Mawdudi recognized that the modern-educated intellectuals in the league were not well grounded in Islamic scholarship and that their program was more a pragmatic one of survival than a step further in Islamic ideological development. The heat of the debate can be seen in Mawdudi's description of the league's leadership. "Not a single leader of the Muslim League from Jinnah himself to the rank and file has an Islamic mentality or Islamic habits of thought, or looks at political and social problems from the Islamic standpoint. . . . Their ignoble role is to safeguard merely the material interests of Indian Muslims by every possible political manoeuvre or trickery."[7]

Although Mawdudi was well known and membership in his organization grew, he was unable to counter the overwhelming appeal of the idea of an independent Islamic state. His proposals were relatively vague ant idealistic, and they did not provide a means for implementing the hope that modernism and nationalism could be eliminated as major factors in Islamic society simply by faithful actions of pious men. After the creation of Pakistan, he moved there, and his movement became an important political force in the state whose creation he had opposed.

Mawdudi advocated Islamic renewal and revival. He was not opposed to modern ideas so long as the individual placed them in the proper context of the dominant sovereignty of God. For Mawdudi, the man who has chosen the right path of Islamic faith will not be misled by fantasies. In scientific investigation, he will work to "explore all avenues of knowledge and power and to harness all that exists in earth and heavens in the interests of mankind. . . . The deeper his [a Muslim scientist's] insight into the world of science, the stronger will be his faith in God."[8] However, thought and analysis were not to be pursued to the point where faith might be questioned. Mawdudi said: "You may not be able fully to grasp the wisdom and usefulness of this or that order, but the very fact that an instruction has emanated from the Prophet is sufficient guarantee for its truth and there can be no room for doubt or suspicion. Your inability to understand it is no reason for its having flaw or defect, for a common man's understanding is not flawless."[9]

Fundamentalism in British India took its most visible form in Mawdudi's Jama'at. It was not a *tariqah* or a traditional grouping of ulama; it was one of the new-style associations that manifested the fundamentalist style in a number of areas. As an organization in a relatively modern format, it was in a position to become active in the new state of Pakistan.

In general, the Islamic experience in British India was rich and varied. In dealing with the political issue of nationalism, some Muslim modernists moved toward an Islamic nationalism, and others joined forces with conservatives to support a composite nationalism, which, in the long run, had secularist implications. It was left to the fundamentalists to reject nationalism altogether. In the issue of defining the relationship of Islam to modern ideas, no one denied the importance of the effort or attempted simply to ignore the existence of the modern world. Instead, the tremendous intellectual diversity that had existed at the end of the nineteenth century continued into the twentieth, and most Indian Muslims both affirmed the validity of their faith, suitably interpreted and expressed, and worked to find a modern expression for that faith in a manner that would not compromise too strongly with secularism or undermine the continued existence of the community.

Islam in Colonial Southeast Asia

In Southeast Asia during the first half of the twentieth century, the issues of winning independence, defining national identity, and creating an ideological basis for modernization were significant. The major factor was the dominance of a European colonial power, but the experience was different from that of India. In both Indonesia and Malaya, the European dominance had been interrupted by the Japanese conquest of the area during World War II, which hastened and also altered the process of the development of nationalism.

Malayan Alternatives. In both Malaya and Indonesia, there were significant alternatives to a modernizing Islamic foundation for nationalism and independence. In Malaya, the British had preserved many of the old local sultanates, and they provided a basis for a Malay political elite that was both experienced and conservative. British policy had left religious affairs in the hands of those rulers, who soon created local religious establishments utilizing old-style religious leaders who represented traditional syncretic and Sufi Islam. The combination of traditional religious and political leadership provided a formidable obstacle to any religious reformism.

Early in the twentieth century, ideas of Islamic modernism were popular in the port cities and the Straits Settlements, which were directly ruled by the British. A lively Muslim reformist intellectual community developed in Singapore, publishing newspapers and establishing schools, which created an informal group of Muslims dedicated to reformist ideas. It came to be called the Young Group (Kaum Muda), as opposed to their conservative opponents, the Kaum Tua (Old Group). In areas of Malaya outside of the coastal cities, the Kaum Muda made little headway, but their influence spread into the islands that became Indonesia.

An important factor in the modern Malayan Islamic experience is that the Muslims there, as in India, do not compose a dominant majority of the society. By the beginning of the twentieth century, Chinese immigrants made up almost half of the population, and there was a significant Indian community. British rule tended to recognize the special position of the original population, and there was little incentive for the religiopolitical Malay elite to encourage nationalism. The Chinese and Indian communities were led by merchants and commercial notables, and they, too, had little interest in major social change. When socioeconomic radicalism emerged, it was in the form of a predominantly Chinese Communist party, which reduced the appeal of radical thought even more for the Malays.

The Muslim community in Malaya was a powerful and established bare majority or minority by the time of World War II. Its basic mood was conservative, and there was little reformist activity. The Japanese conquest destroyed British prestige and opened the door for an upsetting of the old balances. One factor in the change was that the British attempted to create a centralized, unitary government when they returned after the war. Such a government would have removed the Malays from their special position and would have given added power to the Chinese. Rapidly, the old political elite moved to create the United Malays' National Organization (UMNO) in 1946. In the face of a Chinese-dominated communist movement that soon began overt resistance, the UMNO worked to establish effective links with the older conservative leadership in the Chinese and Indian communities, which had formed the Malayan Chinese Association (MCA) and the Malayan Indian Congress (MIC). The result was the formation of the Alliance party as an intercommunal, nationalist movement, basically conservative in its orientation but carefully nonexclusivist in either racial or religious terms.

The Malayan Muslims opted for a non-Islamic nationalism as a matter of internal self-defense. In many ways, they exhibited the same conservative spirit seen in the Deoband ulama who allied themselves with the Indian National Congress in India. The issue of nationalism was resolved by avoiding any connection between it and any of the special communal identities existing in Malaya at the time. The Alliance party was the overwhelming victor in elections held in 1955, and it formed the government that gained independence in 1957. Communal tensions and conflicts were not eliminated by this development, but the dominant style of Islamic experience was a pragmatic conservative adaptationism. Radical secularism would have given too much strength to a competing community, and fundamentalism would have aroused fears and opposition among the necessary non-Muslim partners. Those other types of Islamic experience could only develop in the context of an independent state.

Islam in Indonesia Until Independence. The final pacification of the Southeast Asian islands by the Dutch did not result in Islamic stagnation. The major change was that the older forms of militant resistance were replaced by new approaches and types of organizations; the old *tariqah*-holy war structure was replaced by modern social and political associations.

Within the Dutch East Indies, the Muslims were, at least in theory, a dominant majority, but non-Islamic traditions remained strong in the twentieth century. Although the line of communal demarcation was not as clear as it was between Hindu and Muslim in India or Malay and Chinese in Malaya, there were distinctive alternatives on which a nationalist movement could be based. The old court cultural traditions and special characteristics of local society, especially in the continuation of a Javanese cultural identity, had only been minimally integrated into a more standard Islamic tradition. There was a long history of tension between local syncretistic Islam and a more fundamentalist style of Islam in Indonesia, and a potential division between the more strict Muslims ant the more local, syncretistic Muslims was added to the normal modern division between the relatively modernized and the more traditional.

In this context, conservative Islam meant trying to preserve the special adaptations that had been made to local culture. Fundamentalist Islam was identified with opposition to popular religious customs and to Sufi pantheistic tendencies. In the twentieth century, fundamentalism and Salafiyyah reformism were virtually synonymous. As the modern Indonesian experience evolved, the indigenous, syncretic tradition, especially in the form of pride in the old court cultural traditions, came to be associated first with the colonial administration and then with the most active of the modern-educated classes. Thus, specifically Indonesian nationalism avoided and sometimes opposed a fundamentalist or a reformist Islamic tone. The nationalists who were favorably inclined toward the indigenous culture became the most active spokesmen in the anti-imperialist struggle, and more Islamically oriented groups frequently became their rivals. The nationalists were not, however, the most radical group, since a communist tradition soon developed, and it advocated social revolution. It was a radical secularist tradition with close ties to Moscow, and it began its transformation from a group of Europeans to an Indonesian party with the creation of the Perserikatan Komunis di-India (the Communist Association of the Indies) in 1920.

Explicitly Islamic organizations were largely within the reformist tradition and often concentrated on the problems of purifying Islamic practices. They only gradually became more involved in politics, but because of the potential mass support, they were important political factors. By 1912, a number of small Islamic organizations had been created, and in that year, two organizations were established, the Muhammadiyyah and the Sarekat Islam, which were to develop into movements with nationwide followings.

The Muhammadiyyah was established as a primarily cultural and educational organization and attempted to remain aloof from political struggles as much as possible. Its organizers were inspired by the Salafiyyah ideas coming from the Arab East, and it worked to eliminate "superstitious beliefs" and to bring a full and accurate awareness of the meaning of Islam to Indonesians. It established a large number of schools, trained teachers, and had a wide range of publications and activities related to social welfare. Its schools helped to educate nationalist Indonesians, and its activities opposed the development of communism and radical secularism. The Muhammadiyyah continued as an active educational and cultural association throughout the era of the nationalist struggle for independence. Reformist Islam, in this case, did not provide so much a political organization as a religious dimension for the developing spirit of nationalism.

The Sarekat Islam was an expansion of a Javanese organization of Muslim merchants and businessmen. Part of the initial inspiration for the movement was to protect Muslims from the expanding economic power of the Chinese business community, but the movement grew rapidly into a mass movement for the expression of Indonesian opinion. It opposed the abuses by Dutch administrators and the local chieftains whom they supported, and it was drawn into advocating social as well as moral transformations. One element in the organization's rapid growth was the charismatic appeal of its early leader, H.O.S. Tjokroaminoto (1882–1934), who could appeal to the modern-educated people and at the same time benefit from the messianic expectations that his style aroused in the rural areas. The movement also attracted Marxist youth, and for a brief moment during and immediately following World War I, Sarekat Islam appeared to be laying the foundation for a mass, nationwide nationalist movement. However, the more religiously oriented leaders were forced to expel the communists, who attempted to take control, and the movement soon declined in importance because of internal divisions and loss of momentum.

The leader who had emphasized the religious dimension of the organization was Hajji Agus Salim (1884–1954), and after its decline, he worked to reorganize Sarekat Islam and then established other groups that could appeal more effectively to the modern-educated Muslims. That appeal was especially important because after the collapse of the Sarekat Islam, Indonesian political leadership began to pass into the hands of advocates of a more secularist, or at least less clearly Islamic, nationalism built on a more specifically Indonesian cultural identity. The leading figures in that trend were Sukarno and Muhammad Hatta.

The position of the modernist Islamic activists was that Islam provided the unifying link for Indonesian nationalism. Further, Islam was to lead the way in reforming society. Agus Salim, for example, called himself a socialist Muslim and claimed that the Quran presented socialist principles. Although he led the effort to expel communists from the Sarekat Islam, Salim was not a conservative, and he provided an active link between the early days of Islamic nationalism and the era after World War II.

The divisions among the Muslims made it difficult for a unified Islamic nationalist movement to emerge as an alternative to the more secular nationalism of Sukarno and Hatta, a fact that is illustrated by the experience and impact of the Nahdatul Ulama, an organization established in 1926. That group drew its major support from local ulama who were opposed to both secular nationalism and Islamic modernism. Nahdatul Ulama was opposed to Pan-Islamic ideas, believed that the Wahhabi movement in Saudi Arabia was heretical, and expressed vigorous opposition to both the Muhammadiyyah and the Sarekat Islam. Its activities helped to keep many local ulama out of the nationalist or Islamic activist movements for a relatively long time.

Conservatives and modernists formed a loosely organized alliance in 1937, the Majlisul A'laa Indonesia (MIAI), to combat certain government regulations, but the differences between the two positions were never really reconciled. During World War II, the Japanese created a more effective unification when they formed the Masjumi (Majlisul Sjuro Muslimin Indonesia) to replace the MIAI. Masjumi brought the Muhammadiyyah and the Nahdatul Ulama groups together as well as bringing previously unaffiliated religious leaders into a national association. After the war Masjumi became organized into a political party and was active in the politics of the war for independence. Its party platform combined struggle in defense of the nation with struggle for the faith, and its social programs had wide appeal. Masjumi became, along with the Marxist party and the Partai National Indonesia (PNI) of the secular nationalists, one of the basic poles of Indonesian political life.

During the time of conflict with the Dutch, which led to independence in the period 1945–1949, a variety of small parties and movements emerged. Some of them had a clearly Islamic tone and came to pose problems for the newly established Indonesian nationalist government. One of the most long-lived involved what have been called the Dar al-Islam revolts. In a number of areas, local movements worked vigorously to establish Islamic states. In some cases they were led by men who had cooperated with the nationalist struggle for a brief period but had soon ended up in conflict with the republican government as well as with the Dutch. The programs of those local movements were for the establishment of states based on Islamic law. The longevity of the Dar al-Islam revolts is demonstrated by the fact that the revolt in West Java lasted from 1948 until 1962, in the Celebes from 1950 until 1965, and in North Sumatra from 1953 until 1961. This more fundamentalist style of militance tended to be local in organization, and the national Islamic groups remained largely reformist (with fundamentalist aspects) or conservative.

In Indonesia, there was a wide diversity of activity. The Islamic experience did not resolve the two basic divisions within the country, although compromises seemed to be made. The real difference between conservative and reformist Islam was never fully resolved, although by the time of the struggle for independence, the two major organizations representing those two styles were cooperating in a single political group. The other division was between the more secular style of nationalism and the Islamic orientation. Again, the explicitly Islamic groups cooperated with nationalists after World War II, but the inherent tensions were not eliminated. Although compromises existed, no effective modern Islamic synthesis seemed to be emerging by the time of Indonesian independence. As a result, Indonesian politics would be characterized by instability until a strong leader created a new political regime for the independent country.

Islam in Independence

Pakistan: New Existence as a Majority. The creation of an independent Muslim state in India in 1947 was the culmination of the development of nationalism in South Asia. Although it was a goal whose definition seemed self-evident, the establishment of an Islamic state was clearly an important event that has had profound implications for the modern history of Islam. The Muslims of British India had consciously chosen the option of partition in order to have their own independent state. In other areas of the world, Muslims had achieved independence or were to do so later, but the establishment of Pakistan was the result of the nationalism of Muslims more than of an explicitly Islamic nationalist effort. With the creation of Pakistan, the ability of Muslims to create a clearly Islamic state was put to the test. The basic issue, in both religious and political terms, was, Can a distinctively Islamic state be created and succeed under the conditions of modern history?

The new state received major blows early in its history. Not only was the process of partition bloody and disruptive, leaving Pakistan with little effective governmental structure or personnel, but Pakistan was also deprived of its most effective unifying symbols and leaders with the deaths of the two major leaders of the Muslim League, Muhammad Ali Jinnah in 1948 and Liyaqat Ali Khan, Jinnah's quiet lieutenant in the nationalist struggle who was murdered in 1951. In the absence of a strong leadership that was capable of unifying the diverse elements within the new state, the profound political issue of the meaning of Pakistan became obscured by the personal struggles for political position and power among the remaining politicans.

In the Islamic experience of Pakistan in the two decades following independence, two major themes are important. The first, and most visible, is the continuing failure to create a viable consensus on the meaning of an Islamic state. The long-term evolution was in the direction of political fragmentation rather than national and Islamic consolidation. The second theme, which is too often ignored in view of the political difficulties, is the continuing intellectual vitality of Pakistani Muslims in working to redefine Islam in the modern context.

The new state of Pakistan had only its Islamic identity to unite its diverse elements. The two parts of the country were geographically separated, and there was little convenient access between them. East Pakistan was much more densely populated, although less urbanized, than West Pakistan. The country was composed of geographically compact linguistic units, speaking languages not widely used outside of those areas. Bengali was the language of the overwhelming majority in East Pakistan, and the West Pakistanis were divided into a bare majority of Punjabi speakers and large minorities speaking Pushtu, Sindhi, and Urdu. The language issue illustrates the major difficulties of unification. Although Bengali was spoken by more than half of all Pakistanis, the new government tended to be dominated by people from West Pakistan, and they attempted to make Urdu the only official national language. That attempt failed, but neither section seemed eager to find a compromise.

A significant characteristic of the role of Islam in the politics of Pakistan was that it did not provide a commonly accepted, concrete program of action. Islam was, rather, a vaguely defined sentiment, which was, in different forms, common to virtually all Pakistanis. In British India, Islam, however defined, had provided a distinctive identity in contrast to the Hindu majority, but the process of becoming the dominant majority had eliminated that condition. There was insufficient consensus on the specifics of the meaning of an Islamic state to maintain Islam as the primary focus of loyalty. As a result, other sociocultural identities began to emerge as the basis for political action.

The process of political fragmentation was associated with the decline of the original nationalist elite. As in many countries, the group that achieved independence was displaced by a new generation of political leaders, and the process was a two-step one in Pakistan. The old nationalist leaders were removed first in East Pakistan, where an explicitly Bengali group of leaders defeated the national elite in the 1954 elections. The major group in that defeat was the Awami League, which had been established in 1949 as the first primarily Muslim opposition party. It had soon gained wide support by advocating significant autonomy for East Pakistan and official recognition for the Bengali language. In the period from 1954 until 1958, the Awami League worked with the old national politicians of West Pakistan, but neither group was able to create effective organizations beyond their own regional spheres of influence. The Awami-West alliance did not succeed in providing stable leadership for Pakistan as a whole, and in 1958, the military leadership took control of the government.

The effort to create an Islamic state was part of the problem of instability. The leaders of the Muslim League and the Pakistan movement were largely modern educated and relatively secularist in orientation, and their Muslim identity was more in their communal affiliation than in their intellectual position. Most of the conservative ulama and the fundamentalists had opposed the concept of Pakistan but took an active role in Pakistani politics after independence. They mobilized pressure groups to ensure that the more secularist elite would give real recognition to Islamic principles, but in the debates and struggles, a new synthesis did not emerge out of the interaction of the liberal nationalists, conservatives, and fundamentalists.

One of the major statements of the Islamic position was an official government report that examined some disturbances that occurred in 1953. They had been caused by fundamentalist and conservative agitation that had attempted to force an exclusionary definition of Islam upon the state. The focus had been opposition to the Ahmadiyyah movement and the demand for its suppression. The report, called the Munir Report, clearly identified the dilemmas in defining a modern Islamic state: If it were defined in the exclusive manner proposed by the ulama and the fundamentalists, the state could not be democratic; if the state were theocratic, it could not be a republic based on the will of the people. The conclusion of the report presents a clear expression of modern Islamic individualistic secularism. "The sublime faith called Islam will live even if our leaders are not there to enforce it. It lives in the individual, in his soul and outlook, in his relations with God and men, from the cradle to the grave, and our politicians should understand that if Divine commands cannot make or keep a man a Musalman, their statutes will not."[10]

In many ways, that spirit dominated the constitution that was approved in 1956, although many compromises had been made to accommodate the conservative and fundamentalist positions. It adhered to the principle of complete equality between Muslims and non-Muslims, and rather than imposing Islamic law, it said that the state would be a democracy based on Islamic principles. On the issue of theocracy, God's exclusive sovereignty over the whole universe was affirmed, but the people of Pakistan had a sacred trust to authority in their country. Although the constitution was seen as a successful compromise at the time, it did not make a stable political system possible. In 1958, following political anarchy, the constitution was suspended, martial law was proclaimed, and Muhammad Ayyub Khan took control of the government in a military coup.

The era of Ayyub Khan lasted from 1958 to 1969, and during that time Pakistan was given political stability not on the basis of an ideological consensus but through a strong executive backed by the armed forces. In contrast to other contemporary military regimes, the Ayyub government was relatively conservative in its approach to socioeconomic affairs. It was, however, committed to a relatively secularist concept of a democratic-Islamic Pakistan unified under a strong central government. The 1956 constitution was abrogated, ant a new one was promulgated in 1962.

The Ayyub regime interfered very little with ulama affairs as long as they were not overtly political, an implicitly secularist approach. The government took effective steps to reform Muslim family law along liberal modernist lines and reaffirmed a liberal modernist educational policy in which, as the Commission of National Education reported, "Religion is not presented as a dogma, superstitution or ritual."[11] In the administration of law, the policy of maintaining an independent, modern-style judiciary that recognized the validity of Islamic principles but was not tied to traditional details was continued. The constitution of 1962 established, in general, a regime that was secularist in practice and Islamic modernist in interpretation, but open to compromise with conservatives and fundamentalists on details. It was a workable, pragmatic adaptation rather than a new ideological synthesis, and it was effective as long as the central leader had the power to enforce acquiescence. However, the old regional and ideological differences were not reduced; they were only temporarily submerged.

Pakistan, like many other states in the Muslim world, entered the 1960s under a regime that was moving in the direction of greater Westernization and modernization. In some ways more radical than the White Revolution in Iran and the policies of the Saudis, Ayyub's regime was less committed to a radical position than Nasser in Egypt or the Baʿth party in Syria. In the growing opposition to Ayyub during the decade. the forces that represented a more radical socialist program or a regional-linguistic nationalism appeared to be gaining power rather than the Islamic forces. The fundamentalists under Mawdudi were increasingly becoming another element in the conservative grouping rather than being radical or revolutionary critics of the existing system.

The future, in 1968–1970, appeared to belong to the Pakistani socialists and the regional nationalists, and by 1970, those two themes were being presented by the two major parties. The earliest of those parties was the Awami League, which had been weakened by internal divisions and the death of some of its major leaders. Its efforts to become an effective national party in the 1950s had not been successful and had undermined the party's mass support in East Pakistan. Then, under the leadership of Shaykh Mujib al-Rahman, it reestablished itself as the principle party by advocating East Pakistani autonomy with the promulgation of the Six Point movement in 1966. It is indicative of the problem of defining Islam's role that Islam was not mentioned in that six-point definition of the proposed federal state.

The ideological tradition of the Awami League was consistently more secularist than the thinking of much of the West Pakistani leadership. The Awami leader in 1956, H. S. Suhrawardi, for example, argued in the Pakistan National Assembly against Jinnah's two-nation idea: "The two-nation theory was advanced by the Muslims as justification for the partition of India and the creation of a state made up of geographically contiguous units where the Muslims were numerically in the majority. Once that state was created, the two-nation theory lost its force even for the Muslims."[12] According to that position, Islam was not a basis for the continuing identity of a state, and the new state should now become secular and democratic. Ultimately, the repudiation of the two-nation theory, with its corollary that Pakistan is a single nation, became the basis for Bengali rather than Pakistani or Islamic nationalism in the Awami League. By the late 1960s, the conscious Bengali literary renaissance and increasing pressures for autonomy, if not independence, for East Pakistan produced a movement that was more secular nationalist than Islamic in the Awami League under Shaykh Mujib. Conservative and fundamentalist Islamic forces still had influence, and even Islamic modernist views maintained some popularity, so that Bengali nationalism did not divorce itself fully from its Islamic roots, but it was not an Islamic republic that emerged when East Pakistan became the independent state of Bangladesh after the elections, revolt, and war of 1970–1971.

The emergence of Bangladesh meant that Islam had been the basis for the creation of Pakistan but it could not provide a sufficient basis for long-term national unity. The style of Islam that emerged out of the conflict was a secularist one, associated with but not identical to the nationalist cause. After the experiment of the "Islamic state" in a unified Pakistan, the Muslim community in Bengal adopted a style that was closer to the experience of Islamic communities elsewhere.

The second major movement that had emerged in Pakistan by the end of the 1960s was a more explicitly socialist and democratic one led by Zulfikar Ali Bhutto. That movement took the form of the Pakistan People's party (PPP), which was established in 1967 with the slogan, "Islam is our faith, democracy is our polity, socialism is our economy, all power to the people."[13] In the PPP, a more typical radically oriented socialist party emerged, similar to the Ba'th in Syria or Nasser's Arab socialism. Just as the Pakistan idea had postponed the emergence of an effective secular nationalist movement in Bengal, it appears to have delayed the emergence of radical socialism in West Pakistan. However, by the end of the 1960s, the PPP was gaining strength by building on the unrest created by the relative autocracy of the Ayyub regime and the demand for more activist economic policies. Although the Awami League won the 1970 elections overwhelmingly in East

Pakistan, the PPP won with less strength in the West. After the war and the breakup of the old state, Bhutto became the leader of the new Pakistan, now limited to the old western part.

Bhutto's platform in the 1970 election was socialistic to redress the economic problems of the people. It was called Islamic socialism, but Bhutto did say that his socialism would be of the Scandinavian rather than of the Marxist variety.[14] That statement indicates that the position was not militantly radical, but it certainly was secularist in its basic tone. In its platform of economic justice, the PPP was able to overcome conservative and fundamentalist opposition to win clear mass support. Like the Bengali nationalists, the PPP did not ignore or reject Islam, but Islam was put into a secularist framework that was quite different from the early expectations for an Islamic state.

Independent Pakistan thus passed through a long and difficult evolution. The initial political instability led to a military regime of a more autocratic nature. Neither the early parliamentary government nor the Ayyub regime was able to create a new and satisfactory solution to the problem of creating a modern Islamic state. Instead, after more than two decades of independence, more common lines of political and social evolution developed, and they led to a successful secular nationalist movement in East Pakistan and a dominant radical socialist party in the west. Islam had emerged in a more common, adaptationist form by the end of the 1960s.

In Pakistan, the political evolution is of great importance and dominates the Islamic experience, but in addition to the political activities, Muslim intellectuals have opened new lines of thought. Fundamentalism has remained stable with the restatement of the positions of Mawdudi, and the conservatives have tended to adhere closely to the lines set by the earlier leaders. In these two styles of Islam, there have been no major new dynamic movements of reaffirmation as there were at the end of the nineteenth century, and the organizations and traditions established at that same time remain the dominant modes of conservative and fundamentalist expression.

It is in the area of intellectual adaptationism of the modernist style that the major new activities took place in the two decades following independence. In the area of socioeconomic thought, there were a number of scholars who began the process of defining a specifically Islamic socialism and democracy in terms that were not simply attaching Islamic names to Western concepts. As a result, the effort in the 1950s and 1960s began to shift from showing that all Western ideas are really Islamic, or that all Islamic ideas are really modern, to trying to define the modern Islamic tradition as distinctive. The shift can be seen, for example, in the works of Khalifa Abd al-Hakim, who saw Islamic socialism as the viable alternative to both communism and capitalism.

A similar and more dramatic shift can be seen in the scholarship of Islamic history itself. At the beginning of the century, there were Indian Muslim scholars, such as Amir Ali, who wrote about the history and nature of Islam. Those men were often respected for their sincere faith and vigorous hard work, but they never escaped from the position of being apologists or informed propagandists. However, following World War II, Pakistanis made significant contributions in the world of historical scholarship, and their work is accepted not simply as the product of a sincere faith but as the product of a vigorous scholarly tradition. The works on Islam by scholars such as Fazlur Rahman (b. 1919) and the products of the Islamic Research Institute under his direction are only some of the many scholarly works that combine the continuing modernist effort to define the meaning of the Islamic experience in the perspective of the modern experience.

Muslims in Independent India. It is a measure of the size of the Muslim community in British India that three of the four largest Muslim national groups in the world were originally within its borders. The Muslims that remained within India after independence are only a little more than 10 percent of the population, but they still represent the fourth-largest national community in the Islamic world, twice as large as the Muslim national communities in Egypt or Iran or Turkey and almost twice as large as all the Muslim communities in the Maghrib. Like the Muslims in Pakistan after 1947, the Indian Muslims were involved in an experiment that was unusual for the Islamic tradition, but the basic nature of that experiment was opposite from the Pakistani one. Rather than consciously seeking to create a viable state, the Indian Muslims faced the task of creating a viable Islamic experience voluntarily within a secular context. As one Indian Muslim expressed it: "Those Muslims who on the creation of Pakistan decided to stay on in India also made, through that decision, a choice that is unique in the history of Islam. Till then Muslims had lived as rulers, a persecuted or protected minority, or in unstable co-existence in a non-Muslim society. Never before had they shared power with others in a spirit of equality that transcended religious divisions."[15]

That summary paints an optimistic picture of the situation of the Indian Muslims. Many remained in India because they had no choice or were too poor to make the trip to Pakistan. The picture describes the goal rather than the reality, and the basic issue of the Indian Muslim experiment was whether or not it is possible to create an Islamic experience within a community that transcends religious divisons. The reality is that Indian Muslims have faced many grave problems and even the author who painted the glowing picture of Muslim Indian life felt that most educated Muslims at the time seemed "to be suffering from a feeling of despair and loneliness. They feel alienated from their own community."[16]

Throughout most of the postindependence era, Indian Muslims have been primarily conservative in outlook and have been unwilling to engage in reformist activities or to accept significant reforms for fear that their communal life might be weakened. Even the Indian branch of Mawdudi's fundamentalist organization acted in a primarily conservative manner, working with the traditionalist ulama to prevent changes in personal status law. The argument of the ulama was that although reform of Muslim personal law might be suitable in a country like Turkey, where the reforms were enacted by the Muslims themselves, such actions would not be appropriate for Indian Muslims.

Leadership in the Indian Muslim community went to those Muslims who had cooperated closely with the Indian National Congress, such as Abu al-Kalam Azad. That intellectual elite also contained a number of highly visible public figures who provided manifest proof of the functioning of composite Indian nationalism. Loyal Muslim allies of the Congress in the struggle for independence became the third and fifth presidents of the republic. Zakir Husain (1897–1969), who had been an associate of Mahatma Gandhi and active in the development of national education, was president in 1967–1969. Fakhr al-Din Ali Ahmad (1905–1977), the fifth president, was a British-trained lawyer who had been an active Congress politician in the state of Assam and had served in provincial and national cabinets after independence. However, a new leadership did not develop very rapidly to replace the old politico-intellectual elite that had formulated the ideals of composite nationalism. Although composing at least 10 percent of the population, Muslims held only about 4 percent of the seats in parliament and held an even smaller proportion of government administrative positions.

The ideal of composite nationalism requires a reduction of communal militance, and the Indian Muslims have faced problems in that regard. Although secularism seems to be a necessary corollary of composite nationalism, many of the Muslims have clung to a conservative style that opposes significant change. An even greater problem is that the Hindu majority has also been unable to eliminate communal militancy. Although the Hindu political elite is largely secularist and liberal in approach, the Hindu tradition has experienced a renaissance in the past century and a half that has produced vigorous Hindu activism. For example, Hindu fanatics murdered Gandhi in 1948 when he opposed the massacre of Muslims and the destruction of mosques, and since independence, the threat of communal violence has never been far below the surface of Indian affairs. During the 1960s, there was a resurgence of Hindu militance and communal violence, which increased the problems of the Indian Muslims.

The alternatives for the Muslims were to rebuild communal organization and activism or to reassert the validity of secularism. The followers of

Mawdudi in India had begun to preach the first option with great vigor by the end of the 1960s, and the second alternative was stressed by a small minority of the intellectuals organized in the Indian Secular Forum. Their position was that "the basic cause of communal riots is communal politics. To fight this menace, we should make determined efforts to build up a strong united front of all those who have firm faith in secularism and who hate communal politics."[17] Those alternatives outline the two basic options open to Indian Muslims: maintain a conservative style, which perpetuates the community but keeps it essentially isolated, or accept Islam as an individual and personal faith and not the basis for a community (and hope that the Hindus can move in the same direction). At the end of the 1960s, the resurgence of communalism in India gave little hope for the ultimate success of the secularist experiment.

Communalism and Islam in Malaya. One of the basic elements of the Islamic experience in Malaya was also the problem of the relationship between Islam and communalism and its impact on politics. At independence, the basic spirit was nonreligious nationalism as exemplified by the policies of the Alliance party. The defeat of the Chinese-dominated communist revolutionaries by 1960 and the effective, if conservative, cooperation of the Malay, Chinese, and Indian organizations in the Alliance party gave added strength to the stability of the regime. However, the basis of the new Malay regime was not an elimination of communalism but a maintenance of communal identities with communal interests being carefully balanced. Such a regime requires continuing mutual trust and is always inherently unstable. The creation of the state of Malaysia as a federation of the Malay states, North Borneo, and Singapore in 1963 and the withdrawal of Singapore in 1965 did not change the basic nature of the regime.

In the context of an independent Malaya, and then Malaysia, the major roles of Islam were to be a crucial element in the identity of one of the large communal groups, the Malays, and to be the support for the conservative political elite based on the traditional Malay sultanates. The leading Malay political organization was the United Malays' National Organization (UMNO), which was led by Tungku Abd al-Rahman, and it maintained a moderate policy of cooperative communalism and provided the basis for the stable politics of the first years of independence.

Cooperative communalism required that the Malay Muslim leaders make at least some compromises with the Chinese and Indian groups, which provided the grounds for the emergence of a more militantly Islamic/Malay opposition after independence. In the northern state of Kelantan, the Pan-Malayan Islamic party, or Parti Islam Sa-Tanah Melayu (PMIP, sometimes referred to as the PAS), emerged as a militant Islamic party opposed to any compromise with other communal groups that would undermine the special rights of the Malay Muslims, and it advocated the creation of an Islamic state in which Islamic law would be fully implemented. The PMIP became an active fundamentalist group and gained significant electoral successes, winning control of state governments in the north and gaining a significant number of seats in the federal governments.

The Islamic pressures on the Malay leaders in the Alliance party increased during the 1960s, but the UMNO remained the dominant Malay party in national terms. However, the elections of 1969 posed a significant challenge to the policy of cooperative communalism. During those elections, the Malaysian Chinese Association (MCA) lost a number of seats to more radical groups that demanded greater equality and less communal privilege, and it appeared that the MCA was no longer able to ensure Chinese participation in cooperative communalism. In that situation, Malay/Islamic activism threatened to undermine the UMNO position, and efforts were made to associate the UMNO more visibly with the Malay/Islamic cause. In the process of this reorientation of the political scene, large-scale communal fighting broke out in Kuala Lumpur in May 1969, and the careful structure of balanced trust was broken. The government was placed in the hands of an eight-man National Operations Council under the leadership of Tun Razak. Order was restored, and a new regime was created on the same foundations as those of the Alliance party. Tungku Abd al-Rahman retired, and the new Alliance party leader was Tun Razak. The experiment in cooperative communalism did not totally fail, but it was replaced, after the 1969 riots, by a less optimistic, conservative alliance of communities, which was a fragile balancing of interests challenged by Malay/Islamic activism on the one hand and non-Malay radicalism on the other.

As in the case of India, by the end of the 1960s, it was clear that communalism is a strong force that can create violent confrontations. Neither the optimistic secularism of the Indian Muslims nor the cooperative communalism of the Malaysian Muslims has provided a way to avoid intercommunal conflict, although both outlooks have a significant degree of support. It would appear that the more comprehensive interpretation of the meaning and implications of the Islamic message—the vision of Islam as a community rather than as an individual's faith—remains a strong part of the modern Islamic experience in areas where Islam is a minority faith as well as in those areas where Muslims make up the dominant majority.

Radicalism and Islam in Indonesia. In the years after independence was achieved in Indonesia, four general themes and organizational types interacted. The most important initially was the old secular nationalist group that dominated the early independent governments. A second theme was social radicalism, which was represented most visibly in an active Communist party, the Partai Komunis Indonesia (PKI), and a third was reformist-fundamentalist Islam, which took a number of forms. The fourth element, which was of gradually growing importance, was the armed forces. The military emerged as a well-organized social force that was interested in the modernization and economic development of Indonesia, and it increasingly represented a specific interest group in Indonesian politics.

The interaction of those four elements provided the framework for the developing experience of Indonesian Islam. After the successful conclusion of the war with the Dutch, a parliamentary regime emerged that was dominated by parties representing the two general policy orientations of secular nationalism and the Islamic forces. The secular nationalists were better organized, and divisions were reduced as Sukarno became the dominant national leader by 1959. His prestige was based on his reputation as the leading nationalist and on his dramatic, popular, charismatic appeal.

The Islamic groups were strong more because of the widespread support for Islam than because of effective organization or unified leadership. At the end of World War II, politically active Muslims had been combined in Masjumi, but that unity soon crumbled. In 1947, the old Partai Sarekat Islam Indonesia (PSII), the small, relatively leftist heir of the Sarekat Islam, had already broken away from Masjumi, and, as parliamentary politics became more complex, the old Nahdatul Ulama (NU) group withdrew from Masjumi in 1952. In this way, Islamic political efforts were divided among a number of competing organizations.

After 1952, Masjumi represented the more urban elements and the tradition of the Indonesian modernist reformers, and it included both individuals and some cultural associations. Its main support came from the Muhammadiyyah. The NU, in contrast, continued to represent the more conservative ulama, was willing to accept many of the old syncretic practices, and was sympathetic to local, especially Javanese, cultural traditions. In its conservatism, the NU insisted on adherence to one of the four medieval schools of Islamic law, thus implicitly rejecting the Masjumi-Muhammadiyyah support for *ijtihad*. The PSII was more open to leftist ideas and remained a small minority party.

The platforms of all of those parties called for the creation of a formally Islamic state, but the emphasis varied in terms of defining that goal. The stated goal of Masjumi was "the realization of the doctrine and law of Islam in the life of the individual, in society and in the Republic of Indonesia as a State, directed toward that which pleases God."[18] The NU goal was similar, but there was a more specific emphasis on the teachings of the traditional law schools, and it was less emphatic in its unwillingness to blend its Islamic goals with those of the secular nationalists. Its political practice was aimed at *sulh* ("peaceful reconciliation") as "the normal basis of contact with every kind of group as long as this is not detrimental to Islam and its struggle," and its goal was a state "based on Islam" but also a "state upholding the rule of law and based on the sovereignty of the people in the sense of mutual deliberation."[19]

The Islamic parties and groups did not present a unified front in the major political debate of the era: the definition of the ideological foundations of independent Indonesia. In general terms, the two alternatives were an Islamic state or a state based on the secular nationalists' ideological formulation, which came to be called the Pantjasila (Five Principles). These two positions were not mutually exclusive opposites, but they were different in style and tone. The Muslim parties wanted the state and legal system to recognize formally the dominant position of Islam, and the Pantjasila based the state on a belief in God but with specific religious practice being an individual matter. The latter was a recognition of a secularist position.

The elections of 1955 provided a test of the political strength of the various positions, and altogether, the Islamic parties won 43.5 percent of the votes in the parliamentary elections. That was a substantial achievement, but it came as a disappointment to the Muslim leaders, who had felt that the dominance of Muslims in Indonesia would be translated into an overwhelming majority for their parties. It was clear that the Islamic political scene was dominated by the Masjumi (20.9 percent) and the NU (18.4 percent) and that the other parties had little electoral significance.

On the other side of the Pantjasila-Islam debate, the largest vote was received by the nationalist PNI, which gained 22.3 percent of the votes. Significantly, however, the more radical secularism represented by the communists in the PKI received 16.4 percent. The major elections provided no single party or group of parties with sufficient support to form an effective government, and cabinets had to be compromise arrangements. As a result, the power of the charismatic president, Sukarno, grew rapidly, and in 1957, Sukarno began the creation of an authoritarian political regime, which he came to call guided democracy. Indonesia moved in the direction of an increasingly radical socialism and a growing cooperation between the president and the Communist party.

The new situation created major problems for the Islamic parties. Some of the Masjumi leaders joined with regional revolutionaries in 1958, and they attempted to establish an Indonesian republic in Sumatra. Islamic leaders were also suspected of giving support to the Dar al-Islam revolts, which were continuing. That suspicion brought the Masjumi leaders into direct conflict not only with the Sukarno regime but also with the military, which was beginning to emerge as a separate political force. Although the military was beginning to have doubts about the growing radicalism of Sukarno and his reliance on the PKI, it believed that the support given by the Masjumi leaders to separatist revolts was a threat to Indonesian independence.

The era of guided democracy lasted from around 1957 until 1965, when Sukarno was the dominant figure in Indonesian politics. He and other leaders, such as Nasser, Ben Bella, Kwame Nkrumah, Sékou Touré, and Modibo Keita, became the leading spokesmen for radical Third World socialism, and at the time, that seemed to be the style of rule that would dominate the developing world.

Islam was given a place in the guided democracy, but only the cooperative NU leaders had any visible role in politics. Sukarno frequently maintained that he was a Muslim strongly attached to his faith; he was however, strongly opposed to the idea of an Islamic state whose actions would be subject to veto by the ulama. Islam's role in the state was to be the religious faith of the majority and, if they chose, the active faith of the majority in the nation's parliament. Sukarno believed that fundamentalists and conservatives were oriented toward the past and offered programs that would not aid Indonesia's progress. "Not back to the easy glory of Islam, not back to the time of the caliphs, but run forward, catching up with time, that is the only way to get glory again."[20] Islam in guided democracy was not to compete in glory with the leader and the basic principles of his regime. The socialism of Sukarno was willing to accept religious values as being important in the lives of the people, but it was thoroughly secularist in demanding that religious organizations and leaders refrain from political activities except in clearly subordinate roles.

The overthrow of the Sukarno regime came suddenly in 1965–1966 and was accompanied by a strong reaction against radical secularism. By 1965, the military had emerged as a significant force with sufficient unity to challenge even the great nationalist leader. When six generals were killed in a conspiracy apparently organized by the communists and with the assumed agreement of Sukarno, the army reacted by taking control of the government. Popular opposition to the radical secularism of the PKI was unleashed in a bloodbath in which thousands of communists were killed and the PKI was destroyed as an effective political force. Although the new regime, led by General Suharto, was militantly anticommunist, it was closely associated with the nationalist tradition and was relatively secularist in its approach. The military leaders remembered that Masjumi leaders had supported antigovernment revolts and therefore mistrusted them. The military leaders accepted the NU but were unwilling to open the door for an officially recognized revival of Masjumi. Finally, after long negotiations, a modernist-oriented Muslim party was allowed by the military regime. It could receive support from the old Masjumi people but was not to be identified as a new Masjumi in terms of leadership. The result was the creation in 1968 of the Partai Muslimin Indonesia (PMI) as a highly restricted Islamic party.

The "new order" created by Suharto did not represent a victory for Indonesian Islamic forces as it was a reassertion of the less radical nationalism of the early years of the republic after a detour into the realm of radical socialism under Sukarno. The issue of whether or not Indonesia would be a radical, secularist regime was resolved, but the older debate over the relative merits of a moderate secular nationalism as opposed to an Islamic state were not settled. The Suharto regime inherited the position of the moderate nationalists, although now Indonesia was led by the military rather than by the old parties. By the end of the 1960s, the role of Islam in Indonesia remained unclear.

Muslim Minorities and Nondominant Majorities in Africa

Virtually every country in Africa has at least a small Muslim community. In the parts of the continent south of the states of the Arab East and the Maghrib, these groups range in size and significance from a few thousand and less than one percent of the population in Zimbabwe to virtually the whole population of Somalia. One important feature of African Islam in the twentieth century is the expansion of the world of Islam as the conditions of colonial rule and independence provided opportunities for the conversion of individuals and groups. Non-Muslims found Islam to be an appealing identity in light of the rapid changes that were taking place, and their interest was aided by the modernization of communications and the expansion of the education systems.

Although small Muslim communities have grown in many areas during the twentieth century, the most important region for the development of Islam is the Sudanic area, which stretches from the Atlantic to the eastern shores of the continent through the areas just south of the Sahara. A wide variety of experiences has shaped the development of ideology and social structures in this region. It is not possible to describe the specific local conditions in the many different countries that have emerged during the twentieth century, but certain basic themes can be used to illustrate the main lines of this experience in both the colonial and the independence periods.

Adaptationism: Tranformation of Old Organizations

One of the major themes of the Sudanic Islamic experience in the twentieth century is the remarkable adaptation of a number of the older organizations to the changing conditions of modern times. That adaptation took a number of forms, depending on local conditions and the type of leadership within the movements. Although many of the institutions and structures that had existed in the nineteenth century simply lost effectiveness as a result of unimaginative conservative attitudes, some provide striking examples of the adaptability of the traditional Islamic institutions. Some of them exhibit that characteristic in economic activities, and others became prominent in the political arena and played an important role in nationalism.

The Transformation of Sudanese Mahdism. One of the most remarkable transformations of an earlier Islamic movement is the experience of the Sudanese Mahdist movement, which changed from a nineteenth-century fundamentalist organization led by Muhammad Ahmad into an effectively organized nationalist movement and modern-style political party. The Mahdist state had been destroyed by the Anglo-Egyptian "reconquest" at the end of the nineteenth century, but the religious enthusiasm that had been aroused by the Mahdist era did not end with the defeat of the state. For the first two decades of British rule, there were a number of traditional-style religious revolts against the foreign, infidel rule, and it appeared that the Mahdist momentum would soon be dissipated in those fruitless conflicts. However, a son of the Mahdi, Sayyid Abd al-Rahman (1885–1959), gradually reorganized the followers of the Mahdi, called the Ansar, into an effective sociopolitical force.

Although most of the Ansar were rural tribal people who were still little affected by modern ideas, under Sayyid Abd al-Rahman's leadership, they were brought together with a significant number of the emerging modern-educated Sudanese. By his patronage and interest, Sayyid Abd al-Rahman won the friendship and support of many of those new Sudanese, and the alliance that he forged between the modern-educated Sudanese and the more traditional Ansar became the basis for a nationalist movement that called for the independence of the Sudan. Following World War II, that alliance was the basis for one of the major political groups, the Ummah party.

The gradual modernization of the Ansar can be seen in the vision of the sayyid's role in an independent Sudan. Initially he was the Ansar imam or religious leader, but in the political activity following World War I, it was thought that he could become the king of an independent Sudan. However, after the formation of the Ummah party, many suggested that Sayyid Abd al-Rahman could become Sudan's president.

Under the leadership of Sayyid Abd al-Rahman, the Mahdist movement was transformed from a fundamentalist revolutionary movement into an effective modern political interest group, and after Sudanese independence, Sayyid Abd al-Rahman and then his son became important leaders within the Sudanese parliamentary system. During the 1960s, a grandson of Abd al-Rahman, Sayyid Sadiq, became prime minister. Under Sadiq, an attempt was made to secularize the party, and that attempt caused a split within the Ansar, but Sadiq remained a key leader in the Sudan. After a 1969 revolution overthrew the parliamentary regime, Sadiq became a leading figure in the conservative modernist opposition to the socialist policies of the revolutionary regime.

Within the Sudan, a similar transformation took place among the heirs to the Khatmiyyah Neo-Sufi tradition. The Mirghani family worked through the nationwide organization of the Khatmiyyah Tariqah to become an effective political force and the largest rival to the revived Ansar, and the Khatmiyyah provided the focus and popular support for the nationalism that advocated unity with Egypt. Like the Ansar, the Khatmiyyah became the basis for a major political party that could operate effectively in the arena of modern-style politics.

In this way, the traditional Sudanese Islamic leadership shows that premodern styles of organization can be transformed into vehicles for modern political action. Nationalism in the Sudan rested firmly on the basis of mass Islamic support, and the political parties during the two eras of parliamentary regimes—1956–1958 and 1964–1969—revolved around existing religious loyalties. Even the major "secularist" party, the National Union party, was led by a modern-educated scion of one of the major old religious families, Ismail al-Azhari (1902–1969). Political parties have not been an official part of the government in the Sudan since the 1969 revolution and the development of the Sudanese Socialist Union as the major legal political organization. However, the Ansar and Khatmiyyah political organizations were replaced as the major forces in Sudanese politics not primarily because they were transformed religious organizations but because they shared the fate of other political parties and parliamentary systems with more modern foundations in many African countries.

The Heirs of Uthman Dan Fodio. When the British gained control of northern Nigeria, they adopted a policy of indirect rule that preserved the political structures that had been created during the time of the holy war of Uthman Dan Fodio. The royal courts of northern Nigeria had become established and conservative princedoms rather than maintaining the militant fundamentalist spirit of their founders, but they were still solid symbols of Islamic rule in the region. In this way, the British control preserved a clearly Islamic, if now relatively conservative, political regime.

During the first half of the twentieth century the northern areas of Nigeria remained relatively untouched by nationalist activism, and Nigerian nationalism, when it developed, was largely the creation of the modern-educated Nigerians in the southern cities. Following World War II, the situation began to change. The British began the process of creating institutions of Nigerian self-government, and political parties and interest groups were formed. Northern leaders soon realized that if they did not take action, an independent Nigeria would be created in which they would have little influence.

The leading figure in the northern Muslim political structure was the sardauna of Sokoto, al-Hajj Ahmadu Bello (d. 1966), who had been a district head and was quick to sense the changing nature of the political scene after World War II. In 1949, a small party, the Northern Elements Progressive Union, was organized by younger, modern-educated northerners, and it was soon allied with one of the southern nationalist parties. The sardauna quickly created the Northern People's Congress (NPC), which rapidly became the party of the northern princes and conservative leaders. The NPC was able to mobilize large-scale support in the region, which was still relatively untouched by more modern political ideas.

During the 1950s, Nigeria moved toward self-rule and independence within the framework of a federal system containing three separate regions. The northern region was the largest, containing about half of the population and covering the northern two-thirds of the country. In this region, the NPC was the clearly dominant force. Each of the other two regions were similarly dominated by regionally based parties, the National Council of Nigeria and the Cameroons (NCNC) in the eastern region and the Action Group in the western region. Because of the size of the northern region, the NPC emerged as the largest party in the federal parliament after Nigeria became independent.

The NPC worked to preserve the more traditional structures of the northern areas and followed a relatively conservative policy in the legislature of that region. One of its early actions after independence was to revise the criminal code to bring it more in line with Islamic practices, and it reinforced the power of the Muslim law courts. The sardauna was an important figure in these developments and served as the prime minister of the northern region in the era of self-government from 1955 until he was murdered in 1966 after independence.

On the national scene, the sardauna was a powerful influence, but the NPC leader who served on the national level was al-Hajj Abu Bakr Tafawa Balewa (1912–1966), the first federal prime minister of Nigeria. Balewa was a modern-educated northerner who did not come from one of the ruling families but had become one of the leading men in the NPC. He recognized the need for significant modernization but hoped to accomplish this through gradual reform. He was able to act as a link between the more aristocratic and conservative northern leaders and the modern-educated southern politicians.

None of the three major political parties was able to break through the restrictions of regional interests, and the federal regime soon foundered on the provincial perspectives of the parties and the personal ambitions of many of the political leaders. The result was increasing political instability and regional rivalry. Early in 1966, eastern military officers revolted against the apparently northern-dominated federal regime, and they killed most of the high-ranking northern military officers and many of the major northern political leaders, including the sardauna and Balewa. During the following year, another coup occurred, and the possibility of northern secession was narrowly averted. Order was briefly restored by Lt. Col. Yakubu Gowon, a soldier of northern origin, but then the eastern region seceded and declared itself the independent state of Biafra. It was not until 1970 that unity was restored.

In this tumultuous context, the NPC presents a mixed example of Islamic adaptationism. It shows that traditional Islamic forces based on organizations created in the eighteenth and early nineteenth centuries could adapt to the changing political conditions involved in the emergence of Nigerian nationalism, but the adaptation was a structural adaptation made to preserve a conservative and traditional order. The NPC did not represent a modernization of the style or content of Islam in Nigeria as it tried to adopt the forms of modern politics in order to preserve traditional privileges. As a result, the NPC became identified as a parochial, conservative force that, in the end, failed to protect its patrons. Following the unrest of 1966, the old leadership and the traditional structures were significantly weakened as influential forces in Nigeria. The experience of the NPC illustrates that simply adapting forms and structures may not be sufficient as a means of providing continuity in the Islamic experience.

The Muridiyyah of Senegal. Some traditional Islamic organizations have effectively adapted themselves to modern economic conditions as well as changing their political roles. In Senegal, a branch of the Qadiriyyah emerged at the beginning of the twentieth century as a major economic force, and it was able to operate within the context of economic modernization. The leading figure in this transformation was Ahmad Bamba (d. 1927), who came from a family of religious teachers that had ties with the nineteenth-century militant, Ma Ba. Bamba had studied in Mauritania and had soon gained a reputation for both learning and piety. He had established the Muridiyyah branch of the Qadiriyyah in 1886, and for many years, the French suspected him of planning a holy war. However, under Ahmad Bamba, the old *tariqah* holy war tradition was transformed into a vigorous economic enterprise.

Followers of Bamba were encouraged to establish agricultural settlements, and those became the focal points for the *tariquah's* activity. By hard work and the ability of the order to provide investment capital, the settlements became major peanut producers. Since that was Senegal's major cash crop export, the order was rapidly integrated, as an order, into the emerging modern sector of the Senegalese economy. In a context in which French rule reduced the major tribal leaders to subservient civil servants, the active order also was able to become an influential political force, although it took few major political initiatives.

The Muridiyyah is conservative in style, maintaining the old marabout structure of a "saint-dominated" *tariqah* and considerable tolerance in enforcing the rules of the faith. The emphasis in the *tariqah* is on hard work and obedience to the leader rather than on performing the five prayers or strict adherence to what fundamentalists would consider essential Islamic practices. In this way, the order maintains the old style of Islam while being active in modern life.

The transformation has been an effective one during most of the twentieth century, and it has only recently been challenged by the development of agricultural resources and industry along more modern lines and by the growing proportion of Senegalese workers who are inspired more by self-conscious economic interests than by a pious desire to serve an order. The order has also been challenged by the emergence of fundamentalist Islam among some of the modern-educated Senegalese. It is worth remembering, however, that the Muridiyyah was able by adaptation and transformation to survive the changes that were involved in the French imperial control, in the emergence of nationalism, in the modernization of the Senegalese economy, and in the change from colony to independent state. If the order was able to cope with all those changes, it may be that this type of adaptable traditional institution will be able to maintain its "tradition" of coping in the next stage of development.

That organization illustrates the vitality of some of the traditional Islamic organizations in the contexts of both colonial rule and independence. By reorganizing structures and assuming modern functions, older Muslim groups have effectively adapted to the changing conditions of the twentieth century. That adaptation was not a universal experience, and many such groups have played a decreasing role in the life of Islamic society in Africa. However, in most areas, there have been at least some groups that have made the transition relatively successfully.

Adaptationism: New Associations and Movements

A second type of adaptation has been the development of new organizations, sometimes building on past traditions and at other times creating new structures for the expression of the Islamic experience. When Islam can be identified with the emerging modern and national identities, it has a special appeal, and it has played an important role in the development of nationalist feelings. In spirit and style, many such groups have been reformist or fundamentalist, often mixing support for modern-oriented social reform with a fundamentalist reaffirmation of Islam. In Africa, as in other parts of the modern Islamic world, this adaptation has often taken the form of new associations.

Islam and Political Parties. One common type of modern association in Africa is the political party, and one interesting feature of the African experience is that few of the parties have been explicitly Islamic, in contrast to the experience in Indonesia or India. Muslims have been politically active, and Islam is seen as having relevance to political life. Islam has played a significant role in defining nationalist sentiments and shaping political programs, but parties have been influenced by Islam more than they have been created as the vehicles for implementing a specifically Islamic program.

That situation is at least partially the result of the political context in which the parties emerged in the twentieth century. In most of the Sudanic countries, Muslims are not a dominant majority. They are usually a bare majority or a strong minority, which means that explicitly Islamic parties would have real difficulty in achieving nationwide support. That fact is certainly illustrated by the experience of those political parties that were the product of a transformation of the older Islamic organizations. The NPC in Nigeria and the Ummah party in the Sudan could not gain significant support among the non-Muslim peoples in their country, which hindered their effective development as leading parties. The NPC was crushed by the factional and regional strife to which it had contributed, and the Ummah leadership was unable to create an operable solution to the civil war in the Sudan. In addition, those parties were not so much explicitly Islamic parties as they were parties formed by specific groups of Muslims to represent their particular interests.

When Muslim parties were formed, they often remained small and were viewed by many as being divisive. The nationalist leadership in Ghana, for example, strongly opposed the Muslim Association party because it introduced religion into politics, and such parties were banned in 1957 when Nkrumah came to power. It is only in an area like Mauritania, where Muslims are a dominant majority, that a party like the Union Socialiste des Musulmans Mauritaniens was possible. Even in Gambia, with a similar Muslim majority, the Muslim Congress party formed in 1952 was unable to succeed on the basis of appealing to common religious faith.

The common and most effective organizational participation of Muslims in politics was through cultural and religious associations that allied them-

selves with broader political parties rather than forming separate parties
themselves. This type of structure provided a vehicle for presenting Muslim
views and influencing political development. In the pluralist societies of
Sudanic Africa, this mode of operation seems to have been the most effective means of representing and defending the political interests of the Muslim communities.

West African Wahhabis. One of the best examples of the interaction between a Muslim association and the general political scene is the experience
of the West African "Wahhabis,"[21] a group of Islamic modernist reformers
who were active in the area following World War II. For centuries, Muslim
students from West Africa had studied in the Arab East, although never in
very large numbers. The common pattern in the eighteenth and nineteenth
centuries was for a scholar with a sound Islamic education gained in West
Africa to go on pilgrimage and study in the holy cities and often at al-Azhar.
This experience often had the effect of inspiring the scholar to work for
Islamic reform when he returned to his homeland. This pattern has continued during the twentieth century.

West African Muslim students in Cairo during the first half of the twentieth century often had close contact with the Salafiyyah tradition and often
learned much from members of the Muslim Brotherhood. A small group of
such students returned to West Africa during World War II and settled in
Bamako, where they felt there was a receptivity to ideas of Muslim reform
among some of the population and the power of more conservative religious
leaders was limited.

The young Azharis (former al-Azhar students) soon became active in organizing informal discussion groups and evening lectures. They advocated
ideas and practicies similar to those of Salafiyyah groups elsewhere, and
they opposed the popular local religious practices that seemed to recognize
the *tariqah* leaders as special intermediaries to God. They upheld the right
of *ijtihad* and opposed blind adherence to the traditional schools of law and
thought. They strongly urged their listeners to study the Quran and the Sunnah and to base their lives on those sources and the examples of the *salaf.*

The young teachers gained a substantial following and soon requested
permission from the French to establish a school. That request was denied
for a time, although their popularity increased. In 1949, the teachers organized a formal association called the Subannu al-Muslimin, which was identified by its ideological position rather than by a particular ethnic group or
social class. It rapidly expanded in French West Africa, and its schools were
well attended and respected, although the French authorities were not helpful, and the association encountered the resistance of prominent conservative
religious leaders. The Subannu revived interest in locally led education and

interest in religious studies and the Arabic language outside of the traditional conservative schools.

This was an era of growing political activism in French West Africa and the emergence of elective political offices and parties. Members of the Subannu were involved in that activism as individuals. One of the major political issues of the 1950s was whether French West Africa would emerge as a single political unit or as a series of separate states. The Subannu, as a organization working to build a broader sense of Islamic community, supported the goal of the larger political entity and came to ally itself with a similar group within the largest party in the region, the Rassemblement Democratique Africain (RDA), which worked for the same goal. As the RDA began to utilize a more Islamic political vocabulary, this cooperation continued. The result, however, was not the creation of a Subannu political organization but, rather, the creation in 1957 of a large cultural association, which included the leaders of the Subannu, called the Union Culturelle Musulmane (UCM). The UCM attracted many well-known political leaders and influenced party platforms.

The goals of the UCM as stated in its statutes provide a good example of the mode of action of associations of its type.

> The association will not intervene in political affairs except for that which affects Islamic education and cult. It must not follow upon the heels or be under the dependence of any specific party, yet may accept assistance and the support of the elected representatives and of all those who hold authority. The association will have no link with any of the legal schools or sects within Islam. It will trace its patterns of behavior on the moderate judgment of the first companions of the Prophet. . . . The oral motto of the association will be "We worship but Allah" and the practical motto: "The obligation to conform to the Sunna."[22]

In this way, the history of the West African Wahhabis shows a reformist experience with a fundamentalist tone.

Hamallism. Another West African Islamic movement mixed the themes of social reformism and traditional organization. This movement, often called Hamallism, had its origins in a reform group within the Tijaniyyah Tariquah. It began with the teaching of Shaykh Sidi Muhammad ibn Abd Allah (d. 1909), who attempted to restore Tijaniyyah devotional practice to a form that had been initially set by Ahmad al-Tijani. That restoration involved reciting a particular prayer eleven rather than twelve times and thus utilizing a prayer "rosary" with eleven instead of twelve beads. Although seemingly a minor matter, this reform attacked the authority of the leading Tijaniyyah teachers in the region, and it ultimately became a political matter since the Tijaniyyah establishment was recognized by the French authorities.

The movement did not gain wide support until after Sidi Muhammad's death, when it was led by his disciple, Hamah Allah ibn Muhammad Haydara (or Shaykh Hamallah, 1883–1943), from whose name the movement came to be called the Hamalliyyah or Hamallism. Under Hamallah, the movement became an advocate of social and religious reform. Although he had had a sound Islamic education, Hamallah soon became more respected for his mysticism and asceticism than for his scholarship. He lived a secluded life of meditation and taught only a selected few students, through whom his influence spread rapidly. Through his personal life he was a challenge to the more worldly and wealthy religious teachers, and the contrast in their life-styles gave added emphasis to his reformist teachings.

Athough no evidence was ever found to link Hamallah directly to anti-French action, the French administration mistrusted him and periodically deported him. However, that mistrust only spread his teachings to those places he was sent to, first in Mauritania and then in the Ivory Coast. Under this kind of pressure, Hamallah adopted a shortened version of the prescribed prayers, which is permissible in times of war or great personal danger. He gradually became a symbol for Muslims who opposed the rule of the French.

The Hamallists, as their numbers grew, came into increasing conflict with the followers of conservative teachers. This tension was strengthened by the social reform programs advocated by the Hamallist movement, which stressed the full equality of all people, supported the liberation of women, and opposed the materialism of the established religious leaders. Although Hamallah did not openly oppose the French, he condemned those Muslims who cooperated with them. The movement appealed to many in the lower classes and other people of more humble origins, and it can be considered as being a socioreligious protest movement in the prenationalist era.

Both Hamallah's aloof style and the French policy of sending him into exile meant that his followers were subject to little organizational discipline, and the movement tended to become a series of local, uncoordinated factions. Those factions had a tendency to become extremist, some adopting clearly heterodox practices such as facing west, toward the ocean across which Hamallah would return, rather than toward Mecca while praying and sometimes altering the profession of faith to state, "There is no god but God, and Hamallah is our shaykh." One of the most extreme of Hamallah's followers was Ya'qub Sylla, who developed an even more extreme egalitarianism by rejecting all traditional authority of the tribal chiefs and marabouts and the authority of Islamic law. His followers established separate commu-

nities in which property and earnings were held in common under the local
head of the group. Although Sylla's extremism was rejected by Hamallah,
his faction continued to have influence in many areas, and after World War
II, that influence was utilized by some in the RDA to help undermine the
position of those chiefs who supported the French.

A more intellectual tradition of "orthodox" Hamallism also had a long-
term impact. Hamallah had converted a major Tijaniyyah leader, Tierno
Bokar Salif Tall (d. 1940), who "derived from the intellectual and mystical
content of Hamallah's teaching the notion that Islam—or perhaps more precisely, reformed Tijanism—was a religion that an African could be proud of
qua African."[23] That tradition represented an African Islam that opposed
colonial rule and stressed equality and social reform. Through Tierno Bokar,
Hamallism influenced a number of significant political leaders, like Modibo
Keita, later president of Mali, and Diori Hamani, later president of Niger.

Hamallism was one of the factors that helped to prepare the way for African socialism in the region. It provided a justification in Islamic terms for
egalitarianism and social reform, and it began the process of mobilizing
people outside of the small group of educated elite in support of nationalist
and socialist programs.

The Republicans of Mahmud Muhammad Taha. The most common Islamic associations in Sudanic Africa are not large movements or interregional organizations. Instead, the dynamism of regular religious activity and
the expansion of Islam are usually centered in numerous smaller associations
and clubs in the cities and towns of the region. These groups are often built
around an individual intellectual whose special ideas form the basis for the
organization's activities. In ideological content, the associations range from
conservative Quranic study groups to radical secularists studying the latest
liberation movement. Some of the groups have a formal organization, and
others are little more than a group of people who regularly share a table in a
coffeehouse. Groups of this type are not all religious in orientation, and
those that are, are similar to informal groups that may meet regularly for
playing musical instruments or dancing.

The smaller associations are the continuation of some more traditional
Islamic groups that were similarly organized. They provide regular meeting
places and are the center of informal social and intellectual life for many
people. For the modern-educated Muslims, the regular weekly meeting of
the local *tariqah* and the discussions and teachings of the local shaykh are
no longer relevant or satisfying, and many such Muslims have formed their
own club or found their own guide, whose activities and message relate
more directly to the lives of people living in the conditions of modern change.

An excellent example of a well-organized small association is the Republican Brothers and Sisters in the Sudan, led by Mahmud Muhammad Taha. It is primarily centered in Khartoum and Omdurman, although people from many parts of the Sudan who live in the capital are members. At the end of World War II, an informal discussion group centered around Mahmud favored Sudanese independence rather than unity with Egypt but was unsatisfied with the political parties that were emerging. As a result, its members formed the Republican party in 1945. The party did not become a significant element in Sudanese politics, but Mahmud's vigor and hard work succeeded in gathering a group of followers that survived the era of party politics.

The Republicans became a group dedicated to the revival of a reformed Islam. The heart of Mahmud's teaching was that Muslims should apply the basic principles of Islam rather than work to perpetuate forms and structures that developed as a result of specific historical circumstances. He distinguished within the Quran itself between the Meccan message, when universal principles were presented as the guide for religious faith, and the message after the establishment of the community in Medina. The second message prescribed rules that were designed specifically for the needs of that particular time and place, and as such, it is an important part of the message because it shows how the basic principles can be applied, but it is the example of that period, not its specific rules, that should be followed. Islam, properly understood, is the true basis for a society that is based on justice and equality and rejects all aspects of inequality. In this framework, the Republicans support full equality for women and oppose the special role of traditional religious leaders. Republicans are active in speaking at local cultural clubs, and they have won a small following among university students. Republican Sisters as well as Brothers take an active part in presenting the message of the group, often acting as street-corner preachers.

The Republicans were opposed by traditional Islamic groups as being heretical, and radicals and communists felt they were too tied to a fundamentalist style of thought. At times, the vigorous speeches of Mahmud and his followers resulted in public disturbances and created difficulties with the authorities, both before and after independence. But the organization managed to survive all the political changes and to bring a message of Islamic reform and revival in the Sudan. As such, it represents an important type of modern Islamic association: the small, dedicated association that, in functional terms, is the successor to the *tariqahs* in providing a vehicle for the expression of Islamic faith and for small-group social cohesion.

Islam and the Political Development of African States

Two important features of the political development of those African states in which Muslims form a significant proportion of the population are the general evolution of a state-supported ideology and the consolidation of national unity. In each of those areas, the states both were part of broader African trends and had distinctive characteristics influenced by Islam.

Development of National Ideology. It has been noted that in many areas of the Muslim world, Islam was a factor in providing popular support for the nationalist efforts to eliminate imperialist control and that support was often more in terms of providing a non-European identity than in specific doctrines or institutions. However, nationalism before independence was a general sentiment more than a concrete ideology. It is possible to unite most people in a country in the struggle for independence; it is after gaining independence that the real task of formulating a national ideology and program has to be faced.

In terms of the development of an ideology, it has been said that "Africa had to debate on Europe's terms before she could debate on her own."[24] That statement does not mean simply that Africans had to achieve political independence before they could develop their own perspectives; it means that on a more profound intellectual level, Africans first had to work through and out of perspectives that they had developed by receiving modern European educations and inheriting European-style political structures.

In independent Africa a common, though not universal, pattern is that the new states were first dominated by the politicians and structures that had been created by the imperialist-nationalist experience. The new political elite was Western educated and often more European than African in basic sentiments, and the new political systems were usually multiparty parliamentary systems. However, during the 1960s, in virtually every African state, that initial structure was significantly modified if not overthrown.

The second phase in the political evolution was also in many ways dominated by Western ideas. The parliamentary systems were liberal in ideology and often conservative in their socioeconomic views, and the first challenge came from the more radical, usually Marxist, European traditions. The result was that during the 1960s, many one-party regimes advocating various types of radical socialism replaced the earlier government structures. Often this change was accomplished by the actions of one of the early nationalist leaders, who turned his party into the dominant party and gained for himself an apparent monopoly of political power. That is what happened in Ghana under Kwame Nkrumah, Chad under Francois Tombalbaye, Mali under Modibo Keita, Guinea under Sékou Touré, and Tanzania under Julius Nyerere. As was the case in other parts of the Islamic world, the early 1960s was a time of the growing dominance of radical socialism in Africa. The major opposition groups in the states that did not come under this type of leadership were the representatives of this new force in African politics. It was only in a few, though sometimes major, states that the initial parliamentary period was not succeeded by a radical socialist phase—in Nigeria, the Sudan, and Upper Volta, it was the less radical military officers who gained control.

Radical socialism did not succeed in establishing permanent regimes in many areas. Its ideological vigor, and sometimes its doctrinaire inflexibility, roused considerable opposition. In addition, there was the vague feeling, sometimes more explicitly expressed than at other times, that radical socialism, like liberal parliamentarianism before it, was an "imported" dogma that was not directly suited to the African context. Many of its ideas were recognized as sound, but the total package was not considered appropriate for the sentiments and needs of the various countries. Radical socialism tended to create large-scale bureaucracies and dominating central political regimes that, however much the socialist leaders might talk about African socialism, did not fit the African traditions of tribal communalism and gentle decentralization.

As a result, in many areas, a third phase in the development of national ideologies had emerged by the end of the 1960s. The primary theme in this new phase was the effort to create a true synthesis of African and modern elements, not just a haphazard adoption of a few African symbols by basically European-oriented intellectuals and politicians. In addition, the new ideologies were to attempt to break down the long-standing division between the ruling elite and the general population. The bureaucracies of the era of independence had been fundamentally no closer to the masses than the imperial administration had been, and the new politicians had been no less jealous of their prerogatives than the old imperialists.

What was required was a convergent development of both the elite and the masses. As one sympathetic observer has explained:

> A new politics began to emerge. This proposed that the leaders in power would have to turn their backs on elitist self-promotion: would have to abandon, that is, the project of becoming a ruling class. . . . This politics looked for a comparable movement of cultural convergence from the direction of the masses. Just as the ruling few must break with the colonial heritage, so must the many begin to win clear of handicaps imposed by the precolonial heritage. No one need be asked to abandon the shrines of the ancestors; but the ancestors must learn to speak the language of modern reality, or else accept retirement into cultural decay.[25]

One of the pioneers in this new mood of African ideology was Julius Nyerere in Tanzania, a remarkably durable political leader who has survived and helped to shape the major transitions in his country. He was a major nationalist leader whose party emerged as the strongest in the multiparty stage of self-government. After independence, that party formed the one-party regime and was committed to a relatively radical socialist program, which began to create a large government bureaucracy. The new era was initiated in Tanzania by the Arusha Declaration in 1967, which set in motion movements of economic decentralization and popular participation that are characteristic of the emerging, more African ideological and political structures. In other areas, the rejection of radical socialism was less successful in its results and more violent in its implications. The Authenticity movement in Chad, initiated in 1973, and the national redemption and national renewal policies in Ghana and Upper Volta were attempts to create a new synthesis that were not as successful.

The role of Islam in this changing context is diverse and changing. In the days of parliamentary politics, Islam frequently provided at least one element of the identity of political action groups. On the whole, it was a conservative and more traditional Islam assuming a modern format, as was the case with the NPC in Nigeria and the Ansar and Khatmiyyah parties in the Sudan.

Islam also had a part in the emergence of radical socialism. In the early days of partisan politics, groups like the Hamallists had prepared the way for a popular acceptance of the more radical programs. During the second era, reformist styles of Islam came into prominence. Older leaders and traditional structures were rejected by the new radicals, and both reformist modernism and fundamentalism could provide popularly acceptable reasons for the radicals' attacks on traditional Islam. Although the radical socialists attacked the institutions of traditional Islamic society, they did not attack basic Islamic principles and often were careful to identify the new ideology as being in accord with the fundamentals of Islam. Although there was not as much effort to expound Islamic socialism in Africa as there was in the Arab East, some of the same sentiments existed.

In the emerging radical socialism, Islam was clearly a subordinate feature. As was the case of Touré's socialism in Guinea, "Islam was disciplined in the interests of a unified national development."[26] Although secularist in the sense of working to destroy the political relevance of the traditional Islamic institutions, there was less secularism than in the liberal ideology of the separation of religion and politics that had been frequently expressed in the parliamentary era. Radical socialism opened the way for a more radical modernist Islam and began the process of the reintegration of Islam into national ideologies.

In the emerging third phase, this new style of Islam was to play a role of growing importance. During the second phase, observers often spoke of the politicization of religion, a phrase that reflects both the subordination of

Islam in a broader ideological framework and the secularist assumptions of the observer. By the end of the 1960s, a reverse process was beginning, but it went largely unnoticed. It is only since the rise of the Islamic revolutions of the 1970s that it is possible to recognize the beginnings of the "religioniz- ation" of politics in the preceding decade. Although the attempt to build a more authentically African ideology in the late 1960s was not confined to Muslim areas, in those areas, Islam was a part of the process.

In areas with strong Muslim populations, the transition took a number of forms. In Guinea, as in Tanzania, the transition was made by the ruling group itself under the leadership of Sékou Touré, and by 1967, doctrinaire radical socialism was being replaced. It had created a large bureaucracy rather than a successful socialist state, and the regime moved in the direction of what can be called African populism. In 1967 a "cultural revolution" was launched to bring the state closer to the people. The state was no less radical than before, but now it was more distinguishably Guinean. In an exchange quoted in 1968, some of the spirit of that transition can be seen. A young, educated Guinean complained that inflation had made it impossible for him to afford the price of a pair of trousers, and a revolutionary intellectual responded, "We did not take our independence just for trousers." At the same time, even one of the most fervent supporters of the government noted that "Guineans want to be as realistic as possible. We don't want to live on slogans."[27]

In the effort to stress the authentically local nature of the radicalism, there was a great celebration in Guinea in 1968 to accompany the return of the remains of Alfa Yaya, a religious leader in Futa Jallon who had been exiled by the French in 1911 and had died in Mauritania. The regime was seen as the true heir of the religious radicalism of Futa Jallon, which had been the source of holy wars in the eighteenth and nineteenth centuries, Although often viewed at the time as an example of the influence of Maoism, the transformation of Guinean radicalism, like the Arusha Declaration in Tan- zania, was more the beginning of an authentically indigenous radical tradi- tion that was more closely tied to local culture than the previous radical socialism had been.

In many areas, the debate was shifting, and Africa was beginning to de- bate "on its own terms" rather than on "Europe's terms." Revolutions in the Sudan and Somalia in 1969 and evolution elsewhere brought the end of both parliamentary "liberalism" and ideologically Western radical socialism. There was a revival of emphasis on religious values and the Islamic tradi- tion, although that revival did not mean a restoration of old-style Islamic leadership and institutions.

Islam and Consolidation of National Unity. Achieving a sense of national unity within the boundaries created by the imperial experience has been a major problem for many African governments as sectional, tribal, and ethnic loyalties have provided the basis for sentiments that have undermined a broader sense of national integration. Islam's role in this area is varied and depends upon local conditions. At times, it represents an important vehicle for supratribal or sectional ideas, and at other times, it reinforces the identity of the divisive elements.

In areas where Muslims are a relatively dominant majority, the strength of the Islamic influence has varied. In some countries like Guinea, it has been combined with other nationwide sentiments to be a factor in national unification. However, in areas where internal social and ethnic divisions are strong, Islam has not been a sufficient unifying force for those divisions to be overcome. The experience of Pakistan has been repeated on a much smaller scale in Zanzibar, for example, where the appeal to the common Islamic faith of all Zanzibaris was not sufficient to overcome the divisions among the Arabs, Shirazis, and mainland Africans. The era of party politics leading up to independence was marked by a vigorous and sometimes violent conflict among groups of Muslims for whom ethnic identity was more important than the common faith.

The problem of the relation of Islam to national unity has been most frequently discussed in a number of states in the Sudanic area where a significant proportion of the population is not Muslim. In those states, Muslim and non-Muslim groups tend to be geographically concentrated, mixing only in some of the larger urban areas. Under these conditions, Islam has reinforced sectional and ethnic divisions by being identified with one particular group or section of a country, which has frequently resulted in tensions and, at times, major civil wars. The largest of these conflicts have been in the Sudan, Chad, and Ethiopia.

Those civil wars have been identified in a number of different ways. Some people have seen them as basically religious conflicts, and others have described them as essentially cultural-ethnic clashes. Another feature of the wars is that they can be seen as conflicts between central governments and regional or peripheral forces in countries with insufficiently integrated political systems. No single explanation of the conflicts is sufficient, but, to some extent, each of the dimensions of the conflicts must be considered if the wars are to be understood. Islam is not the sole cause, nor can it be ignored as it played a role in giving form to the conflicts as they developed.

In the Sudan, Ethiopia, and Chad, Islam provided a unifying feature for regions that were ethnically and tribally divided, and thus it helped to define the conflicts as interregional ones within the countries rather than being simply wars of tribal or ethnic separatism. In the Sudan, the Islamic groups were the dominant forces in the central government, and in Chad and Ethiopia, they were fighting against the established governments.

The Sudanese civil war had long-standing historical roots. An Arab-Islamic civilization was firmly established in the northern part of the country, and in the nineteenth century, various attempts were made by the governments in Khartoum, both the Turko-Egyptian regime and then the Mahdists, to extend their control into the non-Muslim southern areas. Those attempts were accompanied by exploitative commercial relations and the development of the slave trade. By the end of the century, the southern tribes had developed a tradition of mistrusting outsiders. The British in the twentieth century kept the southern provinces isolated from northern influence, and the process of modernization and economic development was much slower in the south. When nationalism developed, it was largely a northern phenomenon, and the independent state of the Sudan was dominated by northern politicians. The southern Sudanese feared northern domination, and the "Sudanization" of government services favored northerners to an extent that aroused suspicion in the southern region. A mutiny of southern soldiers in 1955 set the stage for a long conflict that rose and fell in intensity until 1972, when a new constitutional regime, which recognized southern autonomy within the Sudan, was created as a settlement for the war.

During the era of conflict, the early northern nationalists had difficulty in dealing with the problem. Political activity had developed within a framework of Muslim institutions and ideas, and Islam seemed to most Sudanese leaders to be a natural part of the concept of a unified Sudan. As a result, the leaders of both nationalist traditions—those advocating unity with Egypt and supported by the Khatmiyyah and those advocating an independent Sudan and supported by the Ansar—developed a national consciousness in which Islam was a key element. The idea of a fully secular state was not a part of their political vocabulary, which made compromise with the southern leaders difficult. Similarly, the southerners viewed every attempt at national unification as an attack upon the southern region, and they also had difficulty in accepting compromises. It was not until a new generation of leaders emerged in both regions that the 1972 settlement was possible. At that time, pragmatic military commanders and politicans were able to work out a special arrangement. The settlement occurred in the era of the third phase of the development of national ideology, in which the search for authenticity opened the way for an acceptance of the special traditions of the southern region, and the destruction of many of the institutions of traditional Sudanese society freed the ideology from dependence on Mahdist symbols as well as from the restrictions of the perspectives of the old parliamentary regimes.

Neither Chad nor Ethiopia has been as fortunate in resolving its conflicts. In Chad, the Muslims are largely in the northern part, and they remained relatively aloof from modernizing developments during the colonial era. It was the southerners who had become the best educated and the most developed by the time of independence in 1960. Although the initial parliamentary regime provided a careful balance between Muslims and southerners, it was the latter, under Francois Tombalbaye, who were the clearly dominant force. The awareness of this domination was strengthened with the creation of Tombalbaye's one-party regime in 1962–1963. Increasing taxes and inefficient, sometimes corrupt, administrators soon led to some rural revolts, which were scattered and disorganized.

Muslim politicians opposed to the Tombalbaye regime created an organization and a basic ideology when they established the Front de Libération Nationale du Tchad (FROLINAT) in 1966. French military intervention on the side of the government did not succeed in crushing the militant opposition, and FROLINAT gained more support internationally because of that interference. The liberation group represented a variety of opponents of the regime, but most of them had a common Islamic identity. Along with the calls for social justice, FROLINAT also demanded the recognition of Arabic as an official language. The group received substantial support at various times from Libya and the Sudan. Primarily, FROLINAT was more of a liberation group composed of Muslims than an Islamic movement. Its programs were not distinctively Islamic in character and were aimed at giving the Muslim sections of the population appropriate influence in the government and its policymaking processes. That distinction means that the Chadian civil war was a sectional struggle for power with overtones of personal religious identity rather than a religious holy war. However, as a conflict between Muslims and non-Muslims, the war attracted the attention of the rest of the Islamic world, and the religious dimension of the conflict was a means by which FROLINAT could obtain international aid.

In Ethiopia, there is a substantial Muslim population and a long tradition of conflict between the Muslims and the independent Christian state. During the twentieth century, Ethiopian Muslims have faced non-Muslim control from two directions. In the latter part of the nineteenth century, Christian forces had consolidated control over a wide area to form the Ethiopian empire, which came to include many Muslim areas. In addition, Italian imperial control was established on the Red Sea coast in the colony of Eritrea. In that province, most of the coastal population was Muslim, and the highland population was primarily Christian. The Italians conquered all of Ethiopia in 1936 and then, in 1941–1942, lost control to the British. Following World War II, the future of the whole region was defined in a series of major diplomatic settlements, and the Ethiopian empire under Haile Selassie, who had come to power in 1916, once again became an independent state. However, there was difficulty in defining the status of Eritrea.

In Eritrea itself, Muslim leaders and tribal notables formed the Muslim League, which demanded independence. That demand was not the product of a long-standing nationalist movement but, rather, emerged out of the desire of Muslim Eritreans to avoid coming under Ethiopian imperial control. Although there were a number of significant tribal divisions and factions, Islam provided a basis for a regional unity of goals. Great power and UN negotiations did not, however, lead to Eritrean independence, the argument being that almost half of the population was Christian and desired some form of union with Ethiopia. A federal system was created in 1950–1952 that would guarantee Eritrean autonomy but place it within the Ethiopian state. Haile Selassie soon worked to reduce the separate arrangements for the province and, in 1962, abolished the federal system, making Eritrea an integral part of Ethiopia.

Opponents of the federation left the country and, during the 1950s, were active in trying to gain the support of Arab and Muslim states for their cause. The Eritrean Liberation Front (ELF) emerged out of this activity and by 1961 was an established group with offices in various Arab capitals. The 1962 annexation of Eritrea gave the ELF added impetus. It began to organize sporadic local resistance among Muslim tribes in the province, and in the early 1960s, the ELF continued along the lines of the earlier Muslim League as a primarily Muslim separatist movement led by conservative tribal and religious leaders. Its major theme was Muslim opposition to Christian control. Its primary goal was Muslim independence, and it did not advocate programs of social reform or significant modernization.

Because of its limited goals, the ELF made relatively slow progress during the 1960s. It was unable to appeal to the Christian half of the Eritrean population, and its younger, modern-educated members became increasingly dissatisfied with its conservative policies. However, through its diplomacy, the ELF gained increasing support within the Arab world, in terms of both diplomatic support and direct material aid for the war effort.

The repressive regime of Haile Selassie aroused growing opposition among the Christian Eritreans, and they gradually joined forces with the ELF. That combination strengthened the more radical groups within the organization, and finally, in 1969, a separate, more radical group called the Eritrean People's Liberation Front (EPLF) was formed. With the creation of the EPLF, the Eritrean movement passed beyond the stage of Muslim separatism into a phase of working for a more unified, Eritrean national resistance. The cement for this broadening of the movement was a more radical ideology, which was acceptable to both Christians and Muslims. The movement for Eritrean liberation still retains a strong thread of Muslim separatism, but Islam by itself was not able to provide a basis for a unified national movement. Since the creation of the EPLF, a great deal of effort has been expended in trying to build effective cooperation between the two branches, with varying degrees of success. In that effort, conservative Islam represents an obstacle, but a more radical Islam may be emerging as a product of ELF–EPLF interaction.

Summary

Islam is a dynamic force in Africa, manifesting itself in many ways, and the twentieth-century Islamic experience shows a mixture of the basic styles in coping with the changing conditions of the modern world. In a sense, all Muslims have been adaptationists to a significant degree. Conservatives have continued, as best they can, to maintain existing structures and thought patterns, but often their effort has involved a degree of activism and adaptationism. Old-style organizations have been reshaped to meet new challenges, and even traditional religious figures like village holy men have been involved in a subtle transformation of life-style—as is illustrated by the village saint in the Sudan clinging to old customs but able to offer visitors Pepsi Cola cooled in his refrigerator.

Fundamentalism has been more a tone within movements than a foundation for distinct organizations. The West African Wahhabis, for example, were modernists in the Abduh tradition more than fundamentalists of the Saudi type. Individualism is also emerging as a modern style. The intellectual efforts to redefine the faith in a personally satisfying way, such as those by the Republicans in the Sudan, are a common part of the life of modern African Muslims. Islam can be said to be emerging as a religion as well as a way of life for many people of the continent. That idea does not involve a rigorous secularism so much as a redefinition of the meaning of faith in the context of modernizing societies.

Special Experiences of Islamic Minorities

More than one-fifth of the world's Muslims live as small minorities of less than 25 percent of the population of their countries. In some cases, they are the remnants of larger groups whose power has declined in the past century, and in other areas, they are new groups resulting from the expansion of Islam or the migration of Muslims. In either case, the experience of being a weak minority presents special problems not faced by Muslims elsewhere.

The real options for these minority communities are assimilation or a struggle to maintain a special, separate identity. Often, if the latter course is followed, Islam is part of an ethnic-communal identity that sets the Muslims off from the dominant majorities. Among the larger Muslim minorities, different groups follow different lines of adjustment, and intracommunal tensions arise. In this context of diversity, one can identify certain common programs that result. The first of those is the struggle for full independence, but although many Muslim minority groups have attempted to achieve independence, their position makes that goal unattainable unless there is a strong "outside" force willing to aid their struggle. A second program is to work for special recognition and autonomy within the home country. Formal arrangements of this type have often emerged, but there are always pressures on the autonomous groups as the dominant group or ideology continually works to reduce the special privileges of the Muslim minority, creating the conditions for both a more militant Muslim response and a gradual assimilation of Muslims. The third response to the minority situation is to maintain Islam as a personal faith, practiced in private, while conducting public life in conformity with the public life of the majority. This course of action is the one that is usually most strongly supported by the dominant majority leaders.

It is possible to discuss the experience of only a few of the many Muslim minority groups in a general survey of this type. However, by looking at some of those groups, the main lines of the minority Muslim experience can be seen.

Muslims in the Soviet Union

For Muslims in the old Russian Empire, the time of revolution and the overthrow of the imperial system came too soon. The tremendous vitality of the Muslim communities under the czar during the nineteenth and early twentieth centuries created a growing sense of Muslim identity and an increasingly effective synthesis of traditional and modern themes, but those activities had not crystallized into large-scale, effective Muslim movements or organizations by the time of the 1917 revolution.

In the process of revolution and counterrevolution that redefined the whole Russian Empire in the early days of the revolutionary regime, Muslims were actively involved in trying to shape their own future, and there were revolts against Russian control that succeeded in establishing independent Muslim states for short periods of time. Among the most important of those was the Basmachi movement. In 1917, Muslims sympathetic to the revolution had gathered in Khokand, in Central Asia, and announced the formation of an autonomous government, but that government soon clashed with a Russian Bolshevik republic that had been established in Tashkent and was better armed. The Khokand republic was crushed, and many of the Muslims of Turkestan moved into a position of more active and militant revolt against the new regime.

By 1919, Turkestani Muslim opposition had crystallized in the Basmachi movement, which was a nationalist movement built on the assumption that the new Bolshevik regime was as oppressive as the old imperial order. It was not, however, a traditionalist movement but a product of the emerging radical modernism that could be found in the Muslim intellectuals of the time. According to one of the leading intellectuals in the group, the struggle was waged for the defense of Islam and its task was "to strengthen in the East tendencies which conform to the structure of the East; working together with the Moslem people, to liberate them . . . and to give Eastern affairs into the hands of organizations possessing real vitality in the East."[28] The Basmachi attracted many of the active intellectuals of Russian Islam and also gained the support of Young Turk leaders like Enver Pasha, who fled to Central Asia after the defeat of his government in World War I and became active in supporting Muslim Turkish groups in a spirit of Pan-Turkish nationalism. Bolshevik forces were able to crush effective Basmachi resistance by 1923, but sporadic Basmachi fighting continued for more than a decade. Although the Basmachis had mounted a significant movement for Muslim independence and had gained popular support, the Muslim communities of Central Asia were ultimately unable to organize an effective opposition to the establishment of communist control.

For a period of time, it appeared possible to create an alliance between radical social reformers and Muslim nationalists as the emerging Muslim intellectual class, influenced by the ideas of Jadidism and other Muslim reformist movements, welcomed the goal of modernizing social transformation and became an active part of the communist movement. As the movements of open revolt were defeated and Moscow adopted a nationalities policy that resulted in the creation of various "autonomous" socialist republics in Central Asia, it was the young Muslim communist intellectuals who emerged as the leading spokesmen for the Islamic communities.

The leading figure of those spokesmen was Sultan Galiyev (d. 1930), who fully accepted the program of the Russian Communist party but developed a special interpretation of the application of communism in a Muslim context. He believed that it was necessary to establish revolutionary national governments before it would be possible to move into a stage of proletarian rule. He declared: "Since almost all classes in Muslim society have been oppressed formerly by the colonialists, all are entitled to be called proletarian. . . . It is therefore legitimate to affirm that the national movement in the Muslim countries is in character a socialist revolution."[29]

"Sultangaliyevism" became a rallying point for Muslim nationalist sentiments and soon was declared by the major communist leaders to be a "nationalist deviation." Its exponent was expelled from the party in 1923, and after imprisonment and exile, he disappeared and was probably executed. Nationalist deviation was a continuing part of the position of most Muslim communists, and they were all purged in the era leading up to World War II. Sometimes they had been part of movements of local resistance and, at other times, had simply continued the effort to revise communist dogma to adapt it to Islamic conditions. Their leaders were "double-adaptationists," attempting to create a synthesis by transforming both communism and Islam. By 1939, the old Muslim communist leadership had been effectively replaced by a new generation of intellectuals and administrators who were more fully in accord with the "orthodox" communist doctrine.

Following World War II, the primary styles of Islam were a conservative and a radical adaptationism. For the conservatives, the necessary adaptation was to create a personalized Islam that maintained the faith and participated in state-regulated religious activities. For the radicals, Islam was at most a part of a cultural heritage. The Islamic tradition continues to survive in the Soviet Union, but it does not have the visible dynamism of the late ninteenth century. Preserved in many ways by the conservative habits of personal life, it survives also as "a social bond of union which enables the Muslims to differentiate themselves from the Russians."[30]

Muslims in China

At the beginning of the twentieth century, the Muslims in China came into increasing contact with modernizing elements within and outside the country. They faced the choice of resistance or cooperation with the emerging political forces in China, particularly the republican and then later the communist movements. The basic issue was the survival of identifiable Muslim communities.

The Muslims in China have faced a variety of government policies. The nineteenth-century revolts brought direct suppression by the Manchu imperial forces, and the old imperial servants mistrusted Muslims. That situation meant, however, that the Muslims could be allies of the nationalist and republican movement that came to power early in the twentieth century. The new republican regime under Sun Yat-sen proclaimed that the republic was composed of five great peoples, one of whom was the Hui, or Chinese Muslims. Muslims participated actively in the nationalist cause, and some also joined the emerging communist movement. When the communists established the People's Republic in 1949, they continued to give recognition to the Muslim communities, but they emphasized that there were a large number of ethnic groups who were Muslim minorities, rather than a single people. The communist regime gave recognition to the various Muslim groups without emphasizing religion, since they hoped to reduce, if not eliminate, its influence.

The political history is reflected in the establishment of a large number of Muslim associations and groups. There were some that attempted to provide expression for an Islamic identity that was not tied to ethnic groups. In 1913, the Ahund Wang Hao-nan established the Muslim Progressive Society of China after he returned from a pilgrimage to the Middle East. He was impressed by the Islamic modernist movement and worked to strengthen Islamic education in China, emphasizing instruction in Arabic for children. The group became allied with the nationalist leader, Yuan Shih-kai. When he attempted to restore the monarchy with himself as emperor during World War I, he was defeated, and the Muslim Progressive Society also disappeared.

Other pre-World War II groups that illustrate the adaptationist and reformist trends are the Muslim Literary Society, founded in 1926, and the Chinese Muslims Association, established in 1938. The Literary Society was an educational group that encouraged the study of the Quran and the *hadith*s and began a project of translating the Quran into Chinese. The Muslims Association was initiated by the government under a Muslim military commander to organize Muslim resistance to the Japanese.

In the civil war following World War II, the Muslims were not united in their participation, although most of the established leadership supported the Nationalist cause. With the establishment of the Nationalist government on Taiwan and the People's Republic on the mainland, the Muslim communities were divided. On Taiwan, the Chinese Islamic Association provides an organization for the Muslims who fled with the rest of the Nationalists. They maintain mosques and educational institutions and, for all practical purposes, have adopted an assimilationist style of religious life.

The People's Republic has maintained a dual line of policy, giving some recognition to special ethnic identities but following a vigorous line of limiting religious institutions and undermining traditional religious faith. The officially sponsored China Islamic Association maintains mosques and reading rooms and helps to organize pilgrimages to Mecca. It has provided a vehicle for passive assimilationism, which maintains a basis for Islamic identity while reforming or eliminating traditional Islamic structures. Land reform programs brought lands of religious endowments under government control, and independent Islamic schools were closed. Muslim education was placed in the hands of an Islamic institute, which is responsible for training Muslim leaders in the context of an appropriate communist ideology.

Many Muslims have accepted this transformation, but the option of direct resistance has also been chosen. In the perspective of the communists, these Muslim revolts were reactionary and antirevolutionary efforts to block the progress of the people, but according to the opponents of Chinese communism, the movements show the continuing opposition to the People's Republic. At no time since 1949 have Muslim revolts been a major challenge to the government although they, like the nineteenth-century revolts, have often had local significance. One anticommunist pamphlet lists communist-suppressed Muslim movements in 1946, 1950, 1952, 1957, and 1958 and refers to many more.[31] In nature, those movements were attempts to preserve a distinctive Muslim identity, often within the Chinese system, rather than movements for national independence. However, there were movements to establish an independent Islamic state in Honan in 1953, and another with the goal of establishing a Chinese Muslim republic with the slogan of "Glory to Islam."[32]

In China, the Muslim minorities have faced the same choices as elsewhere: assimilationism, cooperation, or militant separatism. Clearly, the militant option has failed, and cooperation, in China, is very one-sided. The Muslims cooperate in order to survive. The major form of Islam is increasingly a personalized assimilation with some government recognition of a special Islamic identity.

Muslim Minorities in the Middle East

Although Muslims are the dominant majority in most states in the Middle East, there are three areas in which that is not the case—Cyprus, Lebanon and Palestine/Israel—and the situation of the Muslims in those countries is very different from that of the Muslim minorities in China or Russia. Although minorities or weak majorities in their own countries, these Muslims live in a region in which all the neighboring countries are strongly Muslim. As a result, it is possible for them to engage in Islamic affirmation with at least potential strong support from outside their own country.

In each of these three Middle Eastern cases, Islam is part of an ethnic or cultural identity that helps to characterize the Muslim groups. On Cyprus, the Muslims are Turks as well, and the interaction with the majority population is on the grounds of both Turkish-Greek and Muslim-Christian identities. Similarly, in Lebanon and Palestine/Israel, the Muslims are also clearly identifiable as Arabs.

In each of the countries, attempts have been made to create systems of balanced toleration and communal survival, with varying degrees of success. In the long run, no arrangement so far developed has eliminated potential conflict. On Cyprus, the Greek majority was inspired by the idea of unity with Greece, and the Turks feared it. When independence came, it was as an independent republic. The new regime had carefully outlined safeguards for the Turkish Muslim minority, but those did not work effectively. Increasingly, the two communities became geographically separated, with the Turks leaving most of the "mixed" areas under Greek pressure. The government itself was dominated by the Greek community, and the end result was a de facto communal partition of the island, which was solidified by the intervention of armed forces of the Turkish republic in 1974. Turkish military occupation of the northern third of the island continued throughout the decade. Communal autonomy is possible for the Turkish Muslim minority in Cyprus because outside assistance is available when the balanced federal system of the Cyprus republic fails to ensure Turkish communal survival.

The relationships among the religious (confessional) communities in Lebanon is more complex because of the large number of different communities within a single, small country. Because of historical conditions and the national development of Lebanon, when that country became independent at the end of World War II, it contained a number of clearly identifiable religious communities, with the largest being Maronite Christian Greek Orthodox, and Shi'i and Sunni Muslim. A careful distribution of political power was worked out on the basis of those communal divisions, and until the 1970s, that distribution provided a basis for stability.

The Lebanese confessional political system depended on mutual confidence and trust among the various religious communities. It was based on the informal agreement that no group would attempt to disrupt the operation of the system and that none of them would call upon outside support to gain advantage within Lebanon. The agreement meant, in particular, that the Maronites and other Christians would not tie Lebanon too closely to the West and the Muslims would not attempt to integrate Lebanon into Pan-Arab unification schemes. The major crisis of the system before its breakdown came in 1958. At that time, a Maronite president attempted to gain an unconstitutional second term and was viewed as relying too much on Western support, and Lebanese Christians became fearful of the rising tide of Pan-Arab enthusiasm built up by the growing popularity of Nasser. However, after a brief civil war, the system was restored.

Although the confessional system was effective, it was inflexible, and it could not cope with the significant demographic and ideological changes that took place in Lebanon. The most important of those changes were the relative growth of the Muslim communities compared with the growth of the Christian ones; the emergence of a more secularist or leftist viewpoint, which was popular among younger Lebanese but could not be integrated into the confessional structure; and the growing importance of Palestinian revolutionary groups operating within Lebanon. By 1975, the pressures had built to the extent that a large number of religious and private groups organized small militias and began fighting in a multisided conflict, which destroyed the old Lebanese political system.

The Muslim communities reacted to the developments in a variety of ways. The Sunni community was most important in the major urban areas, and its leadership was associated with the compromise confessional structure. Although it was concerned about obtaining benefits for Muslims, it was largely conservative in terms of ideology and social programs. The Sunni conservative position was, however, conservative in that it was attempting to preserve the existing institutions, but those institutions themselves were the product of substantial modernization as the major Sunni associations in the late nineteenth and twentieth centuries had been influenced by the thinking of Abduh. The Sunni majority under this leadership adopted the option of maintaining a special religious communal identity within the confessional state.

There was a significant upsurge of effective communal organization among the Shi'i Muslims during the 1960s. The Shi'i community was largely rural and had little power within the confessional system, which was dominated on the Muslim side by the Sunni politicians. However, that situation changed when the Shi'i leadership passed into the hands of Imam Musa al-Sadr (disappeared in 1978). Imam Musa was born in Iran, went to Lebanon in 1959 as a teacher, and soon became the center of an active organizing of Shi'i communal life throughout the country. Through his charismatic personality, he was able to provide a link between the small Shi'i upper class and the mass of poor peasants. With the new organization and leadership, the Shi'i community was able to assert itself as a political force. This revival did not involve the development of a new ideological position but was the product of communal reorganization for effective survival.

The second Lebanese communal leader who reoriented the role of his community was Kamal Jumblatt (killed 1977). Jumblatt came from a leading family in the Druze community, a Muslim group that had emerged out of the Shi'i tradition in medieval times and was prominent in the rural mountain areas in southern Lebanon. Jumblatt's basic political base was his traditional Druze following, but he emerged in the 1960s as one of the leading leftist politicians in Lebanon, and his Progressive Socialist party was one of the few groups to bridge the gap between confessional politics and the developing nonconfessional generation. This political activity did not, however, affect the nature of the religious community.

The Muslim communities in Lebanon were remarkably conservative in their adaptationism. Many Lebanese Muslims active in those communities were significantly modern in their orientations as individuals, but the communities themselves exhibited great continuity in their style and structure. Because of the virtually unique confessional structure, the Muslim communities adopted neither an assimilationist nor a separatist mode but remained basically communal in style, making alliances for pragmatic reasons. That position allowed them to survive but contributed to the inflexibility that led to the collapse of the system during the Lebanese civil war of 1975–1976.

The third major Muslim group in the Middle East that has faced the problem of being a minority is the Palestinian group. The complex history of the Arab-Israeli conflict has many dimensions and has been described in detail by many authors, but the Palestinians are not, strictly speaking, a Muslim minority. For the first half of the twentieth century, they represented the majority of the population in the territory of Palestine, but they came into conflict with the Zionist movement, which created the state of Israel in 1948. In a series of conflicts, the Palestinians became a minority in the Jewish state of Israel and established minority refugee communities in surrounding Arab states. Although the majority of the Palestinians are Muslim, a significant proportion of them are Christian. As a result of these factors, the experience of the Palestinians varies greatly from that of the more clearly Islamic minority groups.

There are two aspects of the Islamic dimension of the Palestine experience, and the first is internal. In the days before the establishment of the state of Israel, much of the leadership for the Palestinians came from Muslim notables, the best known of whom was al-Hajj Amin al-Husseini, the grand mufti of Jerusalem. The Palestinian leadership represented local power groups and often expressed itself in relatively cosmopolitan terms, appealing to Pan-Islamic and Pan-Arab support. As a result of repression and defeat, much of that leadership was eliminated as an effective force among the Palestinians.

During the 1960s, a new type of leadership emerged among the Palestinians, and it was drawn from the more modern-educated, younger generation. Some of the new leaders were Christian in background, and few had any significant religious training. The new leadership created the militant Palestinian organizations like Fatah under Yasir Arafat and the Arab National movement (later the Popular Front for the Liberation of Palestine) under George Habbash. With these organizations, the Palestinians moved in the direction of a nationalist movement. They rejected thoroughly the idea of assimilation, either in Israel or in the various Arab states in which they found themselves. In establishing movements of national liberation, the Palestinians became secular in orientation, although many as individuals were firmly committed Muslims.

The second aspect of the Islamic dimension of the Palestine question is the impact of the issue upon Muslims elsewhere. Because of the central location of Palestine in the Islamic world and the special affection of Muslims for the shrines in the city of Jerusalem, the establishment of a non-Islamic state in Palestine roused great emotions, and opposition to Zionism became a rallying cry for many Muslim peoples. Ayatollah Kashani in Iran and the Muslim Brotherhood in Egypt organized volunteers in 1948 to fight the new state of Israel, and Muslim militants as far away as Indonesia and West Africa frequently included opposition to the establishment of a Jewish state in Palestine in their activist programs. The struggle with Israel became one way of measuring the success of the *ummah* in the modern world. As a result, many Muslim countries took a special interest in the Palestinian cause, and it became one aspect of modern Pan-Islamic ideas.

The experience of the Middle Eastern Muslim minorities presents aspects that are similar to such experiences elsewhere. However, because of their central position in the Islamic world, their experience has often varied significantly from that of minority Muslims elsewhere. The option of nationalist separatism is more viable in the Middle East, and assimilation not as easily imposed or accepted.

Muslim Minorities in the West

During the twentieth century, Islam has spread beyond the more traditional arena of Islamic activities in Africa and Asia, and in a variety of ways, Islam has been established in European and Western communities. Some Muslim communities, like those in the Balkan Peninsula, are the result of early Muslim expansions. In countries like Yugoslavia and Albania, they remain a significant part of the population and face the prospects of separatism or assimilation. However, as a result of the migration of peoples and ideas, Muslims have also created communities in other parts of the West. By the end of the 1960s, for example, Muslims were the second-largest religious group in France as a result of the Algerians who live in that country.

In most cases, these Muslim communities are basically immigrant ones and are identified with people who came from some Muslim land. However, one major Muslim movement is of a different origin, the Nation of Islam or the Black Muslim movement in the United States. Under the pressures of racial discrimination in the United States, some black leaders began to create separatist movements built on a variety of ideologies. One such movement came under the leadership of Elijah Muhammad (1897–1975) in 1934. Inspired by some contact with Islamic ideas, Elijah Muhammad developed an ideology of black separatism utilizing a particular interpretation of Islamic teachings. The organization insisted upon a strict moral code for its members and called for the creation of a separate black Islamic nation within the United States.

In its early history, the movement was limited to blacks and rejected white members, but changes were taking place within the movement by the 1960s. A leading figure in those changes was Malcolm X, who advocated a less racially exclusive organization. Malcolm and others in the movement had come into close contact with other Muslims and believed that Elijah Muhammad was in error in his doctrines on race. One leader in the organization described Malcolm's influence: "The primary influence in terms of changes was he foresaw the natural evolution of the movement. Malcolm saw the way Muslims were in the east. He came back with the description of what was supposed to be an Islamic community. He visualized the ultimate form of the organization was more like the Orthodox Islamic world."[33]

The inherent universalism of the Islamic revelation had its impact on the Nation of Islam movement, and it was being transformed from an ethnic separatist movement into a more cosmopolitan, nationalist liberation movement by the 1960s. Following Elijah Muhammad's death in 1975, his son Wallace Muhammad led the movement into the next step of a movement for cultural autonomy based on the special message of Islam. In this way, in the very different context of American society, the U.S. Muslim minority experiences many of the same problems and faces the same options as Muslim minorities elsewhere.

Conclusion

The first two-thirds of the twentieth century were years of great changes in the world of Islam. Utilizing conservative, fundamentalist, adaptationist, and individualist styles of Islamic experience, Muslims lived in the context of the vast transformations of modern history. Local conditions set limits to the options in many cases, but the great issues of the interaction of elements of continuity within the Islamic tradition with the ideas and structures presented by the West were a common theme.

At the beginning of the century, virtually all of the Islamic world was under European domination, and it was European power as well as European ideas that had to be faced. However, the diverse dynamism seen in the nineteenth century continued into the twentieth. Through movements of reform and nationalism, through redefinition and revival, Islamic societies not only survived, but most of them overcame foreign domination to emerge as independent states by the 1960s. By that time, intellectual adaptationism had created popular ideologies of a more radical style that were displacing the more conservative or religiously oriented ideologies. However, the more radical ideologies, too, were, in at least some ways, "imported" methods and concepts.

By the end of the 1960s, it was becoming clear that modernization was not simply adoption of Western ideologies and institutions, and indigenous forms of political organization and ideology were emerging. Those were clearly the product of the experience of modernization, but they were also, and just as clearly, tied in profound ways to the premodern heritage. It was this new development that dominated the Islamic experience of the 1970s.

6

The Resurgence of Islam

The Spirit of the New Century

Introduction: Main Features of Change

The last quarter of the twentieth century is a time of global transformation and reorientation, and in the early years of its fifteenth century, beginning in 1979–1980, Islam was in the midst of a new surge of dynamism. In this vigorous reaffirmation, there are elements of both continuity and change, and the resurgence is a product of both developments within global modern society and within the global Islamic experience.

The Transformation of the Modern

The impact of the "modern transformation" on the Islamic world is often noted, but an equally important part of the Islamic resurgence is the impact on Islamic experiences of the "transformation of the modern" which has taken place in the final decades of the twentieth century. The nature of modernity itself has changed, with profound implications for all human societies. This can be seen in the changing nature of secularism, in the broader postmodern redefinitions of contemporary life, and in the transformation of radicalism.

Secularism has long been assumed to be an inherent part of the process of modernization. If this means simply that traditional religious concepts will be less important in a modernized society, it is valid. If, however, this assumption means that religion will no longer be a vital force in the political and social life of modernized people, it is clearly not valid. Even the most antireligious worldviews are now recognized as functioning as religious belief systems, and the struggle is between belief systems rather than between belief and unbelief. In addition, even religions traditionally defined exhibit significant signs of vitality in modernized societies as seen in the resurgence of the Christian churches in eastern Europe after decades of communist rule.

289

The renewed vitality of traditional belief systems is clearly visible in the Islamic world. One prominent scholar, Ernest Gellner, is willing to state that "no secularization has taken place in the world of Islam. . . . Islam is secularization-resistant, and the striking thing is that this remains true under a whole range of political regimes."[1] This whole range includes relatively modernized as well as more traditional societies. Modernization clearly has not meant an end of religion as a major force. On the contrary, by the beginning of the 1990s, the renewed vitality of Islam was one of the most important forces even in the most modernized areas.

In this new context, the old modernist adaptationism of liberal Muslim intellectuals is less important than in the first half of the twentieth century. Islamic modernism now seems to have been the phase of intellectual development in the era of Western domination, which was a time of transition between the traditional and contemporary affirmations of a more authentic Islamic thought.

A postmodern redefinition of the Western and modern experiences has played an important role in this change. By the end of the 1960s, people in many modern societies were becoming convinced that modernization as it had been experienced up to that time had not solved the major problems of humanity and had created new problems. In many societies there was an effort to redefine or transcend the modern and to identify new goals for human life.

In the Islamic world, this redefinition started from the concrete base of experience. The first waves of modernization had produced liberal constitutional regimes that had become vehicles for corruption and oppression. The conviction that Western liberalism had failed was part of the incentive for Muslims to turn to more radical ideologies in the 1960s. However, by the beginning of the 1970s, in many areas, growing numbers of people also became convinced that the Western-inspired radical socialisms of people like Nasser, Ahmad Ben Bella, and Sukarno had also failed. The record of conservative modernizing regimes such as the Pahlavi state in Iran or Ayyub Khan's Pakistan was not notably better. As a result of these experiences and the experiences in Western societies, it became possible for Muslims to conclude that the West had failed as a model for modernization and as an inspiration for reform and social revolution.[2]

The experience of the 1960s opened the way for experimentation with new options that were more authentically local. In the Islamic world, the search involved a reassessment of the Islamic tradition and an increasing willingness to use Islam, rather than an imported ideology, as the basis for policies and plans. This effort does not mean an abandonment of transformation efforts or attempts to revert to a premodern social order; it means an attempt to build a postmodern society utilizing traditions that are deeply rooted within society as well as in modern experiences. This situation gives a special character to the Islamic resurgence at the end of the fourteenth Islamic century.

Radicalism takes on a new meaning as a result of these changes. The advocacy of revolutionary change in the social and political order was, for much of the twentieth century identified with Marxist ideology. The evolution of this type of radicalism in the Islamic world reflected the more global development of Marxist radical alternatives. Marxism-Leninism had provided the foundation for revolutionary ideologies in many parts of the world. In the Soviet Union, Eastern Europe, and elsewhere it also became the ideological foundation for the state and society. Radical socialism as an ideology for a sociopolitical establishment came to mean the creation of large bureaucracies and highly centralized structures of power and control. In the Middle East, the radicalism that was tied to large-scale bureaucratic structures, political elite domination, and centralized political control was being widely rejected by radicals and conservatives alike. In some ways, this rejection was a precursor to the democratization in the Soviet Union and Eastern Europe in the late 1980s.

The rejection of the old radicalism involved the emergence of a new style of advocacy of radical social transformation. The new radicalism, beginning in the 1960s and continuing into the 1990s in societies around the globe, emphasized the importance of effective mass participation in the political processes and looked to smaller cultural and ethnic units for identity. The new radicalism became more of a radical populism, stressing the great themes of national liberation rather than class struggle or supraethnic national identity, and of popular participation and authentic cultural continuity.

As radicalism became more populist, it incorporated the effective belief systems of the masses, and in the Islamic world, this process meant the increasing importance of Muslim symbols and terms. By moving away from elite radical socialism, radicalism in the Muslim world became more Islamic in its discourse.

This development was strengthened by the process of modernization. Until the mass media and communications systems were effectively modernized, much of the population lived in relative isolation, and it was possible for a political elite to speak "in the name of the people" without any significant mass participation. However, as the masses began to be more informed through the networks of modern communications, public opinion came to be a growing political force. As the revolution in Iran in 1978–1979 illustrates, even in a carefully controlled police state, antigovernment mass resistance can be generated through the use of modern means of communication. The potential for mass mobilization that has resulted from modernization has been significant in the Islamization of radicalism in the Muslim world.

Revivalist Responses to the Modern

A revival of traditional themes of personal and group identity and a restructuring of basic social and political discourse in accord with these themes has taken place on a global scale in the 1970s and 1980s. The context of this revival is the emergence of what has been called postindustrial society or the beginning of the technotronic age. In both the industrialized and the industrializing world, modernization created large-scale social, economic, and political structures with an emphasis on economies of scale and the virtues of mass production and consumption. In social and cultural terms, this process involved great pressures for global homogeneity. There was an expectation that modernization would produce similar, if not identical cultures and societies throughout the world. Beginning in the 1960s, there were important responses to these developments.

The giant structures of modern and modernizing societies are too large to provide a satisfying identity for many individuals. The globalization of politics, economics, and culture opened up visions for some of universalized groups that could appeal to human hopes for unity but the actual forms and structures for this vision were inadequate. The large structures created by modernism were neither effectively universal enough nor intimate enough to meet the desires of many through the world.

In response, there was a revival of interest in and a growing attachment to ethnic and religious traditions which could appeal to universal ideals while providing authentic intimacy in a community. By the end of the 1980s the most visible example of this process was the revival of ethnic and religious loyalties in the Soviet Union and Eastern Europe, where large scale and universalist structures of Marxism were challenged by a renewed sense of national ethnic and religious identity on the part of the constituent groups. In the Islamic world, these developments combined with the strong continuity of traditional themes to create a resurgence of religion and ethnicity.

One complex element in the modern Islamic experience is the relationship between faith and ethnic loyalties. In the central parts of the Islamic world, the Middle Eastern countries, society has been described as a mosaic of peoples and cultures, with the smaller units maintaining special identities while being integrated into a larger social framework.[3] Because of the universalist implications of the Islamic message, Islam is often considered to be an opponent of ethnicity, but the relationship is more complex. For most major ethnic groups in the Islamic world, religion is a key factor in the definition of the ethnic identity. No Kurd, Malay, Uzbek, Turk, or other group would envision a definition of their special identity without some reference to Islam.

A revival of ethnic consciousness frequently involves a resurgence of religion rather than its negation, as can be seen, for example, in Malaysia. What is in conflict is not Islam and ethnic loyalty but, rather, differing identifications and interpretations of Islam. Kurds who opposed the Khomeini regime in the 1980s may have opposed a particular interpretation of Islam but remained vigorously Islamic. In concrete terms, the competing patterns are a universalized Islam opposed to a pluralist Islam.

The religious revival in the Islamic world is not a totally new feature in the modern Islamic experience. An Egyptian analyst noted this in protesting against the alarmist coverage of the Islamic revolution in Iran in 1979: "They publish news, articles, and figures on the danger of the new Islamic movement as if there had never been, a century or so before, movements in the Islamic world much bigger than the present movement in Iran. The awakening of the Islamic world has not just begun. It began a long time ago."[4] This is a valid objection in terms of the dynamic history of Islam in the past two centuries. However, in the post-World War II era, many movements have tended to subordinate Islam to other causes. The early Westernizing and secularist reformers had this effect as did the nationalist and radical socialist ideologies. The resurgence of the 1970s and 1980s involved an effort to affirm the primacy of Islam in the efforts of social transformation and communal identity. In the global context of the transformation of the modern, the resurgence is the effort to modernize without Westernizing, to create social structures that are both modern and authentically Islamic. It is not an effort simply to recreate old institutions and a premodern social order.

The eighteenth century Muslim experience assumes importance in this context. During that century Muslims were also actively engaged in redefining what was authentically Islamic. The results of that effort were the creation of Neo-Sufism and the mood of socio-moral reconstruction. Specific structures created at that time have not been perpetuated, but the spirit of the movements has remained a part of the "subconscious heritage" and provides an important foundation for contemporary developments.

The eighteenth century revival was fundamentalist and not conservative, which gives the legitimacy of preimperialist development to fundamentalism today. The fundamentalist style was firmly established long before it was called upon to oppose imperialism, and it did not die when the direct control of the imperialists passed. Fundamentalism is not simply a "reactionary" style, reacting to immediate conditions, and this gives contemporary fundamentalism a strength which is not found in the Westernizing modernist traditions, whose appeal is diluted by the disappearance of the need for the old type of apologetics and polemics.

The eighteenth century movements also provided a successful basis for combining the universalist Islamic message with an appeal to the noncosmopolitan masses. The Neo-Sufi orders took Sufism and Islamic universalism out of the hands of the cosmopolitan intellectual elite and created relatively effective mass movements. These movements had an awareness of the larger *ummah* while operating within the context of specific local conditions. These eighteenth century *tariqah*s are not themselves the structures of the recent revival, but they helped to prepare the popular Islamic consciousness for the present resurgence.

The basic theme of the revived Islamic experience in the 1970s and 1980s is well expressed by Sadiq al-Mahdi, a leader of the Ansar in the Sudan and a descendant of the Sudanese Mahdi. He stated, "In the context of Sudanese and indeed Third World countries generally, there are two urgent quests: to satisfy the quest for identity and for modernisation. The communists and secularists want modernization at the expense of identity. The Muslim Brothers are concerned with identity at the expense of modernisation. We satisfy the two quests."[5] Although the specific groups named by al-Mahdi reflect the particular religio-political divisions in the Sudan, the issue is clearly presented: What Muslims want is a faith and programs that do not sacrifice their fundamental Islamic identity to a secularizing modernization nor adhere to old forms so that an authentic modernization is not possible. This search is the key to the Islamic experience of the final quarter of the twentieth century.

Although many of the themes and developments in the Islamic world during the 1970s and 1980s were transnational in character, the state and political boundaries remain one of the major frames of reference for religious developments. Within each state there are different styles of Islamic experience and organizations, and they interact within the framework defined by the political boundaries. As a result, it is useful to examine the experience in the final decades of the twentieth century in terms of the developments within the separate states, organizing the material on the basis of the Islamic style represented by the political leadership.

Traditional and Radical Fundamentalism

The fundamentalist style has the potential for leading in many different directions. Although it is sometimes thought of as an effort of preservation, it is, in reality, more often profoundly revolutionary. Fundamentalists criticize existing institutions and ideas of society, judging them on the basis of an independent analysis of the Quran and the Sunnah, and the radical potential of this approach was seen in the nineteenth century by the speculative fundamentalism of Chiragh Ali in India. The fundamentalist spirit provides a means for rejecting communal tradition in a legitimate way, which can appeal to the beliefs of the masses.

In the current resurgence there are two general streams of Islamic fundamentalism. One is more traditional in its tone, with direct lines of continuity to earlier militant fundamentalist movements. The most visible of this type is the Saudi monarchy, but many of the fundamentalist associations also have continued in established formats and maintained ideological positions that have been defined and upheld for a long time. The shift in emphasis back to more purely Islamic themes has given these groups greater visibility and prestige.

Fundamentalism has also assumed a radical form in the contemporary resurgence. Expressing allegiance to the Quran and the Sunnah and rejecting existing institutions and medieval tradition, the radical fundamentalists engaged in a profound reorientation of the Islamic tradition. This radicalism is a synthesis of the transformed radicalism of the 1960s and the fundamentalist Islamic spirit. It emphasizes mass participation, participatory control, small unit identity, and the elimination of old sociopolitical distinctions. To many observers, this tendency is confusing because there are no appropriate terms in the modern political lexicon. The expression *radical fundamentalists* seems to some to be a contradiction in terms, yet Islamic fundamentalism can provide the basis for advocating a radical transformation of society. The success of radical fundamentalism shows that semantic problems of analysts may not be a helpful indicator of the viability of a movement.

Saudi Arabia: The Traditional Fundamentalist State

During the 1970s Saudi Arabia assumed an increasingly important position in Middle Eastern and global affairs. The Saudi monarchy had been the major opponent of the radical socialist regimes in the Arab world in the 1960s. However, after the Arab-Israeli War of 1967, Saudi Arabia provided support for Nasser's Egypt and King Faysal's pragmatic approach to international affairs opened the way for increasing international Saudi influence. Saudi Arabia's leadership position was made much stronger by the dramatic increases in oil prices and profits during the 1970s and Saudi Arabia came to be seen as an economic superpower able to provide substantial aid to allies as well as initiate ambitious domestic development efforts. At the same time, Saudi leaders provided significant financial support for many different Islamic groups throughout the world, adding to their prestige as leading representatives of global Islam.

The basic nature of the Saudi monarchy continued along the pragmatic lines set by the programs of King Faysal. The aim was to blend modernization with fundamentalist Islam. On the Islamic side, the enforcement of Islamic rules regarding gambling and drinking, limitations on the public activity and dress of women, and compliance with Islamic regulations regarding punishments prescribed in the Quran for such crimes as theft and adultery continued through the 1970s and 1980s to be an important part of Saudi social and legal policies. The constitution is the Quran, and the basic legal system is the Islamic court structure presided over by ulama of the Wahhabi tradition. The modernizing aspects of the Saudi program involve vast investments in education, industrial development, and a modern military.

The process of blending these two elements is difficult and the situation requires constantly maintaining a balance between the demands of the fundamentalists and the expectations of the modern educated elements in the society. The balancing process was successful into the 1990s despite a variety of challenges to the system. The monarchy survived the murder of King Faysal in 1975 and the death of his successor, King Khalid, in 1982, when rule passed smoothly into the hands of King Fahd. Each of these sons of Abd al-Aziz "Ibn Saud" maintained the monarchy created by their father. It is said that this survival was made possible by the vast wealth available to the royal family. Wealth is an important element, but oil wealth did not preserve the Libyan or Iranian monarchies nor a series of radical regimes in Iraq in the 1960s. A key element in Saudi Arabia has been the integrative value of the faith as defined by the Wahhabi tradition and applied within the flexible limits of a pragmatic approach to fundamentalism.

The issues and challenges faced by the monarchy in the 1980s and early 1990s show the strengths and weaknesses of this approach. The ability to manage the potential problems of a transfer of power under crisis conditions shows the strength of the Saudi system in 1963–64, 1975, and 1982. The transitions required maintaining an effective if informal consensus among the leading members of the royal family, the ulama, and the modern educated technocrats necessary to manage the administration and enterprises of the state.

The strongest challenges to the Saudi state in the final decades of the twentieth century have come from the forces of Islamic resurgence rather than from the old radical socialism which seemed to be the major threat in the 1960s. Internal opposition and international developments have combined to confront the monarchy on the very grounds of its legitimacy, its commitment to fundamentalist Islam. This process can be seen in a series of incidents in the 1980s and early 1990s.

In November 1979, at the beginning of the fifteenth Islamic century, a group of militants under the leadership Juhayman ʿUtaybi took control of the holy sanctuary in Mecca and proclaimed the coming of the Mahdi and the end of the Saudi state. Juhayman charged the Saudi leaders with having departed from the true faith and becoming corrupt. The group was defeated only after a bloody battle in the central sanctuary of Islam. Juhayman and many others were executed in the following weeks. Although the messianic message of the Meccan militants was extreme, it reflected a growing dissatisfaction with the materialism of the Saudi state which was expressed even by some of the most notable ulama in the country, like Shaykh Abd al-Aziz ibn Baz, the head of the Supreme Religious Council.[6]

Through the decade of the 1980s Saudi leaders had to balance their active involvement in Middle Eastern and global politics as an economic superpower with their continuing need to reinforce their position as leaders of a truly Islamic state. There was a continuing debate with the Islamic revolutionary leaders in Iran, who challenged the Saudi rulers both by providing inspiration for the Shiʿite minority in the kingdom and by attacking the ideological legitimacy of the monarchy itself. Shiʿite demonstrations in eastern Arabia during 1979 posed a potential threat to oil production in the major Saudi fields, and the possibility of similar expressions of Shiʿite opposition remained into the 1990s. In ideological terms, the Iranian leaders preached that there should be no monarchs in Islam and advocated resistance to Saudi rule.

The tensions with Iran found violent expression in the issue of Iranian participation in the pilgrimage. Saudi authorities had placed restrictions on the activities of Iranian pilgrims but despite these rules, there were various kinds of political demonstrations in which Iranian pilgrims engaged. In the course of such a demonstration during the pilgrimage of 1987, hundreds of pilgrims were injured when security forces attempted to bring it under control. The Iranian leaders condemned the Saudis and even in 1991, a leading Iranian official stated, "we cannot forgive Fahd and his house, because he slaughtered hundreds of pilgrims beside God's house [Mecca] and violated Kabah's sanctity."[7] In response, the Saudis charged Khomeini with "desecrating Mecca to preserve his power" and said that the "Iranian regime's desecration of the Islamic Holy Places is just an extension of its incessant interference in the affairs of the Kingdom of Saudi Arabia."[8]

The Iraqi invasion of Kuwait in August 1990 raised a number of issues for Saudi leaders which reflect the challenges facing the Saudi state in the

1990s. There are issues of modernization which continue to be unresolved and gained some visibility during the Gulf crisis of 1990–1991. The limitations on public activities of women in Saudi Arabia received much attention in Western media as women in the American military began service in the country. There was speculation that the American military presence would have some impact on public opinion in Saudi Arabia, but few incidents of cross cultural tension received any attention.

There was, however, a demonstration by professional Saudi women protesting the prohibition against women driving in the country when more than fifty women from prominent families drove their own cars in November 1990. In a rapid response, the government issued a ruling written by Shaykh Abd al-Aziz ibn Baz, a leading fundamentalist scholar, reaffirming the driving restriction. The Ministry of Interior announced that "driving by women contradicts the Islamic traditions followed by Saudi citizens."[9] The incident reflects the fact that there are groups within Saudi Arabia who hope for a less strict fundamentalism and a more open modernism as a basis for society, but the real power to determine social policy remains with the more actively fundamentalist people like Shaykh Ibn Baz.

The fundamentalist identity of the state was also challenged in some ways by the Gulf crisis. Saudi Arabia had for a long time cooperated with the United States but had been careful to maintain some clear distance in policy to avoid being charged with cooperating too closely with an ally of Israel and a non-Islamic state. After August 1990, the potential for an Iraqi invasion of Saudi Arabia and the developing dynamics of the crisis caused the Saudis to accept the idea of a major non-Muslim and non-Arab military presence on Saudi soil. The Saudi government became an active member of the coalition which was formed against Iraq. Saddam Hussein charged that the Saudis had made Mecca "the captive of the spears of the Americans and Zionists" and called upon all Muslims to rise in *jihad* to defend the holy cities.[10] Criticism of the alliance with the U.S. also came from some important members of the Saudi ulama establishment like Dr. Safar al-Hawali, a leading teacher in Mecca, who argued that it is contrary to Islamic law "to join with non-Muslims in a battle against Muslims."[11] However, while this type of criticism gained some support for Saddam Hussein throughout the Islamic world, it had virtually no practical impact on Saudi policies during the crisis and, as the crisis continued, even some religious leaders were willing to accept the need to have American help.[12]

The experience of Saudi Arabia into the early 1990s suggests that Islamic fundamentalism in its traditional form is a viable Islamic style. The international influence of Saudi Arabia and its support for Islamic causes around the world have given added prestige to Islamic fundamentalism. The real threats to the Saudi system have come not so much from modernizing forces as from those who feel that Saudi leaders have not been strict enough in their fundamentalism. The development of this type of criticism reflects the changing nature of the Islamic resurgence. In the 1970s, the resurgence was a revolutionary force and, in Saudi Arabia, could be seen in the revolt of Juhayman ʿUtaybi. However, by the 1990s, this insistence on greater rigor came from established figures in the political system like Shaykh Ibn Baz rather than peripheral figures like Juhayman. The normalization of this fundamentalism is reflected in the petition presented to the King in May 1991 from leaders of the educational and religious establishment which called for a consultative assembly and protection of human rights as well as elimination of bank interest rates and revision of existing laws to bring them into conformity with the Quran.[13] Even in a fundamentalist state like Saudi Arabia, the new resurgence is influenced by the process of normalization.

Iran and Radical Fundamentalism

For many people the Iranian revolution is the major event of the Islamic resurgence in the 1970s and 1980s. It showed the continuing strength of traditional fundamentalism and marked the emergence of an ideologically radical fundamentalism. It showed that modernization programs that ignore the profound Islamic base of society are insufficient, even when backed by strong coercive forces. The experience of Iran presents a microcosm of the developments and great issues facing Muslims in the final quarter of the twentieth century. During the 1970s, there was a buildup of the effort of adaptationist modernization, which ultimately failed. By the end of the decade, the revolutionary forces of the Islamic resurgence gained such power that they destroyed the monarchy and took control in early 1979. In the early 1980s, Islamic fundamentalism in Iran was a revolutionary and radical force but by the early 1990s, the normalization of the resurgence can be seen in the pragmatic policies of the Islamic republic. The great revolutionary leader, the Ayatollah Khomeini, died in 1989, and the transition to new leadership was made in a manner which reflected the established character of the political system of the Islamic republic.

The Failure of the Monarchy. The basic power of the Iranian monarchy rested on the tradition of monarchical rule, which was accepted by the essentially conservative Iranian population. Rulers and dynasties had been opposed because of bad policies or tyrannical rule, but during the 1970s, opposition to the Shah gradually became opposition to the principle of monarchy itself.

At the beginning of the 1970s, the monarchy appeared to be virtually impregnable. The opposition was weak and divided and the White Revolution appeared to be successfully modernizing Iran. It was assumed, reflecting the conditions of the 1960s, that the major opposition to the Shah's adaptationism came from the secularists and radical leftists. This assumption ignored the development of significant links between the Islamic and secularist opposition groups which began in the 1960s.

The underlying continuity of the oppositional role of Islam in Iran remained strong, and a perceptive analyst could write already in 1969, "Despite all the inroads of the modern age, the Iranian national consciousness still remains wedded to Shi'i Islam, and when the integrity of the nation is held to be threatened by internal autocracy and foreign hegemony, protest in religious terms will continue to be voiced, and the appeals of men such as Ayatollah Khomeini to be widely heeded."[14] During the 1970s the old coalition of forces that had resulted in the constitutional movement of 1905–1906 was rebuilt, bringing together the religious leadership, the modern educated groups, the traditional merchants, and representatives of the ethnic groups in Iran. As the monarchy grew increasingly autocratic the incentives for more effective opposition grew until the revolution burst forth in 1978–1979. By that time the leading element in the alliance was the Islamic leadership, which provided the symbols and terminology for the revolution.

The Shah worked to expand the absolute power of the monarchy and through the utilization of the wealth which came from oil sales and of the power of an expanded military and police system, he was able to co-opt or coerce many potential rivals. This repressive power enabled him to undermine the power of the nationalist and radical secularist groups. He was not, however, able to destroy the influence and organization of the ulama and they became a critical core of effective opposition.

Muhammad Shah recognized the power and influence of Islam and tried to mobilize it in support of his autocracy. However, his attempt to create a set of state controlled religious institutions had little impact on the religious loyalties of most Iranians because of the ineffective and insensitive ways in which the policies were implemented.[15] The coercive power of the state made the independent ulama appear to be heroes of the faith and the shah seemed to be undermining the very reasons for the actual existence of the monarchy. In this way, the shah destroyed the basis for a conservative acceptance of the Iranian monarchical tradition.

Traditional Shi'i Fundamentalism. The development of the repressive monarchy made religious conservatism difficult during the 1970s. Although it is possible to speak of conservative Islam in terms of local village practices or rural attitudes, even these were affected by the modernization programs of the Shah and the extension of state institutions into rural and village life. The conservative ulama were also increasingly forced to choose between accepting a role as supporters or opponents of the Shah's state. For most practical purposes, the conservative style of Islam was submerged during the 1970s, and in its place, the dominant styles became an acquiescing adaptationism on the part of a minority and more visible fundamentalism inspired by either a relatively traditional worldview or a more radical one.

The revival of ulama activism in 1963 was primarily a reaffirmation of Shi'i fundamentals. The *mujtahids* were asserting a traditional position as the chief moral guides of the country. Until the mid-1970s, theirs was the most visible style of Islamic opposition to the Shah, but then a broader spectrum of Islamically-inspired opposition began to emerge. Although all groups were united in their opposition to the Shah and most expressed their opposition in the framework of Islamic discourse, the diversity of views created the basis for divisions within the revolutionary movement after it came to power in early 1979. In this context, the older ulama groupings played a less important role in the actual events of the revolution but by 1982 had emerged as the dominant force within the new system.

Ayatollah Ruhollah Khomeini is clearly the most promient leader to emerge from the revolutionary process, and his position in the revolution and subsequent state is complex because he filled a number of roles. Sent into exile after demonstrations in 1963, he was a vocal opponent of the Shah, and as other centers of opposition were crushed or co-opted, he emerged as the symbol of opposition for virtually every Iranian group. In this way he became the symbol and focus of the revolutionary movement. Following the overthrow of the Shah he became the dominant political force in the Islamic republic, and he was able to command respect and obedience even from those groups that did not agree with his ideological position. In this situation, it was his basic group, the militantly organized ulama, who came to dominate the Islamic Republic while other groups from the original revolutionary movement were displaced from positions of power.

Khomeini was the chief representative of militant but traditional Iranian fundamentalism. He had long advocated an active political role for the ulama. In his discussion of Islamic government, he stated that "it is necessary that the *fuqaha* [jurists] proceed, collectively or individually, to establish a government in order to implement the laws of Islam and protect its territory. . . . Even if it is impossible to fulfill the task, the authority vested in the *fuqaha* [jurists] is not voided, because it has been vested in them by God. . . . The fact that we are are presently unable to establish a complete and comprehensive form of government does not mean that we should sit idle."[16] In early writings, Khomeini had not opposed the monarchical system as such but by the 1970s the manifest program of Khomeini became the destruction of the monarchy and its replacement by an Islamic republican system. In carrying out the first part of this program, he led all elements of the revolution; in implementing the second, he operated as the leader of a particular group within the new regime.

The specific organizational following of Khomeini was made up of many of his own students and of formerly conservative ulama who were mobilized by the revolutionary cause. Their goal became the establishment of a clearly Islamic regime, one that conforms to the Quran and the Shi'i traditions. Their ideology and program are fundamentalist in the traditional sense. They oppose gambling, alcohol, and the corruptions of luxury; they advocate the full implementation of Islamic law in terms of Quranically prescribed punishments for crimes and other matters; and they oppose the modernization of the role of women in society. These are standard themes of fundamentalism and the ulama followers of Khomeini have been careful not to open themselves to charges of heretical innovation.

Since the revolution this group has become the dominant force in the Islamic Republic. The opposition movement and the government for the first two or three years of the Republic was a coalition of forces, with many of the most visible leaders, like Mahdi Bazargan and Abu al-Hasan Bani Sadr, the first prime minister and the first president of the Islamic Republic, being drawn from other groups. However, these leaders were forced out and by 1983, the party of Khomeini, by that time organized as the Islamic Republican Party (IRP) was the dominant force in the new state.

The IRP emerged as the group presenting the program of the more loosely defined "party of God," the general supporters of Khomeini who could be mobilized in the cities and towns. The IRP was organized by a former student of Khomeini, Ayatollah Muhammad Bihishti, who was a leading intellectual and political organizer among the fundamentalist ulama. He had seen the need in the 1970s for a "distinct Islamic ideology" and had been influenced by Islamist intellectuals but ultimately "was suspicious of the modernist lay ideologues and considered them somewhat contaminated by secular ideologies of liberalism, nationalism, and socialism."[17] Bihishti rejected efforts to "reconcile nationalism, liberal democracy, and socialism with Islam as 'syncretic thought'" and affirmed that Khomeini's principle of the rule of the jurist was "the purely Islamic alternative."[18] He led the IRP to a major victory in the parliamentary elections of 1980 and was a key figure in the consolidation of the ulama fundamentalist group in political power.

The nature of the IRP leadership changed dramatically when a series of terrorist attacks organized by former allies in the revolutionary coalition killed Bihishti and many other ulama leaders. In 1979, Ayatollah Murtaza Mutahhari, another major leader, had already been killed, so that the more traditional fundamentalist ulama led by Khomeini lost their most visible proponents.

A more collective leadership emerged with many key figures assuming specific roles within the republic. These included Ayatollah Husayn Ali Muntaziri who often spoke for the more militant traditional fundamentalists and was, until he was relieved of his positions by Khomeini in 1989, the designated successor to Khomeini as the guide for the republic. Another key figure among ulama in Khomeini's party was Hojat al-Islam Hashimi Rafsanjani, who became the Speaker of the parliament and emerged as a leading articulator of the more pragmatic fundamentalist views. He was credited with aiding Ayatollah Khomeini in the decision to accept a ceasefire in the war with Iraq in 1988 and became the president of the republic following Khomeini's death in 1989.

Although important figures can certainly be identified in the Islamic republic, after a decade it was possible to state that "Khomeini and his lieutenants have put in place a working, collective system of power"[19] based on interactions among people who shared a primary commitment to Khomeini's fundamentalist worldview and program and disagreed mostly on matters of tactics and methods. The "pragmatic" and "purist" groups were not separate factions or parties and their collective leadership survived even the trauma of Khomeini's death, although both the new president, Rafsanjani, and Khomeini's successor as Guide of the Revolution, Ali Khamenei, are identified with the more pragmatic approach. In the early 1990s, it seemed clear that the more traditional Shiʻi fundamentalists had established the Islamic Republic in accord with their vision and interpretation and that this republic has successfully survived many profound challenges. The revolution became institutionalized in a way that reflects the normalization of the resurgence by the 1990s.[20]

Liberal and Radical Fundamentalism. The Islamic groups in the original revolutionary coalition included a broad spectrum of revivalist groups, each with roots in Iranian history and in the dynamics of the new resurgence. By the 1970s, the main fundamentalist perspectives in addition to the more traditional one of Khomeini were a liberal tradition and a more radical one.

The liberal nationalist followers of Mosaddiq became disorganized in the years following the collapse of the Mosaddiq government and the most active group in that tradition was the Freedom Movement which emerged in the 1960s. This group was a synthesis of the religious and liberal opposition to the shah, and the more secularist liberals ceased to be an effective force. In the Freedom Movement there was a high level of commitment to Islam and the goals of the movement included a restoration of Islamic values in society. The group's members were fundamentalist in style but influenced by the liberal nationalist ideals. The political system envisaged by these liberal fundamentalists was a government managed by believing lay professionals under the spiritual guidance of the major religious leaders who would not be directly involved in the political process.

At least two senior ayatollahs were part of this group and they provided a balance to the influence of Khomeini and his more active vision of the role of the ulama. Ayatollah Mahmud Taliqani cooperated with the Freedom Movement and had ties to the more radical opposition groups. He was the leading ayatollah in Tehran and was often in jail in the time of the Pahlavis. He was first imprisoned by Reza Shah in 1939 for opposing the expanding power of the monarchy. He advocated an active role for the ulama in opposing tyranny but, after the revolution, he argued that it was time for the ulama to withdraw from direct political participation. This view brought him into conflict with the more traditional fundamentalists and when he died in September 1979 the liberal fundamentalists lost a powerful figure.[21]

A second major leader within the liberal fundamentalist grouping was the Ayatollah Muhammad Kazim Shariat Madari. Born in 1905, he was an older ayatollah whose position as a scholar was senior to that of Khomeini. Although Shariat Madari had been arrested for involvement in the 1963 demonstrations, he was not a political activist. During the events of the revolution in 1977–1978, he became a leading advocate of the religious opposition to the Shah from within Iran.

Shariat Madari's position was a relatively liberal affirmation of the Islamic tradition. He believed that the ulama were the appropriate guides for government but that ulama, especially leading ayatollahs, should not assume political office.[22] In general terms, Shariat Madari did not see modernization as conflicting with Islam and advocated an openness to more liberal views on the role of women in society. The major disagreement between Shariat Madari and the traditional fundamentalists arose over the issue of cultural diversity within the new Islamic republic. Many of his followers were among the Azeri-speaking population in western Iran who had joined the revolution because of the centralizing oppression of the Shah's government. They were not secularists and were committed to the ideal of an Islamic society but hoped that the new regime would recognize their special ethnic identity. When the Khomeini regime imposed a more centralized system, Azeri separatist opposition developed. Although Shariat Madari did not support this movement, many of his followers were involved. In 1982 he was accused of supporting antirevolutionary conspiracies and was officially divested of his titles and remained isolated from public affairs until his death in 1986.

The major political activists among the liberal fundamentalists were the lay professionals, many of whom were major figures in the initial revolutionary government. Mehdi Bazargan, one of the founders of the Freedom Movement, was the first prime minister after the fall of the Shah. Bazaragan was an engineer by profession who had worked closely with Mosaddiq in the early 1950s. He became active in the opposition to the Shah in the 1960s and wrote and spoke on the need for Islamically based reform. He "sees Islam as in accord with democracy, reason and science," but rejects secular assumptions and was "one of the most important politico-religious leaders of the revolution."[23] As prime minister, Bazargan faced the growing power of the traditonal fundamentalists and his position was weakened by the death of Ayatollah Taligani in 1979. When militants occupied the U.S. embassy and held hostages, Bazargan found himself unable to have an impact on policy or events and resigned.

The next major interaction between the liberal and traditional fundamentalists came with the constitutionally defined presidential elections in 1980. The winner in that election, by a substantial margin, was Abu al-Hasan Bani Sadr, a prominent liberal fundamentalist. He had been a student activist in the Mosaddiq era and was wounded in the 1963 demonstrations. He came from a religious family and received a Western education, studying economics in France. He became closely associated with the Ayatollah Khomeini while Khomeini was in exile in France and served in early cabinets of the revolutionary republic. He is a major political theorist in the movement, and as president he faced the growing power of the more traditional fundamentalists and was driven from power and into exile by the end of 1981. During the 1980s, he joined forces with other exiled groups from the original revolutionary coalition but his exile reflects the fundamental peripheralization of the liberal tradition of the Freedom Movement within the Islamist experience of Iran.

A remarkable feature of the Iranian Islamic experience in the 1970s was the emergence of groups which affirmed a fundamentalist style of rigorism but did so in the context of developing a thoroughgoing ideology of radical socialist revolution. This radical fundamentalist perspective developed as a part of the reorientation of radicalism and the revival of religious activism. The movement had its roots in the Freedom Movement of the 1960s, but it soon moved away from the liberal tone of that movement to create a new fundamentalist affirmation of Islam manifesting itself intellectually in the thought and influence of Ali Shariati and organizationally in the Mujahidin-i Khalq or People's Mujahidin Organization of Iran (PMOI).

Ali Shariati (1933–1977) came from a notable family of religious scholars. His father, Muhammad Taqi Shariati, was a well-known scholar of Quranic commentary, and he gave his son a firm grounding in Islamic studies. Father and son both supported Mosaddiq, and Ali Shariati spent much of his life in jail or in exile and died in England under suspicious circumstances. He studied in France and was familiar with a wide range of Western thought as well as being committed to the Shiʿi Islamic tradition. He lectured and taught in Iran at various times. His most famous lectures were given in the Husayniyyah Irshad, a private institution established in Tehran in 1965 as a religious studies center and an Islamic education center for the general public. Shariati's lectures in the late 1960s drew large audiences, and he attracted much attention for his wide-ranging and vigorous interpretations and for his reaffirmation of Islam.[24]

The foundation of Shariati's analysis is *tawhid,* the concept of the divine oneness, and in his interpretation of *tawhid,* he created the foundation for a thoroughly Islamic, radical ideology. He wrote, "My world-view consists of *tauhid. Tauhid* in the sense of oneness of God is of course accepted by all monotheists. But *tauhid* as a world-view in the sense I intend in my theory means regarding the whole universe as a unity."[25] The full implication of this theory for society is that accepting social contradictions or discrimination, accepting unnatural divisions among humans as valid, is a form of polytheism or *shirk* and should be opposed. Within the truly Tawhidi Islamic society, there is a full unity that is not just a legal construct.

> All men are not simply equal: they are brothers. The difference between equality and brotherhood is quite clear. Equality is a legal concept, while brotherhood proclaims the uniform nature and disposition of all men; all men originate from a single source, whatever their color. Secondly, men and women are equal. . . . Man and woman were created out of the same substance and material at the same time and by the same Creator.[26]

Expanding from this foundation, Shariati developed a broad range of concepts that defined a general Islamic philosophy of society and history. He was committed to building a modern ideology based on the Quran and the Shiʿi tradition, but he did not accept the current religious institutions and leadership as meeting the basic needs of Islam, and he was an advocate of new educational programs and social reform. His teachings had important political implications as well. One supporter wrote: "He fought on two fronts simultaneously. He opposed the extreme traditionalists who had spun a web around themselves, separated Islam from society, retreated into a corner of the mosque and madrasa, and often reacted negatively to any kind of intellectual movements within society. . . . He also opposed the rootless and imitative intellectuals who had made the 'new scholasticism' their stronghold. Both groups had severed their relations with society and the masses of the people."[27]

Shari'ati worked with a wide range of people, especially while teaching at the Husayniyyah Irshad. He was on the board of directors with Seyyed Hossein Nasr, whose ideas of mystical unity were similar to Shari'ati's concept of *tawhid,* although Shari'ati went further in drawing the social implications of that unity. Also on the board of the school at that time was Ayatollah Murtaza Mutahhari, a leading intellectual among the more fundamentalist ulama but one who worked closely with Shari'ati in the mission of Islamic revival in Iran.[28] In general terms, Shari'ati was an active and influential teacher and the "natural consequence of Shari'ati's sense of the high ultimate destiny of Islam was to regenerate the revolutionary and reformative aspect of early Islam"[29] His was a revolutionary call for a return to the fundamentals of Islam, and his views provided an important foundation for the radical fundamentalism of the Iranian revolution.

Shari'ati did not create an organization but he did help to provide ideological inspiration for a radical fundamentalism that did assume organizational form. The most significant of these groups was the Mujahidin (PMOI). The PMOI was created by young men who had originally been associated with the Freedom Movement but who, after 1963, became convinced that more militant means were necessary if the Shah's regime was to be overthrown. Although they maintained ties with people like Ayatollah Taliqani, they created their own separate, secret organization.

The PMOI worked to provide a radical Islamic alternative in Iran. In a summary of its history and ideology, the PMOI defined its position in this way in 1979: "After years of extensive study into Islamic history and Shi'i ideology, our organization has reached the firm conclusion that Islam, especially Shi'ism, will play a major role in inspiring the masses to join the revolution. It will do so because Shi'ism, particularly Hussein's historic act of resistance, has both a revolutionary message and a special place in our popular culture."[30] In its ideological work, the PMOI "stressed the use of the fundamental works of Islam, particularly the Qoran and the Nahjol-balagheh [the major Shi'i collection of traditions]. . . . However, the method involved is concerned not with that view of religion and the Qoran which ignores social factors but with the renewed attention to Islam as a social, even as a historical phenomenon."[31] The Quran is "a set a guidelines to praxis based on the ideological values which it presents in terms of the background of the Towhidi world outlook from which the particular practical principles are inferred."[32] The goal of this program is "leading the society to the complete obliteration of exploitation and the establishment of the Towhidi system," which means an emphasis of popular participation and a rejection of existing lines of social discrimination.[33]

The Mujahidin worked hard within the opposition coalition and were active in the early days of the Islamic Republic. However, their strong criticisms of the social policies of the developing state soon led to conflict with the more traditional fundamentalist forces and by the end of 1981, Mujahidin leaders were in formal opposition to the Islamic Republic and began to organize in exile. During the 1980s they became the core of an opposition coalition made up of former participants in the anti-Shah opposition. Under the leadership of Massoud Rajavi the PMOI had some success in creating armed resistance to the Iranian government and gaining international visibility. In 1988 the PMOI's National Liberation Army staged a major raid into eastern Iran, and this was seen by some observers as an indication of the relative weakness of the Iranian government following the end of the long war with Iraq. In the summer of 1990, Rajavi could confidently describe the movement as powerful and as a significant threat to the existing Iranian government.[34]

The government of Rafsanjani emerged in the early 1990s as significantly stronger than was expected by the leaders of the PMOI. The regime survived, with minimal upheaval, both the ending of the war with Iraq, which was an effective defeat of Iran, and the death of Khomeini. In addition, the major regional crisis initiated by the Iraqi invasion of Kuwait changed many of the dynamics of regional power and pushed the PMOI efforts to the periphery. Rafsanjani's policies during the crisis and war added strength to the international position of the Islamic Republic and, in the early 1990s, the threat from the radical fundamentalists, who had sometimes depended upon the strength that Iraq had before the 1990–1991 war, seemed diminished.

Secular Radicalism. The established organizations of secular radicalism in Iran, like the Tudeh Party, were greatly weakened by the Shah's repressive measures. They had less impact on the development of the revolution than the emerging new style of secular radicalism represented by groups like the Fedaʿ-i Khalq-i Iran (Organization of Iranian People's Fedaii Gurrillas, commonly called the Fedayan).

The overthrow of the monarchical regime was a point on which the Islamic groups and the secularist radicals could agree. Old and new style secular radicals recognized revolutionary Islam as an ally in the transformation of society. However, they did not make a significant effort to present their radicalism as a synthesis of Muslim and radical secularist ideas and, as a result, their proclamations and programs were increasingly irrelevant to the concerns and discourse of most Iranians who could express their radical concerns in Islamic terms.

The secularist radical groups worked within the coalition opposing the Shah, but the Fedayan were among the very early targets of Islamic activists in the new republic. The Tudeh Party managed to cooperate with Khomeini's government for a longer time but the party's secretary general, Nureddin Kianuri, was arrested in early 1983 and executed in June of that year. Both new and old style secular radicals seemed to be only a minimal force in Iranian affairs, either inside the country or among the exiles. The fate of the secular radicals reflects the shift in the basis political and social discourse away from the old radical concerns of the 1960s to the concerns and issues of the normalized Islamic resurgence of the 1990s.

Summary. The Islamic Republic of Iran is an important part of the global Islamic resurgence. The movement that came to power in 1979 was made up of many divergent groups but the traditional fundamentalists soon were able to consolidate their positions of control. The mission and experiment represented by the Islamic Republic was the challenge to create an authentically Islamic state which could survive and grow in the modern and postmodern world. To a remarkable degree, Iran has succeeded in creating a longterm, successfully operating state which is accepted by many as being clearly Islamic at least in principle and mission. Even as early as 1983 an informed observer could note that, despite the problems of the economy, a war with Iraq, and issues of political consolidation, Iran had "achieved stability on its own terms," and one could speak of "Iran's durable revolution."[35] In assessing the revolution after a decade, scholars could conclude that Iranian revolutionary leaders had "largely achieved" the goal of "institutionalizing the revolution. . . . In fact as well as in theory, the revolution has profoundly altered the political and social landscape of Iran."[36]

This transformation of state and society does not mean that all problems have been resolved. However, the problems of the regime seem to be those of maintaining an effectively institutionalized Islamic republic rather than creating a continuing revolution. The Islamic resurgence in Iran has, in other words, become normalized in the new postmodern world of nonsecular politics and Islamic discourse.

Libya: The Radical Fundamentalist Revolution

The revolutionary regime in Libya is associated with the emergence of a form of radical fundamentalism as the basis for government policy. The system was created when a group of young military officers led by Muʿammar al-Qadhafi (spelled in a variety of ways in Western sources, including Gaddafi and Qaddafi) overthrew the Sanusi-Libyan monarchy in 1969. In some ways the Libyan revolutionaries seemed to be heirs to the Nasserite tradition of Arab socialism, but even their early pronouncements indicated that the fundamental tone of the new revolution would be different. There was a much greater emphasis on the Islamic basis of the revolutionary program and a willingness to experiment in organizational format.

In more than two decades of experience, the Libyan revolution has shown itself to be consistent in its fundamentalist commitment to Islam but willing to develop a variety of new institutions to put that commitment into practice. In this history of the revolution, the first years appear to be years of experiment which reached a climax with the publication of the three volumes of *The Green Book* in the late 1970s. The 1980s was a period in which the basic ideas of *The Green Book* were put into practice. By the early 1990s, the new socio-political order, called the Jamahiriyyah, had become the normal structure within which action and discourse took place.

In developing the new approach, Qadhafi advocated independent study of the Quran and rejection of the rigid formulations of the past in favor of an active adherence to the Quran as a source of liberation and progress in the modern world. He regularly lectured ulama on the need for this study and, in supporting it, Qadhafi is soundly within the fundamentalist tradition of support for *ijtihad,* even though the results of his own independent study have led him to disagree with most contemporary fundamentalists.

A second element in the emerging ideology was an emphasis on Islamic unity. Qadhafi has given a religious and radical rather than a nationalist orientation to the Libyan fundamentalist experiment. Although the Libyan people are often called a vanguard in the world revolution, there was little sense in the 1970s of an emerging Libyan national awareness.

The Libyan revolutionary identity reaches beyond itself. In its ideology, the state is ignored as much as possible as a basic operating unit. In the perspective of *The Green Book,* the state should be replaced by populist associations, and the borders of the existing state are to be transcended. Qadhafi has worked for a variety of unity plans with a number of states and intervened directly in Chad to form a short-lived union with that country. In addition, Libya has provided support for revolutionary causes throughout the Islamic world and has identified Libyan interests with groups from the Moros in the Philippines to the Palestinians.

It is in the evolution of domestic social and political structures that the radicalism of Libyan fundamentalism is most evident. At first the organizational structures seemed to follow the standard Arab socialist lines of the 1960s. Political parties were banned; a single organization, the Arab Socialist Union, was created, with the Revolutionary Command Council remaining the final authority. However, even at this stage of development, the unusual character of the Libyan revolution was visible. It was described as a "perverse revolution" in that "it claims a social revolution that will bring Libya into the company of the great twentieth-century revolutions for social liberation, yet it zealously pursues a revival of Islamic fundamentalism."[37] It was not yet clear to many observers that a socially radical fundamentalism was a possibility.

The radical fundamentalist ideology began to be more clearly defined in 1973. At that time, Qadhafi announced a major revision of national policy. In a five point program, all existing laws were abrogated, and Islamic law provided the basis for the new legal system. The revolutionary masses were to be armed and all deviationists purged. A cultural revolution was proclaimed in which "all bourgeois and bureaucratic ideas shall be eliminated as they create an insular class which handicaps social progress,"[38] and books and writing that deviated from the Quran were to be eliminated from libraries and the school curricula. In administrative terms, the new national policy aimed at turning the government over to the masses through the creation of people's committees which would run government agencies, schools, and large-scale private enterprises.

Qadhafi defined the new regime as a clear alternative to both communism and capitalism. This approach was called the Third Universal Alternative and was defined in the three volumes of *The Green Book*. The first volume appeared in 1976, and it explained the political dimension of the Third Universal Alternative. The goal was the direct rule by the people through people's participatory committees. The spirit of this approach is captured in the slogan, "No Representation in Lieu of the People," and parliamentary systems are rejected as denials of democracy. "Parliaments are the backbone of traditional democracy as it exists today. A parliament is a misrepresentation of the people. . . . A parliament is originally founded to represent the people, but this in itself, is undemocratic as democracy means the authority of the people not an authority acting on their behalf. . . . True democracy exists only through the participation of the people."[39] The solution recommended is rule by popular congresses and people's committees. Although news reports at the time emphasized the rather chaotic nature of administration by people's committees, the system has in fact survived and expanded. A study of the experience of one oasis community concluded, for example, that the new political structures had resulted in "increased community participation in the decision-making process."[40]

The second volume of *The Green Book,* issued in 1977, outlines the reorganization of economic life. Popular participation is carried further: wages were abolished, workers became full partners in production, and workers' committees took control of economic enterprises. Although private ownership was recognized, it was only for the satisfaction of an individual's needs and did not involve exploitation of others. Rent was seen as a form of exploitation and was abolished. People could own only the homes in which they lived and rental properties passed out of the hands of the old owners. The guiding principle in this area was that "man's legitimate economic activity is solely the satisfaction of his needs. No person has the right to economic activity that provides him with more than is necessary to satisfy his needs, as any amount he acquires in excess of his needs is actually taken from the needs of others."[41]

During 1979 the social basis of the Third Universal Theory was explained in the third volume of *The Green Book,* which discusses the role of minorities, women, and popular unity. Although there is emphasis on the proper roles for women in terms of maintaining households and raising children, women are seen as having the same rights as men in divorce and should not be forced to marry against their will. The rights of ownership for women are confirmed, and women are the owners of the residential homes because of their necessary and natural duties.

The Libyan political system, declared to be the Socialist People's Libyan Arab Jamahiriyyah [people's democracy] in 1977 represents an active experiment in the total reconstruction of society, and the conscious ideological foundation for this effort is the Quran. This is a manifestation of radical populism in a fundamentalist form. While some have pointed to the shortcomings of Qadhafi's ideology, "they should not mask its political effectiveness in Libya. His success at building legitimacy is all the more impressive given the low level of national identity and the lack of a congruous relationship between ruler and ruled that he inherited in 1969."[42]

During the 1980s the experiment became more stable and normalized. There were opposition groups that developed by the middle of that decade, but they were "fragmented, poorly institutionalized, and . . . ideologically divided"[43] and posed no effective challenge to the Jamahiriyyah. The major challenges faced by Qadhafi in the 1980s came primarily in terms of foreign issues. His many attempts to unite with other countries continued to fail, and such efforts reflected his lack of international power. He engaged in a long struggle with the United States during the Reagan administration, with the issues being Libyan claims to territorial waters in the Mediterranean and Libyan support for groups labeled by President Reagan as terrorists. The most serious military confrontation was a major bombing raid in 1986 by U.S. forces against Libya in retaliation for reported Libyan involvement in terrorism against Americans. The struggle and these raids only seemed to strengthen Qadhafi's resolve to oppose American interests, and by 1988 U.S. counterterrorist officials were reporting that Libya continued to act in ways that had brought the 1986 U.S. attack.[44]

By the end of the 1980s, relations with Western states appeared to be improving and some observers were even speaking of "a mellow Qaddafi," and he was widely reported to have great support within a firmly established political system.[45] The complexity of Libya's position by the early 1990s is reflected in Qadhafi's response to the Gulf Crisis. He strongly condemned the Iraqi invasion of Kuwait as a violation of the principles of Arab unity, but he also condemned the attacks by the American-led coalition against Iraq. In an interview after the beginning of the airwar in January 1991, he stated that "he regarded all the warring quarters as stupid and mad. . . . He said he was against the Iraqi invasion of Kuwait and against the aggression launched by the international coalition against the people of Iraq."[46]

Libyan radical fundamentalism emerged during the 1970s as a significant venture in the modern Islamic experience. It is both radical and eccentric, and the special conditions of Libya make the experiment difficult if not impossible to repeat anywhere else. However, the radical populism of the Jamahiriyyah reflects an important dimension of the broader Islamic resurgence. The long-term durability of the Libyan system by the early 1990s illustrates the ability of radical fundamentalism not only to inspire revolutions but also the maintain systems in a relatively stable way.

Conservative Adaptationism and Islamic Revival

The more conservative political regimes in the Islamic world had varying success in coping with the changes of the 1970s, ranging from the total collapse of the Shah's regime to the continuing strength of the Jordanian monarchy. Most of these governments had committed themselves to programs of adaptationist modernization in the 1960s, and the "white revolutions" were seen as the major alternative to radical socialism. The monarchical regimes had been successful at that time, at least to the extent that none of them were directly overthrown by opposition radical socialists. However, the new populist radicalism and revived Islam presented challenges that are more difficult to meet.

Surviving Adaptationist Monarchies

During the 1970s and 1980s a number of adaptationist monarchies survived the challenges and crises. The key to survival seems to be combining an appeal to the authentic sense of identity with a continued commitment to economic modernization. The more closely identified the political system was with the primary popular identities of religion and national culture, the stronger the system was. By the end of the 1970s the threat of radical secularism had been minimized by suppression and by the growing apparent

irrelevance of the old radical programs. Political opposition was not eliminated but, by the 1990s, challenges were more likely to come from those
who could appeal on some religious or national basis.

The effectiveness of the appeal to religion and national culture is clear in
Morocco, where the Islamic validity of the monarchy was firmly established. Hasan II faced a number of challenges, including attempts by the
military to take control of the government. These were defeated by a combination of effective suppression and the psychological unwillingness of even
the participants in the coup attempts to take the final step of overthrowing
the person who was the symbol of communal cultural identity. For many
Moroccans, "the aborted coups [of the 1970s] were a concrete verification of
the legitimacy of their ruler and their form of rule."[47]

Hasan was able to strengthen the appeal of the monarchy to the population
by, from the Moroccan perspective, achieving a major nationalist victory
when he brought Western Sahara, the former Spanish Sahara, into Morocco.
During the 1970s and 1980s there was a continuing struggle with a local
nationalist group, Polisario, but gradually the conflict lessened in intensity.
Some founders of Polisario, like Omar Hadrami, left the organization and by
1990 Polisario had agreed to a ceasefire and the United Nations administered
referendum in the region.

The situation in Morocco was complicated by growing economic difficulties in the 1980s. Riots in 1981, 1984, and 1990 reflected the severity of
economic conditions but in the early 1990s, there was little effectively organized opposition to the monarchy. Significant Islamic fundamentalist groups
among university students and popular preachers condemned the king, but
not usually the monarchy, for the country's problems. The leading articulator of activist fundamentalism is Abd al-Slam Yasin (b. 1928), an educational administrator whose central message is opposition to foreign
domination and socio-economic inequality. Although this Islamic opposition
is divided, populist Islam is a "powerful mode of political discourse," and
opposition to the current system would "have to justify the elimination of the
monarchy in terms of a return to a more righteous and egalitarian Islam
similar to that depicted by people like Abd al-Slam Yasin."[48] In Morocco by
the 1990s both the regime and the opposition were articulated in Islamic
terms.

Jordan presents a remarkable record of monarchical survival during the
1970s and 1980s. The country had faced the major problems created by the
loss of the West Bank during the 1967 War and the challenge of activist
Palestinian organizations. However, by the end of the 1970s, the master
adaptationist, King Husayn had become recognized as an Arab advocate and
ally of many of his former enemies. He worked with the Palestine Liberation

Organization (PLO), and in the Iran-Iraq War that began in 1980, he became a major ally of the radical regime in Iraq. He succeeded in neutralizing potential secularlist radical oppositions by these measures.

In the era of increasing Islamic activism, King Husayn followed a low-key Islamic policy. Although the monarchy could be considered a British creation, the king has sound Islamic credentials as a descendant of the Prophet and the great grandson of one of the last Grand Sharifs of Mecca. The religious prestige of the royal family is kept in the public eye by events which emphasize the pious foundations of the family without committing the government to a fundamentalist Islamic program.

King Husayn recognized the importance of providing opportunities for expression of Islamic fundamentalism as growing numbers of Jordanians became part of the Islamic resurgence in the 1980s. However, because of this recognition, Islamic activists participated within the political system in a normal way rather than adopting antimonarchical revolutionary programs. The process of democratization of Jordan is part of the process of normalization of the Islamic resurgence in that country. The king began the process of lifting martial law and holding elections following riots over economic issues in 1989. In the subsequent parliamentary elections, Islamist candidates won 32 out of the 80 seats and in 1990 a member of the Muslim Brotherhood was elected Speaker of the national parliament. This was in the context of the Gulf Crisis when there was great popular opposition to the non-Muslim military intervention in the region. The monarchy survived by adapting to the growing power of Islamic fundamentalist forces in the country and by being able to include those forces within the normal political processes.

The small monarchical states in the Persian Gulf region—Kuwait, Bahrain, Qatar, and the United Arab Emirates—also faced a variety of challenges in the 1970s and 1980s. Basically conservative in mood and attempting to preserve their monarchical systems, the greatest transformation involved the rulers' encouragement of the development of the oil industry. The states remained politically conservative in a context of rapid socio-economic transformation, creating the problems of growing desires for political participation. The small monarchies reduced the demands for radical change in the political arena by programs of social welfare and economic development. However, this did not eliminate opposition, and parliaments, which had been created earlier, were suspended in Kuwait in 1976 and 1986 and in Bahrain in 1975, and were never created elsewhere. By the end of the 1980s, the expectation, or fear, was that democratization would involve a growing expression of support for Islamic groups as a result of the reduced appeal of both secularist radicalism and conservativism and the growing populist appeal of the various Islamic movements. However, in the early

1990s these tensions seemed to be manageable in most of the small monarchies.

In the Gulf region fundamentalism took both Sunni and Shiʻi forms. Part of the flexibility of the monarchies' responses involved an encouragement of Sunni groups, who then cooperated with the emerging institutions of the Islamic establishment, and a limitation on Shiʻi groups, who were suspected of being supported by the Iranian Islamic Republic. In the mid-1980s this approach seemed to be effective although it contained many risks. The potential danger was that, if the ruling elites would "abandon their time-proven techniques of flexible rule and instead adopt a repressive policy, major upheaval could ensue."[49] The greatest test of this was the experience of Kuwait, where the monarchy was driven out by Saddam Husayn's invasion in August 1990 and restored by American military action early in 1991. After the restoration, Kuwaiti rulers adopted a conservative position to preserve their power, but strong prodemocratic pressures developed and elections were held for a new parliament late in 1992. Despite a carefully limited electorate (only males over 21 whose families were in Kuwait before 1921), candidates critical of the regime won 31 of the 50 seats. The opposition reflected views of conservative business groups and secular elements, but the largest single group was nineteen winners from explicitly Islamic organizations like the Islamic Constitutional Movement which advocated more active implementation of Islamic law. However, the Islamists made it clear that they were not advocating a revolutionary overthrow of the social order, and their success reflected the Islamization of political discourse and the appeal of Islam in the conservative context of Kuwait.

During the 1960s Oman had faced the most active radical challenge of the region's small monarchies. A radical liberation movement, initially called the Dhofar Liberation Front (DLF), emerged in the southernmost province. The movement was able to mobilize considerable popular opposition to the regime as long as the ruler was Sultan Said ibn Taymur, who was repressive and attempted to stop all modernization in the country. However, in 1968, the sultan was overthrown by his son, Qabus, who acted quickly to develop a program of visible, if conservative, modernization. As the appeal of radical socialism in the region as a whole declined, Qabus was able to undermine the appeal of the movement and then, with important military help from Iran, he crushed the opposition.

In this struggle and after the victory, Sultan Qabus mobilized religious symbols as well as military force, development programs, and worked to build a greater acceptance of the legitimacy of the existing political system in contrast to what he called atheistic radicalism. A careful combination of suppression and flexibility of policy meant that during the 1980s, while the country faced some economic problems and internal discontent, opposition appeals were weak. This gradualism was reflected in the creation of a consultative assembly in 1990 which replaced a less representative assembly of notables and government officials. In the Gulf Crisis of 1990–1991, Oman provided active support for the international coalition against Iraq but the crisis had little immediate impact on the country itself.

By the early 1990s, there were still many tensions between populist and establishment Islamic groups, and the nature of the outcome was unclear. What was clear, however, was that Islam had become one of the most important bases of normal as well as revolutionary political discourse in the region. In the Gulf Crisis of 1990–1991, for example, Saddam Husayn did not appeal for support against the United States in the old Ba'th rhetoric of radical secularism; the appeal was made primarily in Islamic terms. The fears and expectations of Islamic revolutions in the Gulf region of the early 1980s were not fulfilled, but the whole political scene, political establishments and oppositions alike, had become increasingly Islamic in identification and discourse with more populist Islamic themes assuming greater importance.

Afghanistan: Kings, Radicals, and Islamic Revolt

Conservative adaptationism did not preserve the monarchy in Afghanistan. The cautious implementation of modernization programs by King Muhammad Zahir in the 1960s failed to provide a basis for a unified political system. The parliamentary system begun in 1962–1963 did not provide effective leadership for the country, and this vacuum opened the way for Daoud Khan to lead the army in a coup which established the republic of Afghanistan in 1973. From 1973 to 1978, Daoud Khan ruled as president, continuing a program of relatively gradual modernization but in the context of working to establish a stronger centralized control over the various regional and ethnic divisions in the country.

Daoud had to rely on foreign assistance because of the relative poverty of Afghanistan and received considerable support from the Societ Union. This helped to strengthen leftist groups in the country, and a radical opposition emerged. Daoud also faced conservative resistance by ethnic and religious leaders who opposed parts of his centralizing and modernizing reforms. This resistance led to an ethnic-religious revolt in Panjsher in 1975. Although the revolt was crushed, the emergence of a conservative resistance led by ethnic and religious notables calling for the overthrow of the "godless, communist dominated regime" was an indication of future trends. When Daoud began a major suppression of the leftist groups, they mobilized civilian and military support and took control of the government in April 1978.

The conservative adaptationism of the monarchy and the Daoud regime had failed, and a doctrinaire leftist regime came to power. That regime provides the background for what many observers call the resurgence of Islam in Afghanistan. However, the struggles which developed were not simply a conflict between secularist radicals and a resurgent Islam. A more complex pattern of conflicts emerged which reflects the pattern of the normalization of Islamic revivalism by the 1990s.

The struggles in Afghanistan after the 1978 revolution represent a number of concurrent conflicts. The new regime, which proclaimed the formation of the Democratic Republic of Afghanistan, was led by a coalition of leftists. The communist party, the People's Democratic Party of Afghanistan (PDPA), had split during the 1960s into the Khalq faction led by Nur Muhammad Taraki and the Parcham faction led by Babrak Karmal. The new government in April 1978 included both Karmal and Taraki, along with another important Khalq figure, Hafizullah Amin. These groups soon became involved in a struggle for power. The Parcham faction was pushed out of the government and Karmal driven into political exile in eastern Europe. Then Taraki and Hafizullah Amin came into conflict and Taraki was killed in October 1979. Amin, facing mounting opposition on a variety of fronts, was himself overthrown and killed as a part of the Soviet invasion of Afghanistan in December 1979. Babrak Karmal returned from exile to lead a new communist government backed by Soviet troops. The central government became relatively firmly established in Kabul under Karmal's leadership as a Soviet-dominated and supported communist regime with potential factional divisions between Khalq and Parcham continuing to surface.

The most visible conflict was the opposition to this regime by noncommunist Afghan forces, who are usually collectively labeled the Mujahidin.[50] By the time of the Soviet invasion in 1979 at least sixty different opposition groups had formed, but under the pressure of the Soviet military campaign, there was considerable consolidation. However, despite the shared goal of the overthrow of the central government and the looming Soviet military threat, profound divisions existed among the opposition. Some of these divisions were based on historic ethnic identities, others reflected different Muslim perspectives and programs, and still others were the result of differences between guerrilla military commanders inside of the country and leaders of refugee political groups based outside of the country.

Through the decade of the 1980s, seven political groups survived and became the most visible in terms of international politics. They formed the core of the Afghan Interim Government (AIG) which was formed in exile early in 1989 after the completion of the withdrawal of Soviet troops, and six of these had been important in the developing resistance in the early 1980s. All of the major groups identified with the AIG are committed to the creation of an Islamic government in Afghanistan and are Sunni. Most draw much of their support from the Pashtuns, the largest ethnic-cultural group in Afghanistan. Pashtuns, comprising almost half of the population, have dominated Afghan politics for a long time.

Three of these groups are more conservative in their orientation, representing older established tribal and religious leadership. The National Islamic Front is led by Sayyid Ahmad Gaylani. Gaylani is a leading member of the Qadiriyyah Tariqah and is respected by his followers for his religious prestige as well as his political abilities. He was a close associate of the deposed king, Muhammad Zahir, and is sympathetic to a program of moderate modernization. He was a wealthy businessman before the revolution, owning the Peugeot dealership in Kabul, and has considerable international experience and exposure. A similar but somewhat more conservative group is the National Liberation Front led by Sibghat-ullah Mujaddidi, also an important figure in an significant tariqah, the Naqshbandiyyah. His family had ties with the anticommunist Basmachi revolutionaries in Central Asia in the 1920s and was an important force in the opposition to the reforms of King Amanallah. His support reflects the continuing popularity of the older conservative forces in Afghan society. The third conservative group is the Movement of Islamic Revolution led by Muhammad Nabi Muhammadi. This group receives much of its support from more traditionalist Sunni ulama who have been less concerned with formal state structures while supporting a stricter application of Islamic law in the life of society.

Four major opposition groups are more overtly identifiable as Islamist or fundamentalist. Fundamentalist opposition to the reform programs of the monarchy and Daoud had developed in an organized manner by the mid-1970s and engaged in a major revolt in 1975. The brutal suppression of the fundamentalists by Daoud provided the context for the emergence of two major Islamist organizations. The more radical activists followed the lead of Gulbuddin Hekmatyar, a former engineering student who formed the Hizb-i Islami in the late 1970s. This group was unwilling to be accommodating with other social forces, declaring all others to be unbelievers (*takfir*), and adopting a relatively traditional fundamentalist program whose spirit is reflected in Hekmatyar's statement that "a pure Islamic system was established 14 centuries ago, and any regime that differs from that ideal is unacceptable."[51] The second Islamist group to emerge in the late 1970s was the Jamiat-i Islam led by Burhanuddin Rabbani, a scholar educated at al-Azhar in Egypt, where he also was influenced by the ideas of the Muslim Brotherhood. He hoped to create a more broadly-based movement dedicated to fundamentalist goals but bringing together more tribal and traditional elements as well as modern intellectuals.

The Hizb-i Islami of Yunis Khalis was created in 1979 when Khalis broke with Hekmatyar over tactics. The group gradually grew in influence during the following decade. The fourth group, Ittihad-i Islami, emerged as a product of the shifting political alliances of the 1980s under the leadership of Rasul Sayyaf. Sayyaf had been a student fundamentalist activist in the 1970s who had studied in Egypt and Saudi Arabia. He helped to organize Arab financial support for the mujahidin and provided arms and money to a number of guerrilla bands.

In addition to the primarily Sunni opposition groups, the Shi'i Muslims, who represent around fifteen percent of the population of Afghanistan, also organized opposition to the Kabul regime, with varying degrees of support from the Islamic Republic of Iran. Most Afghan Shi'is are Hazaras, an ethnically distinct group living primarily in the central part of the country. Their resistance to the Kabul regime tended to take the form of a communal ethnic organization with some ulama leadership, although it is within a longer tradition of Islamic political protest among Afghan Shi'is.[52]

Commanders of opposition forces within Afghanistan frequently were associated with the political groups but many represented essentially separate organizations. Local commanders assumed increasing importance as the military struggle against the Kabul regime continued. Among the best-known of these is Ahmad Massoud, a commander whose loose structure of forces operated in the seven northeast provinces, particularly centered in the Panjshir valley. Massoud had been part of the Islamist youth groups in the 1970s and had taken the lead in Panjshir in the 1975 revolt. His military successes in the early 1980s against Soviet forces gave him special prestige. His structure was associated with Rabbani's political organization but like most military commanders within the country, he operated independently. Following the Soviet withdrawal in 1989, the conflicts between commanders like Massoud and some of the political groups became visible, with open fighting occurring between the forces of Massoud and those of Hekmatyar in 1989–1990. Such conflicts were frequent as mujahidin forces began to capture major cities like Khost.[53] These tensions became a major source of instability as the new political system emerged in 1992.

The communist government remained in power for almost three years even though many predicted its almost immediate collapse after the withdrawal of Soviet forces. Its survival, to some extent, was the result of the divisions among the opposition but it was also related to significant changes in the government's approach and image. The communist government following the coups in 1978 and 1979 was basically a Marxist regime whose radicalism and secularism (or atheism) alienated large segments of Afghan society. In the early 1980s, "Karmal took several purely symbolic but conciliatory steps to clean the tarnished religious image of the PDPA . . . [and this] blurred the regime's image as radically anti-religious."[54] In 1986, Karmal resigned and was replaced by Mohammad Najibullah, a student party activist in the 1960s who had served as the head of the secret police from 1979 until 1985. Najibullah worked to broaden the base of popular support and reduce the radical image of the regime. This involved increasing use of Islamic modes of political discourse and opening the door to some non-PDPA participation in politics. Following the Soviet withdrawal, these lines of effort were intensified, and in 1990 Najibullah created a new political party, the Hizb-i Watan, and agreed to an international plan to hold elections to determine the future of the country. In the statements and policies of Najibullah in 1990–1991, there is clear recognition of the need to express political positions within the framework of discourse which is significantly influenced by Islam. For example, he told a gathering of notables in Pakhtia Province that the "proud, clean Afghan Islamic blood is running through my veins" and that "we are only worshippers of God," and in his address to the nation on the proposed elections he emphasized that the government "has pursued its course on this great national matter in line with the teachings of the sacred religion of Islam and the traditions of the people of Afghanistan, and will continue to do so."[55] Najibullah even invited the former king, Muhammad Zahir, to become involved in the peacemaking process, and it was fundamentalists like Hekmatyar, not the communists, who opposed the idea of the reinvolvement of Muhammad Zahir.[56] The normalization of the Islamic resurgence clearly had become a part of the political and social scene in Afghanistan when even the rhetoric of the old radical secularism of the PDPA became expressed in the discourse of believing Muslims.

Najibullah's adaptations ultimately did not work and by April 1992, much of the country had fallen under the control of various groupings of Mujahidin organizations, opposition armies, and local commanders of government forces who allied themselves with Mujahidin groups. A chaotic struggle for power ensued with most of the groups agreeing only on a temporary transitional arrangement whereby Sighat-ullah Mujaddidi served a two-month term as president and then was replaced by Rabbani. Rabbani then organized his formal election for a two-year term by a "national assembly" that was boycotted by five of the nine factions and organizations involved in ruling the country. Hekmatyar opposed all of the arrangements;

throughout 1992 his armed forces attacked various other groups and regularly shelled Kabul, and regional alliances tended to emerge out the the general conflict.

The old adaptationist monarchy could never be restored by the early 1990s, but neither could a radical secularist regime, however it might adapt its mode of discourse. Some observers have cited the chaos following the Mujahidin victory as proof of the "failure of political Islam," and the Afghan experience clearly shows that neither fundamentalists like Hekmatyar nor more adaptationist Islamic leaders like Rabbani and Mujaddidi have the key to automatic political success. However, what the Afghan experience also shows is that whether or not the fundamentalists win, the terms of political discourse and the basic definition of the socio-political groundrules were Islamized by the early 1990s. The power of the Islamic resurgence does not mean the victory of particular styles of Islamic organizations; it means that the foundations of social and political action for all actors have shifted from the secular, modernist competitions of the 1960s to competitions in which Islamic framework are essential.

Islam in Radical and Secular Regimes

Islamic themes gained increasing importance in the policies and politics of the major regimes that were more socialist or secular in their identity. During the 1970s and 1980s, the gradual Islamization of the basic political discourse within many of these states represents a significant change in approach. This evolution is a natural product of the efforts to create more authentically indigenous ideologies of modernization, and also it represents a practical reorientation of policies in line with popular feeling.

In most of these states, this religionizing of politics provides greater recognition for fundamentalist ideas, but the general official tone continues to be as much modernist as clearly fundamentalist. It is not a context in which conservative Islam plays a significant role other than providing confirmation for the emerging mood after it is established. The basic goal of this effort in most of the regimes is to provide an ideological framework and basis for socio-political discourse which is both manifestly modern and authentically Islamic.

By the early 1990s this new ideological style represented a clear transformation of the radical ideals and programs of the 1960s into an effectively postmodernist set of programs and policies. Secularism had little role as a basis for policies, and old socialist slogans were replaced by the Islamically articulated appeals for popular participation and mobilization. In the early

1970s, these changes were begun in a context where fundamentalism frequently represented a revolutionary challenge to the established radical socialist regimes. As a result, the early Islamization of the politics of radical socialism represented a defensive effort to preempt opposition. However, by the 1980s, Islamically based politics were becoming the normal mode of operation and Islamic discourse, even in very fundamentalist forms, became a significant part of the social and political mainstream. By the early 1990s, this normalization of the Islamic resurgence was one of the dominant features of the social and political scene in many of the countries that had been in the vanguard of radical socialism and secularism in the 1960s.

This transformation was, however, neither uniform nor universal among the major examples of socialist and secular states at the beginning of the 1970s. Special local conditions as well as different regional contexts created a broad spectrum of Islamic experiences, which ranged from the active participation of fundamentalists in the political system in Egypt to their almost total suppression in Syria. Underlying these more visible features was the more broadly based reaffirmation of the importance of Islam in society and daily life, whether or not the style was fundamentalist. The normalization of the resurgence means that it takes forms that are not identifiable simply as revolutionary fundamentalism. Instead, the adaptationist style has become less identified with Westernizing reform and secularism and is itself now more likely to initiate programs of Islamization. In contrast to the early 1970s, the Islamic resurgence is now a significant part of the programs and policies of adaptationists as well as fundamentalists.

Egypt: Arab Socialism and the Revival of Islam

The death of Nasser in 1970 marked the beginning of a new era in Egyptian history. The movement away from the activist socialism of Nasser, which had begun after the Arab-Israeli War of 1967, was intensified under Nasser's successor, Anwar al-Sadat. In state policy, de-Nasserization involved a replacement of socialist economic policies by ones that encouraged a mixed economy through utilizing local private enterprise and foreign investment. It also involved a major reorientation in foreign policy, moving away from close ties with the Soviet Union to firm and cooperative relations with the United States. A third major policy transformation entailed peace with Israel. At first Sadat opposed Israel and provided leadership in planning and executing the 1973 war against that country. In the postwar negotiations, Sadat worked vigorously for a negotiated settlement, resulting in a dramatic trip to Jerusalem in 1977, the Camp David Accord in 1978, and the Egyptian-Israeli peace treaty in 1979.

De-Nasserization also represents a reorientation of popular life and politics. The traditions of Nasserism have not disappeared, and there are still some people who advocate the old policies. However, Nasser is more honored as a symbol of national assertion and pride than as a model for policy, and the dominant tone is increasingly one in which Islamic themes have priority while the socialist themes of the 1960s represent an ideology of opposition. By the late 1980s it was possible to say that the "religious populism" of groups like the Muslim Brotherhood "is proving to be the functional equivalent to Nasser's national socialism."[57]

Official Policy. Sadat's government gave greater official recognition to Islamic themes. In the early 1970s it permitted Islamic student organizations to operate with fewer restrictions, and the Muslim Brotherhood was allowed to publish magazines, although the organization itself remained officially illegal. The fundamentalist activists provided a useful balance to the Nasserite groups in Sadat's de-Nasserization efforts. Sadat also emphasized themes of personal faith. There were pragmatic political reasons for this Islamization of official politics, both as a way of countering potential opposition groups and as a recognition of the general revival of Muslim consciousness in Egypt, especially among the educated elite.

From the beginning of the 1970s, observers and Egyptians alike noted the visible signs of a reaffirmation of Islam among educated Egyptians as well as others. Administrators were more regular in their prayers, the Friday prayer services were much better attended, and growing numbers of educated women were adopting Islamically suitable clothing. This reaffirmation has set the tone for government policies that are less secularist and more Islamic.

The general style of the official revival is modernist in content, although by the 1990s, positions that would have been described as "fundamentalist" in 1970 were accepted as a regular part of moderate, adaptationist discourse. Discussions of changes in the constitution reflect this evolution. In 1971, a new constitution was promulgated after much debate regarding the role of Islam in the state. The text that was approved in the popular referendum stated that "the principles of the Islamic shariʿah are a principle source of legislation," which meant not only that the Shariʿah was not the sole source of legislation, but also that it was the basic "principles" of Islamic law rather than medieval legal specifics that received constitutional recognition.[58] In 1980, the wording was amended to indicate a stronger role for Islamic law by referring to the Shariʿah as *the* principle source of law. By the early 1990s, many steps had been taken in the direction of the Islamization of the Egyptian legal system, and debates were over interpretation and methods of implimentation rather than the issue of Islamization itself.

The great watershed experience in the changing role of official Islam was the murder of Sadat by Muslim militants in 1981. Sadat had encouraged fundamentalist groups as a counter to leftist political influence and identified the government more clearly with Islamic symbols. However, by the mid-1970s, the emergence of extremist fundamentalist groups in addition to the more cooperative Muslim Brotherhood led Sadat to oppose religious extremism. He was sharply critical of the Islamic Revolution in Iran and provided asylum for the deposed shah in 1980, despite strong local opposition. In September 1981, he initiated a strict suppression of Islamic and other opposition groups and was murdered by people from one of the suppressed groups. By the late 1970s, Sadat had come to the point where he made little distinction among the various Muslim organizations, mistrusting, and therefore suppressing, them all.

Husni Mubarak, Sadat's successor as president of Egypt, faced the challenge of potential Islamic revolution and mass disorder in the country. He acted quickly to quell the unrest with quick arrests and trials but then adopted a balanced long-term policy which was relatively successful by the 1990s.

> By gradually shifting its posture toward the religious opposition from indiscriminate confrontation to selective accommodation, the Mubarak government has accomplished important objectives that would have seemed inconceivable at the beginning of the 1980's. It has more effectively isolated and discredited the extremist fringes of the Islamic movement. . . . It has allowed the many groups representing the moderate mainstream of the Islamic movement to compete more openly in the political system and in the economy.[59]

In many ways, the ideas and movements of Islamic revival have moved from the periphery to the mainstream of Egyptian politics and society. In the process, the old modernist and secularist elites have become more open to fundamentalist styles of Islamic experience. At the same time, it is also true that formerly fundamentalist groups and individuals have become more adaptationist in their approaches to the problems of contemporary Egypt. There are now "radical and moderate Islamists" and "legalist and radical Islamists"[60] in a much broader spectrum of affirmation of Islam than was visible in the 1970s.

This broadened spectrum is reflected in the gradual opening of the official political institutions to participation by a greater diversity of organizations. Following Nasser's death, Sadat had continued the one party political system but late in the 1970s had permitted the organization of different tendencies within the single party. By the early 1980s this had become a limited multiparty system with effectively contested elections. The National Democratic Party (NDP) was created out of the old single-party Arab Socialist Union and is the party of the government, winning substantial parliamentary majorities in the elections of 1984, 1987, and 1990. However, other parties won significant numbers of seats in those elections, with the parties supported by the Muslim Brotherhood and other Islamists emerging as the largest opposition bloc in the parliaments. The Brotherhood did not create its own party but worked through coalitions, with its Muslim Alliance list winning almost twenty percent of the vote in 1987.[61] In the general elections of 1990, the results were less clear since three of the major opposition parties boycotted the election, protesting changes in the election laws. The NDP won about the same proportion of the votes (eighty percent) as it had in 1987, giving it comfortable control of the parliament but, despite the boycott, there was a significant number of nongovernment members elected. The political opposition continued to be strong, and the Gulf Crisis provided it with many opportunities to express its disagreement with government policy, both within and outside of parliament. The major part of this opposition continued, however, to be expressed within the framework of mainstream politics rather than peripheral radicalism.

Revived Fundamentalism and Resurgence. The tradition of fundamentalist associations in modern Egypt has deep roots, identified with the Muslim Brotherhood. In the 1970s, however, many of the emerging groups shared a common spirit with the Brotherhood but were not organizationally tied to it. All advocated the establishment of an Islamic state and the enforcement of Islamic law. They were articulated in terms that had been set by Hasan al-Banna and expanded by Sayyid Qutb. In the 1970s, the major differences among the activist fundamentalists were more in terms of method and degree of militance than in content of ideology.

The critical argument for tactics and strategy was the nature of Egyptian society. In the terms of Sayyid Qutb, existing society had departed so far from the faith of Islam that it had become part of the *jahiliyyah,* or force of ignorant unbelief. The obligation of the remaining believers was, in this situation, to engage in the struggle (*jihad*) against unbelief. The necessary decision was to judge whether it was only the Egyptian state which was part of the jahiliyyah or if the whole society had departed from the faith.

One of the earliest of the radical groups to gain visibility was "Takfir wa al-Hijrah," led by Shukri Mustafa (1942–1977).[62] He proclaimed the rejection of Egyptian society as a whole and advocated withdrawal into a separate, pious community. However, in the mid-1970s, the group became involved in a clash with the police and killed a former minister whom they had taken as a hostage. The group was crushed and its leaders executed. Although the group was small, its teachings, clearly expounded during the trial of the leader, provided a new, Islamic base for a critique of the corruption and failures of Egyptian society. No major group emerged after the execution of Shukri Mustafa, but this basic rejectionist position appears to have continued among some smaller groups. "Saved from the Fire," sometimes accused of involvement in violent opposition in the early 1990s, may be one such group.

A second radical fundamentalist tendency argued that the real enemy was the government, rather than the society as a whole. These groups organized attempts to take over the government or to inspire broader mass Islamic revolutions. While they attracted great attention through their militance, they always remained small and were regularly suppressed by the police. In 1974 an early group attempted to take over the Technical Military Academy in a complicated plot to kill Sadat and gain control of the government. By the late 1970s, a movement called "Jihad" emerged as a major radical force and organized the killing of Sadat in 1981. Its basic ideas were most clearly presented by Abd al-Salam Faraj, who argued that Muslims have ignored the duty of jihad. He taught that this duty was incumbent upon all believers and called upon them to revolt against the rule of wicked and unbelieving leaders.[63] Jihad was actively suppressed by the Mubarak government but branches continued to be active throughout the 1980s. In the early 1990s, various groups in the Jihad tradition remained the most important militant fundamentalist groups in Egypt. Members of Jihad were arrested, for example, in 1991 for attempts to bomb government buildings in upper Egypt, and leaders of Jihad confessed to organizing the killing of the Speaker of Parliament, Rifaat al-Mahjub, in 1990.[64]

Some of the earlier militant groups became more mainstream during the 1980s. In the 1970s, student Islamic Societies were organized as visible centers of protest. However, as the political system became more open, many of the former student militants became part of the legal political opposition. On campuses the Islamic groups had moved from the periphery to the mainstream of student life, reflecting broader trends in society.

This change is also visible in the role of the major public preachers. During the 1970s, some scholars emerged as popular teachers and preachers with wide influence. Many of these had been restricted if not jailed under Sadat but were given greater freedom to present their ideas in the 1980s. As a result, they became popular media figures and were defining the boundaries of political discourse by the early 1990s, representing a broad spectrum of Islamic views from relatively traditional fundamentalism to modernism expressed in more fundamentalist terms.

A good example of this trend is Shaykh Umar Abd al-Rahman, who had been arrested after the killing of Sadat on charges of inciting the murder but was released because of lack of evidence. During the 1980s he was detained a number of times but never tried and convicted. In 1990 he came to the United States where he preached his fundamentalist message in Brooklyn amd then in New Jersey. He was not regarded as a particular threat until some people from his mosque were charged with the bombing of the International Trade Center in New York early in 1993. Despite intensive investigation looking for links between him and the bombing, he was not arrested. While not "mainstream," his militant message was a part of the broader activist, but relatively common discourse of both urban America and Mubarak's Egypt.[65] Another highly visible critic of Egyptian society and government is Shaykh Abd al-Hamid Kishk, who has been described as "the great tenor of the Islamist movement."[66] Cassettes and printed collections of his sermons and teachings are available in many parts of the Islamic world.

Popular revivalism is not only an opposition force. A number of very popular revivalist preachers who emerged in the 1970s and 1980s are seen as part of the government-supported religious establishment. Some important figures in this group, like Mustafa Mahmud, a former communist intellectual, present positions which are close to older modernist positions, while others, like Shaykh Muhammad Matwalli al-Shaʿrawi, present more traditional fundamentalist positions. The fact, however, that al-Shaʿrawi can be described as part of the government establishment shows the great changes that have taken place since the 1960s. Under Nasser he would have been jailed for saying the things which he regularly preaches today. The message that "we have tried capitalism and socialism and both failed us . . . but Islam was already there as a middle road,"[67] would have been seen as part of the revolutionary fundamentalist opposition in the 1960s.

The experience of the best-known fundamentalist group, the Muslim Brotherhood, is an important indicator of these trends as well. Although the organization was not yet legally allowed to operate in the early 1990s, for two decades it had functioned as a visible force, publishing magazines and, in the 1980s, supporting candidates and parties in elections. Although under Sadat the Brotherhood expressed strong opposition to some government policies, especially the peace settlement with Israel, it never moved to the militant extreme. In the context of the teachings of Shukri Mustafa and Abd al-Salam Faraj, Muslim Brotherhood positions are moderate and increasingly identified with the broader movement of Islamic revival rather than the radical fringe. Many came to see the Brotherhood as the continuation of the movement of Islamic renewal begun by al-Afghani and Abduh, and thus as much modernist as fundamentalist.[68] By the early 1990s, the formal organization of the Brotherhood had become in many ways an important part of the adaptationist Islamic revivalist mainstream rather than the fundamentalist periphery.

The Broader Spectrum. The revivalist mainstream extends beyond official Islam and the expanded realm of revived fundamentalism. There have been important efforts to rearticulate the vision of the left in Islamic terms. Many of the major figures of the old secularist or socialist elite have come to adopt more openly Islamic positions. Khalid Muhammad Khalid, whose book from the 1940s, *From Here We Begin,* was the classic statement of the Egyptian secularist position, publically supported the establishment of an Islamic state by the 1980s. Perhaps the most thorough effort to define the foundations for a nonfundamentalist but Islamic ideology is the work of Hasan Hanafi. His many writings represent the emergence of an Islamic Liberation Theology defined as the Islamic Left (*al-Yasar al-Islami*).[69]

There has also been a significant revival of more nonpolitical Islamic activities, especially in the continuation of Sufi devotional traditions. Between 1970 and 1985, for example, the number of officially registered Sufi orders tripled, and Sufi devotional meetings represent an important part of the lives of many Egyptians who are not involved in more activist associations.[70]

Activist fundamentalism is an important part of the Islamic revival in Egypt, but by the 1990s it was clear that the reaffirmation of Islam in the late twentieth century was more than an expression of the fundamentalist style. Adaptationists, conservatives, and those reflecting more individualist styles had all come to reflect the broader Islamization of discourse in all areas of Egyptian life.

Arab Socialist and Secularist States

A major ideological transformation took place in the Arab world during the final third of the twentieth century. Arab socialism, which appeared to be the emerging dominant ideology in the middle of the 1960s, changed from a radical and often secularist orientation to a more pragmatic and frequently clearly Islamic stance. Opposition, which was initially expressed in terms of greater leftist radicalism, came increasingly to be expressed in Islamic terms. By the early 1990s, the regimes which had been originally established on the foundations of radical socialism had become the establishments, with both opposition and government policies being expressed in terms compatible with the reaffirmation of Islam.

In Algeria, the overthrow of Ahmad Ben Bella in 1965 was already accompanied by a greater emphasis on Islamic values and Arabic culture.

Houari Boumedienne, who led the country from 1965 until his death in 1978, maintained a commitment to a socialist program, but it was more closely tied to Islam and Arabism than to secularist radicalism. The transition of power at Boumedienne's death was smooth and his successor, Chadli Benjedid (b. 1929) continued the balanced position that Boumedienne had formalized in the constitution of 1976, in which Algeria is described as a socialist state whose religion is Islam. The political system remained a one party state under the control of the Front de Liberation Nationale (FLN).

Demonstrations by fundamentalist students in 1980 reflected the beginnings of Islamist opposition which grew in intensity during the following decade. At first the movement was not tightly organized but a continuing cycle of demonstrations and suppression produced greater cohesion and visibility.[71] General popular opposition grew as Algeria faced increasing economic problems and major riots in many parts of the country in 1988 emphasized the unpopularity of the FLN government. In response Benjedid began a process of democratization and in nationwide provincial and local elections in 1990 the FLN lost significantly, with the opposition Front Islamique du Salut (FIS) winning more than 55 percent of the votes and control in thirty-two of the forty-eight provinces.

The Islamic Front (FIS) emerged as the most significant voice of opposition, although there were many other parties and groups. FIS leaders had organized demonstrations earlier in the decade, and many had been jailed. The president of FIS's governing council is Shaykh Abassi Madani (b. 1931), a philosopher with a doctorate from a British university and strong nationalist credentials, having been a fighter in the FLN against the French from the very beginning of the Algerian Revolution in 1954.[72] Madani and others in the FIS proclaimed that their goal was an Islamic state and society in Algeria which would be achieved through democratic means.

The Algerian government announced national elections for the spring of 1991 but postponed them when FIS demonstrations protesting new election procedures led to violent clashes. When they were finally held late in the year, FIS again won a major victory and it seemed clear that FIS would almost have a two-thirds majority of parliament. Faced with the clear probability of the establishment of an Islamic state, the Algerian military intervened and began an active suppression of FIS. In this way the political dilemmas of the old socialist regimes were highlighted. The old radical socialism no longer represented the most effective vehicle for populist mobilization. In the era of the normalization of the Islamic resurgence, Islamist movements had great appeal and could possibly gain control of governments through democratic means. The participation of Islamist forces within the democratic processes came to be seen by some, especially among the old socialist ruling elites, as a greater danger than that posed by the earlier marginal Islamic fundamentalist militants.

Tunisia experienced a similar evolution with the transformation of the Westernizing secularism of Bourguiba. After the excursion into more radical socialism in the 1960s, Tunisia returned to a less ideological secularist program. Bourguibism continued to stress cultural modernity and Tunisia's role as a bridge between Arab and Western civilizations. However, by the late 1970s, economic problems and repressive political policies led to growing opposition. At first this opposition came from the left, culminating in major labor unrest in 1978. However, during the 1980s, antiregime views were articulated increasingly in Islamic terms. This reflected a growing awareness of their Islamic identity among professionals and younger educated Tunisians.

This Islamic awareness manifested itself in the emergence of a number of groups, the largest and most important being the Mouvement de la Tendance Islamique (MTI). By 1981 the MTI had developed local and regional structures, and its leadership could proclaim its program of a return to the fundamental principles of Islam.[73] Members of MTI soon clashed with police, and during the 1980s many were arrested and served terms in prison. Bourguiba became increasingly concerned with this challenge and initiated severe repressive measures.

In 1987, Bourguiba was forced to retire in a coup led by the Prime Minister Zein al-Abidine Ben Ali, who became president. Ben Ali remained committed to the relatively secularist approach of Bourguiba, although with a more visible commitment to a modernist Islam. He announced measures of democratization, and national elections were held in 1989. Although some secular opposition parties were allowed to participate, the MTI's party, al-Nahdah, was not certified as a legal party. In the elections, however, Islamists running as independents won at least 15 percent of the vote and in the large cities won as much as 30 percent of the vote. This was in sharp contrast to the results of the leading secularist opposition party, which won less than 4 percent of the vote. By 1989, most significant opposition, both democratic and radical, was articulated in Islamic terms, and the major vehicle for its expression was the MTI led by Rashid Ghanoushi.

Ghanoushi was educated in the Zaytuna school in Tunis and then completed his university education in Damascus in the early 1960s. Initially he was a supporter of Arab socialism but soon rejected it in favor of an Islamist position. After a year's study in France, he returned to Tunisia where he became a secondary school teacher. He gradually organized the core of what was to become the MTI. He advocated a "realistic fundamentalism" in which Islamists would "stop repeating a bundle of ideas worked out by a former generation of men of Islamic *dawa* [mission]" and would involve efforts to transfer "Islamic ideology to the level of every day struggle in the life of Muslims."[74]

After the overthrow of Bourguiba, MTI leaders advocated cooperation with the new government and participation in the democractic system. Although Ben Ali had suggested that al-Nahdah, MTI's party, would be legalized, this had not happened by the early 1990s. The Gulf Crisis of 1990–1991 was the occasion for renewed direct clashes between Nahdah members and government forces. Militant members became involved in violent demonstrations and the movement split, with some leaders like Abd al-Fattah Mourou condemning the resort to violence and withdrawing from active involvement in the party. Divisions within the formal Islamist movement reflect organizational weaknesses and the diversity of people involved, but they do not mean that the general popular appeal of Islamic alternatives was weakening in the early 1990s. A return to secularist Bourguibism was not possible, and strong repressive measures were necessary for the Ben Ali regime to avoid further significant Islamization of Tunisian politics and society.

Major transformations in the nature of Arab socialist regimes also occurred in both North and South Yemen, culminating in their unification in May 1990. The Zaydi imamate had been overthrown in 1962, and a long civil war followed between tribal-royalist forces and supporters of the new socialist republican government. By 1970 a compromise was reached in which the conservative forces accepted the principle of a republican regime and the end of the imamate while the socialists agreed to a more conservative orientation for the new Yemen Arab Republic (YAR). In the politics of the 1970s, this balance was maintained through some periods of political instability and military coups and by the 1980s even the radical opposition groups presented their programs in the framework of Islamic symbols and traditions.[75]

During the 1980s, relative stability was achieved under the leadership of Ali Abdallah Salih, who became president of the YAR in 1978 following the murder of President Ahmad al-Ghashmi by an envoy from the People's Republic of South Yemen (PRSY). Salih succeeded in reducing internal tensions by policies of increasing democratization. The influence of forces of the Islamic revival was reflected in the Consultative Assembly where about a quarter of the members were Islamists. However, the government itself continued to maintain a balance of conservative and modernist positions rather than adopting more fundamentalist policies. The threat of continuing conflict with the PRSY was countered by active movement toward the unification of the two Yemens, which was achieved in 1990.

Following its achievement of independence in 1967, South Yemen created a radical people's republic which "adhered consistently and publically to a Marxist-Leninist ideology" in both domestic and international affairs.[76] PRSY's foreign policies brought it into conflict with most of its regional neighbors while internal divisions among the radical groups led to a series of coups and civil wars. In the mid-1980s it remained the last bastion of the old radicalism in the Arab world, supported by Cuba and the Soviet Union. However, a major civil war in 1986 and the changing global context brought a reorientation of policies, and more friendly ties were established with conservative neighbors, and union with the YAR was actively pursued.

In the new Republic of Yemen, Salih of the YAR became president and Haidar Abu Bakr al-Attas, the former president of the PRSY, became prime minister. The new Yemen departed significantly in mood from the old radicalism of the PRSY and proclaimed a multiparty democracy in which Islam, Arabism, and Yemeni traditions were to be the key elements in the new national identity. The major opposition came not from the left but from a combination of some tribal leaders with Islamic fundamentalist groups in the Yemeni Grouping for Reform under the leadership of Abdallah al-Ahmar, head of a great tribal confederation. Al-Ahmar cooperated with the new government, but his group advocated a more active Islamization of laws and the state.

The problems of this carefully balanced system were dramatically illustrated, in terms of international policies, during the Gulf Crisis of 1990–1991, when Yemen condemned the Iraqi attack on another Arab country and agreed to abide by the United Nations sanctions but refused to become a part of the anti-Iraqi military coalition. The united Yemen is a dramatic new development. The 1962 revolution and subsequent events destroyed the most visible traditional Islamic institution in Yemen, the Zaydi imamate. Similarly, the chronic instability of the radical experience in the south led to the demise of the one Marxist regime in the Arab world. The most successful efforts of national integration were those that combined modernizing adaptationism with a recognition of the more conservative Islamic traditions of Yemen and of the importance of the transformation of secularist radicalism into a social republicanism that recognized Islamic principles and Yemeni experiences.

In both Syria and Iraq, leaders of the Ba'th Party remained in control of the countries from the late 1960s into the 1990s, maintaining the symbols of the old Arab socialism but adapting the policies and discourse to the changing regional and global conditions. In Syria a new pragmatic tone was set in 1970 when Hafiz al-Asad emerged in control and his "corrective movement" shifted away from the earlier dogmatic radicalism of the Ba'th Syrian regime. He emphasized a less vigorous socialization of the economy and worked to build a broader base of popular support through a national front.

Although Asad initially faced some opposition from leftist forces, the most effective popular opposition came from groups appealing to a revived Sunni Muslim consciousness. Asad came from a Shi'i community in Syria, the Alawites, and relied heavily on Alawites to fill important political and military positions. This aroused fears among Sunnis of an Alawite domination of Syria. Debates over a new constitution in 1973 reflected these sensitivities, and Asad made a special effort to define his political authority in Islamic terms.

The core of organized opposition to Asad came from the Syrian Muslim Brotherhood. In the early 1970s, Asad, like Sadat, allowed the Brotherhood greater freedom as a way of countering threats to the regime from the left. However, by the mid-1970s the Syrian Brotherhood had begun a major campaign of violent opposition to Asad, culminating in the killing of more than sixty Alawite cadets at a military school in Aleppo in 1979 and an almost successful attempt to kill Asad himself in 1980. In contrast to developments in Egypt, Asad began a major suppression of the Syrian Brotherhood and other Islamist forces. Conflicts led to a major revolt in the city of Hama in 1982, which Asad crushed with the destruction of much of the city and as many as thirty thousand people killed.[77] Although there was some further fundamentalist opposition in the early 1990s, there was limited Islamist challenge to the regime and little opportunity for overt participation in Syrian politics.

The rigorous suppression of the Syrian Brotherhood did not mean that Asad adopted a simply secularist, anti-Islamic stance. Asad was one of the major supporters within the Arab world of the Islamic Revolution in Iran and was an ally of Iran in the Iran-Iraq War of the 1980s. This policy opened him to accusations of breaking Arab unity but was based on Asad's possible empathy with Shi'ite aspirations in the region as a whole and his sense that the Islamic Revolution represented the new effective challenge to imperialist efforts to control the Middle East.[78]

The Gulf Crisis of 1990–1991 and the new global political context opened the way for a significant reorientation of Syrian policy. The long-term rivalry with Iraq led to Syrian condemnation of Iraq's invasion of Kuwait in 1990 and to active Syrian participation in the United Nations coalition forces. At the same time, Asad acted to bring an end to the civil war in Lebanon by using the Syrian army to assist a new national government to regain control of much of the country from the militias that had emerged during the years of fighting. Asad worked closely with conservative Arab regimes and cooperated with efforts by the United States to bring an end to the Arab-Israeli conflict. In all of this, Asad remained the closest of all the Arab leaders to the pragmatic radicalism of the early 1970s. Too much utilization of Islamically based political discourse would open the way for his Sunni opposition within Syria. Instead, he continued to base his policies and calls for popular mobilization on the older ideals of Arab unity, a greater Syria, and a socialist vision of a relatively secular society only somewhat tempered by the emerging populist Islamic discourse of the region as a whole.

In Iraq, the Baʿth Party gained control in 1968 after a decade of turmoil. Under the leadership of Ahmad Hasan al-Bakr, the Iraqi Baʿth took a more pragmatic and nondoctrinaire approach, although it maintained its long rivalry with the Syrian branch of the party. Despite many problems, the Baʿth regime continued in power into the early 1990s, successfully surviving the transfer of leadership when al-Bakr retired in 1978 and Saddam Husayn became president. During these years Iraq became one of the strongest military powers in the region with the help of close ties to the Soviet Union. Because of the revenues from the sale of petroleum, while Iraq had many economic problems, it was among the economic powers of the region as well.

Iraq became involved in two major wars in the era of Saddam. Following the Iranian Revolution, tensions between Iran and Iraq mounted, with Iraq invading Iran in the fall of 1980. In the long and bloody conflict that followed, Saddam used a combination of Arab nationalist and Islamic symbols to mobilize popular support. The war was frequently called "Qadisiyyat Saddam," referring to the battle of Qadisiyyah in 636 CE when the Muslims forces, then almost exclusively Arab, defeated the Persian empire of the day and opened Persia to Arab-Muslim conquest. "Qadisiyyat Saddam" provides a key to the mood and tone of Iraqi policy at the time and may even help to explain why the Shiʿi soldiers in the Iraqi army were willing to fight the Shiʿi, but Persian, Islamic republic.[79]

The second major war began when Iraq invaded Kuwait in August 1990. In proclaiming this "second Qadisiyyah," Saddam Husayn continued to combine the themes of Islam and Arabism and he ultimately identified the war as a jihad against unbelievers.[80] In these positions, Saddam reflects the significant Islamization of radical discourse that had taken place by the early 1990s. The mobilizing call was to jihad, not, as would have been the case in the 1960s, a call to radical revolution. The secular Arabism of the early Baʿth rhetoric became a claim for Arab priority within Islam, with Saddam proclaiming that the "Arabs are the leaders of the Islamic religion. When non-Arabs become the leaders, then Islam will deviate from its meanings and concepts."[81] In the Gulf Crisis of 1990–1991, Saddam received support from a variety of fundamentalist and other explicitly Muslim groups throughout the world, despite his record of secularist radicalism and persecution of Iraqi Muslim activists. He had succeeded in transforming his image among these groups into that of an opponent of anti-Islamic imperialism.

Opposition to the Baʿth regime came from a number of sources but was relatively ineffective. Communist and other leftist groups remained isolated and, in the context of the global failure of Marxist regimes and the Islamic resurgence, had limited impact. Kurds in northern Iraq had a long tradition of resistance to the Arabizing efforts of Iraqi central governments, and appeals to Islam and national unity were insufficient grounds for a settlement; neither side had sufficient armed force to impose a permanent settlement. Following the crushing defeat of the Iraqi army by the United States in 1991, Kurds revolted but were almost defeated. The creation by the United States and its allies of a Kurdish safe zone made it possible for Kurdish leaders to hold elections in 1992 and establish structures of self-government. The key themes of politics were Kurdish survival rather than Islamic resurgence.

Shiʿi movements represented the greatest potential threat to the Baʿth regime. The Sunni Arabs of Iraq dominate the political system centered in Baghdad, although Shiʿi Arabs are the majority of the population. The great Shiʿi holy sites of Najaf and Karbala are centers of scholarship and piety for Shiʿi Muslims throughout the world. In the 1960s and 1970s, important scholars interacted and developed a new sense of intellectually revolutionary Shiʿism. This group of scholars included the Ayatollah Khomeini as well as prominent Iraqis. During the 1960s, the key Iraqi figure was Muhammad Bakr al-Sadr (1930–1980) whose writings presented important explanations of how *tawhid* could provide the foundations for modern systems of politics, economics, and philsophy. He was a compelling speaker and a lucid writer, emphasizing rational analysis as well as piety. He provided a major Islamic critique of both communism and capitalism and worked to define the Islamic alternative to these systems in the modern context.[82]

Shiʿi opposition groups developed in the late 1970s inspired by the teachings of al-Sadr. The largest of these were al-Daʿwah al-Islamiyyah and al-Mujahidin.[83] However, the execution of al-Sadr in 1980, the subsequent repression of the opposition groups and the absence of a major leader to replace al-Sadr meant that Shiʿi opposition had limited impact on Saddam's policies in the 1980s. When there was a major Shiʿi revolt following Saddam's military defeat in 1991, the central government was able to restore control even in the holy cities of Najaf and Karbala by crushing military measures. Although the Shiʿi resistance was unable to provide effective opposition to the Ba'th regime, its intellectual leadership, especially al-Sadr, made a significant contribution to the contemporary Islamic revival in intellectual and conceptual terms.

The evolution of Arab socialist and secularist regimes by the early 1990s showed the power of the Islamic resurgence. In some countries fundamentalists had become the major effective opposition groups and in most areas, Islamic discourse had replaced the older discourse of radical socialism as the basis for policy and political mobilization. Although radicalism continues to be a crucial part of the ideological development of the Arab world, it became less secularist and more Islamic in tone by the early 1990s.

Modernizing Adaptationism in Asia Muslim States

Islam became an increasingly important social and political factor in the major Asian Muslim states during the 1970s and 1980s. In those countries in which Muslims were the dominant majority—Turkey, Pakistan, Bangladesh, and Indonesia—the dominant style continued to be modernizing adaptationism. However, by the early 1990s, this style was no longer solely identified with secular and socialist approaches. The normalization of the Islamic resurgence is reflected in the growing place of Islamic symbols and ideals in the programs and discourse of adaptationism. In this new situation, the reaffirmation of Islam in the modern context was no longer simply a fundamentalist response; it was also emerging as part of the articulation of modernizing adaptationism.

Turkey

Throughout the 1970s and 1980s, Turkey remained committed to the ideals of Kemalism, but the gradual withdrawal from the extreme secularism of the early republic, which had begun after World War II, continued. Turkish political leadership worked to maintain a balance between Turkish goals of modernization in identification with western Europe and ideals of a growing nationalist and religious reaffirmation.

During the 1970s there was a polarization of politics and an increasing resort to terrorism on the part of the extremes of both the left and the right. The two major parties, then the Republican Peoples Party (RPP) and the Justice Party (JP), represented the majority of the population and were the heirs of pragmatic Kemalism, but this moderate center was unable to control effectively the extremist forces. Both parties preferred to form coalitions with groups like the National Salvation Party (NSP) rather than working together in coalition governments. As a result, the NSP, which had won almost 12 percent of the votes in 1973, joined the RPP and then the JP in government coalitions. This brought a vigorously Islamic and antisecularist party into the middle of Turkish politics.

Extremism became a major factor during the 1970s. Both radical leftists and ultranationalists, like the National Action party led by Alparslan Turkes, created militant groups which clashed with each other and governmental authorities. Groups from both extremes engaged in terrorism and murder campaigns in efforts to disrupt the existing political system. The militant left was both radical and secularist and made little attempt to incorporate Islamic themes in their pronouncements. On the right, National Action members often clashed with NSP groups and were more nationalist than fundamentalist. Violence sometimes involved religious communal tensions as well as ideological divisions, and serious Sunni-Shi'i fighting took place in Kahramanmaras (in 1978) and Corum (in 1980). Similarly, unrest among Turkish Kurds in eastern Turkey was strengthened both by the growing general resort to political violence and by Islamic revivalism. In 1979, for example, demonstrators in eastern region supported the NSP and called for an "independent Islamic state."[84]

In the face of growing violence and instability, the military leaders took control of the government in September 1980. Military and civilian leaders worked together in creating a new constitution which maintained the traditions of Kemalism and aimed at a more controlled expression of democracy. This constitution provided the basis for restoration of civilian parliamentary politics and elections in 1983. Politicians from older parties were excluded from the elections, and the Motherland Party, which brought together a variety of centrist, conservative, and Islamically-oriented groups, defeated the moderate party believed to be supported by the military. Motherland Party's leader, Turgut Ozal, became prime minister and the leading Turkish political figure in the 1980s.

In the Turkish elections of 1987 a broader spectrum of political forces was involved. The old JP was revived under the leadership of Demirel as the True Path Party (TPP), getting about 20 percent of the votes, while the old RPP tradition appeared in the Social Democratic Populist Party (SDPP) of Erdol Inonu (which gained about 25 percent of the vote) and a smaller splinter group, the Democratic Left Party (DLP), led by Ecevit. Erbakan again recreated a fundamentalist party, the Welfare Party, which obtained about 6 percent of the votes. The winner was the Motherland Party, with 36 percent of the votes and a clear parliamentary majority.

The political influence of Islamic fundamentalism in Turkey remains limited. In national and local elections over the years, fundamentalist parties organized by Erbakan have won between 5 and 15 percent of the votes and such groups have more influence in particular areas. Some of the most visible fundamentalist leaders now stress the need to work through the mosque rather than through political parties. In the 1980s this view was most forcefully expressed by Jemaleddin Kaplan (Hojaoglu), a Turkish preacher living in Germany who hoped to inspire an Islamic revolution "by following Khomeini's strategy of infiltrating sound and video cassettes of his sermons into the country, exposing the masses to the ideas of the Islamic state."[85] Although people like Hojaoglu have not yet gained mass followings, in the early 1990s there were people in both government offices and the armed forces who were charged with propagating fundamentalism. The murder of a prominent secularist scholar in 1990 by a group calling itself "Islamic Revenge" showed that the extremist fundamentalist fringe continued to exist. However, the murder of a police officer by members of the revolutionary leftist group, Dev Sol, in the same year was a reminder that violent extremism was not simply a fundamentalist phenomenon.

The broader strength of the Islamic resurgence goes beyond the relatively small fundamentalist groups. Virtually all political parties in significant ways now articulate their programs in Islamic terms. The government under the Motherland Party encouraged Islamic financial institutions, enforced compulsory religious education in secondary schools, and supported (and received the support of) the revived Naqshbandiyyah Tariqah in Turkey.[86] In a continuing controversy over women's dress, in 1988, Ozal's government legalized the previously prohibited wearing of Islamic headdress by women on university campuses. Although the law was declared unconstitutional by the supreme court, the popularity of the law illustrated the strength of the Islamic resurgence outside of purely fundamentalist circles.

Most of the social and political leaders of Turkey in the early 1990s are more "cultural Islamists" or "modern-minded Muslims" than fundamentalists in terms of their approach to social policies and political programs.[87] While they are committed to the reformist tradition of Kemalism and see Turkey as having an important role in Europe, they also identify directly with the Turkish Islamic heritage. This double focus was clear by the early 1990s when Turkey actively sought admission to the European Community at the same time that it assumed full membership in the Islamic Conference Organization. In the Gulf Crisis of 1990–1991 Turkey was an important partner in the coalition of forces led by the United States, despite domestic fundamentalist opposition. Direct Turkish involvement in the crisis was explained both in terms of ties with the West and the sense that Turkey's "Islamic heritage links it to the Arab world."[88] Islam had become a normal part of the politics of modernizing adaptationism as well as the banner for fundamentalist opposition in Turkey by the 1990s.

Muslim South Asia

In the major Muslim states in south Asia, problems of political instability and national integration provided the context for the Islamic resurgence of the late twentieth century. The original state of Pakistan was divided in the war of 1970–1971, with two independent states emerging, Pakistan (in the old West Pakistan) and Bangladesh. The failure of Islam to provide a sufficient basis for national unity provided an opening for more secularist and radical leaders in the new states. Chronic political instability, however, led to rule by military officers who found the official reassertion of the Islamic identity of the states to be politically important.

The leader of the new Pakistan in 1971, Zulfikar Ali Bhutto, was committed to programs which were more radical socialist than Islamic in their emphasis. In domestic policy, he initiated programs of agrarian reform and nationalization of industries. Conservative religious forces opposed these policies but their opposition was reduced as Bhutto adopted a more Islamically oriented foreign policy. The Islamic summit conference at Lahore in 1974 helped to give an Islamic luster to his government. When Bhutto and his Pakistan Peoples Party (PPP) won an overwhelming victory in the 1977 elections, charges of election fraud and illegal suppression of the opposition led to widespread unrest. Bhutto attempted to win additional support by enacting more explicitly Islamic legislation but increasing political instability led senior military officers under General Zia al-Haq to take control of the government in July 1979.

Bhutto was executed in 1979 and the new military government promised a rapid return to civilian rule. However, the Soviet invasion of Afghanistan in 1979 changed Pakistan's strategic situation and encouraged the continuation of military rule in the face of the flood of Afghan refugees and attacks from the Afghan communist government. The civilian opposition within Pakistan was divided and ineffective so that Zia was able to consolidate his regime in the early 1980s. Zia's major domestic policy initiatives involved a vigorous effort to make the legal and political systems more clearly Islamic. By the middle of the 1980s this had become a formally proclaimed policy of comprehensive Islamization. Parallel to this, Zia initiated a process of associating civilians with the government, with the stated long-term goal of a return to civilian rule. The proposed power-sharing structure led to elections in

1985, the creation of a national consultative assembly, and the appointment of a civilian prime minister with limited powers.

In 1988 a series of events transformed the political scene in Pakistan. In May, Zia dissolved the assembly and dismissed the prime minister, bringing an end to process of civilianization. He then issued a formal decree making the Shari'a the supreme law of Pakistan and ordered all courts to begin its implementation. Before the full implications of this decree could be worked out, General Zia was killed in a plane crash in August 1988. The legal process of transfer of power worked smoothly, and the acting president, Ghulam Ishaq Khan, organized national elections rapidly.

The post-Zia era opened dramatically with hotly contested elections at the end of 1988. Civilian parties had begun to operate in a limited way after 1985 and moved to the forefront of the political scene in the new era. The PPP had emerged as the major party of opposition under the leadership of Bhutto's daughter, Benazir. In the 1988 elections, the PPP won a plurality of seats in the new parliament, and Benazir Bhutto became prime minister. Benazir Bhutto was educated in Radcliffe College and Oxford and attempted to balance the more secularist tradition of the PPP with careful appeals to the more modernist Islamic elements in the country. She was opposed by conservatives and fundamentalists, many of whom objected to having a woman as ruler, as well as old associates of Zia. After twenty months in office, she was dismissed by the president who charged her with corruption and contravention of the constitution.

In elections late in 1990, the Islamic Democratic Alliance (IDA), a coalition of the political heirs of Zia, conservatives, and fundamentalists, won a major victory over the PPP and gained clear control of parliament. The new prime minister was Nawaz Sharif who appealed more directly to Islamic sentiments but also supported the coalition led by the United States in the Gulf War of 1991. He initiated programs to restructure Pakistan's economy through privatization and faced major problems of widespread violence and public disorder.

The development of legal Islamization in the years immediately following Zia's death illustrates the political importance of Islam. During the 1980s, Pakistan became firmly committed to some form of political, legal, and social Islamization. In the elections of 1988 and 1990, no major party advocated a secularist reversal of Islamization, although women's rights activists actively opposed expansion of Zia's Islamization programs. Instead, the debates concerned the content and method of Islamization. Zia's 1988 decree had not been ratified by the parliament so passage of Islamization laws was a major issue in the politics of the early 1990s. Sharif finally "finessed approval of a bill that places Pakistan under the *sharia,* or Islamic law, but blunts the Muslim clergy's powers and fundamentalist dictates."[89] The emerging mainstream position was Islamically based but was more adaptationist than fundamentalist in style.

The experience of Bangladesh runs parallel in some ways to that of Pakistan with a transition from a more radical regime to a military regime with a more Islamic tone and then the reestablishment of civilian party politics. The leader of the new state in 1971 was Mujib al-Rahman, head of the Awami League (AL). Mujib renounced the idea of an Islamic state and declared the new nation to be secularist and socialist. The programs of Mujib were unable to resolve the country's many problems and early in 1975, Mujib assumed dictatorial powers. He was overthrown and killed by a group of military officers. Despite his initial popularity as "father" of the new country, his secular socialism had not solved the country's problems.

There were other radical alternatives in Bangladesh, but they were not in a position to assume power in 1975. The National Socialist Party led by Major Muhammad Abd al-Jalil represented secular radicalism which maintained that Mujib's socialism had been largely a middle-class program and was doomed to fail. There were also Islamic radical groups, the best known of which was led by Mawlana Abd al-Hamid Bhashani. He had formed a party as early as 1957 and represented a continuation of the tradition of Bengali peasant radicalism that had produced the nineteenth-century revivalist movements. His program was a combination of an appeal to Islamic principles and programs of radical agrarian reform.

In the transition regime following the killing of Mujib, Major General Zia al-Rahman, the chief of army staff and martial law administrator, gradually assumed control. He worked for the creation of a civilian administration supported by the military and assumed the office of president in 1977, with this being confirmed in direct elections in 1978. When martial law was lifted in 1979, parliamentary elections were held and Zia al-Rahman's party, the Bangladesh Nationalist Party (BNP), won a substantial majority of seats. The transition from Mujib to Zia was a clear move from a self-consciously secular regime to a system with an Islamic orientation. Bangladesh was proclaimed to be an Islamic republic, and Zia emphasized the importance of Islam in national unity and society. However, in contrast to Zia al-Haq's program in Pakistan, Zia al-Rahman did not initiate a formal program of legal Islamization, and the general tone was that of an Islamically committed adaptationism rather than fundamentalism. Government policy was sufficiently radical and Islamic so that the BNP received the support of Mawlana Bhashani and yet sufficiently traditional so that it did not arouse the opposition of conservative Muslims or the fundamentalist groups.

The era of Zia came to an abrupt end in May 1981 when Zia was killed in an unsuccessful military coup. Zia had created a civilian political system with sufficient strength to achieve the legally defined transfer of power to his civilian vice president, Abdus Sattar (d. 1985), who then was elected president later in the year. However, Abdus Sattar was overthrown in 1982 by a military leader, Hussein Muhammad Ershad, who reestablished a more authoritarian military regime. Although Ershad proclaimed his intention of restoring civilian government, he never secured a significant level of support from civilian political leaders. His own political party, the Jatiya Party, was divided, and during the nine years of Ershad's rule, he "shuffled his cabinet" more than 60 times.[90] Opposition came from the two major established parties, the AL led by Hasina Wajid, the daughter of Mujib, and the BNP led by Khaleda Zia, the widow of Zia al-Rahman.

Ershad attempted a more fundamentalist style Islamization program in 1987–1988 as a way of building legitimacy and support for his regime. In this way he reflected the importance of Islam as a social and political force in Bangladesh, but even fundamentalist supporters of application of Shariʿa as the law of the land mistrusted Ershad's motives, and he did not get the support of the Jamaat-i Islami. The adaptationist approach of Zia al-Rahman had been popular, but the more rigid fundamentalist approach did not have great appeal in Bangladesh.

Opposition to Ershad was strongly divided, and it was not until younger members of the major opposition groups united that Ershad was overthrown. In the face of major demonstrations late in 1990, Ershad resigned and an interim president quickly arranged for national elections, which were held in early 1991. In the election campaign, the major themes were elimination of corruption and resolving the grave economic problems of the day. The old debates over secularization and Islamization were muted, with most groups accepting the concept of Bangladesh as a modernizing, adaptationist Islamic state. In the elections, the Jamaat-i Islam won eighteen seats in the three hundred seat parliament, but radical secularists like the Communist Party only won five seats. The winner was Khaleda Zia and the BNP who won 138 seats and were able to build a coalition with the Jamaat-i Islam to form a government. The BNP victory opened the way for a return to the more adaptationist style of Islamic policy of Zia al-Rahman rather than either the old style secularism of the days of Mujib or the fundamentalism of Ershad. In the early 1990s Islam was simply a normal part of the political scene rather than a subject for major debate.

Indonesia

In Indonesia, the long dialogue between secular nationalism and more explicitly Islamic perspectives continued into the early 1990s. The government remained under the control of modernizing adaptationists led by the

344   The Resurgence of Islam

major military leaders, and the major potential opposition came from Islamic groupings. Secular radicalism had not reemerged as a major force after the crushing of the Indonesian Communist Party in 1965–1966 and by the 1990s radicalism in any form was more likely to be expressed in Islamic terms.

The evolution of the political system under the direction of President Suharto allowed for significant military control but also opened the way for important civilian participation. Suharto organized a political party, Golkar, which won all of the elections in the 1970s and 1980s, but those elections were not simply rubber-stamp referendums, and opposition parties received a significant proportion of the votes. The basic ideological position of the government was articulated within the framework of the old Pantjasila, which by the mid-1980s became the only legal ideological base for the platform of any political party.

Legal Islamic political activity was increasingly restricted in the 1970s and 1980s. The four major Islamic parties were required to join together in a single party in 1973 and were given a name which made no direct reference to Islam, Partai Persatuan Pembangunan (PPP, "United Development Party"). The proportion of the vote for the Muslim parties had been 27 percent in the 1971 elections and for PPP was almost 30 percent in 1977, but declined to 16 percent in the 1987 elections. By the early 1990s, the activities of the legal political party had limited impact, although it maintained the potential for influence in the post-Suharto era.

The spectrum of Muslim activity spread far beyond the realm of the PPP. Fundamentalist opposition had taken a number of forms. The old Dar-al-Islam movement continued to inspire some rural opposition and terrorist activity, as was clear in the trials of members of Komando Jihad in 1978. In 1990–1991 revolts in Atjeh, in western Sumatra, may also reflect this old opposition spirit. Such continuing militant opposition means that the country's leaders, especially among the military, maintain a general mistrust of Islamic movements.

The real strength of the Islamic resurgence in Indonesia has not, however, been fundamentalist in style. The new generations have been active through student groups and a variety of other organizations in reviving local institutions and building new social and economic foundations on an Islamic basis. The new generation of Muslim intellectual-activists has actively accepted the "challenge to make Islam a dynamic force for modernization and national advancement"[91] and came to play an important political as well as social role by the early 1990s. This intellectual productivity has been paralleled by a broader popular reaffirmation of Islamic identity, especially among professionals and educated Indonesians, which is manifested in growing numbers of people participating in public Muslim rites.

One of the most visible figures in this resurgence is Abdurrahman Wahid, a grandson of a founder of Nahdatul Ulama (NU) who became the organization's leader in the 1980s. NU had been the largest party in the PPP, but in 1984 Wahid led NU's withdrawal from the PPP, emphasizing that NU had a social, religious, and educational mission. Wahid has cooperated with the Suharto regime while maintaining a position which is critical of many of its policies. He has concentrated on making the rural educational system controlled by NU more effective and has directed NU's energies in the direction of community development, establishing a system of people's banks in villages and towns, while Wahid has also made important contributions to the intellectual interpretation of Islam in the Indonesian context.[92]

Fundamentalism is a peripheral part of the Islamic resurgence in Indonesia. The heart of the resurgence is the large, populist activities like those of the NU under Wahid and others who are more adaptationist than fundamentalist in style. The Suharto government tolerates and sometimes encourages this approach, and modernizing adaptationism assumes an increasingly Islamic form in the early 1990s.

Summary

In the four large Asia Muslim states of Turkey, Pakistan, Bangladesh, and Indonesia, the final third of the twentieth century is a time of significant interaction between the forces of modernizing adaptationism and the Islamic resurgence. In each of these states the military played an important role in working to create political stability but did not develop radical socialist programs. Such programs were initiated by civilian leaders such as Sukarno, Bhutto, and Mujib, while in Turkey the emphasis was more on continuing the older traditions of Kemalism. The military intervened in each country in reaction to ineffective civilian rule and maintained a style of modernizing adaptationism which gradually came to include significant Islamic elements by the early 1990s.

In each country, fundamentalist groups provided some challenge to the political establishments but these represented a decreasing part of the Islamic revivalist experience by the early 1990s. Instead, the resurgence emerged as a broader spectrum of experiences, and Islam became a significant part of the modernizing adaptationist style. The most effective Muslim organizations in these states were groups like NU in Indonesia rather than the small, extremist fundamentalist ones. Old conflicts over secularism and religion were often replaced by debates about how the process of Islamization of public and private life should proceed. Rather than being reduced to a pe-

ripheral role, Islam had become a major social and political force in each
country by the early 1990s.

Nondominant Majority Communities and the Islamic Revival

The Islamic experiences of those Muslim communities that are not dominant majorities represent many different expressions of the Islamic resurgence. One key issue was the role of Islam in the process of national
integration. In countries where Muslims comprise less than 85 percent of the
population, but still formed a significant group, the possibility of establishing an Islamic state was limited. In this context, the modernizing transition
from emphasis on community to emphasis on state played a significant role.
Many Muslims in religiously pluralist societies accepted the importance of a
state-defined national identity, although growing numbers worked for the
eventual recognition of Islam as the "national religion." As a result, debates
concerning secularism and the role of religion in society and politics were
an important part of the continuing experience of nondominant Muslim
majorities.

In the religiously pluralist states, Islam was important on two levels. As a
world view that was part of local culture, it provided general support for the
emergence of ideologies that were not manifestly "imported." It could be
recognized as a source of law and ideals and could, in that way, provide at
least part of the sense of national identity. However, on another level, in
those states in which there was significant tension among different ethnic
groups, Islam could become an obstacle to national unity by reinforcing the
special identity of a part of society. When groups were inspired by the Islamic revival to assert their special Islamic identity, Islam became an element of national disunity. Islam could be a force for unity or division,
depending upon the local circumstances.

Malaysia: Islam and Ethnic Tensions

In Malaysia, Islam is identified with the Malay ethnic groups which are
politically dominant but which make up barely half of the population. Following independence the state was led by a broad coalition of parties representing the major groups: the United Malays' National Organization
(UMNO), the Malaysian Chinese Association (MCA), and the Malaysian
Indian Congress. This alliance balanced group interests and maintained a
modernizing and secular adaptationism. By the early 1970s, the coalition
government had become an entrenched political establishment open to

charges of corruption. It had failed to prevent the outbreak of major communal conflict in 1969 and was unable to prevent many Malays from believing that they were not benefiting from programs of development as much as the Chinese and Indians.

During the 1970s a vigorous spirit of missionary activity emerged as a powerful force among Malay Muslims, and it took the form of activities aimed both at winning converts to Islam and at purifying the practices of those already Muslim. This *dakwah* ("mission" or "call") spirit resulted in the creation of many religiously active groups, and soon government policy also reflected this spirit.[93] One of the early groups in this effort was Jamaat Tabligh which had spread to Malaysia from India in the 1950s. Tabligh emphasized personal devotion and was not politically involved. Another relatively nonpolitical movement was Darul Arqam, which had been established in 1969 and advocated the establishment of an Islamic social community. It created three Islamic communal settlements and a small system of schools for younger children. It articulated a purist critique of Malaysian society and the other Muslim organizations, although by the 1980s government leaders recognized its apolitical stance and gave it some support.

The most politically active and influential of the dakwah movements was the Malaysian League of Muslim Youth (ABIM, Angkatan Belia Islam Malaysia), which was formally established in 1971. It was an outgrowth of the National Muslim Students' Association of Malaysia (PKPIM), and provided an organization for graduates as well as students and could engage in more political activities than the PKPIM, which was restricted by laws which banned political organizations on campuses. ABIM leaders were influenced by the ideas and experiences of the Jamaat-i Islami in Pakistan and the Muslim Brotherhood in Egypt, and by scholars in the emerging global network of Muslim revivalists like Ismail al-Faruqi, a Palestinian teaching in the United States, and a noted Malaysian scholar, Syed Naguib al-Attas.

ABIM called for a more moral political and economic system based on the principles of Islam and a rejection of capitalism and socialism. Anwar Ibrahim, the leader of ABIM during the 1970s, emphasizes that the Islamic resurgence is not essentially anti-Western but is part of the long historical process of bringing Islamic practice into line with the demands of the Quranic revelation and would be taking place whether or not the West had expanded. For him, the ideal of *tawhid* means that there must be a constant effort to improve human society. He notes that in a pluralist society like Malaysia, Islamic political action must involve cooperation with non-Muslims, and he emphasizes that a truly Islamic society will be democratic and tolerant.[94]

The most active explicitly Muslim political party in Malaysia is Parti Islam SeMalaysia (PAS), which had been established in 1951 by members of UMNO who felt that UMNO was moving in too secular a direction. The party had strength in the more rural states through support from local ulama, but it always remained a relatively small opposition party on the national scene. ABIM cooperated with PAS during the 1970s, and in the early 1980s ABIM members gained most of the leadership positions in PAS. However, the situation was dramatically changed when Anwar Ibrahim joined forces with UMNO in 1982 and rapidly became one of the major national UMNO leaders, holding important cabinet posts throughout the decade and frequently being mentioned as a possible future prime minister.

The complexities of Muslim politics in Malaysia in the early 1990s reflect the evolution of the Islamic resurgence in general. By the time of the general elections of 1990, UMNO had been under the leadership of Mahathar Mohamad, who had once been expelled from the party for his Malay ethnic radicalism, for almost a decade. During this time, the government became an active supporter of many aspects of dakwah and moderate adaptionist style Islamization was an important part of government policy. UMNO itself had moved significantly away from its earlier secularist positions. This trend was emphasized by the incorporation of Anwar Ibrahim and his ABIM allies into the mainstream of national politics.

Even the fundamentalist opposition had moved clearly into the mainstream as PAS became a major member in the opposition coalition which challenged the UMNO alliance in the 1990 elections. To do this, PAS worked closely with an anti-Mahathir faction of the old UMNO and also with the leading party of the Chinese community, the Democratic Action Party (DAP). While PAS remained committed to the ideal of Islamization of Malaysian society, it excluded its traditional call for the establishment of an Islamic state from its election platform and a party leader explained that the terms were dropped because "it was more practical and in line with the times."[95] Although the opposition coalition lost in the 1990 elections, PAS gained control of one of the state governments and, although all other opposition groups ended up with reduced numbers of parliamentary seats, PAS won seven seats, compared with only one in the previous 1986 elections.

The evolution of the Islamic resurgence in the 1970s and 1980s was from reflecting the views of relatively fringe opposition groups to being the primary basis for the agendas of mainstream politics. Former activist fundamentalists like Anwar Ibrahim and leaders of PAS remain committed to their Islamic visions but have become more open to adaptationist styles of operation in both the political and social realms. However, as long as Islam in Malaysia remains primarily related to the Malay ethnic identity, it is a potentially divisive force.

Islam and National Disunity: Eritrea and Chad

In some areas Islam was a factor in defining opposition to national unity and encouraging separatism. Islam was not always the determining factor in the nature of such opposition, as can be seen in the evolution of civil wars in Ethiopia and Chad. These internal conflicts developed during the 1960s and, at least initially, one side in the struggle was identified in some way with Islam. However, as these conflicts developed, the identifying visions were altered, and the role of Islam was changed and possibly reduced.

In Ethiopia, the Eritrean liberation movement continued to fight the central government during the 1970s. Although initially a Muslim separatist movement, it received a broader base of support as a result of the repressive policies of the Ethiopian emperor, Haile Selassie, and by 1970, support for Eritrean independence came from virtually all elements in the province, both Muslim and Christian. This situation did not change following the overthrow of the emperor by a radical military regime in 1974. Although the new government, under the leadership of Mengistu Haile Mariam initiated many radical programs, it was as firmly committed as the old imperial government in its opposition to secessionist movements, and the struggle in Eritrea was intensified.

During the 1970s, the Eritrean national movement was divided. The original organization had been the Eritrean Liberation Front (ELF), but by 1970 the Eritrean People's Liberation Front (EPLF) had come into existence. The EPLF rejected the conservative Muslim separatism of the ELF and advocated an ideologically radical program which appealed to many of the younger generation and provided a common vision for both Muslim and Christian Eritreans. The two groups came into conflict, and the ELF was defeated by both the Ethiopian army and the EPLF. By 1980, the EPLF, with its more consciously secular program, emerged as "the sole major nationalist movement in Eritrea fighting Ethiopia's army."[96] Although it faced some setbacks, the EPLF gradually took control of virtually all of Eritrea, capturing the major urban centers of Afabet (1988), the port of Massawa (1989), and Asmara in 1991 as the central government was collapsing. When the regime of Mengistu was overthrown, the EPLF controlled Eritrea and could demand Eritrean self-determination.

As a result of the long conflict, an Eritrean identity had emerged by the early 1990s which brought together the different ethnic and religious groups in the province. The EPLF succeeded on the basis of its superior organization and the unity created by the repressive policies of the Ethiopian central government. It did not appeal explicitly to Muslim sentiments and maintained at least some of the rhetoric of its Marxist beginnings. The Eritrean national identity had to be able to include both Muslims and Christians, and the EPLF provided a secular and radical basis for this. It did not, however, emphasize explicitly antireligious ideas.

The Mengistu regime was defeated by a coalition of regionally based opposition movements, with the capital and institutions of the central government coming under the control of the Ethiopian People's Revolutionary Democratic Front (EPRDF), a radical group whose primary support was drawn from the Tigre people. The EPLF had supported the EPRDF and secured a guarantee of a referendum on Eritrean independence by 1993. In this situation, the victorious liberation fronts faced the challenge of defining the nature of the state or states which would emerge. In Eritrea, one important issue was the place of Islam and specific ethnic identities. One important ethnic group in Eritrea, the Afars, had organized their own liberation front, the Afar Liberation Front, and also claimed the right of self-determination. When the Afar leader, Sultan Alimirah, returned from exile in 1991, he announced his hope of uniting Afars in Ethiopia and Eritrea in an independent Afar state which would be based on Islamic law.[97] Similarly, within central Ethiopia, liberation groups among the Oromos, a predominantly Muslim people who comprise about 40 percent of Ethiopia's population, worked to gain greater strength within the national Council. The role of Islam in defining Oromo aspirations was not clear in the early 1990s. However, Islam in Ethiopia and Eritrea continued to be a potentially important divisive force.

In Chad, the civil war begun in the 1960s continued in different forms into the early 1990s. Initially the conflict was between northern Muslim groups and the southern, non-Muslim government of François Tombalbaye. Tombalbaye's regime was increasingly repressive and imposed an program of "authenticity," in which local Chadian customs were imposed. Tombalbaye was overthrown and killed in a military coup in 1975 and a southern Christian general, Felix Malloum, became president.

Northern Muslim opposition to the central government continued but it was divided. The main Muslim organization, FROLINAT, split into a faction led by Goukouni Oueddei and the Forces Armees du Nord (FAN), a new group created by Hissen Habre. Oueddei was the son of a major tribal religious leader with a reputation for piety. It was his fellow tribesmen that brought him to power in FROLINAT in 1976. Under Oueddei's leadership, FROLINAT received significant aid from Libya in the name of Islamic unity. In contrast, Habre was a French-educated soldier who was northern but not explicitly traditional or Islamic in his orientation.

The 1980s was a time of continued fighting with a confusing near-anarchy emerging. Malloum attempted to created a "national government of reconciliation" in 1978 which included Habre, but conflict among the various armed groups continued. Negotiations aided by major African states like Nigeria and Sudan resulted in a new national government led by Oueddei in 1979 but fighting continued. Libyan military intervention in 1980 in support of Oueddei and the announcement, in 1981, of the union of Libya and Chad as Muslim states created a major international reaction. In response, Libya agreed to withdraw, opening the way for Habre to gain control of the capital in 1982. From 1982 until late 1990, Habre remained the formal leader of the country in the capital but faced military opposition from Libyan and Chadian forces throughout that time. However, by 1990, it seemed that he had finally brought an end to the era of chronic instability as the Libyans had been defeated and the remaining opposition groups seemed divided and weak. Then, in a very rapid reversal, Idris Deby, a military officer who had fled to Sudan after being involved in a failed coup attempt, led a military force from western Sudan and drove Habre out of the capital and assumed control of the government in December 1990. The chronic instability continued.

By the 1990s, civil conflict in Chad had moved far beyond the original north-south conflict to become simply struggle for power among northern Muslim leaders. While the Islamic resurgence had some impact through the rhetoric and support of Libya in the name of Islamic unity, this was not a significant force. Instead of an Islamization of politics, there was a continued militarization of politics with the state simply being the tool of the military group that happened at any given moment to control N'Djamena, the capital. Islam has the potential for providing some basis for an ideology of national unity and for a continuing regional division, but in the political discourse of the early 1990s it was simply a source of slogans in the continuing struggle for power among military leaders.

National Unity and Islam: Nigeria and Sudan

Efforts to establish an Islamic basis for national unity in the religiously pluralist states of Nigeria and Sudan tended to increase tensions by the early 1990s. Great national conflicts in these two countries appeared to be resolved by the late 1970s on the basis of settlements in which religious and ethnic rivalries were subordinated to the demands of national unity. However, these more secular solutions disintegrated in the early 1980s, and efforts by activist Muslims to create systems of national unity on Islamic foundations increased. This was one important element involved in the continuing political instability in both Sudan and Nigeria during the 1980s and early 1990s.

Nigeria experienced violent coups and a major civil war in the first years after independence in 1960. Then in 1966 a military regime under the leadership of Yakubu Gowon brought an end to the civil war involving the attempted secession of the southeastern region. In the 1970s, Gowon made major strides in the direction of restoring a sense of national unity with the aid of growing revenues from the sale of oil and popular sentiments in favor of ending internal conflict. However, as people began to doubt that he would fulfill his promise of restoration of civilian rule, unrest grew and Gowon was overthrown in 1975 by Brigadier Murtala Mohammed. Mohammed was a Hausa soldier from Kano in the north who had initially favored northern secession but had become an important advocate of federal unity.

Mohammed initiated a rigorous anticorruption campaign and began a phased program for return to civilian rule. Although he was killed in an abortive coup attempt in 1976, his associate and successor, Olusegun Obasanjo, continued his policies. A new constitution was drafted and approved by a constituent assembly, national elections were held in 1979, and a constitutional civilian regime assumed leadership of the country under the newly elected president, Shehu Shagari. Shagari was a northern Muslim but had campaigned on a platform of national unity and was committed to the continuation of a nonreligious federal state as defined by the new constitution. Although Shagari was reelected in 1983, military officers led by Mohammed Buhari took control of the government at the end of that year. The civilian leadership of the Second Republic could not solve Nigeria's grave economic problems and was tainted by corruption and profiteering. Religious issues played little role in the failure of the second attempt at civilian rule in Nigeria.

Buhari's regime imposed stricter controls over the press and freedom of expression as well as failing to improve the economic situation and was itself overthrown in 1985 by a new Armed Forces Ruling Council led by Ibrahim Babangida. The new government made significant commitments to avoid political repression, improve the economy, and restore civilian rule. By the early 1990s, Babangida's government had made important progress in all of these areas, although the restoration of civilian rule remained problematic.

Throughout the 1970s and 1980s, Islamic issues came to play increasingly important roles in Nigerian politics and life. On the extremes, there was a long series of violent confrontations involving Muslim activist groups. In Kano, in northern Nigeria, a messianic Muslim group developed around a popular teacher, Alhaji Mohammad Marwa, often called Maitatsine.[98] During 1980 his followers began a millenarian revolt against existing social conditions in the name of a messianic Muslim vision. In the suppression of the revolt as many as ten thousand people may have been killed and Maitatsine was executed. However, his followers were involved in major revolts later in other northern cities in 1982 and 1984. This unrest reflected the distintegration of the traditional northern economy and the continuing, and apparently growing, ability of Islam to provide the terms for the expression of discontent and revolt.

Intercommunal violence reflected the continuing importance of religious identities in Nigeria. There were major riots between Christians and Muslims in a number of places with some of the most serious taking place in Kafanchan in 1987 and Bauchi state in 1991. Both Muslim and Christian mission efforts and activism were involved in these conflicts, illustrating the strength of religious feeling among all communities.

In a broader sense, there was a growing effort among Muslims to define Nigeria in more clearly Islamic terms, and this created new tensions in the unstable political context. A major crisis in the Constituent Assembly debates in 1978 was disagreement over whether or not to establish a Federal Sharia Court of Appeal. The issue was resolved only by the direct intervention of Obasanjo and the creation of a compromise allowing for the creation of a special committee of Supreme Court justices knowledgable in Islamic law to hear cases involving Sharia court appeals. In constitutional discussions in 1988, debate on this issue became so heated that the military declared the earlier compromise to be the final solution to the problem.[99] These tensions had been heightened in 1986 when it became public knowledge that the federal government had applied for full membership in the Organization of the Islamic Conference, the major international association of Muslim states, rather than maintaining its former special observer status.

Muslim positions were increasingly effectively articulated. In the 1960s, the most visible representatives of Islamic views were conservative northern leaders like the Sardauna of Sokoto. However, by the 1990s, while leaders of the traditional establishments maintained some real influence, significant fundamentalist voices had emerged. Abubakar Gumi had been a close associate of the old northern Muslim political leaders but, after their downfall in the late 1960s, gradually emerged as a leading presenter of a politically conservative fundamentalist perspective. He became a very popular radio star and is similar in some ways to preachers like Shaykh Kishk in Egypt. He was strongly critical of the traditional Sufi orders and local religious practices as well as being opposed to modernizing secularism. A more radical fundamentalist position is presented by Ibraheem Sulaiman, a university lecturer who became especially popular among Nigerian Muslim students in the 1980s. He actively presented the case for Islam as an alternative to the Western ideologies of capitalism and communism. His goal was to separate Islam from communal divisions in Nigeria so that it could become the basis for Nigerian national unity. He believes that Islam "offers the best and most reliable possibility for Nigeria to secure the total and all embracing freedom it requires to become a nation in earnest."[100] An additional person with increasing visibility in the early 1990s was Ibrahim el Zakzaky, a religious teacher in Zaria who preached a radical puritanism and whose followers were involved in the riots of 1991. He and others were reported to have received some support from the Islamic Republic of Iran, and this caused some of them to be called "Shi'ites" by their critics.

Across this broad spectrum, fundamentalism

> is essentially about the reform of Islam for the purpose of creating a more just society along Islamic lines. It is not only a moral response to what it sees as the corrupting influence of Western libertarianism and exploitation, and godless socialism, but also a reaction to the failure of Western, secular (which to many Muslims means Christian) political, economic and educational systems to provide solutions to the country's problems.[101]

In this context, the Islamic experience in Nigeria entered a new phase. Islam was competing as an ideology of national identity rather than simply as a communal identity. As such, it opened the way for increasing tensions within Nigeria.

Sudan experienced a sequence of civilian and military regimes following independence in 1956. The periods of civilian rule in 1956–1958, 1964–1969, and 1985–1989 showed remarkable continuity of political organization. In each of these periods the largest political organizations were those supported by the two largest Muslim associations in the country, the Ansar (the Sudanese Mahdist movement) and the Khatmiyyah Tariqah. In addition, there were smaller parties representing southern, primarily non-Muslim groups and other groups like the Muslim Brotherhood and the Sudan Communist Party. In the three periods of civilian rule, no party was strong enough to rule alone, so parliamentary politics was an unstable sequence of coalitions which were unable to resolve the basic problems of the economy or national unity.

The various military regimes represent more authoritarian approaches to these problems. The first military regime (1958–1964) was more conservative, while the second, led by Ja'far Numayri, attempted to create national unity on a variety of bases. When Numayri came to power in 1969, he worked to establish a relatively typical Arab socialist regime in the framework of a radical socialist ideology. He clashed with the traditional Muslim forces in the Sudan, like the Ansar, but soon also was involved in a struggle for power with the Communists in his regime. By 1972 he moved to a more pragmatic approach and succeeded in bring an end to the long civil war in the southern Sudan through recognition of southern autonomy as defined in the Addis Ababa agreement of 1972 and the subsequent constitution. He continued this policy of national unity through compromise and recognition of diversity in a policy of national reconciliation with many of his northern political opponents. Sadiq al-Mahdi, a great-grandson of the Sudanese Mahdi and leader of the Ummah Party, and Hasan Turabi, the leader of the Sudanese Muslim Brotherhood, accepted the idea of reconciliation in 1977–1978, and Turabi became actively involved in the government. In this phase, there was recognition of the importance of Islam in Sudanese life, but groups like the Muslim Brotherhood emphasized the desirability of a gradual evolution rather than an Islamic revolution to achieve Muslim goals in Sudan.

The situation changed significantly in the early 1980s. Numayri undermined the effectiveness of the Addis Ababa agreement by dictatorial interference in southern affairs, and armed southern resistance emerged by 1983 in the form of the Sudan People's Liberation Movement under the leadership of John Garang. Then, beginning with the "September Laws" of 1983, Numayri began the enforced Islamization of the political, legal, and economic systems of the Sudan. This program tended to be a relatively arbitrary collection of rules and regulations which were intregrated by the general concept of the president as an imam to whom people would give an oath of allegiance. Although the intellectual content was in some ways inspired by the programs of the Muslim Brotherhood, the organization of Numayri's Islamization program was closer to the model of the small Sufi orders built around a single holy man's charisma. Numayri's program received its strongest support from these smaller orders, especially those in the central part of the country like the followers of Abu Qurun whose son was a presidential advisor for Islamization.

The September Laws were opposed directly by the Ansar and their leader Sadiq al-Mahdi was jailed. The Khatmiyyah were less open in their criticism but essentially withdrew from major involvement in the political arena. The small but articulate Republican Brothers were active in their criticism, and their leader, Mahmud Muhammad Taha, was executed in January 1985 for his opposition. The opposition to Numayri's Islamization gave added strength to the SPLM, whose relatively radical socialist program increasingly emphasized a strict secularism. Garang was able to mount a strong challenge in military terms in the south, and the movement won some support among northern intellectuals. Even the Muslim Brotherhood had reservations about Numayri's program, since the specific ordinances were drafted without Brotherhood involvement and the September Laws came as a surprise to the Brotherhood. When the Brotherhood appeared to be gaining strength in the context of the developing Islamization program, Numayri suppressed that group as well in early 1985.[102]

Numayri attempted to establish a comprehensive Islamization in Sudan, in economic and social areas as well as legal and political. This effort to resolve the problems of disunity by an imposed Islamization only emphasized the divisions in the country, both among Muslims themselves and between non-Muslims and Muslims. However, the establishment of a formally Islamic state created a context which continued after Numayri's overthrow in 1985. Debate and conflict centered on two key issues: whether or not the state should be Islamic or secular and, second, among those supporting some form of Islamic state, how that Islamic nature would be defined.

Islamic issues were the heart of the struggle for national unity in the regimes that followed Numayri's. Numayri was overthrown in 1985 by military officers committed to a restoration of civilian politics. Their transitional regime suspended implementation of some aspects of Numayri's program but postponed any major actions until the election of a civilian parliament. In the election campaign of 1986, all parties, even the National Islamic Front (NIF) supported by the Muslim Brotherhood, promised significant modifications of the September Laws, and most pledged their abrogation. The SPLM did not participate in the elections or the new civilian state but maintained its strongly secularist position. The new government was again dominated by the older Ansar and Khatmiyyah-based parties, but the Muslim Brotherhood emerged as a major political force. The prime minister from 1986–1989 was Sadiq al-Mahdi, who lead a constantly shifting array of political groups in an unstable coalition. He was unable to resolve the grave economic problems facing the country and could not bring an end to the civil war. Despite the fact that he had been imprisoned for his opposition to the September Laws, he was never able to formally and fully abrogate them. It seemed impossible for any northern Muslim politician to advocate the de-Islamization of the state, even if it simply meant the replacement of the September Laws by some other means of recognizing an Islamic identity.

The third period of civilian politics was brought to an end when a group of military officers led by Omar Hassan al-Bashir took control of the government in 1989. The new government became increasingly identified with the National Islamic Front, and government programs of full Islamization were being implemented by the early 1990s. This brought the new government into increasing conflict with the SPLM but Bashir received growing support from Hasan Turabi and a broad base of the Muslim Brotherhood. In international terms, the new government adopted activist Islamist positions and during the Gulf Crisis of 1990–1991 opposed American military intervention. Turabi became a leader in an Islamist coordinating group which included Madani of Algeria and Ghanoushi of Tunisia. By the early 1990s, Sudan had become the leading Islamist state in the Arab world and, along with Iran, was emerging as one of the two activist models of an essentially fundamentalist state. However, while in Iran revolutionary Islamic program could be the basis for a national sense of unity, in Sudan, the emergence of a fundamentalist government has emphasized the major divisions within the society.

Summary

In countries where Muslims were a majority but where there were significant non-Muslim elements, Islam can be a divisive element. In Nigeria and Sudan, moves to create relatively fundamentalist style Islamic national identity have created conflicts and tensions. Although some Muslim thinkers, like Mahmud Muhammad Taha in Sudan, have made special efforts to articulate a pluralistic Islamic perspective, most major activist movements have been less able to create a persuasive form of inclusive social identity based on Islam. At the same time, it is also clear that secularists have been equally unable to cope with the reaffirmation of religious loyalties. In the early 1990s this made societies like Nigeria and Sudan potentially unstable.

Muslim Minorities and Islamic Revival

Muslim minority communities which made up less than 25 percent of the population of their countries were also clearly affected by the resurgent affirmation of Islam and the normalization of the Islamic resurgence by the early 1990s. At times, groups in the minority communities were inspired to increasing activism, and at other times they received more careful attention from the dominant groups. In general, most minority Muslims followed a line of moderation or adaptation, but there was a growing sense of pride in the Islamic heritage and a growing public participation in the global Muslim community.

Major Minority Communities: Soviet Union, China, and India

The reaffirmation of Islam as a basis for communal identity was an important element in the experiences of major Muslim minority communities like those in the Soviet Union, China, and India. Although these communities were a relatively small proportion of the total population in their countries, in terms of numbers these communities were among the largest in the Islamic world. In different ways, changing social and political environments opened the way for stronger affirmations of separate identity as well as the continuation of the older responses of adaptation.

In the Soviet Union, the visible Muslim militancy of the early twentieth century was not revived. However, communist efforts to eliminate the influence of traditional religions had failed, and as the structures of the Soviet Union collapsed in the early 1990s, the central Asian republics were in good positions to reaffirm their national identities. In this context, debates heard elsewhere about the relationships between Islam and special ethnic identities and the nature of an Islamic state began to have importance among Muslims in the former Soviet Union.

The various Muslim groups within the Soviet Union had experienced significant societal changes during the period of communist rule. There had been a social transformation involving literacy rates, the status of women, and the influence of Russian culture. At the same time, the federal character of the Soviet Union had allowed for the development of distinctive cultural identities. The Soviet Union had supported an official Muslim establishment with four (after 1990, five) directorates with Muftis and a restricted education system. Parallel to this establishment, a structure of popular Islamic organizations existed, usually representing continuations of Sufi orders, like the Naqshbandiyyah, or maintenance of special shrines. These popular groups were criticized as appealing to the superstitions of rural peoples but this "parallel" Islam represented a powerful force for Islamic continuity within the Soviet Union.

During the 1970s, there was evidence of Islamic revival both among urban intellectuals and in rural areas. This involved more widespread and visible participation in public Islamic acts like prayer and fasting during Ramadan as well as the production of writings reflecting greater emphasis of traditional themes.[103] In the late 1980s, during the era of Gorbachev, there were major demonstrations and riots relating to reassertions of local national sentiments. By the early 1990s, these efforts involved activist participation within the emerging new political systems as well as opposition. This greater sense of activist involvement was visible in the struggles of the leaders in the official Muslim establishment in 1989 and in 1991 because of popular protests and criticisms of their behavior. A more populist Mufti emerged in Kazakhstan at this same time was able to involve the establishment more directly in popular Muslim community affairs.

Leaders of the central Asian republics played important roles in the restructuring of the Soviet Union in late 1991. In the rapidly changing conditions, Muslim communities were faced with important choices regarding the nature and future of their republics. In making those decisions, Islam remains a very important element in national identity but there is a broad range of responses. In Kazakhstan, where the Kazakhs comprise less than half of the population and there is a large Russian minority, the draft constitution of 1992 explicitly prohibited the establishment of a state ideology based on a religious organization, and the major Islamic opposition party, Alash, had in the early 1990s, "limited potential appeal."[104] However, in Tajikistan, Islamic leaders were important in the civil war which erupted in 1992 after independence. The official head of the Muslim establishment, Kazi Akbar Turajonzoda, supported the Islamic Renaissance Party which acted in coalition of three parties opposed to Rahmon Nabiev, the former Communist Party leader who had been elected president of the republic late in 1991. Turajonzoda emphasized that the opposition was working to establish a secular democratic government and that while, in the distant future, Tajikistan would become an Islamic state, "introducing any ideology by force is a mistake."[105] The opposition coalition forced the former Communist Party group out of power briefly in 1992, but by the end of that year they returned through a bloody coup, while regional groups engaged in open warfare throughout most of the year. Early in 1993 Turajonzoda and other leaders were formally charged with treason. Similar but not so dramatic tensions developed in the other newly independent Central Asian republics. In each of them, explicitly Islamic political organizations gained some visibility and significance but in none did an overtly Islamic government emerge in the first year of independence.

It was clear that Islam had successfully survived the seventy-five years of Soviet Communist rule as well as the earlier imperial Russian rule. Explicitly Islamic political groups like the Islamic Renaissance Party of Tajikistan developed throughout the region, and they did not represent simply the extremist fringe. In an interesting reversal of position, it was the old Communist groups that were the "conservative" forces, while the Islamic elements worked with the secular democratic and more radical groups. The most important transformation was, of course, that Muslims were no longer a minority community in a much larger unit, and the politics of a majority community are different from that of a minority.

In China, the 1970s had been a time of important transitions for Muslims. After the upsets of the Cultural Revolution, which had actively attacked all traditional religious institutions, the Chinese communist government began a policy of allowing greater religious freedom and cultural autonomy among the various minority peoples. This resulted in the increasingly open practice of Islam, with thousands of new mosques being built in Muslim areas, especially Xinjiang, and the establishment of new Islamic educational institutions in major cities.[106] This revival tended to take the form of greater open expression of religion rather than of activist opposition to the government or communism. While there may have been some fundamentalist activist groups, the primary mode was adaptationist, taking advantage of new opportunities as the Chinese communist system developed.

The restrictions on political freedoms following the crushing of the democratic movement in Peking in the spring of 1989 set limits on Muslim political actions, but nonpolitical expressions of cultural autonomy continued. There were reports of activist opposition as well. Possibly encouraged by nationalist affirmations in the Soviet republics, Islamic separatists formed an organization called the Islamic Party of East Turkestan in Xinjiang Autonomous Region and soon clashed with government forces in April 1990.[107] In the early 1990s, it was clear that Muslim communities had successfully survived the challenges of Maoist China and were emerging as distinctive elements in Chinese society with possibly important international implications.

Muslims in India face the longstanding options of a cautious conservatism or active support for official secularism in India. The conservative mode preserves communal identity but at the cost of relative stagnation and isolation within Indian society, while the secularist approach depends for its success on a corresponding secularism on the part of the Hindu majority. By the early 1990s, it seemed clear that an upsurge of Hindu fundamentalism as well as the growth of activist Islamic cultural assertions were significant developments which undermined peaceful communal relations and secular politics for Muslims in India. Major conflicts in the 1970s and 1980s reflected the tensions which afflicted Indian Muslims.

The inherent problems of the conservative approach came to the fore in 1985 when the Supreme Court ruled that a divorced Muslim woman, Shah Bano, should receive maintenance. This decision raised the issue of a uniform civil code, which many Muslims opposed as interference in their religious life. The Shah Bano case resulted in major riots and demonstrations and, ultimately, the passage of special legislation recognizing Muslim regulations regarding civil status of women.[108] This response emphasized Muslim communal isolation and the conservative nature of the continuing Muslim identity in India.

The Shah Bano affair was only one reflection of growing intercommunal tensions. During the 1980s, more than 4000 people were killed in communal riots, which was almost four times the number for the 1970s.[109] In the early 1990s, the focus of intercommunal conflict was the dispute over a shrine in Ayodhya, where a four century old mosque was identified by Hindu fundamentalists as being a specially holy Hindu site. Communal fighting broke out in 1990 and the government of V. P. Singh fell over the issue. In December 1992, Hindu fundamentalist mobs destroyed the Ayodhya mosque and major rioting broke out throughout the country. The conflict provided the context for growing demands from Hindu extremists that the official policy of secularism be abandoned. In the face of these challenges there was a growing demand among Muslims for strengthened communal defenses and serious doubts were raised about the viability of the long-standing Indian Muslim position of cooperation with secular Indian governments. The early 1990s witnessed the most serious threat to the Indian Muslim minority since the days of the partition after World War II.

An additional area of tensions for Indian Muslims was Kashmir, the only Muslim-majority province in India. Kashmiri Muslim opposition to the inclusion of Kashmir into the Republic of India was an old issue which received new life at the end of the 1980s when Kashmiri militants began open opposition to Indian control. Muhammad Abdallah, the old "Lion of Kashmir" who had advocated Kashmiri autonomy and had worked with Indian leaders as well as being arrested by them, died in 1982. His son, Faruq Abdallah served as head of the government of Kashmir during much of the 1980s and at times in the early 1990s, but Kashmiri activists did not accept his compromising leadership. In 1989 the daughter of a Muslim member of the Indian cabinet was kidnapped by members of the Jammu and Kashmir Liberation Front (JKLF). She was freed after five JKLF militants were released from detention, but a period of active conflict between government forces and Kashmiri nationalists followed.

The JKLF and its leader Amanullah Khan were relatively secularist, but a more actively Islamic tone developed in Kashmiri opposition to Indian control. There were some differences over whether the goal was an independent Kashmir, as advocated by the JKLF, or a more Islamic state tied closely to Pakistan but growing numbers accepted the need from secession from India. The opposition and repression increased with the murder in May 1990 of a leading Muslim figure, Maulvi Mohammed Farooq, who had established the Awami Action Committee, a pro-Pakistan self-defense group. By mid-1990 a well-informed journalist, Barbara Crossette, could state that "small groups of armed Muslim separatists, who 15 months ago were described as a radical fringe attractive mostly to unemployed youth, now apparently have the support of an alienated, influential middle class."[110] Kashmiri Muslim separatism had become the main political force. Its programs were not defined in fundamentalist terms, but the Islamic revival, as elsewhere, had moved from the periphery to the mainstream in Kashmir.

In most of India, political separatism was neither desired nor practical, but the issues of cultural separatism and its corresponding vulnerability to intercommunal violence were the most important challenges facing Muslim

Indians. Most Muslim Indians remained basically conservative in their style, although their sensitivities have been raised by the broader forces of global Islamic resurgence. However, voices of a more activist affirmation of Islam were increasingly heard in the early 1990s.

Great transformations took place in the three largest Muslim minority communities during the 1970s and 1980s. In the Soviet Union, Muslims became a majority in a series of smaller independent states rather than a minority in a large one. In India and China there were increasing opportunities to affirm the Islamic message publically and occasional militant activism, as in Kashmir and Xinjiang, but the general mood was one of continuing the adaptationist style of minority life.

Minorities and Islamic Affirmation

Muslim minority communities throughout the world were more actively involved in their public affirmation of Islam. These actions took many forms, ranging from open revolt against central governments to an intensification of cultural and religious activities. One common feature in all of these efforts was an affirmation of the continuing validity of the Islamic message in the context of the contemporary world. It is in these minority communities that it is especially clear that by the 1990s, the Islamic resurgence of the late twentieth century was not simply the product of militant fundamentalism. As the resurgence moved from the radical periphery to the mainstreams of minority Muslim communal life, adaptationist forms of active Islamic assertion are also visible. Often Muslim actions were in the context of the major global transformations that characterized the late 1980s.

The end of the world of communist states not only transformed the status of Muslims in the former Soviet Union, it also created new situations for Muslims in eastern Europe. In Bulgaria, the communist regime had attempted a forced cultural assimilation of Bulgaria's ethnic Turk and Muslim groups (comprising 7–8 percent of the population). Restoration of rights of Muslims and other minorities was an important part of the democratic reformers' program. A largely Muslim party, the Movement for Rights and Freedoms, contested the elections of 1990 and 1991, gaining the position of the third largest party in the country. Its program concentrated on cultural rights in a secular society rather than on creating an Islamic society or state.

The collapse of the communist regime in Albania also opened the way for new Islamic activity. Before the establishment of communist rule, about 70 percent of the population was Muslim. However, all forms of religion were actively suppressed under communist rule and antireligion laws only began to be relaxed after the death in 1985 of Enver Hoxha, the long-ruling Stalinist dictator. In 1990 the right to practice religion was restored, and the first legal Muslim public prayers were said in the main mosque of the capital in 1991. By 1992 older Muslim leaders who had been released from prison began the task of rebuilding communal organizations. Again, the concern was not the implementation of a fundamentalist program; it was the reaffirmation of the basic Muslim communal identity. This was also apparent among the Albanians in the Kosovo district of the former Yugoslavia. They created their own parliament, in defiance of the governing Serbs, through secret elections in 1992 and were developing autonomous cultural and educational institutions to preserve their communal identity.

Basic issues of communal survival faced other Muslims in Yugoslavia where they made up almost 20 percent of the population. In 1971 citizens were able to identify themselves as Muslims, and the Yugoslav government gave increasing recognition to the Muslim nationality. Although it was possible for some critics to accuse, in 1979, some Muslim leaders of spreading "Khomeini ideology," the basic efforts of Yugoslav Muslims were to create and maintain communal cultural structures and traditions. As the old Yugoslav federation disintegrated in 1990–1992, Muslims found themselves struggling to preserve even these basics. When former federal republics declared their independence, they came under attack from the Serbian-dominated federal government and from local Serbian groups. Bosnia and Herzegovina, where 40 percent of the population is Muslim, became independent in 1992 but immediately faced major conflict and the seige of Sarajevo, the Bosnia capital, gained international attention. Serbian campaigns of "ethnic purification" in resulted in large numbers of Muslim refugees.

The Muslim leaders of independent Bosnia advocated a multiethnic state and were secularist in orientation. However, indecisive European and American responses to Bosnian losses led some Muslim communal leaders to say, "We feel betrayed by Europe," and raise the question of whether or not Western leaders were hoping for the elimination of a Muslim community in Europe.[111] The plight of the Bosnians attracted attention throughout the Muslim world, and aid came, sometimes in the form of small groups of fighters. Under the pressures of vicious conflict, more militant Muslim responses were emerging by the end of 1992.

Muslim minority militance made some major gains in the Philippines. Strong Muslim communities in the southern islands had long opposed attempts to control the region by outsiders—having opposed the Spanish, the Americans, the Japanese, and finally the independent central government. Tensions increased by the late 1960s as a result of efforts by central governments to control the region and increasing immigration of non-Muslims into Muslim areas. President Ferdinand Marcos declared martial law in 1972 as open Muslim revolt broke out. The major group leading the revolt was the Moro National Liberation Front (MNLF) headed by Nur Misuari. The demand was for recognition of Muslim autonomy, and some advocated Muslim independence. After bloody fighting an agreement which promised autonomy was signed in 1976 through the mediation of the Organization of the Islamic Conference. Divisions among the Muslims allowed Marcos to avoid implementation of the agreement, and sporadic fighting continued for the next decade.

With the overthrow of Marcos in 1986, a new effort was made to resolve the conflict by President Corazon Aquino. This led to a major referendum in the Muslim areas in 1989, when four regions—two provinces on the island of Mindanao, the Tawi Tawi island group, and Sulu—approved inclusion in a newly created Autonomous Region of Mindanao. In 1990 elections Zacaria Candao was elected to head the government of the autonomous region. The MNFL opposed the new arrangement as insufficient, and fighting between local factions in the region created instability. However, the Philippine president elected in 1992, Fidel Ramos, created a National Unification Commission which seemed in early 1993 to be making progress in discussions with the MNLF. Muslim efforts had succeeded in securing significant recognition in the Philippines.

In other areas, efforts by Muslim minorities to gain some recognition were not as successful. In Thailand, separatist sentiments based especially in the Patani region of southern Thailand resulted in a series of revolts in the years after World War II. In the 1970s there were some demonstrations, and in the late 1980s an activist from the very small Shi'i community in the area who had studied in Iran articulated Muslim demands. However, government forces had little difficulty in suppressing opposition although they could not eliminate Muslim aspirations for greater recognition. Muslims seeking autonomy or recognition in Myanmar (Burma) had even less success, although there was some organized Islamic activity for recognition in the 1980s. Perhaps the most surprising effort of a Muslim minority community came in 1990 in Trinidad. For years the small Muslim community, which is divided between South Asians and African-Americans, had engaged in missionary and cultural activities. However, in 1990, Yasin Abu Bakr, the head of a local fundamentalist group called the Jamaat al-Muslimeen, organized a significant coup attempt to gain control of the government. Even though the attempt failed, the movement was able to bring together younger radical elements from both communities of Muslims and was emerging as a significant force by 1992.[112] Throughout the Caribbean, Muslim minority activism grew in intensity during the 1970s and 1980s, although not as dramatically as in Trinidad.[113]

Most Muslims in small minority communities worked to defend their human rights and maintain some special communal identity but were not militantly active in seeking structural autonomy. By the 1980s, however, virtually no minority community was primarily characterized by a conservative acceptance of existing conditions and a hidden identity behind an assimilationist mode. Differences arose primarily over issues of adaptation to special conditions in their societies and choosing between adaptationist and fundamentalist approaches to maintaining Islamic identity and public affirmation of the faith and message. The move away from a conservative approach to a more assertive mood is well illustrated in the history of the Muslims in the Republic of South Africa in the 1970s and 1980s.[114] The established leadership of the South African Muslims was basically conservative for many years, cooperating with the government even as apartheid became more actively imposed. However, in the 1970s more activist groups like the Muslim Youth Movement (MYM) emerged. These combined a growing awareness of and participation in the international Islamic resurgence with a growing involvement in the antiapartheid struggle. By the early 1990s, a full spectrum of active movements had emerged, ranging from Qiblah, which advocated an Iranian-style Islamic revolution in South Africa, to the Call of Islam, "the most prominent of the organisations in the Muslim community who look to the South African experience rather than to external Islamic tendencies for their inspiration."[115] The majority of active Muslims in South Africa maintain an adaptationist style, believing that affirmation of their Islamic identity involves the attempt to "ensure that *ʿAllahu Akbar* becomes an integral part of that non-racial, non-sexist and democratic South Africa which will arise out of the ashes of apartheid."[116] This is a clear example of the emerging activist adaptationism among Muslim minorities (and others) which showed that, by the 1990s, it was not only the militant fundamentalists who represented the resurgence of Islam.

In Western Europe and North America, Muslim immigrant, refugee, and native communities were increasingly active in the visible affirmation of their Islamic faith during the 1970s and 1980s. In the former West Germany, for example, officials noted that by 1980 Islamic centers were organized throughout the country, especially among immigrant Turkish workers, and that much of this activism was of a fundamentalist style.[117] In France a dispute during 1989 over permitting Muslim female students to wear Islamically identifiable "scarves" reflected important issues of Muslim life in the West. A government school principal expelled three students because they insisted upon wearing Muslim scarves in school, in violation, he said, of the official policy of separation of religion and state. The result was a major public debate in which French popular resentment against "non-

French" immigrants came into conflict with assertions of immigrant communal identities within France. "By making demands to participate in political life in France, while maintaining distinct cultural identities, immigrants, even if they are citizens, challenge the cultural basis of French politics."[118] While this was an issue involving a broader affirmation of communal identity, the controversy gave added strength to Muslim fundamentalists who opposed cultural assimilation. Similar developments took place in the 1980s and 1990s in other countries with strong Muslim communities. Pressures grew among Muslim groups in Great Britain and the United States for developing separate communal schools and gaining recognition for them. Active centers like the Islamic Center of Southern California in Los Angeles developed in many major urban centers and national associations and societies like the American Muslim Council indicated the growing influence of Muslims in the United States and other Western societies. In the United States, distinctively African-American Muslim groups grew dramatically in size and significance, and this growth was reflected in many ways, including a renewed interest during the 1990s in the life and thought of Malcolm X. The appeal of the teachings of the Egyptian Islamist, Shaykh Umar Abd al-Rahman, who lived in exile in New York and New Jersey after 1990,[119] show the potential popularity of a more militant fundamentalist approach in Western societies. However, the alarm caused by the bombing of the International Trade Center in New York obscured the fact that most Muslim communities are strongly adaptationist in style. It seemed clear that virtually no significant Muslim individual or group in Western societies maintained a conservative position of preserving the old style quiescent and passive minority mode of living.

Summary

Among the many Muslim minority communities there was an increasing sense of communal identity in the 1970s and 1980s. Sometimes this was in opposition to trends in their larger communities and sometimes aided by policies relaxing previous restrictions. It was a tendency which received support in many ways from resurgent Islamic sentiments elsewhere.

By the early 1990s, the basic options of separatist militance or assimilationism remained, but a new style of assimilationism developed that involved a willingness to accept existence in a religiously pluralistic society without forgoing public affirmation of Islam. In the global context of an increasing recognition of the validity of expressions of cultural pluralism, it became possible for Muslims to operate in a new style of minority life. This was essentially integration without full assimilation.

Palestinians and Lebanese: Special Cases

The Palestinians continued to represent a special set of experiences as Muslim minority communities in the final quarter of the twentieth century. Following the Israeli victory in the 1967 war, there was no place where Palestinians represented a governing majority, and the relationship between their national identity and Islam was complex. Their community identity was not strictly Muslim because of the significant minority of Christian Palestinians, but the Palestinian cause increasingly became a concern of Muslim groups around the world following the 1967 War. In general, Palestinian experiences reflected the broader trends of the era, characterized by increasingly strong affirmations of Islam, often in a more fundamentalist style. In the 1970s and 1980s, Palestinian communities were in three different types of contexts which effected the evolution of their experiences as "Muslim minorities."

One important context was as citizens of the state of Israel. Sunni Muslims of Palestinian origin comprise almost 15 percent of the population of pre-1967 Israel, and they had accepted their status as a minority, showing little sign of Islamic or Palestinian activism for the first two decades of Israel's history. However, one of the consequences of the 1967 War was to bring Israeli Arabs into more direct contact with other Muslims and open the way for them to undertake, in West Bank Islamic learning centers, advanced Islamic studies not available in Israel. Then, after the Egyptian-Israeli Peace Treaty of 1979, it became possible for Israeli Muslims to study in the great Muslim schools in Egypt. Initially, the interest in Islam was primarily cultural, but this interest began in the late 1970s to assume, among a very small minority, a more activist political tone. A group called Usrat al-Jihad ("The Family of Holy War") was formed by Shaykh Abdallah Nimr Darwish, a young scholar from a village near Tel Aviv. They called for a holy war against Israel and for the establishment of an Islamic state. Darwish was soon imprisoned and, on his release in 1984, he helped to form the Islamic Movement to work for peaceful change in Muslim life in Israel, working "only through education, culture and social reform to give every Moslem here back his identity."[120]

In Israel, full assimilation is not an option for the Muslim minority unless they convert to Judaism. As the longstanding political organizations of Arab Israelis like the communist party and other groups appeared increasingly ineffective, especially in lessening a sense among Israeli Arabs that they were subject to government neglect and seeming discrimination, dynamic Islamic organizations had growing appeal. By the late 1980s, the Islamic Movement and other groups had successfully organized effective community welfare and cultural programs in many areas and in the country wide municipal elections of 1989, Islamic movement candidates won in five Israeli Arab municipalities, the largest of which is Umm al-Fahm, near Tel Aviv. Darwish and other leaders emphasize that "they reject violence and are willing to accept Israel for the sake of peaceful coexistence, . . . [noting that] an Islamic state . . . can be proclaimed only in a land where Muslims are the majority, so that it is not appropriate in Israel."[121] It was clear by the early 1990s that the Muslim minority response within Israel reflected the power of the broader Islamic resurgence but was similar to those other minorities who accepted integration while affirming a authentic Islamic identity rather than assimilation.

A second context of Palestinian experiences in the 1970s and 1980s is the broader global one of refugee and immigrant groups and the major Palestinian organizations which operate on an international scale. At the beginning of the 1970s, expressions of Palestinian aspirations and identity were dominated by radical secularist and nationalist themes, reflecting the prominence of leaders like Yasir Arafat and George Habbash. However, by the 1980s, there was a more clearly Islamic element in those expressions. Iranian Islamic revolutionary leaders gave strong support to Palestinian groups and developed strong ties to Yasir Arafat and other Palestine Liberation Organization (PLO) leaders. Palestinian Muslims around the world were also affected by the dynamics of the Islamic resurgence and were often an important part of it. One of the leading intellectuals in the global network of Islamic scholar-activists, for example, was Ismail R. al-Faruqi (1921–1986), a Palestinian who had been forced to leave in 1948 and who became one of the leading theorists of the Islamic revival.[122] However, although Palestinians as individuals were active in the resurgence, the major organizations which were specifically identified as Palestinian, like the PLO and its constituent groups, remained largely within the framework of their initial perspectives, either nationalist or leftist in orientation rather than advocating explicit programs of Islamization. By the early 1990s the problems of balancing traditional perspectives with the emerging strength of Islamic themes became apparent, as Arafat expressed his Palestinian nationalism in increasingly religious terms while operating within the context of active negotiations with Israel for the creation of an autonomous or independent *national* Palestinian state.

Explicitly Islamic Palestinian movements emerged in the third context of Palestinian experience, that of living under Israeli occupation the the West Bank and Gaza areas. In these areas there had long been small groups of the Muslim Brotherhood with ties to Egypt and Jordan. After the Israeli occupation in 1967, the nationalist and leftist Palestinian movements received massive popular support, and it was not until the late 1970s that more explicitly

Islamic groups began to have some significance. At that time there was a growing trend of Islamic revivalism reflected increased popular participation in religious activities.[123] This resulted in increased support for Islamic groups and a growing tension, and sometimes conflict, between these groups and the Palestinian nationalist organizations. The Muslim Brotherhood benefited initially but was supplanted in the early 1980s by more violent and activist fundamentalist groups which sometimes received support from Israeli occupation forces as a way of weakening the PLO and the dominant more secular Palestinian nationalist leadership.[124] By the late 1980s the new Islamic militant resistance was usually identified with an group called Islamic Jihad, but all of the older forms of opposition to Israeli control were overtaken by local and international developments. In December 1987 a local form of popular resistance, which came to be called the "Intifada," broke out which was apparently initiated by new, younger elements and not controllable by leadership of the existing organizations.

At this same time a new militant fundamentalist group, the Movement of Islamic Resistance (*Harakah al-Muqawamah al-Islamiyyah*), known by its acronym, Hamas, was formed as a "militant outgrowth of an Islamic community association that had already gained wide popularity by providing educational and welfare services to Palestinians."[125] It soon became the major rival of the PLO and Arafat throughout the occupied territories. Hamas-supported candidates won elections in a number of different organizations, ranging from student and labor unions to chambers of commerce and syndicates of physicians and engineers. In Gaza, Hamas's stronghold, open fighting between Hamas and PLO supporters took place and could not be controlled by the organizations' leaders.

In 1989, Shaykh Ahmad Yassin of Gaza, a major leader in Hamas, was imprisoned for ordering the killing of Arabs who collaborated with Israel but this did not stop the growing influence of Hamas. In December 1992 a group of Hamas extremists kidnapped an Israeli soldier, demanding the release of Shaykh Yassin in return for the soldier's release. When the soldier's body was found, the Israeli government captured and attempted to expel more than four hundred people identified in some way with Hamas or Islamic Jihad, but Lebanon did not accept the deportees, leaving them in a no-man's land encampment at the heart of an international incident. The incident gave Hamas a high level of international visibility and backing, even among supporters of Arafat and the PLO. The long term implications of this were not clear in early 1993, but it was clear that militant fundamentalism had become a significant force among Palestinians, weakening the more moderate adaptationists who were in the process of negotiating with Israel.

In terms of minority options, among the Palestinians, those within Israel were effectively creating a situation of integration without assimilation, while the refugee groups and communities under occupation were working for varieties of separatism, either negotiated autonomy or the militant separatism of the fundamentalists.

Lebanon's traditional political system had been based on a carefully balanced structure of integration without assimilation for the major religious communities in the country, the Maronite Christians and the Sunni and Shi'i Muslims. However, the system collapsed in the mid-1970s under pressure from changes in the relative sizes of the communities, the emergence of new centers of social and political power, and internal and international problems created by growing militance among Palestinians in Lebanon and increasing military pressures from Israel. Many different communal groups created militias, and a major civil war broke out. In 1976, Syria intervened and the Syrian army became the largest single military force in the country. Israel invaded the country in 1978 and in 1982 and established an Israel-controlled "security zone" in the southern part of the country. The country's experience went beyond simply civil war to near total social and political chaos.

By the early 1990s, however, substantial stability had been restored, and a new political system began to operate, although still in the context of significant foreign military occupation by Syria and Israel. In 1988 conflict over election of a president brought successful outside mediation, and in 1989 in al-Taif, Saudi Arabia, the surviving members of the last elected parliament created the basis for establishing a new, modified political system. The system created by the 1989 agreement continued to be based on religious communities but created a different balance of power. Seats in the new parliament were divided equally between Christian and Muslim (instead of the old 6:5 ratio in favor of the Christians) and the parliament had greater power and responsibility. This reduced the power of the President, who is traditionally a Maronite Christian, and gave significant additional power to the Speaker of parliament, who is customarily a Shi'i Muslim. The prime minister, usually a Sunni Muslim, emerged as "the single most important position."[126] On the strength of the agreement, the central government with Syrian military assistance was able to establish control over much of the country and accomplish the disarming of most of the communal militias. Following much negotiation, parliamentary elections were held in 1992 and, despite a boycott by significant numbers of hard-line Maronites and difficulties with holding elections in the Israeli-controlled zone in the south, a new government was created. By 1993, under the leadership of an activist and highly respected prime minister, Rafiq al-Hariri, it was clear that while Lebanon still faced very grave problems, the long era of the civil war was over.

The new political situation reflected important changes within the major Lebanese Muslim communities. Before the civil war, all of the communities had been dominated by conservative notables, usually from a small group of major families. By the early 1990s, the communities were led, in political and social terms, by new styles of leaders. The experiences of the Shiʿi and Sunni communities in the 1970s and 1980s reflect the broader trends within the Islamic world. Conservative options were weakened in the face of fundamentalist responses to crises, and gradually the mainstream of thought and politics became significantly Islamized. The Islamic resurgence became normalized in the emergence of Islamically oriented adaptationist leaders and groups.

The transformation of Shiʿi leadership and organization is the most dramatic. In the early 1970s, the Shiʿi communities were dominated by a few old, conservative families. Gradually, Amal, the organization created by Imam Musa al-Sadr (disappeared in 1978) emerged, in the context of the civil war, as the largest and most effective Shiʿi organization in the country. In the reorganization following the disappearance of al-Sadr during a visit to Libya, Nabih Berri became the leader of Amal in 1980. Amal was basically reformist rather than revolutionary and emphasized Lebanese national themes rather than Pan-Islamic programs. It did not advocate the establishment of an Islamic republic in Lebanon, and under Berri's leadership, Amal "developed as a Shii nationalist organization, pursuing the redressing of Shii grievances although accepting the framework of a united, Arab multiconfessional Lebanon."[127] It was also an active military force in the civil war, defending Shiʿi areas.

During the Israeli invasion of Lebanon in 1982, Shiʿi radicals became impatient with Amal's adaptationism and more radical fundamentalist groups emerged. Islamic Amal was created by Husayn al-Musawi, who rejected Berri's moderation and advocated the goal of an Islamic republic with the support of the Iranian Islamic Republic. Islamic Amal's center was in Baʿalbek, in northern Lebanon, where it received the support of a contingent of the Iranian Revolutionary Guard which had come to Lebanon. Islamic Amal's ideology reflected the influence of the Ayatollah Khomeini, but the group was a part of an emerging radical fundamentalist tendancy in Lebanon known as Hizballah ("Party of God").

The intellectual inspiration of the Hizballah came from Shaykh Muhammad Husayn Fadlallah, a prominent Iraqi-born teacher whose writings and sermons were well-known throughout Shiʿi communities in the Arab world. In the mid-1970s he wrote *Islam and the Logic of Force* (*al-Islam wa al-Matiq al-Quwwa*), which received considerable international attention in the 1980s. He provided an incentive and a justification for active and militant, if necessary, involvement in society. Like Khomeini, he engaged in "a power-ful reinterpretation of Shii belief and history, emphasizing political activism and social reform. Muslims were not passively to await the return of the Twelfth Imam but instead to revolt against injustice."[128] Although Fadlallah had no direct organizational role in the emerging Hizballah organization, he was acknowledged as an important inspiration for the emerging Shi'i funda-mentalist movement in the 1980s.

Throughout the 1980s there were frequent clashes, both political and mili-tary, between Amal and Hizballah as the struggle for control of the Shi'i community developed. In this struggle, the old religious establishment and notable families had little role except to ally themselves from time to time with one group or the other. However, by the 1992 parliamentary elections, both Amal and Hizballah accepted the need for the political settlement and frequently presented joint slates. The result was that the Shi'i activist organi-zations emerged as the largest single group in the new parliament and Berri became the Speaker of parliament, and thus politically the most powerful Shi'i leader in the country. Representatives of some of the old notable fami-lies were elected, but "unlike the past, representatives of the traditional fam-ilies needed Mr. Birri [Berri] to secure their re-election."[129] It was suggested that the two organizations had received significant support in the Shi'i south through "having provided basic services to one of the poorest and most neglected parts of the country."[130] Amal and Hizballah had become the main-stream of Shi'i politics not marginal actors. The normalization of the Islamic resurgence was clearly visible in the Shi'i politics of Lebanon by the early 1990s.

A similar but less dramatic process seems to have taken place among the Sunnis. Like the Shi'is, Sunni politics before the civil war had been domi-nated by a small elite of powerful notable families. No major Sunni commu-nal organization similar to Amal emerged in the 1970s but a number of smaller radical fundamentalist groups developed in the large cities in the context of the civil war. These challenged the political and religious estab-lishment of the old families and the Sunni Mufti. Sunni fundamentalist mili-tias did not fare well in Beirut but were better organized in the cities of Tripoli and Sidon and emerged out of the trials of the Israeli invasion in 1982 as major forces. By the time of the elections of 1992 it was clear that Sunni fundamentalists represented a very significant force within the Sunni community.

Al-Jama'ah al-Islamiyyah ("The Islamic Society") emerged as a major group in the Sunni community. It had been organized in the early 1960s in Tripoli, which has remained its major center, but expanded into other cities. In the instability following the Israeli invasion of 1982, a number of new militant Sunni groups emerged, including the Movement of Islamic Tawhid led by Shaykh Saʿid Shaʿban, which advocated support for Islamic revolution.[131] However, the more broadly based al-Jamaʿah al-Islamiyyah, under the leadership of Shaykh Fathi Yakan emerged as the major Sunni fundamentalist force in the electoral politics of the early 1990s. In 1992 the electoral monopoly of the old families was broken with the election of Yakan in Tripoli. Similarly in Beirut, the fundamentalist Association of Islamic Charitable Works succeeded in getting one of its candidates elected. Again, as well the Shiʿi organizations, the successes of the Sunni fundamentalists were attributed not to their revolutionary ideology but to their work in "building grass-roots support through educational, health, and other welfare programs . . . [and the Sunni fundamentalists] deny any sweeping political goals and concentrate instead on neighborhood-based social, economic, and religious reform."[132]

The fundamentalists did not dominate the Sunni political scene. While the old families suffered major losses in power, they still maintained significant influence. While the new prime minister, al-Hariri, was not from one of the old elite families, neither was he a fundamentalist. He had, in fact, established relatively close ties with Berri and Bahiyyah al-Hariri, who was elected to a Sunni seat from Sidon, ran on the electoral list organized by Birri and Amal. The old militant Sunni fundamentalists had, however, been drawn into the political mainstream and show the power of the trend of normalization in the Islamic resurgence.

In Lebanon, the conservative mode, as reflected in the previous power of elite families, was severely weakened by the early 1990s. Secularist adaptation was also less powerful as the old groups from the left were weakened in the civil war. While militant fundamentalism was an active force in the early 1980s, the dynamics of the broader popular Islamic resurgence and the developments of specific local conditions made an Islamically committed adaptationism the most appealing option in the final years of the century. For all of its distinctive turmoil, Lebanon reflects the broader trends of the contemporary Islamic experience.

Conclusion

Throughout the Islamic world, the final quarter of the twentieth century was a period of dramatic developments. Clearly, Islam was not a dying force, and its vitality was shown in a variety of ways that ranged from major revolutions to the reorientation of dominant ideologies. This vitality was visible in all three of the major dimensions of the contemporary experience.

On the local level, rapidly changing conditions provided the context for a reaffirmation of Islam in many ways. The forms of this reaffirmation varied with the diversity of local conditions, and what came to be called the Islamic resurgence was not a single, monolithic experience. However, in country after country, Islam came to be an increasingly important factor in the evolution of local conditions.

In the broader dimension of modern global history, the failure of many modern approaches to the problems of contemporary society led to many postmodern efforts which included a resurgence of allegiance to nonmodern worldviews. The standard modern ideology of secularism, rationalist science, and mass production had proved inadequate for the needs of human societies in the last decades of the twentieth century. As late as the 1960s, it had been possible to predict that traditional religions would gradually disappear as effective forces in the modern world and to claim that the major task for adherents of such religions was to come to terms with modernity. However, by the 1970s, it was becoming clear that even the modern world view was having to change and come to terms with the new conditions which were increasingly best described as postmodern. In this context, a postmodern revivalist Islam, especially in fundamentalist forms, could emerge as a competing world view—and did so with much success in the 1970s and 1980s.

In the dimension of Islamic continuity and change, the 1970s and 1980s was a time when the dominant modernist adaptationism was significantly challenged by a more fundamentalist style of Islam. One of the significant developments of the 1970s was the emergence of a new radical style of fundamentalism, which began at first on the revolutionary fringes of society. However, by the early 1990s, this revolutionary fundamentalist impulse had combined with a broader popular reaffirmation of Islamic piety and practice. The result was that the formerly modernist mainstream had become Islamized in many ways and, similarly, the mood of the radical fundamentalist fringe had become normalized. In this process a new adaptationism gradually began to emerge which departed from the old modernist and secularist perspectives and assumed a more Islamically committed viewpoint. The foundations of the Islamic experience that had been laid in the eighteenth century became more clearly visible in the dynamic historical developments of the final quarter of the twentieth century. At the beginning of its fifteenth century, the Islamic world was in the midst of major transformations in all dimensions of its experience. In those transformations, elements of both continuity and dramatic change are clearly evident.

7

Perspectives and Prospects

The Islamic Resurgence and Contemporary History

The Iranian Revolution and the murder of Anwar Sadat by members of Jihad provided the immediate framework for interpretations of the Islamic resurgence in the early 1980s. Efforts to interpret the resurgence then concentrated upon explaining the rise of militant Islamic fundamentalism. In the 1990s, this is still in many ways the major focus of attention, emphasized by the attention given to the bombing of the International Trade Center in New York by people identified as Muslim fundamentalists. However, more than a decade of experience creates a much broader perspective for viewing the resurgence. In many ways, what was a peripheral concern in the 1960s became during the 1970s an awareness of marginalized but significant revolutionary forces. However, in the decade and a half after the Iranian revolution, the revival of activist Islam moved from the periphery of society and politics to the mainstream and, in the process, transformed the scope both of the nature of the movements involved and of the nature of analysis necessary for understanding those movements.

These developments reflected some broader, global trends which provide the foundations for much that is found in the experiences of the adherent to resurgent faith as well as of those engaged in studying those experiences. Perhaps the most important trend was the resurgence itself in the context of world societies in the modern era. Much of the understanding of the conditions of modernity involved an assumption that modernization involved secularization. Some challenges to this assumption were already being raised in the late 1970s by scholars dealing with religion in the West, especially in the United States. Two scholars, writing in 1979, looked back at a symposium on the state of the sociological study of religion that had been published in a major journal in 1970.[1] They observed that "much of the literature assessed there pointed to the declining importance of religion itself in secular society. . . . In the context of religion's presumed demise, sects and cults held

375

little interest for sociologists of religion. . . . More important than sects and cults were questions of religion's future without its traditional functions."[2] However, by the end of the 1970s, they were able to speak of the "unexpected return of religion to social prominence,"[3] even without mentioning the Iranian Revolution which was contemporary with the discussion.

Two important characteristics of this "return of religion" are the globalization of religious resurgence and its normalization or emergence in the mainstreams of societies. While the diverse experiences of Muslims in the late twentieth century cannot simply be equated with religious developments in other traditions, it is also a mistake to view the Islamic developments as isolated phenomena.

Many people recognized common features of religious resurgence in many different global contexts as they emerged by the 1990s. Often this was simply a recognition of a shared willingness to engage in violent actions to support the particular cause. Even in these cases, however, there was a clearly recognizable difference between the old violent radical revolutionaries of the left and the emerging religious radicals. The new movements were specifically *religious* in character as they affirmed the main traditions of their particular cultures. Many scholars went beyond this similarity of means to discussing broader similarities among the fundmentalist movements that provide the most visible manifestations of the resurgence. The volumes of the Fundamentalism Project sponsored by the American Academy of Arts and Sciences show that "what were once viewed as unrelated religious movements . . . are increasingly recognized as sharing a set of fundamentalist 'family resemblances' that cut across religious traditions."[4]

In this comparative perspective, the various religious resurgences are seen as parallel processes taking place in different societies. This represents a religious resurgence on a global scale but in separate contexts. Some scholars go beyond this and identify the fundamentalist resurgence in the late twentieth century as being interactively affected by the emerging global situation. They affirm that the "resurgence of 'fundamentalistic' promotion of particularist ideologies and doctrines," seen as the "recent globe-wide assertion of particularist ideas," can best be understood in the context of "increasing *globality*."[5]

Although it is interpreted in many different ways, most people now see the Islamic resurgence of the final quarter of the twentieth century as part of a global context. This resurgence has distinctive characteristics but it takes place on a world context in which there is also the rise of activist assertions of faith in Christian, Jewish, Hindu, Buddhist, and other major world traditions of religion. The resurgence in each of these cases is better understood when seen in the context of the "virtually worldwide eruption of religious and quasi-religious concerns and themes."[6] The Islamic resurgence, in this context, can be seen as a dynamic response to the modern historic transformations. It is not a rare and pathological response but rather an effectively articulated response in tune with some of the major global developments of the end of the twentieth century.

By the early 1990s, violent militancy was clearly manifested among Hindu fundamentalists, Buddhists in Sri Lanka, Jewish fundamentalists in Israel, and others elsewhere. As a result, analyses that interpret the militancy of Islamic fundamentalism as being somehow directly caused by distinctively Islamic doctrines and traditions are increasingly out of touch with the realities of the global religious resurgence of the late twentieth century. The globalization of the resurgence reflects the new realities of what can be seen as a postsecular era. The renewed role of religion casts doubt upon the simple assumption that modernity involves the decline of religion in human life.

The normalization of the religious resurgence, or the emergence of the resurgence in the mainstream of societies, is a second important trend. The religious resurgence emerged by the 1990s as something more than a militant response to modernity or to the problems of modern social transformations. Even many of those who benefited from, and participated, in the manifestations of modernity are actively involved in the resurgence. For much of the twentieth century, religious fundamentalists were viewed as being people from the margins of society who were unable to participate directly in modern life. Observers tended to assume that fundamentalists were uneducated, rural, poor, and conservative. This was true for analysts of the American religious experience[7] as well as for those discussing Muslim fundamentalists. This made it difficult to identify the fundamentalist religious resurgence as it developed in the 1970s because analysts sometimes simply would not be able to conceive of middle class educated urban professionals as fundamentalists. This conceptual barrier was aided by the fact that in the 1960s and early 1970s the activists of the religious resurgence represented a small proportion of the population and were marginal in many ways to the systems of social and political power. They only gradually assumed greater significance.

In the United States this process may have begun among the youth counterculture of the 1960s but in the following decade produced a major religious resurgence. This evolution in the United States, as summarized by Theodore Long and Jeffrey Hadden, exhibits many similarities to the phases of the Islamic resurgence:

the youth counterculture of the late 1960s became infatuated with the possibility of new consciousness through religion. The counterculture itself barely survived the sixties, but the plethora of new religions—and old ones rediscovered—spawned in its wake made a substantial impact on religion and society alike. As the sects and cults of the seventies penetrated conventional life, they rejuvenated religious consciousness throughout society. And as they clashed with established institutions, they brought religion once more to center stage as a public issue of political, legal, and economic significance.[8]

In Muslim countries, the clash with established institutions usually was direct and in the political arena. As a result, the sectarian movements of the early 1970s often represented revolutionary political opposition to established secularizing and modernizing regimes. However, even when the majority of the population did not agree with their violent methods or even their specific goals, these movements helped to "rejuvenate religious consciousness throughout society" in many countries. By the 1980s, educated professionals were active participants in the developing nonviolent religious resurgence. In this way, the Islamic resurgence came to have many different dimensions by the 1990s. There were still the extremist and violent marginal groups, but the majority of society had been significantly involved in the active reaffirmation of Islam. The resurgence was part of the normal life of most of society, and this process of normalization is a significant aspect of the resurgence of Islam as it is manifested in the 1990s.

Interpretations of the Resurgence

The Islamic resurgence has been interpreted in many different ways. In the late 1970s, most interpretations concentrated on specific details and particular cases and then identified a somewhat broader pattern. However, by the early 1990s, the perspectives of many analysts broadened in the generality of the conceptual bases for their presentations. The resurgence was seen, for example, as a clash of civilizations rather than simply the emergence of some militant groups.

From the mid-1970s until the early 1990s, however, there was one common issue which continued to be debated, and that was the long-term significance of the Islamic resurgence. One position was that the resurgence was fundamentally the last stand "of the adherents of a great religion which has yet to come to terms theologically and convincingly with today's world."[9] In this perspective, the resurgence represented a passing phase and would soon lose its impetus. One finds constant evidence of this view in the statements of analysts in the period: "Many Middle East watchers believe the newness of the Islamic revolution and its force have now passed [1981];"[10] "Islamic Fundamentalism—an idea whose time has gone [1985];"[11] "The political phenomenon we here identified as 'Islamic fundamentalism' is a spent force now" (in 1989, just before the Rushdie affair began).[12]

At the other extreme were those participants in the resurgence who became convinced that the immediate victory of Islamic forces on a global scale was at hand. Shi'i enthusiasm was aroused by the success of the Iranian revolution and, in the years following, the conviction of imminent triumph was exhibited in many ways, ranging from the remarkable letter from Ayatollah Khomeini presented to Gorbachev, urging him to study Islam, to the announcement of the near coming of the Imam on student bulletin boards at the London School of Economics in 1992. There were fewer apocalyptic pronouncements in the Sunni world, but the occupation of the Holy Sanctuary in Mecca at the beginning of the new Islamic century reflected a similar spirit.

Between these two extremes of interpretation of the resurgence, there were many different approaches, and it is not possible to mention them all. Discussions of the Islamic resurgence are numerous, with one selective bibliography listing more than 1200 recent books and major articles on the revival.[13] Although there was great variety, there had also emerged by the early 1990s, some agreement among most interpreters on certain basic themes.

One area of relative agreement is that the Islamic resurgence arose in a context of crisis where existing social and political options were perceived as having failed. An early assessment by R. Hrair Dekmejian stated that "at the most general level of analysis, the recent quest for a return to the Islamic ethos appears to be a natural response to the successive pathological experiences which have buffeted Islamic societies in contemporary times."[14] In different forms, this crisis continues to be seen as an important dimension of the resurgence, and many analysts would agree with John L. Esposito's observation that "modernization has not led to the triumph of secular political and economic ideologies. Liberal nationalism, Arab nationalism and socialism, capitalism and Marxism have, in fact, come to be viewed [by Muslims] as the sources of Muslim political and economic failures."[15] The failure of existing institutions and regimes to cope with the challenges of late twentieth century experiences is accepted by most as an important dimension of the resurgence.

There are, however, a number of different, and sometimes contradictory, analytical perspectives that relate to broad issues of interpretation. Three important approaches illustrate some of the most important issues involved. One approach sees the resurgence in broad world historical terms as a continuation of the clash between two great civilizations, Islam and the West. A second identifies the resurgence with fundamentalism and views it as a uniquely modern development, while a third emphasizes the postmodern dimensions of the success of Islamic fundamentalism in the late twentieth century.

The first line of analysis views the resurgence as the most recent phase in the long interaction between Islamic and Western civilizations. One of the most effective presenters of this world historical approach is Bernard Lewis, who has written many influential studies of Islamic history. From the early 1960s until the 1990s, Lewis placed his interpretation of the modern Islamic experience in the context of the continuities of history. In this view, "in its long confrontation with the civilization of the West, the Islamic world has gone through successive phases of revival and resistance, response and rejection."[16] In this context, the potential for Islamic resurgence always exists, and even in the early 1960s, when most scholars were describing the decline of Islam, Lewis wrote, "Until very recently, it was in religious terms that the problems were formulated [in the Islamic confrontation with the West], and the different solutions propounded and argued. Even today [lecture in 1963], it would be very rash to assert that the secularization of Islamic sentiment has passed the point of no return."[17] In one of the earliest major discussions of the emerging resurgence in the 1970s, Lewis identified the Islamic revival as a significant force, before the Iranian revolution brought it to the attention of most people. He observed that the various ideologies of nationalism and socialism were the product of a small elite, and that "Islam is still the most effective form of consensus in Muslim countries, the basic identity among the masses. . . . As regimes come closer to the populace, even if their verbiage is left-wing and ideological, they become more Islamic."[18]

As the strength of the resurgence grew in the 1980s, Lewis emphasized the confrontational nature of the Islamic resurgence, and, in presenting an explanation of the resurgence, he spoke of the "roots of Muslim rage," concluding that the West is "facing a mood and a movement far transcending the level of issues and policies and the governments that pursue them. This is no less than a clash of civilizations—the perhaps irrational but surely historic reaction of an ancient rival against our Judeo-Christian heritage, our secular present, and the worldwide expansion of both."[19] This Muslim reaction, in this view, becomes increasingly militant, viewing the conflict as being with the "enemies of God," and "for those who wage war against the enemies of God, their struggle can end only in death or victory," and the result, in Lewis's view, is the impossibility of "even a prospect of peace" based on "dialogue and compromise" with them.[20]

This ultimately pessimistic view recognizes the power and the authenticity of the Islamic resurgence and places it firmly in the context of broader trends of world history. One critique, however, notes that "emphasis upon the clash of civilizations reinforces the tendency to downplay or overlook specific political and socioeconomic causes for Muslim behavior, to see Muslim actions as an irrational reaction rather than a response to specific policies and actions. . . . The primacy of competing political interests, policies, and issues is dismissed or eclipsed by the vision of an age-old rivalry."[21] The specific aspects of particular cases are important, even in understanding the current manifestations of the world historical continuities.

A second approach emphasizes the discontinuities involved in the rise of contemporary Islamic fundamentalism. Rather than seeing the resurgence as part of a long pattern of interaction between Western and Islamic civilizations, scholars like Bruce Lawrence insist fundamentalisms of all types, including Islamic fundamentalism, are direct products of the modern era: "Without modernity there are no fundamentalists, just as there are no modernists. The identity of fundamentalism, both as a psychological mindset and a historical movement, is shaped by the modern world. Fundamentalists . . . are at once the consequence of modernity and the antithesis of modernism."[22] In contrast to the approach by Lewis, this perspective sees contemporary fundamentalists as accepting modernity in some ways, with an important distinction being made between modernity and modernism. Lawrence says that fundamentalists "accept implicitly the benefits of modernity, often thriving through their use of technology, while explicitly rejecting modernism as a holistic ideological framework. They are moderns but not modernists."[23] In this analysis, the resurgence of Islam represents a particular case of the broader dynamics of modern history and the resurgence is identified with Islamic fundamentalism. It is the operation of the religious forces utilizing the modern instrumentalities of technology, communication, and mobility to accomplish "the enormous task" of being "fully authentic Muslims in a world that cares little about religion and less about Islam but whose principal actors nonetheless possess the means to control the one and define the other."[24] In this situation, Muslim fundamentalism is "not unimportant" but is "doomed to failure."[25]

A third approach also places the Islamic resurgence in a broader global perspective but sees it more in the context of the emergence of postmodern thought and the historical internal evolution of Islamic experience. This analysis, as presented by Ernest Gellner, sees "three fundamental and irreducible positions" on "questions of faith" in the contemporary world, with each expressing "a fundamental option of the human spirit, when facing the world as it is now."[26] These three options are religious fundamentalism, relativism as currently exemplified by postmodernism, and enlightenment rationalism (or "rationalist fundamentalism").[27] In Gellner's view, secularization is a major part of the contemporary experience but "to say that secularization prevails in Islam is not contentious. It is simply false. Islam is as strong now as it was a century ago. In some ways, it is probably stronger," and, as a result, "in our age, fundamentalism is at its strongest in Islam."[28]

Gellner concentrates on the long-term historical dynamics of Islamic experience. In this long history, he states that "the really central, and perhaps most important, feature of Islam is that it was internally divided into a High Islam of the scholars and the Low Islam of the people."[29] There was a latent tension between these two styles of Islam which at times resulted in conflicts, with representatives of High Islam leading fundamentalist movements of purification and revival. In the premodern world, this resulted in an often-repeated cycle. From time to time, the reformers would prevail and, "having re-established a purified order, things slowly returned to normality . . . Literate, rule-abiding scripturalist puritanism is practicable for urban scholars, but not so for the masses, or for the rural tribesmen . . . And so the rival style re-affirms itself."[30] However, in the modern era, this cycle is not repeated as the socio-cultural foundations for Low or Folk Islam have been significantly weakened, while increasing literacy, urbanization, and other factors have strengthened the bases for High Islam.

The very experiences and developments of the modern era opened the way for increasing importance for reform-oriented High Islam which could, in the colonial context, provide an identity for reactive nationalism. In addition, "the urge to reform, ever present in Islam, acquired a new vigour and instensity. No doubt it also acquired some new themes and additional motivation . . . But the dominant and persuasive answer recommended neither emulation of the West, nor idealization of some folk virtue and wisdom. It recommended a *return* to, or a more rigorous observance of, *High* Islam."[31] Gellner paints a picture of an Islam that is far from being "doomed to failure" in his conclusion:

> on the evidence available so far, the world of Islam demonstrates that it is possible to run a modern, or at any rate modernizing, economy, reasonably permeated by the appropriate technological, educational, organization principles, *and* combine it with a strong, pervasive, powerfully internalized Muslim conviction and identification. A puritan and scripturalist world religion does not seem necessarily doomed to erosion by modern conditions. It may on the contrary be favoured by them.[32]

These major perspectives reflect some of the diversity of interpretation. Each in different ways deals with the profound issues of continuity and change as they emerge in the history of the modern Islamic world. These interpretations also show the awareness of the importance of a broad and inclusive, actually global, perspective, as well as the need to understand the specifics of particular cases.

Views from Within the Resurgence

In the late 1970s much of the analytical discussion of the Islamic resurgence was presented by people from outside of the movements, and possibly even more from outside of the Islamic community. At that time there were many publications by individuals and movements directly involved in the resurgence, but these were primarily presentations of positions as a part of the movements' activities rather than reflections on the resurgence. However, by the 1990s, there was a growing body of interpretations of the resurgence written by Muslims who were directly involved in the dynamics of the resurgence itself, either as advocates or opponents. In this growing literature there are many different approaches and perspectives. Examples of three of the most important viewpoints—the committed fundamentalists, the nonfundamentalist but actively Islamic, and the secularist—can provide some understanding of the Muslim self-consciousness of the resurgence.

Some of the fundamentalists who have been most actively engaged in the process of self-examination and the interpretation of the broader resurgence are in the Sudanese Muslim Brotherhood under the leadership of Hasan Turabi. Two volumes by Hasan Makki outlining the history of the Muslim Brotherhood in Sudan from 1944 to 1985 present a carefully documented account which goes beyond the confines of a partisan propaganda piece even though the perspective of the author is a clear commitment to the movement.[33] An account of the movement in English by Abdelwahab El-Affendi is based on a dissertation accepted by a Western university. Even a scholar with a very negative evaluation of the Islamist movement in Sudan, described the book as "not an idiosyncratic theological tract, but a metaphysical monograph on the importance and dynamism of Islam in the modern world, meticulously researched with an excellent bibliography."[34] Hasan Turabi himself has written a remarkably frank account of the development of the Islamic movement in Sudan, providing a critique of policies and approaches of himself and others.[35]

It is clear that all of these accounts are written by people who are committed to the movement and its goals, and they are, in this sense, partisan accounts. However, they also make a major effort to present analysis which is more than partisan polemic. At times this means that basic questions get rephrased in useful and interesting ways. El-Affandi opens his study, for example, with such a restatement: "The central question habitually asked about the present wave of Muslim self-assertion is why did it happen? However, a more appropriate question would be why was it necessary to remind Muslims to abide by the faith they profess? Simple inertia should have dictated that Muslims should stick to their own life styles unless pressured to abandon them."[36] Sudanese Islamists have also studied the Islamic resurgence in broader historical and geographic perspectives. Hasan Makki, for example, has written studies of the late eighteenth-century revivalist, Ahmad ibn Idris, as well as of the Islamic movement in Iran in the twentieth century.[37] Turabi has presented broader interpretations of the Islamic resurgence to a variety of audiences, including a subcommittee of the United States House of Representatives.[38]

The analyses of the resurgence presented by Sudanese and other Islamists have many points of similarity with the views of other scholars. There is a tendency to view the broader historical context in terms of the historical clash of civilizations. "Underlying most [of the themes in the revivalist literature] . . . is the already acknowledged tension in which Muslims perceive their culture and religion to be in conflict with the west."[39] In fundamentalist presentations, there is a greater inclination to describe this confrontation in religious terms, as a clash between Islam and Christianity, than is the case in the works of Western non-Muslim scholars. Fundamentalist interpreters also emphasize the special conditions in the modern era which gave rise to the resurgence, especially the emergence in the Muslim world of Western secularist movements and thought. Many of the accounts of the establishment of activist Islamist groups stress the importance of the contest with communists or leftist radicals in the emergence of fundamentalist organizations among students.[40] In broader terms, the fundamentalist literature on the resurgence is also "clearly focused on issues of modernity,"[41] but, in contrast to the conclusions of people like Lawrence, fundamentalists conclude that Islam will ultimately win rather than being ultimately doomed to failure. Fundamentalist analysts also emphasize the long traditions of renewal in Islam, viewing the current resurgence as a new phase in a deeply rooted heritage of continual or cyclical renewal, thus reflecting important continuities within Islamic history.[42]

In general terms, the fundamentalists' studies of the resurgence are remarkably similar to other studies in terms of the main themes examined and the dimensions of the context which are seen as important. It is primarily in terms of the interpretive conclusions that the major differences arise. Often these differences arise more from the fundamental assumptions which underlie the intellectual paradigms of the analysts than from the logic of the analysis itself. If one starts with a position of faith in an almighty God, your conclusions about the ultimate destiny of religion in the world are going to be different from a person whose starting assumptions are basically secular and who hypothesizes the ultimate disappearance of religion.

The interpretation of the resurgence itself has become a point of debate among Muslims, involving opponents of the fundamentalists as well as the fundamentalists. As the resurgence spread beyond the confines of militant fundamentalist minorities, many nonfundamentalists became more visible as significant parts of the resurgence. Hasan Hanafi, the Egyptian philosopher, provides a comprehensive interpretation of the resurgence from the perspective of the Islamic Left.[43] The emergence of an Islamic alternative is seen as arising out of the failure of the contemporary ideologies of modernization—Western Liberalism, State Socialism, and Traditional Marxism—and a context of identity crisis caused by the domination of Muslims by the West. At the same time, Hanafi sees a growing awareness of the failures of the West and of the potential power of the Islamic heritage. The distinctive aspect of Hanafi's analysis is his strong criticism of most of the fundamentalist movements, which he describes as engaged in sterile ritualism. In his critique of the Islamist student groups in Egypt in the early 1980s, for example, he says that they "confine themselves to pure ritualism without entering into the sociopolitical drama of the country."[44] The conclusion is pessimistic because the most viable alternative, the Islamic left, is not as powerful as the ritualists and secularists. However, in his vision, "in the remote future, when conservation as a historical mood paves the way to progressivism, Islam can be carried on as progress."[45]

Another perspective from a nonfundamentalist protagonist of an Islamic resurgence is provided by Bassam Tibi, who argues for the secularization of Islam. He views the current resurgence as the product of major crises and as dominated by the fundamentalist orientation. "The preoccupation with modern Islam in its current phase arises from the fact that the contemporary Islamic Middle East finds itself in a crisis—actually, in a double crisis produced by the pauperization of the Muslim peoples and the identity crisis brought on by Westernization. In their despair Muslims are turning to Islam as the promise for a better future and as the basis for a cultural identity. The product of this development is a repoliticization of Islam."[46] Like Hanafi, Tibi opposes the currently influential fundamentalism, but he sees the long-term survival of Islam requiring its effective secularization.

Another committed Muslim understanding of the resurgence is to view fundamentalism in the context of the postmodern world situation. Akbar Ahmad starts with a global perspective in which the revival of ethnicity and religious fundamentalism is linked to postmodernism. "Fundamentalism is the attempt to resolve how to live in a world of radical doubt. It is a dialogue with the times, a response to it . . . [A]n argument can be made that ethno-religious revivalism is both cause and effect of postmodernism."[47] Like many others, Akbar sees the resurgence taking place in the context of the failure of modernist ideologies and conflict between Islam and the West. The danger is in the restrictive negativism of many of the revivalists: "Muslim leaders have pushed themselves into a hole dug by themselves in viewing the present upsurge simplistically as a confrontation with the West. They are in danger of rejecting features central to Islam—such as love of knowledge, egalitarianism, tolerance—because they are visibly associated with the West."[48]

He sees continuities with past revivalist impulses and distinctive new approaches.

> The test for Muslims is how to preserve the essence of the Quranic message . . . without it being reduced to an ancient and empty chant in our times; how to participate in the global civilization without their identity being obliterated. . . . Into the predicament that postmodernism plunges us there is also promise. . . . [The Islamic vision] has much to offer a world saturated with disintegration, cynicism and loss of faith. However, this will only be possible if there is a universal tolerance of others among Muslims and non-Muslims alike, an appreciation of their uniqueness and a willingness to understand them.[49]

The broad diversity of perspectives on the resurgence among Muslims reflects the changing nature of the resurgence itself. This is a manifestation of the arrival of the power of the resurgence into the mainstream of Muslim societies. It reflects the wide ranging debate within the Muslim world, just as the different perspectives of non-Muslim observers reflect the broader debates over the nature of global interactions in the twenty-first century, and in particular, debates over the nature of the relations between Islam and the West.

The Islamic Threat?

By the 1990s much of the discussion of the relations between Islam and the West revolved around the issue of whether or not Islam in some significant way posed a threat to the West. This debate itself was a product of the significant changes that had occurred since the late 1960s. At that time few would have argued that the small groups of fundamentalist militants were more than a terrorist nuisance. At most they represented a problem for some governments in the Islamic world but few, outside of the militants themselves, would have identified Islamic fundamentalism as a major threat to the global interests of the United States. However, by 1989, Patrick Buchanan, the well-known conservative author and politician could write a column entitled "Rising Islam May Overwhelm the West," and in 1993 a respected scholar of modern Muslim affairs could speak of the potential of an armed Islam which could "create a world order based not on American hegemony but on a restored balance of power—and terror."[50] Following the bombing of the International Trade Center in New York, the representative of Israel to the United Nations could announce: "The free world must act to curb and fight this menacing phenomenon [of militant Islamic fundamentalism]. We must act now, before it is too late."[51] Others argued that this image of Islamic fundamentalist as the new menacing superpower was primarily a product of the search for super-enemies following the end of the Cold War. While all recognized that some fundamentalists were dangerous and violent, the disagreement was over the magnitude of the threat that they posed, and the degree to which the violence was characteristic of the Islamic resurgence as a whole.

The major issues in this debate were clearly defined by John L. Esposito in a study entitled *The Islamic Threat: Myth or Reality*. Even those who disagreed with Esposito's conclusions recognized that he had raised and defined the crucial questions.[52] These issues are not simple disagreements over the operations of abstract models. The positions taken determine the nature of important policies undertaken by many governments. Just as the Western interpretations of the Islamic resurgence have their parallels in the Muslim world, the debate over "the Islamic threat" has its parallel in the debate over the "threat of the West" to Islam. The results of these debates over the nature and existence of mutual threats will shape the relations between Islamic and Western societies for a significant period.

Conclusions and Prospects

The general portrait presented in this book is the evolution of Islamic communities through the interaction of the styles of Islamic experience. These styles are identified not so much by the content of ideas expressed as by modes of dealing with historic change and of interpreting the Islamic message. These styles take different forms in the various eras of Islamic history, and their special roles and programs are related to local conditions.

The great dynamic of this interaction of styles follows a pattern seen in the diversity of Islamic experiences. As Islamic communities are created or expand, adaptation to local conditions is necessary, and such adaptations were the foundations for the great syntheses of Islamic history. New social and political structures were created, which provided the basis for expanding Islamic life, and intellectual adaptationism enabled Islamic thought to meet challenges such as those posed in the medieval era by the Hellenistic philosophical traditions.

With the great successes of Islamic adaptationism came a sense of the need to preserve the achievements, and a conservative style of Islamic action worked to preserve the gains that had been made and became a brake upon conscious changes adaptationists wished to make. However, at various times and in different places, the process of adaptation appeared to introduce such flexibility or so many compromises that the clearly Islamic nature of the community seemed to be threatened. In that situation, the process of renewal would take a fundamentalist form. The Quran and the Sunnah provide an absolute standard for judging the "Islamicness" of society, and those fundamentals have been used by activists throughout Islamic history as the basis for criticism of the status quo and for programs of Islamic renewal. This fundamentalism produced movements that sometimes were revolutionary and at other times were able to encourage a less militant affirmation of the Islamic fundamentals within the existing structures. Following this effort at "re-Islamization," which was often actually a further step in the initial Islamization of a society, the process of adaptation and conservative preservation would continue, with the basic Islamic nature of the community being affirmed.

The individualist style emphasized the more personal and individual aspects of Islam and interacted with the more communal orientation of the other three. In individual terms, this style often meant an emphasis on individual piety rather than on communal obligation, and in terms of the community as a whole, the style stressed the charismatic nature of leadership. In medieval Islamic civilization, the interaction of the community and individual helped to provide the basis for the Islamic tradition of mysticism in contrast to the conservative and fundamentalist emphasis upon the law and communal obligation. In the modern Islamic experience, the tradition of the individualistic style has opened the way for an acceptance of secularism in its nonradical forms. In all periods, the potential within the Islamic experience for the emergence of religiously oriented charismatic leadership provided a vehicle for a reaffirmation of Islam in the context of messianic expectations.

Since the eighteenth century, all of these styles have continued to be visible within Islamic life, and the interaction of these styles has provided the dominant modes of Islamic expression. The eighteenth century experience helped to provide the definition of the fundamentalist style as it was to interact in the modern era. Modernizing adaptation and fundamentalist reaction provided the major vehicles for Islamic expression during the nineteenth century, and in the twentieth century modernizing adaptation supported by a secularist individualism became the dominant style under the influence of the special conditions of modernizing societies. However, as the compromises involved in these styles appeared to threaten the authentic Islamic nature of the community, fundamentalist pressures began to build, and because of factors like the oil boom of the 1970s, the reassertion of the fundamentalist style became an important force in the Islamic world.

Clearly, as discussed in Chapters 4, 5, and 6, many different factors shaped the Islamic experience in the twentieth century. However, in addition to the local dimension and the dimension of the relationship of the Islamic movements to the main elements of modern history, the continuing evolution of Islamic society in the framework of the Islamic dimensions of styles and faith is also significant.

The rich diversity of the modern Islamic experience bears testimony to the continuing ability of the Islamic message to inspire people in many different ways. Although some may simply be using Islam for other purposes, the experiences of Muslims since the eighteenth century make it impossible to speak of contemporary societies in the Islamic world as "post-Muslim" in the same way that people sometimes speak of Western society as post-Christian. In this book, the diversity and conflict as well as the continuity and consensus have been explored as a way to understand the modern Islamic experience.

History is not a predictive science, and the social scientists have had little success in devising an accurate method of foretelling the future of humanity. However, it is possible to speculate about the future of the Islamic revival on the basis of its continuities with the past.

At the beginning of the fifteenth Islamic century, Islamic communities were engaged in a vigorous reaffirmation of the Islamic message. Since adaptationism had been identified with Westernizing modernization and could be seen to be threatening the authentic Islamic nature of the community, it is not surprising that this reaffirmation was initially made in a fundamentalist style. In the revival of the 1970s, a new type of fundamentalism was emerging which combined traditional themes with radical methods. It represented a revolutionary challenge to the existing regimes and to modernist and secularist approaches. In the 1980s, this spirit of reaffirmation became accepted by increasing proportions of society to the extent that it is possible to speak of the resurgence entering the mainstream of Muslim societies. In this context, many revivalists faced the challenge of adapting the fundamentalist message to the specific conditions of their particular societies, and a new adaptationism, not tied to the Westernizing agenda, was visible.

By the 1990s, the resurgence had achieved much, and the old dynamic of attempting to preserve gains was beginning to be visible. A decade and a half after the success of the Islamic revolution in Iran, for example, a major concern of the leaders of the Islamic Republic was to preserve the achievements of the revolution. The Islamic Republic was less a challenge to the existing conditions than it was simply a distinctive element in the "status quo of the emerging new world order." In this way, one might also be able to speak of the new conservatism.

Similarly, the highly visible conflicts and issues of the fundamentalist resurgence had hidden the activities of the quieter groups like the Sufi orders. By the early 1990s, there were also indications that the orders had not disappeared but rather had been winning increasing support. They reflected an important emerging aspect of the reaffirmation of Islam at the beginning of the fifteenth Islamic century.[53] In the continuing strength of the tariqahs, it is possible to see the continuing vitality of the individualist style of Islamic experience as it went beyond the confines of Western secularist individualism.

The Islamic resurgence has developed in the context of the contemporary world which might helpfully be thought of as post-modern. An activist fundamentalism was the first phase of that resurgence, and it continues to be an important part of it. The degree to which the future of the reaffirmation of Islam continues to be militant and violent depends upon the strength of the desire to preserve gains and the ability of committed resurgent Muslims to adapt to the special conditions of the postmodern world, possibly in ways suggested by Akbar Ahmad. Whatever happens, it is clear that with its unity and variety, its consensus and conflict, its continuity and change, Islam will continue in its fifteenth century to be a vital force in the world.

Notes
Glossary of Non-English Terms
Bibliographical Essay
Index

Notes

Chapter 1. Introduction

1. Donald Eugene Smith, *Religion, Politics, and Social Change in the Third World* (New York: Free Press, 1971), p. 3.

2. Isma'il R. Al Faruqi, *Islam* (Niles, Ill.: Argus Communications, 1979), p. 13.

3. Mazheruddin Siddiqi, *The Qur'anic Concept of History* (Karachi: Central Institute of Islamic Research, 1965), p. 1.

4. Fazlur Rahman, *Islam,* 2d ed. (Chicago: University of Chicago Press, 1979), p. 25.

5. James A. Bill and Robert Springborg, *Politics in the Middle East,* 3rd ed. (Glenview, Ill.: Scott, Foresman/Little, Brown Higher Education, 1990), p. 138.

6. Ross E. Dunn, *The Adventures of Ibn Battuta* (Berkeley: University of California Press, 1986), p. 7.

7. Clement Henry Moore, "Authoritarian Politics in Unincorporated Society," *Comparative Politics* 6 (1974):216.

8. Arthur Goldschmidt, Jr., *A Concise History of the Middle East,* 3d ed. (Boulder, Colo.: Westview Press, 1988), p. 120. See also the discussion in William H. McNeill, *The Age of Gunpowder Empires, 1450–1800* (Washington: American Historical Association, 1989), pp. 33–40.

9. Stanford J. Shaw, *History of the Ottoman Empire and Modern Turkey,* vol. 1 (Cambridge, Eng., Cambridge University Press, 1976), p. 59.

10. Halil Inalcik, *The Ottoman Empire: The Classical Age 1300–1600,* trans. Norman Itzkowitz and Colin Imber (London: Weidenfeld and Nicolson, 1973), p. 176.

11. The contrasts and similarities in the transition from more adaptationist to more fundamentalist styles in these two parts of the Islamic world are suggested in the sometimes controversial but always thoughtprovoking study, Clifford Geertz, *Islam Observed: Religious Development in Morocco and Indonesia* (Chicago: University of Chicago Press, 1968).

12. Marshall G. S. Hodgson, *The Venture of Islam,* 3 vols. (Chicago: University of Chicago Press, 1974), 3:14–15.

13. Quran, 17:88. (Personal translation.)

14. Ibid., 3:144.

15. Abdallah Laroui, *The Crisis of the Arab Intellectual,* trans. Diarmid Cammell (Berkeley: University of California Press, 1976), p. 16.

16. For a broad spectrum of views on this issue, see Lisa Appignanesi and Sara Maitland, ed., *The Rushdie File* (Syracuse, N.Y.: Syracuse University Press, 1990).

17. Seyyed Hossein Nasr, *Ideals and Realities of Islam* (London: George Allen and Unwin, 1966), p. 29.

18. Isma'il Raji al Faruqi, *Tawhid: Its Implications for Thought and Life* (Herndon, Va.: International Institute of Islamic Thought, 1402/1982), p. 18.

19. Abdulaziz Abdulhussein Sachedina, *The Just Ruler (al-sultan al-'adil) in Shi'ite Islam* (New York: Oxford University Press, 1988), p. 4.

20. Ibid., p. 5.

21. Ibn Khaldun, *The Muqaddimah: An Introduction to History,* trans. Franz Rosenthal, 3 vols. (New York: Pantheon Books, 1958), 2:163.

22. D. B. MacDonald, "Al-Mahdi," in *The Shorter Encyclopaedia of Islam,* ed. Hamilton A. R. Gibb and J. H. Kramers (Leiden: E. J. Brill, 1953), pp. 311, 313.

Chapter 2. The Foundations of the Modern Experience: Revival and Reform in the Eighteenth Century

1. Evelyn Baring, first earl of Cromer, *Modern Egypt,* 2 vols. (New York: Macmillan, 1909), 2:184.

2. H.A.R. Gibb, *Modern Trends in Islam* (Chicago: University of Chicago Press, 1947), p. 105.

3. Fazlur Rahman, "Revival and Reform in Islam," in *The Cambridge History of Islam,* ed. P. M. Holt, Ann K. S. Lambton, and Bernard Lewis, 2 vols. (Cambridge: Cambridge University Press, 1970), 2:640.

4. Fazlur Rahman, *Islam* (Garden City, N.Y.: Doubleday, Anchor Books, 1968), p. 239.

5. Stanford J. Shaw, *History of the Ottoman Empire and Modern Turkey,* Vol. 1 (Cambridge, Eng.: Cambridge University Press, 1976), p. 223.

6. Richard Repp, "Some Observations on the Development of the Ottoman Learned Hierarchy," in *Scholars, Saints, and Sufis,* ed. Nikki R. Keddie (Berkeley: University of California Press, 1972), p. 30.

7. Ibid., p. 32.

8. Norman Itzkowitz, "Men and Ideas in the Eighteenth Century Ottoman Empire," in *Studies in Eighteenth-Century Islamic History,* ed. Thomas Naff and Roger Owen (Carbondale, Ill.: Southern Illinois University Press, 1977), p. 16.

9. Ibid., pp. 19–20.

10. Niyazi Berkes, *The Development of Secularism in Turkey* (Montreal: McGill University Press, 1964), p. 52. See also Robert W. Olson, "The Esnaf and the Patrona Halil Rebellion of 1730: A Realignment in Ottoman Politics?" *Journal of the Economic and Social History of the Orient* 17(1974):329–332.

11. Stanford J. Shaw, *Between Old and New: The Ottoman Empire Under Sultan Selim III, 1789–1807* (Cambridge, Mass.: Harvard University Press, 1971), p. viii.

12. Joan E. Gilbert, "The Ulama of Medieval Damascus and the International World of Islamic Scholarship" (Ph.D. diss., University of California, Berkeley, 1977), Chapter 2.

13. See Albert Hourani, "Shaikh Khalid and the Naqshbandi Order," in *Islamic Philosophy and the Classical Tradition,* ed. S. M. Stern, Albert Hourani, and Vivian Brown (Columbia, S.C.: University of South Carolina Press, 1973), pp. 89–103.

14. Ibid., pp. 99–100.

15. Afaf Lutfi al-Sayyid Marsot, "The Political and Economic Functions of the 'Ulama in the 18th Century," *Journal of the Economic and Social History of the Orient* 16 (1973):132.

16. Peter Gran, *Islamic Roots of Capitalism: Egypt, 1760–1840* (Austin: University of Texas Press, 1979), p. 11.

17. Marsot, "Political and Economic Functions," p. 134.

18. Afaf Lutfi al-Sayyid Marsot, "The Ulama of Cairo in the Eighteenth and Nineteenth

Centuries," in *Scholars, Saints, and Sufis,* ed. Nikki R. Keddie (Berkeley: University of California Press, 1972), pp. 161–162.

19. Ibid., p. 157.

20. Abd al-Rahman al-Jabarti, *'Aja'ib al-'Athar fi al-Tarajim wa al-Akhbar,* ed. Hasan Muhammad Jawhar et al., 7 vols. (Cairo: Lajnah al-Bayan al-'Arabi, 1958–1967), 1:131–134.

21. Gran, *Islamic Roots,* pp. 48–49.

22. *Encyclopaedia of Islam,* 2d. ed., s.v. "Ibn Hadjar al-'Askalani."

23. Gran, *Islamic Roots,* Chapters 2 and 3.

24. J. Spencer Trimingham, *The Sufi Orders in Islam* (London: Oxford University Press, 1971), p. 85.

25. Rahman, *Islam,* p. 245.

26. Abdallah al-Salih al-'Uthaymayn, *al-Shaykh Muhammad bin Abd al-Wahhab, Hayyatuhu wa Fikruhu* (Riyadh: Dar al-'Ulum, n.d.), p. 125.

27. *Majmu'ah al-Rasa'il wa al-Musa'il al-Najdiyyah,* 4 vols. (Cairo: Mataba'ah al-Manar, 1928–1931), 1:3.

28. Quoted in Abul A'la Maududi, *A Short History of the Revivalist Movement in Islam,* trans. al-Ash'ari (Lahore: Islamic Publications, 1976), p. 93.

29. Aziz Ahmad, *Studies in Islamic Culture in the Indian Environment* (Oxford: Clarendon Press, 1964), pp. 202–203.

30. *Encyclopaedia of Islam,* 2d ed., s.v. "Hind, Growth of Muslim Religious Thought."

31. Salih ibn Muhammad al-Fulani, "Al-Kitab Qatf al-Thamar fi Raf' Asanid al-Musannafat fi al-Fanun wa al-'Athar," Dar al-Kutub (National Library), Cairo, Egypt, Tal'at 195.

32. J. C. van Leur, *Indonesian Trade and Society* (The Hague: W. van Hoeve, 1955), p. 289.

33. Clifford Geertz, *Islam Observed: Religious Development in Morocco and Indonesia* (Chicago: University of Chicago Press, 1968), p. 65.

34. G.W.J. Drewes, *Directions for Travellers on the Mystic Path* (The Hague: Martinus Nijhoff, 1977), p. 37.

35. Andrew C. Hess, "The Forgotten Frontier: The Ottoman North African Provinces During the Eighteenth Century," in *Studies in Eighteenth-Century Islamic History,* ed. Thomas Naff and Roger Owen (Carbondale, Ill.: Southern Illinois University Press, 1977), p. 86.

36. Charles-André Julien, *History of North Africa,* trans. John Petrie (New York; Praeger, 1970), p. 332.

37. Jamil M. Abun-Nasr, "Religion and Politics in Eighteenth-Century Tunisia," *Zeitschrift der Deutschen Morgenlandischen Gesellschaft,* Supp. 3:1 (1977), pp. 304–315.

38. Andre Raymond, "North Africa in the Pre-Colonial Period," in *The Cambridge History of Islam,* ed. P. M. Holt, Ann K. S. Lambton, and Bernard Lewis, 2 vols. (Cambridge, Eng.: Cambridge University Press, 1970), 2:280.

39. Ibid., 2:269.

40. *Encyclopaedia of Islam,* 2d ed., s.v. "Barakat."

41. Trimingham, Sufi Orders, p. 115.

42. John Voll, "Two Biographies of Ahmad Ibn Idris al-Fasi (1760–1837)," *International Journal of African Historical Studies* 6 (1973):637.

43. J. S. Trimingham, "The Phases of Islamic Expansion and Islamic Culture Zones in Africa," in *Islam in Tropical Africa,* ed. I. M. Lewis (London: Oxford University Press, 1966), p. 128.

44. Humphrey Fisher, "The Western and Central Sudan," in *The Cambridge History of Islam,* ed. P. M. Holt, Ann K. S. Lambton, and Bernard Lewis, 2 vols. (Cambridge, Eng.: Cambridge University Press, 1970), 2:364.

45. C. C. Stewart, *Islam and Social Order in Mauritania* (Oxford: Clarendon Press, 1973), p. 39.

46. Hamid Algar, "Shi'ism and Iran in the Eighteenth Century," in *Studies in Eighteenth-Century Islamic History,* ed. Thomas Naff and Roger Owen (Carbondale, Ill.: Southern Illinois University Press, 1977), p. 299.

47. Ibid., p. 301.

48. Nikki R. Keddie, "The Roots of the Ulama's Power in Modern Iran," in *Scholars, Saints, and Sufis,* ed. Nikki R. Keddie (Berkeley: University of California Press, 1972), p. 224.

49. Hamid Algar, "The Oppositional Role of the Ulama in Twentieth-Century Iran," in *Scholars, Saints, and Sufis,* ed. Nikki R. Keddie (Berkeley: University of California Press, 1972), p. 235.

Chapter 3. European Domination and Islamic Response

1. Wilfred Cantwell Smith, *Islam in Modern History* (Princeton: Princeton University Press, 1957), p. 41.

2. L. Carl Brown, *The Tunisia of Ahmad Bey, 1837–1855* (Princeton: Princeton University Press, 1974), p. 358.

3. Ibid., pp. 356–369.

4. Ibid., p. 366.

5. Richard L. Chambers, "The Ottoman Ulema and the Tanzimat," in *Scholars, Saints, and Sufis,* ed. Nikki R. Keddie (Berkeley: University of California Press, 1972), p. 46.

6. Norman Itzkowitz and Joel Shinder, "The Office of Seyh ul-Islām and the Tanzimat—A Prosopographic Enquiry," *Middle Eastern Studies* 8 (1972):93–101.

7. Richard L. Chambers, "The Education of a Nineteenth Century Ottoman *Alim,* Ahmed Cevdet Pasa," *International Journal of Middle East Studies* 4 (1973):463.

8. Quoted in Bernard Lewis, *The Emergence of Modern Turkey* (London: Oxford University Press, 1961), p. 166.

9. Ibid., p. 169.

10. Stanford J. Shaw and Ezel Kural Shaw, *History of the Ottoman Empire and Modern Turkey,* Vol. 2 (Cambridge, Eng.: Cambridge University Press, 1977), p. 212.

11. Afaf Lutfi al-Sayyid Marsot, "The Ulama of Cairo in the Eighteenth and Nineteenth Centuries," in *Scholars, Saints, and Sufis,* ed. Nikki R. Keddie (Berkeley: University of California Press, 1972), p. 163.

12. Quoted in Albert Hourani, *Arabic Thought in the Liberal Age, 1798–1939* (London: Oxford University Press, 1962), pp. 140–141.

13. Quoted in Nadav Safran, *Egypt in Search of Political Community* (Cambridge, Mass.: Harvard University Press, 1961), p. 90.

14. Leon Carl Brown, *The Surest Path, The Political Treatise of a Nineteenth-Century Muslim Statesman* (Cambridge. Mass.: Harvard University Press, 1967), pp. 74–75.

15. Jamil M. Abun-Nasr, *The Tijaniyya* (London: Oxford University Press, 1965), Chapters 2 and 3.

16. Hamid Algar, *Religion and State in Iran, 1785–1906* (Berkeley: University of California Press, 1969), p. 136.

17. Hamid Algar, "The Oppositional Role of the Ulama in Twentieth-Century Iran," in *Scholars, Saints, and Sufis,* ed. Nikki R. Keddie (Berkeley: University of California Press, 1972), pp. 238–240. This whole discussion of Iran relies heavily upon the works of Hamid Algar and Nikki Keddie. In addition to the works already cited, see Hamid Algar, *Mirza*

Malkum Khan (Berkeley: University of California Press, 1973), and the following works by Nikki R. Keddie: *Religion and Rebellion in Iran: The Tobacco Protest of 1891–92* (London: Frank Cass, 1966); *Sayyid Jamal ad Din al-Afghani: A Political Biography* (Berkeley: University of California Press, 1972); and *Iran: Religion, Politics, and Society, Collected Essays* (London: Frank Cass, 1980). For a statement of the more fundamentalist position in the crisis of constitutionalism, see Abdul-Hadi Hairi, "Shaykh Fazl Allah Nuri's Refutation of the Idea of Constitutionalism," *Middle Eastern Studies* 13 (1977):327–339.

18. Fazlur Rahman, *Islam* (Garden City, N.Y.: Doubleday, Anchor Books, 1968), p. 267.

19. Aziz Ahmad, *Islamic Modernism in India and Pakistan, 1857–1964* (London: Oxford University Press, 1967), p. 61.

20. Ibid., p. 62.

21. Peter von Sivers, "The Realm of Justice: Apocalyptic Revolts in Algeria (1849–1879)," *Humaniora Islamica* 1 (1973):53.

22. Ibid., p. 60.

23. C. Snouck Hurgronje, *Mekka in the Latter Part of the 19th Century,* trans. J. H. Monahan (Leiden: E. J. Brill, 1970), pp. 207–208.

24. R. Bayly Winder, *Saudi Arabia in the Nineteenth Century* (New York: St. Martins Press, 1965), p. 228.

25. Ibid., pp. 222–223.

26. B. G. Martin, *Muslim Brotherhoods in 19th-Century Africa* (Cambridge, Eng.: Cambridge University Press, 1976), p. 125.

Chapter 4. Twentieth-Century Islam: Dominant Majorities in the Middle East and Africa

1. The figures for Muslim populations and their proportions of the total populations used in this chapter are based on information appearing in Richard V. Weekes, ed., *Muslim Peoples: A World Ethnographic Survey* (Westport, Conn.: Greenwood Press, 1978).

2. Albert Hourani, *Arabic Thought in the Liberal Age, 1798–1939* (London: Oxford University Press, 1962), p. 343.

3. Majid Khadduri, *Political Trends in the Arab World* (Baltimore: Johns Hopkins Press, 1970), p. 69.

4. Hourani, *Arabic Thought,* p. 299.

5. Arnold J. Toynbee, *Survey of International Affairs 1925, Volume I: The Islamic World Since the Peace Settlement* (London: Oxford University Press, 1927), p. 426.

6. Sylvia G. Haim, ed., *Arab Nationalism: An Anthology* (Berkeley: University of California Press, 1962), p. 176.

7. Ibid., p. 56.

8. Hourani, *Arabic Thought,* p. 172.

9. Hisham Sharabi, *Arab Intellectuals and the West: The Formative Years, 1875–1914* (Baltimore, Md.: Johns Hopkins Press, 1970), p. 94.

10. Taha Hussein (Husayn), *The Future of Culture in Egypt,* trans. Sidney Glazer (Washington, D.C.: American Council of Learned Societies, 1954), p. 136.

11. Charles D. Smith, "The 'Crisis of Orientation': The Shift of Egyptian Intellectuals to Islamic Subjects in the 1930's," *International Journal of Middle East Studies* 4 (1973):406–407.

12. Nadav Safran, *Egypt in Search of Political Community* (Cambridge, Mass.: Harvard University Press. 1961), p. 142.

13. Khadduri, *Political Trends,* p. 231.

14. Hanna Batatu, *The Old Social Classes and the Revolutionary Movements of Iraq* (Princeton: Princeton University Press, 1978), p. 390.

15. Ibid. p. 397.

16. For these views see Haim, *Arab Nationalism,* p. 63, and Kamel S. Abu Jaber, *The Arab Ba'th Socialist Party: History, Ideology, and Organization* (Syracuse N.Y.: Syracuse University Press, 1966), p. 129.

17. Tareq Y. Ismael, *The Arab Left* (Syracuse, N.Y.: Syracuse University Press, 1976), p. 91.

18. A full text of the program is reprinted in Gerald De Gaury, *Faisal, King of Saudi Arabia* (New York: Frederick A. Praeger, 1967), pp. 147–151.

19. See the speech quoted in De Gaury, *Faisal,* p. 167.

20. Muhammad Abdallah al-Samman, *Hasan al-Banna: al-Rajal wa al-Fikrah* (Cairo: Dar al-I'tisam, 1978/1398), p. 62.

21. Richard P. Mitchell, *The Society of the Muslim Brothers* (London: Oxford University Press, 1969), p. 30.

22. Kemal H. Karpat, ed., *Political and Social Thought in the Contemporary Middle East* (New York: Frederick A. Praeger, 1968), p. 125.

23. Ibid., p. 132.

24. Batatu, *Old Social Classes,* p. 25.

25. Richard D. Robinson, *The First Turkish Republic* (Cambridge, Mass.: Harvard University Press, 1963), p. 71.

26. Niyazi Berkes, *The Development of Secularism in Turkey* (Montreal: McGill University Press, 1964), p. 486.

27. Ibid., p. 482.

28. James Alban Bill, *The Politics of Iran: Groups, Classes, and Modernization* (Columbus, Ohio: Charles E. Merrill, 1972), p. 24.

29. Louis Dupree, *Afghanistan* (Princeton: Princeton University Press, 1980), p. 452.

30. George S. Harris, *The Origins of Communism in Turkey* (Stanford, Calif. Hoover Institution, 1967), p. 70.

31. Sepehr Zabih, *The Communist Movement in Iran* (Berkeley: University of California Press, 1966), p. 259.

32. Seyyed Hossein Nasr, *Ideals and Realities of Islam* (London: George Allen and Unwin, 1966), p. 147.

33. *Turkish Daily News,* 4 June 1977.

34. Mohammad Hassa Faghfoory, "The Role of the Ulama in Twentieth Century Iran with Particular Reference to Ayatullah Haj Sayyid Abul Qasim Kashani" (Ph.D. diss., University of Wisconsin, Madison, 1978), p. 172.

35. Ibid., pp. 142–143.

36. Clement Henry Moore, *Tunisia Since Independence* (Berkeley: University of California Press, 1965), p. 33.

37. Ibid., p. 48.

38. Ronald Segal, *African Profiles* (Baltimore: Penguin, 1962), pp. 290–291.

39. Charles F. Gallagher, *The United States and North Africa* (Cambridge, Mass.: Harvard University Press, 1963), p. 95.

40. Segal, *African Profiles,* p. 295.

41. Robert Merle, *Ahmed Ben Bella,* trans. Camilla Sykes (New York: Walker, 1967), p. 43.

42. Frantz Fanon, *Studies in a Dying Colonialism,* trans. Haakon Chevalier (New York: Monthly Review Press, 1965), Chapter 1.

43. Merle, *Ahmed Ben Bella,* p. 133.

44. David C. Gordon, *The Passing of French Algeria* (London: Oxford University Press, 1966), p. 115.

45. Ibid., p. 117.

46. E.I.J. Rosenthal, *Islam in the Modern National State* (Cambridge, Eng.: Cambridge University Press, 1965), p. 320.

47. Leon Carl Brown, "The Role of Islam in Modern North Africa," in *State and Society in Independent North Africa,* et. Leon Carl Brown (Washington, D.C.: Middle East Institute, 1966), p. 119.

48. Abdallah Laroui, *The Crisis of the Arab Intellectual,* trans. Diarmid Cammel (Berkeley: University of California Press, 1976), p. 37.

49. Gordon, *Passing of French Algeria,* p. 117.

Chapter 5. Twentieth-Century Islam: Eastern World, Nondominant Majorities, and Minorities

1. Aziz Ahmad, *Islamic Modernism in India and Pakistan, 1857–1964* (London: Oxford University Press, 1967), p. 166.

2. Ibid., pp. 152–153.

3. Allama Muhammad Iqbal, *The Reconstruction of Religious Thought in Islam* (Lahore: Muhammad Ashraf, 1968), p. 156.

4. Ibid., p. 173.

5. Ahmad, *Islamic Modernism,* p. 175.

6. Abul Aʻla Maududi, *The Process of Islamic Revolution* (Lahore: Islamic Publications, 1977), pp. 17–19.

7. Ahmad, *Islamic Modernism,* p. 214.

8. Abul Aʻla Maududi, *Towards Understanding Islam* (Gary, Ind.: International Islamic Federation of Student Organizations, 1970), pp. 14–15.

9. Ibid., p. 36.

10. Ahmad, *Islamic Modernism,* p. 242.

11. Ibid., p. 245.

12. G. P. Bhattacharjee, *Renaissance and Freedom Movement in Bangladesh* (Calcutta: Minerva Associates, 1973), p. 48.

13. Rounaq Jahan, *Pakistan: Failure in National Integration* (New York: Columbia University Press, 1972), p. 140.

14. Kalim Siddiqui, *Conflict, Crisis, and War in Pakistan* (New York: Praeger 1972), p. 123.

15. A. B. Shah in the foreword to S. E. Hassnain, *Indian Muslims: Challenge and Opportunity* (Bombay: Lalvani Publishing House, 1968), p. 5.

16. Ibid., p. 9.

17. Ibid., in the text by Hassnain, p. 138.

18. B. J. Boland, *The Struggle of Islam in Modern Indonesia* (The Hague: Martinus Nijhoff, 1971), p. 49.

19. Ibid., p. 51.

20. Ibid., p. 126.

21. For the use of this name and a history of the movement, see Lansiné Kaba, *The Wahhabiyya: Islamic Reform and Politics in French West Africa* (Evanston, Ill.: Northwestern University Press, 1974).

22. Ibid., p. 237.

23. Pierre Alexandre, "A West African Islamic Movement: Hamallism in French West Africa," in *Protest and Power in Black Africa,* ed. Robert I. Rotberg and Ali A. Mazrui (New York: Oxford University Press, 1970), p. 508.

24. Peter Worsley, *The Third World,* 2d ed. (Chicago: University of Chicago Press, 1970), p. 120.

25. Basil Davidson, *Let Freedom Come: Africa in Modern History* (Boston: Little, Brown and Co., 1978), pp. 327–328.

26. Claude Rivière, *Guinea: The Mobilization of a People,* trans. Virginia Thompson and Richard Adloff (Ithaca, N.Y.: Cornell University Press, 1977), p. 235.

27. *New York Times,* 16 December 1968.

28. Alexander G. Park, *Bolshevism in Turkestan, 1917–1927* (New York: Columbia University Press, 1957), p. 41.

29. Alexandre Bennigsen and Chantal Lemercier-Quelquejay, *Islam in the Soviet Union,* trans. Geoffrey E. Wheeler and Hubert Evans (New York: Praeger, 1967), p. 112.

30. Ibid., p. 183.

31. Shen Ping-wen, *Chinese Communist Criminal Acts of Persecution of Religions* (Taipei World Anti-Communist League, China Chapter, 1978), Chapter 4.

32. Raphael Israeli, "Muslim Minorities Under Non-Islamic Rule," *Current History* 78 (1980):161.

33. Clifton E. Marsh, "The World Community of Islam in the West: From Black Muslims to Muslims (1931–1977)" (Ph.D. diss., Syracuse University, 1977), p. 203.

Chapter 6. The Resurgence of Islam: The Spirit of the New Century

1. Ernest Gellner, "Islam and Marxism: Some Comparisons," *International Affairs* 67, no. 1 (January 1991):2.

2. See John O. Voll, "Islamic Renewal and the 'Failure of the West'," in *Religious Resurgence, Contemporary Cases in Islam, Christianity, and Judaism,* ed. Richard T. Antoun and Mary E. Hegland (Syracuse, N.Y.: Syracuse University Press, 1987), pp. 127–144.

3. An early statement of this description is found in Carleton S. Coon, *Caravan, The Story of the Middle East* (New York: Henry Holt, 1951).

4. Abd al-Hamid Abd al-Ghani, "Al-harakah al-islamiyyah al-jadidah," *Akhbar al-Yawm,* 3 February 1979, p. 7.

5. "Islamic Revival in Africa," *Africa Currents,* nos. 19/20 (Spring/Summer 1980):53.

6. Joseph A. Kechichian, "The Role of the Ulama in the Politics of an Islamic State: The Case of Saudi Arabia," *International Journal of Middle East Studies* 18, no. 1 (February 1986):58–59.

7. Remarks by Deputy Hojjat ol-Eslam 'Ali Akbar Muhtashemi, 24 Jan. 1991. *Foreign Broadcast Information Service, Near East and South Asia* (FBIS-NES), 90-016 (24 January 1991).

8. *Om El Kora* (Newsletter distributed by Om El Kora Center for Islamic Studies, Washington, D.C.) 1, no. 4 (25 Moharam 1408/18 Sept 1987):1, and *Facts About Iranian Rioting in Holy Mecca 1407 H* (n.p.: Society for the Preservation of Islamic Faith and Holy Places, n.d.; distributed by Om El Kora Center).

9. *New York Times,* 15 November 1990. For additional coverage of the event see *New York Times,* 7 November 1990.

10. "Saddam Calls Arabs, Muslims to 'Save' Mecca," Baghdad, 10 August 1990. FBIS-NES-90-156.

11. Mamoun Fandy, "The Hawali Tapes," *New York Times,* 24 November 1990.

12. Judith Miller, "Saudi and Proud of It," *New York Times,* 13 January 1991.

13. *New York Times,* 26 May 1991.

14. Hamid Algar, "The Oppositional Role of the Ulama in Twentieth-Century Iran," in *Scholars, Saints, and Sufis,* ed. Nikki R. Keddie (Berkeley: University of California Press, 1972), p. 255.

15. George W. Braswell, Jr., "Civil Religion in Contemporary Iran," *Journal of Church and State* 21 (Spring 1979):235–243.

16. Imam Khomeini, *Islam and Revolution,* trans. Hamid Algar (Berkeley: Mizan Press, 1981), p. 64.

17. Said Amir Arjomand, *The Turban for the Crown* (New York: Oxford University Press, 1988), p. 149.

18. Ibid., p. 150.

19. Fouad Ajami, "Iran: The Impossible Revolution," *Foreign Affairs* 67, no. 2 (Winter 1988/89):149.

20. For a helpful discussion of the situation in the years immediately following Khomeini's death, see Shireen T. Hunter, "Post-Khomeini Iran," *Foreign Affairs* 68, no. 5 (Winter 1989/90): 133–149.

21. For some of his views, see Ayatullah Sayyid Mahmud Taleghani, *Society and Economics in Islam,* trans. R. Campbell (Berkeley: Mizan Press, 1982).

22. Shahrough Akhavi, *Religion and Politics in Contemporary Iran* (Albany: State University of New York Press, 1980), p. 174.

23. Nikki R. Keddie, *Roots of Revolution* (New Haven: Yale University Press, 1981), pp. 213–215.

24. Helpful information about Shariati's life and thought can be found in Keddie, *Roots of Revolution,* pp. 215–225.

25. Ali Shariʿati, *On the Sociology of Islam,* trans. Hamid Algar (Berkeley: Mizan Press, 1979), p. 82.

26. Ibid., p. 77.

27. Gholam Abbas Tavassoli, "Introduction," in Shariʿati, *On The Sociology of Islam,* pp. 20–21.

28. For a comparison of the approaches of these two men, see Hamid Algar, "Introduction," in Ayatullah Murataza Mutahhari, *Fundamentals of Islamic Thought,* trans. R. Campbell (Berkeley: Mizan Press, 1985), pp. 15–16.

29. Abdulaziz Sachedina, "Ali Shariati: Idealogue of the Iranian Revolution," in *Voices of Resurgent Islam,* ed. John L. Esposito (New York: Oxford University Press, 1983), p. 212.

30. Ervand Abrahamian, "The Guerrilla Movement in Iran, 1963–1977," *MERIP Reports,* no. 86 (March/April 1980):10.

31. "How to Study the Qoran," *Mojahed* 1:2 (25 February 1980): 17.

32. "How to Study the Qoran," *Mojahed* 1:4 (April 1980):40.

33. "Getting to Know the PMOI," *Mojahed* 1:2 (25 February 1980):10

34. "Rajavi: NLA Heralds Mullah's Overthrow," *Iran Liberation* no. 115 (August 1, 1990):2–4.

35. Elaine Sciolino, "Iran's Durable Revolution," *Foreign Affairs* 61, no. 4 (Spring 1983):893.

36. John L. Esposito and James P. Piscatori, "The Global Impact of the Iranian Revolution: A Policy Perspective," in *The Iranian Revolution, Its Global Impact,* ed. John L. Esposito (Miami: Florida International University Press, 1990), pp. 317–318.

37. Ruth First, *Libya: The Elusive Revolution* (Baltimore: Penguin, 1974), p. 11.

38. "Gadhafi's Important Speech," *Progressive Libya* 2:9 (May 1973):1.

39. Muammar Al Qadhafi, *The Green Book, Part One: The Solution of the Problem of Democracy* (n.p., n.d.), pp. 13–14.

40. John P. Mason, "Qadhdhafi's 'Revolution' and Change in a Libyan Oasis Community," *Middle East Journal* 36, no. 3 (Summer 1982):334.

41. Raymond N. Habiby, "Muʿammar Qadhafi's New Islamic Scientific Society," *Middle East Review* 11:4 (Summer 1979):37.

42. Ronald Bruce St. John, "The Ideology of Muʿammar al-Qadhdhafi: Theory and Practice," *International Journal of Middle East Studies* 15, no. 4 (November 1983):486.

43. Lisa Anderson, "Qadhdhafi and His Opposition," *Middle East Journal* 40, no. 2 (Spring 1986):237.

44. *New York Times*, 3 June 1988.

45. *New York Times*, 9 January 1989.

46. "Urges End to Gulf Crisis 25 Jan," Tripoli, 27 January 1991. FBIS-NES-91-018 (28 January 1991). See also Qadhafi's speech in Tripoli to a union on 26 January in FBIS-NES-91-018.

47. M. E. Combs-Schilling, *Sacred Performances: Islam, Sexuality, and Sacrifice* (New York: Columbia University Press, 1989), p. 309.

48. Henry Munson, Jr., "The Social Base of Islamic Militancy in Morocco," *Middle East Journal* 40, no. 2 (Spring 1986):284.

49. James A. Bill, "Resurgent Islam," *Foreign Affairs* 63, no. 1 (Fall 1984):124.

50. An important source for this discussion of the Afghan opposition is Olivier Roy, *Islam and Resistance in Afghanistan*, 2d ed. (Cambridge, Eng., Cambridge University Press, 1990).

51. *Time*, 4 February 1980, p. 38.

52. David Busby Edwards, "The Evolution of Shiʿi Political Dissent in Afghanistan," in *Shiʿism and Social Protest*, ed. Juan Cole and Nikki Keddie (New Haven: Yale University Press, 1986), pp. 201–229.

53. *New York Times*, 7 April 1991.

54. Eden Naby, "Islam within the Afghan Resistance," *Third World Quarterly* 10, no. 2 (April 1988):799.

55. Najibullah Addresses Paktia Elders, 11 Mar 1990. FBIS-NES-90-049 (13 March 1990), and Najibullah Addresses Nation on UN Statement, 27 May 1991. FBIS-NES-91-102 (28 May 1991).

56. *New York Times*, 3 June 1990.

57. Saad Eddin Ibrahim, "Egypt's Islamic Activism in the 1980s," *Third World Quarterly* 10, no. 2 (April 1988):648.

58. Joseph P. O'Kane, "Islam in the New Egyptian Constitution: Some Discussions in *al-Ahram*," *Middle East Journal* 26 (1972):137–148. Some of the positions taken in these debates are translated in John J. Donohue and John L. Esposito, eds., *Islam in Transition* (New York: Oxford University Press, 1982), pp. 238–245.

59. Robert Bianchi, "Islam and Democracy in Egypt," *Current History* 88, no. 535 (February 1989):93–94.

60. For a discussion of these different perspectives, see Yahya Sadowski, "Egypt's Islamist Movement: A New Political and Economic Force," *Middle East Insight*, pp. 37–45.

61. Mona Makram-Ebeid, "Political Opposition in Egypt: Democratic Myth or Reality?" *Middle East Journal* 43, no. 3 (Summer 1989):423–436.

62. This discussion of the radical Islamist groups in Egypt is strongly influenced by a number of important studies: Gilles Kepel, *Muslim Extremism in Egypt: The Prophet and Pharoah*, trans. Jon Rothschild (Berkeley: University of California Press, 1985; Emmanuel Sivan, *Radi-*

cal Islam: Medieval Theology and Modern Politics (New Haven: Yale University Press, 1985); and the many writings of Saad Eddin Ibrahim, including "Egypt's Islamic Activism in the 1980s," *Third World Quarterly* 10, no. 2 (April 1988):632–657.

63. A translation of Faraj's book and an analysis of it is found in Johannes J. G. Jansen, *The Neglected Duty* (New York: Macmillan, 1986).

64. See, for example, FBIS-NES-91-103 (29 May 1991) and FBIS-NES-91-105 (31 May 1991).

65. *New York Times*, 16 December 1990, and *Wall Street Journal*, 7 January 1993.

66. Kepel, *Muslim Extremism*, p. 173.

67. *New York Times*, 24 March 1991.

68. Bianchi, "Islam and Democracy," pp. 94–95.

69. See, for example, Hasan Hanafi, *al-Yasar al-Islami, Kitabat fi al-Nahdah al-Islamiyyah* (Cairo: al-Markaz al-Arabi, 1981) and also the more comprehensive collection of essays found in Hasan Hanafi, *Min alʿAqidah illa al-Thawrah* [From Creed to Revolution], 5 vols. (Cairo: Maktabah al-Madbuli, 1988).

70. Saad Eddin Ibrahim, "Egypt's Islamic Activism," pp. 638–639.

71. Hugh Roberts, "Radicalism Islamism and the Dilemma of Algerian Nationalism: The Embattled Arians of Algers," *Third World Quarterly* 10, no. 2 (April 1988):575–582.

72. "Who is Abassi Madani?", *North African News* 1, no. 2 (June 1990):3.

73. Susan Waltz, "Islamist Appeal in Tunisia," *Middle East Journal* 40, no. 4 (Autumn 1986):653.

74. "An Abstract of Two Interviews with Rashid al Ghanoushi [from *Arabia*]," *The Movement of Islamic Tendency in Tunisia: The Facts* (n.p.: September 1987), pp. 91–100.

75. See, for example, the statements of the Democratic National Front in 1980, as reported in FBIS, *Daily Report: Middle East and Africa* 5, no. 163 (20 August 1980).

76. Adeed Dawisha, *The Arab Radicals* (New York: Council on Foreign Relations, 1986), pp. 48–50.

77. For a discussion of the Hama revolt, see Fred Lawson, "Social Bases for the Hamah Revolt," *MERIP Reports* 12, no. 9 (no. 110, November–December 1982):24–28. For the broader policy context of the Sunni opposition, see Daniel Pipes, *Greater Syria, The History of an Ambition* (New York: Oxford University Press, 1990), pp. 180–186.

78. Patrick Seale, *Asad of Syria, The Struggle for the Middle East* (Berkeley: University of California Press, 1988), especially chapter 21.

79. Samir Khalil, *Republic of Fear* (New York: Pantheon, 1989), pp. 270–276.

80. See, for example, "Saddam Husayn Issues 'Victory' Day Message," FBIS-NES-90-153 (8 August 1990), and "Saddam Calls Arabs, Muslims To 'Save' Mecca," FBIS-NES-90-156 (13 August 1990).

81. "Saddam Addresses Martyrs' Families, Assails Iran," FBIS-NES-91-145 (29 July 1991).

82. See, for example, Ayatullah Baqir al-Sadr, *Introduction to Islamic Political System*, trans. M. A. Ansari (Karachi: Islamic Seminary, 1982), and Ayatullah Muhammad Baqir Al-sadr, *Islam and Schools of Economics*, trans. M. A. Ansari (Karachi: Islamic Seminary, 1980).

83. Hanna Batatu, "Iraq's Underground Shiʿa Movements: Characteristics, Causes, and Prospects," *Middle East Journal* 35, no. 4 (Autumn, 1981):578. See also Chibli Mallat, "Religious Militancy in Contemporary Iraq: Muhammad Baqer as-Sadr and the Sunni-Shia Paradigm," *Third World Quarterly* 10, no. 2 (April 1988):699–729.

84. *Christian Science Monitor* (International Weekly Edition), 16 April 1979.

85. Feroz Ahmad, "Islamic Reassertion in Turkey," *Third World Quarterly* 10, no. 2 (April 1988):762.

86. Amberin Zaman, "Return of the Fundamentalists," *The Middle East*, no. 185 (March 1990), p. 8.

87. Feroz Ahmad, "Islamic Reassertion," pp. 764–769.

88. James Brown, "Turkey in the Age of Glasnost," *Current History* 89, no. 550 (November 1990), p. 381.

89. *Christian Science Monitor,* 1 August 1991.

90. Craig Baxter, "Bangladesh in 1990: Another New Beginning?" *Asian Survey* 31, no. 2 (February 1991):146–147.

91. Howard M. Federspiel, "Muslim Intellectuals and Indonesia's National Development," *Asian Survey* 31, no. 3 (March 1991):238.

92. See, for example, Michael Vatikiotis, "Indonesia: Practical Piety," *Far Eastern Economic Review,* 14 June 1990, pp. 26–32, and Jon Miller, "Wahid—Fast-Rising Indon Political Leader with Clout," *New Straits Times,* 27 June 1990.

93. Discussions of the various dakwah movements which have been helpful in preparing this section are Zainah Anwar, *Islamic Revivalism in Malaysia* (Selangor Darul Ehsan, Malaysia: Pelanduk, 1987), Judith Nagata, *The Reflowering of Malaysian Islam* (Vancouver: University of British Columbia Press, 1984), and Jomo Kwame Sundaram and Ahmad Shabery Cheek, "The Politics of Malaysia's Islamic Resurgence," *Third World Quarterly* 10, no. 2 (April 1988):843–868.

94. Based on comments and presentations by Anwar Ibrahim at the symposium, "Resurgent Islam: Prospects and Implications," organized by John L. Esposito and held in Durham, New Hampshire, 2–5 October 1980, and also interviews with John Voll and John Esposito during July 1990 in Kuala Lumpur.

95. See various reports in FBIS-EAS-90-200 (16 October 1990).

96. Tekle Mariam Woldemikael, "Political Mobilization and Nationalist Movements: The Case of the Eritrean People's Liberation Front," *Africa Today* 38, no. 2 (1991):33.

97. *Christian Science Monitor,* 8 August 1991.

98. A helpful discussion of this movement is Paul M. Lubeck, "Structural Determinants of Urban Islamic Protest in Northern Nigeria: A Note of Method, Mediation, and Materialist Explanation," in *Islam and the Political Economy of Meaning,* ed. William R. Roff (Berkeley: University of California Press, 1987).

99. Ibrahim A. Gambari, "Islamic Revivalism in Nigeria: Homegrown or Externally Induced?" in *The Iranian Revolution, Its Global Impact,* ed. John L. Esposito (Miami: Florida International University Press, 1990), pp. 306–307.

100. Quoted in Allan Christelow, "Three Islamic Voices in Contemporary Nigeria," in *Islam and the Political Economy of Meaning,* ed. William R. Roff (Berkeley, University of California Press, 1987), p. 240. Christelow provides an excellent introduction to the positions of both Sulaiman and Gumi.

101. Peter Clarke, "Islamic Reform in Contemporary Nigeria: Methods and Aims," *Third World Quarterly* 10, no. 2 (April 1988):527.

102. For the positions of the Republic Brothers at this time, see Abdullahi Ahmed An-Na'im, "Translator's Introduction," in *The Second Message of Islam* by Mahmoud Mohamed Taha (Syracuse, N.Y.: Syracuse University Press, 1987), pp. 9–19; for Garang's views in general, see Mansour Khalid, ed., *John Garang Speaks* (London: KPI, 1987); for the position of the Muslim Brotherhood, see Abdelwahab El-Affendi, *Turabi's Revolution, Islam and Power in Sudan* (London: Grey Seal, 1991), pp. 118–130.

103. These revivals are well discussed in Martha Brill Olcott, "Soviet Central Asia: Does Moscow Fear Iranian Influence," in *The Iranian Revolution, Its Global Impact,* ed. John L. Esposito (Miami: Florida International University Press, 1990), pp. 212–224.

104. Martha Brill Olcott, "Central Asia's Post-Empire Politics," *Orbis* 36, no. 2 (Spring 1992):264. See also Craig H. Baab, "The Draft Constitution of Kazakhstan," *Central Asia Monitor* no. 6 (1992).

105. Justin Burke, "Tajiks Struggle for National Identity," *Christian Science Monitor,* 30 September 1992. Helpful descriptions of events in the Tajik conflict can be found in the "News and Comments" sections of the issues of *Central Asian Monitor.*

106. L. J. Newby, "'The Pure and True Religion' in China," *Third World Quarterly* 10, no. 2 (April 1988):940–942. See also the special issue on "Muslims in China" of *Aramco World Magazine* 36, no. 4 (July–August 1985).

107. Robert Delfs, "Distant Smoke," *Far Eastern Economic Review,* 19 April 1990, pp. 10–11, and Robert Delfs, "Islamic Call to Arms," *Far Eastern Economic Review,* 3 May 1990, pp. 10–11.

108. Discussion of this case from a number of different perspectives can be found in articles which appeared in *Far Eastern Economic Review,* 20 March 1986: Salamat Ali, "A Minority Syndrome," Syed Shahabuddin, "The Crisis of Identity," and K. R. Malkani, "Prisoners of their Past."

109. Mushirul Hasan, "Indian Muslims since Independence: In Search of Integration and Identity," *Third World Quarterly* 10, no. 2 (April 1988):830.

110. Barbara Crossette, "Amid Kashmir 'Paradise,' a Deadly Struggle," *New York Times,* 15 June 1990. See also her articles at that time, especially "Muslim Leader of Kashmir Slain" *New York Times,* 22 May 1990. A clear description of Indian repression and its impact is Sheila Tefft, "Kashmiris Step Up Drive for Secession, as India Tightens Grip," *Christian Science Monitor,* 5 December 1990.

111. *New York Times,* 23 August 1992.

112. See, for example, the description in *New York Times,* 11 November 1992.

113. Abdullah Hakim Quick, "Islands under the Crescent," *Africa Events* 6, no. 2 (February 1990).

114. Helpful discussions of the history of Islam in South Africa can be found in Farid Esack, "Three Islamic Strands in the South African Struggle for Justice," *Third World Quarterly* 10, no. 2 (April 1988); Gorkeh Gamal Nkrumah, "Islam in South Africa," *Review of African Political Economy* no. 52 (November 1991); and Farid Esack, "Islam in South Africa: A Rejoinder to Nkrumah," *Review of African Political Economy* no. 53 (March 1992).

115. Esack, *Third World Quarterly,* p. 488.

116. Ibid, p. 498.

117. *New York Times,* 23 March 1980.

118. David Beriss, "Scarves, Schools, and Segregation: The *Foulard* Affair," *French Politics and Society* 8, no. 1 (Winter 1990):2.

119. A good summary of his activities in Brooklyn can be found in Peter Waldman, "Egyptian Jihad Leader Preaches Holy War to Brooklyn Muslims," *Wall Street Journal,* 7 January 1993.

120. Thomas L. Friedman, "An Islamic Revival Is Quickly Gaining Ground in an Unlikely Place: Israel," *New York Times,* 30 April 1987. This article reflects important research on the background and status of Islamic resurgence within Israel.

121. Joel Greenberg, "Winds of Islam Sweep Israel, Changing Landscape," *New York Times,* 16 September 1992. See also Friedman, "An Islamic Revival" 30 April 1987.

122. John L. Esposito, "Ismail R. al-Faruqi: Muslim Scholar-Activist," in *The Muslims of America,* ed. Yvonne Yazbeck Haddad (New York: Oxford University Press, 1991), pp. 65–79.

123. Mohammed K. Shaddid, "The Muslim Brotherhood Movement in the West Bank and Gaza," *Third World Quarterly* 10, no. 2 (April 1988):662–663.

124. See, for example, the comments by the military governor of Gaza reported in David K. Shipler, "Under Gaza's Calm Surface: Death, Drugs, Intrigue," *New York Times,* 28 March 1991.

125. *New York Times,* 20 December 1992.

126. Augustus Richard Norton, "Lebanon After Taʿif: Is the Civil War Over? " *Middle East Journal* 45, no. 3 (Summer 1991):463.

127. John L. Esposito, *Islam and Politics,* 3d ed. (Syracuse: Syracuse University Press, 1991), p. 248. The charter of the Amal movement is printed as appendix A in the important study, Augustus Richard Norton, *Amal and the Shiʿa: Struggle for the Soul of Lebanon* (Austin, Tex.: University of Texas Press, 1987).

128. Esposito, *Islam and Politics,* p. 251.

129. "Birri List Easily Sweeps South," *The Lebanon Report* 3, no. 10 (October 1992):4.

130. Ibid.

131. See Marius Deeb, *Militant Islamic Movements in Lebanon* (Washington: Georgetown Center for Contemporary Arab Studies, 1986), pp. 7–10.

132. "Controversial Elections Shake System," *The Lebanon Report* 3, no. 9 (September 1992):3.

Chapter 7. Perspectives and Prospects: The Islamic Resurgence and Contemporary History

1. "The Sociology of Religion: Some New Directions and Some Old Directions Reconsidered, Symposium Issue," *Sociological Analysis* 31, no. 3 (Fall 1970) and no. 4 (Winter 1970).

2. Theodore E. Long and Jeffrey K. Hadden, "Sects, Cults, and Religious Movements," *Sociological Analysis* 40, no. 4 (Winter 1979):280.

3. Ibid.

4. Peter Steinfels, "Fundamentalism: Last Spasm of the 20th Century?" *New York Times,* 6 April 1993. The basic thesis of these families resemblances is set out by the directors of the Fundamentalism Project in Martin E. Marty and R. Scott Appleby, "Conclusion: An Interim Report on a Hypothetical Family," in *Fundamentalisms Observed,* ed. Martin E. Marty and R. Scott Appleby (Chicago: University of Chicago Press, 1991).

5. Roland Robertson and JoAnn Chirico, "Humanity, Globalization, and Worldwide Religious Resurgence: A Theoretical Exploration," *Sociological Analysis* 46, no. 3 (1985):233.

6. Ibid, p. 222.

7. See, for example, the discussions in R. Stephen Warner, "Theoretical Barriers to the Understanding of Evangelical Christianity," *Sociological Analysis* 40, no. 1 (1979):1–9, and Susan Harding, "Representing Fundamentalism: The Problem of the Repugnant Cultural Other," *Social Research* 58, no. 2 (Summer 1991):373–393.

8. Long and Hadden, p. 280.

9. *Christian Science Monitor* (International Edition), 18 December 1978.

10. *Christian Science Monitor,* 12 March 1981.

11. Elie Kedourie in an article in *Daily Telegraph* (London), 27 August 1985.

12. Fouad Ajami, "Bush's Middle East Memo," *U.S. News & World Report,* 26 Dec 1988/2 Jan 1989.

13. Yvonne Yazbeck Haddad et al., *The Contemporary Islamic Revival: A Critical Survey and Bibliography* (New York: Greenwood Press, 1991).

14. R. Hrair Dekmejian, "The Anatomy of Islamic Revival: Legitimacy Crisis, Ethnic Conflict, and the Search for Islamic Alternatives," *Middle East Journal* 34 (1980):3.

15. John L. Esposito, *Islam and Politics,* 3d ed. (Syracuse: Syracuse University Press, 1991), pp. 271–272.

16. Bernard Lewis, *The Middle East and the West* (Bloomington, Ind.: Indiana University Press, 1964), p. 96.

17. Ibid.

18. Bernard Lewis, "The Return of Islam," *Commentary*, January 1976, p. 48.

19. Bernard Lewis, "The Roots of Muslim Rage," *The Atlantic*, September 1990, p. 60.

20. Bernard Lewis, "The Enemies of God," *The New York Review of Books*, 25 March 1993, p. 31.

21. John L. Esposito, *The Islamic Threat: Myth or Reality* (New York: Oxford University Press, 1992), p. 179.

22. Bruce B. Lawrence, *Defenders of God* (New York: Harper & Row, 1989), p. 2.

23. Ibid, p. 17.

24. Bruce B. Lawrence, "Muslim Fundamentalist Movements: Reflections Toward a New Approach," in *The Islamic Impulse*, ed. Barbara Freyer Stowasser (London: Croom Helm, 1987), p. 32.

25. Ibid.

26. Ernest Gellner, *Postmodernism, Reason and Religion* (London: Routledge, 1992), p. 1.

27. Ibid, p. 2.

28. Ibid, pp. 4–5.

29. Ibid, p. 9.

30. Ibid, p. 15.

31. Ibid, p. 19.

32. Ibid, p. 22.

33. Hasan Makki Muhammad Ahmad, *Harakah al-Ikhwan al-Muslimin fi al-Sudan 1944– 1969 m.* (Khartoum: Dar al-Fikr, n.d.) and Hasan Makki, *al-Harakah al-Islamiyyah fi al-Sudan 1969–1985 m.* (Khartoum: IRSS, 1990).

34. Abdelwahab El-Affendi, *Turabi's Revolution: Islam and Power in Sudan* (London: Grey Seal Books, 1991). The review quoted is by Robert O. Collins in *Middle East Journal* 47, no. 1 (Winter 1993):134.

35. Hasan al-Turabi, *al-Harakah al-Islamiyyah fi al-Sudan, al-Tatawwur wa al-Kasb wa al-Manhaj* (Cairo: al-Qari' al-Arabi, 1991).

36. El-Affandi, *Turabi's Revolution*, p. 1.

37. Hasan Makki Muhammad Ahmad, *al-Sayyid Ahmad bin Idris al-Fasi* (Khartoum: al-Markaz al-Islami al-Ifriqi, 1986), and Hasan Makki, *Harakah al-Baʿth al-Islami fi Iran* (Omdurman: Bayt al-Maʿrifah, 1990).

38. "Opening Statement of Dr. Hassan al-Turabi," U.S. House Foreign Affairs Africa Subcommittee Hearing on: The Implications for U.S. Policy of Islamic Fundamentalism in Africa, May 20, 1992, published in *Middle East Affairs Journal* 1, no. 1 (Summer 1992/1413):4–10.

39. Yvonne Yazbeck Haddad, "The Revivalist Literature and the Literature on Revival: An Introduction," in Haddad et al., *The Contemporary Islamic Revival*, p. 11.

40. See, for example, the accounts of the origins of the Islamic movement in Sudan in Hasan Makki, *Harakah al-Ikhwan al-Muslimin*, chapter 1.

41. Haddad, "The Revivalist Literature," p. 7.

42. See, for example, Hasan al-Turabi, *Tajdid al-Fikr al-Islami* (Jiddah: al-Dar al-Saʿu-diyyah, 1987). One of the intellectual pioneers of the resurgence, Abu al-Ala Mawdudi, wrote an important study of this tradition: S. Abul Aʿla Maududi, *A Short History of the Revivalist Movement in Islam*, trans. Al-Ashʿari (Lahore: Islamic Publications, 1963).

43. This summary of Hanafi's analysis is based primarily on Hassan Hanafi, "Origin of Modern Conservatism and Islamic Fundamentalism," (Paper presented in Amsterdam, December 1979), Hassan Hanafi, "The Relevance of the Islamic Alternative in Egypt," *Arab Studies Quarterly* 4, nos. 1–2 (Spring 1982):54–74; and Hasan Hanafi, "Madha yaʿni al-Yasar al-Islami," *al-Yasar al-Islami* 1 (1981):5–48.

44. Hanafi, *Arab Studies Quarterly,* p. 73.

45. Ibid, p. 74.

46. Bassam Tibi, *The Crisis of Modern Islam,* trans. Judith von Sivers (Salt Lake City: University of Utah Press, 1988), p. 147.

47. Akbar S. Ahmed, *Postmodernism and Islam: Predicament and Promise* (London: Routledge, 1992), p. 13.

48. Ibid, p. 48.

49. Ibid, pp. 264–265.

50. Patrick J. Buchanan, "Rising Islam May Overwhelm the West," syndicated column which appeared in *New Hampshire Sunday News,* 20 August 1989; and Martin Kramer, "Islam vs. Democracy," *Commentary* 95, no. 1 (January 1993):40.

51. Gad Yaacobi, Letter to the Editors, *New York Times,* 23 March 1993.

52. John L. Esposito, *The Islamic Threat: Myth or Reality* (New York: Oxford University Press, 1992). For a critical response which agrees with the basic questions but gives different answers, see Daniel Pipes, "Fundamental Questions About Muslims," *Wall Street Journal,* 30 October 1992.

53. John Obert Voll, "Conservative and Traditional Brotherhoods," *Annals, AAPSS,* 524 (November 1992):66–78.

Glossary of Non-English Terms

This glossary provides short definitions for some of the technical terms and names that appear in the text. Names of people and groups and other proper names are not included.

ayatollah. Literally, this means a wonder or exemplar of God. It is a title for a high-ranking religious scholar in the Shi'ite tradition.

caliph. The Western form of the Arabic term *khalifah,* which means successor. In Islamic history, the caliphs were the successors of the Prophet as leaders of the Muslim community.

grand vizier. This title was commonly given to the highest administrative official in a premodern Islamic political system. The grand vizier of the Ottoman Empire was one of the most powerful figures in the state.

hadith. A statement or account of an action or saying of the Prophet Muhammad. These accounts were collected in medieval times and provide an authoritative basis for Islamic law, supplementing the text of the Quran.

ijtihad. The action of using informed, independent judgment in a legal or theological issue. A person who uses *ijtihad* is called a *mujtahid.*

imam. There are three significant meanings for this title: (1) the leader of a group of praying Muslims (2) a general title for any Muslim leader with some religious authority; (3) in Shi'ite Islam, the title of the rightful, divinely guided ruler. In the Shi'ite tradition, there is a line of succession to the imamate from the Prophet Muhammad through his cousin and son-in-law, Ali.

jadid. Arabic word meaning "new." It is often used as a label for reforms and reformers. For example, Islamic modernism in Russia was called Jadidism, and the reforms of the Ottoman ruler, Selim III, were called the new order, or *nizam-i-jedid.*

khalifah. See *caliph.*

Kharijites. The name of one of the major traditions of Islam. It began in 657 when a group seceded from the army of the caliph, and later it developed an anarchic interpretation of the equality of all believers.

Koran. See *Quran.*

madhhab. This means an orientation or school of thought and refers to the schools of law, especially in Sunni Islam.

madrasah. An educational institution or school.

409

Mahdi. The title of the divinely guided figure who is expected to come in the last days and establish the rule of God on earth.

Mamluk. Literally meaning "owned," this term is applied to military slaves who were a ruling oligarchy in many parts of the Islamic world in premodern times.

millet. A religious community or social group. In the Ottoman Empire, the various *millet*s were granted semiautonomy under the guidance of their religious leaders.

mujaddid. Arabic word meaning "renewer." A widely accepted hadith reports that the Prophet Muhammad said that God would send a Mujaddid (Renewer) at the beginning of each century to strengthen the faith of the Muslims. Frequently, fundamentalist-style reformers were thought of as *mujaddid*s. The process of this type of renewal is called *tajdid*.

mujtahid. See *ijtihad*.

nizam-i-jedid. See *jadid*.

Quran. Record of the revelations Muslims believe were sent to mankind through the messenger of God, Muhammad. The Quran is thus the heart of the Islamic faith and the foundation for Islamic law and social order. In English usage, it is commonly called the Koran.

Rashidun. The period of the first four caliphs. Sunni Muslims believe that the community of Muslims at this time can provide a model for Muslim life.

salaf. The pious ancestors who lived at the time of Muhammad and the Rashidun caliphs are the *salaf*. They are believed by Sunni Muslims to have had special insight into the requirements of the faith because of their close association with the Prophet Muhammad. As a result, fundamentalist reformers and other renewers frequently call for a return to the attitude or the ways of the *salaf*. In the twentieth century, reformers in the tradition of Muhammad Abduh have been called the Salafiyyah because they called for a return to the principles followed by the *salaf*.

Shari'ah. The structure of Islamic law.

shaykh. This term can apply to a tribal leader, a religious teacher, or a ruler.

shaykh al-Islam. An honorific title for important Muslim scholars. In the Ottoman state, it was the title of the highest official in the government structure of Islamic schools and courts.

Sh'ism. A major tradition within Islam. It has its origins in the faction (*shi'ah*) within the community who believed that Ali was the rightful successor to the Prophet Muhammad.

Sufism. This dimension of Islam stresses the immanence of God. It manifests itself as the Islamic form of mysticism.

sultan. A ruler in later medieval Islamic states. Although the sultans had legitimate authority, they were primarily military commanders and therefore are not the same as caliphs, who led the early Muslim community as direct successors to the Prophet Muhammad.

sunnah. Accepted custom or practice. The Sunnah of the Prophet Muhammad is defined by the *hadith*s and is an authoritative model for Islamic behavior.

Sunni. Sunni Islam is the tradition that accepts the legitimacy of the caliphs who actually succeeded the Prophet, in contrast to Shi'ism. The majority of the Muslims in the world are Sunnis.

tajdid. See *mujaddid*.

Tanzimat. Literally, this means "reorganization." The term is applied to the program of modernizing reforms within the Ottoman Empire in the middle years of the nineteenth century.

taqlid. The action of imitation. The term is applied to the action of following precedents set by earlier thinkers and is the opposite of *ijtihad*.

tariqah. This means "path" and refers to the devotional path developed by Sufi teachers. It also refers to the social organization or Sufi brotherhood formed by followers of such Sufi teachers.

tawhid. Literally, "union or unity." In Islamic thought this is the term applied to the oneness of God and implies the absolute and single sovereignty of God in the universe. In modern Islamic thought, *tawhid* is stressed as the basis for unity of religion and politics and religion and economics.

ulama. Collective term for the learned men in the Islamic tradition.

ummah. This means "community" and refers to the total community of believing Muslims.

vizier. An administrative official, usually of high rank.

wali. A person who is believed to be close to God and has, as a result, special piety and spiritual power.

Bibliographical Essay

It was impossible, even in the first edition of this book, to provide a complete or comprehensive bibliography of works covering the modern Islamic experience. In the past decade, the materials available have come to represent a vast library. What is presented here is simply a series of suggestions for readers who wish to pursue some subject beyond the discussion in this book. This bibliographical essay does not mention all of the sources cited in this book, and many major studies are not discussed. However, the publications noted here do provide the foundation for further study of the issues of continuity and change in the modern Islamic experience. Although significant works have been written in this subject in many languages, this bibliography has been restricted to works in English that are relatively easily available. (Works in other languages are listed in the bibliographies discussed below.) As a convenience for the reader, the works have been grouped into special topic areas rather than simply being presented in alphabetical order.

Interpreting the Interpreters

The starting point for further reading on the subject may be studies that examine works similar to this book. It is very important to understand the perspectives and prejudices of the people who write on the Islamic experience. Popular and scholarly Western attitudes toward Islam in the modern era have been carefully examined by Norman Daniel, *Islam, Europe, and Empire* (Edinburgh: Edinburgh University Press, 1966), and by Edward W. Said in his thought-provoking and sometimes controversial works, *Orientalism* (New York: Pantheon, 1978), *Covering Islam: How the Media and the Experts Determine How We See the Rest of the World* (New York: Pantheon, 1981), and *Culture and Imperialism* (New York: Alfred A. Knopf, 1993). In this growing literature, a very helpful perspective is provided by the North African philsopher-historian Hichem Djait, *Europe and Islam: Cultures and Modernity,* trans. Peter Heinegg (Berkeley: University of California Press, 1985).

Bibliographies

Two very helpful bibliographical sources are *Index Islamicus, 1906–1955* (Cambridge: Heffer, 1958), with supplementary volumes by J. D. Pearson, and the bibliographical section of each issue of *The Middle East Journal*. For an introduction to the literature on the twentieth-century resurgence, see Yvonne Haddad et al., *The Contemporary Islamic Revival: A Critical Survey and Bibliography* (New York: Greenwood, 1991).

General Surveys

An important general reference work for the whole Islamic world in the modern era is *The Oxford Encyclopedia of the Modern Islamic World* (Oxford University Press, 1995). It is also sometimes helpful to use a general interpretation of the whole sweep of Islamic history. Perhaps the most significant such study in recent years is Marshall G. S. Hodgson, *The Venture of Islam,* 3 vols. (Chicago: University of Chicago Press, 1974). Other important broad surveys are Ira Lapidus, *A History of Islamic Societies* (Cambridge: Cambridge University Press, 1988) and Albert Hourani, *A History of the Arab Peoples* (Cambridge, Mass.: Harvard University Press, 1991). Those who need a feeling for the general sweep of Islamic history but would like to have it in concise form will be greatly assisted by Richard M. Eaton, *Islamic History as Global History* (Washington, D.C.: American Historical Association, 1990).

Introductions to Islam

The historical perspective needs to be supplemented by an understanding of the intellectual content and faith of Islam. Many introductions to Islam have appeared in the past century. A recent work which has been well-received by both Muslim and non-Muslim scholars is John L. Esposito, *Islam, The Straight Path,* expanded ed. (New York: Oxford University Press, 1991).

In recent years a number of introductions to Islam written by Muslims have become increasingly available to the English-reading audience. These books provide important sources for understanding the different modern Islamic perspectives. Isma'il R. Al Faruqi, *Islam* (Niles, Ill.: Argus Communications, 1979) is a readable discussion written by a strict Sunni Muslim with substantial teaching experience in the West. Seyyed Hossein Nasr, *Ideals and Realities of Islam* (London: George Allen & Unwin, 1966) is written from the perspective of modern philosophical Sufism within the Shi'i tradition. An introduction by Sayyid Qutb, *This Religion of Islam* (Gary, Ind.: International Islamic Federation of Student Organizations, n.d.) exists in many editions and is by one of the major scholars in the Muslim Brotherhood in Egypt. A more conservative presentation from the perspective of a North American Muslim is provided in Suzanne Haneef, *What Everyone Should Know About Islam and Muslims* (Chicago: Kazi Publications, 1982). Fazlur Rahman, *Islam,* 2d ed. (Chicago: University of Chicago Press, 1979) is by the former director of the Islamic Research Institute in Pakistan who taught for many years in the United States. His scholarly works have had a significant influence on Western scholars. His perspective is that of a contemporary modernist within the Sunni tradition.

Interpretations of Modern Islamic Experiences

There is a long tradition in the West of describing the Muslim world and the modern Islamic experience. Much of this literature is ethnocentrically oriented polemic, which either sees Islam as a reactionary obstacle to progress or describes it as a major threat to the West. However, during the twentieth century, there have been a number of books that present significant insights into the modern Islamic experience, even though many have limitations because of the prejudices of the times. An early work of this type is Lothrop Stoddard, *The New World of Islam* (New York: Scribner's, 1921). This work tends to see Islam as a threatening force but provides a good picture of some aspects of Islamic dynamism during and immediately after World War I. About a decade later, a valuable collection of essays appeared: H. A. R. Gibb, ed., *Whither Islam? A Survey of Modern Movements in the Muslim World* (London: Victor Gollancz, 1932). Although the mood and tone of this work are clearly dated, valuable information is provided.

Two of the most influential works to examine and interpret the modern Islamic experience are H. A. R. Gibb, *Modern Trends in Islam* (Chicago: University of Chicago Press, 1947), and Wilfred Cantwell Smith, *Islam in Modern History* (Princeton: Princeton University Press, 1957). Gibb presents a critique of Islamic modernist thought that shaped both Muslim and non-Muslim views, and Smith discusses the relationship between the experience of the Islamic community in history and the Muslim sense of crisis in the modern world. Although both works reflect the conditions of the 1940s and 1950s, they continue to provide influential frameworks for analysis.

The Islamic resurgence of the late twentieth century produced a very large number of works. Some of the most readily available continue to be in the genre of instant history and the journalistic potboiler. However, now a wide spectrum of scholarly analysis is also available: Daniel Pipes, *In The Path of God: Islam and Political Power* (New York: Basic Books, 1983) takes a global view and places contemporary Islamic developments in the context of both long-term history and the impetus provided by the oil profits of the 1970s, emphasizing potential and actual conflicts between Islam and the West in the contemporary era. John L. Esposito, *Islam and Politics,* 3d ed. (Syracuse: Syracuse University Press, 1991) places contemporary Islamic dynamism in the broader historical context, emphasizing the dimensions of internal developments of Islamic thought and institutions in the context of modern global power relations. Many conferences have been held and some of the resulting volumes of collections of papers are very useful. These include Shireen T. Hunter, ed., *The Politics of Islamic Revivalism: Diversity and Unity* (Bloomington: Indiana University Press, 1988); John L. Esposito, ed., *Voices of Resurgent Islam* (New York: Oxford University Press, 1983); and William R. Roff, ed., *Islam and the Political Economy of Meaning* (London: Croom Helm, 1987).

Specific Areas and Eras

Each of the specific regions and periods discussed in the book are studied in many articles and books. It is not possible to provide even a beginning bibliography for each area and period covered; what follows is a limited list of the books that have been helpful in the preparation of this volume, noting a few more recent publications dealing with the unrevised chapters of this edition. In most cases, these works have bibliographies that can be used as the basis for more intensive study.

Eighteenth Century

Despite its importance for Islamic history, the eighteenth century continues to receive less attention than it deserves. Good collections of materials illustrating important lines of contemporary scholarship are Thomas Naff and Roger Owen, eds., *Studies in Eighteenth-Century Islamic History* (Carbondale, Ill.: Southern Illinois University Press, 1977), and Nehemiah Levtzion and John O. Voll, ed., *Eighteenth-Century Renewal and Reform in Islam* (Syracuse: Syracuse University Press, 1987). The old standard on the eighteenth century Ottoman Empire is H. A. R. Gibb and Harold Bowen, *Islamic Society and the West*, vol. 1, pts. 1–2 (London: Oxford University Press, 1950–1957). An important analysis of a major revivalist tradition and the issues involved in "Neo-Sufism" is R. S. O'Fahey, *The Enigmatic Saint: Ahmad Ibn Idris and the Idrisi Tradition* (London: Hurst, 1990).

The Arab World

The previously mentioned *A History of the Arab Peoples* by Albert Hourani is an important introduction to the great diversity and historical experience of the Arab world. Another useful survey is Arthur Goldschmidt, *A Concise History of the Middle East*, 4th ed. (Boulder, Colo.: Westview Press, 1991). An important introduction from an anthropological perspective is Michael Gilsenan, *Recognizing Islam: Religion and Society in the Modern Arab World* (New York: Pantheon, 1982). Useful specialized studies, whose contents are indicated by the titles, are: Albert Hourani, *Arabic Thought in the Liberal Age, 1798–1939* (London: Oxford University Press, 1962); Hisham Shirabi, *Arab Intellectuals and the West: The Formative Years, 1875–1914* (Baltimore, Md.: Johns Hopkins University Press, 1970); Hanna Batatu, *The Old Social Classes and the Revolutionary Movements of Iraq* (Princeton: Princeton University Press, 1977). Important analyses of changing Arab historical consciousness are Abdallah Laroui, *The Crisis of the Arab Intellectual: Traditionalism or Historicism?*, trans. Diarmid Cammell (Berkeley: University of California Press, 1976) and Yvonne Yazbeck Haddad, *Contemporary Islam and the Challenge of History* (Albany: State University of New York Press, 1982).

For the North African part of the Arab world, two very helpful discussions are Jamil M. Abun-Nasr, *A History of the Maghrib*, 2d ed. (Cambridge: Cambridge University Press, 1975) and Francois Burgat and William Dowell, *The Islamic Movement in North Africa* (Austin, Tex.: University of Texas Press, 1993).

Brief surveys of the history and political development of each country in the Middle East and North Africa, along with special bibliographies for each country, can be found in David E. Long and Bernard Reich, ed., *The Government and Politics of the Middle East and North Africa* (Boulder, Colo.: Westview Press, 1986).

The Northern Tier

The widespread interest in the Islamic revolution in Iran in 1979 sparked great interest and many publications. In preparing the sections on Iran in this book, the works of Nikki Keddie and Hamid Algar were of special help. Good starting points are their chapters in *Scholars, Saints, and Sufis,* ed. Nikki Keddie (Berkeley: University of California Press, 1972). More general studies are Hamid Algar, *Religion and State in Iran, 1785–1906* (Berkeley: University of Calfornia Press, 1969), and, among the numerous books by Keddie, *An Islamic Response to Imperialism: Political and Religious Writings of Sayyid Jamal ad-Din al-Afghani* (Berkeley: University of California Press, 1969) and *Roots of Revolution: An Interpretive History of Modern Iran* (New Haven, Conn.: Yale University Press, 1981). Other very helpful works on modern Iran are Shahrough Akhavi, *Religion and Politics in Contemporary Iran* (Albany: State University of New York Press, 1980); Roy Mottahedeh, *The Mantle of the Prophet: Religion and Politics in Iran* (New York: Simon and Schuster, 1985); and Robin Wright, *In the Name of God: The Khomeini Decade* (New York: Simon and Schuster, 1989). The essential source for Khumayni's writings is *Islam and Revolution: Writings and Declarations of Imam Khomeini,* trans. Hamid Algar (Berkeley: Mizan Press, 1981).

For Turkey, an excellent survey covering Ottoman and modern times is Stanford J. Shaw (and Ezel Kural Shaw for vol. 2), *History of the Ottoman Empire and Modern Turkey,* 2 vols. (Cambridge: Cambridge University Press, 1976–1977). The standard source for the process of modernization remains Bernard Lewis, *The Emergence of Modern Turkey* (London: Oxford University Press, 1961), and the basic issues of the modern Islamic experience are examined in Niyazi Berkes, *The Development of Secularism in Turkey* (Montreal: McGill University Press, 1964). Important recent developments are covered in the essays in Richard Tapper, ed., *Islam in Modern Turkey: Religion, Politics and Literature in a Secular State* (London: Tauris, 1991).

The old standard introduction in English to the modern history of Afghanistan remains Louis Dupree, *Afghanistan* (Princeton: Princeton University Press, 1980). Among the many new studies that have appeared in the past decade, focusing on the development of the Mujahidin groups, a very helpful work is Olivier Roy, *Islam and Resistance in Afghanistan,* 2d ed. (Cambridge: Cambridge University Press, 1990).

South Asia

The works of Aziz Ahmad provide a good starting point for further study on Islam in South Asia. Especially helpful are his *Studies in Islamic Culture in the Indian Environment* (Oxford: Clarendon Press, 1964), and *Islamic Modernism in India and Pakistan, 1857–1964* (London: Oxford University Press, 1967). The appropriate sections on South Asian states in the following are good starting points for more recent developments: Carlo Caldarola, ed., *Religion and Societies: Asia and the Middle East* (Berlin: Mouton, 1982) and John L. Esposito, ed., *Islam in Asia: Religion, Politics, & Society* (New York: Oxford University Press, 1987). Studies presenting important interpretations of the lives and contributions of two leaders who represent the two contrasting modes of Islamic development in South Asia are Khurshid Ahmad and Zafar Ishaq Ansari, ed., *Islamic Perspectives: Studies in Honour of Mawlana Sayyid Abul A'la Mawdudi* (Leicester: The Islamic Foundation, 1979) and Ian Henderson Douglas, *Abul Kalam Azad: An Intellectual and Religious Biography,* ed. Gail Minault and Christian W. Troll (Delhi: Oxford University Press, 1988).

Southeast Asia

The three chapters in volume 2 of *The Cambridge History of Islam,* ed. P. M. Holt, Ann K. S. Lambton, and Bernard Lewis (Cambridge: Cambridge University Press, 1970), which cover Southeast Asia, provide a sound survey of the Islamic history of the region. An important study of the broader issues of the modern and contemporary period is Fred R. Von Der Mehden, *Religion and Modernization in Southeast Asia* (Syracuse: Syracuse University Press, 1986). The essays in the collections of Caldarola, *Religion and Societies,* and Esposito, *Islam in Asia,* provide important interpretations of recent developments. Many special studies provide a basis for understanding the special character of the Islamic experience in Southeast Asia. Some which have been specially helpful in the writing of this book are B. J. Boland, *The Struggle of Islam in Modern Indonesia,* revised (The Hague: Nijhoff, 1982); Zainah Anwar, *Islamic Revivalism in Malaysia: Dakwah Among the Students* (Selanger, Malaysia: Pelanduk, 1987); Judith Nagata, *The Reflowering of Malaysian Islam: Modern Religious Radicals and their Roots* (Vancouver: University of British Columbia Press, 1984).

Saharan and Sub-Saharan Africa

For the study of Islam in Africa one of the best-known scholars is J. Spencer Trimingham. In a number of works, he provided introductions to Islamic history in many parts of Africa. A general summary of his work is presented in *Influence of Islam Upon Africa* (New York: Praeger, 1968). Although his work has been superseded in many particulars, his broader perspectives are still useful. Important special studies include Mervyn Hiskett, *The Sword of Truth: The Life and Times of the Shehu Usuman Dan Fodio* (London: Oxford University Press, 1973); B. G. Martin, *Muslim Brotherhoods in 19th-Century Africa* (Cambridge: Cambridge University Press, 1976); August H. Nimtz, Jr., *Islam and Politics in East Africa* (Minneapolis: University of Minnesota Press, 1980); Peter B. Clarke, *West Africa and Islam: A Study of Religious Development from the 8th to the 20th Century* (London: Edward Arnold, 1982).

Major Muslim Minorities

The histories of the large Muslim communities that are minorities in their countries are complex. The essential source for Muslim minorities studies is *Journal, Institute of Muslim Minority Affairs.* The collections edited by Caldarola, *Religion and Societies* and Esposito, *Islam in Asia,* provide useful introductions to the Islamic communities in India, and an important collection of essays by an Indian Muslim thinker is Syed Vahiduddin, *Islam in India: Studies and Commentaries,* vol. 3, *The Islamic Experience in Contemporary Thought,* ed. Christian W. Troll (Delhi: Chanakya Publications, 1986). For Muslims in China, Raphael Israeli, *Muslims in China: A Study in Cultural Confrontation* (London: Curzon Press, 1980), provides much information but does not fully supersede older works like Marshall Broomhall, *Islam in China: A Neglected Problem* (London: Morgan & Scott, 1910).

The transformation of Muslims of Central Asia from being minorities within the Soviet Union into being the majorities in newly independent states has created a new opening for studies which are only beginning to appear. Among the important studies of Islam in the Soviet Union are Alexandre Bennigsen and Chantal Lemercier-Quelquejay, *Islam in the Soviet Union,* trans. Geoffrey E. Wheeler and Hubert Evans (New York: Praeger, 1967); Alexandre Bennigsen and S. Enders Wimbush, *Mystics and Commissars: Sufism in the Soviet Union* (Berkeley: University of California Press, 1985); and Michael Rywkin, *Moscow's Muslim Challenge,* rev. ed. (Armonk, N.Y.: M. E. Sharpe, 1990). An important source for information about the rapidly changing situation in the new, independent republics of Central Asia is *Central Asia Monitor,* a bimonthly magazine.

Muslim minority communities have gained increasing importance in a number of areas. Important studies of some of these are Tomas Gerholm and Yngve Georg Lithman, *The New Islamic Presence in Western Europe* (London: Mansell, 1988); Yvonne Yazbeck Haddad, ed., *The Muslims of America* (New York: Oxford University Press, 1991); from the Muslim activist perspective: *Muslim Communities in Non-Muslim States* (London: Islamic Council of Europe, 1980) and Syed Abul Hasan Ali Nadwi, *Muslims in the West: The Message and the Mission* (Leicester: The Islamic Foundation, 1983).

Interpretations of Islamic Fundamentalism

One of the special issues raised in this book is the nature of Islamic fundamentalism. There are some very important studies that have shaped the contemporary awareness of the style of Islam that this book calls fundamentalist. A work of critical significance is Richard P. Mitchell, *The Society of the Muslim Brothers* (London: Oxford University Press, 1969; reprint 1993). This book is accepted even by members of the Brotherhood as the standard authority on the history of the organization.

Other scholars whose work has shaped many analyses of Islam in general and of Muslim fundamentalism in particular are Clifford Geertz, *Islam Observed: Religious Development in Morocco and Indonesia* (Chicago: University of Chicago Press, 1968), and the work of Ernest Gellner as seen in *Muslim Society* (Cambridge: Cambridge University Press, 1981) and other works. Recent influential scholarship includes John L. Esposito, *The Islamic Threat: Myth or Reality* (New York: Oxford University Press, 1992); Gilles Kepel, *Muslim Extremism in Egypt: The Prophet and the Pharoah,* trans. Jon Rothschild (Berkeley: University of California Press, 1986); Emmanuel Sivan, *Radical Islam: Medieval Theology and Modern Politics* (New Haven, Conn.: Yale University Press, 1985); and articles and books by Daniel Pipes. In the broader comparative and global terms, the volumes published by the Fundamentalism Project are of increasing importance. The basic analytical framework is set in the first volume: Martin E. Marty and R. Scott Appleby, *Fundamentalisms Observed* (Chicago: University of Chicago Press, 1991).

Keeping Informed

Day-to-day news tends to stress the sensational and violent, but major newspapers such as the *Christian Science Monitor* and the *New York Times* provide continuing coverage. In addition, *The Middle East Journal* publishes a quarterly chronology. There are also now a number of Muslim periodicals available which provide continuing coverage of Islamic subjects and concerns. At the scholarly level, there is *The American Journal of Islamic Social Sciences,* and at the popular level there is the nationally distributed magazine of the Islamic Center of Southern California, *The Minaret*. Translations of speeches and articles from the Muslim world itself are published by the U.S. government through the Foreign Broadcast Information Service (FBIS) and the Joint Publications Research Service (JPRS). The publications of these two organizations are available at any library that is a U.S. government repository.

Index

Guide to Alphabetization and Listings

In determining the order of names and terms in this index, some special practices have been followed:

(1) Names and terms beginning with the Arabic definite article (al- or el-) are indexed under the letter following the article. When in the middle of the name or term, the article (al- or el-) is treated as part of the word.

(2) Compound Islamic names are treated as a single name. Thus, names beginning with "Abd al-" are listed under that initial word rather than the second word in the compound. (Abd al-Qadir will be found under "Abd al-" rather than "Qadir.") Similarly, names ending in "al-din" will be listed under the first word of the compound name. (Hamid al-Din will be found under Hamid.)

(3) Special titles that normally precede personal names (like ayatollah, king, or sayyid) are not treated as part of the name and may appear in parentheses after the name.

(4) Individuals are listed under their family names or personal identification terms (like "Ibn" or a descriptive adjective like "al-Baghdadi") if these names are in common usage. Otherwise, individuals are listed under their personal given names. Thus, it is "al-Mahdi, Sadiq," and "Ibn al-Arabi, Muhyi al-Din," but also "Qabus ibn Said."

al-Banna, Hasan, 135, 159, 180–182, 326.
See also Muslim Brotherhood
Baqi billah, Muhammad, 39
Barakat clan (Mecca), 50
al-Barawi, Uways, 137
al-Bashir, Omar Hassan, 356–357
Basmachi movement, 279, 319
al-Basri, Abdallah ibn Salim, 60
Basyuni, Muhammad, 127
Ba'th party, 174–175, 247, 248, 317,
333–337. See also Iraq; Syria
Baytar, Salah al-Din, 174. See also Ba'th
party
al-Bayyumi, Ali, 45
Bayyumiyyah Tariqah, 45
Bazargan, Mahdi, 206, 302, 305. See also
Freedom movement (Iran)
al-Bazzaz, Abd al-Rahman, 165
Bello, al-Hajj Ahmadu, 260
Ben Ali, Zein al-Abidine, 331
Ben Badis, 220–221
Ben Barka, Mehdi, 229
Ben Bella, Ahmad, 157, 222, 225–226,
256, 290, 329
Bengali (language), 245, 248
Benjedid, Chadli, 330
Bennabi, Malik, 227, 230
Ben Salah, Ahmad, 227
Ben Youssef, Salah, 227
Berber Decree of 1930, 224
Bergson, Henri, 234
Berri, Nabih, 371
Bhashani, Mawlana Abd al-Hamid, 342
Bhutto, Benazir, 341–342
Bhutto, Zulfikar Ali, 248–249, 340, 345
Biafra, 261
Bihbihani, Aga Muhammad Baqir, 82
Bihishti, Muhammad (ayatollah), 302
Black Muslims. See Nation of Islam move-
ment (USA)
BNP. See Bangladesh Nationalist Party
Bonneval, Claude-Alexandre Comte de, 35
Bornu, 143
Bosnia and Herzegovina, 363
Boumedienne, Houari, 226, 330
Bourguiba, Habib, 217–219, 227–229,
331–332
Brelwi, Ahmad, 53, 110–111, 128
Brown, L. Carl, 86

Buchanan, Patrick, 387
Buhari, Mohammed, 352
Bukhara, 122
al-Bukhari, Muhammad ibn Isma'il, 128
al-Bukhari, Murad, 39. See also Muradi
family
Bulgaria, 362
Burujirdi, Ayatollah, 214
Bu Said dynasty (Oman), 66–67, 132–
133. See also Oman
Byzantine Empire, 9

Call of Islam (South Africa), 365
Camp David Accord, 323
Candao, Zacaria, 364
Caribbean region, 364
Central Asian republics, 358–359
Cevdet Pasha, Ahmad, 89, 98, 99
Chad, 271, 273, 274–275, 310, 350–351
China, 147–149, 161, 280–282, 359–360
China Islamic Association (People's Re-
public), 281
Chinese Islamic Association, 281
Chinese Muslim Association, 281
Chinese Muslim republic, 282
Chiragh Ali, 113, 114, 135, 295
Communist Association of the Indies. See
Perserikatan Komunis di-India (PKI)
Communist Party (Afghanistan). See Khalq
(Afghanistan); Parcham; People's
Democratic party of Afghanistan
(PDPA)
Communist Party (Indonesia). See Partai
Komunis Indonesia (PKI); Per-
serikatan Komunis di-India (PKI)
Communist Party (Iran), 203–205. See
also Tudeh party
Communist Party (Iraq), 171–173
Communist Party (Malaya/Malaysia), 240
Communist Party (Syria), 173, 174
Comoro Islands, 136
Conservative mode (Islamic), 8, 10, 22,
83, 87, 149–151, 158–159, 193,
293–294, 313, 365, 374, 387–390
in Afghanistan, 198–201
in Africa, 261, 277
in Arab world, 50, 127, 182–190